Accounting: Systems and Procedures

IBM

McGraw-Hill Accounting 10/12 Series

Accounting: Systems and Procedures

FIFTH EDITION

David H. Weaver, Ph.D.
Educational Consultant
Parsippany, New Jersey

Edward B. Brower, Ed.D.
Professor, Department of Vocational Education, Business Education
Temple University
Philadelphia, Pennsylvania

James M. Smiley, Ph.D.
Formerly Associate Professor of Business Education
University of Georgia
Athens, Georgia

Virginia A. Rose, Ph.D.
Business Education Curriculum Consultant for the State of Ohio
The Ohio State University
Columbus, Ohio

Gregg Division
McGraw-Hill Book Company
New York Atlanta Dallas St. Louis
San Francisco Auckland Bogotá Guatemala
Hamburg Lisbon London Madrid Mexico Milan
Montreal New Delhi Panama Paris San Juan
São Paulo Singapore Sydney Tokyo Toronto

Sponsoring Editor: Elissa M. Pinto
Editing Supervisor: Suzette André
Design and Art Supervisor/ Text and Cover Designer: Karen Tureck
Production Supervisor: Frank P. Bellantoni and S. Steven Canaris
Photo Editor: Rosemarie Rossi

Cover Photographer: Ken Karp

Photo Credits

Pages 2–3, 5, 23, 56, 90, 124, 152, 185, 230, 271, 278–279, 425, 534, 569, and 594: Richard Hackett. Page 8: George Goodman/Monkmeyer Press. Pages 235 and 269 (top): Courtesy of IBM Corporation. Pages 268 and 519: Les Morsillo. Pages 269 (bottom), 274, and 281: Jules T. Allen. Page 270 (left): Courtesy of Sperry Corporation. Pages 270 (right) and 272: Courtesy of Control Data Corporation. Page 273: Chris Hackett/The Image Bank. Page 283: Courtesy of Wilson Jones Company. Page 297 (top): Courtesy of VISA International. Page 297 (bottom): Courtesy of MasterCard International, Inc. Page 306: Moag, Inc. Page 330: Will Faller. Page 379: Barbara Pfeffer/Peter Arnold, Inc. Page 467: Arthur d'Arazien/The Image Bank. Page 530: Courtesy of NCR Corporation.

Library of Congress Cataloging-in-Publication Data

Accounting, systems and procedures.

(McGraw-Hill accounting 10/12 series)
1. Accounting. I. Weaver, David H., date
II. Series.
HF5635.A222 1988 657 87-17234
ISBN 0-07-069356-0

The manuscript for this book was processed electronically.

***Accounting Systems and Procedures,* Fifth Edition**

2 3 4 5 6 7 8 9 0 VNHVNH 8 9 4 3 2 1 0 9 8

ISBN 0-07-069356-0

Contents

Preface

What does the cover of this textbook suggest to you? The chances are that when you looked at it, you saw a group of abstract shapes and figures arranged in a pattern of some sort. That is, you saw it as a piece of ''modern'' art.

While we see the cover as modern, we see it as traditional too. That is because it depicts the strong tradition that has made *Accounting: Systems and Procedures* so successful in the field of accounting education—the systems approach.

As you can see in the diagram on page xi, each of the planes shown on the cover represents an accounting subsystem. As data flows through the various accounting subsystems and is processed, the subsystems are linked together in a general accounting subsystem, and the data becomes meaningful information.

What forges the links in an accounting system? The people, forms, procedures, and equipment that make up the system. This textbook does not teach isolated procedures. Instead, it shows students how the people, forms, procedures, and equipment in an accounting system are related, and it teaches the concepts on which this accounting system is structured. So, whether students go on to further accounting study, or go directly into the business world, *Accounting: Systems and Procedures* can give them the fundamental understanding of the accounting system that they will need in order to succeed.

Teaching Methodology

The *Accounting: Systems and Procedures* program consists of this series as well as the *Accounting: Systems and Procedures, Advanced Course* series. The program is based on up-to-date accounting methodology, systems, and procedures. It can be used as a semester, year, two-year, three-year, or shorter course of instruction. It can also be used in vocational, avocational, or general education courses of instruction. The complete program is best described as holistic in its presentation. That is, it emphasizes the importance of the whole teaching system as well as the independence of its parts, which are described below.

Short Learning Units The learning sequence is structured in a building-block arrangement. Each reading section leads logically to the next. Related reading sections make up a topic. Related topics make up a chapter. Related chapters make up a part. The basic program contains two parts.

Learning Reinforcement and Immediate Feedback Each topic and chapter is followed by appropriate exercises and problems so that at each stage learning is reinforced. Students move on to the next topic or chapter only after they have mastered the present one. The reinforcement exercises also provide students with immediate feedback so that they can check what they have learned at every stage.

Learning Evaluation The evaluation strategy includes performance goals for every topic and chapter that state what students are expected to learn, and progress and comprehensive tests to measure the achievement of those goals. This evaluation strategy enables both the student and the teacher to assess whether the student is ready to proceed to the next topic or chapter.

Recycling The teaching methodology also includes a recycling strategy. That is, students restudy the particular concepts or topics they have failed to master. There are ample problems of all levels of difficulty and complexity, so teachers can assign materials appropriate to the needs of the student until mastery is achieved.

Career Information Instruction in this program is based on a hierarchy of skills and knowledge. The vocational skills and knowledge associated with various accounting, computing, and related office jobs are presented in a progression from the simple to the complex. A photographic scenario introduces each part and each chapter in the textbook. The scenario uses a personal approach. Emphasis is on the aspects of accounting in that part or chapter that involve people, forms, procedures, and/or equipment. Other career education information is included from the *Dictionary of Occupational Titles*.

Vocabulary All accounting terms are in red in the textbook and are defined at that point. Then, they are listed at the end of the chapter under ''The Language of Business'' section in the order in which they appear in the chapter. In this way, students can easily locate the word in the chapter. In addition, such a listing gives a brief outline of the content covered in the chapter. Various vocabulary-building activities, such as crossword puzzles, are included in the *Working Papers*.

Accounting Concepts, Principles, and Controls The program teaches students the fundamental accounting concepts, principles, and controls. The text is based on generally accepted accounting principles, Accounting Principles Board (APB) Opinions, and statements of financial accounting standards. These are accounting principles accepted by the accounting profession. Accounting concepts and accounting principles are included in the topic of the textbook where they are relevant.

The subsystems in Part 2 emphasize internal controls in an accounting system. Students are taught that subsystems are designed to include internal controls for safeguarding assets, checking accuracy, promoting honesty, and encouraging efficiency and speed in processing data.

Equation/Cycle Approach The equation/cycle approach emphasizes the importance of the three basic accounting elements, and then presents accounting content following the sequential steps of the accounting cycle. It presents the analysis of transactions using the common language of increases and decreases.

The equation/cycle approach overcomes the disadvantages and shortcomings of the balance sheet/equation approach, which introduces the financial statements out of sequence and fails to cover the complete accounting cycle. The equation/cycle approach takes students through the entire accounting cycle in sequence, up to closing the ledger. Thus, students' difficulty in understanding closing is greatly reduced since they are presented with the reasoning behind closing the ledger before having to record the closing entries.

VISUALIZING THE ACCOUNTING SYSTEM

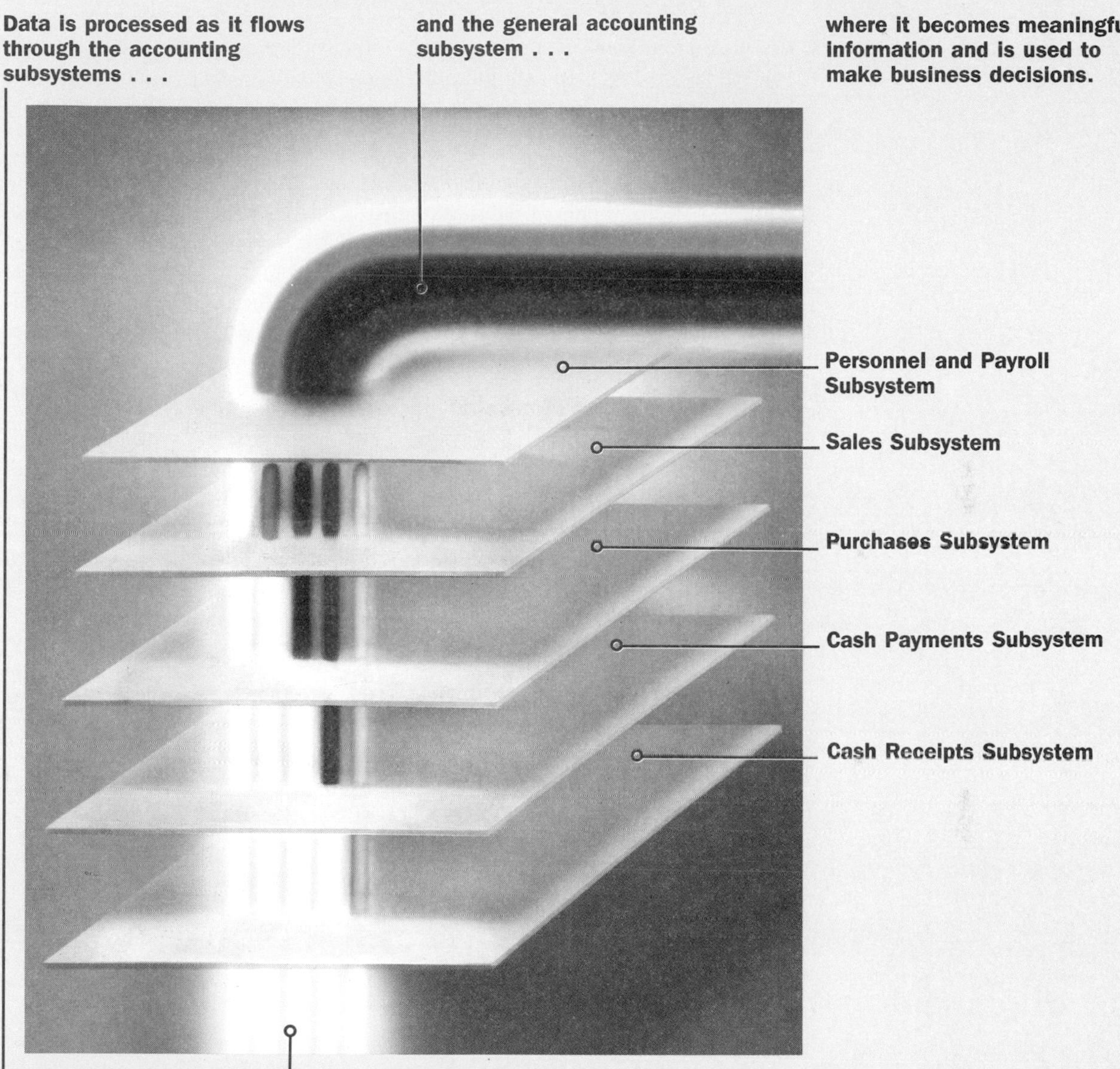
Data is processed as it flows through the accounting subsystems . . .
and the general accounting subsystem . . .
where it becomes meaningful information and is used to make business decisions.
Personnel and Payroll Subsystem
Sales Subsystem
Purchases Subsystem
Cash Payments Subsystem
Cash Receipts Subsystem

This approach also presents the concept of accounts much earlier, including extending accounts into revenue and expenses and the Income Summary account prior to encountering debits and credits. Thus, the equation/cycle approach presents the complete picture of closing entries and accumulating net income in the accounting cycle.

Systems The entire program follows an accounting systems approach. This approach traces the flow of data in a continuous sequence from its origin to its ultimate use. Flowcharts are used to show this sequence and flow of data. No business activity is treated as an isolated event. Coverage is from source documents to financial statements.

The concept of an accounting system is developed throughout. In Part 1, systems are presented in a service business using the equation with increases and decreases, as well as a journal-ledger system. In Part 2, the accounting system involves special journals and subsidiary ledgers in a merchandising business.

Subsystems Most accounting systems have a number of subsystems to process specific kinds of data. Six subsystems are presented in Part 2: cash receipts, including coverage of bank cards; cash payments; purchases on credit; sales on credit; personnel and payroll, including computation of state income tax; and general accounting, emphasizing the interpretation of financial statements and including coverage of control of internal transactions, ratios, and budgeting.

Interpretation of Financial Information The interpretation of financial information is emphasized throughout the program. In Part 1, students first learn to interpret accounting data within the accounting cycle, as well as to interpret the results between two accounting periods. Students learn that accounting cycle activities are continuous from one accounting period to the next. As a result, they study the closing procedures for one accounting period and begin work for the next accounting period. In addition, interpretation of financial information is expanded to include comparative financial statements.

Computerized Accounting New to this edition are two chapters, entitled Computer Explorations, that introduce students to computerized accounting. Students are given an overview of the types of computer equipment and types of programs that they are likely to encounter when they enter the business world. The concept of automated data processing is integrated throughout the textbook. Photographs portray people at work using both manual and automated data processing methods. Notes for the teacher point out other appropriate areas in which automated accounting can be introduced.

Components of the Program

Accounting: Systems and Procedures consists of several components that complement the basic textbook by reinforcing learning. Each component is designed to correlate with teaching and learning stages throughout the instructional period. Also available is a variety of computerized activities designed to give students hands-on experience with microcomputers. All of the computerized activities are based on the methodology used in the textbook. The components supplementing the textbook are described below.

Textbooks The textbook is divided into two parts. In addition to this textbook containing Parts 1 and 2, Part 1 is available by itself in a softcover version. Having both versions available enables teachers to choose the materials best suited to their classroom needs.

Part 1 uses the accounting equation/cycle approach to teach students basic accounting theory and applications. Two accounting periods are used to illustrate the steps of the accounting cycle. Exercise Plus, a single proprietorship, is used as an example of a service business. The role of accounting in business and the economic, social, and consumer aspects of accounting are described. The ten-column worksheet and a simple adjustment are also presented. Banking activities and petty cash activities are also included to help students prepare for employment and to help them in their personal financial management.

Part 2 introduces six accounting subsystems. This is done using a merchandising business, Computer Age. Cash receipts, cash payments, purchases on credit, sales on credit, personnel and payroll, and general accounting are covered. The worksheet and end-of-period adjustments are shown in relation to the complete accounting cycle. Each subsystem describes the people, forms, procedures, and equipment used to control the subsystem. Career titles and *Dictionary of Occupational Titles* reference numbers and descriptions are included. Flowcharts for each subsystem are included so that students can visualize the accounting subsystem. Uncollectible accounts, depreciation, accruals and deferrals, and the combination journal are presented in the last three chapters of Part 2.

Teacher's Edition A teacher's edition, which is new with this edition of the program, should prove to be an invaluable tool. It contains the entire student textbook, page for page, with annotations and cross-references for the teacher overprinted in blue. A special commentary section, which appears only in the teacher's edition, provides teaching assistance in the form of comprehensive material on organizing the accounting course. In addition, an overview of each chapter and teaching pointers for each chapter are included. The answers to the review questions and management cases at the end of each chapter are also located in the commentary section.

Working Papers There are two workbooks, one for each part of the textbook. These workbooks contain the working papers needed to complete the exercises, topic problems, chapter problems, and projects found in the textbook. They also contain selected problems to supplement the extensive problem material in the textbook. The workbooks also include ''Check Your Reading'' exercises and exercises on accounting concepts and principles.

Each *Working Papers* workbook has a teacher's edition, which is an exact copy of the workbook with the solutions printed in bright red.

Manual Accounting Applications There are three manual accounting applications. Two are practice sets to be used by the students individually. The third is a simulation to be used by several students working together.

All-Star Professionals, the service business practice set, involves completing work for an entire accounting cycle. Banking and petty cash activities are also included. This practice set is intended to be used after Part 1.

The Grandstand practice set involves a merchandising business and includes subsystems for cash receipts, cash payments, purchases, sales, personnel and payroll, and general accounting. It is intended to be used after Chapter

14 of Part 2. Both applications have separate teacher's manuals and keys which include teaching suggestions, progress sheets, solutions to the practice set, and suggested solutions to the management cases.

The *Sun-N-Ski* simulation involves a merchandising business that sells athletic equipment. It covers the complete accounting cycle for a merchandising business, special journals and ledgers, and payroll procedures. In the last week of the simulation, the books are closed and financial statements prepared. The accounting information is interpreted and applied in making the decisions called for by the management cases in the simulation. The number of students working in the *Sun-N-Ski* group is flexible and can vary from five to nine. Any number of groups can work on *Sun-N-Ski* in a classroom. *Sun-N-Ski* is intended to be used after Chapters 9 to 14 of Part 2 have been studied. *Sun-N-Ski* has a separate teacher's operating manual.

Microcomputer Tutorial The *Microcomputer Tutorial* provides questions on a chapter-by-chapter basis that test the student's understanding of the material learned in a particular chapter. It gives students immediate feedback about the accuracy of their answers, and refers them to a specific textbook page if they need to study the material further. It is an excellent tool for review and reinforcement.

Computerized Accounting Applications *All-Star Professionals,* the service business practice set, and *The Grandstand,* the merchandising business practice set, are both available in computerized versions. Each computerized version is a continuation of the activities in the manual sets. Any computerized versions can be completed instead of or in addition to the manual set. The practice sets both contain complete instructions for doing the work on a microcomputer, a narrative of transactions, and detachable source documents. Teacher's manuals are available for both that contain teaching suggestions and complete solutions in the form of computer printouts.

Applications Disk The applications disk can be used to complete the two projects in the text. A user's guide provides instructions for running the software, input sheets that can be duplicated for student use, and keys to the projects in the form of computer printouts.

Evaluation Manual An *Evaluation Manual* containing objective tests, progress tests, and comprehensive tests is available. The tests are competency-based, and are correlated with the chapter goals given in the textbook and the topic goals given in the *Source Book*. The tests are used to evaluate the student's performance against the goals. Solutions to the tests are included in the *Evaluation Manual*.

Microcomputer Test Bank A computerized test bank, entitled *Computerized Objective Tests,* contains 25 objective questions for each chapter. These are the questions given in the Objective Tests section in the *Evaluation Manual*. Multiple versions of a test can be printed out, with each version containing the questions in a different sequence. Up to five questions can be added for each chapter. An answer key for each test can be printed out. The user's guide contains complete directions for operating the program.

Source Book The *Source Book* provides a comprehensive guide to teaching the textbook. Complete lesson plans, teaching suggestions, and time schedules for each chapter in the text are included. Transparency masters of commonly used accounting forms are also provided.

Other Teacher's Tools As noted already, there is a teacher's edition of the textbook, a teacher's edition for each of the two *Working Papers,* teacher's manuals and keys for each of the two manual and two computerized practice sets, a guide for the applications disk, a guide for the microcomputer tutorial, and a teacher's operating manual for *Sun-N-Ski*.

Special Features

Included in the special features of *Accounting: Systems and Procedures,* Fifth Edition, are the following.

Readability The authors have used a simple, direct style of writing. All technical accounting vocabulary terms are printed in red and are defined at that point. Marginal notes and illustrations are used to review, illustrate, and provide additional detail to text discussions. Color is used schematically to improve readability.

Vocabulary The authors believe that understanding accounting terms is essential for success in accounting. Therefore, accounting vocabulary is shown in red in the text and defined at that point. It is also listed in ''The Language of Business'' section at the end of each chapter.

Marginal Notes and Illustrations The marginal notes identify key terms, ideas, rules, controls, and formulas. These notes provide a valuable aid for reinforcing reading, completing problems, and reviewing for tests. Students and teachers report that marginal notes are often used to refresh their memories about an accounting control, concept, principle, or procedure. The marginal illustrations visually reinforce the content without interrupting the student's reading of the text. In many instances, marginal illustrations highlight specific areas of larger illustrations, serving as a reference to illustrations previously shown. As a result, students do not have to turn back and forth among pages.

Accounting Concepts and Accounting Principles The basic concepts of accounting and the generally accepted accounting principles from the FASB are included at the end of each topic in the textbook.

Projects Two projects are provided at appropriate intervals in the textbook. These projects enable students to integrate and apply the concepts, principles, and procedures they have learned in preceding chapters. The projects are longer than topic and chapter problems but shorter than the practice sets. They can be completed either manually or by using the software that is available with the program.

Chapter Problems The chapter problems are designed to show business operations as a continuous process. As students learn new accounting concepts and procedures, chapter problems are assigned that tap previous learning and build on learning gained in earlier chapter problems. This unique feature prepares students to work on projects, practice sets, and the accounting simulation.

Management Cases As a further check of mastery, but especially to enable students to understand the purpose of what they have learned, management cases are provided at the end of every chapter. These cases require students to apply their knowledge in a realistic business situation. Students must analyze and interpret financial information and then make a critical decision, in the same way business managers must. These cases also underscore how managers use accounting information to direct and control the operations of a business. Because these cases are sufficiently detailed, answers will usually vary, just as they would in actual business situations.

David H. Weaver
Edward B. Brower
James M. Smiley
Virginia A. Rose

Acknowledgments

The authors want to express sincere thanks to the following accounting educators who provided much useful input during the preparation of *Accounting: Systems and Procedures,* Fifth Edition.

Susan G. Anderson
Portside Vocational-Technical School
Port Allen, Louisiana

Lloyd Beasley
Cabot High School
Cabot, Arkansas

Gerald A. Burton
New Holstein High School
New Holstein, Wisconsin

James Cox
John F. Kennedy High School
San Antonio, Texas

Robert Cox
Corona del Sol High School
Tempe, Arizona

Patricia Fordham
Utah Vocational Education
Salt Lake City, Utah

David E. Gynn
Kent Roosevelt High School
Kent, Ohio

Ralph Heatherington
Wheaton Central High School
Wheaton, Illinois

Mary Jo Jensen
Rutledge College
Springfield, Missouri

Joyce Keefer
Moorpark High School
Moorpark, California

Susanne Mackey
Anchorage Community College
Anchorage, Alaska

Robert M. Marra
Maine South High School
Park Ridge, Illinois

Sheldon R. Mead
Hackensack High School
Hackensack, New Jersey

Judy A. Oglesby
Falls Church High School
Falls Church, Virginia

Scott Peterson
Columbia Heights High School
Columbia Heights, Minnesota

Mildred Polisky
Formerly Milwaukee Area Technical Institute
Milwaukee, Wisconsin

Betty Rice
J. J. Pearce High School
Richardson, Texas

Jacquelin Steinberger
Trimble Technical High School
Fort Worth, Texas

Connie Stubbe-Petlack
Workman High School
City of Industry, California

Sister Margaret Clare Ragel
Boylan High School
Rockford, Illinois

Barbara Trent-Langdon
Franklin Heights High School
Columbus, Ohio

Paul V. Will
Parker Senior High School
Janesville, Wisconsin

Carol Yacht
Beverly Hills High School
Beverly Hills, California

William Zahurak
Community College of Allegheny County
Pittsburgh, Pennsylvania

PART 1

Basic Accounting

¡*Saludos, estudiantes de contabilidad*! Do you know what the last sentence means? It is written in Spanish and means "Greetings, accounting students!" Here is another sentence: Bring me the *income statement* that summarizes *revenue, expenses*, and *net income* for the *accounting period* ended June 30. Did you understand the last sentence? Probably not. Why? Because you have not studied accounting. You have not studied the very special language that includes terms like revenue, expenses, net income, and accounting period.

The above discussion suggests some of what you will study in Part 1 and throughout the course. You will study the language of business—the terms used by owners and managers as they talk about their businesses. The same terms will become a part of your business vocabulary. And, you will learn that accounting is a system used to change data into meaningful information. You will learn that accounting is an information system.

Think for a moment about all the activity completed by a local business—dozens of sales are made each day; merchandise is purchased; bills are paid; employees are paid; equipment is operated; letters are received, written, and filed. Each of these activities causes many numbers and words to be created. The numbers and words created by business activity are called *data*. However, unorganized data is not useful—it is just lots of numbers and words. The system used to change numbers and words from data to something useful is known as an *information system*.

When an information system is processing words, it is known as a *word processing system*. When it is processing numbers, it is known as a *data processing system*. When the numbers are financial data, the information system is known as an *accounting system*. In Part 1, you will learn how to process data through an accounting system.

In Part 1 you will also be introduced to a business owned by Lisa Long that operates under the name of Exercise Plus. This business sells health and physical fitness services to its customers and keeps its accounting records manually. Thus you will begin your study of accounting by learning about a service business that uses a manual accounting system. As you progress, you will study other types of businesses and accounting systems, including computerized accounting systems.

One final comment before you begin: Exercise Plus collects information about its business activity in accounts. (You will learn about accounts in Chapter 1.) To help you find the number for a particular account, the chart of accounts used by Exercise Plus is found below.

Amusez-vous bien, des élèves de comptabilité! The last sentence is in French and means "Have fun, accounting students!"

EXERCISE PLUS
CHART OF ACCOUNTS

Assets

101 Cash
102 Petty Cash
103 Accts. Rec./Carmen Saldi
104 Accts. Rec./Talbot Industries
108 Supplies
111 Furniture
112 Exercise Equipment

Liabilities

201 Accts. Pay./Shone Products
202 Accts. Pay./XYZ Repairs

Owner's Equity

301 Lisa Long, Capital
399 Income Summary

Revenue

401 Sales

Expenses

501 Advertising Expense
502 Delivery Expense
503 Miscellaneous Expense
504 Repairs Expense
505 Salaries Expense
506 Supplies Expense

CHAPTER

1

The Language of Business

Accounting terms, concepts, and principles are the common language used to communicate financial information. This is why accounting is often called the language of business. In this introductory chapter you will learn how the basic elements of accounting and the accounting equation are used to provide financial information.

CHAPTER GOALS

After studying Chapter 1, you will be able to:

1. Define the terms listed in "The Language of Business" section on page 19.
2. Explain the accounting concepts and principles in this chapter related to the elements of accounting and the basic accounting equation.
3. Classify business items as either assets, liabilities, or owner's equity.
4. Use the accounting equation to show the relationship between the assets, liabilities, and owner's equity of a business.
5. Demonstrate the procedure for checking the equality of the accounting equation.
6. Show how a balance sheet follows the form of the accounting equation in reporting the financial condition of a business.

Accounting is the process of recording, classifying, and summarizing financial information. Accounting terms and concepts are used in preparing financial records for businesses. These same terms and concepts are also used in reporting and analyzing the financial results from operating the businesses. In fact, accounting terms and concepts are the common language used to communicate financial information from one person to another. Thus, accounting is often called "the language of business."

Some accounting terms have very specific meanings in accounting. In this textbook, such terms are highlighted to help you understand the language of business. Similarly, the basic concepts and principles of accounting are emphasized and highlighted to help you develop a broad understanding of the field of accounting.

A *profit-making organization* is known as a business. There are three main types of businesses. A *service business* sells services (such as beauty salons, dry cleaners, and airlines). A *merchandising business* sells goods (such as food markets and automobile dealers). A *manufacturing business* produces goods (such as automobiles). Some organizations are nonprofit. A *nonprofit organization* supplies certain benefits to society. Examples of nonprofit organizations are cities and states, schools, and hospitals.

The same terms are used in presenting financial information for any business, regardless of its size or type of organization. Information for a large corporation such as General Motors is presented in the same terms as information for medium or small businesses such as your local grocery store. The terms and concepts you learn in accounting can be applied to any business.

Accounting also plays a role in our personal and social lives. Each of us must keep records for income taxes. Our social organizations, such as clubs and schools, must also have financial information to operate successfully. Citizens are asked to vote on issues that involve accounting terms and concepts. As a result, it is important for everyone to understand the language of business.

TOPIC 1

The Elements of Accounting

Elements of Accounting
- Assets
- Liabilities
- Owner's equity

What are the elements of accounting? Accounting is based on three elements: assets, liabilities, and owner's equity. These three elements are explained in this topic.

Every business needs economic resources to operate. *Economic resources* is a general term that describes the items needed to start and operate a business. (These items might include money, buildings, equipment, and trucks.) In accounting, the term for economic resources is *assets*.

Businesses get their economic resources (assets) from two sources. The owner may invest personal money or goods such as furniture. Or the owner may borrow money from others. In accounting, the term *owner's equity* refers to that portion of the economic resources contributed by the owner. The term *liabilities* refers to that portion of the economic resources obtained by borrowing. You will learn more about assets, liabilities, and owner's equity in the discussion on the following pages.

Concept: Economic Resources
Every business, regardless of type, size, or ownership, needs economic resources to operate. In accounting, these economic resources are called assets.

Assets

What is the meaning of assets, the first accounting element? **Assets** are things of monetary value that a business owns. The assets that a business owns depend on the nature of the business. For example, a department store's assets would include counters, racks, and shelves needed to store and display the goods it has to sell.

Although there are many kinds of assets, accountants generally recognize six major categories. These are cash, receivables, inventories, plant and equipment, natural resources, and intangible assets. The latter two are studied in advanced accounting. The other four categories of assets will be discussed below.

Major Categories of Assets
- Cash
- Receivables
- Inventories
- Plant and equipment

Cash One of the most common assets is cash. **Cash** includes not only coins and currency but also checks and money orders that have been received from others. Cash also includes money deposited in bank accounts.

Receivables Receivables are another common business asset. **Receivables** are amounts of money to be collected in the future. Many businesses do not immediately receive all or part of the money owed to them. Until a receivable is collected, the business has a legal right or claim against someone else's assets. As a result of this claim, all receivables are assets.

The most common types of receivables are accounts receivable and notes receivable. **Accounts receivable** are the total amount to be collected from customers to whom goods and services are sold on credit. In accounting the term *credit* means buying, selling, or borrowing with a promise to pay within a period of time. Thus, selling on credit means that goods or services are given to the customer but the seller will not receive payment until a future date.

Each account receivable is an asset because it is a claim against the customer's property until the customer pays the amount owed. For the same reason, notes receivable are assets. A **note receivable** is a writ-

Goods on hand for sale, such as a store's inventory of clothing, are considered assets of a business.

ten promise signed by the customer to pay the business a sum of money at a future date.

■ Inventories **Inventories** are goods that a business has on hand to sell or goods that will be used to operate the business. For instance, ten-speed bicycles, blue jeans, and roller skates are examples of inventories a department store might have on hand for sale.

Supplies are another important type of business inventory. They are considered inventory because they are materials to be used in the operation of the business. Paper, pencils, and packing crates are examples of supplies. (Another kind of inventory, goods used for the manufacture of other goods, is studied in advanced accounting.)

■ Plant and Equipment **Plant and equipment** are assets used over a long period of time to operate the business. Examples of plant and equipment assets are buildings, land, machinery, office or store equipment, and trucks.

■ Asset Accounts

Every business needs to keep records for each of its assets. For example, a separate record is kept to show how much cash the business has. As you will see in later chapters, the record should also show how the amount of cash changes. Cash will increase and decrease. All of these changes are recorded in an account. An **account** is a record of the financial details for each asset, liability, or owner's equity item.

In accounting, similar items are grouped together in a single account. For example, a record of all the coins, currency, money orders, and checks the business has on hand plus the money it has deposited in banks is recorded in the Cash account. Supplies, such as paper, pencils, and pens, are recorded in the Supplies account. Desks, chairs, and tables are assets that are recorded in the Furniture account.

Assets are only one element of accounting. As you learn more about assets and the other two elements, you will see that accounts are kept for each element.

You are going to learn about the elements of accounting through a small business owned by Lisa Long. The business is called Exercise Plus. This business does not produce or sell goods. It sells services. Specifically, Exercise Plus develops exercise, diet, and health programs for its customers.

EXERCISE PLUS

- DIET/NUTRITION COUNSELING
- EXERCISE PROGRAMS, INCLUDING AEROBIC CLASSES
- HEALTH CLUB
- RELAXATION PROGRAMS FOR TEENS AND ADULTS

"YOUR FITNESS SPECIALISTS"

3010 SOUTH FIFTH STREET
555-1234

The assets of Exercise Plus are shown in four accounts. The Cash account totals $9,000, the Accounts Receivable account $1,000, the Furniture account $3,000, and the Exercise Equipment account $9,000. The monetary value of the total assets the business owns is $22,000, as shown in the margin.

Exercise Plus
Assets

Cash	*$ 9,000*
Accounts Receivable	*1,000*
Furniture	*3,000*
Exercise Equipment	*9,000*
Total Assets	*$22,000*

Concept: Account
A record of the changes in the accounting elements is kept in an account. A separate account is kept for each asset, liability, or owner's equity item.

Exercises A and B on page 11 may be completed at this point.

Liabilities

What is the meaning of liabilities, the second accounting element? Liabilities are debts that a business owes. Some of a business's assets may be obtained by borrowing from others. For example, a business may borrow money from a bank and then use the money to buy assets, such as trucks. When the business borrows the money, it incurs a liability for the amount of the loan.

Borrowing can also take place in other ways. A business may buy a typewriter from a dealer on credit and promise to pay for the typewriter sometime in the future. Buying on credit means that goods or services are received by the buyer but the buyer will pay for them later.

The one to whom the debt is owed is called the *creditor*. In the example just given, the typewriter dealer is the creditor. The creditor has a legal claim against the assets of the business until the business pays its debts. The business, in turn, has incurred liabilities for the amount it owes to the typewriter dealer.

Most businesses have liabilities. They frequently find it easier to buy on credit than to pay cash immediately. For example, most new-car dealerships have liabilities for the cars they hold for sale. Very few dealers could pay cash for the cars before they sell them.

Exercise Plus has liabilities. It bought furniture for $3,000 and equipment for $1,000 from Shone Products on credit. Shone Products accepted a promise from Exercise Plus to pay the $4,000 in the future.

Exercise Plus now owes Shone Products $4,000 for the items bought on credit. Until Exercise Plus pays this debt, Shone Products has a claim of $4,000 against Exercise Plus's assets. Exercise Plus, therefore, has a liability of $4,000.

Liability Accounts

In accounting, liabilities are identified by the word *payable*. **Payables** are amounts owed (debts) to be paid in the future. For example, an amount borrowed from a bank is called a **loan payable**. The amounts owed to creditors for goods or services bought on credit are called **accounts payable**. A written promise to pay a creditor a specific amount in the future is called a **note payable**. A long-term debt that involves the pledge of property as security is called a **mortgage payable**.

Principal Types of Liabilities
- Loan payable
- Accounts payable
- Note payable
- Mortgage payable (long-term debt)

Separate accounts are used to keep a record of each liability. When Exercise Plus bought the furniture and equipment on credit, the liability of $4,000 was recorded in an Accounts Payable account.

Exercise Plus
Liabilities

Accounts Payable *$4,000*

Concept: Claims of Creditors

Economic resources that are obtained by borrowing result in claims of creditors against the economic resources of the business. In accounting, claims of creditors are called *liabilities*.

Exercise C on page 11 may be completed at this point.

Owner's Equity

What is the meaning of owner's equity, the third accounting element? *Equity* (or **owner's equity**) is the financial interest of the owner in a business. It is the owner's claim against the assets.

Creditors, as you learned earlier, have legal claims against the assets of the business. The owner has a legal claim against the remaining assets. Thus, the owner's equity in a business is the difference between the total assets owned and the total liabilities owed.

Types of Owner's Equity

- Single proprietorship—owner's equity
- Partnership—partners' equity
- Corporation—stockholders' equity

In accounting, if there is more than one owner of the business, the term *equity* changes to identify the form of business ownership. How the meaning changes is shown in the following discussion of the three major forms of business ownership: single proprietorship, partnership, and corporation.

Single Proprietorship The **single proprietorship** is a business owned by one person. For example, Exercise Plus is a single proprietorship owned by Lisa Long. Owner's equity here means the financial interest of the owner in a single proprietorship.

Partnership In a **partnership**, ownership of a business is divided among two or more persons. In this case, the term *partners' equity* is used instead of *owner's equity*. Partners' equity is the financial interest of owners in a partnership.

Corporation A **corporation** is a business chartered under state law that has the legal right to act as a person. Usually a corporation is owned by many people. Owners of a corporation are known as stockholders or shareholders. In this case, the term *stockholders' equity* is used. Stockholders' equity is the financial interest of owners in a corporation.

COMPUTING OWNER'S EQUITY

Assets	*$22,000*
Less: Liabilities	*4,000*
Owner's Equity	*$18,000*

Exercise Plus
Owner's Equity

Lisa Long, Capital	*$18,000*

Owner's Equity Accounts

Let's look at the owner's equity of Exercise Plus—a single proprietorship. The total assets are $22,000, and the total liabilities are $4,000. The total liabilities of $4,000 are subtracted from the total assets of $22,000. The remaining $18,000 is the owner's equity.

The owner's equity account used to show the owner's investment in the business is called **capital**. Lisa Long's investment in Exercise Plus is $18,000. This is written as "Lisa Long, Capital $18,000," as shown in the margin.

Concept: Claims of Owner

Economic resources that are invested by the owner or owners result in claims of the owner or owners against the economic resources of the business. In accounting, the claim of the owner against the assets of a business is called *owner's equity*. (The term *owner's equity, partners' equity,* or *stockholders' equity* is used depending on the form of business ownership.)

Exercise D on this page may be completed at this point.

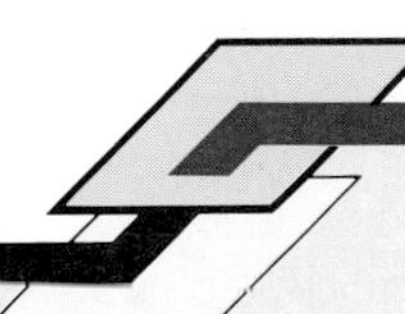

TOPIC 1 EXERCISES

EXERCISE A. Indicate which of the following items are assets. Refer to the text and margin notes on pages 7 and 8.

EXAMPLE: Tools—Yes

1. Furniture
2. Good weather
3. Supplies
4. Notes receivable
5. Good intentions
6. Equipment
7. Deposits in bank
8. Inventories
9. Buildings
10. Accounts receivable

EXERCISE B. Classify each of the following assets as either cash, receivables, inventory, or plant and equipment. Refer to the text and margin notes on pages 7 and 8.

EXAMPLE: Buildings—Plant and equipment

1. Amounts to be collected from customers
2. Money order
3. Store equipment
4. Machinery
5. A check
6. Computers
7. Goods on hand for sale
8. Land
9. Supplies
10. Trucks

EXERCISE C. Classify each of the following items as an asset or as a liability. Refer to the text and margin notes on pages 9 and 10.

EXAMPLE: Note payable—Liability

1. Accounts payable
2. Plant and equipment
3. Notes receivable
4. Supplies
5. Loan payable
6. Amounts due from customers
7. Office building
8. Furniture
9. Trucks
10. Cash

EXERCISE D. Classify each of the following items as an asset, a liability, or owner's equity. Refer to the text and margin notes on pages 10 and 11.

EXAMPLE: Office equipment—Asset

1. Money order
2. Note payable
3. Land
4. Loan payable
5. Accounts receivable
6. Paul Thomas (a customer)
7. Money on deposit with banks
8. Philip Klein (owner's investment)
9. Videodisc Inc. (a creditor)
10. Certified check

TOPIC 1 PROBLEMS

TOPIC PROBLEM 1. Financial Consultants, owned by Mary Costello, has the assets, liabilities, and owner's equity shown below. Compute the total assets and total liabilities. The total owner's equity is given.

Assets		Liabilities		Owner's Equity	
Cash	$6,000	Loans Payable	$2,400	Mary Costello, Capital	$15,100
Accounts Receivable	400	Accounts Payable	1,200		
Furniture	7,300				
Computer Equipment	5,000				
Total Assets	$?	Total Liabilities	$?		

TOPIC PROBLEM 2. Robert Strauss, a doctor, has the assets, liabilities, and owner's equity shown below. List the assets in one column and the liabilities in another column. Give the amounts for total assets, total liabilities, and owner's equity.

Cash	$ 6,000	Land	$20,000
Notes Payable	1,500	Office Equipment	4,000
Accounts Receivable	8,000	Loan Payable	28,000
Building	40,000	Supplies	500
Accounts Payable	2,000	Robert Strauss, Capital	72,000
Medical Equipment	25,000		

Total Assets $? Total Liabilities $? Total Owner's Equity $?

TOPIC 2

The Accounting Equation

How are assets, liabilities, and owner's equity related to each other? Assets represent the things of monetary value that a business owns. Liabilities are the claims of the creditors against those assets. (Creditors always have a claim against the assets of a business until all the liabilities are paid.) Owner's equity is the claim of the owner against the remaining assets of the business. What is not claimed by the creditors is claimed by the owners.

■ Relationship of the Elements of Accounting

Assets	=	**Claims Against Assets**		
Total Assets	=	Creditors' Claims	+	Owner's Claim

The relationship among the accounting elements can be summarized as follows. The total assets always equal the total claims against those assets—creditors' claims and owner's claims. The relationship is expressed in the **accounting equation**:

Assets = Liabilities + Owner's Equity

Left Side		Right Side
A	=	L + OE

The accounting equation states that total assets equal total liabilities plus total owner's equity. Accountants frequently shorten this statement by showing the equation as A = L + OE. Assets (A) are shown on the left side of the equation. Liabilities (L) and Owner's Equity (OE) are shown on the right side of the equation. Mathematically, the total of the left side of the equation must always equal the total of the right side. If no liabilities exist, then total assets equal the owner's equity.

The accounting equation for Exercise Plus on September 1 is as follows.

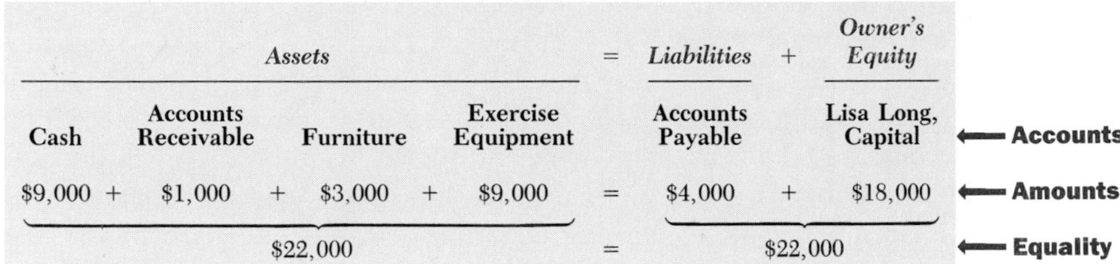

Assets				=	*Liabilities*	+	*Owner's Equity*	
Cash	Accounts Receivable	Furniture	Exercise Equipment		Accounts Payable		Lisa Long, Capital	⟵ **Accounts**
\$9,000 +	\$1,000 +	\$3,000 +	\$9,000	=	\$4,000	+	\$18,000	⟵ **Amounts**
	\$22,000			=		\$22,000		⟵ **Equality**

Assets	=	*Liabilities*	+	*Owner's Equity*
A	=	L	+	OE
\$22,000	=	\$4,000	+	\$?
\$22,000	=	\$4,000	+	\$18,000

The accounting equation shows Lisa Long's equity in Exercise Plus as \$18,000. The total assets of the business are \$22,000. The total liabilities are \$4,000. Thus, Lisa Long's equity in Exercise Plus is \$18,000 because the total liabilities and total owner's equity must equal total assets.

The accounting equation has three elements. As you can see illustrated in the table below, if you know any two elements, you can easily compute the amount of the missing element.

COMPUTING THE AMOUNT OF A MISSING ELEMENT

Cases	**Computation**					**Proof of Equation** A	=	L	+	OE
Know all three elements	A \$22,000	= =	L \$ 4,000	+ +	OE \$18,000	\$22,000	=	\$4,000	+	\$18,000
Know liabilities and owner's equity	L \$ 4,000	+ +	OE \$18,000	= =	A \$?	\$22,000	=	\$4,000	+	\$18,000
Know assets and liabilities	A \$22,000	– –	L \$ 4,000	= =	OE \$?	\$22,000	=	\$4,000	+	\$18,000
Know assets and owner's equity	A \$22,000	– –	OE \$18,000	= =	L \$?	\$22,000	=	\$4,000	+	\$18,000

Concept: Accounting Equation

There is always a relationship between assets and the claims against those assets. This relationship is expressed by the accounting equation: Assets equal Liabilities plus Owner's Equity (A = L + OE).

Exercise E on page 16 may be completed at this point.

Equality of the Equation

Why do total assets equal the total of liabilities plus owner's equity? The totals of the two sides of the accounting equation are always equal because these two sides are two views of the same business. Assets on the left side show what the business owns. Liabilities and owner's equity on the right side tell who supplied the assets and the amount each group supplied. Creditors and the owner have supplied everything that a business owns.

A	=	L	+	OE
$22,000	=	$4,000	+	$18,000
$22,000	=	$22,000		

The order in which the elements are listed in the equation is important. For example, liabilities come before owner's equity. This emphasizes that the claims of the creditors are recognized before the claims of the owner or owners. If a business cannot pay its debts when they become due, the business may be declared bankrupt. In this case, the assets of the business would be sold and the claims of the creditors would be paid before the owner or owners would receive any money.

In accounting, a **proof** is used to "prove" or "check" that the work is accurate. The accounting equation provides one such proof. You recall learning that the total of the left side of an equation must equal the total of the right side of the equation.

The equality of the left- and right-side totals is a proof or check that the totals are mathematically correct. This equality is used as a proof in all accounting work.

Notice, however, that the proof shows only that the totals are mathematically correct. It does not prove that the amounts are in the correct place in the equation. For example, suppose the amounts of the liabilities and owner's equity are switched—that is, liabilities are shown as $18,000 and owner's equity as $4,000. These amounts still equal $22,000 even though each amount is under the wrong element.

There is another expression used for equality in accounting. When two amounts agree, they are said to be *in balance*. Having the equation in balance means that the total of the amounts on the left side equals the total of the amounts on the right side of the equation. When two amounts do not agree in accounting, the amounts are said to be *out of balance*. Thus, if the two sides of the equation do not agree, the equation is said to be out of balance.

Concept: Equality of the Equation

A direct relationship exists between the accounts and the accounting equation. The total of the accounts on the left side of the equation must equal the total of the accounts on the right side of the equation. This keeps the equality of the equation.

Concept: Proving the Equation

The equality of the total assets and the total of the liabilities and owner's equity should be checked at regular intervals.

Exercise F on page 17 may be completed at this point.

The Accounting Equation and the Balance Sheet

What is the relationship between the accounting equation and the balance sheet? The accounting equation shows the relationship between the accounting elements. The **balance sheet** is a formal report, or financial statement, that lists the accounting elements. The balance sheet is easier to read than the accounting equation. It provides an itemized listing of the assets, liabilities, and owner's equity of a business for a specific date. The main purpose of the balance sheet is to present this information in an orderly fashion for the use of owners, creditors, and others interested in the financial standing of a business.

The form of a balance sheet is based on the accounting equation: Assets = Liabilities + Owner's Equity. Study the illustration below. It shows the relationship of the accounting equation and the balance sheet for Exercise Plus on September 1. Assets are shown on the left side of a balance sheet, and liabilities and owner's equity are shown on the right. The word *balance* emphasizes that the total of the figures on the left must equal the total of the figures on the right.

A balance sheet shows the kinds of assets owned. It also shows the kinds and amounts of liabilities and owner's equity.

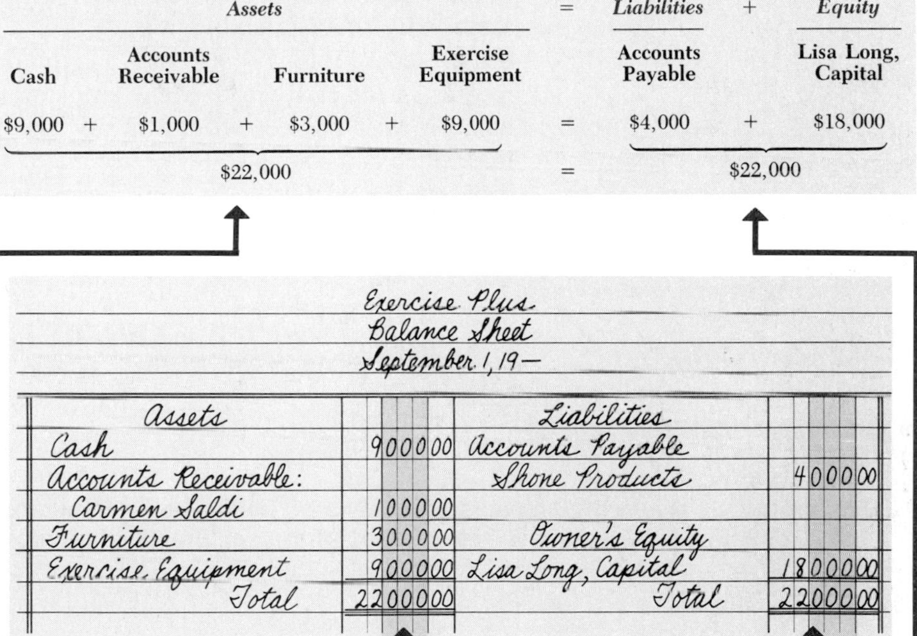

Assets
=
Liabilities
+
Owner's Equity
Cash
Accounts Receivable
Furniture
Exercise Equipment
Accounts Payable
Lisa Long, Capital
$9,000 + $1,000 + $3,000 + $9,000 = $4,000 + $18,000
$22,000 = $22,000

Exercise Plus
Balance Sheet
September 1, 19—

Assets		Liabilities	
Cash	9000 00	Accounts Payable	
Accounts Receivable:		Shone Products	4000 00
Carmen Saldi	1000 00		
Furniture	3000 00	Owner's Equity	
Exercise Equipment	9000 00	Lisa Long, Capital	18000 00
Total	22000 00	Total	22000 00

Notice that the format of a balance sheet differs from the format of the accounting equation in three important ways.

1. A balance sheet contains a heading that answers these questions: WHO? (the name of the business), WHAT? (the name of the statement), and WHEN? (the date of the statement). The date is extremely important because the amounts on the statement show the financial position of the business on that day.
2. The accounts receivable are listed by customer. The accounts payable are listed by creditor.

3. In the Owner's Equity section of a balance sheet, the word *capital* is used with the owner's name, rather than owner's equity. Owner's equity is a general term for the total financial interest of an owner. Capital, however, is the specific term for the investment of an owner. In the Owner's Equity section of the balance sheet for Exercise Plus, the phrase "Lisa Long, Capital" is used for the specific purpose of showing Lisa Long's investment in the business.

The preparation and interpretation of the balance sheet will be discussed in greater detail in later chapters. For now just remember that the balance sheet follows the accounting equation (A = L + OE) and that the total amounts on the left and right sides must be equal. In other words, a balance sheet, like the accounting equation, must balance.

Accuracy and Legibility

In performing accounting tasks, such as the preparation of a balance sheet, only accurate and legible work is acceptable. *Accuracy* means that all records are without error. *Legibility* means that the accounting records can be easily read. Many problems in accounting are caused by numbers that are not written neatly and legibly. Accounts may be misspelled and amounts may be recorded incorrectly. Legibility would decrease the possibility of these errors.

Exercise G on page 17 may be completed at this point.

TOPIC 2 EXERCISES

EXERCISE E. When the amounts of any two of the accounting elements are known, the third can be computed. Compute the missing amounts in the following accounting equations.

Assets	=	*Liabilities*	+	*Owner's Equity*
EX.: $2,000	=	*$ 400*	+	*$ 1,600*
1. $ 700	=	$ 50	+	$?
2. $ 400	=	$ 300	+	$?
3. $ 900	=	$?	+	$ 500
4. $ 850	=	$ 440	+	$?
5. $?	=	$ 98	+	$ 1,200
6. $12,340	=	$8,340	+	$?
7. $11,400	=	$?	+	$ 1,000
8. $?	=	$ 970	+	$11,450
9. $ 8,765	=	$ -0-	+	$?
10. $ 9,000	=	$?	+	$ 5,000

EXERCISE F. Compute the proof of the following accounting equations. Compute the left-side total and then compute the right-side total. Show the equality check.

Assets					=	*Liabilities*	+	*Owner's Equity*	**Equality Check**		
Cash		Accounts Receivable		Supplies		Accounts Payable		Capital	**A**	=	**L + OE**
EX.: $60	+	*$ 30*	+	*$ 10*	=	*$ 20*	+	*$ 80*	**$ 100**	=	**$ 100**
1. $600	+	$400	+	$400	=	$200	+	$1,200	$?		$?
2. $400	+	$500	+	$ 25	=	$370	+	$ 555	$?		$?
3. $620	+	$ 90	+	$ 30	=	$ 40	+	$ 700	$?		$?
4. $700	+	$ 50	+	$ 20	=	$ 30	+	$ 740	$?		$?
5. $800	+	$100	+	$ -0-	=	$ -0-	+	$ 900	$?		$?
6. $680	+	$250	+	$300	=	$500	+	$ 730	$?		$?
7. $700	+	$ -0-	+	$ -0-	=	$ -0-	+	$ 700	$?		$?
8. $750	+	$560	+	$150	=	$200	+	$1,260	$?		$?
9. $820	+	$ -0-	+	$200	=	$150	+	$ 870	$?		$?
10. $999	+	$111	+	$222	=	$332	+	$1,000	$?		$?

EXERCISE G. Answer each of the following questions. Refer to the text and illustration on pages 15 to 16.

1. What three questions does the heading of the balance sheet answer?
2. What group of accounts is shown on the left side of the balance sheet?
3. What groups of accounts are shown on the right side of the balance sheet?
4. Why are accuracy and legibility important in preparing a financial statement such as the balance sheet?

TOPIC 2 PROBLEMS

TOPIC PROBLEM 3. Dr. Robert Jorgen owns the Sawmill Health Center, a clinic that provides medical services. On December 15, 19—, the business had the assets and liability listed in the next column.

Arrange the assets, liability, and owner's equity for the Sawmill Health Center in the form of an accounting equation. Then, compute the figure for the owner's equity. Finally, prove the equality of the accounting equation.

Accounts Payable	$ 725
Cash	2,950
Accounts Receivable	800
Supplies	1,200

TOPIC PROBLEM 4. On November 30, the Willow Garage has the amounts in the accounting equation as shown below. Work through the equation to check for accuracy.

1. Correct any errors.
2. Prove the equality of the equation.

Assets						*Liabilities*	+	*Owner's Equity*	**Equality Check**		
Cash		Accounts Receivable		Supplies		Accounts Payable		Fred Willow, Capital	**A**	=	**L + OE**
$2,500	+	$690	+	$1,050	=	$50	+	$4,190	**$3,680**		**$4,240**
		Total Assets			=	Liabilities	+	Owner's Equity			
		$?			=	$?	+	$?	**$?**	=	**$?**

CHAPTER 1 REVIEW

CHAPTER SUMMARY

Accounting is the language of business. It is the process of recording, classifying, and summarizing financial information.

The three elements of accounting are assets, liabilities, and owner's equity. Assets are things of monetary value that a business owns, such as cash, receivables, inventories, and plant and equipment. Liabilities are the debts that a business owes. Owner's equity (or equity) is the financial interest of the owner or owners in the business. It is the claims of the owner or owners against the assets of the business. The relationship between these three elements is expressed in the accounting equation: A = L + OE.

The accounting equation must always be in balance. In other words, the total of the left side of the equation should always equal the total of the right side of the equation. To determine if the equation is in balance, the equality of the equation must be proved at regular intervals.

The accounting equation for Exercise Plus, a single proprietorship owned by Lisa Long, illustrates the relationship of assets, liabilities, and owner's equity for a business enterprise.

THE LANGUAGE OF BUSINESS

Here are some terms that make up the language of business. Do you know the meaning of each?

accounting
assets
cash
receivables
accounts receivable
note receivable
inventories
plant and equipment
account
liabilities
payables
loan payable
accounts payable
note payable
mortgage payable
owner's equity
single proprietorship
partnership
corporation
capital
accounting equation
proof
balance sheet

REVIEW QUESTIONS

1. What is meant by the statement, "Accounting is the language of business"?
2. What is the difference between a receivable and a payable?
3. Name two types of inventory.
4. Give three examples of liabilities.
5. In what way does the equity section of the equation vary according to the three basic forms of business ownership?
6. Who has first claim against the assets of a business? Who has second claim?
7. What is the accounting equation? Why must it always be in balance?

8. Why do total assets equal the total of liabilities plus owner's equity?
9. What is the purpose of the balance sheet? What information does it contain?
10. How does the balance sheet follow the format of the accounting equation?

CHAPTER PROBLEMS

Problems for Chapter 1 are given below. Write your answers on a separate sheet of paper unless you are using the workbook for this textbook. If you are using the workbook, do the problems in the space provided there.

CHAPTER PROBLEM 1-1. On June 1, 19—, Angela Price signed a contract to buy the Clark Parking Garage from Thomas Hall. For the purchase price of $200,000, Price received the following assets: Land, $50,000; Building, $130,000; and Equipment, $20,000. Price took $70,000 from her personal bank account to invest in the business. With this cash investment, she made a down payment of $40,000 and deposited the rest in Clark Parking Garage's bank account. A long-term loan was obtained from the First National Bank for the balance of the purchase price. Prepare an accounting equation to classify this data. Check the equality of the equation.

CHAPTER PROBLEM 1-2. Marshall's Radio Repairs is owned by Frank Marshall. On July 1, 19—, the business has the following assets and liabilities: Cash, $4,500; Accounts Payable, $600; Office Equipment, $5,000; Note Payable, $1,500; Accounts Receivable, $3,000. Compute the owner's equity. Prepare an accounting equation as of July 1, 19—. Check the equality of the accounting equation.

a. If on July 15 Frank Marshall's cash has increased to $8,500 and there are no changes in other elements of the accounting equation above, what is the amount in his Capital account? Write a new equation. Check the equality of the equation.

b. The accounting equation for Marshall's Radio Repairs on July 25 is shown below. As you can see, the equation has not been completed. Complete the equation by filling in the missing parts. Check the equality of the equation.

MARSHALL'S RADIO REPAIRS, Accounting Equation, July 25, 19—

Assets					*Liabilities*			+	*Owner's Equity*
Cash		Accounts Receivable		Office Equipment	=	Accounts Payable	Note Payable		Frank Marshall, Capital
$?	+	$3,000	+	$5,000	=	$-0-	+ $1,500	+	$14,400

Equality Check

A	=	L + OE
$?	=	$?

c. By July 31 Marshall's Radio Repairs had paid off all its debts. The accounting equation for Marshall's Radio Repairs on July 31 is illustrated below. The equation has not been completed. Complete the equation by filling in the missing parts. Check the equality of the equation.

MARSHALL'S RADIO REPAIRS, Accounting Equation, July 31, 19—

Assets				=	*Liabilities*	+	*Owner's Equity*
Cash		Accounts Receivable		Office Equipment			Frank Marshall, Capital
$8,500	+	$___?___	+	$5,000	= $-0-	+	$14,400

Equality Check		
A	=	**L + OE**
$___?___	=	**$___?___**

CHAPTER PROBLEM 1-3. The December 7 accounting equation for Fort Worth Real Estate contains errors. You have been asked to verify this accounting equation data.

a. Identify all the errors you locate in the equation shown below.

FORT WORTH REAL ESTATE, Accounting Equation, December 7, 19—

Assets					=	*Liabilities*	+	*Owner's Equity*
Note Payable		Office Equipment		Cash		Automobile		Alice Cole, Capital
$5,000	+	$9,000	+	$10,000	=	$9,000	+	$15,000

Equality Check		
A	=	**L + OE**
$24,000	=	**$24,000**

b. Prepare a corrected accounting equation. Check the equality of the equation.

c. After you complete your work, review it for accuracy.

MANAGEMENT CASES

Starting a Business. Many businesses fail because owners do not plan for sufficient cash to cover their costs. An owner needs to have enough money to cover items such as rent and salaries until the business becomes a thriving operation. If more money is needed, the owner must decide how much money can be borrowed and how much money must come from the owner's own investment.

CASE 1M-1. A brother and sister, Joseph and Ruth Chan, are starting separate businesses. Joseph has learned furniture building, repair, and refinishing. For the past three years, he has worked for a furniture refinishing shop. In six months, Joseph plans to open a small business—Joseph's Refinishing Shop. His business will repair and refinish furniture and will also build furniture on special order.

Ruth has passed the certified public accountant's examination and plans to open an accounting office. She will serve as an accountant for small businesses, prepare and file tax returns, and provide consulting services.

Who will need more assets to open a business, Joseph Chan or Ruth Chan? Explain.

CASE 1M-2. Dennis O'Rouke plans to open his own men's clothing shop. He has worked for five years as a salesclerk in Carl's Men's Shop. In addition to gaining sales experience, Mr. O'Rouke learned about men's fashion trends and how to work well with people. Carl Bernstein, the owner of the shop, also taught Mr. O'Rouke how to keep accounting records. Under Mr. Bernstein's guidance, Dennis O'Rouke gained valuable experience.

a. What advantages does Dennis O'Rouke have as an employee that he will not have when he becomes the owner of his own shop?

b. Why might Dennis O'Rouke prefer to own a business rather than be an employee?

c. What assets will Dennis O'Rouke need when he starts his own men's clothing shop?

CHAPTER

2

An Accounting Cycle Using the Accounting Equation

A business follows a sequence of steps to record, classify, and summarize financial information. This sequence is the *accounting cycle*. In this chapter you will study the accounting cycle in its most basic form.

CHAPTER GOALS

After studying Chapter 2, you will be able to:

1. Define the terms listed in ''The Language of Business'' section on page 51.
2. Explain the accounting concepts and principles in this chapter related to the effect of transactions on the accounting equation.
3. Record changes to the accounting equation caused by transactions.
4. Explain how sales and the cost of operating a business affect owner's equity.
5. Calculate net income or net loss for a business.
6. Transfer net income or net loss into the owner's Capital account.
7. Prove the equality of the accounting equation after transferring net income or net loss into the Capital account.
8. Process accounting information through the eight steps of the accounting cycle.

TOPIC 1

Effect of Transactions on Permanent Accounts

Will amounts in the accounting equation change? Yes, the amounts in the accounting equation change as a result of business transactions. A **transaction** is a financial event that affects one or more elements in the accounting equation. The term *financial* means that transactions must be stated in monetary terms (in dollar amounts). Due to the special nature of accounting, each transaction affects one or more elements in the accounting equation. Also, the accounting equation remains in balance after each transaction is recorded.

As you will recall from Chapter 1, Exercise Plus had the following amounts in its accounting equation as it started business on September 1.

	Assets							=	*Liabilities*	+	*Owner's Equity*
Accounts →	Cash		Accounts Receivable		Furniture		Exercise Equipment		Accounts Payable		Lisa Long, Capital
Amounts →	$9,000	+	$1,000	+	$3,000	+	$9,000	=	$4,000	+	$18,000
Equality (Balance) →			$22,000					=		$22,000	

The accounting equation as of September 1.

■ Using Accounts

Businesses use accounts to record the changes caused by transactions over a period of time. Some accounts are permanent accounts. The amounts in **permanent accounts** are carried forward from one period to another. Thus, the amounts in these accounts at the end of a period are the beginning amounts for the next period. Accounts for assets, liabilities, and owner's equity Capital in the accounting equation fit in this category. Thus, the asset accounts, liability accounts, and owner's equity Capital account in the September 1 accounting equation for Exercise Plus are permanent accounts.

Some accounts are temporary accounts. A **temporary account** gathers data for only one period at a time. After a period of time the data is moved out of the temporary account and into a permanent account. At the beginning of any accounting period, therefore, there will be a "zero" amount in a temporary account. Temporary accounts will be discussed at greater length later in this chapter.

Exercise A on page 31 may be completed at this point.

■ Accounting Periods

A typical business is affected by hundreds, even thousands, of business transactions in a week, a month, or a year. Think of the numerous sales and purchases of goods and services that occur daily at a typical department store. The details of each transaction are not important to owners or managers. What is important, however, is a summary of transactions for a day, month, or some other time period. To "summarize" means to present data in condensed form. The September 1 accounting equation for Exercise Plus is one such summary. It lets Lisa Long know the balance of each of Exercise Plus's accounts without a lot of detail. Owners and managers need summaries to make business plans about future business operations. At least once a year a business must also provide a summary to the federal government for tax purposes.

The period of time for which a business summarizes its financial information is called its **accounting period**. The length of an accounting period varies from business to business. Typically, however, a business summarizes its accounts every month, every three months, or once every year.

A business may choose any accounting period to summarize its data. But the Internal Revenue Service and some other agencies require a business to report the results of its operations at least once a year. Once a business selects a specific accounting period, that period of time must be used in all following accounting periods. By using the same time period, managers and owners can compare the results of one accounting period with the results of another.

Exercise Plus has an accounting period of one month. The accounting equation on page 24 shows the amount in each account as it begins its accounting period for September. Any transaction in September will therefore affect the equation for the September accounting period.

Concept: Transaction

Transactions are financial events which cause the amounts in the accounting equation to change. Each transaction affects one or more of the accounting elements.

Concepts: Permanent Accounts; Temporary Accounts

Amounts in permanent accounts are carried forward from one period to another. Amounts in temporary accounts, on the other hand, are not carried forward from one accounting period to the next.

Concept: Accounting Period

The life of a business is divided into a series of accounting periods. The length of these accounting periods varies from business to business.

Asset Transactions

Which business transactions affect only asset accounts? Two transactions that affect only assets are buying an asset for cash and collecting an account receivable.

Buying Assets for Cash

When cash is paid for another asset, only one accounting element is affected—assets. The asset that is received increases and the asset Cash decreases. Let us look at an example of such a transaction.

On September 5, Exercise Plus decides to buy additional equipment for $4,000 in cash. A determination must now be made as to how this transaction affects the accounts. Determining which accounts are affected and how they are affected is called **analyzing a transaction**. The September 5 transaction for Exercise Plus is analyzed below.

Transaction	Analysis	Accounting Entry
September 5: Exercise Plus buys additional exercise equipment from Fitness Supplies Corporation and gives a check for $4,000 in payment.	▪ The asset *Exercise Equipment* increases by $4,000 because the business now owns more equipment. ▪ The asset *Cash* decreases by $4,000 because the business now has less money.	▪ Increase the asset *Exercise Equipment* by $4,000. ▪ Decrease the asset *Cash* by $4,000.

	Assets							=	*Liabilities*	+	*Owner's Equity*
	Cash		Accounts Receivable		Furniture		Exercise Equipment		Accounts Payable		Lisa Long, Capital
Previous Balance →	$9,000	+	$1,000	+	$3,000	+	$ 9,000	=	$4,000	+	$18,000
Effect of Transaction →	−4,000						+4,000				
New Balance →	$5,000	+	$1,000	+	$3,000	+	$13,000	=	$4,000	+	$18,000
Equality of Equation →	$22,000								$22,000		

Buying assets for cash.

The exchange of one asset for another asset does not change the total amount of the assets. Exercise Plus now has more equipment but less cash. The left side of the accounting equation still totals $22,000. The liabilities and owner's equity accounts are not affected by the transaction. Thus, the right side of the accounting equation still totals $22,000. The accounting equation is in balance following the September 5 transaction.

This transaction demonstrates points that apply when analyzing *any* transaction.

- The effects of each transaction are stated in dollar amounts.
- Each transaction affects at least two accounts.

- The accounting equation is in balance after each transaction is recorded.

Collecting Accounts Receivable When a customer pays all or part of a debt, a business is said to receive "cash on account." Cash that is received on account affects only one accounting element—assets. This is shown in the September 6 transaction below. The asset Cash increases, and the asset Accounts Receivable decreases. The accounting equation is still in balance.

Transaction	Analysis	Accounting Entry
September 6: Exercise Plus receives a check for $1,000 from Carmen Saldi on account. The money is to be applied against the amount Carmen Saldi owes Exercise Plus.	▪ The asset *Cash* increases by $1,000 because the business now has more money. ▪ The asset *Accounts Receivable* decreases by $1,000 because that amount is no longer due from customers.	▪ Increase the asset *Cash* by $1,000. ▪ Decrease the asset *Accounts Receivable* by $1,000.

Assets								=	*Liabilities*	+	*Owner's Equity*	
Cash		Accounts Receivable		Furniture		Exercise Equipment			Accounts Payable		Lisa Long, Capital	
$5,000	+	$1,000	+	$3,000	+	$13,000		=	$4,000	+	$18,000	← Previous Balance
+1,000		−1,000										← Effect of Transaction
$6,000	+	$ -0-	+	$3,000	+	$13,000		=	$4,000	+	$18,000	← New Balance
				$22,000				=		$22,000		← Equality of Equation

Collecting accounts receivable.

Liability Transactions

Do liability transactions affect only one element? Liability transactions usually affect more than one accounting element. In the following transactions, both assets and liabilities are affected.

Buying Assets on Credit Assets bought on credit are received when purchased but are not paid for until a future date. Buying an asset on credit creates a liability. This kind of transaction affects two accounting elements—assets and liabilities. Both of the elements increase, as shown in the transaction for September 7 that is analyzed on page 28.

With this increase in furniture, the total assets are now $24,000. Against these assets, the creditor (Shone Products) has a claim of $6,000. Owner's equity, which is not affected, is still $18,000. Thus, Exercise Plus now has total liabilities and owner's equity of $24,000. The accounting equation is in balance.

Transaction	Analysis	Accounting Entry
September 7: Exercise Plus buys additional furniture for $2,000 on credit from Shone Products. The creditor allows 30 days to pay this amount.	▪ The asset *Furniture* increases by $2,000 because the business now owns more furniture. ▪ The liability *Accounts Payable* increases by $2,000 because the business now owes more money.	▪ Increase the asset *Furniture* by $2,000. ▪ Increase the liability *Accounts Payable* by $2,000.

	Assets							=	*Liabilities*	+	*Owner's Equity*
	Cash		Accounts Receivable		Furniture		Exercise Equipment		Accounts Payable		Lisa Long, Capital
Previous Balance	$6,000	+	$ -0-	+	$3,000	+	$13,000	=	$4,000	+	$18,000
Effect of Transaction					**+2,000**				**+2,000**		
New Balance	$6,000	+	$ -0-	+	$5,000	+	$13,000	=	$6,000	+	$18,000
Equality of Equation				$24,000				=		$24,000	

Buying assets on credit.

Exercise B on page 31 may be completed at this point.

■ Returning Assets Bought on Credit When a business returns assets bought on credit and not yet paid for, two accounting elements are affected—assets and liabilities. Both elements decrease, as shown in the September 8 transaction below. Assets decrease be-

Transaction	Analysis	Accounting Entry
September 8: Exercise Plus returns furniture (one cabinet) bought for $500 on credit from Shone Products because it arrived in damaged condition.	▪ The asset *Furniture* decreases by $500 because the business now owns less furniture. ▪ The liability *Accounts Payable* decreases by $500 because the business now owes less money.	▪ Decrease the asset *Furniture* by $500. ▪ Decrease the liability *Accounts Payable* by $500.

	Assets							=	*Liabilities*	+	*Owner's Equity*
	Cash		Accounts Receivable		Furniture		Exercise Equipment		Accounts Payable		Lisa Long, Capital
Previous Balance	$6,000	+	$ -0-	+	$5,000	+	$13,000	=	$6,000	+	$18,000
Effect of Transaction					**−500**				**−500**		
New Balance	$6,000	+	$ -0-	+	$4,500	+	$13,000	=	$5,500	+	$18,000
Equality of Equation				$23,500				=		$23,500	

Returning assets bought on credit.

cause the business now has fewer assets. Liabilities decrease because the creditor has less claim against the assets. The accounting equation is still in balance.

■ Paying Liabilities When a business pays all or part of a debt in cash, the payment is said to be "on account." Note that the term *account* has several meanings in accounting usage. *Account* refers to the record of financial details for each asset, liability, or owner's equity item. However, *cash paid on account* means paying all or part of a debt. *Cash received on account* means receiving cash for all or part of a debt.

Paying a liability affects two accounting elements—assets and liabilities. Both elements decrease.

Transaction	Analysis	Accounting Entry
September 12: Exercise Plus writes a check for $4,000 to Shone Products on account. The payment is applied against the total amount owed to Shone Products.	▪ The asset *Cash* decreases by $4,000 because the business now has less money. ▪ The liability *Accounts Payable* decreases by $4,000 because the business now owes less money.	▪ Decrease the asset *Cash* by $4,000. ▪ Decrease the liability *Accounts Payable* by $4,000.

	Assets							=	*Liabilities*	+	*Owner's Equity*	
	Cash		Accounts Receivable		Furniture		Exercise Equipment		Accounts Payable		Lisa Long, Capital	
	$6,000	+	$ -0-	+	$4,500	+	$13,000	=	$5,500	+	$18,000	← Previous Balance
	−4,000								**−4,000**			← Effect of Transaction
	$2,000	+	$ -0-	+	$4,500	+	$13,000	=	$1,500	+	$18,000	← New Balance
				$19,500				=		$19,500		← Equality of Equation

Paying liabilities.

Owner's Equity Transactions

Can owner's equity increase or decrease at any time? Yes, the owner's equity can be increased or decreased at any time in the accounting period. To illustrate how owner's equity increases or decreases, we will analyze transactions that affect the owner's investment.

Exercise C on page 32 may be completed at this point.

■ Increasing the Owner's Investment Two elements are affected when the owner increases the investment in the business—assets and owner's equity. Both of the elements increase, as shown in the transaction on page 30. This transaction increases assets and owner's equity in the same amounts. Liabilities are unchanged. The accounting equation is in balance.

Transaction	Analysis	Accounting Entry
September 14: Lisa Long decides that Exercise Plus needs more cash for additional exercise equipment and furniture. She withdraws $13,000 from her personal savings account and deposits the cash in the business checking account.	▪ The asset *Cash* increases by $13,000 because the business now has more money. ▪ The owner's equity account *Lisa Long, Capital* increases by $13,000 because the owner now has increased her investment in the business.	▪ Increase the asset *Cash* by $13,000. ▪ Increase the owner's equity account, *Lisa Long, Capital* by $13,000.

	Assets					=	*Liabilities*	+	*Owner's Equity*
	Cash	Accounts Receivable	Furniture	Exercise Equipment			Accounts Payable		Lisa Long, Capital
Previous Balance →	$ 2,000 +	$ -0- +	$4,500 +	$13,000		=	$1,500	+	$18,000
Effect of Transaction →	**+13,000**								**+13,000**
New Balance →	$15,000 +	$ -0- +	$4,500 +	$13,000		=	$1,500	+	$31,000
Equality of Equation →		$32,500				=		$32,500	

Increasing the owner's investment.

■ **Decreasing the Owner's Investment** When the owner withdraws assets from the business, two elements are affected—assets and owner's equity. Both elements decrease. For example, when Lisa

Transaction	Analysis	Accounting Entry
September 21: Lisa Long withdraws $6,000 from the Exercise Plus checking account.	▪ The asset *Cash* decreases by $6,000 because the business now has less cash. ▪ The owner's equity account *Lisa Long, Capital* decreases by $6,000 because the owner now has decreased her investment in the business.	▪ Decrease the asset *Cash* by $6,000. ▪ Decrease the owner's equity account, *Lisa Long, Capital* by $6,000.

	Assets					=	*Liabilities*	+	*Owner's Equity*
	Cash	Accounts Receivable	Furniture	Exercise Equipment			Accounts Payable		Lisa Long, Capital
Previous Balance →	$15,000 +	$ -0- +	$4,500 +	$13,000		=	$1,500	+	$31,000
Effect of Transaction →	**−6,000**								**−6,000**
New Balance →	$ 9,000 +	$ -0- +	$4,500 +	$13,000		=	$1,500	+	$25,000
Equality of Equation →		$26,500				=		$26,500	

Decreasing the owner's investment.

Long withdraws $6,000 for her personal use on September 21, assets and owner's equity decrease by the same amount. Although the amount withdrawn was for Lisa Long's personal use, the transaction was recorded only in the business records for Exercise Plus. In accounting, a business exists separately from its owner. Each business must maintain a set of accounting records separate from other businesses and from the personal affairs of its owner. The individual business for which accounting records are kept is called an **accounting entity** (sometimes also referred to as a "business entity").

Concept: Accounting Entity
Each business must maintain a set of accounting records separate from other businesses and from the personal affairs of its owner or owners.

Exercise D on page 32 may be completed at this point.

TOPIC 1 EXERCISES

EXERCISE A. Answer the following questions about the accounting equation for Exercise Plus shown on page 24. Also, refer to the discussion "Using Accounts" on page 24 in answering the following questions.

1. What is the date of the accounting equation?
2. Name the asset accounts.
3. What is the title of the liability account?
4. What is the title of the owner's equity account?
5. Which accounts are considered "permanent accounts"?
6. What is the amount of the total assets?
7. What is the amount of the total liabilities?
8. Do the total assets equal the total of liabilities plus owner's equity?

EXERCISE B. The accounting equation for Molly's Wallpaper Service on March 31 is given below. Show what happens to the equation below as a result of each of the asset transactions for April. Use this procedure: First record the transaction. Then add or subtract to determine the new balance for each account. Then check the equality of the two sides of the equation. For further assistance, refer to the illustrations on pages 26 and 27.

EXAMPLE: Bought equipment for $200 in cash.

1. Received $500 from a customer on account.
2. Bought equipment for $250 in cash.
3. Returned furniture bought for $300 in cash.
4. Bought furniture for $75 in cash.

	Assets							=	*Liabilities*	+	*Owner's Equity*	**Equality Check**
	Cash		Accounts Receivable		Equipment		Furniture		Accounts Payable		Molly Troy, Capital	**A = L + OE**
	$1,900	+	$1,700	+	$1,400	+	$5,300	=	$3,300	+	$7,000	**$10,300 = $10,300**
EX.:	– *200*				+ *200*							
	$1,700	+	$1,700	+	$1,600	+	$5,300	=	$3,300	+	$7,000	**$10,300 = $10,300**

EXERCISE C. Continue with the accounting equation from Exercise B. Show what happens to the equation as a result of the following liability transactions. Check the equality of the equation after each transaction. For further assistance, review the illustration of liability transactions on page 29.

5. Bought furniture for $900 on credit.

6. Paid $100 to a creditor on account.

7. Bought equipment for $400 on credit.

8. Returned furniture bought for $450 on credit.

EXERCISE D. Continue with your accounting equation from Exercise C. Show what happens to the equation as a result of the following transactions affecting the owner's equity Capital account. Check the equality of the equation after each transaction. For further assistance, review the illustrations of the owner's equity transactions on page 30.

9. Molly Troy invested an additional $3,000 in the business.

10. Molly Troy withdrew $100 from the business for personal use.

TOPIC 1 PROBLEMS

TOPIC PROBLEM 1. Microcomputer Service is a single proprietorship owned by Irene La Rosa. The accounting equation for the business shows the following information.

Assets						=	*Liabilities*	+	*Owner's Equity*	**Equality Check**
Cash		Accounts Receivable		Equipment			Accounts Payable		Irene La Rosa, Capital	**A = L + OE**
$5,000	+	$200	+	$28,000		=	$7,000	+	$26,200	**$33,200 = $33,200**

Show what happens to the accounting equation for Microcomputer Service as a result of each of the September transactions below. Follow this procedure for each transaction. First, record the effects of the transaction. Then determine the account balances. After completing these tasks, check the equality of the accounting equation.

a. Bought equipment for $200 in cash.

b. Owner withdrew $1,000 from the business.

c. Bought equipment for $2,000 on credit.

d. Owner invested an additional $2,000 in the business.

e. Paid $1,000 to a creditor on account.

f. Returned equipment bought for $75 in cash.

g. Received $50 cash from a customer on account.

h. Returned equipment bought for $400 on credit.

TOPIC PROBLEM 2. Each of the following accounting equations was prepared after the completion of a transaction by the Lopez Trucking Company. Explain what happened in each transaction.

EXAMPLE: Donald Lopez started the business with a cash investment of $40,000.

	Assets					=	*Liabilities*			+	*Owner's Equity*
	Cash		Shop Equipment		Trucks		Accts. Pay./ Ace Garage		Accts. Pay./ Central Motors		Donald Lopez, Capital
EXAMPLE:	*+$40,000*										*+$40,000*
Trans. a					+$15,000				+$15,000		
New Balance	$40,000	+		+	$15,000	=		+	$15,000	+	$40,000
Trans. b	− 2,500		+$2,500								
New Balance	$37,500	+	$2,500	+	$15,000	=		+	$15,000	+	$40,000
Trans. c			+$1,000				+$1,000				
New Balance	$37,500	+	$3,500	+	$15,000	=	$1,000	+	$15,000	+	$40,000
Trans. d	− 1,000								− 1,000		
New Balance	$36,500	+	$3,500	+	$15,000	=	$1,000	+	$14,000	+	$40,000
Trans. e			− 500				− 500				
New Balance	$36,500	+	$3,000	+	$15,000	=	$ 500	+	$14,000	+	$40,000
Trans. f	+ 2,000										+ 2,000
New Balance	$38,500	+	$3,000	+	$15,000	=	$ 500	+	$14,000	+	$42,000
Trans. g	− 250						− 250				
New Balance	$38,250	+	$3,000	+	$15,000	=	$ 250	+	$14,000	+	$42,000
Trans. h	− 3,000										− 3,000
New Balance	$35,250	+	$3,000	+	$15,000	=	$ 250	+	$14,000	+	$39,000
Trans. i	− 500		+ 500								
New Balance	$34,750	+	$3,500	+	$15,000	=	$ 250	+	$14,000	+	$39,000
Trans. j	− 1,500								− 1,500		
New Balance	$33,250	+	$3,500	+	$15,000	=	$ 250	+	$12,500	+	$39,000

TOPIC 2

Effect of Transactions on Temporary Accounts

Is owner's equity affected only when the owner increases or decreases the amount of the business investment? No, owner's equity is also affected when a business sells goods and services or has an expense in operating a business. In this topic, we will look at revenue transactions and expense transactions for Exercise Plus for the month of September. You will see how these transactions increase or decrease owner's equity. Then, in Topic 3, you will see how these transactions are important in determining whether a business makes a net income or incurs a net loss.

■ Revenue Transactions

When a business sells goods or services, it receives cash or receivables from its customers. As a result of these sales, the left side of the accounting equation increases. This happens because the asset Cash increases or the asset Accounts Receivable increases. (The receivable that increases can also be a Note Receivable.) Remember that the total claims against the assets must always equal the total of the assets. Thus, the right side of the equation must increase by the same amount. Since liabilities are not affected, owner's equity must increase. The increase in owner's equity resulting from the inflow of assets from sales is called **revenue.**

Revenue From Sales for Cash or on Credit

Assets	= Liabilities +	Owner's Equity
+	0	+

Assets increase.
Liabilities are not affected.
Owner's equity increases.

A business may earn revenue by selling goods or services to customers for cash or credit. For instance, Exercise Plus earns revenue by selling memberships to individuals, families, and businesses for their employees. To analyze the effects of revenue transactions, we will now study the cash and credit sales made by Exercise Plus for September. The following transactions will show how revenue transactions increase owner's equity. Note that revenue is listed separately under owner's equity in the accounting equation. This is to distinguish revenue from capital, the owner's investment.

■ Revenue From Cash Sales Two elements are affected when a business sells services or goods for cash—assets and owner's equity. Both elements increase. For example, on September 26 Exercise Plus receives $4,000 in cash as revenue for sales of its services.

Transaction	Analysis	Accounting Entry
September 26: Exercise Plus receives $4,000 in cash as revenue from the sale of services during September.	▪ The asset *Cash* increases by $4,000 because the business now has more money. ▪ The owner's equity *Income Summary (Revenue)* increases by $4,000 because the business now has earned revenue.	▪ Increase the asset *Cash* by $4,000. ▪ Increase the owner's equity *Income Summary (Revenue)* by $4,000.

	Assets					= *Liabilities* +		*Owner's Equity*	
	Cash		Accounts Receivable	Furniture	Exercise Equipment		Accounts Payable	Lisa Long, Capital	Income Summary (Revenue)
Previous Balance →	$ 9,000 +		$ -0- +	$4,500 +	$13,000	=	$1,500 +	$25,000 +	$ -0-
Effect of Transaction →	+4,000								+4,000
New Balance →	$13,000 +		$ -0- +	$4,500 +	$13,000	=	$1,500 +	$25,000 +	$4,000
Equality of Equation →			$30,500			=		$30,500	

Receiving revenue from cash sales.

This transaction increases cash by $4,000. Thus, the left side of the accounting equation now shows total assets of $30,500. The total claims against the assets must always equal the total assets. Thus, the right side of the accounting equation must also increase by the same amount. Liabilities are not affected by this transaction. The owner's equity must increase by $4,000. Since the sale of services is not an investment, the Capital account is not used. Instead, a new owner's equity account, Income Summary, is used to increase owner's equity.

The Income Summary account is a temporary owner's equity account. As its name suggests, the **Income Summary account** summarizes data about a business's income (revenue less expenses equals net income) for one period at a time. (Expenses are covered later in this chapter.) More about the special function of the Income Summary account will be discussed in Topic 3.

Inflow of Cash

From Investment	From Sales
Increases	Increases
Capital account	Revenue account

Increases Owner's Equity

■ Revenue From Sales on Credit The sales of services on credit affects two accounting elements—assets and owner's equity. Both elements increase. This is illustrated in the analysis of the September 27 transaction.

Transaction	Analysis	Accounting Entry
September 27: Exercise Plus sells a business membership on credit to Talbot Industries for $1,400 and a family membership on credit to Carmen Saldi for $700.	▪ The asset *Accounts Receivable* increases by $2,100 because that amount is due from customers. ▪ The owner's equity *Income Summary (Revenue)* increases by $2,100 because the business has now earned revenue.	▪ Increase the asset *Accounts Receivable* by $2,100. ▪ Increase the owner's equity *Income Summary (Revenue)* by $2,100.

	Assets				=	*Liabilities*	+	*Owner's Equity*		
	Cash	Accounts Receivable	Furniture	Exercise Equipment		Accounts Payable		Lisa Long, Capital	Income Summary (Revenue)	
	$13,000 +	$ -0- +	$4,500 +	$13,000	=	$1,500	+	$25,000 +	$4,000	⟵ **Previous Balance**
		+2,100							**+2,100**	⟵ **Effect of Transaction**
	$13,000 +	$2,100 +	$4,500 +	$13,000	=	$1,500	+	$25,000 +	$6,100	⟵ **New Balance**
					=	$1,500		$31,000		
		$32,600						$32,600		⟵ **Equality of Equation**

Receiving revenue from sales on credit.

The sale on credit increases the left side of the accounting equation because the asset Accounts Receivable increases. The right side of the accounting equation increases by the same amount. Since liabilities are not affected, owner's equity must increase, so that the accounting equation remains in balance.

Revenues are recorded at the time goods are given to the customer or when services are performed. What is received—either cash or the customer's promise to pay in the future—is also recorded at the same time. This is one of many generally accepted accounting principles (sometimes called **GAAPs**). **Accounting principles** or standards guide accountants in their work. Because they are the guides for uniform and acceptable accounting work, major accounting principles are highlighted throughout this textbook.

Concept: Changing Owner's Equity
Owner's equity is affected not only by changes in the investment but also by revenues and expenses.

Principle: Recording Revenue
The generally accepted accounting principle is that revenue is recorded at the point of sale of goods or as services are rendered.

Expense Transactions

Are goods and services needed to operate a business? Yes, goods and services are needed to operate a business and generate revenue. The cost of goods and services used in the operation of a business are called **expenses**. Salaries, telephone, fuel, and electricity are common business expenses.

To see how expenses affect owner's equity, let's look at the expense transactions for Exercise Plus for September. Expense transactions for an accounting period, like revenue transactions, are recorded in the Income Summary account. Thus, you will note that the term *expense* is used under Income Summary in the accounting equation. You will also notice that a minus sign is used between ''Revenue'' and ''Expense.'' This shows that expense amounts are subtracted directly from the amounts received as revenue.

Expenses Paid by Cash

Assets	=	Liabilities	+	Owner's Equity
−		0		−

Assets decrease.
Liabilities are not affected.
Owner's equity decreases.

Paying Expenses With Cash When a business pays cash for an expense, two elements are affected—assets and owner's equity. Both elements decrease. This is illustrated by the September 28 transaction analyzed at the top of the next page. This transaction decreases the left side of the equation because the asset Cash has decreased, as shown in the margin. The right side of the equation decreases by the same amount. Since no liability is affected by the cash transaction, owner's equity must decrease.

The Capital account is not affected at this time since no investment is involved. Revenue is not affected since revenue involves the inflow of assets (cash or receivables). Expenses are affected. Expenses can be viewed as decreases in the owner's equity caused by the outflow of cash. The accounting equation is in balance.

Incurring Expenses on Credit

Assets	=	Liabilities	+	Owner's Equity
0		+		−

Assets are not affected.
Liabilities increase.
Owner's equity decreases.

Incurring Expenses on Credit A business may promise to pay for an expense in the future. In this case, two accounting elements are affected—liabilities and owner's equity. Liabilities increase and

Transaction	Analysis	Accounting Entry
September 28: Exercise Plus pays an expense of $2,900 for salaries.	▪ The asset *Cash* decreases by $2,900 because the business now has less money. ▪ The owner's equity *Income Summary (Expense)* decreases by $2,900 because the business has incurred an expense.	▪ Decrease the asset *Cash* by $2,900. ▪ Decrease the owner's equity *Income Summary (Expense)* by $2,900.

	Assets			=	*Liabilities* +	*Owner's Equity*		
Cash	Accounts Receivable	Furniture	Exercise Equipment		Accounts Payable	Lisa Long, Capital	Income Summary (Revenue − Expense)	
$13,000 +	$2,100 +	$4,500 +	$13,000	=	$1,500 +	$25,000 +	$6,100	← Previous Balance
−2,900							−2,900	← Effect of Transaction
$10,100 +	$2,100 +	$4,500 +	$13,000	=	$1,500 +	$25,000 +	$3,200	← New Balance
					$1,500 +	$28,200		
$29,700				=	$29,700			← Equality of Equation

Paying expenses with cash.

owner's equity decreases. This is illustrated in the margin on page 36 and in the September 29 transaction for Exercise Plus shown below.

Transaction	Analysis	Accounting Entry
September 29: Exercise Plus receives a bill for repairs expense of $200 from XYZ Repairs for repairing some exercise equipment. The creditor allows 30 days to pay this amount.	▪ The liability *Accounts Payable* increases by $200 because the business now owes more money. ▪ The owner's equity *Income Summary (Expense)* decreases by $200 because the business has now incurred an expense.	▪ Increase the liability *Accounts Payable* by $200. ▪ Decrease the owner's equity *Income Summary (Expense)* by $200.

	Assets			=	*Liabilities* +	*Owner's Equity*		
Cash	Accounts Receivable	Furniture	Exercise Equipment		Accounts Payable	Lisa Long, Capital	Income Summary (Revenue − Expense)	
$10,100 +	$2,100 +	$4,500 +	$13,000	=	$1,500 +	$25,000 +	$3,200	← Previous Balance
					+ 200		− 200	← Effect of Transaction
$10,100 +	$2,100 +	$4,500 +	$13,000	=	$1,700 +	$25,000 +	$3,000	← New Balance
					$1,700	$28,000		
$29,700				=	$29,700			← Equality of Equation

Incurring expenses on credit.

The assets (left) side of the accounting equation is not affected. Liabilities are affected because Exercise Plus has made a promise to pay for the repairs expense. Liabilities have increased by $200. Expenses are also affected. They have decreased owner's equity by $200. The Capital account is not affected at this time since no investment is involved. Revenues are not affected because there is no inflow of assets from a sale. The left side of the equation totals $29,700, as does the right side. The equation is still in balance.

Expenses are recorded when costs arise in generating revenue. What is given—cash or an agreement to pay in the future—is also recorded at the same time.

Principle: Expenses

The generally accepted accounting principle is that expenses represent the cost of goods and services used up in the process of generating revenue.

Exercise E on this page may be completed at this point.

TOPIC 2 EXERCISE

look over again

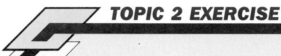

EXERCISE E. McKay's Repair Service is a single proprietorship owned by Frank McKay. The assets, liabilities, and owner's equity for the business on May 1 are shown in the accounting equation below. Indicate what happens in the accounting equation as a result of the following May transactions. Check the equality of the equation after each transaction.

EXAMPLE: Received $200 for the sale of services.

1. Paid $500 to a creditor on account.
2. Received $400 for the sale of services.
3. Sold services for $700 on credit.
4. Bought equipment for $400 on credit.
5. Paid $150 for advertising expense.
6. Received $1,000 from the sale of services.
7. Owes $150 for equipment repair.
8. Sold services for $800 on credit.
9. Paid $600 for rent.

	Assets						=	*Liabilities*	+	*Owner's Equity*			
	Cash		Accounts Receivable		Equipment			Accounts Payable		Frank McKay, Capital		Income Summary (Revenue)	**Equality Check**
	$4,000	+	$600	+	$1,400		=	$500	+	$5,500	+		**A = L + OE**
EX.:	+ 200										+	*$200*	
	$4,200	+	$600	+	$1,400		=	$500	+	$5,500	+	$200	**$6,200 = $6,200**

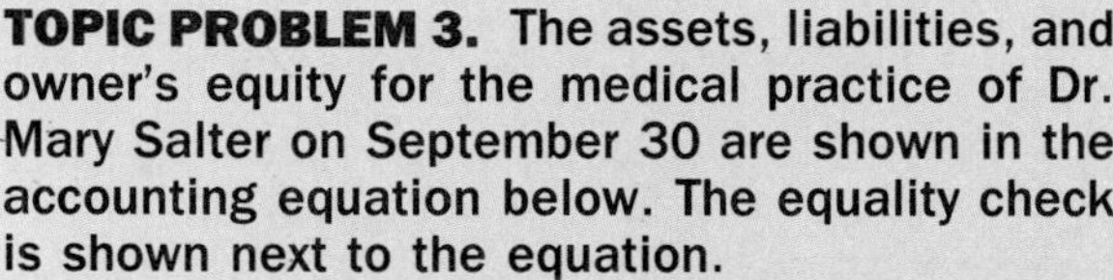

TOPIC 2 PROBLEMS

TOPIC PROBLEM 3. The assets, liabilities, and owner's equity for the medical practice of Dr. Mary Salter on September 30 are shown in the accounting equation below. The equality check is shown next to the equation.

Show what happens to the accounting equation as a result of each of the following transactions, all of which took place in October. Use this procedure for each transaction: First, read the transaction. Then, add or subtract to determine the new balance for each account. Finally, check the equality of the two sides of the equation after the transaction has been recorded.

For further assistance, you may wish to refer to the illustrations of transactions that are shown on pages 34 to 37.

a. Bought additional equipment for $6,000 on credit.

b. Received $900 for the sale of services.

c. Paid $80 for telephone expense.

d. Returned equipment bought for $200 on credit.

e. Received $300 from a patient on account.

f. Dr. Salter invested an additional $5,000 in the business.

g. Paid $450 for rent.

h. Sold services for $950 on credit.

i. Bought additional equipment for $800 in cash.

j. Dr. Salter withdrew $1,200 from the business for personal use.

k. Paid $400 to a creditor on account.

l. Owes $150 for repair expense.

m. Returned equipment bought for $100 in cash.

Assets						*Liabilities*	+	*Owner's Equity*			Equality Check
Cash		Accounts Receivable		Equipment		Accounts Payable		Mary Salter, Capital		Income Summary (Revenue − Expense)	A = L + OE
$5,000	+	$1,000	+	$5,300	=	$1,400	+	$9,900	+	-0-	$11,300 = $11,300

TOPIC PROBLEM 4. Indicate what happens to each of the three accounting elements as a result of the transactions that are listed below. Use a table like that shown below, with the headings Assets, Liabilities, and Owner's Equity. For each element, write in the answer column "+" if there is an increase, "−" if there is a decrease, or "0" if there is no effect.

EXAMPLE: Bought equipment on credit.

Assets	Liabilities	Owner's Equity
+	+	0

a. Bought a truck on credit.

b. Returned equipment bought on credit.

c. Received revenue from sales on credit.

d. The owner invested additional cash in the business.

e. Received cash from a customer on account.

f. Paid cash for an expense.

g. Incurred an expense on credit.

h. Bought equipment for cash.

i. The owner withdrew cash from the business for personal use.

j. Paid cash in payment of a liability.

k. Received revenue from cash sales.

TOPIC PROBLEM 5. Bill Baumann opened Bill's Sporting Goods. Each equation below was done after the completion of a transaction. Explain what happened in each transaction.

EXAMPLE: Bill Baumann started a business with an investment of $50,000 in cash and $45,000 in equipment (total capital of $95,000).

	Assets					= *Liabilities*	+	*Owner's Equity*		
	Cash	Accounts Receivable		Equipment		Accounts Payable		Bill Baumann, Capital		Income Summary (Revenue − Expense)
EXAMPLE:	*$50,000 +*	*$ -0-*	+	*$45,000*	=	*$ -0-*	+	*$95,000*	+	*$ -0-*
Trans. a				+50,000		+50,000				
New Balance	$50,000 +	$ -0-	+	$95,000	=	$50,000	+	$95,000	+	$ -0-
Trans. b		+400								+ 400
New Balance	$50,000 +	$400	+	$95,000	=	$50,000	+	$95,000	+	$ 400
Trans. c	− 200									− 200
New Balance	$49,800 +	$400	+	$95,000	=	$50,000	+	$95,000	+	$ 200
Trans. d	+ 90	− 90								
New Balance	$49,890 +	$310	+	$95,000	=	$50,000	+	$95,000	+	$ 200
Trans. e	+ 1,500									+1,500
New Balance	$51,390 +	$310	+	$95,000	=	$50,000	+	$95,000	+	$1,700
Trans. f	−10,000					−10,000				
New Balance	$41,390 +	$310	+	$95,000	=	$40,000	+	$95,000	+	$1,700
Trans. g						+ 600				− 600
New Balance	$41,390 +	$310	+	$95,000	=	$40,600	+	$95,000	+	$1,100
Trans. h	− 2,500							− 2,500		
New Balance	$38,890 +	$310	+	$95,000	=	$40,600	+	$92,500	+	$1,100
Trans. i	− 900			+ 900						
New Balance	$37,990 +	$310	+	$95,900	=	$40,600	+	$92,500	+	$1,100
Trans. j				− 2,300		− 2,300				
New Balance	$37,990 +	$310	+	$93,600	=	$38,300	+	$92,500	+	$1,100
Trans. k	+ 300			− 300						
New Balance	$38,290 +	$310	+	$93,300	=	$38,300	+	$92,500	+	$1,100
Trans. l	+ 4,000							+ 4,000		
New Balance	$42,290 +	$310	+	$93,300	=	$38,300	+	$96,500	+	$1,100

TOPIC 3

Summarizing and Interpreting Accounting Information

Having recorded and classified business transactions, is the cycle of activities for the accounting period completed? No, there are several additional activities that must be undertaken. In general, what has happened thus far is that transactions occurred and created financial data. Data was recorded as the transactions occurred. The data was also processed. That is, the data was classified and stored in the accounting equation of Exercise Plus. Now the data can be used to satisfy an important goal of accounting—to make business decisions. However, before the goal of decision-making is possible, additional activities are necessary.

At the end of the accounting period, the data must be summarized and the equality of the accounting equation must be checked. If there are accounts with incorrect balances, adjustments must be made to correct the balances before the data is summarized. In this topic you will learn how to do the following.

- Prove the equality of the accounting equation.
- Compute the net income or net loss for the September accounting period.
- Transfer the net income or net loss to the Capital account.
- Prepare a proof of your summarizing work.
- Interpret accounting information.

In Chapter 7 you will summarize and interpret the accounting data for Exercise Plus, using the October accounting period. At that time, you will learn how to make adjustments to accounts that have incorrect balances or that are not up to date.

Proving the Equality of the Equation

Each business transaction completed by Exercise Plus during September is shown on page 42. As you review the transactions, note the following.

1. An account balance is computed after each transaction. That is, amounts in the accounts are totaled after each transaction. An increase (+) is added and a decrease (−) is subtracted. In accounting, the difference between the increases and decreases in an account is called a **balance**, instead of a total. Thus, as shown in the margin, the balance of the Cash account on September 6 was $6,000. The balance of the Accounts Receivable account on September 5 was $1,000. On September 6, however, the Accounts Receivable had a zero balance.

2. The equation is proved at the end of the accounting period.

	Assets	
	Cash	Accounts Receivable
Sept. 1 Balance	$9,000	$1,000
Sept. 5	−4,000	
Balance	$5,000	$1,000
Sept. 6	+1,000	−1,000
Balance	$6,000	$ -0-

Add pluses and subtract minuses to compute account balance.

If all amounts have been recorded correctly, the total of the account balances on the left side of the equation should equal the total of the account balances on the right side of the equation. After completing this proof of the equality of the equation, Exercise Plus can go on to summarize its accounting information for the September accounting period. If Exercise Plus had not checked the equality of the equation at the end of the accounting period, it might have gone on to summarize and interpret information that was inaccurate and misleading.

	Assets				=	*Liabilities* +	*Owner's Equity*	
	Cash	Accounts Receivable	Furniture	Exercise Equipment		Accounts Payable	Lisa Long, Capital	Income Summary (Revenue − Expense)
Sept. 1 Balance	$ 9,000 +	$1,000 +	$3,000 +	$ 9,000	=	$4,000 +	$18,000 +	$ -0-
	− 4,000			+ 4,000				
Sept. 5 Balance	$ 5,000 +	$1,000 +	$3,000 +	$13,000	=	$4,000 +	$18,000 +	$ -0-
	+ 1,000	−1,000						
Sept. 6 Balance	$ 6,000 +	$ -0- +	$3,000 +	$13,000	=	$4,000 +	$18,000 +	$ -0-
			+2,000			+2,000		
Sept. 7 Balance	$ 6,000 +	$ -0- +	$5,000 +	$13,000	=	$6,000 +	$18,000 +	$ -0-
			− 500			− 500		
Sept. 8 Balance	$ 6,000 +	$ -0- +	$4,500 +	$13,000	=	$5,500 +	$18,000 +	$ -0-
	− 4,000					−4,000		
Sept. 12 Balance	$ 2,000 +	$ -0- +	$4,500 +	$13,000	=	$1,500 +	$18,000 +	$ -0-
	+13,000						+13,000	
① **Sept. 14 Balance**	$15,000 +	$ -0- +	$4,500 +	$13,000	=	$1,500 +	$31,000 +	$ -0-
	− 6,000						− 6,000	
Sept. 21 Balance	$ 9,000 +	$ -0- +	$4,500 +	$13,000	=	$1,500 +	$25,000 +	$ -0-
	+ 4,000							+4,000
Sept. 26 Balance	$13,000 +	$ -0- +	$4,500 +	$13,000	=	$1,500 +	$25,000 +	$4,000
		+2,100						+2,100
Sept. 27 Balance	$13,000 +	$2,100 +	$4,500 +	$13,000	=	$1,500 +	$25,000 +	$6,100
	− 2,900							−2,900
Sept. 28 Balance	$10,100 +	$2,100 +	$4,500 +	$13,000	=	$1,500 +	$25,000 +	$3,200
						+ 200		− 200
Sept. 29 Balance	$10,100 +	$2,100 +	$4,500 +	$13,000	=	$1,700 +	$25,000 +	$3,000
Sept. 30 Equality of Equation						$1,700 +	$28,000	
	$29,700				②	$29,700		

Exercise F on page 48 may be completed at this point.

Transactions of Exercise Plus for monthly accounting period ended September 30.

Summarizing Accounting Information

Do owners and managers usually want to know the details of each transaction? No, each transaction is recorded as it occurs to show the effects of the transaction on the accounting equation. Owners and managers, however, usually are not interested in having the details of every transaction. Generally, they want to look at the ''big picture.'' They want the results of transactions summarized for them. Thus, managers and owners are more interested in knowing the account balances, especially at the end of the accounting period. For example, Lisa Long wants to know the balance of the Cash account. She might even want this information on a daily basis. Certainly she wants to know whether the business has earned a profit (net income) for the accounting period. After all, it is the **profit incentive**—the desire to earn a net income—which causes individuals to risk investing in a business. Indeed, Ms. Long has a pressing need for this information since Exercise Plus, like any other private business, must make a profit to survive.

Computing Net Income or Net Loss

Whether a business has a net income or a net loss depends on whether revenue is more or less than expenses for the same accounting period. A **net income** results when revenue is greater than expenses. A **net loss** results when the expenses are greater than the revenue. "Net" means that all deductions have been made. Therefore, *net income* indicates that all related expenses have been deducted from the revenue.

An accounting principle, called **the matching principle**, requires that the revenue earned in one period be matched against the expenses needed to earn that revenue. "Matching" means that total expenses for the accounting period are subtracted from total revenue for the same period. Revenue and expenses are matched in the Income Summary account for an accounting period. If you examine the Income Summary account on page 42, for example, you will see that a minus is used between "Revenue" and "Expenses" to show that the amounts have been "matched," or subtracted.

Exercise Plus has a net income of $3,000 for the accounting period ended September 30. This is shown in the margin. The net income was obtained by matching the total revenue of $6,100 ($4,000 + $2,100) against total expenses of $3,100 ($2,900 + $200). The $3,000 is a net income because total revenue is greater than total expenses. This information is very important for managers and owners. The reason is that net income (or net loss) is one of the benchmarks used by managers and owners to determine whether their businesses are succeeding.

COMPUTING NET INCOME FOR ACCOUNTING PERIOD ENDED SEPTEMBER 30, 19—

Revenue	Expenses
$4,000	$2,900
+2,100	+ 200
$6,100	$3,100

Total Revenue	$6,100
Less: Total Expenses ..	−3,100
Net Income	$3,000

Principle: Matching Revenue and Expenses

The generally accepted accounting principle is that revenue must be matched against the expenses incurred in obtaining that revenue. The result of matching revenue and expenses is net income (or net loss) for the accounting period.

Exercise G on page 48 may be completed at this point.

Transferring Net Income (or Net Loss) to the Capital Account

What happens to the net income (or net loss) at the end of the accounting period? The net income (or net loss) is transferred to the Capital account. During the accounting period, revenue transactions increase the Income Summary account and expenses decrease the Income Summary account. Thus, revenue and expenses are matched in the Income Summary account. The result of this matching is net income (or net loss) for the period.

The Income Summary account is a temporary account whose balance must be transferred to the Capital account at the end of each accounting period. As you know, temporary accounts gather data for one accounting period only. Therefore, the Income Summary account must have a zero balance at the end of each accounting period. This is done by adding net income to the Capital account or by subtracting a net loss from the Capital account. After this is done, the total liabilities plus owner's equity still equal the total assets. The accounting equation is proved and is in balance.

Transferring a Net Income Exercise Plus had a net income of $3,000 for the accounting period ended September 30. The Income Summary account must be zero on October 1 so that revenue and expenses for the next accounting period (October) may be collected. Starting each accounting period with a zero balance in the temporary accounts separates one accounting period from another. This also ensures that revenues and expenses for one accounting period do not get mixed in with revenues and expenses for the next accounting period.

At the end of each accounting period, the net income amount is transferred to the Capital account. The amount of the net income is subtracted from the Income Summary account ($3,000 − $3,000), as shown below. The Income Summary account is now zero. The net income is added to the Capital account. Thus, the Capital account is increased by the amount of the net income ($25,000 + $3,000 = $28,000). The account is now ready to collect data for the next accounting period.

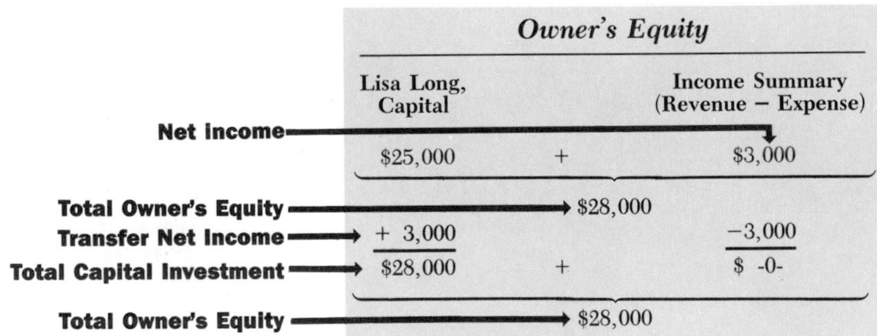

Transferring net income to the Capital account.

The equation on the next page shows that the net income for Exercise Plus is transferred to the Capital account on September 30. Notice how the transfer of net income affects the accounts.

1. The Income Summary account balance is now zero.
2. The Capital account has been increased by the amount of the net income ($3,000).

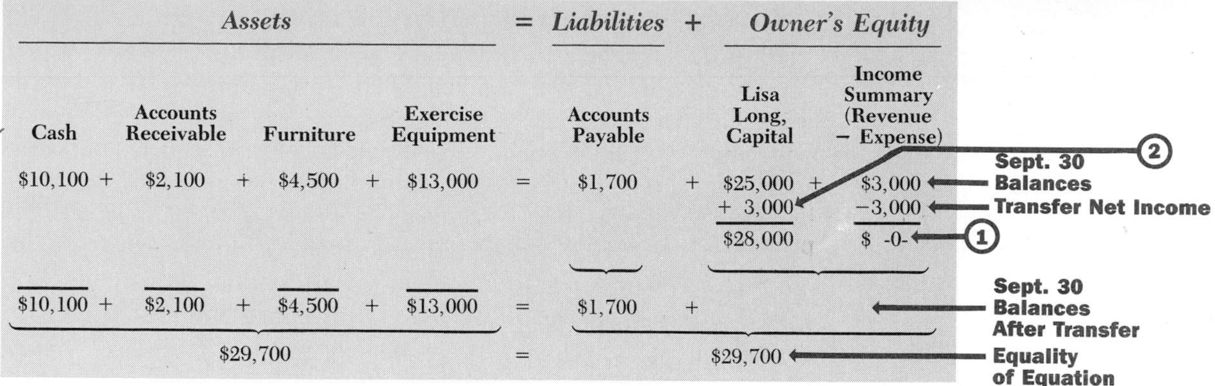

Cash	Accounts Receivable	Furniture	Exercise Equipment	Accounts Payable	Lisa Long, Capital	Income Summary (Revenue − Expense)	
		Assets		= **Liabilities** +	**Owner's Equity**		
$10,100 +	$2,100 +	$4,500 +	$13,000 =	$1,700 +	$25,000 +	$3,000	② Sept. 30 Balances
					+ 3,000	−3,000	Transfer Net Income
					$28,000	$ -0-	①
$10,100 +	$2,100 +	$4,500 +	$13,000 =	$1,700 +			Sept. 30 Balances After Transfer
	$29,700		=		$29,700		Equality of Equation

The net income has been transferred to the Capital account.

Only one element is affected—owner's equity—and the equation is still in balance.

■ Transferring a Net Loss A net loss for an accounting period means that expenses have been greater than revenue. Expenses decrease the Capital account.

Suppose Exercise Plus had a $2,000 loss during September as shown below. (In accounting, parentheses or a circle around an amount means a minus.) The net loss must also be transferred to the Capital account. However, the net loss is subtracted from the Capital account since a net loss decreases owner's equity.

Lisa Long, Capital		Income Summary (Revenue − Expense)	
Owner's Equity			
$25,000	+	($2,000)	Net Loss
	$23,000		Total Owner's Equity
− 2,000		+2,000	Transfer Net Loss
$23,000	+	$ -0-	Total Capital Investment
	$23,000		Total Owner's Equity

Transferring a net loss to the Capital account.

The net loss is transferred by subtracting $2,000 from the Capital account and adding $2,000 to the Income Summary account. The amount is added because the Income Summary account must be zero at the end of the accounting period. Again, only one element—owner's equity—is affected. The equation is still in balance.

Exercises H and I on pages 48 and 49 may be completed at this point.

Interpreting Accounting Information

Why do owners and managers need summaries of accounting information? Owners and managers need summarized accounting information to make business decisions. They need information to judge how well their business is doing and to make decisions about future business operations. For example, looking at the accounting equation for September 30 on page 45, Lisa Long knows that her business has $10,100 in available cash. If she wanted to buy additional equipment for the business, could she pay $5,000 cash for it?

Before Lisa Long can answer the question, she will need to consider such questions as: When does she have to pay the liabilities for Exercise Plus? About how much cash will be received from cash sales in October? In other words, to make a decision to buy equipment for Exercise Plus, Lisa Long will need to interpret the accounting information given to her.

To ''interpret'' accounting information means to clarify the meaning of the information. For example, it appears that a decision by Lisa Long to buy the equipment involves little risk. Even if Exercise Plus pays all its liabilities in October ($1,700), the business will still have $8,400 available in cash to buy the equipment. This would leave Exercise Plus with $3,400 ($8,400 − $5,000 for the equipment) to cover expenses for October. Also, cash sales during October should make additional funds available to help pay October's business expenses.

Suppose, however, the accounting equation for September 30 showed that Exercise Plus had to pay $6,000 in liabilities in October. Also, suppose the business had suffered a net loss during the September accounting period. Lisa Long might have given a much different meaning to this accounting information, and her decision to buy the equipment might be quite different.

Although interpreting accounting information is the last step of the accounting cycle, in terms of making business plans it can be considered one of the most important. Interpreting accounting information will be discussed in later chapters.

The Accounting Cycle

As you have seen, businesses follow a sequence of procedures or steps in keeping their accounting records. This sequence of steps is known as the **accounting cycle**. In this chapter you learned how to analyze transactions and use the equation to process the accounting data. Here is a summary of what you learned so far. Each item is a step in the accounting cycle.

Step 1. Each transaction is recorded.

Step 2. A chronological record is kept of each transaction. (*Chronological* means to keep by date.)

Step 3. The changes that are caused by the transactions are posted to and stored in the accounts, and the balance (total) of each account is updated. (*Update* means to bring up to date.)

Step 4. The equality of the equation is proved at the end of the accounting period.

Step 5. The accounting information is summarized by account balances at the end of the accounting period. (Before the summaries are prepared, any account with an inaccurate or incomplete balance must be adjusted to record the correct balance.)

Step 6. The revenue and expense data is summarized in the Income Summary account and income or loss is transferred to the Capital account at the end of the accounting period.

Step 7. The equality of the equation is proved again after the net income (or loss) is transferred from the Income Summary account to the Capital account.

Step 8. The accounting records provide financial information for managers and owners to interpret and to use for making decisions.

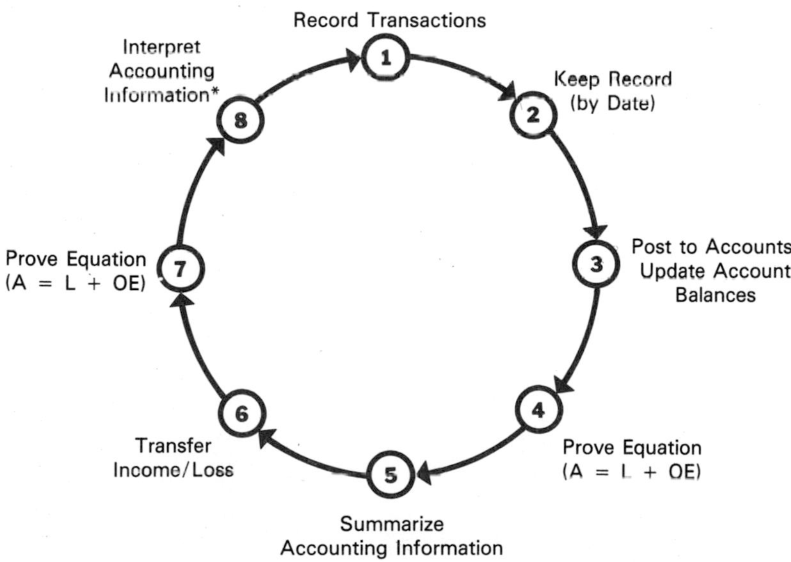

*Interpretation occurs all during the accounting cycle but is most concentrated at the end of the accounting period.

The accounting cycle, illustrated above, and the accounting equation are the foundation of all accounting work.

Exercise J on page 49 may be completed at this point.

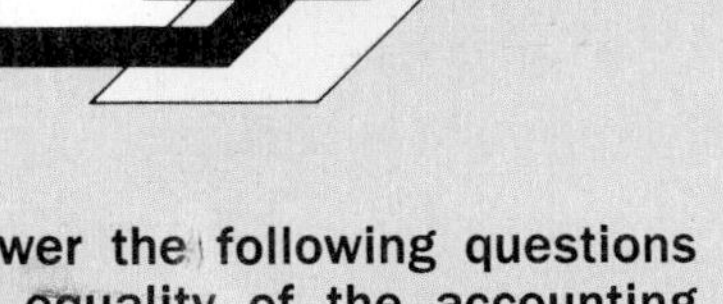

TOPIC 3 EXERCISES

EXERCISE F. Answer the following questions about proving the equality of the accounting equation. Refer to the Exercise Plus equation on page 42.

1. What is the amount of total assets on September 1?
2. What is the balance of the Accounts Payable account on September 12?
3. What is the balance of the Lisa Long, Capital account on September 21?
4. What is the balance of the Accounts Receivable account on September 27?
5. What is the total amount of owner's equity on September 29?
6. What is the amount of total liabilities plus owner's equity on September 30?
7. How many transactions affected the Income Summary account during the accounting period ended September 30?
8. What is the amount of total assets on September 30?

EXERCISE G. Compute the net income (or net loss) for each of the companies below. Show the change in the Income Summary account and the change in owner's equity. The first computation is done as an example. Refer to the table below.

Company	Revenue	Expenses	Income Summary		Amount	Owner's Equity	
			Net Income	Net Loss		Decrease	Increase
***EXAMPLE:* A**	***$17,000***	***$ 4,000***	✓	______	***$13,000***	______	✓
B	8,000	10,000	______	______	$______	______	______
C	19,500	6,500	______	______	$______	______	______
D	12,000	12,500	______	______	$______	______	______
E	18,600	13,500	______	______	$______	______	______

EXERCISE H. Show the transfer of the Income Summary account balance in the Owner's Equity section of the equation. Use a form similar to the one illustrated below.

Owner's Equity July 31, 19—			Owner's Equity August 31, 19—			Owner's Equity September 30, 19—		
Ellen Levine, Capital		Income Summary (Revenue − Expense)	Ellen Levine, Capital		Income Summary (Revenue − Expense)	Ellen Levine, Capital		Income Summary (Revenue − Expense)
$15,000	+	$3,000	$21,000	+	$6,000	$29,000	+	($4,000)
+ 3,000		−3,000	?		?	?		?
$18,000	+	$ -0-	$?	+	$?	$?	+	$?
$18,000			$___?___			$___?___		

EXERCISE I. Answer the following questions about transferring net income (or net loss) to the Capital account. Refer to the accounting equations on pages 44 to 45.

1. What is the amount of the owner's equity before the net income is transferred on September 30?
2. What is the balance of the Income Summary account before net income is transferred on September 30?
3. What amount is transferred to the Capital account?
4. What is the amount of the Income Summary account after the net income is transferred on September 30?
5. What is the amount of owner's equity after the net income is transferred on September 30?

EXERCISE J. Answer the following questions about interpreting accounting information and the accounting cycle. Refer to the text and the illustrations on pages 46 to 47.

1. In terms of making decisions, what is considered one of the most important steps in the accounting cycle?
2. How many steps are described in the accounting cycle?
3. In which step of the accounting cycle are the balances of the temporary accounts transferred to the permanent Capital account?

TOPIC 3 PROBLEMS

TOPIC PROBLEM 6. On October 1, James Will had the assets, liabilities, and owner's equity in his law practice as shown below (refer to the accounting equation and equality check below).

a. Show what happens to the accounting equation as a result of the following transactions taking place during the accounting period ending October 31.

b. Prove the equality of the equation after the last transaction but before the transfer to the Income Summary account.

c. Transfer the Income Summary account balance to the Capital account.

d. Check the equality of the equation after the transfer.

Oct. 1 James Will started the business with an investment of $20,600 in cash and $14,500 in office equipment, which equals total capital of $35,100.
16 Sold services for $750 on credit.
17 Bought office equipment for $195 on credit.
25 Received $600 for the sale of services.
28 Paid $335 for rent expense.

Assets					=	*Liabilities*	+	*Owner's Equity*		
Cash		Accounts Receivable		Office Equipment		Accounts Payable		James Will, Capital		Income Summary (Revenue − Expense)
$20,600	+	$-0-	+	$14,500	=	$-0-	+	$35,100	+	$-0-

Equality Check
A = L + OE
$35,100 = $35,100
Oct. 1 Balance

TOPIC PROBLEM 7. Continue with the equation for Topic Problem 6. Mr. Will continues his law practice during the next accounting period beginning November 1. The account balances as of November 1 are shown in the equation below.

a. Show what happens to the accounting equation as a result of the following transactions, which took place during the accounting period ended November 30.

b. Check the equality of the equation after the last transaction but before the transfer of the Income Summary account balance.

c. Transfer the Income Summary account balance to the Capital account.

d. Check the equality of the equation after the transfer.

Nov. 1 James Will started the new accounting period with $20,865 in cash, $750 in accounts receivable, and $14,695 in office equipment. These assets equal the total of liabilities of $195 plus owner's equity of $36,115.

6 Returned equipment bought for $45 on credit.

14 Received $700 for sale of services.

29 Paid $335 for rent expense.

Assets					=	*Liabilities*	+	*Owner's Equity*			**Equality Check**
Cash		Accounts Receivable		Office Equipment		Accounts Payable		James Will, Capital		Income Summary (Revenue − Expense)	**A = L + OE** **$36,310 = $36,310**
$20,865	+	$750	+	$14,695	=	$195	+	$36,115	+	$-0-	**Nov. 1 Balance**

TOPIC PROBLEM 8. Continue with the equation from Topic Problem 7. James Will continued his law practice during the next accounting period beginning December 1. The account balances of December 1 are shown in the equation below.

a. Show what happens to the accounting equation as a result of the following transactions, which took place during the accounting period ended December 31.

b. Check the equality of the equation after the last transaction but before the transfer of the Income Summary account balance.

c. Transfer the Income Summary account balance to the Capital account.

d. Check the equality of the equation after the transfer.

Dec. 1 Mr. Will started the new accounting period with an investment of $21,230 in cash, $750 in accounts receivable, and $14,650 in office equipment. These assets equal the total of liabilities of $150 plus owner's equity of $36,480.

8 Received $785 for the sale of services.

14 Paid $65 for repair services.

21 Paid $50 on account.

28 Paid $335 for rent expense.

Assets					=	*Liabilities*	+	*Owner's Equity*			**Equality Check**
Cash		Accounts Receivable		Office Equipment		Accounts Payable		James Will, Capital		Income Summary (Revenue − Expense)	**A = L + OE** **$36,630 = $36,630**
$21,230	+	$750	+	$14,650	=	$150	+	$36,480	+	$-0-	**Dec. 1 Balance**

CHAPTER 2 REVIEW

CHAPTER SUMMARY

In this chapter, you were introduced to the sequence of steps that Exercise Plus, or any business, follows in keeping its accounting records. These steps make up the *accounting cycle.* You used an expanded accounting equation to record transactions and to process accounting information through the accounting cycle.

The period of time for which a business summarizes its financial information is called an *accounting period.* One month, three months, and a year are examples of accounting periods.

Throughout the accounting period, after each transaction, the accounting equation must be in balance. At regular intervals, including the end of the accounting period, accountants must prove that the equation is in balance. This means that the total of the account balances on the left side of the equation is equal to the total of the account balances on the right side of the equation.

At the end of the accounting period, the accounting information is summarized by account balances. (Any account balance that is inaccurate or incomplete must be adjusted—that is, corrected—before the financial records are prepared.) Net income or net loss is computed and transferred from the Income Summary account to the owner's Capital account. Finally, the financial records for the business are prepared and the resulting financial information is made available to owners and managers for interpretation and use in making business decisions. The steps in the accounting cycle are outlined and described on pages 46 to 47.

THE LANGUAGE OF BUSINESS

Here are some terms that make up the language of business. Do you know the meaning of each?

transaction
permanent account
temporary account
accounting period
analyzing a transaction
accounting entity
revenue
Income Summary account
accounting principles (GAAPs)
expenses
balance
profit incentive
net income
net loss
matching principle
accounting cycle

REVIEW QUESTIONS

1. How does a transaction affect the accounting equation?

2. What are the most common accounting periods used by a business?

3. What is the effect on the accounting element Assets when an asset is exchanged for another? What is the effect on the element Liabilities? On the element Owner's Equity?

4. What elements of the accounting equation are affected when an owner invests additional funds in a business?

5. Are owners allowed to withdraw assets from the business for their personal use? What is the effect on the accounting elements when assets are withdrawn for personal use?

6. How does a revenue transaction affect the accounting elements?

7. How does an expense transaction affect the accounting elements?

8. Is the Income Summary account a temporary or permanent account? Explain your answer.

9. Does the element Owner's Equity increase or decrease when a business earns a net income? Does it increase or decrease when a business has a net loss?

10. Why do business managers and owners need to interpret accounting information?

CHAPTER PROBLEMS

Problems for Chapter 2 are given below. Write your answers to the problems on a separate sheet of paper unless you are using the workbook for this textbook. If you are using the workbook, do the problems in the space provided there.

CHAPTER PROBLEM 2-1. Match the revenue with related expenses, and compute the net income (or net loss) for each accounting period.

Revenue for the Accounting Period Ended					
Apr. 30	$19,000	Jan. 31	$18,000	Feb. 28	$12,000
Mar. 31	$13,000	May 31	$11,000	June 30	$11,000

Expenses for the Accounting Period Ended					
May 31	$ 8,000	Mar. 31	$14,000	June 30	$13,000
Jan. 31	$15,000	Apr. 30	$16,000	Feb. 28	$11,000

EXAMPLE: Jan. 31, Net Income $3,000

CHAPTER PROBLEM 2-2. The effects of the transactions for Brown's Delivery Service are shown in the equations at the top of the next page. Analyze the changes caused by each transaction. Explain what transactions took place to bring about the changes.

EXAMPLE: May 1 Assets = Owner's equity

Cash + Equipment = Allen Brown, Capital

$10,000 + $2,000 = $12,000

EXPLANATION: On May 1, Allen Brown started the business with an investment of $10,000 in cash and $2,000 in equipment.

a. May 1

Assets			=	Owner's Equity
Cash	+	Equipment	=	Allen Brown, Capital
$10,000	+	$2,000	=	$12,000

b. May 17

Assets					=	Liabilities	+	Owner's Equity
Cash		Equipment		Truck		Accounts Payable		Allen Brown, Capital
$10,000	+	$2,000	+	$7,000	=	$7,000	+	$12,000

c. May 22

Assets							=	Liabilities	+	Owner's Equity	
Cash		Accounts Receivable		Equipment		Truck		Accounts Payable		Allen Brown, Capital	Income Summary (Revenue − Expense)
$10,000	+	$2,000	+	$2,000	+	$7,000	=	$7,000	+	$12,000	$2,000

d. May 28

Assets							=	Liabilities	+	Owner's Equity	
Cash		Accounts Receivable		Equipment		Truck		Accounts Payable		Allen Brown, Capital	Income Summary (Revenue − Expense)
$9,500	+	$2,000	+	$2,000	+	$7,000	=	$7,000	+	$12,000	$1,500

e. May 31

Assets							=	Liabilities	+	Owner's Equity	
Cash		Accounts Receivable		Equipment		Truck		Accounts Payable		Allen Brown, Capital	Income Summary (Revenue − Expense)
$9,500	+	$2,000	+	$2,000	+	$7,000	=	$7,000	+	$13,500	$-0-

CHAPTER PROBLEM 2-3. On May 1, Barbara Sanchez had the assets, liabilities, and owner's equity in her accounting practice indicated in the May 1 transaction below.

a. Show the change to the accounting equation as a result of the following transactions during the month of May. Use a form similar to the one below to record the effect of the May transactions.

b. Check the equality of the equation after the last transaction but before the transfer to the Income Summary account.

c. Transfer the Income Summary account balance to the Capital account.

d. Check the equality of the equation after the transfer.

	Assets					=	Liabilities	+	Owner's Equity		
	Cash		Accounts Receivable		Office Equipment		Accounts Payable		Barbara Sanchez, Capital		Income Summary (Revenue − Expense)
May 1 Balance	$14,900	+	$800	+	$5,000	=	$450	+	$20,250	+	$-0-
	?		?		?		?		?		?
May 4 Balance	$?	+	$?	+	$?	=	$?	+	$?	+	$?

May 1 Barbara Sanchez started the accounting period with $14,900 in cash, $800 in accounts receivable, and $5,000 in office equipment. The assets equaled the total liabilities of $450 plus owner's equity of $20,250.

4 Received $900 for the sale of services.

May 8 Paid $75 for telephone expense.
11 Sold services for $650 on credit.
16 Paid $80 for office equipment.
20 Owes $95 for advertising expense.
26 Received $200 on account.
28 Ms. Sanchez withdrew $1,500 from the business.
31 Returned office equipment bought for $80 in cash.

MANAGEMENT CASES

Comparing Information. One feature of accounting is that it provides information in such a way that each business is uniquely described. One business does not look exactly like another. Each business has its own assets, liabilities, and owner's equity. As a result, accounting data provides information to help owners, managers, and others make informed decisions about a business or businesses.

CASE 2M-1. Marie Ross and Tim O'Brien own separate businesses. Marie's Diner is in its third year of profitable operation. Tim's Coffee Shop just opened last summer. Each owner uses a monthly accounting period.

Ms. Ross and Mr. O'Brien decide to form a business partnership by combining their businesses.

a. Based on the data below, what are the differences in the assets of the coffee shop and the diner?

b. Compare the net income for the month ended June 30.

c. Why do you think Marie's Diner is earning a larger net income than Tim's Coffee Shop?

d. What can Mr. O'Brien do to increase his net income? (*Hint:* Look at his Cash balance.)

MARIE'S DINER, June 30, 19—

Assets						=	*Liabilities*	+	*Owner's Equity*		
Cash		Merchandise for Sale		Store Equipment			Accounts Payable/ Walsh Supplies		Marie Ross, Capital		Income Summary (Revenue − Expense)
$5,000	+	$8,000	+	$12,000		=	$2,000	+	$20,000	+	$3,000 Net Income

TIM'S COFFEE SHOP, June 30, 19—

Assets						=	*Liabilities*	+	*Owner's Equity*		
Cash		Merchandise for Sale		Store Equipment			Accounts Payable/ Brooks Supplies		Tim O'Brien, Capital		Income Summary (Revenue − Expense)
$15,000	+	$1,000	+	$6,000		=	$500	+	$21,000	+	$500 Net Income

CASE 2M-2. Ruth Ward, the owner of the Ward Antique Shop, examines the information below and sees that the business has $2,500 in cash. This is more cash than she believes the business needs. She is considering withdrawing $2,000 in cash to invest in another business. Refer to the equation below.

a. In anticipating the amount of money that her business will need in the near future, what items should Ms. Ward consider?

b. How much money can Ms. Ward expect the business to receive in the near future?

c. Do you feel that Ms. Ward can make a cash withdrawal of $2,000 without placing the business in a difficult financial situation? Why or why not? Include all the reasons why Ms. Ward should or should not make this cash withdrawal.

Assets						=	*Liabilities*	+	*Owner's Equity*		
Cash		Accts. Rec./ Mike Shaw		Merchandise for Sale			Accounts Payable/ Ramero Antiques		Ruth Ward, Capital		Income Summary (Revenue − Expense)
$2,500	+	$1,000	+	$11,800		=	$6,500	+	$6,500	+	$2,300 Net Income

CHAPTER

3

An Accounting Cycle Using Debits and Credits

In Chapter 2 you learned how to process information through the entire accounting cycle using the accounting equation. In this chapter you will record the same transactions again. However, the focus will shift from the accounting equation to recording transactions in a new form of account—the T account. You will also learn to record changes to accounts by using the rules of debiting and crediting.

CHAPTER GOALS

After studying Chapter 3, you will be able to:

1. Define the terms listed in ''The Language of Business'' section on page 86.
2. Explain the accounting concepts and principles in this chapter related to the use of the T form of account, debiting and crediting of accounts, and proving the ledger.
3. Open T accounts for asset, liability, and owner's equity accounts.
4. Analyze business transactions that are related to increasing and decreasing asset, liability, and owner's equity accounts.
5. Record business transactions in asset, liability, and owner's equity accounts, using the rules of debit and credit.
6. Balance T accounts and prepare a trial balance.

TOPIC 1

Forms of Accounts

Is only one form of account used in business? No, several different forms of accounts are used. In Chapter 2 you saw a one-column account. In a one-column account, increases and decreases to account balances are recorded in the same column. In this chapter, a two-sided, or two-column, account is used. Increases to the account are put on one side of the account. Decreases are put on the other side.

Setting Up Accounts

The accounting equation for Exercise Plus has seven accounts: Cash; Accounts Receivable; Furniture; Exercise Equipment; Accounts Payable; Lisa Long, Capital; and Income Summary.

Assets				=	*Liabilities*	+	*Owner's Equity*	
Cash	Accounts Receivable	Furniture	Exercise Equipment		Accounts Payable		Lisa Long, Capital	Income Summary

Using many accounts in an accounting equation is awkward.

Most businesses, however, have many more accounts. For example, Exercise Plus has only one Accounts Receivable account on September 1, even though more than one customer could have purchased its services on credit. Also, Exercise Plus has only one Accounts Payable account on September 1, even though it could have made purchases on credit from more than one business. A business should have a separate account for each individual who owes it money and for each creditor to whom it owes money. Businesses also have many other asset accounts and liability accounts; for example, Delivery Equipment and Loans Payable.

Also, an Income Summary account was used in the equation for Exercise Plus. But most managers and owners want to know more than the amount of net income. They want to know the revenue earned and expenses incurred. They also want to know the types of revenue earned and types of expenses incurred. To provide this information, a separate account is set up for each revenue and each expense item. Since Exercise Plus obtains revenue only from sales of its services, it can use one revenue account—Sales. However, at least two expense accounts—Repairs Expense and Salaries Expense—should be used.

It is difficult to use many accounts in an equation. As a result, a different form of account is generally used in accounting records.

T Accounts

The T account is the simplest form of account with two sides. It looks like a large T, as shown in the margin. All increases to the account are written on one side. All decreases are written on the opposite side.

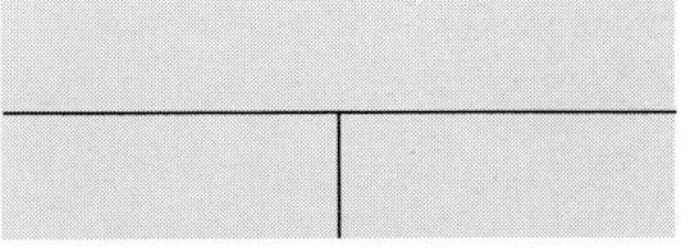

The T account separates increases and decreases to an account.

A T account has four parts.

1. Account title and, usually, an account number
2. Debit, or left, side
3. Credit, or right, side
4. Account balance (can be either a debit or a credit balance)

Account balance can be either a debit balance or a credit balance.

	Account Title		Account Number	
				①
②	*Debit side (left)*		*Credit side (right)*	③
④	*Debit balance*	*or*	*Credit balance*	④

The T account does the following.

- It keeps a record of each transaction by account title.
- It separates the increases and decreases to the account.
- It stores the amounts for future use.
- It shows the account balance.

A separate T account is set up for each account in the accounting equation. Thus, a T account is set up for each asset, each liability, and each owner's equity account.

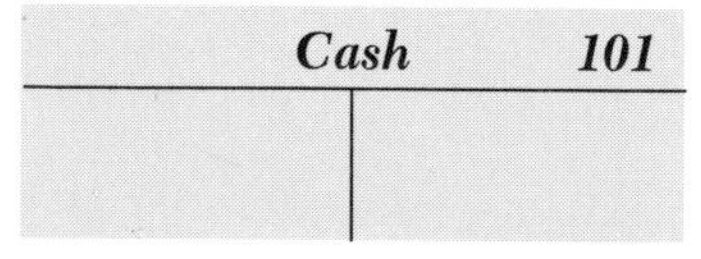

Account title is written in the center. Account number is written at the right.

■ Account Title and Number Each T account is given a title that clearly identifies that account. The account title is the specific name of the account. Examples are Cash; Furniture; or Lisa Long, Capital. The account title is written on the top line of the T account, as shown in the margin.

In addition to a title, accounts are usually assigned account numbers. The account number is the specific number assigned to an account. The account number is a code. *Coding* is a means of abbreviating (shortening) data. The numbers are used to code accounts so that it is easier and quicker to locate a specific account. For example, the Cash account can be assigned an account number, such as 101. It would be easier to find Account 101 than it would be to look through a group of account titles. The account number is written at the right along the top line of the T account, as shown in the margin.

PLAN FOR A CHART OF ACCOUNTS

Account	Number
Asset accounts	101 through 199
Liability accounts	201 through 299
Owner's Equity accounts	301 through 399
Revenue accounts	401 through 499
Expense accounts	501 through 599

Account numbers are assigned to each account according to a chart of accounts. A **chart of accounts** is a listing of all account titles and numbers used by a business. The account numbers and titles identify the accounts as asset, liability, or owner's equity accounts. Exercise Plus uses a three-digit plan for numbering its accounts. The plan is shown in the margin. Other numbering plans may call for more digits, but in general, they operate the same way.

The first digit in any account number indicates the group to which that account belongs. For example, account numbers beginning with 1 are asset accounts. Those beginning with 2 are liability accounts, and those with 3 are owner's equity accounts. Revenue accounts are assigned numbers beginning with 4, and expense accounts are assigned numbers beginning with 5. Revenue and expense accounts are temporary owner's equity accounts and are given separate numbers.

The next two digits in the account number indicate the sequence of the account within its group. Refer to the chart of accounts for Exercise Plus in the margin. Note that gaps have been left. This will allow new Accounts Receivable accounts to be inserted when necessary. Most businesses leave gaps in the sequence of numbers assigned to accounts so that new accounts can be inserted within the sequence later on.

Using alphabetic abbreviations is another form of coding. "Accts. Rec.," for example, is the abbreviation for "Accounts Receivable." "Accts. Pay." is the abbreviation for "Accounts Payable." These abbreviations also keep account titles as short as possible. Note that "Accts. Rec." comes before the name of each customer in the account title. Also, "Accts. Pay." is used before the name of each creditor.

EXERCISE PLUS
CHART OF ACCOUNTS

Assets
101 Cash
103 Accts. Rec./Carmen Saldi
104 Accts. Rec./Talbot Industries
111 Furniture
112 Exercise Equipment

Liabilities
201 Accts. Pay./Shone Products
202 Accts. Pay./XYZ Repairs

Owner's Equity
301 Lisa Long, Capital
399 Income Summary

Revenue
401 Sales

Expenses
504 Repairs Expense
505 Salaries Expense

■ Debit Side The left side of a T account is always called the **debit side**. An amount on the debit side of an account is called a **debit**, or abbreviated as **Dr.** Recording data on the debit side is known as "debiting the account." In the T account below, the $200 is a debit.

Debit side (Dr.) 200	*Credit side (Cr.)* 50

The $200 is a debit. The $50 is a credit.

■ Credit Side The right side of the T account is always called the **credit side**. An amount on the credit side of an account is called a **credit**, or abbreviated as **Cr.** Recording an amount on the credit side is known as "crediting the account." The $50 illustrated above is a credit.

■ Account Balance The **account balance** is the difference between the total debits and the total credits in an account. The procedures used to compute the balance of a T account are shown below and on the next page.

1. Total all debits ($90 + $10 = $100).
2. Total all credits ($50 + $20 = $70).

COMPUTING AN ACCOUNT BALANCE

Account Not Showing Balance

Cash	*101*
90	*50*
10	*20*

Account Showing Balance

Cash	*101*
90	*50*
10	*20*
(3) *30* (1) *100*	(2) *70*
(4) *Debit Balance*	

3. Subtract the smaller amount from the larger amount. The difference is the account balance ($100 − $70 = $30).
4. Show the balance on the side of the account with the larger total.

In the Cash account shown, the debit total ($100) is larger than the credit total ($70). Therefore, the Cash account has a debit balance ($30). When the credit total is larger than the debit total, the account has a credit balance, as illustrated below. Notice that the balance is written to the left of the totals. If there are amounts on only one side of the account, that total is the balance and it is not necessary to enter the balance to the left of the total.

The credit total is greater than the debit total. Thus, the account has a credit balance.

Accts. Pay./Shone Products	*201*
50	*70*
10	*20*
60	*30 90*
	Credit Balance

The terms *debiting* and *crediting* should not be confused with *increasing* and *decreasing*. Debiting simply means entering an amount on the left side of an account. Crediting means entering an amount on the right side of an account. You will see later that a debit increases some accounts and decreases others. Likewise, a credit will increase some accounts and decrease others.

Exercises A and B on pages 64 and 65 may be completed at this point.

Rules for Debiting and Crediting

How are increases and decreases shown in an account? Some accounts are increased on the debit side. Other accounts are increased on the credit side. The reason some accounts are increased on the debit side and others are increased on the credit side is based on the position of the elements in the accounting equation. Refer to the accounting equation below and the illustration on page 61 as you read the rules for debiting and crediting.

Assets = Liabilities + Owner's Equity

Assets appear on the left side of the equation. Liabilities and owner's equity appear on the right side of the equation. As a result, asset accounts increase and decrease differently than liabilities and owner's equity accounts. The three basic rules for debiting and crediting accounts are as follows.

- The balance of an account normally appears on the same side of the account as the element appears in the accounting equation.
- The balance of an account is *increased* on the same side of the account as the element appears in the accounting equation.
- The balance of an account is *decreased* on the opposite side of the account as the element appears in the accounting equation.

Rules for Debiting and Crediting
- To increase an asset, debit the account.
- To decrease an asset, credit the account.
- To increase a liability, credit the account.
- To decrease a liability, debit the account.
- To increase owner's equity, credit the account.
- To decrease owner's equity, debit the account.

Assets A	=	Liabilities L	+	Owner's Equity OE

+ Asset Accounts −		− Liability Accounts +		− Owner's Equity Accounts +	
Increase on the debit side.	*Decrease on the credit side.*	*Decrease on the debit side.*	*Increase on the credit side.*	*Decrease on the debit side.*	*Increase on the credit side.*

The rules for debiting and crediting are based on the accounting equation.

■ Showing Opening Balances The beginning amount in each account is called an **opening balance**. The opening balance for each account relates to the position of that account in the accounting equation. Since assets appear on the left side of the accounting equation, the opening balance of an asset account is shown on the debit, or left, side of the account. For example, the opening balance of the Cash account shown below is a debit of $90.

Cash			*101*
Opening Balance	*90*	*Decrease*	*50*
		Decrease	*20*
Increase	*10*		
30	*100*		*70*
Debit Balance			

Asset accounts are increased by debits and decreased by credits.

Liabilities and owner's equity appear on the right side of the accounting equation. Thus, the opening balances of liability accounts and the owner's equity Capital account are shown on the credit, or right, side of the accounts.

■ Increasing Accounts An increase to an account is recorded on one side of the account only. Since assets appear on the left side of the accounting equation, any increase to an asset account is recorded on the debit, or left, side of the account. For example, in the illustration above, a transaction occurred that increased the Cash account by $10. This increase is recorded by debiting the account for $10.

Since liabilities appear on the right side of the accounting equation, all liabilities are increased on the credit, or right, side. Thus, liability accounts are increased by crediting the accounts.

Owner's equity also appears on the right side of the accounting equation. Thus, owner's equity accounts are increased on the credit side.

Decreasing Accounts A decrease to an account is recorded on the opposite side of the account as the element appears in the accounting equation. As a result, asset accounts are decreased on the credit side. For example, in the illustration on page 61, a transaction occurred that decreased the Cash account by $50. The decrease is recorded in the Cash account by crediting the account.

Since liabilities appear on the right side of the equation, liability accounts are decreased on the opposite side. Thus, liability accounts are decreased on the debit side. The debit side is the side opposite to that in which the liability element appears in the accounting equation.

Owner's equity also appears on the right side of the equation. Thus, owner's equity is decreased by debiting the owner's equity accounts.

Showing Normal Balances The difference between the two sides of an account is the account balance. The account balance normally appears on the same side as the element appears in the accounting equation. Thus, asset accounts normally have debit balances. Liability accounts and owner's equity accounts normally have credit balances.

Principle: Increasing an Account Balance
The generally accepted accounting principle is that the balance of an account is increased on the same side as the element appears in the accounting equation.

Principle: Decreasing an Account Balance
The generally accepted accounting principle is that the balance of an account is decreased on the side opposite to that on which the element appears in the accounting equation.

Exercise C on page 65 may be completed at this point.

Opening the Accounts

Is a separate account opened for each asset, liability, and owner's equity item? Yes, a separate account is used for each asset, liability, and owner's equity item. The T accounts shown on page 63 were opened for Exercise Plus. All the data was taken from the September 1 accounting equation.

The following procedure is used to open an account.

1. Write the account title at the center and the account number at the right.
2. Enter the date and the opening balance on the same side as the account as shown in the accounting equation.

Opening Asset Accounts Assets appear on the left side of the accounting equation. Thus, asset account balances are recorded on the debit (left) side of the T accounts. The first asset listed in the accounting equation is Cash, which has a balance of $9,000. Thus, the Cash

Cash	Accounts Receivable	Furniture	Exercise Equipment	=	Accounts Payable	Lisa Long, Capital
Assets				=	*Liabilities* +	*Owner's Equity*
$9,000 +	$1,000 +	$3,000 +	$9,000	=	$4,000 +	$18,000
$22,000				=	$22,000	

Accounting equation as of September 1.

① *Cash* 101

19—	
Sept. 1 9,000	

② *Accts. Pay./Shone Products* 201

	19—
	Sept. 1 4,000

Accts. Rec./Carmen Saldi 103

19—	
Sept. 1 1,000	

Lisa Long, Capital 301

	19—
	Sept. 1 18,000

Furniture 111

19—	
Sept. 1 3,000	

Exercise Equipment 112

19—	
Sept. 1 9,000	

To open an account, write the title at the center and the number at right. Enter the date and the opening balance on the proper side.

Assets		*Liabilities* + *Owner's Equity*
$22,000	=	$4,000 + $18,000
Total Debits = $22,000	=	Total Credits = $22,000

Proof

account is debited for $9,000. The second asset in the equation is Accounts Receivable. A separate account is opened for each business or individual who owes a debt. The business or individual who owes a debt is called a debtor. Carmen Saldi is the debtor who owes $1,000 to Exercise Plus. Therefore, an account is opened for Accts. Rec./ Carmen Saldi. The account is debited for $1,000.

■ **Opening Liability Accounts** Liabilities appear on the right side of the accounting equation. Thus, liability account balances are recorded on the credit (right) side of the T accounts. The first liability is Accounts Payable. A separate account is opened for each creditor (business or individual to whom a debt is owed) so that the amount owed to each can be found quickly. The Accts. Pay./Shone Products account is credited for $4,000.

■ **Opening Owner's Equity Accounts** Owner's equity also appears on the right side of the accounting equation. Therefore, owner's equity account balances appear on the credit (right) side of the

T accounts. Since the total owner's equity on September 1 is $18,000, the Lisa Long, Capital account is credited for $18,000.

■ Ledger

A group of accounts is called a **ledger**. A business can maintain a record of financial transactions with a ledger. Such records can also be organized conveniently according to account titles. For example, the Exercise Plus ledger on September 1 is made up of the six accounts shown on page 63.

The asset accounts have debit balances. The debit side of the accounts in the ledger totals $22,000. The liability and owner's equity accounts have credit balances. The credit side of the accounts also totals $22,000. According to the accounting equation, the total debit balances (assets) in the ledger must always equal the total credit balances (liabilities and owner's equity). Thus, the equality of the accounting equation is maintained in the ledger.

Exercises C and D on page 65 may be completed at this point.

Concept: Ledger

Records of the changes caused by transactions should be available according to account titles. These records are kept in a ledger.

TOPIC 1 EXERCISES

EXERCISE A. Compute the account balances for the following T accounts. Refer to the text, margin notes, and illustrations on pages 59 to 60. An example is illustrated below.

EXAMPLE:

Accts. Rec./Pride Stores 103

	Debit	Credit
	100	25
	50	
	75	
200	225	

Dr. Balance 200 or Cr. Balance ___

Furniture 111

Debit	Credit
200	350
300	
500	

Accts. Pay./Anne's Shop 201

Debit	Credit
200	850
	300
	200

Alan Ramirez, Capital 301

Debit	Credit
2,000	5,000

Sales 401

Debit	Credit
	700
	500

Delivery Expense 501

Debit	Credit
400	
50	
75	

EXERCISE B. Find the balance for each of the following T accounts. Then show the debit balance or credit balance using a form similar to the one shown in the example at the right. Then total all debits and credits to prove their equality.

	Balance	
EXAMPLE:	Dr.	Cr.
Cash 101	$1,750	____

Cash 101		*Accts. Rec./Joyce Levy 102*		*Supplies 103*		*Furniture 112*	
1,550	30	200	250	30		300	300
50	20	300		200		20	
200		500				100	

Truck 114		*Accts. Pay./Mark Gibbs 201*		*Rhonda Todero, Capital 301*	
3,200		10	400	20	5,680

EXERCISE C. Indicate which of the following items would appear on the debit side and which would appear on the credit side of an account.

EXAMPLE: Balance of a liability account—Credit

1. Decrease to an asset account

2. Increase to an asset account

3. Balance of an owner's equity account

4. Increase to a liability account

5. Decrease to a liability account

6. Decrease to an owner's equity account

7. Increase to an owner's equity account

EXERCISE D. Open a T account for each asset, liability, and owner's equity item that is listed in the chart of accounts below.

Enter the account title, the account number, the account balance, and the date. Refer to the accounting equation for April 1, below, which contains the balance for each of the accounts.

CHART OF ACCOUNTS

Assets
101 Cash
102 Accts. Rec./Philip Kim
103 Accts. Rec./Janet Manero
111 Truck

Liabilities
201 Accts. Pay./King Motors

Owner's Equity
301 Sally Ross, Capital

	Assets							=	*Liabilities*	+	*Owner's Equity*
	Cash		Accts. Rec./ Philip Kim		Accts. Rec./ Janet Manero		Truck		Accts. Pay./ King Motors		Sally Ross, Capital
April 1 balances	$800	+	$610	+	$215	+	$9,000	=	$3,000	+	$7,625

TOPIC 1 PROBLEMS

TOPIC PROBLEM 1. Open a T account for each asset, liability, and owner's equity account that is listed in the chart of accounts at the right.

Enter the account title, the account number, the date, and the account balance. If there is no account balance for a particular account, do not record the date or an amount. Check that the total debit balances equal the total credit balances in the ledger. Refer to the accounting equation below.

CHART OF ACCOUNTS

Assets
101 Cash
103 Accts. Rec./Rita Holt

Liabilities
201 Accts. Pay./Brian Butler

Owner's Equity
301 Alice Kaliski, Capital
399 Income Summary

Revenue
401 Sales

Expenses
501 Rent Expense

Assets			=	*Liabilities*	+	*Owner's Equity*			
Cash		Accts. Rec./ Rita Holt		Accts. Pay./ Brian Butler		Alice Kaliski, Capital		Income Summary (Revenue − Expense)	
$4,260	+	$120	=	$190	+	$4,190	+	$-0-	**Aug. 1 balances**

TOPIC PROBLEM 2. Open a T account for each asset, liability, and owner's equity item for the following accounts. Use appropriate account numbers according to the chart of accounts at the right. Check that the total debit balances equal the total credit balances. The May 1 balances are as follows.

Accts. Pay./Eastern Corporation	$ 9,000
Cash	6,750
Shop Equipment	15,000
Robert McCall, Capital	12,750
Repairs Expense	-0-
Sales	-0-
Income Summary	-0-

CHART OF ACCOUNTS

Assets
101 Cash
111 Shop Equipment

Liabilities
201 Accts. Pay./
Eastern Corporation

Owner's Equity
301 Robert McCall, Capital
399 Income Summary

Revenue
401 Sales

Expenses
501 Repairs Expense

TOPIC 2

Debiting and Crediting Asset and Liability Accounts

How does an accountant analyze a business transaction? In Chapter 2 you recorded the effect of business transactions on the accounting equation. You learned the following three basic rules of double-entry accounting.

- Each transaction affects at least two accounts.
- Each transaction is stated in dollar amounts.
- The accounting equation is in balance after each transaction is recorded.

Now you will find out how business transactions are recorded in accounts. But first, you must analyze the transaction.

Analyzing Business Transactions

An accountant studies each business transaction and asks three questions. These questions will help you to analyze the changes caused by a transaction.

- *What happens?* For each business transaction, name all accounts affected, classify the accounts, determine if the accounts are increased or decreased, and determine the amounts.
- *Which accounting rules apply?* Apply the accounting rules of debiting and crediting to each part of the transaction. Use the summary of accounting rules for increasing and decreasing accounts shown in the margin.
- *What entry is to be made?* State the business transaction as an accounting entry. An **accounting entry** is (1) the date of the transaction, (2) the debit account title and the amount, and (3) the credit account title and the amount. The debit part of the entry is always stated before the credit part.

Accounting Rules

Assets:	Debits increase Credits decrease
Liabilities:	Credits increase Debits decrease
Owner's Equity:	Credits increase Debits decrease

Assume that Exercise Plus buys additional exercise equipment for $4,000 in cash. *What happens?* would be answered as follows. The asset Exercise Equipment *increases* by $4,000, and the asset Cash *decreases* by $4,000.

The accounting rules that apply to this transaction are the following. *To increase an asset, debit the account. To decrease an asset, credit the account.* Thus, the entry is as follows. Debit the Exercise Equipment account for $4,000, and credit the Cash account for $4,000.

This transaction illustrates double-entry accounting. **Double-entry accounting** means that each transaction affects two or more accounts and that the total debit amounts always equal the total credit amounts.

Exercises E and F on pages 70 and 71 may be completed at this point.

Recording Changes in Asset Accounts

How are changes in asset accounts recorded? To answer this question, we will enter the September transactions of Exercise Plus in the T accounts already opened. The beginning balances were taken from the accounting equation of September 1. Each transaction will be analyzed to show the following.

- Which asset account is increased or decreased.
- Which rules of debiting and crediting apply to these increases or decreases.
- What the accounting entry should be.

The following transactions illustrate the accounting rules for increasing and decreasing asset accounts.

Exercise Plus buys additional exercise equipment from the Fitness Supplies Corporation and issues a check for $4,000 in payment. The asset account Exercise Equipment is increased. Therefore, Exercise Equipment is debited for $4,000. The asset account Cash is decreased. Therefore, Cash is credited for $4,000.

SEPTEMBER 5: EXERCISE PLUS BUYS ADDITIONAL EXERCISE EQUIPMENT FOR $4,000 IN CASH.

What Happens	Accounting Rule	Accounting Entry
The asset *Exercise Equipment* increases by $4,000.	To increase an asset, debit the account.	Debit: Exercise Equipment, $4,000
The asset *Cash* decreases by $4,000.	To decrease an asset, credit the account.	Credit: Cash, $4,000

Cash 101

19—		*19—*	
Sept. 1	*9,000*	*Sept. 5*	**4,000**

Exercise Equipment 112

19—			
Sept. 1	*9,000*		
5	**4,000**		

Buying assets for cash.

Exercise Plus receives a check for $1,000 from Carmen Saldi on account. The asset account Cash is increased. Therefore, it is debited for $1,000. The asset account Accts. Rec./Carmen Saldi is decreased. Therefore, it is credited for $1,000.

SEPTEMBER 6: EXERCISE PLUS RECEIVES $1,000 FROM CARMEN SALDI ON ACCOUNT.

What Happens	Accounting Rule	Accounting Entry
The asset *Cash* increases by $1,000.	To increase an asset, debit the account.	Debit: Cash, $1,000
The asset *Accts. Rec./Carmen Saldi* decreases by $1,000.	To decrease an asset, credit the account.	Credit: Accts. Rec./Carmen Saldi, $1,000

Cash 101

19—		*19—*	
Sept. 1	*9,000*	*Sept. 5*	*4,000*
6	**1,000**		

Accts. Rec./Carmen Saldi 103

19—		*19—*	
Sept. 1	*1,000*	*Sept. 6*	**1,000**

Collecting an account receivable.

Exercises G and H on page 71 may be completed at this point.

Recording Changes in Liability Accounts

How are changes in liability accounts recorded? The steps used to record changes in liability accounts are the same as those for asset accounts. Remember, however, that liability accounts increase on the credit side and decrease on the debit side.

Exercise Plus buys additional furniture for $2,000 on credit from Shone Products. The asset account Furniture is increased. Therefore, it is debited for $2,000. The liability account Accts. Pay./Shone Products is also increased. Therefore, it is credited for $2,000.

SEPTEMBER 7: EXERCISE PLUS BUYS ADDITIONAL FURNITURE FOR $2,000 ON CREDIT FROM SHONE PRODUCTS.

What Happens	Accounting Rule	Accounting Entry
The asset *Furniture* increases by $2,000. The liability *Accts. Pay./Shone Products* increases by $2,000.	To increase an asset, debit the account. To increase a liability, credit the account.	Debit: Furniture, $2,000 Credit: Accts. Pay./Shone Products, $2,000

Furniture 111

Debit		Credit	
19—			
Sept. 1	3,000		
7	**2,000**		

Accts. Pay./Shone Products 201

Debit		Credit	
		19—	
		Sept. 1	4,000
		7	**2,000**

Buying assets on credit.

Exercise Plus returns furniture to Shone Products because it arrived damaged. Exercise Plus now owes Shone Products $500 less because of the return. The liability account Accts. Pay./Shone Products is decreased. Therefore, it is debited for $500. The asset account Furniture is decreased. Therefore, it is credited for $500.

SEPTEMBER 8: EXERCISE PLUS RETURNS FURNITURE BOUGHT FOR $500 ON CREDIT FROM SHONE PRODUCTS.

What Happens	Accounting Rule	Accounting Entry
The liability *Accts. Pay./Shone Products* decreases by $500. The asset *Furniture* decreases by $500.	To decrease a liability, debit the account. To decrease an asset, credit the account.	Debit: Accts. Pay./Shone Products, $500 Credit: Furniture, $500

Furniture 111

Debit		Credit	
19—		19—	
Sept. 1	3,000	Sept. 8	**500**
7	2,000		

Accts. Pay./Shone Products 201

Debit		Credit	
19—		19—	
Sept. 8	**500**	Sept. 1	4,000
		7	2,000

Returning assets bought on credit.

The transaction for September 12 illustrates how a liability account is decreased when a liability is paid. On September 12 Exercise Plus writes a check for $4,000 to Shone Products on account. The liability account Accts. Pay./Shone Products is decreased. Therefore, it is debited for $4,000. The asset account Cash is decreased. Therefore, it is credited for $4,000.

SEPTEMBER 12: EXERCISE PLUS PAYS $4,000 TO SHONE PRODUCTS ON ACCOUNT.

What Happens	Accounting Rule	Accounting Entry
The liability *Accts. Pay./ Shone Products* decreases by $4,000. The asset *Cash* decreases by $4,000.	To decrease a liability, debit the account. To decrease an asset, credit the account.	Debit: Accts. Pay./Shone Products, $4,000 Credit: Cash, $4,000

Cash 101

19—			*19—*		
Sept.	*1*	*9,000*	*Sept.*	*5*	*4,000*
	6	*1,000*		*12*	**4,000**

Accts. Pay./Shone Products 201

19—			*19—*		
Sept.	*8*	*500*	*Sept.*	*1*	*4,000*
	12	**4,000**		*7*	*2,000*

Paying liabilities.

This topic has explained how changes are recorded for two types of permanent accounts—assets and liabilities. In Topic 3, you will see how changes are recorded for owner's equity accounts—the permanent Capital account and the temporary revenue and expense accounts.

Exercises I and J on page 72 may be completed at this point.

TOPIC 2 EXERCISES

EXERCISE E. Decide whether the account is increased or decreased in each of the following.

EXAMPLE: Cash account is debited—Increased

1. Accts. Pay./Ronald Towne is credited.
2. Mortgage Payable account is credited.
3. Accts. Rec./Helen Parks is debited.
4. Accts. Pay./Crown Supplies is credited.
5. Capital account is credited.
6. Equipment account is credited.
7. Mortgage Payable account is debited.
8. Furniture account is credited.

EXERCISE F. Analyze the following transactions in sentence form. Use the example as a guide.

EXAMPLE: The Kalli Company received $600 from Sage Clothes on account.

The asset account Cash is increased; therefore, it is debited for $600. The asset account Accts. Rec./Sage Clothes is decreased; therefore, it is credited for $600.

1. The Katz Company bought additional equipment for $400 on credit from the Echo Furniture Store.
2. O'Neill and Associates returned office furniture bought for $300 on credit from the Office Supplies Store.
3. Karen Burton invested an additional $4,000 in her single proprietorship, Burton's Bakery.

EXERCISE G. For each of the following transactions, determine: (1) what happens to the basic elements, (2) which accounting rule of debiting or crediting applies, and (3) what accounts should be debited and credited. Use a form similar to the one shown in the example at the right. Use the signs A+ to indicate increases and A− to indicate decreases in the asset accounts.

1. Received $230 from a customer on account.
2. Bought tools for $600 in cash.
3. Bought a typewriter for $800 in cash.
4. Returned tools bought for $50 in cash.
5. Received $25 from sale of equipment.

NOTE: Save your form for further use in Exercise I.

EXAMPLE: Received $550 in cash from a customer on account.

	Accounting Rule		Accounting Entry	
What Happens	**Debit**	**Credit**	**Account Debited**	**Account Credited**
Example: A+	√		Cash	
A−		√		Accounts Receivable

EXERCISE H. Analyze each of the transactions at the right. Then record the debit and the credit amounts in the appropriate T accounts.

EXAMPLE: Bought supplies for $30 in cash.

1. Bought office equipment for $500 in cash.
2. Received $100 from Mary Souza on account.
3. Bought shop equipment for $300 in cash.
4. Returned shop equipment for $150 in cash.

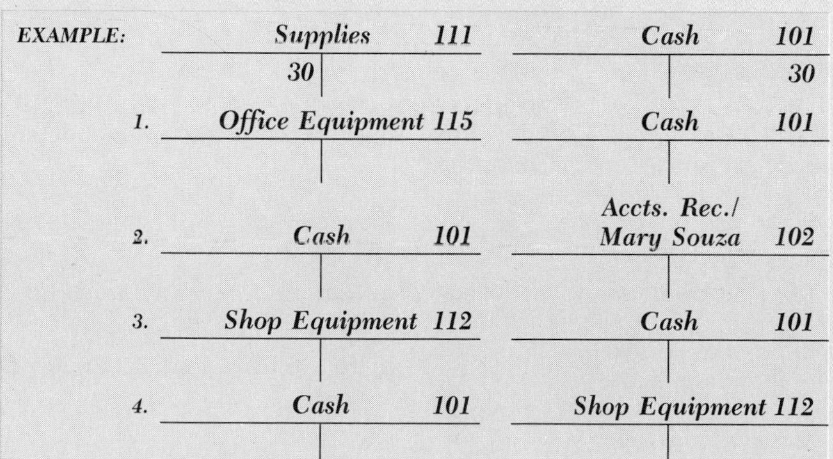

EXERCISE I. Use your form from Exercise G to analyze the following transactions. For each transaction, determine (1) what happens to the basic elements, (2) which accounting rule of debiting or crediting applies, and (3) what accounts should be debited and credited. Use the signs A+, A−, L+, and L− to indicate increases and decreases in the asset and liability accounts.

1. Bought tools for $200 on credit.
2. Returned tools bought for $75 on credit.
3. Paid $150 to a creditor on account.
4. Bought furniture for $175 on credit.
5. Bought tools for $85 in cash.

EXERCISE J. Set up two T accounts for each of the following transactions. Give an appropriate title and account number to each account. Then record the amount on the correct side of each account.

EXAMPLE: Bought equipment for $250 on credit from the Star Equipment Company.

1. Bought equipment for $600 in cash.
2. Returned equipment bought for $90 in cash.
3. Returned equipment bought for $100 on credit from the Star Equipment Company.
4. Paid $150 to the Star Equipment Company on account.
5. Bought supplies for $95 on credit from Micro Supplies.
6. Received $135 from Suzanne's Salon on account.
7. Borrowed $6,000 from State Savings Bank as a loan to be paid in 120 days.
8. Bought an adding machine for the office for $250 on credit. Gave a note to Office Machine Company.
9. Bought land for $10,000 on credit and gave a mortgage to Tri-City Savings Bank.
10. Bought a chair for $350 in cash.

Equipment	*111*
250	

Accts. Pay./ Star Equip. Co.	*203*
	250

TOPIC 2 PROBLEMS

TOPIC PROBLEM 3. Set up two T accounts for each of the following transactions. Give an appropriate title and account number to each account, and record the amount on the correct side of each account.

a. Received $900 from Diane Hoffman on account.
b. Bought a second-hand truck for $5,000 on credit from Capital Trucks.
c. Bought a desk and chair for $500 on credit from Office Supply Company.
d. Paid $700 to Capital Trucks on account.
e. Bought two tables for $450 cash.
f. Received $400 from Linda Jacobs on account.
g. Returned the chair bought for $100 on credit from Office Supply Company.
h. Paid $100 to Office Supply Company on account.

TOPIC PROBLEM 4. The T accounts below show the results of seven transactions for Alex Murphy's business. Explain what happened in transactions *a, b, c, d, e, f,* and *g*. The debit and credit entries for a transaction are identified by the same letter. The first transaction is done as an example. Refer to the T accounts below.

EXAMPLE: *a.* Alex Murphy started a business with an investment of $7,500 in cash, $800 in accounts receivable, $8,000 in equipment, and $1,400 in Accts. Pay./Ann Fields.

Cash 101

	Debit		Credit
a.	7,500	*c.*	900
e.	200	*d.*	1,400
g.	800	*f.*	500

Accts. Rec./Sandra Tobin 102

	Debit		Credit
a.	800	*g.*	800

Equipment 111

	Debit		Credit
a.	8,000		
b.	3,000		

Furniture 112

	Debit		Credit
c.	900	*e.*	200

Accts. Pay./Ann Fields 201

	Debit		Credit
d.	1,400	*a.*	1,400

Accts. Pay./Allied Stores 202

	Debit		Credit
f.	500	*b.*	3,000

Alex Murphy, Capital 301

	Debit		Credit
		a.	14,900

TOPIC PROBLEM 5. Set up two T accounts for each transaction below. Give a title and account number to each account. Then record the amount on the correct side of each account.

Hint: Transactions *a* and *d* involve expanding on concepts you learned in this topic.

a. Borrowed $2,500 from Diamond Savings Bank as a loan to be paid in 90 days.

b. Bought an adding machine for the office for $575 on credit. Gave a note to McBride Office Machines promising to pay in 60 days.

c. Paid $600 to Diamond Savings Bank as part payment of its loan.

d. Paid $5,000 to First Savings Bank in full payment of mortgage.

TOPIC PROBLEM 6. Set up two T accounts for each of the transactions below. Set up all accounts to be debited in Column A. Set up all accounts to be credited in Column B. Give an appropriate title and account number to each account. Then record the amount on the correct side of each account.

Hint: Transactions *b* and *i* involve expanding on concepts you learned in this topic.

a. Bought a truck for $6,000 in cash.

b. Borrowed $10,000 from Trust Savings Bank as a loan.

c. Paid $400 to City Supplies on account.

d. Received $250 from Hughes Company on account.

e. Paid $450 to Thomas LaSalle on account.

f. Returned shop equipment bought for $400 on credit from City Supplies.

g. Bought shop equipment for $900 in cash.

h. Returned tools bought for $50 in cash.

i. Paid $2,000 on a loan.

j. Bought supplies for $250 on credit from Williams Company.

k. Returned shop equipment bought for $450 in cash.

l. Bought shop equipment for $1,000 on credit from Maynard Company.

m. Paid $250 to Trent Company on account.

n. Bought tools for $525 on credit from Nelson Tool Company.

TOPIC 3

Debiting and Crediting Owner's Equity Accounts

Which accounts are used to record changes in owner's equity? The capital, revenue, and expense accounts are used. The permanent account Capital is used when the owner makes additional investments or withdrawals. The temporary owner's equity accounts are used when the business obtains revenue and has expenses. In all cases, two basic rules govern the increases and decreases in owner's equity.

- *To increase owner's equity, credit the account.* Additional investments and revenues increase owner's equity. Therefore, credit the Capital account when investments are made, and credit the revenue accounts when revenue is earned.
- *To decrease owner's equity, debit the account.* Withdrawals of investment and incurring expenses decrease owner's equity. Therefore, debit the Capital account when investments are withdrawn, and debit the expense accounts when expenses occur.

Lisa Long, Capital 301	
Record withdrawals on the debit side.	*Record investments on the credit side.*

■ Recording Changes in the Capital Account

The Capital account shows the owner's investment in the business. This account increases when the owner makes an additional investment. The Capital account decreases when the owner withdraws an asset, such as cash or equipment. The Lisa Long, Capital account had a balance of $18,000 on September 1. During September the following transactions caused changes in the Capital account.

On September 14 Lisa Long invested more money in Exercise Plus. The asset account Cash is increased. As you can see in the analysis on

SEPTEMBER 14: LISA LONG INVESTS AN ADDITIONAL $13,000 IN EXERCISE PLUS.

What Happens	Accounting Rule	Accounting Entry
The asset *Cash* increases by $13,000. The owner's equity *Lisa Long, Capital* increases by $13,000.	To increase an asset, debit the account. To increase owner's equity, credit the account.	Debit: Cash, $13,000 Credit: Lisa Long, Capital, $13,000

Cash 101

Date		Debit	Date		Credit
19—			*19—*		
Sept.	*1*	*9,000*	*Sept.*	*5*	*4,000*
	6	*1,000*		*12*	*4,000*
	14	**13,000**			

Lisa Long, Capital 301

Date		Debit	Date		Credit
			19—		
			Sept.	*1*	*18,000*
				14	**13,000**

Increasing owner's investment.

the previous page, therefore, the Cash account is debited for $13,000. Owner's equity is also increased. Thus, the Lisa Long, Capital account is credited for $13,000.

On September 21 Lisa Long decides to withdraw $6,000 in cash from Exercise Plus. This results in a decrease in owner's equity. Therefore, the Lisa Long, Capital account is debited for $6,000. The asset Cash also decreases. Thus, the Cash account is credited for $6,000.

SEPTEMBER 21: LISA LONG WITHDRAWS $6,000 FROM EXERCISE PLUS.

What Happens	Accounting Rule	Accounting Entry
The owner's equity *Lisa Long, Capital* decreases by $6,000.	To decrease owner's equity, debit the account.	Debit: Lisa Long, Capital, $6,000
The asset *Cash* decreases by $6,000.	To decrease an asset, credit the account.	Credit: Cash, $6,000

Cash — *101*

19—		19—		
Sept. 1	9,000	Sept. 5	4,000	
6	1,000	12	4,000	
14	13,000	21	**6,000**	

Lisa Long, Capital — *301*

19—		19—	
Sept. 21	**6,000**	Sept. 1	18,000
		14	13,000

Decreasing owner's investment.

Recording Changes in Revenue Accounts

How are changes in revenue accounts recorded? Owner's equity increases when the owner makes an additional investment of cash or other assets in the business and when revenue is earned by the business. The way in which most businesses earn revenue is through the sale of goods or services.

Revenue Accounts	
	Record revenue on the credit side.

To increase owner's equity, credit the account.

The amount of a sale is recorded in a revenue account called Sales. Since revenue increases owner's equity, the Sales account is credited for the amount of the sale. Exercise Plus sold services for cash and on credit during the September accounting period.

On September 26 Exercise Plus received $4,000 cash from the sale of its fitness services during the month of September. The asset Cash increases. Therefore, the Cash account is debited for $4,000. The revenue also increases owner's equity. Therefore, the owner's equity account Sales is credited for $4,000. This is analyzed in the table shown on the next page.

SEPTEMBER 26: EXERCISE PLUS RECEIVES $4,000 IN CASH FROM THE SALE OF SERVICES DURING SEPTEMBER.

What Happens	Accounting Rule	Accounting Entry
The asset *Cash* increases by $4,000. The revenue *Sales* increases owner's equity by $4,000.	To increase an asset, debit the account. To increase owner's equity, credit the account.	Debit: Cash, $4,000 Credit: Sales, $4,000

Cash 101

19—			19—		
Sept.	1	9,000	Sept.	5	4,000
	6	1,000		12	4,000
	14	13,000		21	6,000
	26	**4,000**			

Sales 401

			19—		
			Sept.	26	**4,000**

Receiving revenue from cash sales.

In the transaction for September 27, sales are made on credit to two customers. As a result, two accounts receivable accounts are affected—an account for Carmen Saldi and an account for Talbot Industries.

The asset account Accts. Rec./Carmen Saldi is debited for $700. The asset account Accts. Rec./Talbot Industries is debited for $1,400. The owner's equity account Sales is credited for $2,100. Although this transaction involves two debits ($700 + $1,400) and one credit ($2,100), the total of the debits equals the total of the credits. Any transaction involving more than one debit or credit is called a **compound transaction**

Exercises K and L on pages 78 and 79 may be completed at this point.

SEPTEMBER 27: EXERCISE PLUS SELLS SERVICES ON CREDIT TO CARMEN SALDI FOR $700 AND TO TALBOT INDUSTRIES FOR $1,400.

What Happens	Accounting Rule	Accounting Entry
The asset *Accts. Rec./Carmen Saldi* increases by $700, and the asset *Accts. Rec./Talbot Industries* increases by $1,400. The revenue *Sales* increases owner's equity by $2,100.	To increase an asset, debit the account. To increase owner's equity, credit the account.	Debit: Accts. Rec./Carmen Saldi, $700 Accts. Rec./Talbot Industries, $1,400 Credit: Sales, $2,100

Accts. Rec./Carmen Saldi 103

19—			19—		
Sept.	1	1,000	Sept.	6	1,000
	27	**700**			

Accts. Rec./Talbot Industries 104

19—					
Sept.	27	**1,400**			

Sales 401

			19—		
			Sept.	26	4,000
				27	**2,100**

Receiving revenue from sales on credit.

Recording Changes in Expense Accounts

What transactions decrease owner's equity? Owner's equity decreases when the owner makes a withdrawal of an asset for his or her personal use. Owner's equity also decreases when expenses occur in operating the business. A business normally has many different types of expenses. Common expenses for a business include rent, salaries, and utilities. A separate account is opened for each kind of expense. Since an expense decreases owner's equity, the amount is recorded as a debit to the expense account. Expenses can either be paid in cash or incurred on credit.

Expense Accounts	
Record expenses on the debit side.	

To decrease owner's equity, debit the account.

To see how expenses affect owner's equity, let us look at the expense transactions of Exercise Plus for September.

On September 28 Exercise Plus pays salaries to its employees. The salaries are an expense of $2,900 to the business. The expense decreases owner's equity. As a result, the Salaries Expense account is debited for $2,900, thus decreasing owner's equity. The asset account Cash is also decreased. Therefore, the account Cash is credited for $2,900. The effect of this transaction is shown below.

SEPTEMBER 28: EXERCISE PLUS PAYS AN EXPENSE OF $2,900 FOR SALARIES.

What Happens	Accounting Rule	Accounting Entry
The expense *Salaries Expense* decreases owner's equity by $2,900.	To decrease owner's equity, debit the account.	Debit: Salaries Expense, $2,900
The asset *Cash* decreases by $2,900.	To decrease an asset, credit the account.	Credit: Cash, $2,900

Cash			*101*		
19—			*19—*		
Sept.	*1*	*9,000*	*Sept.*	*5*	*4,000*
	6	*1,000*		*12*	*4,000*
	14	*13,000*		*21*	*6,000*
	26	*4,000*		*28*	**2,900**

Salaries Expense			*505*
19—			
Sept.	*28*	**2,900**	

Paying expenses.

On September 29 Exercise Plus receives a bill for $200 from the XYZ Repairs for repairs to exercise equipment. The Repairs Expense account is debited for $200, thus decreasing owner's equity. The liability account Accts. Pay./XYZ Repairs is credited for $200, thus increasing liabilities. This transaction is illustrated at the top of page 78.

SEPTEMBER 29: EXERCISE PLUS OWES A REPAIRS EXPENSE OF $200 TO XYZ REPAIRS FOR REPAIRS TO EXERCISE EQUIPMENT.

What Happens	Accounting Rule	Accounting Entry
The expense *Repairs Expense* decreases owner's equity by $200. The liability *Accts. Pay./XYZ Repairs* increases by $200.	To decrease owner's equity, debit the account. To increase a liability, credit the account.	Debit: Repairs Expense, $200 Credit: Accts. Pay./XYZ Repairs $200

Accts. Pay./XYZ Repairs	*202*
	19— *Sept. 29* **200**

Repairs Expense	*504*
19— *Sept. 29* **200**	

Incurring expenses on credit.

Exercise M on page 79 may be completed at this point.

TOPIC 3 EXERCISES

EXERCISE K. The T accounts below show the results of six transactions for Pulaski's Dental Service. Indicate whether each transaction increases or decreases the accounts. Then explain what happened in each transaction.

EXAMPLE: *1.* Cash account increases. Mary Pulaski, Capital account increases. Mary Pulaski started the business with an investment of $6,000 in cash.

Cash			*101*
1.	*6,000*	*2.*	*2,000*
5.	*8,000*	*6.*	*600*

Office Equipment			*111*
3.	*800*	*4.*	*200*

Mary Pulaski, Capital			*301*
2.	*2,000*	*1.*	*6,000*
4.	*200*	*3.*	*800*
6.	*600*	*5.*	*8,000*

EXERCISE L. Analyze each of the following transactions. Then record the debit amount and the credit amount in the appropriate T accounts.

EXAMPLE: Iris Cohen started the business with $37,000 in cash.

1. Sold services for $490 in cash.

2. Sold services for $440 on credit to Juan Martinez.

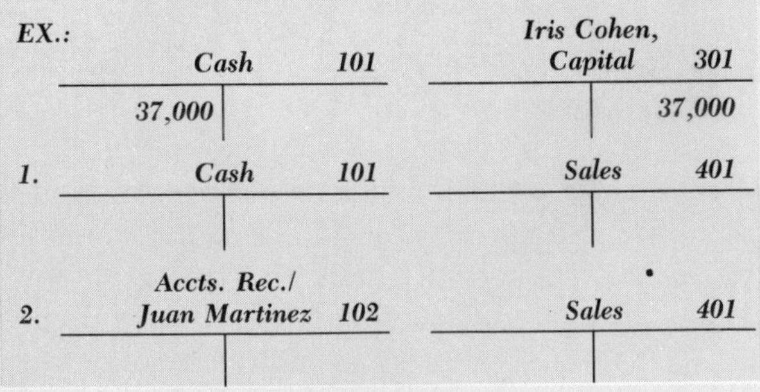

3. Owner withdrew $300 from the business for her personal use.

4. Owner invested another $2,000 in the business.

5. Sold services for $510 on credit to Sandra LaMont.

6. Bought office equipment for $475 cash.

7. Received $350 from Barbara Ryan on account.

8. Owner withdrew $40 of office equipment from the business.

3.	*Iris Cohen, Capital 301*	*Cash 101*
4.	*Cash 101*	*Iris Cohen, Capital 301*
5.	*Accts. Rec./ Sandra LaMont 104*	*Sales 401*
6.	*Office Equipment 111*	*Cash 101*
7.	*Cash 101*	*Accts. Rec./ Barbara Ryan 103*
8.	*Iris Cohen, Capital 301*	*Office Equipment 111*

EXERCISE M. For each of the transactions below, determine (1) what happens to the basic elements, (2) which accounting rule of debiting or crediting applies, and (3) what accounts should be debited and credited. Use the signs A+, A−, L+, L−, OE+, and OE− to indicate increases or decreases in the accounts. Use a form like the one shown below.

EXAMPLE: Norman Pappas started the business with $7,000 in cash.

1. Received $300 from sale of services.
2. Norman Pappas withdrew $200 from the business.
3. Sold services for $600 on credit to Marie Jackson.
4. Bought tools for $90 in cash.
5. Received $40 from sale of services.
6. Norman Pappas invested an additional $4,000 in the business.
7. Sold services for $800 on credit to Ralph Phillips.
8. Received $300 from Marie Jackson on account.
9. Sold services for $500 on credit to the Carter Company.
10. Received $20 from sale of tools.
11. Norman Pappas withdrew $600 from the business.
12. Paid $300 for rent.
13. Sold services for $400 on credit to Sylvia Huff.
14. Paid $60 for telephone expense.
15. Norman Pappas withdrew $335 from the business.
16. Owes $50 to Pike Garage for gasoline.
17. Received $95 from sale of services.

	Accounting Rule		Accounting Entry	
What Happens	**Debit**	**Credit**	**Account Debited**	**Account Credited**
A+	√		Cash	
OE+		√		Norman Pappas, Capital

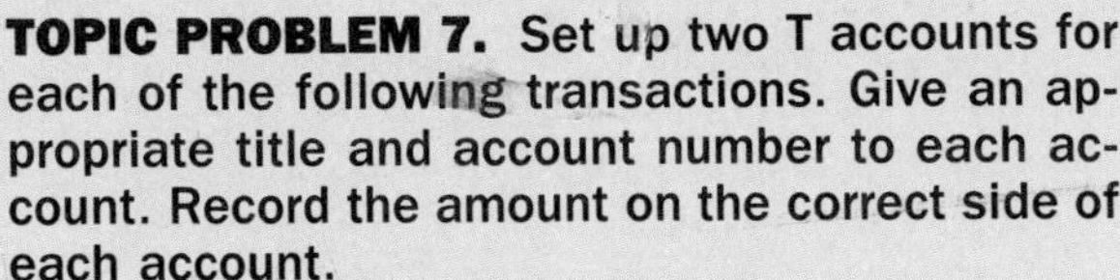

TOPIC 3 PROBLEMS

TOPIC PROBLEM 7. Set up two T accounts for each of the following transactions. Give an appropriate title and account number to each account. Record the amount on the correct side of each account.

EXAMPLE: Frank Drake started a business with $6,500 in cash.

a. Bought equipment for $3,000 on credit from the Reed Company.

b. Sold services for $670 on credit to Rose Sanders.

c. Frank Drake withdrew $1,000 from the business for his personal use.

d. Returned equipment bought for $500 on credit from the Reed Company.

e. Received $475 from Rose Sanders on account.

f. Paid $350 for rent.

g. Sold services for $550 in cash.

h. Paid $350 to the Reed Company on account.

i. Sold services for $800 on credit to Herman Hughes.

j. Paid $55 for utilities.

k. Frank Drake invested an additional $2,000 in the business.

l. Bought additional equipment for $260 in cash.

Cash	*101*
6,500	

Frank Drake, Capital	*301*
	6,500

TOPIC PROBLEM 8. Althea Brooks bought Deluxe Decorators on April 1. Complete the following accounting activities for the business.

a. Open the following T accounts: Cash; Accts. Rec./Beck Stores; Automobile; Office Fixtures; Accts. Pay./Barlow Auto; Althea Brooks, Capital; Fees; Automobile Expense; and Rent Expense. Assign appropriate account numbers to the accounts.

b. Record the transactions for April in the appropriate T accounts. Enter both the date and the amount of each transaction.

Apr. 1 Althea Brooks invested the following assets in Deluxe Decorators: Office Fixtures, $19,000.
2 Althea Brooks invested an additional $6,000 in the business.
3 Bought an automobile for $10,000 on credit from Barlow Auto.
4 Sold services for $6,000 on credit to Beck Stores.
5 Paid $560 for rent.
10 Paid $4,000 to Barlow Auto on account.
15 Sold services for $2,500 in cash.
18 Received $400 from Beck Stores on account.
18 Bought an office lamp for $95 in cash.
24 Owes $40 to Barlow Auto for repairs expense.
28 Sold services for a fee of $2,900 in cash.
29 Althea Brooks withdrew $1,000 from the business for her personal use.

TOPIC 4

Proving the Ledger

How does the accountant prove that the ledger is in balance? One way is to make sure that for each transaction, the total debits equal the total credits. Also, at regular intervals the accountant prepares a proof to show that the total debit balances in the ledger equal the total credit balances. (The term *proof* means a test to show that something is true.) The proof that the ledger is in balance is called a **trial balance**.

■ Computing Account Balances

Before a trial balance can be prepared, the balance of each account must be determined. In Topic 1, you learned that an account balance is the difference between the total debits and the total credits in an account.

Computing an Account Balance

- Total all debits.
- Total all credits.
- Subtract the smaller amount from the larger amount.
- Show balance on the side of account with the larger amount.

If entries appear on both sides of the account, draw a single rule under the last amount in the column with the most entries. Then draw a single rule directly across in the other column. Enter the totals of each column below the single rule. Then record the account balance to the left of the total in the column with the larger total. (The Cash account on page 82 is an example of ruling an account with debit and credit entries.)

If all the entries are on one side of the account, draw a rule and record the total. Also, draw a rule directly across in the other column and enter a zero below the rule. Write the balance, which is the same as the total, in the appropriate column. (See the Exercise Equipment account and the Sales account on page 82.)

If an account has only one entry, no total needs to be written because the amount of the entry is the total and also the account balance. (See the Accts. Rec./Talbot Industries account on page 82.)

Each type of account usually has a "normal" balance. For example, an asset account, such as Exercise Equipment, should have a debit balance. Likewise, a liability account, such as Accts. Pay./Shone Products, should have a credit balance. Capital and revenue accounts normally have credit balances and expense accounts normally have debit balances. The types of accounts and the normal balances are listed in the margin.

Account	Normal Account Balance
Asset	Debit
Liability	Credit
Capital	Credit
Revenue	Credit
Expense	Debit

The process of computing account balances is referred to as **balancing the accounts**. The ledger on page 82 shows the accounts for Exercise Plus at the close of business on September 30.

Concept: Trial Balance

The equality of the total debits and total credits in the ledger should be proved at regular intervals.

Exercises N and O on page 84 may be completed at this point.

EXERCISE PLUS LEDGER

Assets = *Liabilities* + *Owner's Equity*

Cash 101

Date	Debit	Date	Credit
19—		19—	
Sept. 1	9,000	Sept. 5	4,000
6	1,000	12	4,000
14	13,000	21	6,000
27	4,000	28	2,900
10,100	27,000		16,900

Accts. Rec./Carmen Saldi 103

Date	Debit	Date	Credit
19—		19—	
Sept. 1	1,000	Sept. 6	1,000
27	700		
700	1,700		1,000

Accts. Rec./Talbot Industries 104

Date	Debit	Date	Credit
19—			
Sept. 27	1,400		

Furniture 111

Date	Debit	Date	Credit
19—		19—	
Sept. 1	3,000	Sept. 8	500
7	2,000		
4,500	5,000		500

Exercise Equipment 112

Date	Debit	Date	Credit
19—			
Sept. 1	9,000		
5	4,000		
13,000	13,000		

Accts. Pay./Shone Products 201

Date	Debit	Date	Credit
19—		19—	
Sept. 8	500	Sept. 1	4,000
12	4,000	7	2,000
	4,500	1,500	6,000

Accts. Pay./XYZ Repairs 202

Date	Debit	Date	Credit
		19—	
		Sept. 29	200

Lisa Long, Capital 301

Date	Debit	Date	Credit
19—		19—	
Sept. 21	6,000	Sept. 1	18,000
		14	13,000
	6,000	25,000	31,000

Sales 401

Date	Debit	Date	Credit
		19—	
		Sept. 26	4,000
		27	2,100
		6,100	6,100

Repairs Expense 504

Date	Debit	Date	Credit
19—			
Sept. 29	200		

Salaries Expense 505

Date	Debit	Date	Credit
19—			
Sept. 28	2,900		

Preparing a Trial Balance

When is a trial balance prepared? A trial balance may be prepared at any time to ensure that the accounts are in balance. Generally, a trial balance is prepared at the end of each month. A trial balance must be prepared at the end of each accounting period.

In Chapter 2 we proved the equality of the accounting equation as each transaction was recorded. When T accounts are used, the equation is not proved as each transaction is recorded.

A trial balance can be prepared in several ways. In this topic, we use what accountants call a quick trial balance. A **quick trial balance** is a listing of the account balances to check the equality of the debits and credits in the ledger. The account titles and account numbers are not shown. The next chapter uses a formal trial balance. A **formal trial balance** is a summary that lists the account titles and account numbers in addition to the debit and credit balances.

A trial balance may be prepared on an adding machine or a calculator with a tape. Simply add all the debits and get a total. Then add all the credits and get a total. The two totals must be equal for the ledger to be in balance.

There is another way of doing a quick trial balance. Each account balance is entered in the order in which the account appears in the ledger. Each debit balance is added. Each credit balance is subtracted. Since the total debits (amounts added) must equal the total credits (amounts subtracted), when the last account balance has been entered the final result must be zero. If the total is zero, the ledger is in balance. If the total is not zero, an error has been made. The calculator tape can be used to check the amounts back to the accounts to find the error.

The above procedure is called a zero proof. A **zero proof** is a test in which the difference is zero if two amounts are equal. The difference between the total debit amounts added and the total credit amounts subtracted must be zero.

If a calculator is not available, the amounts can be written on a sheet of paper and computed manually.

Whether the proof is written on a sheet of paper or is prepared on a calculator tape, the proof should be identified by writing a heading on the paper. Answer these three questions: WHO? (the name of the company), WHAT? (the name of the accounting proof), and WHEN? (the date when the proof was made).

Exercise Plus
Trial Balance
September 30, 19–

```
     0.00T
10,100.00
   700.00
 1,400.00
 4,500.00
13,000.00
   200.00
 2,900.00
32,800.00T

     0.00T
 1,500.00
   200.00
25,000.00
 6,100.00
32,800.00T
```

Quick trial balance of total debits and total credits.

Exercise Plus
Trial Balance
September 30, 19–

```
     0.00T
10,100.00
   700.00
 1,400.00
 4,500.00
13,000.00
 1,500.00-
   200.00-
25,000.00-
 6,100.00-
   200.00
 2,900.00
     0.00T
```

Quick trial balance with zero proof.

■ Summarizing the Use of T Accounts

This chapter covered the procedure for using T accounts for recording the changes caused by transactions. The procedure made no change to the accounting cycle that is discussed in Chapter 2. Here is a summary of Steps 1 through 4 of the accounting cycle.

Step 1. Each transaction was recorded.

Step 2. A chronological record was kept of each transaction.

Step 3. The changes caused by the transactions were available for each account and the account balance was updated.

Step 4. The equality of the equation was proved at the end of the accounting period.

The next chapter discusses different ways for completing Steps 5 through 8 of the accounting cycle.

Exercise P on page 84 may be completed at this point.

TOPIC 4 EXERCISES

EXERCISE N. Answer the following questions about Exercise Plus's accounts. Refer to the account balances shown on page 82.

1. What is the Cash account balance?
2. Is the Cash account balance the total amount of cash received during the month? Explain.
3. What is the balance of the Accts. Rec./Carmen Saldi account on September 15? On September 30?
4. Does the Sales account have a debit or credit balance? Why?
5. Why is the balance of the Accts. Pay./Shone Products account on the credit side?
6. What does the balance in the Exercise Equipment account show?
7. Does the Salaries Expense account have a debit balance or a credit balance? Why?
8. What is the total amount of cash paid out during the month?
9. What is owed to Shone Products on September 8?
10. What is the balance in Lisa Long's Capital account on September 1? On September 15? On September 30?

EXERCISE O. Compute the debit total and credit total for the following accounts. Then show the debit balance or credit balance. Use a format similar to the one shown in the example.

EXAMPLE: Cash
Debits: $400, $500, $800, $250, $150
Credits: $725, $85, $45
Debit Total $2,100 Credit Total $855
Debit Balance $1,245 Credit Balance ______

a. Rent Expense
Debits: $555
Credits: $0

b. Accts. Pay./Sky Motors
Debits: $90, $45, $35, $130
Credits: $205, $345

c. Fees
Debits: $0
Credits: $150, $170, $85, $100, $45

d. Equipment
Debits: $3,000, $6,000
Credits: $4,000

e. Loans Payable
Debits: $0
Credits: $4,500

f. Alice Barker, Capital
Debits: $500
Credits: $3,000

EXERCISE P. Take a quick trial balance of the accounts for the Southern Company and for the Robotics Repair Company. Total all debits. Total all credits. State if there is equality of debits and credits.

1. Accounts for the Southern Company: LaVonna Jack, Capital, $5,933; Cash, $4,500; Accts. Rec./Madeline Barnes, $24; Accts. Rec./Dale Wilson, $14; Equipment, $3,750; Accts. Pay./Office Supplies, $150; Loans Payable, $2,200; Rent Expense, $250; Salaries Expense, $375; Utilities Expense, $55; Sales, $685.
2. Accounts for the Robotics Repair Company: Equipment, $1,600; Utilities Expense, $55; Accts. Pay./Wayne Supplies, $900; Brad Kennedy, Capital, $2,255; Cash, $1,000; Supplies, $2,600; Accts. Rec./Thurman Auto Service, $600; Sales, $3,100; Rent Expense, $400.

TOPIC 4 PROBLEMS

TOPIC PROBLEM 9. Prepare a quick trial balance for the Hi-Tech Company on November 30 for the data given below. Check that the total debits equal the total credits.

Account No.	Account Title	Balance	Account No.	Account Title	Balance
101	Cash	$ 6,000	201	Accts. Pay./Radio Supplies	$ 7,000
102	Accts. Rec./Banner Stores	8,000	202	Accts. Pay./Sound Company	-0-
103	Accts. Rec./Slater Stores	3,500	301	Timothy Conner, Capital	21,700
104	Accts. Rec./Warren Company	-0-	401	Sales	9,000
111	Furniture	3,000	501	Rent Expense	1,000
112	Office Equipment	4,300	502	Repairs Expense	-0-
113	Radio Supplies	11,900	503	Salaries Expense	-0-

TOPIC PROBLEM 10. Prepare a trial balance for the Star TV Repair Service on December 31 from the following data. List the accounts by account number as they would appear in the chart of accounts. Check that there is a zero proof.

Account No.	Account Title	Balance	Account No.	Account Title	Balance
101	Cash	$ 7,500	103	Accts. Rec./Ann White	$ 100
111	Television Equipment	17,000	301	John Spiegel, Capital	21,650
118	Office Furniture	3,000	401	Sales	11,000
102	Accts. Rec./Joyce Grello	50	501	Salaries Expense	5,000

CHAPTER SUMMARY

The T account is the simplest form of an account with two sides. T accounts are kept in a ledger, which is a book, file, or other record of the changes caused to the accounts by transactions.

When you debit an account, you enter an amount on the left side of the T account. When you credit an account, you enter an amount on the right side. The basic rules for debiting and crediting accounts are covered in this chapter so that you can use T accounts to record transactions through the first four steps of the accounting cycle.

As part of Step 4, you learned how a trial balance is prepared to check the equality of the ledger.

THE LANGUAGE OF BUSINESS

Here are some terms that make up the language of business. Do you know the meaning of each?

T account
chart of accounts
debit side
debit (Dr.)
credit side
credit (Cr.)
account balance
opening balance
ledger
accounting entry
double-entry accounting
compound transaction
trial balance
balancing the accounts
quick trial balance
formal trial balance
zero proof

REVIEW QUESTIONS

1. What are accounts? What are T accounts?
2. Name the four parts of a T account.
3. List the rules for debiting and crediting.
4. Does debit always mean increase and credit always mean decrease? Why or why not?
5. What are the three steps in analyzing business transactions?
6. What are the three basic rules of double-entry accounting?
7. Name two revenue accounts. Name three expense accounts.
8. Why are revenue accounts credited to increase owner's equity? Why are expense accounts debited to decrease owner's equity?
9. What is the normal balance of asset accounts? Liability accounts? The Capital account? Revenue accounts? Expense accounts?
10. What is the purpose of the trial balance?

CHAPTER PROBLEMS

Problems for Chapter 3 are given below. Write your answers on a separate sheet of paper unless you are using the workbook for this textbook. If you are using the workbook, do the problems in the space provided there.

CHAPTER PROBLEM 3-1. Analyze the transactions in the T accounts shown below. Corresponding debit and credit entries are identified by the letters *a* through *n*. In the space provided in your workbook or on a separate sheet of paper, describe the transaction indicated by each set of entries. Transaction *a* is given as an example below.

EXAMPLE: *a.* Erica Mees started the business with $20,000 in cash.

Cash			*101*
a.	*20,000*	*b.*	*400*
f.	*400*	*g.*	*175*
i.	*235*	*h.*	*675*
k.	*450*	*j.*	*850*
		m.	*105*

Accts. Rec./ James Paterno			*102*
e	*450*	*f.*	*400*

Accts. Rec./ Lucas Stowe			*103*
l.	*950*		

Equipment			*111*
c.	*3,150*	*d.*	*50*
g.	*175*		

Accts. Pay./ Dora Thomas			*201*
d.	*50*	*c.*	*3,150*
h.	*675*	*n.*	*86*

Erica Mees, Capital			*301*
j.	*850*	*a.*	*20,000*

Sales			*401*
		e.	*450*
		i.	*235*
		k.	*450*
		l.	*950*

Advertising Expense			*501*
m.	*105*		
n.	*86*		

Rent Expense			*502*
b.	*400*		

CHAPTER PROBLEM 3-2. Roman Garcia started his own delivery service. Open a T account for each of the following accounts: Cash, 101; Accts. Rec./Alice Fisher, 102; Furniture, 111; Accts. Pay./Bates Store, 201; Accts. Pay./Turner Fuels, 202; Roman Garcia, Capital, 301; Sales, 401; Fuel Expense, 501; and Rent Expense, 502.

a. Analyze each transaction given below and record the debit and credit amounts in the appropriate T accounts. Identify each entry by the date of the transaction. Then, determine the balance of each account and indicate whether each is a debit or credit balance.

Mar. 1 Roman Garcia invested $18,000 in the business.
4 Bought furniture for $800 in cash.
5 Sold services for $875 in cash.

Mar. 9 Paid $450 for rent.
10 Returned furniture bought for $100 in cash.
11 Bought furniture for $1,800 on credit from Bates Store.
13 Sold services for $950 on credit to Alice Fisher.
16 Roman Garcia withdrew $800 from the business.
23 Owes $365 to Turner Fuels for gasoline.
24 Received $450 from Alice Fisher on account.
25 Returned furniture bought for $250 on credit from Bates Store.
27 Paid $500 to Bates Store on account.
28 Roman Garcia invested an additional $5,000 in the business.

b. Prepare a quick trial balance.

CHAPTER PROBLEM 3-3. Roberta Kaplan started a business on June 1 with a cash investment of $12,000. The account balances of her company on June 30 are given below. Open a T account for each account. Enter all the transactions that took place in June, including sales of services for $625 cash, plus sales on credit to Peter Kirk for $650 and to Sarah Carr for $475. Then prepare a quick trial balance.

Assets
101 Cash, $12,175
102 Accts. Rec./Peter Kirk, $650
103 Accts. Rec./Sarah Carr, $475
111 Equipment, $5,000

Liabilities
201 Accts. Pay./Lee Equipment, $5,000

Owner's Equity
301 Roberta Kaplan, Capital, $12,000

Revenue
401 Sales, $1,750

Expenses
501 Rent Expense, $370
502 Telephone Expense, $80

MANAGEMENT CASES

Fitting Records to the Business. No two businesses will have the same number of accounts or use the same account titles. The kind of information that is needed by management determines what accounts are used.

CASE 3M-1. Louis and Eunice Kingston operate an automobile service station and an attached diner. Mr. Kingston sells gasoline, oil, tires, and other automobile supplies. He also fixes flat tires, lubricates cars, and does repair work. Mrs. Kingston operates the diner. She has a breakfast and luncheon menu, and she keeps the diner open the same hours as the service station—from 8 A.M. to 5 P.M.

Mr. Kingston had enough time in the past to do the repair work. When Mrs. Kingston had extra time, she helped out in the service station with customer services while Mr. Kingston did the repair work. Recently, business has increased. Mr. Kingston now finds that he cannot do the repair work and also attend to customer services. Mrs. Kingston's diner has become a favorite place for breakfast and lunch. They must decide whether they should employ a full-time helper, limit the repair work, reduce customer services, or close the diner.

No separate records of revenue from the various phases of the business have been kept. All revenue from customer service and repairs, as well as from the diner, is shown in one revenue account. How can the records be organized to help the Kingstons decide what to do?

CASE 3M-2. Carl's Clock Repair Shop cleans and repairs antique clocks. Carl Irving is the owner and manager of the business, and he has two employees. Carl's Clock Repair Shop cleans and repairs clocks in the shop and also provides a pickup and delivery service to businesses and residences. Customers like this service.

Mr. Irving keeps his own accounting records. He uses one revenue account to record all revenue. Mr. Irving uses one expense account to record all expenses. However, he believes that his system is not giving him the information needed about revenues and expenses.

a. What are the various expenses that such a business might have?

b. Why would it be useful to the manager to know the amount received from each source of revenue and spent for each type of expense?

c. What plan would you suggest to make the financial records show the total of each major item of revenue and expense?

CHAPTER

4

Summarizing the Accounting Cycle Activities

You learned how to record business transactions in Chapter 3, covering Steps 1 to 4 in the accounting cycle. In Chapter 4 you will learn how to complete Steps 5 to 8. You will find out how the trial balance is used to prepare financial statements, how the ledger is prepared for the next accounting period, and how accounting information is interpreted.

CHAPTER GOALS

After studying Chapter 4, you will be able to:

1. Define the terms listed in "The Language of Business" section on page 120.
2. Explain the accounting concepts and principles in this chapter related to preparing financial statements, closing the ledger, and preparing a postclosing trial balance.
3. Prepare a formal trial balance from account balances.
4. Prepare an income statement from revenue and expense account balances.
5. Prepare a balance sheet from asset, liability, and owner's equity account balances.
6. Apply the procedures for closing temporary owner's equity accounts.
7. Prepare a postclosing trial balance.

TOPIC 1

The Trial Balance and the Income Statement

How is the accounting data in the ledger summarized for managers and owners? The accountant summarizes accounting data by preparing financial statements. There are a number of financial statements that can be prepared. However, the two most common statements are the income statement and balance sheet.

The income statement and the balance sheet are prepared at the end of each accounting period. These statements must also be prepared for income tax purposes at the end of each year. Each statement is prepared from the trial balance.

■ The Formal Trial Balance

In Chapter 3 you prepared an informal trial balance and a quick trial balance. You will now find out how to prepare a formal trial balance. A formal trial balance lists account titles and account numbers in addition to debit and credit balances.

A formal trial balance lists the account titles and account numbers in addition to the debit and credit balances.

The formal trial balance for Exercise Plus prepared on September 30 is shown on page 92. The account balances were obtained from the ledger. Several important purposes are served by the formal trial balance.

- It lists the balance of each account in the ledger, according to the chart of accounts. Asset accounts are listed first, followed by liabilities and the owner's equity capital account. Next, the revenue and expense accounts are listed.
- It proves that the ledger is in balance (Step 4 in the accounting cycle).
- It provides the data needed to prepare the income statement and balance sheet (Step 5 in the accounting cycle).
- It provides the data needed to transfer the net income or net loss to the Capital account at the end of the accounting cycle (Step 6 in the accounting cycle).

■ Preparing the Formal Trial Balance

A trial balance is usually prepared in pencil because it is not a formal statement. However, it can also be prepared in ink. The steps to prepare a formal trial balance are as follows.

■ Heading Center the heading at the top of the trial balance. The heading answers these questions: WHO? (the name of the company), WHAT? (the name of the statement), and WHEN? (the date of the statement).

Exercise Plus
Trial Balance
September 30, 19—

Heading for trial balance.

EXERCISE PLUS LEDGER

Assets = *Liabilities* + *Owner's Equity*

Assets

Cash 101

19—		19—	
Sept. 1	9,000	Sept. 5	4,000
6	1,000	12	4,000
14	13,000	21	6,000
26	4,000	28	2,900
10,100	27,000		16,900

Accts. Rec./Carmen Saldi 103

19—		19—	
Sept. 1	1,000	Sept. 6	1,000
27	700		
700	1,700		1,000

Accts. Rec./Talbot Industries 104

19—			
Sept. 27	1,400		

Furniture 111

19—		19—	
Sept. 1	3,000	Sept. 8	500
7	2,000		
4,500	5,000		500

Exercise Equipment 112

19—			
Sept. 1	9,000		
5	4,000		
13,000	13,000		

Liabilities

Accts. Pay./Shone Products 201

19—		19—	
Sept. 8	500	Sept. 1	4,000
12	4,000	7	2,000
	4,500	1,500	6,000

Accts. Pay./XYZ Repairs 202

		19—	
		Sept. 29	200

Owner's Equity

Lisa Long, Capital 301

19—		19—	
Sept. 21	6,000	Sept. 1	18,000
		14	13,000
	6,000	25,000	31,000

Sales 401

		19—	
		Sept. 26	4,000
		27	2,100
		6,100	6,100

Repairs Expense 504

19—			
Sept. 29	200		

Salaries Expense 505

19—			
Sept. 28	2,900		

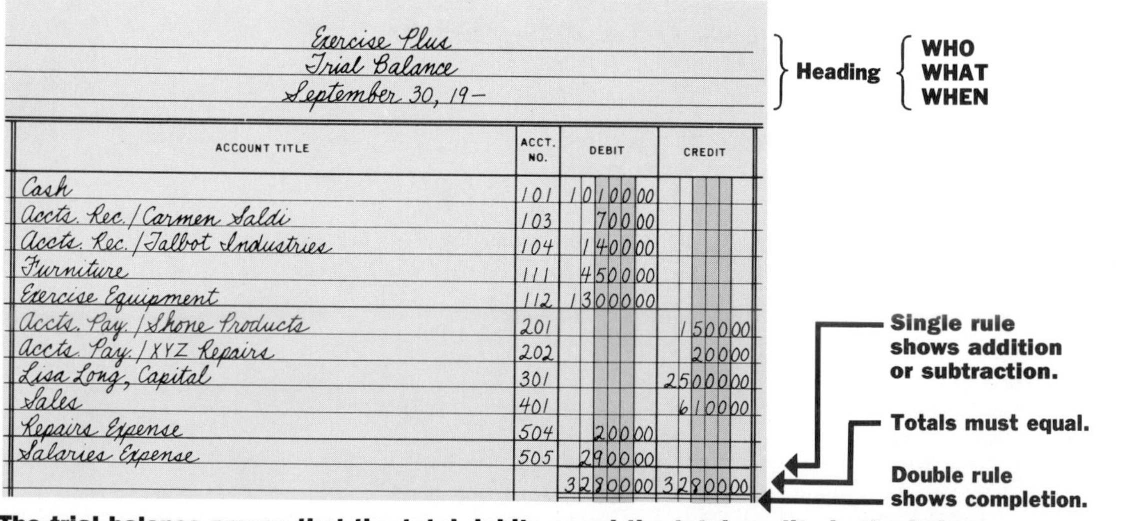

Exercise Plus
Trial Balance
September 30, 19—

ACCOUNT TITLE	ACCT. NO.	DEBIT	CREDIT
Cash	101	10100 00	
Accts. Rec./Carmen Saldi	103	700 00	
Accts. Rec./Talbot Industries	104	1400 00	
Furniture	111	4500 00	
Exercise Equipment	112	13000 00	
Accts. Pay./Shone Products	201		1500 00
Accts. Pay./XYZ Repairs	202		200 00
Lisa Long, Capital	301		25000 00
Sales	401		6100 00
Repairs Expense	504	200 00	
Salaries Expense	505	2900 00	
		32800 00	32800 00

Heading
WHO
WHAT
WHEN
Single rule shows addition or subtraction.
Totals must equal.
Double rule shows completion.

The trial balance proves that the total debits equal the total credits in the ledger.

■ List the Accounts List the accounts in numeric (number) order, just as they appear in the ledger. Write the account title in the first column and the account number in the second column. Write the account balance in the proper money column (Debit or Credit). List all accounts whether or not they have balances. This will ensure that you have not missed an account. Some accountants, however, prefer to list only accounts with balances.

ACCOUNT TITLE	ACCT. NO.	DEBIT		CREDIT	
Cash	101	10,100	00		
Accts. Rec./Carmen Saldi	103	700	00		
Accts. Rec./Talbot Industries	104	1,400	00		
Furniture	111	4,500	00		
Exercise Equipment	112	13,000	00		
Accts. Pay./Shone Products	201			1,500	00
Accts. Pay./XYZ Repairs	202			200	00
Lisa Long, Capital	301			25,000	00
Sales	401			6,100	00
Repairs Expense	504	200	00		
Salaries Expense	505	2,900	00		

Trial balance data taken from ledger.

■ Dollar Signs and Decimal Points When the trial balance is prepared on ruled accounting paper, dollar signs, commas, and decimal points are not used with amounts in money columns. The vertical lines in the money columns take the place of commas and decimal points. The money columns also show that you are working with dollars. Use dollar signs, commas, and decimal points when writing amounts in columns other than ruled money columns.

■ Proving a Trial Balance Prepared in Pencil After all the account balances have been entered, the trial balance is totaled and ruled. Complete the trial balance as follows when it is prepared in pencil.

- Draw a single rule across both money columns.
- Add the amounts in the money columns.
- Record the totals on the line below the single rule.
- Check that the total of the Debit column equals the total of the Credit column. If the total debits do not equal the total credits, then there is an error. All errors must be corrected before the trial balance can be completed.
- Draw a double rule across both money columns beneath the totals when the totals balance. The double rule shows that the Debit and Credit columns are equal.

		32,800	00	32,800	00

Ruling column totals.

In general, rules are drawn across all columns in financial statements except explanation columns. In the trial balance, the account title and account number columns are considered explanations. In accounting, single rules show computations (addition or subtraction). Double rules across columns indicate that the work is accurate and completed. Single and double rules are always drawn with a ruler.

Proving a Trial Balance Prepared in Ink A trial balance can be prepared in ink, and the steps are similar to those for preparing one in pencil. There is one difference. The totals of the money columns are written in small pencil figures directly under the last entry. The small pencil total is called a **pencil footing**. The pencil footing is used to double-check the equality of the debit and credit totals before the amounts are written in ink. The portion of the trial balance shown below illustrates pencil footing.

Salaries Expense	505	2,900	00		
		32,800	00	32,800	00
		32,800	00	32,800	00

Pencil footings are used to check the equality before totals are written in ink.

Exercise A on page 98 may be completed at this point.

The Income Statement

What is the income statement? The **income statement** is a financial statement reporting the revenue, expenses, and net income or net loss for a specific period of time. It is sometimes referred to as a *statement of profit and loss*, a *statement of revenue and expenses*, a *statement of earnings*, or a *statement of operations*. The preferred title, however, is income statement.

Income, as you recall, is the difference between the revenue earned from the sale of goods and services and the expenses needed to operate the business. A completed income statement is shown on page 95. The information on the income statement is a summary of the Income Summary section of the accounting equation you studied in Chapter 2.

The income statement is important for several reasons.

- It lists and summarizes all sources of revenue for an accounting period.
- It lists and summarizes all expenses for an accounting period.
- It matches the summarized expenses against the summarized revenues. Thus, it reports the net income (or net loss) for an accounting period.
- It is the basis for many business decisions made by managers, owners, and creditors. Examples of the decisions are described later in this chapter.

Assets				= Liabilities +	Owner's Equity	
Cash	Accounts Receivable	Furniture	Exercise Equipment	Accounts Payable	Lisa Long, Capital	Income Summary (Revenue – Expenses)
$10,100 +	$2,100 +	$4,500 +	$13,000 =	$1,700 +	$25,000 +	**$3,000**
				$1,700 +	$28,000	
$29,700			=	$29,700		

Sept. 30 Balance

Transfer Net Income

Equality of Equation

Exercise Plus
Income Statement
For the Month Ended September 30, 19–

Revenue:		
Sales		6,100.00
Expenses:		
Repairs Expense	200.00	
Salaries Expense	2,900.00	
Total Expenses		3,100.00
Net Income		3,000.00

Heading { **WHO** **WHAT** **WHEN**

Revenue Section

Expense Section

Net Income or Net Loss Section

The income statement reports the revenue, expenses, and net income or net loss for a specific period of time.

■ Preparing an Income Statement

An income statement is a permanent record that is written in ink, typewritten, or printed on a press or by a computer. It is for the use of managers, owners, and outsiders, such as creditors. The income statement, as you know, is prepared at the end of each accounting period. It is prepared by using data directly from the trial balance. The steps to prepare an income statement follow.

■ Heading Center the heading at the top of the income statement, as shown below. The heading answers these questions: WHO? (the name of the company), WHAT? (the name of the statement), and WHEN? (the accounting period the statement covers).

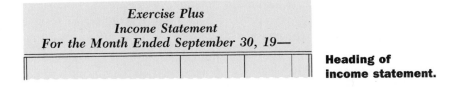

Exercise Plus
Income Statement
For the Month Ended September 30, 19—

Heading of income statement.

The time covered by an accounting period is an important part of the heading of an income statement. The time period can be a month, a quarter (three-month period), a year, or any length of time that a business decides is best for its needs. As noted earlier, however, a business must prepare an income statement at least once a year. In this regard, accountants distinguish between a fiscal year and a calendar year. Any twelve-month period is called a **fiscal year**. For example, an accounting period that runs from July 1 to June 30 is a fiscal year. A twelve-month period that begins on January 1 and ends on December 31 is considered a **calendar year**.

The time period covered in an income statement is important for another reason. If the length of time is not included in the heading, one would not know if the income was earned in a month, a quarter, a year, or some other period of time. Notice, for example, that the heading of the income statement on page 95 reads "For the Month Ended September 30, 19—." Thus, Exercise Plus earned a net income of $3,000 for one month—the month of September. The third line of the heading will vary depending on the time period in question. Here, for example, is how the heading would read for the most common accounting periods.

- For one month: "For the Month Ended September 30, 19—" (use the last day of the month).
- For three months: "For the Quarter Ended March 31, 19—" (use the last day of the third month).
- For a calendar year: "For the Year Ended December 31, 19—."
- For a fiscal year: "For the Year Ended June 30, 19—" (use the last day of the twelve-month period).

■ Revenue Section After the heading is written, the revenue information must be entered on the income statement. Write the title "Revenue" followed by a colon on the first line at the left margin, as shown. Indent one-half inch and list the revenue items beneath the title. Begin each word with a capital letter. When there is only one revenue account, as shown below, enter the amount in the second money column. If there are several accounts, the individual amounts are listed in the first money column, a single rule is drawn across the money column under the last entry, and the total amount is listed in the second money column. (Notice that the money columns are not indicated as debit or credit columns.)

Revenue section of income statement.

Revenue:				
Sales			*6,100*	*00*

■ Expense Section Next, the expense information must be entered. At the margin on the line beneath the last entry in the Revenue section, write the title "Expenses" followed by a colon. Indent one-half inch and list the expenses beneath the title. List the accounts in the order in which they appear in the ledger. Begin each word with a capital letter. The illustration below shows how the expenses should be listed. The individual amounts are listed in the first money column. The total amount is entered in the second money column. Write the words "Total Expenses" immediately following the last expense listed. If there is only one expense account, enter that amount in the second money column.

Expenses:				
Repairs Expense	200	00		
Salaries Expense	2,900	00		
Total Expenses.......			3,100	00

Expenses section of income statement.

■ Net Income or Net Loss Section

Finally, the net income or net loss must be entered. Draw a single rule across the money column under the amount of total expenses, as shown. Subtract the total expenses from the total revenue and enter the difference on the next line in the second money column. Write either "Net Income" or "Net Loss" on the same line at the left margin. Then draw a double rule across both money columns to show that the money columns are completed.

Net Income............			3,000	00

Net Income section of income statement.

Remember that the temporary revenue and expense accounts listed on the lower portion of the trial balance are used to prepare an income statement. The temporary revenue and expense accounts are called **income statement accounts** or nominal accounts.

Exercise Plus
Trial Balance
September 30, 19—

ACCOUNT TITLE	ACCT. NO.	DEBIT		CREDIT	
Cash	*101*	*10,100*	*00*		
Accts. Rec./Carmen Saldi	*103*	*700*	*00*		
Accts. Rec./Talbot Industries	*104*	*1,400*	*00*		
Furniture	*111*	*4,500*	*00*		
Exercise Equipment	*112*	*13,000*	*00*		
Accts. Pay./Shone Products	*201*			*1,500*	*00*
Accts. Pay./XYZ Repairs	*202*			*200*	*00*
Lisa Long, Capital	*301*			*25,000*	*00*
Sales	*401*			*6,100*	*00*
Repairs Expense	*504*	*200*	*00*		
Salaries Expense	*505*	*2,900*	*00*		
		32,800	*00*	*32,800*	*00*

Exercise Plus
Income Statement
For the Month Ended September 30, 19—

Revenue:				
Sales			*6,100*	*00*
Expenses:				
Repairs Expense	*200*	*00*		
Salaries Expense	*2,900*	*00*		
Total Expenses			*3,100*	*00*
Net Income			*3,000*	*00*

The income statement accounts listed in the lower portion of the trial balance are used to prepare the income statement.

Concept: Income Statement

Revenues, expenses, and net income or net loss for an accounting period are summarized in a financial report called an income statement.

Exercise B on page 98 may be completed at this point.

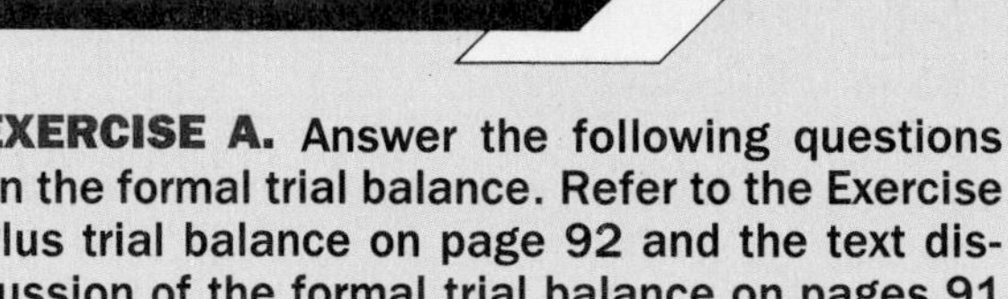

TOPIC 1 EXERCISES

EXERCISE A. Answer the following questions on the formal trial balance. Refer to the Exercise Plus trial balance on page 92 and the text discussion of the formal trial balance on pages 91 to 94.

1. When was the formal trial balance for Exercise Plus prepared?
2. Where does the accountant obtain the amounts listed in the debit and credit columns?
3. In what order are accounts listed in the trial balance?
4. Are the debit and credit balances placed in the same column in the trial balance? Why or why not?
5. What does the total $32,800 in the debit and credit columns represent?
6. Does the trial balance provide sufficient data to compute the net income or net loss for the accounting period? Why or why not?

EXERCISE B. Answer the following questions on the income statement. Refer to the income statement for Exercise Plus on page 95.

1. What is the length of the accounting period?
2. Where does the accountant obtain the amounts listed for the revenue and expenses?
3. What is the total revenue?
4. What is the total of the expenses?
5. What kinds of expenses does Exercise Plus have?
6. What is the net income for the accounting period?

TOPIC 1 PROBLEMS

TOPIC PROBLEM 1. Prepare a trial balance for Parkside Taxi Service on July 31. The account balances are given below. Assign appropriate numbers to the accounts. Follow the chart of accounts on page 58.

Accts. Pay./Rapid Motors	$1,000
Accts. Rec./King Corporation	2,275
Cash	$ 5,500
Vehicles	11,500
Fare Revenue	5,000
Rent Expense	525
Salaries Expense	2,540
Maintenance Expense	255
Andrew O'Malley, Capital	16,980
Gas and Oil Expense	385

TOPIC PROBLEM 2. The Hollywood Cinema had the following revenue and expenses during the month of September. Prepare an income statement for the month ended September 30, 19—.

Paid for Advertising	$ 700
Film Rental Expense	9,000
Admissions (Revenue)	$16,000
Rent Expense	3,000
Food Sales (Revenue)	2,500
Miscellaneous Expense	25
Salaries Paid	6,300
Paid for Heat and Light (Utilities)	250

TOPIC PROBLEM 3. Arlene Caro owns the Hair Style Shop. On December 31 the business's financial records show the data given below. Set up an accounting equation like the one on page 95 to classify the financial data for this business. Then prepare an income statement for the three-month period ended December 31, 19—.

Shop Equipment Owned	$ 6,400
Sales to Customers	12,000
Utilities Expense	$ 350
Arlene Caro, Capital (October 1)	5,900
Advertising Costs	75
Salaries Paid	6,300
Cash in Bank	6,200
Due From Customers	75
Rent Expense	500
Owed on Equipment	2,000

TOPIC 2

The Balance Sheet

How do managers and owners learn about the financial position of a business? A second financial statement, the balance sheet, provides this information. A **balance sheet** (also known as a *statement of financial position*) is a financial statement reporting the assets, liabilities, and owner's equity of a business on a specific date.

A balance sheet is prepared from the trial balance after the income statement has been prepared.

The balance sheet is prepared after the income statement because the net income or net loss will change owner's equity.

A balance sheet must be prepared at the end of each accounting period. However, like the income statement, the balance sheet may be prepared at other times during the accounting period.

The balance sheet serves the following purposes.

- It lists and summarizes business assets on a specific date.
- It lists and summarizes the claims of creditors (liabilities) against the assets.
- It shows the owner's claim (owner's equity) against the assets.
- It provides data from which managers, owners, and outsiders can make business decisions.

Preparing a Balance Sheet

The balance sheet is based on the accounting equation. The accounting equation shows the relationship among the accounting elements, and the balance sheet reports that relationship.

Look at the balance sheet for Exercise Plus shown on the next page. Notice the relationship between the accounting equation for Exercise Plus and the balance sheet. Note also that the balance sheet consists of a heading and these four sections.

1. Assets section
2. Liabilities section
3. Owner's Equity section
4. Proof of Equality section

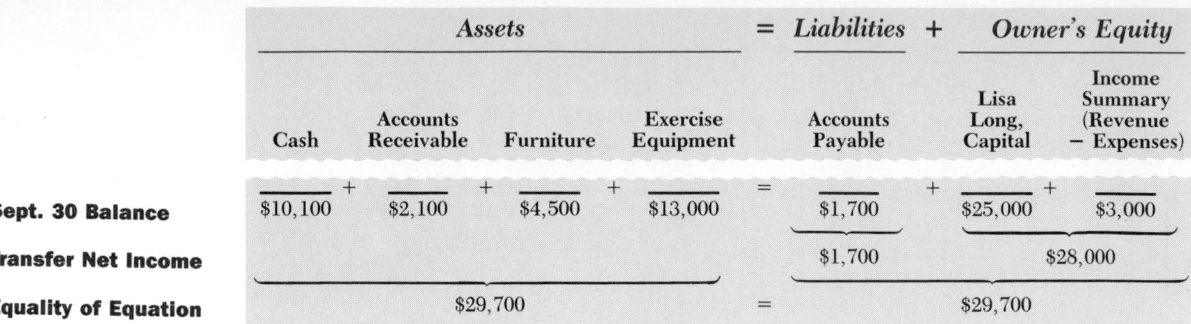

	Assets				=	Liabilities	+	Owner's Equity	
	Cash	Accounts Receivable	Furniture	Exercise Equipment		Accounts Payable		Lisa Long, Capital	Income Summary (Revenue − Expenses)
Sept. 30 Balance	$10,100	$2,100	$4,500	$13,000	=	$1,700	+	$25,000	$3,000
Transfer Net Income						$1,700		$28,000	
Equality of Equation	$29,700				=	$29,700			

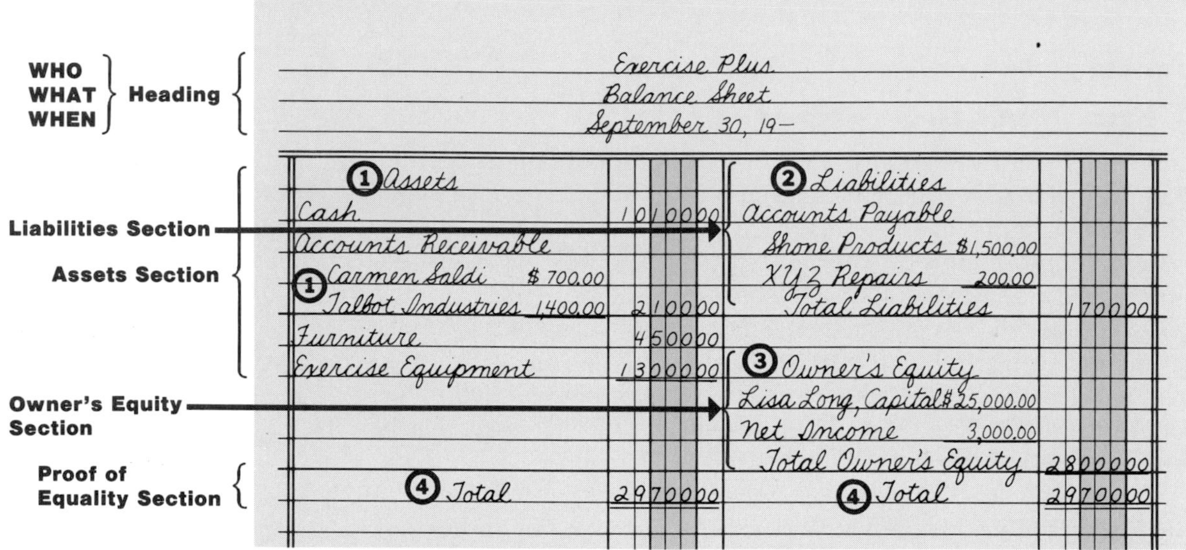

Exercise Plus
Balance Sheet
September 30, 19—

① Assets			② Liabilities		
Cash		10 100 00	Accounts Payable		
Accounts Receivable			Shone Products	$1,500.00	
① Carmen Saldi	$ 700.00		XYZ Repairs	200.00	
Talbot Industries	1400.00	2 100 00	Total Liabilities		1 700 00
Furniture		4 500 00			
Exercise Equipment		13 000 00	③ Owner's Equity		
			Lisa Long, Capital	$25,000.00	
			Net Income	3,000.00	
			Total Owner's Equity		28 000 00
④ Total		29 700 00	④ Total		29 700 00

The balance sheet reports the assets, liabilities, and owner's equity of the business on a specific date.

■ Heading Center the heading at the top of the balance sheet as shown below. The heading answers these questions: WHO? (the name of the company), WHAT? (the name of the statement), and WHEN? (the date of the statement). Notice that the date is different on the balance sheet and the income statement. The income statement summarizes revenues and expenses and states the net income earned, or the net loss incurred, *during a period of time*. The balance sheet states the assets, liabilities, and owner's equity *on a specific date*.

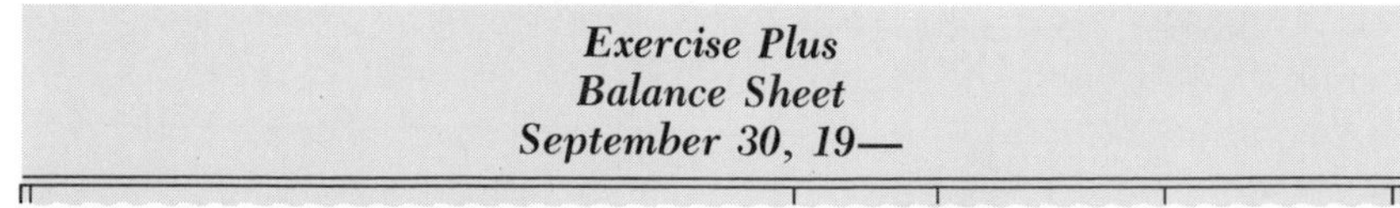

Exercise Plus
Balance Sheet
September 30, 19—

Heading of balance sheet.

Concept: Financial Position
The financial position of a business or individual is expressed through its assets, liabilities, and owner's equity.

Concept: Balance Sheet
The accounting equation is summarized in a financial statement called a balance sheet.

Concept: Financial Statements
An income statement summarizes the revenues and expenses for a period of time. A balance sheet summarizes an accounting equation on a given date.

Exercise C on page 105 may be completed at this point.

Assets Section

How is the Assets section prepared? Center the title "Assets" on the first line of the left side of the balance sheet. Then list each asset along the left margin, starting with Cash. Begin each word with a capital letter. Record the amount of each asset in the left money column.

If there are several accounts receivable, list them alphabetically with their balances in the Assets section. Since the amounts are not written in the ruled money columns, use dollar signs, commas, and decimal points. Draw a single rule below them. Then list the total in the left money column, as shown below. If there is only one account receivable, list the debtor's name and enter the amount in the money column.

ONE ACCOUNT RECEIVABLE

Assets		
Cash	10,100 00	
Accounts Receivable:		
Carmen Saldi	700 00	
Furniture	4,500 00	
Exercise Equipment	13,000 00	

SEVERAL ACCOUNTS RECEIVABLE

Assets			
Cash		10,100 00	
Accounts Receivable:			
Carmen Saldi	$ 700.00		
Talbot Industries	1,400.00	2,100 00	
Furniture		4,500 00	
Exercise Equipment		13,000 00	

Accounts receivable and other assets.

Assets are usually listed in the order in which they are expected to be exchanged for cash or used. The ease with which assets can be exchanged for cash is called **liquidity**. Cash is the most liquid of all assets and is listed first. Receivables—accounts receivable and notes receivable—usually follow cash because the money is expected to be received shortly. Then the other assets, such as buildings, furniture, and office equipment, follow. These assets are not normally converted into cash.

Liabilities Section

How is the Liabilities section prepared? Center the title ''Liabilities'' on the first line of the right side of the balance sheet, as shown below. Liabilities are listed before owner's equity because the claims of creditors come before the claims of the owner.

List each liability at the margin, beginning each word with a capital letter. Record each amount in the money column at the right. Note that there are several ways of presenting the Liabilities section.

ONE ACCOUNT PAYABLE

Liabilities		
Accounts Payable:		
Shone Products	*1,500*	*00*

SEVERAL ACCOUNTS PAYABLE

Liabilities		
Accounts Payable:		
Shone Products *$1,500.00*		
XYZ Repairs *200.00*		
Total Liabilities	*1,700*	*00*

Accounts payable only.

Liabilities		
Loans Payable	*600*	*00*
Accounts Payable:		
Shone Products	*1,500*	*00*
Mortgage Payable	*25,000*	*00*
Total Liabilities	*27,100*	*00*

Liabilities		
Loans Payable	*600*	*00*
Accounts Payable:		
Shone Products...... *$1,500.00*		
XYZ Repairs *200.00*	*1,700*	*00*
Mortgage Payable	*25,000*	*00*
Total Liabilities	*27,300*	*00*

Accounts payable and other payables.

Liabilities are usually listed in the order in which they must be paid. That is, debts that must be paid first are listed first. Accounts Payable are usually listed after Loans Payable because paying an account is more flexible than paying a bank loan. Debts paid over long periods of time, such as a Mortgage Payable, are listed last in the Liabilities section.

Owner's Equity Section

How is the Owner's Equity section prepared? The steps to prepare the Assets and Liabilities sections of the balance sheet were rather easy. You simply obtained the asset and liability account balances from the trial balance. The Owner's Equity section is not quite so easy. Why? Because the accountant must obtain information from both the trial balance and the income statement.

Refer to the trial balance on page 104. Note that the balance of the Lisa Long, Capital account is $25,000. This balance shows the beginning capital balance, plus any new investments for the accounting period, minus any withdrawals. What the balance does not show is the results of operating Exercise Plus for the month; that is, it does not show the net income or net loss for the month. The accountant must add the net income ($3,000) to the Lisa Long, Capital account ($25,000) to show total owner's equity on September 30. The steps to complete the Owner's Equity section of the balance sheet are discussed below.

Single Proprietorship
- Owner's Equity

Partnership
- Partners' Equity

Corporation
- Stockholders' Equity

Skip a line after the Liabilities section is completed. Then center the title "Owner's Equity" on the next line, as shown on the balance sheet on page 104. The title of the section identifies the type of business ownership. For example, a single proprietorship uses Owner's Equity, a partnership uses Partners' Equity, and a corporation uses Stockholders' Equity.

On the line after the title, write at the margin "Lisa Long, Capital." Write the amount of the capital as shown on the balance sheet on page 104. Since the amount is not written in a ruled money column, use a dollar sign, comma, and decimal point. This quickly identifies the numbers as dollar amounts.

On the next line, write "Net Income" and then the net income amount under the capital amount. Draw a single rule under the net income amount. On the next line, indent one-half inch from the margin and write the words "Total Owner's Equity." Total the capital amount and net income amount. Then write the total in the money column on the same line as total owner's equity.

In a single proprietorship like Exercise Plus, the name of the one owner appears in the Owner's Equity section. As you recall from Chapter 1, there are other forms of business ownership. If Exercise Plus were a partnership, the financial interest of each owner would be shown. If Exercise Plus were a corporation with hundreds or thousands of owners, the total stockholders' equity would be shown.

■ **Proof of Equality** After all items are entered on a balance sheet, the amounts must be totaled and ruled to prove the equality of the statement.

Draw a single rule across both money columns, as shown in the balance sheet on page 104, and total the amounts in the columns. Center the word "Total" and enter the totals of each column on the line immediately below the single rule. The totals of each column must be equal. In other words, total assets must equal the total of liabilities plus owner's equity. If the totals are equal, draw a double rule across both money columns beneath the totals. The double rule indicates that the columns are equal and the balance sheet is complete.

A balance sheet, like an income statement, is a permanent record. It can be written in ink, typewritten, or printed on a press or by a computer. The accounts that appear on the balance sheet are listed on the upper portion of the trial balance. These accounts are called **balance sheet accounts** or *permanent accounts*. (Some accountants also call these accounts *real accounts*.)

One final comment about the balance sheet. The balance sheet just described was prepared in account form. In the **account form balance sheet**, assets are listed on the left side and liabilities and owner's equity are listed on the right side. (If you look at the balance sheet, you will see that it looks like a big T account.) In a later chapter, you will learn about another form of balance sheet.

Earlier in this chapter, you learned how to prepare a formal trial balance, an income statement, and a balance sheet. The relationship between these three statements is shown below. Note that the trial balance is prepared first. Next, the income statement is prepared from the lower portion of the trial balance. Finally, the balance sheet is prepared. The balance sheet is prepared last because the figure for the net income (or net loss) is needed to prepare the Owner's Equity section.

Exercise D on page 105 may be completed at this point.

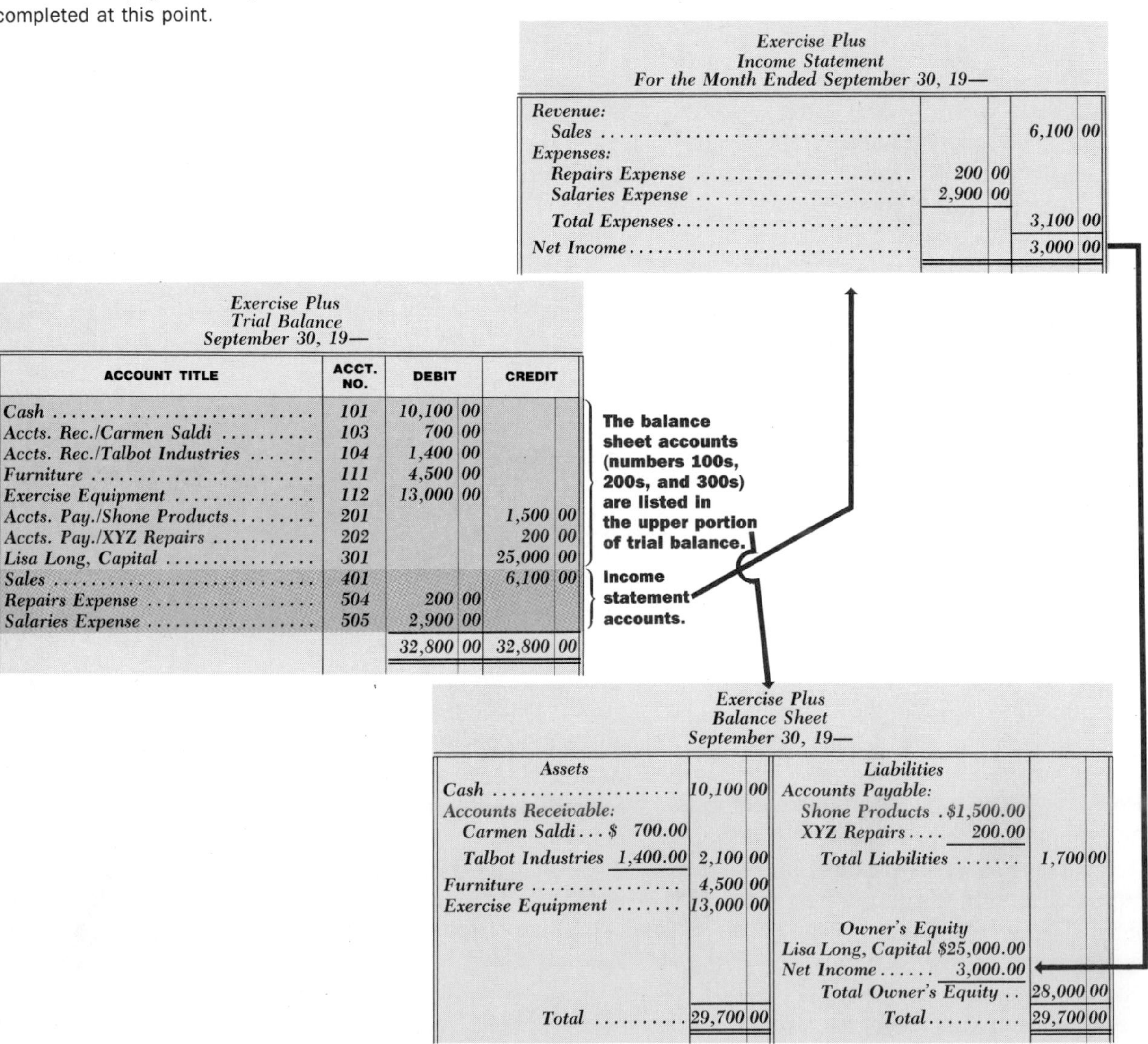

Exercise Plus
Income Statement
For the Month Ended September 30, 19—

Revenue:		
Sales		6,100 00
Expenses:		
Repairs Expense	200 00	
Salaries Expense	2,900 00	
Total Expenses		3,100 00
Net Income		3,000 00

Exercise Plus
Trial Balance
September 30, 19—

ACCOUNT TITLE	ACCT. NO.	DEBIT	CREDIT
Cash	101	10,100 00	
Accts. Rec./Carmen Saldi	103	700 00	
Accts. Rec./Talbot Industries	104	1,400 00	
Furniture	111	4,500 00	
Exercise Equipment	112	13,000 00	
Accts. Pay./Shone Products	201		1,500 00
Accts. Pay./XYZ Repairs	202		200 00
Lisa Long, Capital	301		25,000 00
Sales	401		6,100 00
Repairs Expense	504	200 00	
Salaries Expense	505	2,900 00	
		32,800 00	32,800 00

Exercise Plus
Balance Sheet
September 30, 19—

Assets		*Liabilities*	
Cash	10,100 00	*Accounts Payable:*	
Accounts Receivable:		*Shone Products . $1,500.00*	
Carmen Saldi . . . $ 700.00		*XYZ Repairs 200.00*	
Talbot Industries 1,400.00	2,100 00	*Total Liabilities*	1,700 00
Furniture	4,500 00		
Exercise Equipment	13,000 00		
		Owner's Equity	
		Lisa Long, Capital $25,000.00	
		Net Income 3,000.00	
		Total Owner's Equity	28,000 00
Total	29,700 00	*Total*	29,700 00

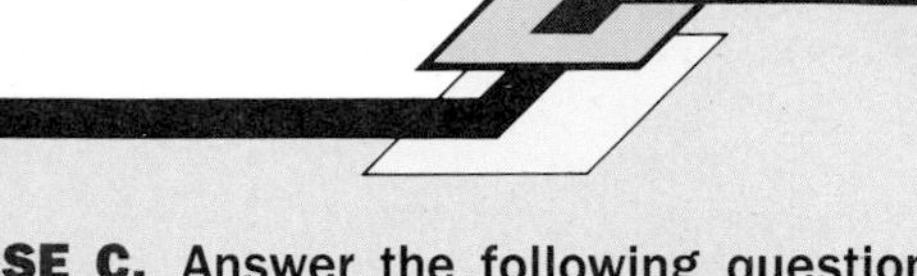

TOPIC 2 EXERCISES

EXERCISE C. Answer the following questions on the balance sheet. Refer to the balance sheet for Exercise Plus shown on page 100.

1. Who is the owner of the business?
2. The balance sheet shows the financial position of the business for what date?
3. How much cash does the business have?
4. Who owes money to the business? How much money is owed by each customer?
5. What equipment does the business own?
6. What is the recorded cost of the furniture?
7. What is the total amount of the assets owned by the business?
8. To whom does the business owe money?
9. What is Lisa Long's equity in the business?
10. Using the balance sheet, solve the accounting equation.

$? = $? + $?

EXERCISE D. The data given at the right shows the financial position of the Sports Supply Company on March 31.

1. Complete the heading and Assets section of a balance sheet in account form.
2. Complete the Liabilities section of the balance sheet.
3. Complete the Owner's Equity section and the remainder of the balance sheet.

Cash	$ 6,250
Accounts Receivable/Sally Davis	55
Building	8,000
Equipment	6,000
Land	12,000
Accounts Payable/Toro Company	5,000
Accounts Payable/Wilson Company	7,000
Laura Solomon, Capital	17,305
Net Income	3,000

TOPIC 2 PROBLEMS

TOPIC PROBLEM 4. Indicate whether each of the following items appears on the income statement, the balance sheet, or both. Use IS for income statement and BS for balance sheet. If the item appears on both statements, write IS and BS.

a. The total revenue
b. The amount owed to the business by customers
c. The net income
d. The amount owed to creditors by the business
e. The accounting period
f. The total liabilities
g. The net loss
h. The financial position of the business on a specific date
i. A list of the assets owned by the business
j. A list of the expenses
k. The owner's investment
l. The Capital account amount
m. Total assets
n. Name of the statement
o. Name of the company
p. Proof of equality

TOPIC PROBLEM 5. Quick Cleaners, owned by Lionel White, has the following assets, liabilities, and income as of September 30.

Has $7,000 in cash
Owns equipment that cost $22,000
Owes $2,500 to Best Machinery
Judy Reich owes $300
Net income is $4,500

a. Set up an accounting equation like the one on page 100 to classify this financial data. Once you have determined the kind and amount of each asset and liability, use the equation to determine the capital.

b. When the accounting equation is in balance, prepare a balance sheet.

TOPIC PROBLEM 6. The following assets and liabilities are for Cora's Beauty Salon on June 30, 19—. The shop is owned by Cora Thomas. Set up an accounting equation to determine the capital. Prepare a balance sheet to present this information.

Has $6,000 in cash
Lynn Alvarez owes her $40
Owns a building that cost $40,000
Owes $900 to Jones' Beauty Supply
Owns land that cost $6,000
Owes $21,000 on a mortgage
Owns shop equipment that cost $9,000
Owns supplies that cost $500
Owes $3,000 to Clark Corporation
Wendy Blake owes her $60
Net income is $2,500

TOPIC 3

Updating the Owner's Equity Accounts

What happens to the temporary account balances after the financial statements are prepared? After the financial statements are prepared, the next step in the accounting cycle is to transfer the revenue and expense data to the Capital account. The process of transferring revenue and expense data to the Capital account is called **closing the ledger**. The entries required to close the ledger are known as **closing entries**. The process of closing the ledger ensures that the revenue and expense data for one accounting period is clearly distinguished from the revenue and expense data for another accounting period.

The ledger must be closed for two reasons.

- The temporary accounts (the revenue and expense accounts) must be prepared to collect the revenue and expenses for the next accounting period. Net income or loss has been computed on the income statement, so the temporary accounts are no longer needed to collect revenue and expense data for the accounting period that has just ended.
- The permanent Capital account balance must be updated to agree with the total owner's equity amount shown on the balance sheet. Net income from the income statement is added to, or the net loss subtracted from, the Capital account on the balance sheet. This must also be done in the ledger.

After all temporary account balances have been transferred to the Capital account, the ledger will show the following.

- The temporary accounts will have zero balances.
- The Capital account will contain the owner's investment and the net income or the net loss for the accounting period.

■ Transferring a Net Income or a Net Loss

In Chapter 2, transactions were recorded in accounts in an accounting equation. The net income (or net loss) was transferred from the Income Summary account to the Capital account. The following equation reviews how the net income for Exercise Plus was transferred to the Capital account on September 30. (You may want to refer back to Chapter 2, Topic 3 to review the entire procedure.) Note the following.

1. The Income Summary balance is now zero.
2. The Capital account has increased by the amount of net income ($3,000).

Assets				=	*Liabilities* +	*Owner's Equity*		
Cash	Accounts Receivable	Furniture	Exercise Equipment		Accounts Payable	Lisa Long, Capital	Income Summary (Revenue − Expenses)	
$10,100 +	$2,100 +	$4,500 +	$13,000	=	$1,700 +	$25,000 +	$3,000	(2) **Sept. 30 Balance**
						+ 3,000	−3,000	**Transfer Net Income**
						$28,000	$ -0-	(1)
					$1,700 +	$28,000		
$29,700				=	$29,700			**Equality of Equation**

In Chapter 3, the transactions were recorded in T accounts in a ledger instead of in an equation. On September 30, the T accounts in the ledger for Exercise Plus appear as shown on page 108.

Transferring the net income in a ledger differs from transferring the net income in the equation. Note these differences for Exercise Plus.

- The revenue is recorded in a Sales account. (See Account 401.)
- The expenses are recorded in various expense accounts. (See Accounts 504 and 505.)
- The Income Summary account has not been used yet. (See Account 399.)
- The net income amount does not appear in the ledger.
- The figure in the Capital account does not yet equal the total amount for owner's equity shown on the balance sheet. (The balance sheet shows total owner's equity of $28,000; the Capital account balance shows $25,000.)

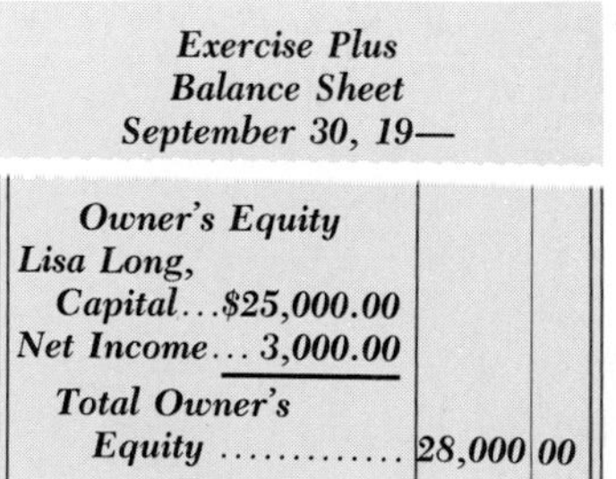

Exercise Plus
Balance Sheet
September 30, 19—

Owner's Equity		
Lisa Long, Capital...$25,000.00		
Net Income... 3,000.00		
Total Owner's Equity	*28,000*	*00*

Capital account does not show total owner's equity.

EXERCISE PLUS LEDGER

Assets = *Liabilities* + *Owner's Equity*

Assets

Cash 101

19—		19—	
Sept. 1	9,000	Sept. 5	4,000
6	1,000	12	4,000
14	13,000	21	6,000
26	4,000	28	2,900
10,100	27,000		16,900

Accts. Rec./Carmen Saldi 103

19—		19—	
Sept. 1	1,000	Sept. 6	1,000
27	700		
700	1,700		1,000

Accts. Rec./ Talbot Industries 104

19—			
Sept. 27	1,400		

Furniture 111

19—		19—	
Sept. 1	3,000	Sept. 8	500
7	2,000		
4,500	5,000		500

Exercise Equipment 112

19—			
Sept. 1	9,000		
5	4,000		
13,000	13,000		

Liabilities

Accts. Pay./Shone Products 201

19—		19—	
Sept. 8	500	Sept. 1	4,000
12	4,000	7	2,000
	4,500	1,500	6,000

Accts. Pay./XYZ Repairs 202

		19—	
		Sept. 29	200

Owner's Equity

Lisa Long, Capital 301

19—		19—	
Sept. 21	6,000	Sept. 1	18,000
		14	13,000
	6,000	25,000	31,000

Income Summary 399

Sales 401

		19—	
		Sept. 26	4,000
		27	2,100
		6,100	6,100

Repairs Expense 504

19—			
Sept. 29	200		

Salaries Expense 505

19—			
Sept. 28	2,900		

Exercise Plus ledger on September 30.

Before you see how to transfer the net income to the Capital account, it may help you to learn how to transfer any amount from one T account to another.

■ The Transfer Process

An amount is transferred from one account to another by means of a debit entry in one account and a credit entry in another account. Remember that the double-entry accounting principle requires that the debits equal the credits for each transaction.

■ **Transferring a Debit Amount From One Account to Another** Debit the account to which you want to transfer the amount. Credit the account containing the amount you want to transfer. Suppose you want to transfer a $200 debit from Account *A* to Account *B*. You debit Account *B* for $200 and credit Account *A* for the same amount.

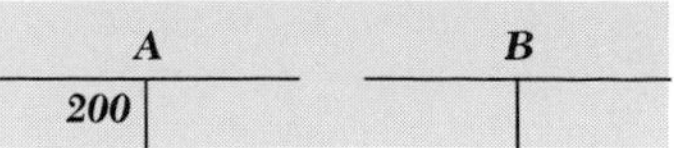

Before transfer.

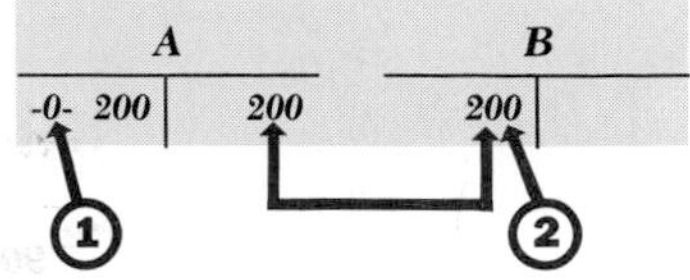

After transfer.

1. Account *A* now has a zero balance. A **zero balance** occurs when the debits equal the credits in an account. The zero balance in Account *A* shows that the amount was transferred out of the account.
2. Account *B* has a debit balance of $200 showing that the amount was transferred to this account.

An account that has a zero balance is called a **closed account**.

■ **Transferring a Credit Amount From One Account to Another** Debit the account containing the amount you want to transfer. Credit the account to which you want to transfer the amount. The following is done to transfer a $400 credit from Account *C* to Account *D*. Debit Account *C* for $400 and credit Account *D* for $400.

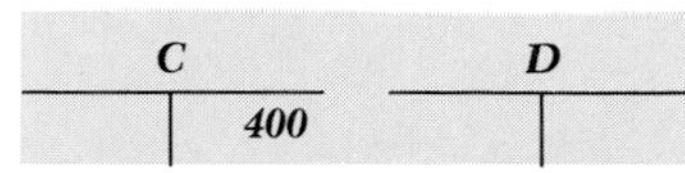

Before transfer.

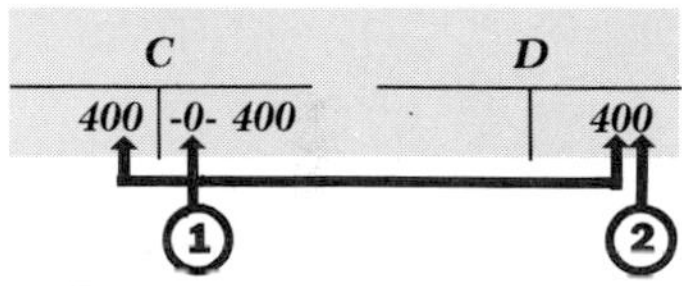

After transfer.

1. Account *C* now has a zero balance.
2. Account *D* has a credit balance of $400.

The $400 credit amount has been transferred from Account *C* to Account *D*.

■ Transferring Amounts

There are several reasons for transferring an amount from one account to another.

- *Correcting an error*. An amount may have been entered in the wrong account. To correct the error, the amount must be transferred to the correct account. For example, a $700 debit may have been entered in the Furniture account instead of the Exercise Equipment account. To correct this error, the Exercise Equipment account is debited for $700 and the Furniture account is credited for $700.

Furniture			*111*	*Exercise Equipment*			*112*
Error	*700*	*Correcting Entry*	*700*	*Correcting Entry*	*700*		

The correcting entry transfers amount to correct account.

- *Transferring the revenue and expense data to the Capital account*. This process is explained in the next segment.

Concept: Closing the Ledger

The revenue and expense data for one accounting period must be clearly distinguished from that of another accounting period.

Exercise E on page 117 may be completed at this point.

Transferring the net income (or net loss) to the Capital account closes the temporary Income Summary account.

Closing the Temporary Accounts

Is the revenue and expense data transferred (closed) directly to the Capital account? No, the balances of the revenue and expense accounts are transferred to the Income Summary account. The Income Summary account will then summarize the revenue and related expenses in the ledger. The balance of the Income Summary account will be the net income or net loss for the accounting period. The net income or net loss is then transferred from the Income Summary account to the Capital account. Three entries are required to transfer the revenue and expense data to the Capital account.

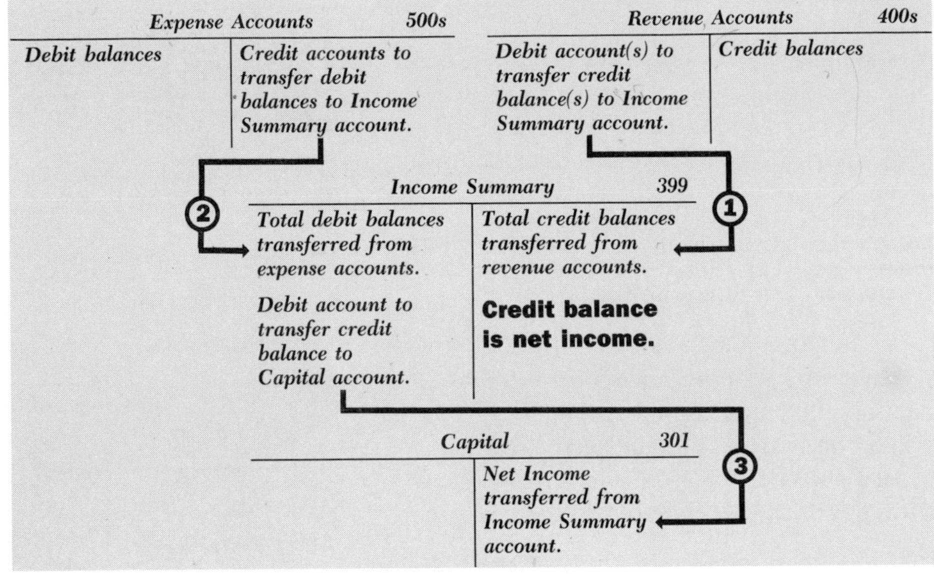

Expense Accounts 500s
Debit balances
Credit accounts to transfer debit balances to Income Summary account.
Revenue Accounts 400s
Debit account(s) to transfer credit balance(s) to Income Summary account.
Credit balances
Income Summary 399
Total debit balances transferred from expense accounts.
Debit account to transfer credit balance to Capital account.
Total credit balances transferred from revenue accounts.
Credit balance is net income.
Capital 301
Net Income transferred from Income Summary account.
1
2
3

Transferring net income to Capital account.

1. The revenue account balances are transferred to the Income Summary account.

2. The expense account balances are transferred to the Income Summary account.

3. The balance of the Income Summary account (net income or net loss) is transferred to the Capital account.

■ Purpose of the Income Summary Account

The Income Summary account is a temporary account and is used at the end of each accounting period. It serves several purposes.

- It summarizes the total revenue and the total expenses for each accounting period. That is why the title "Income Summary" is used.
- It shows the net income or net loss for each accounting period.
- It allows one amount (the net income or net loss) to be entered in the Capital account. As a result, the Capital account shows only investments, withdrawals, and net income or net loss.

■ Transferring a Net Income

Remember that amounts are transferred from one account to another account by means of debit and credit entries. Also remember that the total debits must equal the total credits for each entry.

1. *Transferring revenue account balances*. The first step to transfer the net income is to transfer the revenue for the accounting period from the revenue account(s) to the Income Summary account. This is done by debiting the revenue accounts and crediting the Income Summary account. On September 30, the revenue account Sales has a credit balance of $6,100. (Exercise Plus uses only one revenue account.) The

Sales			*401*
19—		*19—*	
Sept. 30	*6,100*	*Sept. 26*	*4,000*
		27	*2,100*
		6,100	*6,100*

Income Summary			*399*
		19—	
		Sept. 30	*6,100*

First closing entry transfers revenue account balance.

credit balance is transferred by debiting the revenue account for $6,100 and crediting the Income Summary account for the same amount.

The revenue account Sales now has a zero balance. The Income Summary account has a credit balance. Thus, the revenue of $6,100 for the accounting period has been transferred to the Income Summary account.

2. *Transferring expense account balances*. The second step is to transfer the expenses from the expense accounts to the Income Summary account. The expense accounts have debit balances. Therefore, the expense accounts are credited and the Income Summary account is debited. This transfers the expense account balances.

On September 30, the Repairs Expense account has a $200 balance and the Salaries Expense account has a $2,900 balance. The debit balances are transferred by crediting each expense account and debiting the Income Summary account for the total expenses.

Repairs Expense			*504*
19—		*19—*	
Sept. 29	*200*	*Sept. 30*	*200*

Salaries Expense			*505*
19—		*19—*	
Sept. 28	*2,900*	*Sept. 30*	*2,900*

Income Summary			*399*
19—		*19—*	
Sept. 30	*3,100*	*Sept. 30*	*6,100*

Second closing entry transfers expense account balances.

Notice that the expense accounts now have zero balances. The expenses for the accounting period have been transferred to the Income Summary account.

In this entry, the credits to the expense accounts ($200 + $2,900) equal the total debit ($3,100) to the Income Summary account. As a result, the ledger is still in balance.

3. *Transferring the Income Summary account balance*. The third entry is to transfer the balance of the Income Summary account to the permanent Capital account.

In the Income Summary account, the total expenses ($3,100) are listed on the debit side. The total revenue ($6,100) is listed on the credit side. The revenue is greater than expenses. Thus, the business earned a net income for the accounting period ended September 30.

If the expenses had been greater than the revenue, the balance would be on the debit side. This would be a net loss.

Net income, as you know, increases owner's equity. The net income of $3,000 must be added to the Lisa Long, Capital account to update owner's equity. The net income, therefore, is transferred from the Income Summary account to the Lisa Long, Capital account. The credit balance in the Income Summary account is transferred by debiting the Income Summary account for $3,000 and crediting the Lisa Long, Capital account for the same amount.

Lisa Long, Capital				*301*
19—		*19—*		
Sept. 21	*6,000*	*Sept. 1*		*18,000*
		14		*13,000*
	6,000		*25,000*	*31,000*
		30		*3,000*
	6,000		*28,000*	

Income Summary				*399*
19—		*19—*		
Sept. 30	*3,100*	*Sept. 30*		*6,100*
30	*3,000*		*3,000*	

Third closing entry transfers Income Summary account balance.

The Income Summary account now has a zero balance. In fact, after the net income or net loss is transferred to the Capital account, all the temporary accounts have zero balances. The Lisa Long, Capital account now has a balance of $28,000. Thus, the Capital account shows the total owner's equity at the end of the September accounting period: the investment plus the net income.

■ Transferring a Net Loss

If the business suffers a net loss, the Income Summary account shows a debit balance at the end of the accounting period. To transfer a debit balance, you would credit the Income Summary account and debit the Capital account. The debit to the Capital account would then decrease the owner's equity by the amount of the net loss.

Suppose the Income Summary account for Exercise Plus had shown a net loss of $500 instead of a net income of $3,000. The balance of the

Income Summary account would have been transferred as follows. The Income Summary account would be credited for $500 and the Lisa Long, Capital account debited for the same amount.

Lisa Long, Capital			*301*	*Income Summary*			*399*
19—		*19—*		*19—*		*19—*	
Sept. 21	*6,000*	*Sept. 1*	*18,000*	*Sept. 30*	*6,600*	*Sept. 30*	*6,100*
		14	*13,000*		*500*	*30*	*500*
	6,000	*25,000*	*31,000*				
30	*500*	*24,500*					

Transferring a net loss from the Income Summary account.

The net loss would be subtracted from the balance of the Capital account. The Lisa Long, Capital account would now have a balance of $24,500 ($25,000 − $500).

Exercises F and G on pages 117 and 118 may be completed at this point.

The Postclosing Trial Balance

How does the accountant prove the closed ledger? The closed ledger is proved by preparing a postclosing trial balance. A **postclosing trial balance** is the proof that the ledger is in balance after all the temporary accounts have been closed to the Capital account. (The prefix *post* means *after*.) Proving the closed ledger is the seventh step in the accounting cycle.

Updating Account Balances Before a postclosing trial balance can be prepared, the account balances must be updated; that is, the current balance for each account in the ledger must be shown.

The closing entries did not affect the permanent asset and liability accounts. Thus, these account balances did not change. The permanent Capital account and the temporary accounts have changed and must be updated. The ledger on page 114 illustrates updated accounts.

- *To update the Capital account, draw a single rule under both money columns.* Total the amounts and compute a new account balance. (See the Lisa Long, Capital account.)
- *To update a closed account with two or more entries on either side of the account, draw a single rule across both money columns and total the columns.* Then draw a double rule across both money columns. (See the Income Summary account.) Remember that a double rule means that the amounts are equal and the work is completed.
- *To update a closed account with only one debit and one credit amount, draw a double rule across both money columns.* (See the Repairs Expense account.)

EXERCISE PLUS LEDGER

Assets = Liabilities + Owner's Equity

Assets

Cash 101

19—		19—	
Sept. 1	9,000	Sept. 5	4,000
6	1,000	12	4,000
14	13,000	21	6,000
26	4,000	28	2,900
10,100	27,000		16,900

Accts. Rec./Carmen Saldi 103

19—		19—	
Sept. 1	1,000	Sept. 6	1,000
27	700		
700	1,700		1,000

Accts. Rec./Talbot Industries 104

19—			
Sept. 27	1,400		

Furniture 111

19—		19—	
Sept. 1	3,000	Sept. 8	500
7	2,000		
4,500	5,000		500

Exercise Equipment 112

19—			
Sept. 1	5,000		
5	4,000		
13,000	13,000		

Liabilities

Accts. Pay./Shone Products 201

19—		19—	
Sept. 8	500	Sept. 1	4,000
12	4,000	7	2,000
	4,500	1,500	6,000

Accts. Pay./XYZ Repairs 202

		19—	
		Sept. 29	200

Owner's Equity

Lisa Long, Capital 301

19—		19—	
Sept. 21	6,000	Sept. 1	18,000
		14	13,000
	6,000	25,000	31,000
		30	3,000
	6,000	28,000	34,000

Income Summary 399

19—		19—	
Sept. 30	3,100	Sept. 30	6,100
30	3,000		
	6,100		6,100

Sales 401

19—		19—	
Sept. 30	6,100	Sept. 26	4,000
	6,100	27	2,100
		6,100	6,100
			6,100

Repairs Expense 504

19—		19—	
Sept. 29	200	Sept. 30	200

Salaries Expense 505

19—		19—	
Sept. 28	2,900	Sept. 30	2,900

Account balances updated after closing temporary accounts.

■ Preparing the Postclosing Trial Balance A postclosing trial balance is prepared like a formal trial balance but only permanent accounts are listed. The balance of each account is listed in the order in which it appears in the ledger. A quick postclosing trial balance can be prepared with a print/display calculator. A postclosing trial balance, like a formal trial balance, is usually prepared in pencil. It may, however, be prepared in ink. The postclosing trial balance prepared for

Exercise Plus on September 30 is shown below. As you review the postclosing trial balance note these points.

- It contains only balance sheet accounts. The temporary accounts have been closed to the permanent Capital account.
- It contains the accounts and balances that agree completely with the balance sheet. The balance of Lisa Long, Capital is the same as the total owner's equity on the balance sheet. It shows the owner's investment *plus* the net income for the accounting period.
- The ledger is now ready to receive entries for the next accounting period.

Owner's Equity

Lisa Long, Capital — *301*

19—		19—	
Sept. 21	6,000	Sept. 1	18,000
		14	13,000
	6,000	25,000	31,000
		30	3,000
		28,000	34,000

Updated Capital account.

Exercise Plus
Postclosing Trial Balance
September 30, 19—

ACCOUNT TITLE	ACCT. NO.	DEBIT	CREDIT
Cash	101	10 100 00	
Accts. Rec./Carmen Saldi	103	700 00	
Accts. Rec./Talbot Industries	104	1 400 00	
Furniture	111	4 500 00	
Exercise Equipment	112	13 000 00	
Accts. Pay./Shone Products	201		1 500 00
Accts. Pay./XYZ Repairs	202		200 00
Lisa Long, Capital	301		28 000 00
		29 700 00	29 700 00

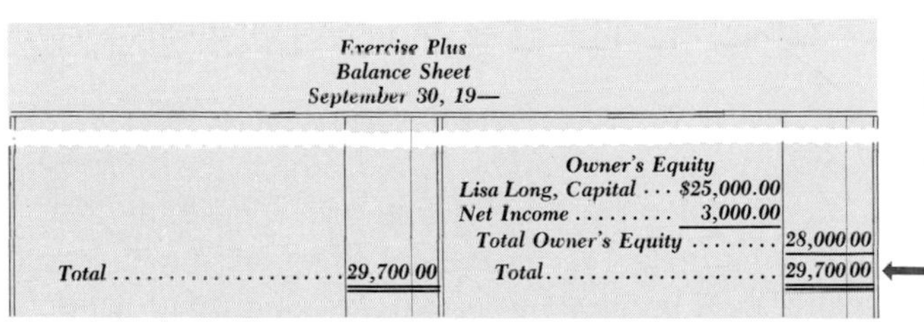

Exercise Plus
Balance Sheet
September 30, 19—

		Owner's Equity	
		Lisa Long, Capital · · · $25,000.00	
		Net Income · · · · · · · · 3,000.00	
		Total Owner's Equity · · · · · · · ·	28,000 00
Total ·	29,700 00	*Total* ·	29,700 00

The account balances on the trial balance now agree with the balances shown on the balance sheet.

Concept: Postclosing Trial Balance

The equality of the total debits and the total credits in the ledger should be verified after the ledger has been closed.

Exercise H on page 118 may be completed at this point.

Interpreting Accounting Information

Do owners and managers use accounting information only at the end of the accounting period? No. To operate a business successfully, owners and managers require a constant flow of information. Much of this information is provided by financial statements such as those that have been discussed.

Management interprets financial information on a continuous basis.

Interpreting (or using) accounting information is often considered the last step in the accounting cycle. This is because people often think of the income statement and the balance sheet as being the only sources of accounting information for owners and managers.

Actually, accounting information must be interpreted constantly and must often be obtained from sources besides the financial statements. For example, suppose Lisa Long wants to know the details of the total revenue she received from sales from September 1 to September 26. She will look at the Sales account in the ledger. The income statement shows the revenue for the entire period from September 1 to September 30, and not for parts of the period.

Suppose that on September 14 Lisa Long wants to know the amount of cash she has available. She must look at the Cash account in the ledger. The balance sheet will not be prepared until September 30. When it is prepared, the balance sheet will show the amount of cash available on September 30 only. Similarly, if Lisa Long wants to know to whom she sold services for $700 on credit on September 27, she must look at the ledger, not the income statement, for that information. Thus, while you learned that the interpretation of accounting information is the eighth step of the accounting cycle, remember that it is a process that goes on constantly.

■ Review of Accounting Cycle Activities

The eight steps of the accounting cycle can be reviewed as follows.

Step 1. *Record each transaction.* The data for each transaction is recorded in the accounting equation and in the ledger.

Step 2. *Keep a chronological record of each transaction.* The transactions are shown by date in the accounting equation and the ledger.

Step 3. *Store the changes caused by the transactions in each account and update the accounts.* In the ledger, the debits and credits are recorded for each account in T accounts.

Step 4. *Prove the equality of the accounts.* Formal and informal trial balances are prepared to prove the equality of the debits and credits in the ledger.

Step 5. *Summarize the accounting information at the end of the accounting period.* The accounting information is summarized by account balances at the end of the accounting period. Any accounts that have incorrect balances must be adjusted or corrected before the summaries are prepared. Otherwise, the financial statements will present an inaccurate or incomplete picture of the operations of a business for the accounting period. (The procedure for making adjustments will be discussed in Chapters 5 to 7.) Next, two financial statements are prepared—an income statement and a balance sheet.

Step 6. *Transfer net income (or net loss) to the permanent Capital account at the end of the accounting period.* The revenue and expense data is transferred to the Capital account at the end of the accounting period. This is done by the closing entries, which close the temporary accounts.

Step 7. *Prove the equality of the accounts after the net income (or net loss) has been transferred.* A postclosing trial balance is prepared to prove the equality of the closed ledger.

Step 8. *Interpret the accounting information.* The financial information is used to make business decisions.

Exercise I on page 118 may be completed at this point.

TOPIC 3 EXERCISES

EXERCISE E. Refer to the T accounts below and indicate which accounts would be debited and credited in order to do the following.

1. Transfer balance of Account *A* to Account *B*.

2. Transfer balance of Account *C* to Account *D*.

3. Transfer balance of Account *F* to Account *E*.

4. Transfer balance of Account *H* to Account *G*.

Account A	
900	

Account B	

Account E	
300	

Account F	
	600

Account C	
400	
300	

Account D	

Account G	
600	300
300	

Account H	
700	1,000
200	

EXERCISE F. Indicate which of the following is a permanent account and which is a temporary account that is closed.

EXAMPLE: Delivery Expense: temporary—closed

1. Accts. Pay./Doris Guzman

2. Sales

3. Equipment

4. Income Summary

5. Fees (Revenue)

6. Electricity Expense

7. Henry Chen, Capital

8. Salaries Expense

9. Postage Expense

EXERCISE G. Analyze each of the transactions listed below. Then record the debit amount and the credit amount in the appropriate T accounts.

1. Close the Sales account.

2. Close the expense accounts.

3. Close the revenue and expense accounts.

4. Close the Income Summary account.

1.

Sales 401 (Debit)	*Sales 401* (Credit)
	3,000

Income Summary 399 (Debit)	*Income Summary 399* (Credit)

2.

Rent Expense 501 (Debit)	*Rent Expense 501* (Credit)
700	

Utilities Expense 502 (Debit)	*Utilities Expense 502* (Credit)
500	

Income Summary 399 (Debit)	*Income Summary 399* (Credit)

3.

Advertising Expense 501 (Debit)	*Advertising Expense 501* (Credit)
600	

Rent Expense 502 (Debit)	*Rent Expense 502* (Credit)
200	

Salaries Expense 503 (Debit)	*Salaries Expense 503* (Credit)
1,000	

Sales 401 (Debit)	*Sales 401* (Credit)
	4,000

Income Summary 399 (Debit)	*Income Summary 399* (Credit)

4.

Anne Warren, Capital 301 (Debit)	*Anne Warren, Capital 301* (Credit)
1,000	*5,000*

Income Summary 399 (Debit)	*Income Summary 399* (Credit)
3,000	*4,000*

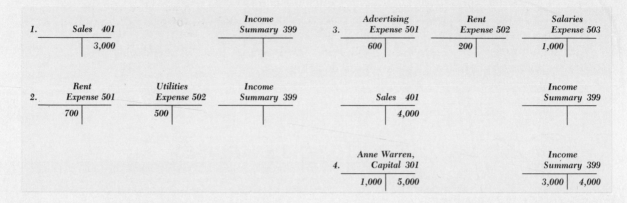

EXERCISE H. Arrange the following accounting activities in the correct order. The accounting period is for the month ended on December 31, 19—. Refer to the text, margin notes, and illustrations on pages 113 to 115.

1. Update owner's equity

2. December 31 trial balance

3. Enter transactions for the December accounting period

4. December 1 account balances

5. Prove equality—postclosing trial balance

6. January 1 account balances

7. Prepare balance sheet

8. November 30 postclosing trial balance

9. Prepare income statement

EXERCISE I. Indicate in which step of the accounting cycle each of the following activities is performed. Refer to the accounting cycle steps on pages 116 to 117.

EXAMPLE: 1. Recording the original data: Step 1.

1. Recording the original data

2. Preparing a statement showing total assets, liabilities, and owner's equity

3. Proving that the closed ledger is in balance

4. Closing the revenue and expense accounts

5. Using the accounting data to make decisions

6. Proving that the ledger is in balance before preparing the financial statements

7. Updating the Capital account with Income Summary data

8. Preparing a statement showing total revenue, expenses, and net income or net loss

TOPIC 3 PROBLEM

TOPIC PROBLEM 7. The T accounts for the revenue accounts, expense accounts, Income Summary account, and Capital account of the Howard Bates Company are shown below. Transfer the amounts to close all revenue accounts and expense accounts. Close the Income Summary account. These end-of-accounting-period activities occur on June 30, 19—. Refer to the illustrations on pages 110 and 114.

Howard Bates, Capital 301

Debit		Credit	
19—		19—	
June 10	500	June 1	20,500
		8	1,200

Income Summary 399

Debit	Credit

Sales 401

Debit	Credit	
	19—	
	June 10	9,500
	20	650

Advertising Expense 501

Debit		Credit
19—		
June 5	250	

Delivery Expense 502

Debit		Credit
19—		
June 27	700	

Rent Expense 503

Debit		Credit
19—		
June 26	1,500	

Salaries Expense 504

Debit		Credit
19—		
June 30	3,000	

Income Summary

Debit		Credit	
19-		19-	
June 30	5,450	June 30	10,150
30	4,700		
	10,150		10,150

CHAPTER SUMMARY

In this chapter you saw how to prepare a formal trial balance, financial statements, and a post-closing trial balance. You also saw how to close temporary accounts so that the accounting records are ready to receive information for the next accounting period.

The accountant prepares a formal trial balance to show that the debits and credits in the ledger are equal before going on to other end-of-the-period accounting work. Once the trial balance is prepared, the accounts can be sorted and classified for preparation of the income statement and the balance sheet.

The income statement shows the net income or net loss from operating a business for a period of time. The balance sheet shows the financial condition of a business by assets, liabilities, and owner's equity on a specific date. Both the income statement and the balance sheet provide information which managers, owners, and others can use to make business decisions.

After preparing the income statement and the balance sheet, the accountant closes the ledger or books for the accounting period.

The closing procedure clears the books to receive data about business transactions for the next accounting period. It therefore helps divide the activities for one accounting period from the activities carried out for another period.

Interpreting the information provided by the income statement, the balance sheet, and other financial sources is often regarded as the last step in the accounting cycle. However, owners and managers require a constant flow of information all during the accounting period. For that reason, interpretation should be regarded as an ongoing process.

THE LANGUAGE OF BUSINESS

Here are some terms that make up the language of business. Do you know the meaning of each?

pencil footing
income statement
fiscal year
calendar year
income statement accounts
balance sheet
liquidity
balance sheet accounts
account form balance sheet
closing the ledger
closing entries
zero balance
closed account
postclosing trial balance

REVIEW QUESTIONS

1. What is the source of information used to prepare the trial balance?
2. What is the order of accounts listed on the trial balance?
3. What is the purpose of an income statement?
4. Describe the steps necessary to prepare an income statement.

5. What would be the effect on net income if the accountant failed to record a sales transaction made on the last day of the accounting period? If the accountant recorded the same expense transaction twice? Would the trial balance totals be equal if neither of the two errors were discovered?
6. What is a balance sheet?
7. What portion of the balance sheet is prepared from the trial balance? What portion of the balance sheet is prepared from the income statement? Why must the income statement be used to prepare the balance sheet?
8. Why are revenue and expense accounts transferred (closed) at the end of the accounting period? Describe each of the closing entries.
9. How would the accountant know if one of the expense accounts was not included in the closing entries?
10. At what point(s) in the accounting cycle is accounting information used to make decisions? Explain.

CHAPTER PROBLEMS

Problems for Chapter 4 are given below. Write your answers on a separate sheet of paper unless you are using the workbook for this textbook. If you are using the workbook, do the problems in the space provided there.

CHAPTER PROBLEM 4-1. The ledger for Gilbert's Computer Service is shown below.

a. Compute the account balances for Gilbert's Computer Service.

b. Prepare a trial balance to prove the equality of Gilbert's Computer Service's ledger.

Cash 101

Date	Debit	Date	Credit
19—		*19—*	
Apr. 1	*16,000*	*Apr. 8*	*3,000*
5	*50*	*18*	*55*
15	*2,325*	*25*	*250*
		27	*1,500*
		29	*1,000*

Accts. Rec./Computer Supplies Co. 102

Date	Debit	Date	Credit
19—		*19—*	
Apr. 3	*250*	*Apr. 5*	*50*
10	*1,475*		

Equipment 103

Date	Debit	Date	Credit
19—			
Apr. 1	*5,000*		
8	*3,000*		
9	*7,000*		

Accts. Pay./Star Co. 201

Date	Debit	Date	Credit
19—		*19—*	
Apr. 29	*1,000*	*Apr. 9*	*7,000*

Joyce Gilbert, Capital 301

Date	Debit	Date	Credit
19—		*19—*	
Apr. 27	*1,500*	*Apr. 1*	*21,000*

Income Summary 399

Date	Debit	Date	Credit

Sales 401

Date	Debit	Date	Credit
		19—	
		Apr. 3	*250*
		10	*1,475*
		15	*2,325*

Rent Expense 501

Date	Debit	Date	Credit
19—			
Apr. 25	*250*		

Utilities Expense 502

Date	Debit	Date	Credit
19—			
Apr. 18	*55*		

CHAPTER PROBLEM 4-2. Using the trial balance which you prepared for Gilbert's Computer Service in Chapter Problem 4-1, do the following.

a. Prepare an income statement for Gilbert's Computer Service.

b. Prepare a balance sheet for Gilbert's Computer Service.

CHAPTER PROBLEM 4-3. Using the account balances which you computed for Gilbert's Computer Service's ledger in Part *a* of Chapter Problem 4-1, do the following.

a. Update and close the appropriate ledger accounts for Gilbert's Computer Service.

b. Prepare a postclosing trial balance for Gilbert's Computer Service.

CHAPTER PROBLEM 4-4. Examine and analyze the balance sheet for the Mary Allen Real Estate Agency shown below. The balance sheet was prepared by an inexperienced accounting clerk on April 30 and contains errors. You have been asked to check the accuracy of the balance sheet. You should do the following.

a. Find the errors in the balance sheet.

b. Prepare a corrected balance sheet.

Mary Allen Real Estate Agency, Balance Sheet

Office Equipment	*5,700.00*		
Automobile	*11,200.00*	*Accts. Rec./Pam Wells*	*1,550.00*
Loans Payable	*16,400.00*	*Accts. Pay./Ad Agents*	*1,440.00*
Cash	*7,000.00*		
Building	*49,000.00*		
		Mary Allen, Capital	*?*
		Net Income	*4,680.00*
	89,300.00		*89,300.00*

MANAGEMENT CASES

The Need for Information. Each day a manager must make important business decisions. Examples include buying new equipment or granting a loan to an applicant. Information for these decisions can come from the records either of the manager's business or of other businesses. All these records must provide accurate information quickly.

CASE 4M-1. Linda Shaw has been giving ceramic lessons in her home to family and friends. Recently, Linda decided to go into business and advertised to give lessons for a fee. She seeks your help in setting up accounting records. What financial information would you need from her to determine the business's assets, liabilities, and owner's equity? What accounts would you suggest? What other advice would you give her? Where can she find additional information?

CASE 4M-2. Clarence Boston owns a successful restaurant. Since new housing is being built nearby, he expects an increase in business. He wants to add more seating and a larger kitchen so that his customers will not have to wait. In order to expand, Clarence wants to borrow $50,000 from a bank and makes an application for a loan. With the application he includes a letter saying that his business is estimated to be worth $150,000. The bank replies that it cannot make a decision about the loan. It needs information about the revenue and expenses of the business and a list of the assets and liabilities of the business.

a. Why would the bank want a list of the assets and liabilities of the business before making a decision about the loan?

b. What financial statements should Clarence have sent with his loan application?

c. Why would the bank be interested in the income statement?

d. What factors other than those shown on the financial statements do you think the bank will consider in determining whether or not to approve the loan?

e. What other factors should Clarence consider before he decides whether or not to expand?

CHAPTER

5

Origination and Input of Accounting Data

All of the topics that you studied in Chapters 1 to 4 provide a basic framework for understanding accounting. To see how accountants actually put this framework to use in supplying financial information to businesses, you will now study the steps in the accounting cycle again.

CHAPTER GOALS

After studying Chapter 5, you will be able to:

1. Define the terms listed in "The Language of Business" section on page 147.
2. Explain the accounting concepts and principles in the chapter related to originating data and journalizing transactions.
3. Analyze source documents.
4. Use source documents to analyze transactions and determine the debit and credit entries.
5. Journalize entries in a two-column journal.
6. Create an audit trail.
7. Describe the relationship between the accounting and data processing cycles.

TOPIC 1

Originating Data

What is the first step in the accounting cycle? The first step in the accounting cycle, as you learned, is to record the data about each transaction. In accounting terms, the starting point for recording the data about a business transaction is called **originating data**.

ACCOUNTING CYCLE

1
Originate data

In Chapters 5 to 7, the accounting cycle will be examined in greater detail. As each step of the accounting cycle is reexamined, you will study actual business forms and procedures used by accounting personnel. In this topic, you will begin with the first step of the accounting cycle—originating data.

Source Documents

In previous chapters, the transactions were given in narrative form. That is, the details of the transactions were described in words. You were told that on a certain date a certain transaction took place. For example, on page 28 a transaction for Exercise Plus is given as follows.

Sept. 7 Exercise Plus buys additional furniture for $2,000 on credit from Shone Products. The creditor allows 30 days to pay this amount.

A source document provides information and evidence about a transaction.

In actual practice, the details of this transaction would be recorded on a business form. Businesses use forms to record the data about business transactions. The forms are called source documents. A **source document** is a business form containing data about a transaction. In this way, a separate record of each transaction is available. For example, the details of the transaction to purchase the additional furniture on credit would be recorded on a business form called a *purchase invoice,* or *bill.* The details of a sale are recorded on a *sales invoice*.

Look at the purchase invoice at the right and note the following information. The purchase invoice lists the details of the transaction on September 7 described above.

1. The number of the invoice. Note that the number is preprinted on the purchase invoice.

2. The date of the transaction.

3. The name of the seller (creditor).

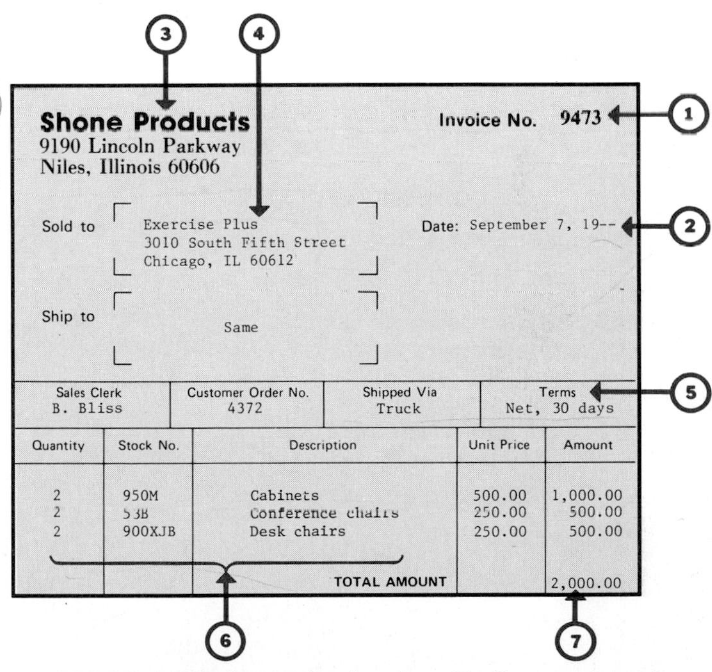

Shone Products
9190 Lincoln Parkway
Niles, Illinois 60606

Invoice No. 9473

Sold to: Exercise Plus
3010 South Fifth Street
Chicago, IL 60612

Date: September 7, 19--

Ship to: Same

Sales Clerk	Customer Order No.	Shipped Via	Terms
B. Bliss	4372	Truck	Net, 30 days

Quantity	Stock No.	Description	Unit Price	Amount
2	950M	Cabinets	500.00	1,000.00
2	53B	Conference chairs	250.00	500.00
2	900XJB	Desk chairs	250.00	500.00
		TOTAL AMOUNT		2,000.00

To the seller, this is a sales invoice. To the purchaser, this is a purchase invoice.

4. The name of the purchaser (buyer).
5. The terms of the credit granted by the creditor.
6. The quantity, stock number, and description of the items or service purchased.
7. The dollar amount of the transaction. Note that all extensions appear in the Amount column. An **extension** is the product of multiplying the quantity by the unit price. The extensions are then totaled.

The accounting clerk uses this purchase invoice to analyze the transaction and determine the debit entry and the credit entry. Since the transaction can be traced back to this purchase invoice, the invoice is a source document for the transaction. It originates the data and supplies evidence that the transaction took place.

Use of Source Documents

Source documents usually consist of paper forms with data written on them. The purchase invoice on page 125 is a source document.

Chapters 2 and 3 give the transactions for September in narrative form. The transactions for October are now listed on pages 127 to 130 using source documents. An example is given of a source document that would be used for each transaction.

Once a source document is prepared, it will be used to communicate the data about a transaction through additional steps in the accounting cycle. It is also used to communicate the data to other parts of the business. For example, a salesclerk in the store writes out a sales invoice for a sale on credit. The salesclerk then sends the sales invoice to the accounting clerk in the accounting office. The sales invoice is the source document that provides the accounting office with the data needed to record the transaction in the accounting records. The source document makes it easier to determine the debit and credit entries. This is Step 2 of the accounting cycle—journalizing the transactions.

Purposes of a Source Document:

- Gives proof the transaction occurred
- Makes a transaction easier to trace through the accounting cycle
- Provides information for recording the transaction in a journal (Step 2 in the accounting cycle)

Frequently, the salesclerk will be located in a store in one city and the accounting clerk will be located in an accounting office in another city. The important accounting details of the transaction must be communicated from the store to the office.

In some cases, there is more than one business form to support a transaction. For example, Exercise Plus issues a check for $2,000 to pay salaries. In this case, there are more details to the transaction than are recorded on the checkbook stub. As you will learn later, a payroll summary is prepared to summarize the payroll data for all employees. Thus, the complete details of this transaction are supplied by the checkbook stub and the payroll summary. It is good accounting practice to have a source document support each check that is written. In this way, the reason the check was issued can be traced back to the invoice or other authorization.

Some other terms used in place of *source documents* are *business papers, original papers,* and *supporting documents*.

OCTOBER TRANSACTIONS FOR EXERCISE PLUS

Narrative Transactions	Source Documents

October 1: Exercise Plus started a new set of records.

Balance Sheet: A financial statement reporting the assets, liabilities, and owner's equity for a specific date.

Exercise Plus
Balance Sheet
September 30, 19—

Assets			*Liabilities*		
Cash	10,100	00	*Accounts Payable:*		
Accounts Receivable:			*Shone Products . . . $1,500.00*		
Carmen Saldi . . . . . $ 700.00			*XYZ Repairs 200.00*		
Talbot Industries . . 1,400.00	2,100	00	*Total Liabilities*	1,700	00
Furniture	4,500	00			
Exercise Equipment	13,000	00			
			Owner's Equity		
			Lisa Long, Capital . . $25,000.00		
			Net Income 3,000.00		
			Total Owner's Equity	28,000	00
Total	29,700	00	*Total*	29,700	00

October 5: Exercise Plus received a check for $700 from Carmen Saldi on account.

Remittance Slip: A record listing details of cash received.

Exercise Plus — REMITTANCE SLIP 104
3010 South Fifth Street
Chicago, Illinois 60612

NAME: *Carmen Saldi*

AMOUNT RECEIVED	CHECK NUMBER	CHECK DATE
$ 700.00	773	10/5/—

EXPLANATION: *Received on account.*

DATE RECEIVED	RECEIVED BY
10/5/	L.L.

Carmen Saldi

PAY TO THE ORDER OF *Exercise Plus* $ *700 00/100*
Seven hundred and 00/100 DOLLARS
TRADERS BANK
Chicago, Illinois 60601
Carmen Saldi
:0710-0436: 204-1997-0773

October 6: Exercise Plus bought supplies to last several months from the Webster Corporation and issued a check for $600 in payment.

Checkbook Stub: A record in a checkbook giving details of each check issued.

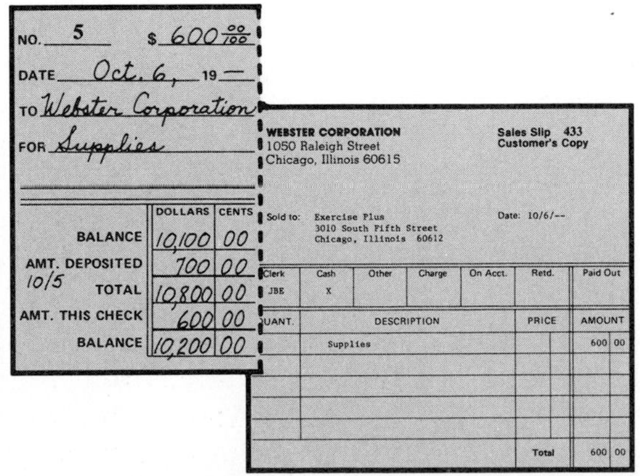

NO. 5 $ *600 00/100*
DATE *Oct. 6,* 19 —
TO *Webster Corporation*
FOR *Supplies*

	DOLLARS	CENTS
BALANCE	10,100	00
AMT. DEPOSITED 10/5	700	00
TOTAL	10,800	00
AMT. THIS CHECK	600	00
BALANCE	10,200	00

WEBSTER CORPORATION — Sales Slip 433, Customer's Copy
1050 Raleigh Street
Chicago, Illinois 60615

Sold to: Exercise Plus, 3010 South Fifth Street, Chicago, Illinois 60612 — Date: 10/6/--

Clerk	Cash	Other	Charge	On Acct.	Retd.	Paid Out
JBE	X					

QUANT.	DESCRIPTION	PRICE	AMOUNT
	Supplies		600 00
		Total	600 00

OCTOBER TRANSACTIONS FOR EXERCISE PLUS

Narrative Transactions	Source Documents
October 7: Exercise Plus bought additional furniture for $700 on credit from Shone Products. The creditor allowed Exercise Plus 30 days to pay this amount.	*Purchase Invoice*: A bill listing the items or services purchased, the amounts, the terms, and the date.

Shone Products Invoice No. 9822
9190 Lincoln Parkway
Niles, Illinois 60606

Sold to: Exercise Plus, 3010 South Fifth Street, Chicago, Illinois 60612 Date: October 7, 19--

Ship to: Same

Sales Clerk	Customer Order No.	Shipped Via	Terms
B. Bliss	4375	Truck	Net, 30 days

Quantity	Stock No.	Description	Unit Price	Amount
2	4398	Conference tables	350.00	700.00
		TOTAL AMOUNT		700.00

Narrative Transactions	Source Documents
October 8: Exercise Plus returned furniture (one table) bought for $350 on credit from Shone Products because it arrived in damaged condition.	*Credit Memorandum*: A form granting credit to the purchaser for a purchase return or allowance.

Shone Products
9190 Lincoln Parkway
Niles, Illinois 60606

CREDIT MEMORANDUM
Copy 1: Customer

No. CM-67

To: Exercise Plus, 3010 South Fifth Street, Chicago, Illinois 60612

Date October 8, 19--
Sold on Invoice No. 9822
Your Order No. 4375

We have credited your account as follows:

QUANTITY	DESCRIPTION	PRICE	AMOUNT
1	Conference table, Model 4398	350.00	350.00

Narrative Transactions	Source Documents
October 12: Exercise Plus issued a check for $1,500 to Shone Products on account.	*Checkbook Stub*: A record in a checkbook giving details of each check issued.

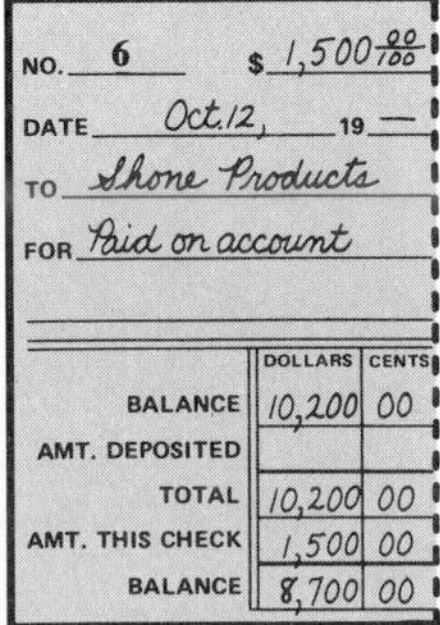

NO. 6 $ 1,500 00/100
DATE Oct. 12, 19—
TO Shone Products
FOR Paid on account

	DOLLARS	CENTS
BALANCE	10,200	00
AMT. DEPOSITED		
TOTAL	10,200	00
AMT. THIS CHECK	1,500	00
BALANCE	8,700	00

Narrative Transactions	**Source Documents**

October 12: Lisa Long invested an additional $6,000 in Exercise Plus. She withdrew $6,000 from her personal savings account and deposited the cash in the business checking account.

Remittance Slip: A record listing details of cash received.

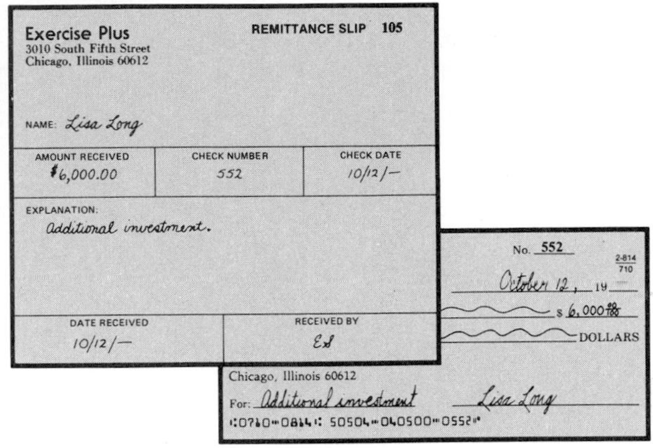

Exercise Plus
3010 South Fifth Street
Chicago, Illinois 60612

REMITTANCE SLIP 105

NAME: Lisa Long

AMOUNT RECEIVED	CHECK NUMBER	CHECK DATE
$6,000.00	552	10/12/—

EXPLANATION: Additional investment.

DATE RECEIVED	RECEIVED BY
10/12/—	E.L.

No. 552
2-814
710
October 12, 19—
$ 6,000 00/100
DOLLARS
Chicago, Illinois 60612
For: Additional investment
Lisa Long
⑆0710⑈0814⑆ 50504⑈040500⑈0552⑈

October 21: Lisa Long withdrew $2,000 from the Exercise Plus checking account and deposited it in her personal savings account.

Checkbook Stub: A record in a checkbook giving details of each check issued.

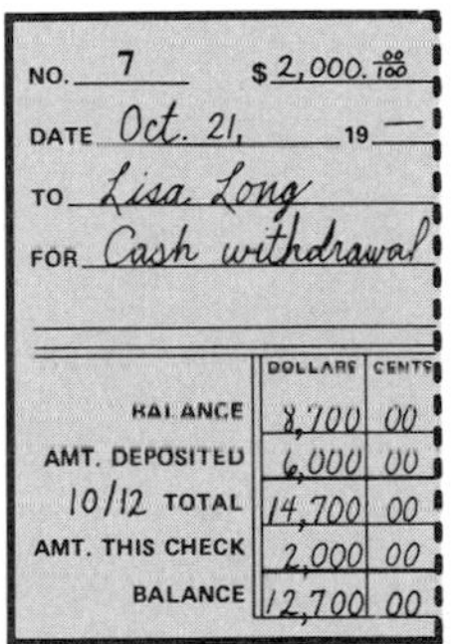

NO. 7 $ 2,000. 00/100
DATE Oct. 21, 19—
TO Lisa Long
FOR Cash withdrawal

	DOLLARS	CENTS
BALANCE	8,700	00
AMT. DEPOSITED	6,000	00
10/12 TOTAL	14,700	00
AMT. THIS CHECK	2,000	00
BALANCE	12,700	00

October 26: Exercise Plus received $1,400 in cash from the sale of fitness and exercise services during October.

Sales Invoice: A bill listing the items or services sold, the amounts, the terms, and the date.

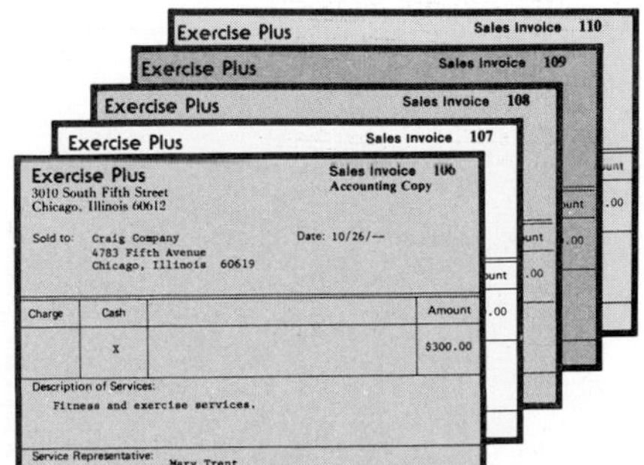

Exercise Plus — Sales Invoice 110
Exercise Plus — Sales Invoice 109
Exercise Plus — Sales Invoice 108
Exercise Plus — Sales Invoice 107

Exercise Plus
3010 South Fifth Street
Chicago, Illinois 60612

Sales Invoice 106
Accounting Copy

Sold to: Craig Company
4783 Fifth Avenue
Chicago, Illinois 60619

Date: 10/26/—

Charge	Cash		Amount
	X		$300.00

Description of Services:
Fitness and exercise services.

Service Representative: Mary Trent

OCTOBER TRANSACTIONS FOR EXERCISE PLUS

Narrative Transactions	**Source Documents**

October 27: Exercise Plus sold exercise services on credit to Carmen Saldi for $1,200 and to Talbot Industries for $1,000.

Sales Invoice: A bill listing the items or services sold, the amounts, the terms, and the date.

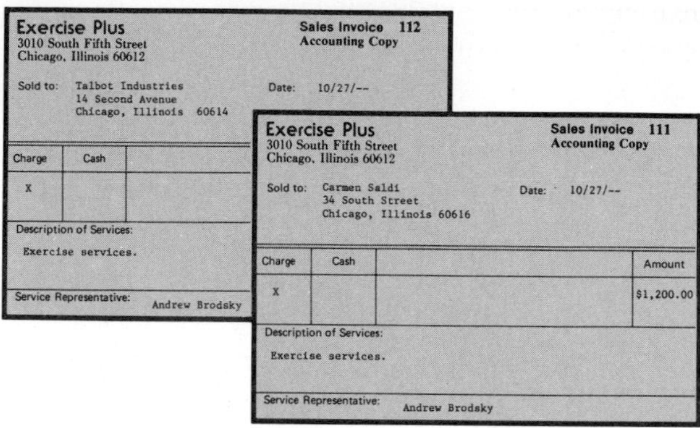

Exercise Plus
3010 South Fifth Street
Chicago, Illinois 60612
Sales Invoice 112
Accounting Copy
Sold to: Talbot Industries
14 Second Avenue
Chicago, Illinois 60614
Date: 10/27/--

Charge	Cash	
X		

Description of Services:
Exercise services.
Service Representative: Andrew Brodsky

Exercise Plus
3010 South Fifth Street
Chicago, Illinois 60612
Sales Invoice 111
Accounting Copy
Sold to: Carmen Saldi
34 South Street
Chicago, Illinois 60616
Date: 10/27/--

Charge	Cash		Amount
X			$1,200.00

Description of Services:
Exercise services.
Service Representative: Andrew Brodsky

October 28: Exercise Plus paid an expense of $2,000 for salaries.

Checkbook Stub: A record in a checkbook giving details of each check issued.

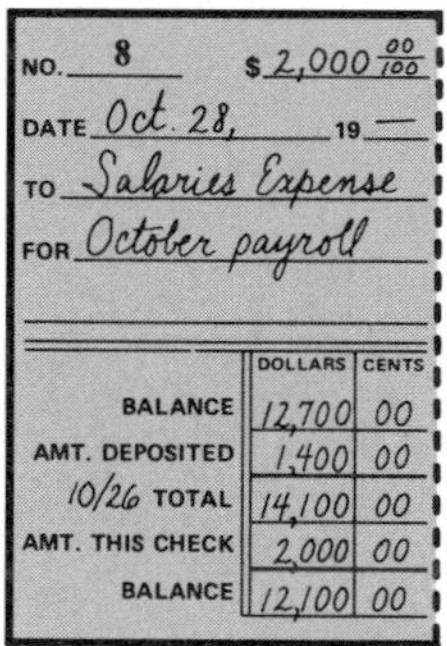

NO. 8 $ 2,000 00/100
DATE Oct. 28, 19 —
TO Salaries Expense
FOR October payroll

	DOLLARS	CENTS
BALANCE	12,700	00
AMT. DEPOSITED	1,400	00
10/26 TOTAL	14,100	00
AMT. THIS CHECK	2,000	00
BALANCE	12,100	00

October 29: Exercise Plus received a bill for repairs expense of $200 from XYZ Repairs for making repairs to the gym. The creditor allowed Exercise Plus 30 days to pay this amount.

Purchase Invoice: A bill listing the items or services purchased, the amounts, the terms, and the date.

XYZ REPAIRS
126 Mountain Road
Lakeville, Illinois 60610

Invoice No. 212

Date: 10/29/--

To: Exercise Plus
3010 South Fifth Street
Chicago, Illinois 60612

Terms: Net, 30 days

Repairs to gym.	$200.00

Sources of Transaction Data

Some source documents are originated inside the business. Data collected inside the business is called *internal data*. Sources of internal data for Exercise Plus are its checkbook stubs and sales invoices. The data comes from business forms originated within Exercise Plus.

Other source documents are originated outside the business. Data that comes from outside the business is called *external data*. Sources of external data for Exercise Plus include the checks from customers, the owner's personal checks, and purchase invoices. The data from these transactions comes from forms originated outside the business.

Business forms that come from outside businesses may provide the data for "internal" source documents. For example, a check received from a customer is a source document for a remittance slip, an "internal" source document. When the check from the customer is deposited in the business's checking account, the business will no longer have possession of it. In order to have a record of the transaction based on the check, the business must fill out a remittance slip. A **remittance slip** is a record listing the details of cash received. It is a receipt showing *the amount* received, *from whom* the amount was received, and *by whom* the amount was received.

A business form may be a source of internal data for one business and a source of external data for another.

Some source documents provide internal data to one business and external data to another. For example, the invoice from Shone Products to Exercise Plus serves both purposes. To Shone Products, which originated the invoice, it provides internal data. To Exercise Plus, which received the invoice from Shone Products, it provides external data. Shone Products considers the invoice a sales invoice because it documents a sale of goods. Exercise Plus considers the invoice a purchase invoice because it documents a purchase of goods.

Concept: Source Document
A record of the original data about each transaction should be available. This record is commonly called a source document.

Exercise A on page 133 may be completed at this point.

Methods of Processing Data

How does a business process data? A business may use manual and/or electronic methods of processing its accounting data. **Manual data processing** is a method of processing data manually (by hand) with the use of some equipment, such as calculators and cash registers. **Electronic data processing (EDP)** is a method of processing data using a computer. Computers and computerized accounting systems are discussed elsewhere in special chapters later in this book.

The accounting concepts and principles you learned apply to either method of processing data. However, the procedures, or ways of doing things, vary. For example, both methods rely on source documents for the origination of data. But the source documents may look somewhat

Accounting concepts and principles apply to both manual and electronic data processing.

different. In manual data processing systems, for example, the source documents are usually paper business forms with preprinted information. In electronic systems, the source documents might consist of magnetic tapes with magnetized spots on them.

■ Manual Data Processing Several different business forms are used as source documents in manual data processing, as shown here.

RECORDED DATA IN MANUAL DATA PROCESSING

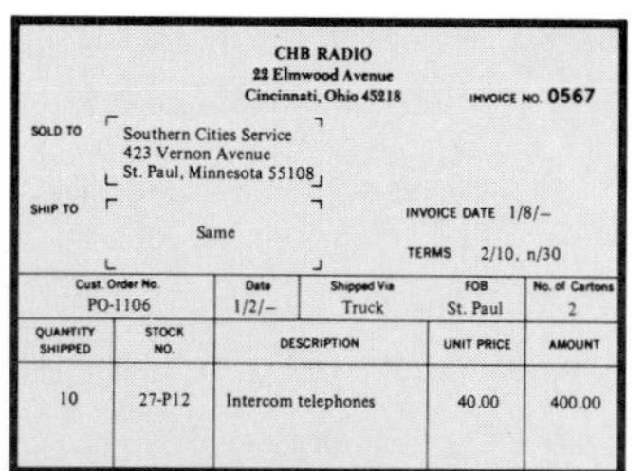

CHB RADIO
22 Elmwood Avenue
Cincinnati, Ohio 45218

INVOICE NO. 0567

SOLD TO Southern Cities Service
423 Vernon Avenue
St. Paul, Minnesota 55108

SHIP TO Same

INVOICE DATE 1/8/–
TERMS 2/10, n/30

Cust. Order No.	Date	Shipped Via	FOB	No. of Cartons
PO-1106	1/2/–	Truck	St. Paul	2

QUANTITY SHIPPED	STOCK NO.	DESCRIPTION	UNIT PRICE	AMOUNT
10	27-P12	Intercom telephones	40.00	400.00

Paper form with typewritten data.

NO. 6 $ 1,500 00/100
DATE Oct. 12, 19 –
TO Shone Products
FOR Paid on account

	DOLLARS	CENTS
BALANCE	10,200	00
AMT. DEPOSITED		
TOTAL	10,200	00
AMT. THIS CHECK	1,500	00
BALANCE	8,700	00

Check stub with handwritten data.

No. 6 2-814/710
October 12, 19 –
PAY TO THE ORDER OF Shone Products $ 1,500.00/100
One thousand five hundred and 00/100 DOLLARS
Lincoln Bank
Chicago, Illinois 60612
Exercise Plus
By Lisa Long
⑆0710⑈0814⑆ 5050⑈020600⑈0006

Check with handwritten and printed data.

■ Electronic Data Processing You are probably familiar with several business forms designed for use with electronic data processing equipment. Several examples are shown here.

SOME BUSINESS FORMS USED IN ELECTRONIC DATA PROCESSING

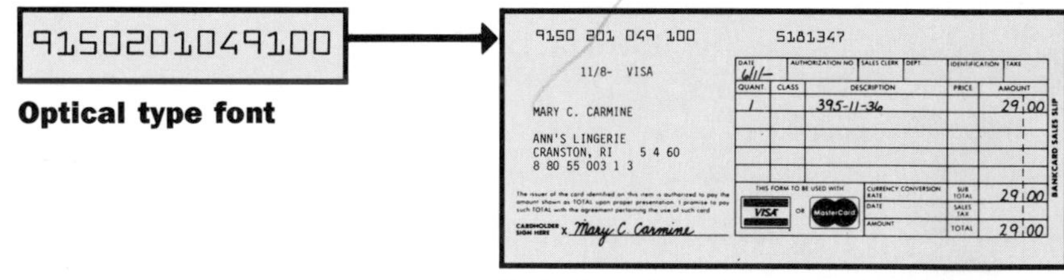

Optical type font

Data is printed in optical type fonts.

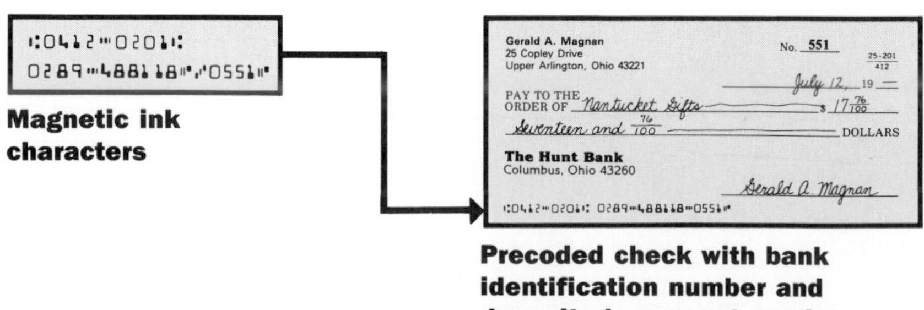

Magnetic ink characters

Precoded check with bank identification number and depositor's account number.

Universal Product Code

Data printed in Universal Product Code.

```
        GIANT FOOD - MCLEAN

  1.03b 2b/.89BK/POT      .46 B
        HN     FRANKS    2.69 B
        BR MILK BALL      .45 B
        SERVICE DELI     1.12 B
        SERVICE DELI     1.43 B
        HOT DOG ROLL      .32 B
        HALF&HALF PT      .65 B
        CHOC MILK 2*      .41 B
        SOFTSOAP         1.99 T
        TRAY PUZZLE       .99 T
        TAX   .42 BAL 10.93
        CHK 30.00 CHG 19.07
07/12/XX 18:52 005839      2121
          THANK YOU
```

Receipt tape.

These forms contain all the data about a business transaction. Such data is read and processed automatically by electronic data processing equipment. For example, some electronic cash registers can read universal product codes, which consist of numbers and lines of various thicknesses. At the checkout counter, the salesclerk passes the coded label on the product over an optical scanner. The data is automatically entered into the cash register, which is connected to a computer.

The computer relays the price back to the cash register. The cash register then prints the data on a cash register tape. One copy of the tape is given to the customer, and another remains locked inside the cash register. The cash register tape becomes the source document.

A variety of source documents are used in business. Each source document is designed to fit the specific needs of a business as well as the way the business processes data.

Exercises B and C on this page and page 134 may be completed at this point.

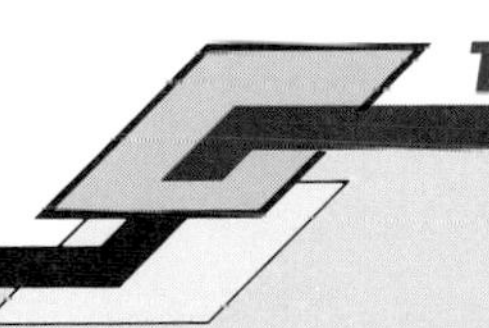

TOPIC 1 EXERCISES

EXERCISE A. Decide which of the following is a source document. Write "yes" or "no" after the item, as appropriate.

EXAMPLE: Sales invoice—yes

1. An order placed by telephone
2. Employee's conversation
3. Checkbook stub
4. Balance sheet
5. Newspaper
6. Cash register receipt

EXERCISE B. Match the electronic data processing items in Column A with the business forms in Column B.

Column A	Column B
1. Universal product code	a. Check from a checkbook
2. Magnetic ink characters	b. Credit card account
3. Optical scanner	c. Cash register tape
4. Optical type font	d. Label on a candy bar

EXERCISE C. The following are ways of processing data. Identify the method being used as either manual or electronic.

EXAMPLE: Paychecks printed by a computer—electronic data processing

1. Report cards printed by a computer

2. Sales recorded on a cash register

3. Invoices typed on a typewriter

4. Amounts added on an adding machine

5. Amounts added by a computer

6. Invoices written by hand

TOPIC 1 PROBLEMS

TOPIC PROBLEM 1. Renee Hess is a new employee in the accounting department. Her supervisor asks her to select all the source documents from a stack of forms, correspondence, and other records.

The stack of source documents that was given to Renee Hess contains the items shown at the right. Prepare a list of the items in the stack that are accounting source documents.

3 remittance slips
1 utility bill
5 unsigned letters
10 checks received today
4 telephone messages
2 memos from the company president
1 gas bill
2 shopping lists
45 invoices

TOPIC PROBLEM 2. For each of the following transactions, name an appropriate source document.

a. David Hernandez started a new set of accounting records on March 1.

b. Bought a new truck from Citrus Motors for $18,000, Check 389.

c. Sold services to Leann Monson for $700 on credit.

d. Received a check for $300 from White's Repair on account.

e. Paid monthly payroll.

f. Sold services for $600 in cash.

g. Bought supplies on credit.

h. Returned a defective adding machine purchased on credit.

TOPIC 2

Journalizing Data

Is it practical to enter debits and credits directly into accounts? In Chapter 3, the debits and credits for each transaction were entered directly into T accounts in the ledger. This may be done easily when there are only a few transactions. However, entering debits and credits directly into accounts is not practical when many transactions are involved.

There are several reasons why data from source documents is not recorded directly into the ledger.

- It is difficult to locate a complete transaction in the ledger. The record of each transaction exists in the form of a debit entry in one or more accounts and a credit entry in one or more different accounts. The debits and credits for a transaction do not appear together. Thus, you would have to search through the entire ledger to locate all parts of a specific transaction.
- It is difficult to compare the volume of transactions by day. Debits and credits of transactions for a specific date are not stored in one account in the ledger. Instead, the transactions are scattered throughout the ledger by account title. Thus, you would have to search again through the entire ledger to determine the volume of transactions for a specific date.
- It is difficult to locate an error in an entry. The debits and credits for each transaction do not appear together. Again, you would have to search tediously through the entire ledger to check that the debits equal the credits for each entry.

These difficulties can be avoided by recording the transactions from source documents into a record called a journal before transferring the debits and credits to the accounts in the ledger.

■ Journals

A journal is a daily record of the important facts and amounts of every transaction. In a journal, the transactions are recorded in chronological order. That is, transactions are recorded according to the date on which they occur. This makes it quite easy to trace any transaction. A **journal** is, therefore, a chronological listing of all transactions analyzed in terms of the accounts to be debited and credited.

After the data about a transaction is originated, it is recorded in a journal. **Journalizing** is the recording of transactions in a journal. It is the second step in the accounting cycle. Several items should be emphasized before you learn how to journalize transactions.

ACCOUNTING CYCLE

1 Originate data

↓

2 Journalize transactions

- There are many different types of journals used in business. The first journal that will be described is the two-column journal, which is the basic type of journal. It is illustrated here.

JOURNAL Page

DATE	ACCOUNT TITLE AND EXPLANATION	POST. REF.	DEBIT	CREDIT

The two-column journal has one money column for debits and one money column for credits.

- Journalizing does not change the accounting rules of debiting and crediting. The only difference between this procedure and the one followed in Chapter 3 is that a transaction is recorded in the journal before it is recorded in the accounts.
- The transaction will be journalized using the manual method for processing data. The same details are present whether the transactions are recorded manually or by some machine or computer.
- The details of the transactions are obtained from source documents.

Concept: Journal

A record of all transactions should be available in chronological order. This record is commonly called a journal.

Exercise D on page 144 may be completed at this point.

The Journalizing Procedure

What must be done before a transaction can be journalized? Before the data from a source document is recorded in a journal, the transaction must be analyzed. **Analyzing a transaction** means determining the effects the transaction has on the various asset, liability, and owner's equity accounts. This analysis determines the journal entry to be recorded. A **journal entry** is a recording in a journal of a transaction showing the date, the accounts, and the amounts to be debited and credited, and, if necessary, an explanation. A journal entry contains the following data.

- The date
- The title of the accounts to be debited and credited
- The amounts of the debits and the credits
- The source document number and/or a brief explanation

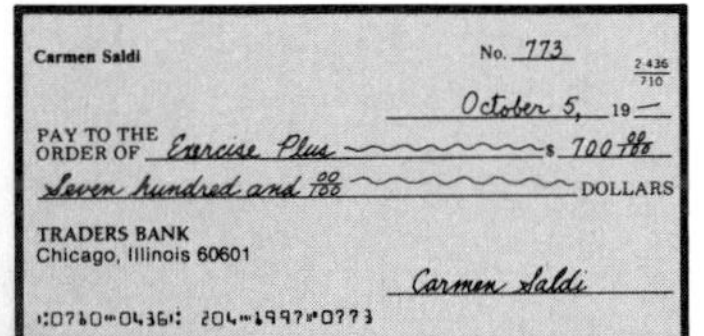
Carmen Saldi   No. 773   2-436/710
October 5, 19—
PAY TO THE ORDER OF Exercise Plus $ 700 00/00
Seven hundred and 00/100   DOLLARS
TRADERS BANK
Chicago, Illinois 60601
Carmen Saldi
⑆0710⑈0436⑆ 204⑈1997⑈0773

Check received from debtor.

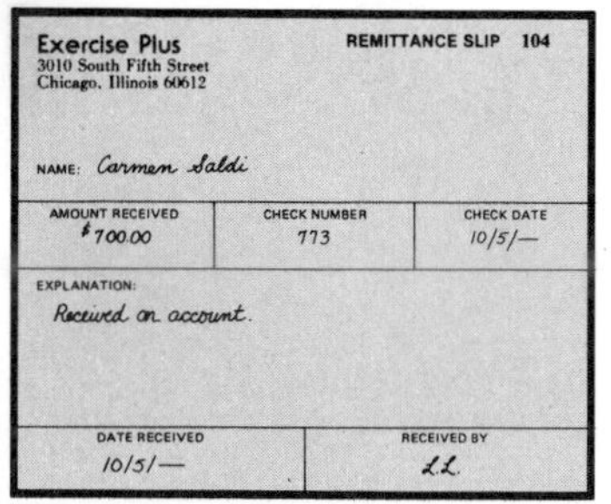
Exercise Plus   REMITTANCE SLIP 104
3010 South Fifth Street
Chicago, Illinois 60612

NAME: Carmen Saldi

AMOUNT RECEIVED	CHECK NUMBER	CHECK DATE
$700.00	773	10/5/—

EXPLANATION:
Received on account.

DATE RECEIVED	RECEIVED BY
10/5/—	L.L.

Remittance slip is a source document.

The basic guidelines for making a journal entry will be illustrated by using the October 5 transaction. On October 5, Exercise Plus received a check for $700 from Carmen Saldi on account.

Lisa Long prepared a remittance slip as a record of the transaction. The remittance slip becomes the source document because it is a record of the amount of cash received from each customer.

Here are the basic guidelines to follow in recording the journal entry.

Analyzing the Transaction Analyze the effects of the transaction in the usual way. Determine what happens, the accounting rule to apply, and the debit entry and the credit entry. You may find it helpful to use T accounts in determining the entry. (When using T accounts to analyze transactions, you do not have to write the date. You are just analyzing the debits and credits of the transaction and checking the equality of debits and credits.)

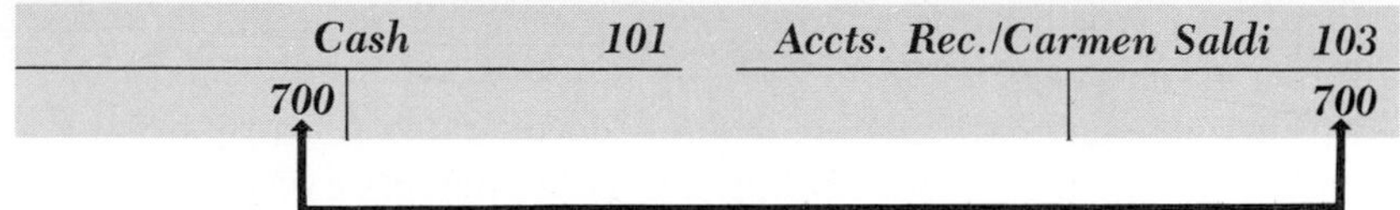

Cash 101
700
Accts. Rec./Carmen Saldi 103
700

T accounts help in analyzing transactions.

■ Recording the Date of the Transaction Record the date of the transaction in the Date column. When starting a page of a journal, write the year in small figures at the top of the page in the left part of the divided Date column, as shown in the margin. Abbreviate the month and enter it below the year. Then write the day of the month in the right part of the Date column. Write the date when recording the first debit of each journal entry. Do not repeat the day for other debits and credits of the same journal entry.

For the next transaction, record only the day of the month. Do not repeat the month and the year. Write the year and month only in these three instances: when starting a new page, when the month changes, or when the year changes.

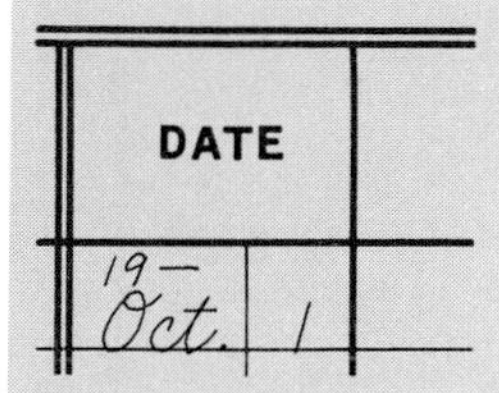

The year and month are written at the top of a page.

■ Recording the Debit Entry To record the debit entry, write the title of the account that is to be debited in the next column. Use the same line as the date. Start writing the title at the vertical rule of the Account Title and Explanation column. Then enter the amount of the debit in the Debit money column, on the same line. Since this is a ruled form, it is not necessary to use dollar signs, commas, or decimal points.

The month is written when the month changes.

■ Recording the Credit Entry Record the credit entry on the line below the debit entry. Indent about a half inch from the Date column, and write the title of the account that is to be credited. On the same line, enter the amount of the credit in the Credit money column.

The credit entries are indented so that they can easily be distinguished from the debit entries. Remember that debit means left and credit means right. Thus, the debit is written to the left and the credit to the right.

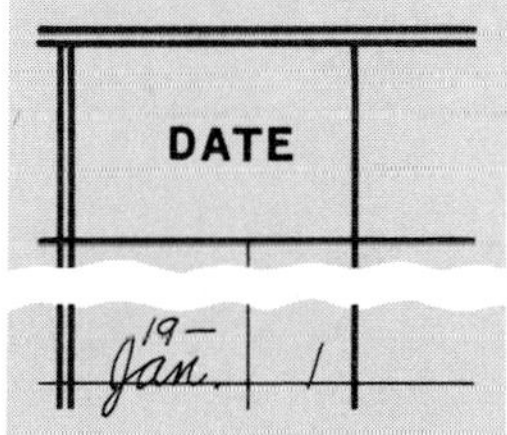

The year and the month are written when the year changes.

■ Writing an Explanation On the line below the credit entry, indent about an inch from the Date column and record an explanation of the transaction. The source document number, if one is available, should be entered as part of the explanation. When the account titles or the source document numbers reveal the reason for an entry, a further explanation is frequently omitted.

Explanations are used when transactions are unusual or complicated or when additional data is needed. The explanations should be short but clear. The type of source document should be identified, such as an invoice (Inv.), check (Ck.), remittance slip (RS), or credit memorandum (CM). Note that these words have been abbreviated in the journal in order to save space.

In this chapter, explanations have been included for all journal entries. However, they will be omitted in later chapters except where the journalized transaction is unusual or complicated in nature.

JOURNAL Page

DATE		ACCOUNT TITLE AND EXPLANATION	POST. REF.	DEBIT	CREDIT
19— Oct.	5	Cash		700 00	
		Accts. Rec./Carmen Saldi			700 00
		Received on account, RS-104			

Debit Entry → Credit Entry → Explanation →

Journal entry for October 5 transactions.

■ **Posting Reference** The Posting Reference (Post. Ref.) column is not used in journalizing. This column is used when the data is transferred from the journal to the ledger. This procedure is known as posting, and is explained later.

The following illustration shows how the October 5 transaction would be recorded in the journal. This example shows a transaction in which Exercise Plus received $700 in cash from Carmen Saldi on account.

■ **The Audit Trail** When data is recorded, a cross reference is usually given to show the source of the data. **Cross-referencing** involves entering the date and journal page number on the source document and the source document number, if one is available, in the journal. The reference can be a date, a name and address, or a number such as the journal page number. These references form an audit trail. An **audit trail** is a cross-referencing of items that makes it possible to trace the details of a transaction from the source document to the financial statements.

An audit trail involves cross-referencing each step of the accounting cycle.

Making the audit trail involves cross-referencing the source documents and the journal. Anyone can then trace the entry from the source document to the journal. The source document can also be traced from the journal.

A cross-referencing number on the source document shows that the entry has been journalized. If you are interrupted while journalizing, you can tell from the cross-reference number on the source document which ones have been journalized. If a cross-referencing number were omitted after a source document had been journalized, you might journalize the transaction a second time by mistake. Thus, it is very important to record all cross-referencing numbers on the source documents during the journalizing procedure.

■ Journalizing Typical Transactions

In Chapter 3, transactions were entered directly into the T accounts for the month of September. The transactions that are illustrated on page 140 are the October transactions for Exercise Plus. The journal entries on pages 141 and 142 show how the October transactions would be recorded in a general journal.

■ Summarizing the Journalizing Procedure

Here are some points to remember in journalizing.

- The data actually originates on source documents.
- The first entry is an opening entry. An **opening entry** opens the accounts in a new set of books. The source document for Exercise Plus's opening entry is the balance sheet. If Exercise Plus were a new business and the owner invested only cash, the Cash account and the owner's Capital account would be the only accounts shown.

  Exercise Plus opens a new set of books on October 1. Therefore, the opening entry records the permanent account balances as of October 1. The source document for the opening entry is the September 30 balance sheet. The balance sheet is prepared after all transactions for September 30 are recorded. Thus, the balance sheet for September 30 and the accounts in the ledger would be the same.
- No blank lines are left between entries. Since the explanation is indented an inch, each journal entry clearly stands out.
- Within any one entry, there is at least one debit and one credit. However, there may be more than one debit and more than one credit. In such a case, this entry is called a compound journal entry. A **compound journal entry** is an entry that contains more than two accounts. For example, the journal entry dated October 1 requires more than one debit and more than one credit. In every compound journal entry, the total debits for the transaction must always equal the total credits.
- Each source document is cross-referenced to the journal so that the audit trail is available.
- Only complete journal entries are recorded on a journal page. Do not begin recording a transaction at the bottom of a page unless there are enough lines to journalize the complete entry. Note that in the journal on page 141 only two blank lines remain at the bottom of the page, which is not enough to journalize a complete entry. The pages of the journal are numbered consecutively; that is, the pages are numbered in numeric sequence. The year and the month are repeated at the top of the Date column on each page. In each entry, the debits are always recorded before the credits.

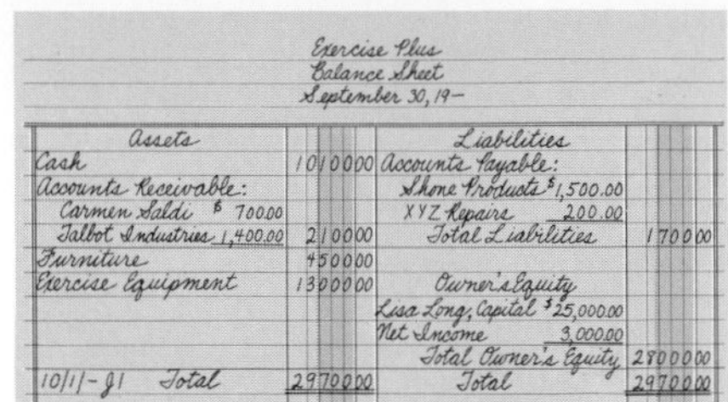

Exercise Plus
Balance Sheet
September 30, 19--

Assets			Liabilities		
Cash		10,100.00	Accounts Payable:		
Accounts Receivable:			Shone Products	1,500.00	
Carmen Saldi	700.00		XYZ Repairs	200.00	
Talbot Industries	1,400.00	2,100.00	Total Liabilities		1,700.00
Furniture		4,500.00			
Exercise Equipment		13,000.00	Owner's Equity		
			Lisa Long, Capital	25,000.00	
			Net Income	3,000.00	
			Total Owner's Equity		28,000.00
10/1/-- J1 Total		29,700.00	Total		29,700.00

October 1: Account titles and balances for the opening entry are taken from the September 30 balance sheet.

Carmen Saldi — No. 773 — October 5, 19--
PAY TO THE ORDER OF Exercise Plus $700 00/100
Seven hundred and 00/100 DOLLARS
TRADERS BANK, Chicago, Illinois 60601 — Carmen Saldi

Exercise Plus — REMITTANCE SLIP 104
3010 South Fifth Street, Chicago, Illinois 60612
NAME: Carmen Saldi
AMOUNT RECEIVED: $700.00 | CHECK NUMBER: 773 | CHECK DATE: 10/5/--
EXPLANATION: Received on account.
10/5/-- J1
DATE RECEIVED: 10/5/-- | RECEIVED BY: LL

October 5: Received $700 from Carmen Saldi on account.

WEBSTER CORPORATION — Sales Slip 433, Customer's Copy
1050 Raleigh Street, Chicago, Illinois 60615
Sold to: Exercise Plus, 3010 South Fifth Street, Chicago, Illinois 60612 — Date: 10/6/--

Clerk	Cash	Other	Charge	On Acct.	Retd.	Paid Out
JBE	X					

QUANT.	DESCRIPTION	PRICE	AMOUNT
	Supplies		600 00
	10/6/-- J1		
		Total	600 00

NO. 5 — 10/6/-- J1 — $600 00/100
DATE Oct. 6, 19--
TO Webster Corporation
FOR Supplies

	DOLLARS CENTS
BALANCE	10,100 00
AMT. DEPOSITED 10/5	700 00
TOTAL	10,800 00
AMT. THIS CHECK	600 00
BALANCE	10,200 00

October 6: Bought supplies for $600 in cash.

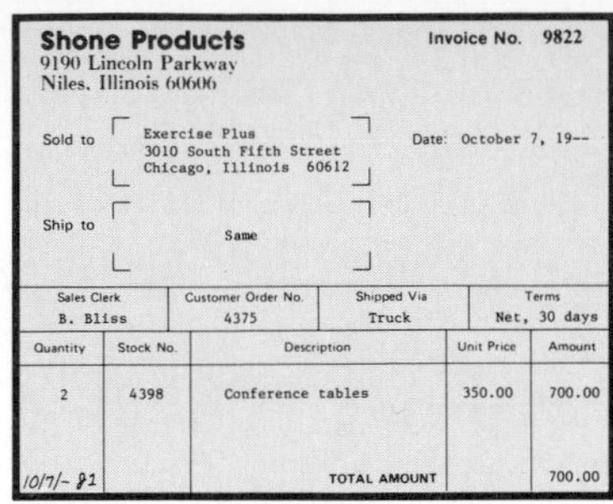

Shone Products — Invoice No. 9822
9190 Lincoln Parkway, Niles, Illinois 60606
Sold to: Exercise Plus, 3010 South Fifth Street, Chicago, Illinois 60612 — Date: October 7, 19--
Ship to: Same

Sales Clerk	Customer Order No.	Shipped Via	Terms
B. Bliss	4375	Truck	Net, 30 days

Quantity	Stock No.	Description	Unit Price	Amount
2	4398	Conference tables	350.00	700.00
10/7/-- J1		TOTAL AMOUNT		700.00

October 7: Bought furniture (conference tables) for $700 on credit from Shone Products.

Shone Products — CREDIT MEMORANDUM, Copy 1: Customer
9190 Lincoln Parkway, Niles, Illinois 60606
No. CM-67
To: Exercise Plus, 3010 South Fifth Street, Chicago, Illinois 60612
Date October 8, 19--
Sold on Invoice No. 9822
Your Order No. 4375
We have credited your account as follows:

QUANTITY	DESCRIPTION	PRICE	AMOUNT
1	Conference table, Model 4398	350.00	350.00
	10/8/-- J1		

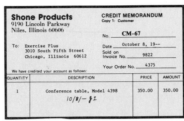

October 8: Returned furniture (conference table) bought for $350 on credit from Shone Products.

NO. 6 — 10/12/-- J1 — $1,500 00/100
DATE Oct. 12, 19--
TO Shone Products
FOR Paid on account

	DOLLARS CENTS
BALANCE	10,200 00
AMT. DEPOSITED	
TOTAL	10,200 00
AMT. THIS CHECK	1,500 00
BALANCE	8,700 00

October 12: Paid $1,500 to Shone Products on account.

Lisa Long, 1000 Lake Drive, Chicago, Illinois 60601 — No. 552 — October 12, 19--
PAY TO THE ORDER OF Exercise Plus $6,000 00/100
Six thousand and 00/100 DOLLARS
Lincoln Bank, Chicago, Illinois 60612
For: Additional investment — Lisa Long

Exercise Plus — REMITTANCE SLIP 105
3010 South Fifth Street, Chicago, Illinois 60612
NAME: Lisa Long
AMOUNT RECEIVED: $6,000.00 | CHECK NUMBER: 552 | CHECK DATE: 10/12/--
EXPLANATION: Additional investment.
DATE RECEIVED: 10/12/-- | RECEIVED BY: LL
10/12/-- J1

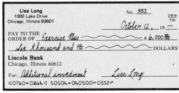

October 12: Received $6,000 from Lisa Long as an additional investment.

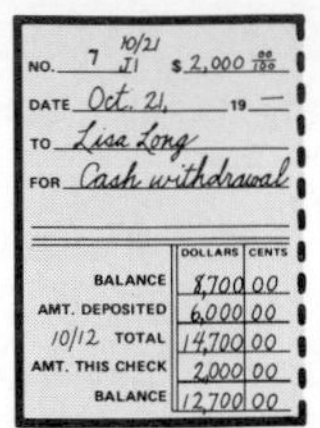

NO. 7 — 10/21/-- J1 — $2,000 00/100
DATE Oct. 21, 19--
TO Lisa Long
FOR Cash withdrawal

	DOLLARS CENTS
BALANCE	8,700 00
AMT. DEPOSITED	6,000 00
10/12 TOTAL	14,700 00
AMT. THIS CHECK	2,000 00
BALANCE	12,700 00

October 21: Paid $2,000 to Lisa Long as a withdrawal from business.

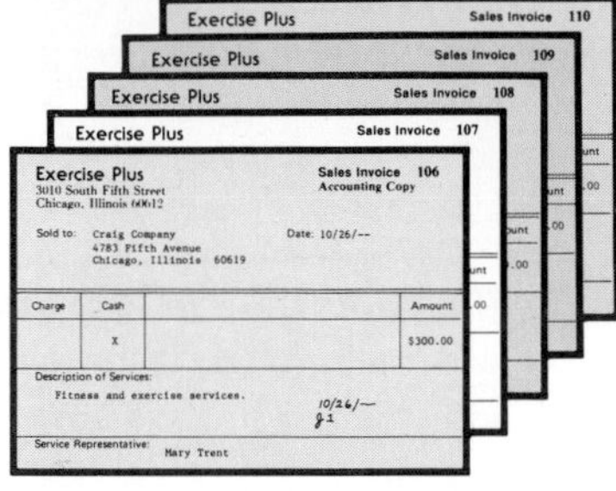

Exercise Plus — Sales Invoice 110; Sales Invoice 109; Sales Invoice 108; Sales Invoice 107
Exercise Plus — Sales Invoice 106, Accounting Copy
3010 South Fifth Street, Chicago, Illinois 60612
Sold to: Craig Company, 4783 Fifth Avenue, Chicago, Illinois 60619 — Date: 10/26/--

Charge	Cash		Amount
	X		$300.00

Description of Services: Fitness and exercise services.
10/26/-- J1
Service Representative: Mary Trent

October 26: Received $1,400 cash for sale of services.

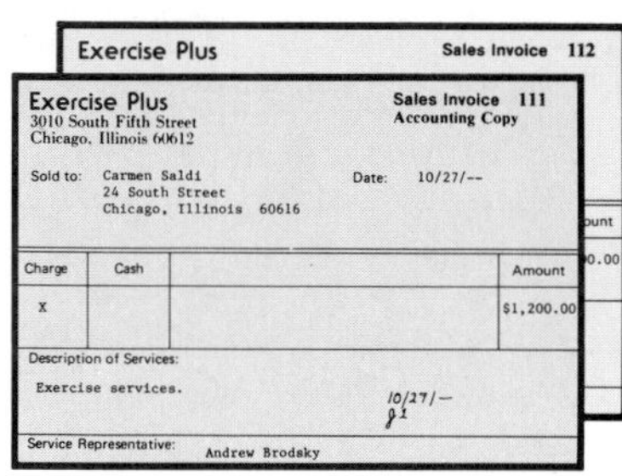

Exercise Plus — Sales Invoice 112
Exercise Plus — Sales Invoice 111, Accounting Copy
3010 South Fifth Street, Chicago, Illinois 60612
Sold to: Carmen Saldi, 24 South Street, Chicago, Illinois 60616 — Date: 10/27/--

Charge	Cash		Amount
X			$1,200.00

Description of Services: Exercise services.
10/27/-- J1
Service Representative: Andrew Brodsky

October 27: Sold services on credit to Carmen Saldi for $1,200 and to Talbot Industries for $1,000.

NO. 8 — 10/28/-- J2 — $2,000 00/100
DATE Oct. 28, 19--
TO Salaries Expense
FOR October payroll

	DOLLARS CENTS
BALANCE	12,700 00
AMT. DEPOSITED	1,400 00
10/26 TOTAL	14,100 00
AMT. THIS CHECK	2,000 00
BALANCE	12,100 00

October 28: Paid an expense of $2,000 for salaries.

XYZ REPAIRS — Invoice No. 212
126 Mountain Road, Lakeville, Illinois 60610
Date: 10/29/--
To: Exercise Plus, 3010 South Fifth Street, Chicago, Illinois 60612 — Terms: Net, 30 days

Repairs to gym. 10/29/-- J2	$200.00

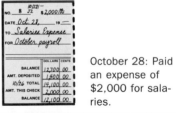

October 29: Recorded an expense of $200 to XYZ Repairs for making repairs to the gym.

JOURNAL					Page 1
DATE		**ACCOUNT TITLE AND EXPLANATION**	**POST. REF.**	**DEBIT**	**CREDIT**
19— Oct.	1	Cash		10100 00	
		Accts. Rec./Carmen Saldi		700 00	
		Accts. Rec./Talbot Industries		1400 00	
		Furniture		4500 00	
		Exercise Equipment		13000 00	
		Accts. Pay./Shone Products			1500 00
		Accts. Pay./XYZ Repairs			200 00
		Lisa Long, Capital			28000 00
		Opening entry, Sept. 30 balance sheet.			
	5	Cash		700 00	
		Accts. Rec./Carmen Saldi			700 00
		Received on account, RS-104.			
	6	Supplies		600 00	
		Cash			600 00
		Bought supplies, Ck. 5.			
	7	Furniture		700 00	
		Accts. Pay./Shone Products			700 00
		Bought conference tables, Inv. 9822.			
	8	Accts. Pay./Shone Products		350 00	
		Furniture			350 00
		Returned table, CM-67.			
	12	Accts. Pay./Shone Products		1500 00	
		Cash			1500 00
		Paid on account, Ck. 6.			
	12	Cash		6000 00	
		Lisa Long, Capital			6000 00
		Additional investment, RS-105.			
	21	Lisa Long, Capital		2000 00	
		Cash			2000 00
		Cash withdrawal, Ck. 7.			
	26	Cash		1400 00	
		Sales			1400 00
		Cash sales, Inv. 106-110			
	27	Accts. Rec./Carmen Saldi		1200 00	
		Accts. Rec./Talbot Industries		1000 00	
		Sales			2200 00
				45150 00	45150 00
		Credit sales, Inv. 111-112			

This journal page does not have enough lines remaining for a complete entry, so a new journal page must be started.

JOURNAL Page 2

DATE		ACCOUNT TITLE AND EXPLANATION	POST. REF.	DEBIT	CREDIT
19— Oct.	28	Salaries Expense		2000 00	
		Cash			2000 00
		October payroll, Ck. 8.			
	29	Repairs Expense		200 00	
		Accts. Pay./XYZ Repairs			200 00
		Repair of gym, Inv. 212.			

Pages are numbered consecutively. Year, month, and day are entered in the date column.

- The journal form illustrated on page 141 and above is a two-column journal. A **two-column journal** is a journal that has two money columns—one for debits and one for credits. The two-column journal helps to prevent errors because the equality of the debits and credits for each transaction can be checked at a glance. The **journal proof** is the equality of the total debits and total credits. This is shown with pencil footings on page 1 of the journal.
- Listing transactions in chronological order makes it quite easy to locate any specific transaction. The complete entry is located in one place. It is easy to compare the volume of transactions from day to day.

Exercises E and F on page 145 may be completed at this point.

Other Methods of Keeping the Journal

A journal is a chronological listing of transactions that can be prepared in a variety of ways.

Are all journal entries recorded in a paper-based journal? No. A journal can be a bound book, it can be a group of loose-leaf sheets, or it may not be a paper form at all. The journal can be maintained on a computer. In this case, transaction data may be entered into the computer from a keyboard or directly from a cash register connected with the computer. The data does not have to be printed on a business form. Instead, it may be entered in the computer and stored on magnetic disks, magnetic tapes, or other forms of electronic storage. The journal may be printed later or may not be printed at all. Data may remain stored in the computer until it is needed. Today, businesses frequently use machines to make listings of transactions instead of doing so by hand.

The method of preparing a journal varies from business to business. The form of the journal also varies. Businesses may use journals with only one money column or more than two money columns. These types of journals are explained in future chapters. Regardless of the method or the form, the function of the journal is the same in all businesses. It provides a chronological record of the transactions.

Concept: Audit Trail
References should be provided so that the data can be traced from its origination (beginning) to its use (end).

The Data Processing Cycle

Does the accounting cycle change when using electronic data processing? No. Whether data is processed manually or electronically, the same accounting concepts and principles apply. The basic differences between the manual and the electronic accounting cycles are the speed and types of equipment and materials used.

Every business processes data to provide information that will meet the needs of managers and owners who use accounting information to make business decisions. However, before any data is processed, a business must decide what information is needed, where to get the information, and how to process it. Managers and owners make decisions concerning needed information in logical order similar to the following.

- *What information is needed?* In data processing, *output* is the term used for information needed. It has the same meaning in accounting. Managers and owners need information shown on financial statements, such as the income statement and the balance sheet. This information in accounting is called output.
- *What data is required to supply output?* In accounting and data processing, data needed to supply output is called *input*. Transactions recorded in a journal are input into the accounting system.
- *Where is the input data collected?* In accounting, input data is collected on source documents. All accounting information originates on some sort of source document. This data enters the accounting cycle as transactions in a journal. Transactions, therefore, become input data for the needed output.
- *What should be done to the input data to provide the needed output?* Specific procedures are used to process input to get the desired output. This is called *processing data*. In accounting, processing input data involves these activities: journalizing, updating the accounts, proving the ledger, preparing financial statements, closing the ledger, and proving the closed ledger. You are learning about these activities. You know that these accounting cycle activities can be processed through manual data processing or through electronic data processing. In either instance, the same accounting cycle activities, accounting concepts, and principles are used. But the data is manipulated differently in a manual process and an electronic process. This is because of the differences in materials and equipment used, such as the use of paper and pen versus the use of computers.

DATA PROCESSING CYCLE

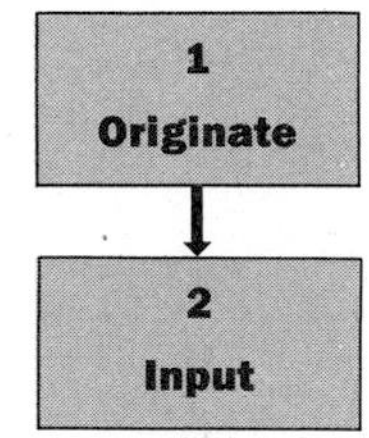

ACCOUNTING CYCLE

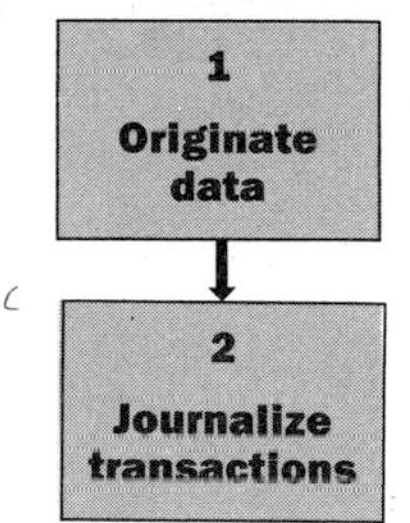

The answers to these four questions are called the data processing cycle. The **data processing cycle** is the series of steps taken to process data and provide information.

Now we compare the first two steps in the data processing cycle with the steps in the accounting cycle. (Note that the order in which data is processed is different from the order in which the questions are asked.)

Step 1. *Origination of data.* The origination step involves collecting the data. The data is collected on source documents. This step may or may not involve a computer. If a computer is used, some accountants consider this step combined with Step 2 to be the first step in the data processing accounting cycle.

Step 2. *Input of data.* After the data has been collected, it must be entered into the system so that it can be processed—this step accomplishes the same thing as journalizing in the manual cycle. The data to be processed is called **input data**. In accounting, the input data is taken from source documents and arranged in the manner needed for processing. When a computer is used, this is the step where the input data is put into the computer.

It is very important that you learn data processing terms when studying accounting. Accounting systems and procedures use a variety of data processing equipment to complete accounting activities. However, as you learned earlier, the same accounting concepts and principles are used both in manual and electronic data processing. The title of this chapter is "Origination and Input of Accounting Data." Thus, you can begin to see from this discussion how accounting relates to electronic data processing.

Exercise G on page 146 may be completed at this point.

TOPIC 2 EXERCISES

EXERCISE D. Answer the following questions about the journal. Refer to the text and illustrations on pages 135 to 136.

1. What are the first two steps in the accounting cycle?
2. How can the difficulties of entering debits and credits directly into accounts be avoided?
3. In what order are transactions recorded in journals?
4. What type of journal is described in this topic?
5. What are the three reasons why data from source documents are not recorded directly into the ledger?

EXERCISE E. Answer the following questions about journalizing. Refer to Exercise Plus's journal on pages 141 and 142.

1. What assets are recorded on October 1?
2. Are supplies bought with cash or on credit on October 6?
3. What is the source of the $6,000 cash received on October 12?
4. Which customer paid on October 5? How much?
5. From whom is the furniture purchased on October 7?
6. For what item is $2,000 in cash spent on October 28?
7. To whom are sales on credit made on October 27?

EXERCISE F. The journal below contains the entries for the first two weeks of February for Lin Legal Services.

On a form like the one shown, analyze each journal entry in terms of an increase or decrease in the accounting elements. State what occurred in each transaction. Use the signs A +, A −, L +, L −, OE +, and OE − to show the increases and decreases.

Date	Debit	Credit	Transaction
Feb. 1	A +	L +, OE +	Margaret Lin started the business with an investment of $1,650 in cash, $2,700 in a law library, and an account payable of $800.

GENERAL JOURNAL Page *10*

DATE		ACCOUNT TITLE AND EXPLANATION	POST. REF.	DEBIT	CREDIT
19—					
Feb.	*1*	*Cash*		*1650 00*	
		Law Library		*2700 00*	
		Accts. Pay./Robert Myers			*800 00*
		Margaret Lin, Capital			*3550 00*
	2	*Utilities Expense*		*65 00*	
		Cash			*65 00*
	3	*Equipment*		*550 00*	
		Accts. Pay./Robert Myers			*550 00*
	4	*Accts. Rec./Robin Davis*		*800 00*	
		Sales			*800 00*
	5	*Law Library*		*85 00*	
		Cash			*85 00*
	7	*Cash*		*650 00*	
		Accts. Rec./Robin Davis			*650 00*
	8	*Cash*		*1050 00*	
		Sales			*1050 00*
	9	*Accts. Pay./Robert Myers*		*50 00*	
		Equipment			*50 00*
	11	*Margaret Lin, Capital*		*600 00*	
		Cash			*600 00*
	14	*Accts. Pay./Robert Myers*		*450 00*	
		Cash			*450 00*

EXERCISE G. Answer the following questions about journalizing and data processing. Refer to the text and illustrations on pages 142 to 144.

1. Is there only one way to keep a journal? Explain.
2. What are the differences between the manual and electronic accounting cycles?
3. Name the first two steps of the data processing cycle.

TOPIC 2 PROBLEMS

TOPIC PROBLEM 3. Ventura Travel Service, owned by John Daniel, had the following transactions during September and October. Journalize these transactions. Provide a brief explanation for each journal entry.

Sept. 1 John Daniel started the business with $20,000 in cash.
14 Bought office equipment (adding machine and file cabinets) for $1,100 in cash (Check 101).
21 Bought supplies for $700 on credit from Freeway Sales (Invoice 321).
28 Sold services for $725 on credit to Linda Michaels (Invoice 001).
Oct. 3 Paid $65 for telephone expense (Check 102).
Oct. 5 Returned office equipment (file cabinet) bought for $350 in cash (Remittance Slip 001).
15 Received $400 from Linda Michaels on account (Remittance Slip 002).
17 Sold services for $1,020 in cash (Invoice 002).
18 Paid $85 to Freeway Sales on account (Check 103).
29 Paid $250 to John Daniel as a withdrawal (Check 104).

NOTE: Save your work from this problem for further use in Topic Problem 1, Chapter 6.

TOPIC PROBLEM 4. The Carson Clinic, owned by Ann Carson, had the following transactions during December. Journalize these transactions. If the account titles do not reveal the reason for an entry, provide a brief explanation.

Dec. 2 Ann Carson started the business with an investment of $25,000 in cash and $6,000 in medical equipment.
5 Bought used medical equipment for $15,000 on credit from the Medi-Vac Company.
8 Bought office equipment (word processor and adding machine) for $1,800 in cash.
9 Sold services for $450 on credit to Workman High School for medical examinations.
Dec. 11 Paid $600 for December rent.
12 Returned medical equipment (scales) bought for $1,250 on credit from the Medi-Vac Company.
14 Paid $875 to Ann Carson as a withdrawal from the business.
18 Returned office equipment (adding machine) bought for $250 in cash.
19 Paid $2,200 to the Medi-Vac Company on account.
20 Received $225 from Workman High School on account.
26 Owes $200 to TriCities Tribune for advertising during December.
30 Sold services for $1,800 in cash.

NOTE: Save your work from this problem for further use in Topic Problem 2, Chapter 6.

CHAPTER 5 REVIEW

CHAPTER SUMMARY

The first step in the accounting cycle is originating data. A source document is a form containing data about a transaction. The source document may originate within a business (internal data) or outside the business (external data). The information from source documents is used to determine the debit and credit parts of the various business transactions. It is the basis of journal entries.

Journalizing represents the second step of the accounting cycle. Journal entries are day-to-day listings of business transactions in terms of accounts debited and credited. The basic form of a journal contains two money columns: one for debit amounts and one for credit amounts. In a journal, all transactions are summarized with their debit and credit parts in chronological order. Because a journal entry allows an accountant to record an explanation of a transaction, it is possible to create an audit trail. This is the descriptive or explanatory information in the entry that allows one to trace each transaction back to a source document and verify whether a transaction has been recorded accurately.

The examples you studied in this chapter are based on the manual accounting system. However, whether an accounting system is based on manual or electronic methods, the concepts and procedures are fundamentally the same.

THE LANGUAGE OF BUSINESS

Here are some terms that make up the language of business. Do you know the meaning of each?

originating data
source document
extension
remittance slip
manual data processing
electronic data processing (EDP)
journal
journalizing
analyzing a transaction
journal entry
cross-referencing
audit trail
opening entry
compound journal entry
two-column journal
journal proof
data processing cycle
input data

REVIEW QUESTIONS

1. Name four different types of source documents.
2. Describe the data contained in a journal.
3. What are the differences between a journal and a source document?
4. Describe two purposes for which source documents are used.
5. What is the difference between internal data and external data?
6. Describe the procedure followed in journalizing a transaction.

7. Give reasons why data from source documents is not recorded directly in the ledger.
8. How can the equality of debits and credits be proved in the two-column journal?
9. Why is an audit trail necessary in accounting?
10. What are the first two steps in the data processing cycle? How do they compare with the first two steps in the accounting cycle?

CHAPTER PROBLEMS

Problems for Chapter 5 are given below. Write your answers on a separate sheet of paper unless you are using the workbook for this textbook. If you are using the workbook, do the problems in the space provided there.

CHAPTER PROBLEM 5-1. On October 1, 19—, Joseph Malone started the Metro Copy Center.

Journalize the transactions below. (Do not give explanations.) Use the following account titles when journalizing the entries: Cash; Accts. Rec./Jordan Brothers; Accts. Rec./National Real Estate; Supplies; Copy Equipment; Trucks; Accts. Pay./Buy Rite Paper Company; Accts. Pay./Clean Copy Company; Joseph Malone, Capital; Sales; Supplies Expense; Truck Expense.

Oct. 1 Joseph Malone started the Metro Copy Center by investing $40,000.
2 Purchased on account two used copy machines for $11,500 from the Clean Copy Company.
3 Bought a used delivery truck for $8,000 in cash.
5 Sold services for $650 on credit to Jordan Brothers.
7 Recorded $7,100 in cash sales for the week.
9 Purchased gas and oil for $75 in cash.
10 Received purchase invoice from Buy Rite Paper Company for paper supplies for $1,100 on account.
14 Recorded $6,800 in cash sales.
18 Sold services for $1,500 on credit to National Real Estate.
21 Recorded cash sales of $7,020 for the week.
26 Received check for $650 from Jordan Brothers in payment of account.
28 Recorded cash sales of $6,200 for the week.
31 Joseph Malone withdrew $1,000 from the business for personal use.

NOTE: Save your work from this problem for further use in Chapter Problem 6-1.

CHAPTER PROBLEM 5-2. You have been hired as an accounting clerk for Yvette's Veterinary Clinic. Until you came to the veterinary clinic, the accounting records were handled by an accounting service. Record the information from the source documents you receive for the month of May in a journal. Record the opening entry for May 1 on page 1 of the journal using the information from the balance sheet below. Then record the other transactions described in this problem. Omit all explanations from the journal. Use the account numbers and titles listed below. (You will not use the Supplies Expense account until Chapter Problem 6-2.)

101 Cash
102 Accts. Rec./Holly's Kennels
103 Accts. Rec./Holsum Pet Service
104 Supplies
111 Office Furniture
201 Accts. Pay./Abbey Furniture
202 Accts. Pay./Craig Medical Supplies
301 Yvette Lewis, Capital
401 Fees
501 Supplies Expense
502 Utilities Expense

Yvette's Veterinary Clinic
Balance Sheet
April 30, 19—

Assets			*Liabilities*		
Cash	7,600	00	Accounts Payable:		
Accounts Receivable:			Abbey Furniture $1,025.00		
Holly's Kennels $1,700.00			Craig Medical Supplies 480.00		
Holsum Pet Service 850.00	2,550	00	Total Liabilities	1,505	00
Supplies	765	00			
Office Furniture	3,700	00	*Owner's Equity*		
			Yvette Lewis, Capital $12,000.00		
			Net Income 1,110.00		
			Total Owner's Equity	13,110	00
Total	14,615	00	Total	14,615	00

May 1 Received Remittance Slip 102 showing a $250 payment on account by Holly's Kennels.

5 Issued Check 347 to Konig Stationery to pay for supplies of $526.

10 Received Purchase Invoice 2307 from Abbey Furniture for new office furniture for $680.

12 Received Credit Memorandum 22 from Abbey Furniture for $250 for damaged goods.

15 Received Remittance Slip 103 showing cash sales of $2,360 for fees for the first half of the month.

17 Issued Sales Invoice 4995 to Holly's Kennels for services on credit for $720.

19 Issued Check 348 for $135 to SoCal Electric for utilities expense.

May 20 Issued Check 349 for $500 to Abbey Furniture.

23 Received Purchase Invoice 79A from Craig Medical Supplies for supplies for $325 on credit.

25 Issued Sales Invoice 4996 to Holsum Pet Service for services sold on credit for $750.

28 Received Remittance Slip 104 showing payment of $1,700 from Holly's Kennels on account.

30 Issued Check 350 for $1,000 to Yvette Lewis for withdrawal from business.

31 Received Remittance Slip 105 showing cash receipts of $2,945 for fees for the second half of the month.

NOTE: Save your work from this problem for further use in Chapter Problem 6-2.

SUPPLEMENTAL CHAPTER PROBLEM 5-3. If you are using the workbook for Part 1, do Supplemental Chapter Problem 5-3 in the space provided there.

NOTE: Save your work from this problem for further use in Supplemental Chapter Problem 6-3.

MANAGEMENT CASES

Keeping Appropriate Records. When starting a business, owners often decide to keep their own accounting records. Sometimes they will not have had a course in accounting. Even if they have, they may not recall exactly the procedures to follow. Thus, owners may be getting inaccurate information and missing information that they need.

There is no single way of keeping accounting records. However, accurate records must be kept to provide the information that is needed for making decisions.

CASE 5M-1. Patrick Lane owns and operates a pet store. He keeps a bank account into which he deposits cash received and from which he pays invoices. His checkbook is the only accounting record he maintains. If there is a larger balance in the bank account at the end of the year than at the beginning, he assumes that his business has had a net income. If there is a smaller balance in the bank account, he assumes that his business has had a loss. For example, at the beginning of last year the bank account had a balance of $8,600. At the end of the year the balance was only $6,000. Thus, Mr. Lane assumed that his business had lost $2,600 during the year.

a. Do you agree that the business had a net loss for the year?

b. Would it be possible for the bank account to have decreased and yet for the business to have had a net income during the year? Explain.

c. What information would Mr. Lane need in order to learn whether or not the owner's equity actually increased or decreased during the year?

d. What types of transactions are not shown in the checkbook?

e. Does Mr. Lane need a journal? Give your reason.

CASE 5M-2. Christine Acosta has excellent accounting knowledge. She is the accountant for Gale's Auto Repair, a gas station and auto repair shop. Her work involves all phases of accounting processes using manual data processing.

Gale's Auto Repair is expanding its repair services in March. As a result of the expansion, the present manual method of processing accounting data is inadequate. Ms. Acosta, recognizing the need to keep appropriate accounting records, recommended to the owner that electronic data processing equipment should be purchased. As a result, Ms. Acosta was given approval to purchase the electronic accounting equipment and to make any changes in business forms.

a. Will the accounting concepts and principles change when electronic data processing equipment is used? Why or why not?

b. Which step in the accounting cycle (originating data or journalizing transactions) will show the greatest change in business forms? Explain your answer.

c. Is an opening entry necessary when Gale's Auto Repair converts to electronic data processing equipment for accounting records? Why or why not?

CHAPTER

6

Processing Accounting Data

You have learned that source documents provide the information necessary to keep a chronological listing of the transactions of a business. This listing makes it easier for the accountant to record changes in the ledger accounts. You will now learn to process data. You will learn to post data to the ledger, prepare a trial balance, and prepare a document called a worksheet. The worksheet is a useful tool for preparing end-of-period accounting work.

CHAPTER GOALS

After studying Chapter 6, you will be able to:

1. Define the terms listed in "The Language of Business" section on page 182.
2. Explain the accounting concepts and principles in this chapter related to posting data to the ledger and preparing a worksheet.
3. Post journal entries to general ledger accounts.
4. Prepare a trial balance, using account balances from the general ledger.
5. Locate trial balance errors when the trial balance is not in balance.
6. Prepare a worksheet with one adjustment.

TOPIC 1

Posting Data to the Ledger

What is the third step in the accounting cycle? The third step in the accounting cycle is to transfer the accounting data from the journal to the ledger. This procedure is called posting. **Posting** is the process of transferring data from the journal to the ledger.

In posting, data is classified according to account titles, and the amounts are sorted according to debits and credits. Each amount listed in the Debit column of the journal will be posted to the Debit money column of an account in the ledger. Each amount listed in the Credit column of the journal will be posted to the Credit money column of an account in the ledger.

1 Originate data → 2 Journalize transactions → 3 Post entries

Forms of Ledger Accounts

As you know, a *ledger* is a group of accounts. In Chapter 3 you used T accounts in a ledger. The T account is only one of many different forms of accounts. Any account used to show the increases and decreases for each asset, liability, and owner's equity item is called a **ledger account**.

T accounts are useful when learning accounting and when analyzing transactions. However, businesses need more information than the T account provides.

They want such information in an account to show:

- The balance of the account at all times
- The order in which the debits and credits occurred in an easily readable format
- Where one accounting period ends and a new one begins

To provide the additional information needed, businesses use more detailed forms of ledger accounts.

Concept: Ledger
Records of the changes caused by transactions should be available according to account title and account number. These records are kept in a ledger.

Cash				*101*
19—		*19—*		
Oct. 1	*10,100*	*Oct. 6*		*600*
5	*700*	*12*		*1,500*
12	*6,000*	*21*		*2,000*
26	*1,400*	*28*		*2,000*
12,100	*18,200*			*6,100*

Balances are not constantly available in T accounts. Also, it is time-consuming to obtain the balances.

Balance Ledger Form In this chapter, a balance ledger form will be used. The **balance ledger form** is an account form that shows the current balance of the account after each entry is posted. It is the type of ledger that is most commonly used today.

The balance ledger form has a Heading section, a Date column, an Explanation column, a Posting Reference column, and four money columns. The first two money columns are used to record the amounts for the entries. The last two money columns are used to record the account balance as each entry is posted.

Advantages of Using the Balance Ledger Form

- Constantly shows the current account balance
- Easily identifies the balances as either debit or credit balances
- Provides the account balances for preparing the trial balance

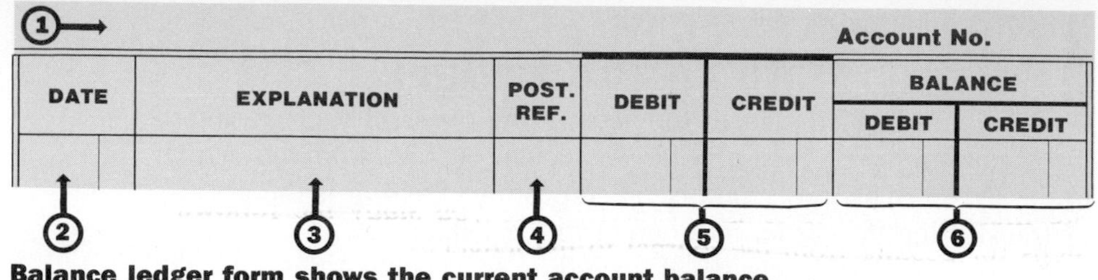

Balance ledger form shows the current account balance.

EXERCISE PLUS CHART OF ACCOUNTS

Assets
101 Cash
103 Accts. Rec./Carmen Saldi
104 Accts. Rec./Talbot Industries
108 Supplies
111 Furniture
112 Exercise Equipment

Liabilities
201 Accts. Pay./Shone Products
202 Accts. Pay./XYZ Repairs

Owner's Equity
301 Lisa Long, Capital
399 Income Summary

Revenue
401 Sales

Expenses
504 Repairs Expense
505 Salaries Expense
506 Supplies Expense

1. *Heading*. When a ledger account is opened, the title of the account is written at the top left of the account and the account number is written at the top right. Numbers are assigned to each account in the order in which the account is listed in the chart of accounts for the business.

2. *Date column*. The date the transaction was recorded in the journal is listed.

3. *Explanation column*. An explanation of the transaction may be given.

4. *Posting Reference (Post. Ref.) column*. The page number of the journal in which the transaction is recorded is listed.

5. *Debit and Credit columns*. The amount of each debit and credit entry is listed in the appropriate money column.

6. *Balance (Debit/Credit) columns*. The current balance of the account is listed in the appropriate balance money column.

The money columns for the entries follow the T account format. The Debit column is the left money column. The Credit column is the right money column. The money columns in the Balance section also follow this format. A debit balance is recorded in the balance column on the left. A credit balance is recorded in the balance column on the right.

When a ledger is opened, a heading and account number are entered for each account listed in the chart of accounts. The chart of accounts for Exercise Plus is shown in the margin. An account is opened for each of the items in the chart of accounts, regardless of whether it has a balance or not. If this is done, an account will be available when it has to be used.

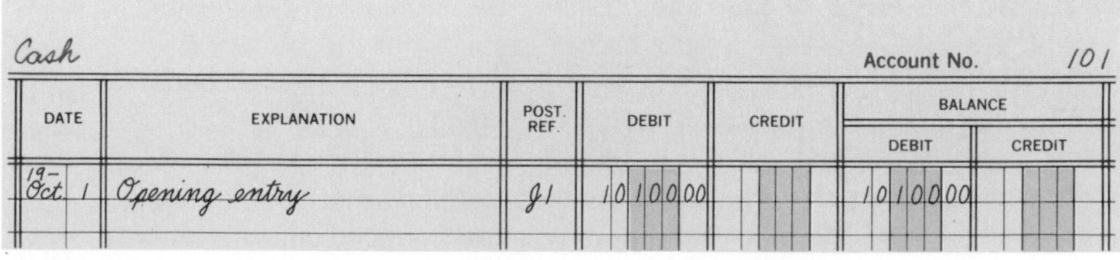

An account is established for each account on the chart of accounts.

Exercise A on page 165 may be completed at this point.

The Posting Procedure

What is the procedure followed for posting data from the journal to the ledger? The procedure for posting from the journal to the ledger accounts can be illustrated by posting the October 1 entry for Exercise Plus. The journal entry and the accounts to which it is posted are illustrated. Refer to this illustration as you study the following steps for posting from the journal to the ledger.

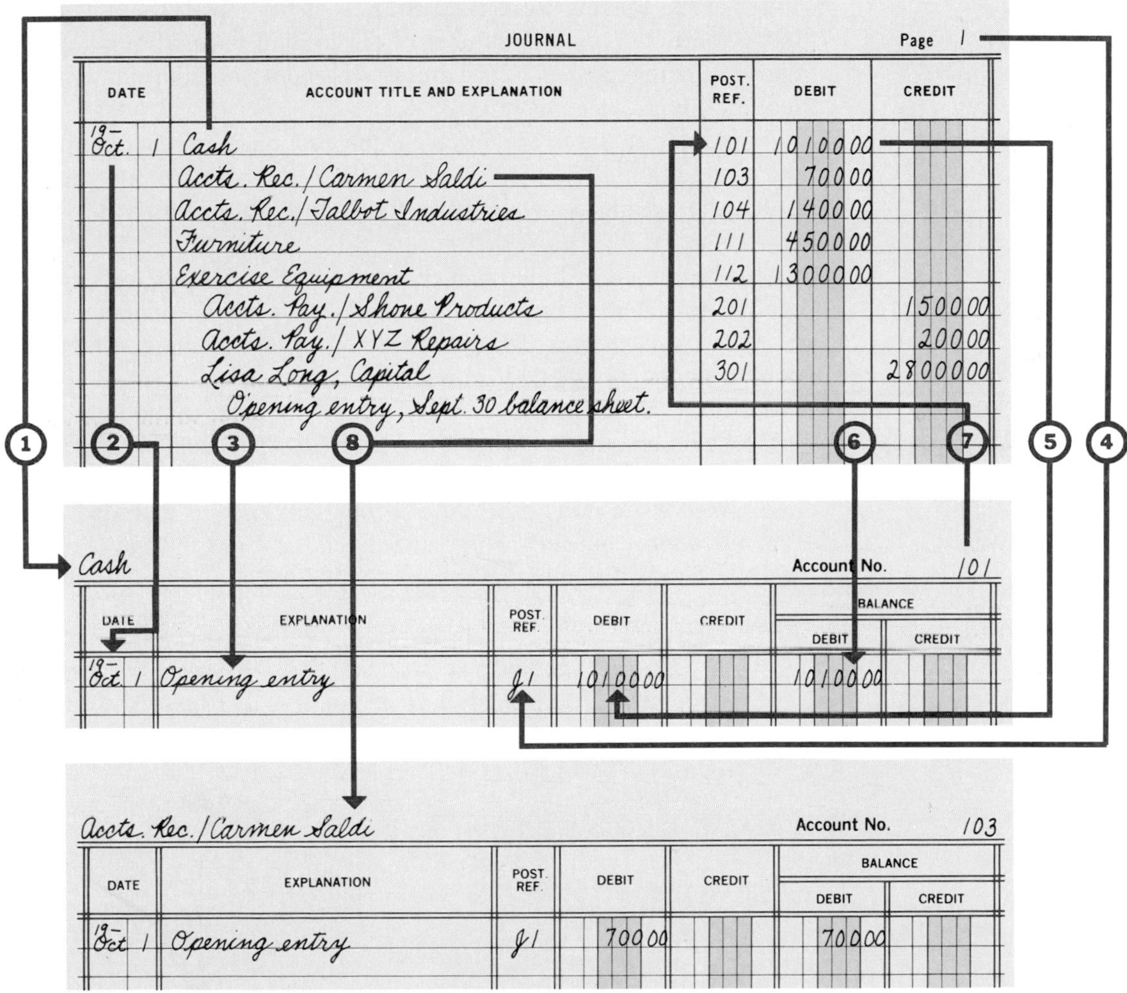

1. Locate the ledger account for the first debit listed in the journal.

2. Record the date in the Date column. The date in the ledger should be the same as the date in the journal entry. For the first line only, record the year, the month, and the day of the first entry. In the following entries, record the day of the month only. Do not repeat the month or the year except when either changes or when the account is continued on another page.

3. Enter an explanation if one is needed to explain the entry. In the ledger accounts shown here, the words "Opening entry" are written as the explanation. This means that this is an opening balance and not a change caused by a transaction. In later accounts we show the source document written out. To save time, these are often abbreviated. Explanations other than source document numbers are seldom used. To find a complete explanation of the entry, the entry is traced back to the journal or to the source document.
4. Enter in the Posting Reference column of the ledger the letter "J" (for "journal") and the number of the journal page from which the entry is being posted. This cross-references the journal with the ledger. Thus, an audit trail exists.
5. Record the amount in the correct Debit or Credit money column. In the transaction illustrated, Cash has been debited in the journal. Thus, the amount is recorded in the Debit column of the Cash account.
6. Compute and record the balance in the correct Balance money column. Since there is only one debit amount in the Cash account and no previous balance, the debit amount is the balance. Thus, the debit amount is repeated in the Debit Balance column.
7. Enter in the Posting Reference column of the journal the number of the ledger account to which the journal entry has been posted.
8. Locate the ledger account for the next entry. If the next entry is a debit, repeat the same procedure. If the next entry is a credit, apply this procedure, but record the amount in the Credit money column and the Credit Balance column.

Additional debits will be added to the Cash account balance and additional credits will be subtracted. In this way, the current balance of the Cash account is always shown.

Other ledger accounts after October 1 entry is posted.

Accts. Rec./Talbot Industries — Account No. 104

DATE		EXPLANATION	POST. REF.	DEBIT	CREDIT	BALANCE DEBIT	BALANCE CREDIT
19— Oct.	1	Opening entry	J1	1400 00		1400 00	

Supplies — Account No. 108

DATE		EXPLANATION	POST. REF.	DEBIT	CREDIT	BALANCE DEBIT	BALANCE CREDIT

Furniture — Account No. 111

DATE		EXPLANATION	POST. REF.	DEBIT	CREDIT	BALANCE DEBIT	BALANCE CREDIT
19— Oct.	1	Opening entry	J1	4500 00		4500 00	

Exercise Equipment — Account No. 112

DATE		EXPLANATION	POST. REF.	DEBIT	CREDIT	BALANCE DEBIT	BALANCE CREDIT
19— Oct.	1	Opening entry	J1	13000 00		13000 00	

Accts. Pay./Shone Products — Account No. 201

DATE		EXPLANATION	POST. REF.	DEBIT	CREDIT	BALANCE DEBIT	BALANCE CREDIT
19— Oct.	1	Opening entry	J1		1500 00		1500 00

Accts. Pay./XYZ Repairs — Account No. 202

DATE		EXPLANATION	POST. REF.	DEBIT	CREDIT	BALANCE DEBIT	BALANCE CREDIT
19— Oct.	1	Opening entry	J1		200 00		200 00

Lisa Long, Capital — Account No. 301

DATE		EXPLANATION	POST. REF.	DEBIT	CREDIT	BALANCE DEBIT	BALANCE CREDIT
19— Oct.	1	Opening entry	J1		28000 00		28000 00

Income Summary — Account No. 399

DATE		EXPLANATION	POST. REF.	DEBIT	CREDIT	BALANCE DEBIT	BALANCE CREDIT

Sales Account No. 401

DATE		EXPLANATION	POST. REF.	DEBIT	CREDIT	BALANCE	
						DEBIT	CREDIT

Repairs Expense Account No. 504

DATE		EXPLANATION	POST. REF.	DEBIT	CREDIT	BALANCE	
						DEBIT	CREDIT

Salaries Expense Account No. 505

DATE		EXPLANATION	POST. REF.	DEBIT	CREDIT	BALANCE	
						DEBIT	CREDIT

Supplies Expense Account No. 506

DATE		EXPLANATION	POST. REF.	DEBIT	CREDIT	BALANCE	
						DEBIT	CREDIT

Account	Normal Balance
Asset accounts	Debit balance
Liability accounts	Credit balance
Capital accounts	Credit balance
Revenue accounts	Credit balance
Expense accounts	Debit balance

■ Computing New Balances Computing and recording the new balance in the Cash account was simple because there was no previous balance. When there is a previous balance, however, you must compute the new balance. Remember that the balance of an account normally appears on the same side as the account appears in the accounting equation.

■ Computing Debit Balances The Cash account will be used to illustrate how to compute the account balance after posting amounts to an account with a debit balance. Refer to the Cash account on page 159.

1. The opening entry on October 1 shows a debit balance of $10,100. The balance is identified as a debit by entering the amount in the Debit Balance column.

Cash					Account No.	*101*
DATE	EXPLANATION	POST. REF.	DEBIT	CREDIT	BALANCE DEBIT	BALANCE CREDIT
19— Oct. 1	*Opening entry*	*J1*	*10,100 00*		*10,100 00*	
5	*Remittance Slip RS-104*	*J1*	*700 00*		*10,800 00*	
6	*Check 5*	*J1*		*600 00*	*10,200 00*	
12	*Check 6*	*J1*		*1,500 00*	*8,700 00*	
12	*Remittance Slip RS-105*	*J1*	*6,000 00*		*14,700 00*	
21	*Check 7*	*J1*		*2,000 00*	*12,700 00*	
26	*Invoices 106–110*	*J1*	*1,400 00*		*14,100 00*	
28	*Check 8*	*J2*		*2,000 00*	*12,100 00*	

(1) (2) (3) (4)

Debits are added to a debit balance. Credits are subtracted from a debit balance.

2. The second posting is on October 5. This shows a debit of $700 from the receipt of cash on Remittance Slip RS-104. The account previously had a debit balance of $10,100. The debit entry of $700 must be added to the previous debit balance. The new balance is $10,800 ($10,100 + $700). Since this is still a debit balance, the amount is again entered in the Debit Balance column.

3. The third entry is a credit posted on October 6. Exercise Plus issued Check 5 for $600. Since this payment decreases the amount of cash, the Cash account is credited and the new balance must be computed. The credit entry of $600 is subtracted from the previous debit balance. The new balance is $10,200 ($10,800 − $600). Since the account still has a debit balance, the amount is again entered in the Debit Balance column.

4. Additional debits are added to the previous debit balance. Additional credits are subtracted. In this way the current balance is always shown in the account.

■ Computing Credit Balances Computing the new balance for an account with a credit balance is basically the same. Additional credits are added to the previous credit balance. Additional debits are subtracted from a previous credit balance. The Accts. Pay./Shone Products account will be used to illustrate this procedure.

Accts. Pay./Shone Products					Account No.	*201*
DATE	EXPLANATION	POST. REF.	DEBIT	CREDIT	BALANCE DEBIT	BALANCE CREDIT
19— Oct. 1	*Opening entry*	*J1*		*1,500 00*		*1,500 00*
7	*Invoice 9822*	*J1*		*700 00*		*2,200 00*
8	*Credit Memorandum CM-67*	*J1*	*350 00*			*1,850 00*
12	*Check 6*	*J1*	*1,500 00*			*350 00*

(1) (2) (3) (4)

Credits are added to a credit balance. Debits are subtracted from a credit balance.

1. The first entry shows a credit balance of $1,500. This balance is identified as a credit balance by being placed in the Credit Balance column.
2. The second entry is a credit of $700 on October 7 from Invoice 9822. This credit amount is added to the previous credit balance because it increases the account balance. The new balance is $2,200 ($1,500 + $700). It is recorded in the Credit Balance column.
3. The third entry is a debit of $350 on October 8 from Credit Memorandum CM-67. Since a debit decreases liabilities, the debit is subtracted from the previous credit balance. The new balance is $1,850 ($2,200 − $350). The balance is still a credit balance.
4. Additional debits are subtracted. Additional credits are added to the previous credit balance. Thus, the current balance is always shown.

Computing Zero Balances In some instances, the computation results in a zero balance. When there is no balance, a dash and zeros are written in the last balance column used. The Accts. Rec./Carmen Saldi account, for example, has a zero balance after the remittance on October 5 is posted.

Accts. Rec./Carmen Saldi **Account No.** *103*

DATE		EXPLANATION	POST. REF.	DEBIT	CREDIT	BALANCE DEBIT	BALANCE CREDIT
19—							
Oct.	1	Opening entry	J1	700 00		700 00	
	5	Remittance Slip RS-104	J1		700 00	— 00	
	27	Invoice 111	J1	1,200 00		1,200 00	

A dash and zeros are written in the last balance column used.

1. The first entry shows a debit balance of $700.
2. The second entry is a credit of $700 from Remittance Slip RS-104 on October 5. A credit reduces a debit balance. Thus, the new balance is $0 ($700 − $700). To show a zero balance, write a dash and zeros in the Debit Balance column—the last balance column used. If a zero balance occurs in an account with a credit balance, enter the dash and zeros in the Credit Balance column.
3. Additional debits and credits are added or subtracted. The current balance is always shown.

Exercise B on page 165 may be completed at this point.

Audit Trail

Why is it important to complete the Posting Reference columns in the journal and the ledger? Cross-referencing the journal and the ledger in posting continues the audit trail. **Cross-referencing in**

posting means entering the journal page number in the ledger and the ledger account number in the journal.

JOURNAL					Page 1
DATE		ACCOUNT TITLE AND EXPLANATION	POST. REF.	DEBIT	CREDIT
19— Oct.	1	Cash	101	10,100 00	

Cash					Account No. 101	
DATE		EXPLANATION	POST. REF.	DEBIT	CREDIT	BALANCE	
						DEBIT	CREDIT
19— Oct.	1	Opening entry	J1	10,100 00		10,100 00	

Cross-referencing the journal and the ledger.

The journal page number and the ledger account number are called **posting reference numbers**. There are two advantages to cross-referencing the journal and the ledger.

- It allows anyone to trace an entry from the journal to the ledger.
- It allows anyone to locate the journal entry from which an item was posted to the ledger. Thus, you can easily go back to the complete journal entry to obtain more information about the transaction.

If the audit trail is continued, an entry can be traced from the source document to the journal and to the ledger. Or, it can be traced from the ledger to the journal and to the source document.

It is very important to show all posting reference numbers in the journal and in the ledger. A posting reference number in the journal shows that the journal entry has been posted to the ledger. If you are interrupted while posting, you can identify your last posting by the posting reference numbers in the journal. If a posting reference number is omitted after an entry has been posted, you could post the entry a second time by mistake.

■ The Ledger After Posting

After the October transactions are posted from the journal, the ledger for Exercise Plus should appear as shown on the following pages. Remember that the account number is entered in the Posting Reference column of the journal after each entry is posted.

LEDGER

Cash — **Account No.** *101*

DATE		EXPLANATION	POST. REF.	DEBIT		CREDIT		BALANCE DEBIT		BALANCE CREDIT	
19—											
Oct.	1	Opening entry	J1	10,100	00			10,100	00		
	5	Remittance Slip RS-104	J1	700	00			10,800	00		
	6	Check 5	J1			600	00	10,200	00		
	12	Check 6	J1			1,500	00	8,700	00		
	12	Remittance Slip RS-105	J1	6,000	00			14,700	00		
	21	Check 7	J1			2,000	00	12,700	00		
	26	Invoices 106–110	J1	1,400	00			14,100	00		
	28	Check 8	J2			2,000	00	12,100	00		

Accts. Rec./Carmen Saldi — **Account No.** *103*

DATE		EXPLANATION	POST. REF.	DEBIT		CREDIT		BALANCE DEBIT		BALANCE CREDIT	
19—											
Oct.	1	Opening entry	J1	700	00			700	00		
	5	Remittance Slip RS-104	J1			700	00	—	00		
	27	Invoice 111	J1	1,200	00			1,200	00		

Accts. Rec./Talbot Industries — **Account No.** *104*

DATE		EXPLANATION	POST. REF.	DEBIT		CREDIT		BALANCE DEBIT		BALANCE CREDIT	
19—											
Oct.	1	Opening entry	J1	1,400	00			1,400	00		
	27	Invoice 112	J1	1,000	00			2,400	00		

Supplies — **Account No.** *108*

DATE		EXPLANATION	POST. REF.	DEBIT		CREDIT		BALANCE DEBIT		BALANCE CREDIT	
19—											
Oct.	6	Check 5	J1	600	00			600	00		

Furniture — **Account No.** *111*

DATE		EXPLANATION	POST. REF.	DEBIT		CREDIT		BALANCE DEBIT		BALANCE CREDIT	
19—											
Oct.	1	Opening entry	J1	4,500	00			4,500	00		
	7	Invoice 9822	J1	700	00			5,200	00		
	8	Credit Memorandum CM-67	J1			350	00	4,850	00		

Exercise Equipment **Account No.** *112*

DATE		EXPLANATION	POST. REF.	DEBIT	CREDIT	BALANCE DEBIT	BALANCE CREDIT
19—							
Oct.	1	Opening entry	J1	13,000 00		13,000 00	

Accts. Pay./Shone Products **Account No.** *201*

DATE		EXPLANATION	POST. REF.	DEBIT	CREDIT	BALANCE DEBIT	BALANCE CREDIT
19—							
Oct.	1	Opening entry	J1		1,500 00		1,500 00
	7	Invoice 9822	J1		700 00		2,200 00
	8	Credit Memorandum CM-67	J1	350 00			1,850 00
	12	Check 6	J1	1,500 00			350 00

Accts. Pay./XYZ Repairs **Account No.** *202*

DATE		EXPLANATION	POST. REF.	DEBIT	CREDIT	BALANCE DEBIT	BALANCE CREDIT
19—							
Oct.	1	Opening entry	J1		200 00		200 00
	29	Invoice 212	J2		200 00		400 00

Lisa Long, Capital **Account No.** *301*

DATE		EXPLANATION	POST. REF.	DEBIT	CREDIT	BALANCE DEBIT	BALANCE CREDIT
19—							
Oct.	1	Opening entry	J1		28,000 00		28,000 00
	12	Remittance Slip RS-105	J1		6,000 00		34,000 00
	21	Check 7	J1	2,000 00			32,000 00

Income Summary **Account No.** *399*

DATE		EXPLANATION	POST. REF.	DEBIT	CREDIT	BALANCE DEBIT	BALANCE CREDIT

Sales **Account No.** *401*

DATE		EXPLANATION	POST. REF.	DEBIT	CREDIT	BALANCE DEBIT	BALANCE CREDIT
19—							
Oct.	26	Invoices 106–110	J1		1,400 00		1,400 00
	27	Invoices 111–112	J1		2,200 00		3,600 00

Repairs Expense **Account No.** *504*

DATE		EXPLANATION	POST. REF.	DEBIT		CREDIT		BALANCE DEBIT		BALANCE CREDIT	
19— Oct.	29	Invoice 212	J2	200	00			200	00		

Salaries Expense **Account No.** *505*

DATE		EXPLANATION	POST. REF.	DEBIT		CREDIT		BALANCE DEBIT		BALANCE CREDIT	
19— Oct.	28	Check 8.	J2	2,000	00			2,000	00		

Supplies Expense **Account No.** *506*

DATE		EXPLANATION	POST. REF.	DEBIT		CREDIT		BALANCE DEBIT		BALANCE CREDIT	

The procedure of posting a transaction and computing the new balance is frequently referred to as updating the account. In general, the term *updating the account* is used in data processing systems and refers to the posting of any current data to an account or file.

The frequency of posting depends on the needs of the business.

The information in every account must be kept up to date. Some businesses post daily, some post once or twice a week, and others post once every two weeks. The frequency depends upon the needs of the business. Regardless of the type of business, however, most businesses update their ledger accounts at least monthly so that a set of financial statements can be prepared.

Concept: Audit Trail

References should be provided so that data can be traced from its origination (beginning) to its use (end).

Exercise C on page 166 may be completed at this point.

Other Methods of Keeping the Ledger

Are several accounts kept on one page in a ledger? No. In actual practice each ledger account is usually kept on a separate page or separate card. However, the accounts illustrated in this topic show several ledger accounts on one page in order to save space.

A ledger is a group of accounts that can be maintained in a variety of ways.

Some businesses keep their accounts in a bound "book." But most businesses keep their accounts on individual, loose-leaf forms printed on paper or cards. The accounts can then be stored in a loose-leaf binder, a filing cabinet, a ledger tray, or an open tub file. The accounts can then be removed easily so that entries can be made manually, mechanically, or electronically. The accounts can also be rearranged to add new accounts or to remove accounts to be stored in other areas.

The procedures shown for posting were those followed in posting by hand. The actual method used to post data will depend on the method of data processing used in that business. Thus, posting may be done manually, by machines, or by computers. The ledger form, however, does not vary greatly from method to method, nor does the type of data kept in the ledger account. The accounting theory is the same no matter how the posting is done.

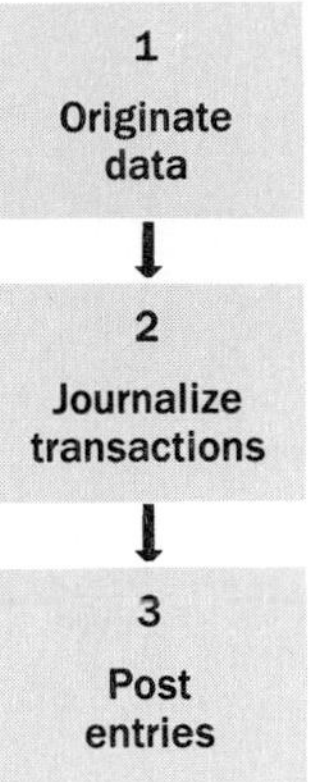

■ The Accounting Cycle

Posting the journal entries to the ledger accounts is the third step in the accounting cycle. The steps discussed up to this point are as follows.

Step 1. *Originating the data.* Recording the original data on a source document

Step 2. *Journalizing the transactions.* Recording the transactions in a journal

Step 3. *Posting the entries.* Transferring the journal entries to the ledger accounts

Exercise D on page 166 may be completed at this point.

TOPIC 1 EXERCISES

EXERCISE A. Answer the following questions about the balance ledger form. Refer to the balance ledger form on page 154.

1. What two items identify an account?
2. What type of account is commonly used in learning accounting and in analyzing transactions?
3. How many money columns are there on a balance ledger form?
4. What date is posted to the ledger?
5. What number is in the Posting Reference column?
6. What amounts are recorded in the first two money columns?
7. How is a ledger opened?

EXERCISE B. Answer the following questions about the procedure for posting from the journal to the ledger. Refer to the text and illustrations on pages 155 to 160.

1. Is the debit or the credit part of the journal entry posted first?
2. What date is used in posting a transaction?
3. In the ledger account, what data is written in the Posting Reference column?
4. What data is written in the Posting Reference column of the journal?
5. Is a debit entry added to or subtracted from a debit balance? From a credit balance?

dr / cr

EXERCISE C. Arrange the following steps of the posting procedures in the correct order. Refer to pages 155 to 160.

Compute and record the balance
Record account number in journal
Locate ledger account
Record explanation, if needed, in account
Locate the next ledger account
Record journal page number in account
Record date in account
Record amount in account

EXERCISE D. Answer the following questions about keeping the ledger. Refer to the text, margin notes, and illustrations on pages 164 to 165.

1. How often should a business post to the ledger?
2. Does the ledger form vary greatly from posting method to posting method?
3. What are the first three steps in the accounting cycle?

TOPIC 1 PROBLEMS

TOPIC PROBLEM 1. Refer to the journal entries in Topic Problem 3 in Chapter 5. Open ledger accounts for Cash; Accts. Rec./Linda Michaels; Supplies; Office Equipment; Accts. Pay./Freeway Sales; John Daniel, Capital; Sales; and Telephone Expense. Number each account according to the plan at the right. Post the journal entries made in Topic Problem 3 in Chapter 5 to the accounts.

PLAN FOR THE CHART OF ACCOUNTS	
Asset accounts	101 through 199
Liability accounts	201 through 299
Owner's Equity accounts	301 through 399
Revenue accounts	401 through 499
Expense accounts	501 through 599

NOTE: Save your work from this problem for further use in Topic Problem 3.

TOPIC PROBLEM 2. Refer to the journal entries made in Topic Problem 4 in Chapter 5. Open ledger accounts for Cash; Accts. Rec./Workman High School; Medical Equipment; Office Equipment; Accts. Pay./Medi-Vac Company; Accts. Pay./TriCities Tribune; Ann Carson, Capital; Sales; Advertising Expense; and Rent Expense. Number each account according to the plan given in Topic Problem 1 above. Post the journal entries made in Topic Problem 4 in Chapter 5 to the accounts.

TOPIC 2

Preparing Accounting Proofs

Is there a way to check that the journal entries have been posted accurately to the ledger? Yes. As you learned in Chapter 4, a proof is made to verify the equality of the ledger at the end of each accounting period. Proving the equality of the ledger is the fourth step in the accounting cycle. A trial balance is used to do this.

■ Preparing a Trial Balance

If financial statements are not being prepared, a quick trial balance can be done. However, if the financial statements are being prepared, then a formal trial balance is needed. An example of a formal trial balance for Exercise Plus on October 31 is shown here.

A trial balance is a proof that can be made in a variety of ways.

Exercise Plus
Trial Balance
October 31, 19—

ACCOUNT TITLE	ACCT. NO.	DEBIT	CREDIT
Cash	101	12,100 00	
Accts. Rec./Carmen Saldi	103	1,200 00	
Accts. Rec./Talbot Industries	104	2,400 00	
Supplies	108	600 00	
Furniture	111	4,850 00	
Exercise Equipment	112	13,000 00	
Accts. Pay./Shone Products	201		350 00
Accts. Pay./XYZ Repairs	202		400 00
Lisa Long, Capital	301		32,000 00
Sales	401		3,600 00
Repairs Expense	504	200 00	
Salaries Expense	505	2,000 00	
		36,350 00	36,350 00

A trial balance is prepared to check that the total of the debit balances in the ledger is equal to the total of the credit balances.

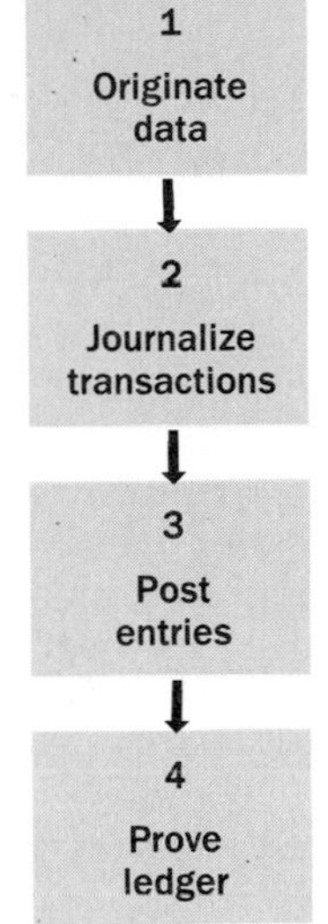

Concept: Trial Balance
The equality of the total debits and the total credits in the ledger should be verified at regular intervals.

Exercise E on page 173 may be completed at this point.

Trial Balance Errors

How can you tell if there is an error in the trial balance? When the debit total equals the credit total, a trial balance is in balance. However, when the two totals are not equal, the trial balance is out of balance. If the trial balance does not balance, one or more errors have been made.

To locate the error or errors, start with the last step in preparing a trial balance. Then work back, step by step, through the accounting cycle until the error or errors are found. This means that you should start with the trial balance first, and then go to the ledger, the journal, and finally the source documents.

■ Check-Marking

When searching for errors, follow an orderly procedure. The procedures should let you know the records you have checked and not checked, or what records have been checked twice. One procedure is to use a check mark (✓) and a check mark with a line through it (✗). Check marks are written in pencil.

- The check mark (✓) is placed at the right of the amount or entry after it is checked for an error. The check mark shows that this item has been compared with its source and has been verified as being correct. The audit trail is extremely helpful in searching for errors.
- A line is made through a check mark (✗) when an item has been checked again. This means that the item has been checked a second time and has been verified as being correct. Additional lines can be placed through the check mark if more rechecking is needed.

WRONG: ✓176.30
RIGHT: 176.30✓

Place a check mark to the right of amount.

When using check marks, be careful that you do not deface the accounting records. Use check marks that are small and legible. Be consistent in using them, and place them to the right of the amounts, as shown in the margin. (Placing the check marks to the right avoids running the check mark through the first digit of an amount. For example, a 1 with a line through it could be confused with a 7.)

Reread

■ Locating Trial Balance Errors

Follow this procedure to trace errors in the trial balance.

- *Check the addition of both money columns of the trial balance.* Use a calculator and check the amounts on the tape against those on the trial balance. Put check marks at the totals you checked. If there is no error, go to the next step.
- *Compare the balance of each ledger account with the amount entered for that account on the trial balance.* An account balance may have been copied incorrectly or entered in the wrong column. An account balance may have been omitted, or it may have been included more than once. Place a check mark after each item on the trial balance and in the ledger as you examine it.
- *Check that each account listed on the trial balance has a check mark beside it.* The absence of a check mark may indicate that an account was listed more than once.
- *Check entries for the amount of difference.* Compute the difference between the two totals on the trial balance. Then search the ledger accounts and the journal for entries of this exact amount. For example, if the difference is $50, check each entry of $50 to see whether it has been journalized and posted correctly. If only the debit entry for a $50 transaction is posted and not the credit entry, a $50 error will appear. Likewise, if a debit entry for $50 is posted twice, the debits would be $50 greater than the credits. In

Trial Balance
October 31, 19–

```
     0.00T
12,100.00
 1,200.00
 2,400.00
   600.00
 4,850.00
13,000.00
   200.00
 2,000.00
36,350.00T✓

     0.00T
   350.00
   400.00
32,000.00
 3,600.00
36,350.00T✓
```

Check addition of both money columns.

the journal, perhaps the $50 debit and not the credit may have been journalized.

- *Check entries for one-half of the amount of difference*. Divide the difference between the two totals on the trial balance by 2. Search the ledger accounts and the journal for an entry of this amount. For example, if the difference is $50, check entries of $25 ($50 ÷ 2). An account with a debit balance of $25 could have been placed in the Credit column of the trial balance. This would throw off the trial balance by $50, twice the amount of the difference. The debit total would be $25 less than it should be, and the credit total would be $25 more.

DEBIT			CREDIT	
12,100	00	√		
1,200	00	√		
2,400	00	√		
600	00	√		
4,850	00	√		
13,000	00	√		
			350	00 √

Check amounts on the trial balance.

- *Check entries for a transposition*. Divide the trial balance difference by 9. If the difference can be divided evenly by 9, two digits in an amount may have been transposed. A **transposition** means that the digits or numbers were placed in reverse order. For example, if $32 were posted as $23, there would be a difference of $9 on the trial balance. If $4,680 were posted as $4,860, there would be a difference of $180. Each of these differences can be evenly divided by 9. This procedure of dividing by 9 is an excellent way to uncover the possibility of transposed digits.

Correct amount	$ 32	$4,860
Transposed amount	23	4,680
Difference	$ 9	$ 180
Differences are evenly divisible by 9	$9 ÷ 9 = $1	$180 ÷ 9 = $20

Check for transpositions.

- *Check entries for a slide*. If the trial balance difference can be divided by 9 but the error is not located, then look for a slide. A **slide** is an error caused by the misplacement of a decimal point. For example, recording $123.40 as $12.34 will give an error of $111.06. This amount is evenly divisible by 9.

Correct amount	$123.40
Slide number	12.34
Difference	$111.06
Difference is evenly divisible by 9	$111.06 ÷ 9 = $12.34

Check for slides.

Locating Ledger Errors

If the error is not discovered by checking the trial balance, then go to the ledger. This is the next step in the reverse order of the accounting cycle.

- *Check that each account balance has a check mark*. When you checked the account balances on the trial balance, you should have put a check mark after each account that was shown correctly on the trial balance. Remember that the absence of a check mark indicates that the account balance was not listed in the trial balance.
- *Verify the balance of each ledger account*. An account balance may have been computed incorrectly. Check the addition and subtraction in each account. An example of how to use an adding machine to check the balance of an account is shown in the margin.

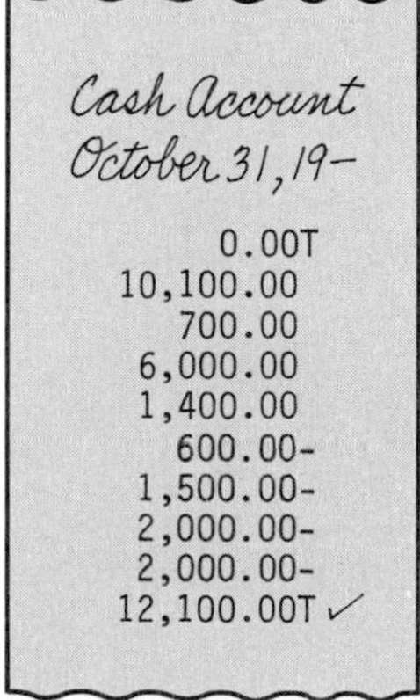

Cash Account
October 31, 19–
0.00T
10,100.00
700.00
6,000.00
1,400.00
600.00-
1,500.00-
2,000.00-
2,000.00-
12,100.00T

Check account balance.

Locating Journal Errors

If the error is not located in the ledger, go to the journal.

Journal Proof
Page 1
October 27, 19—

0.00T
10,100.00
700.00
1,400.00
4,500.00
13,000.00
700.00
600.00
700.00
350.00
1,500.00
6,000.00
2,000.00
1,400.00
1,200.00
1,000.00
45,150.00T

0.00T
1,500.00
200.00
28,000.00
700.00
600.00
700.00
350.00
1,500.00
6,000.00
2,000.00
1,400.00
2,200.00
45,150.00T

Check journal page proofs.

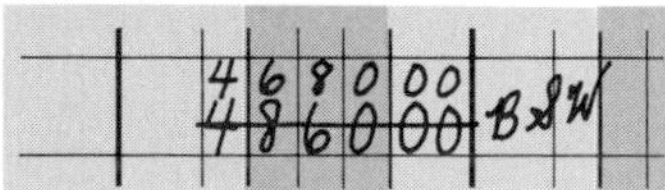

Initial all changes.

- *Check that each entry has been posted.* Examine the Posting Reference column in the journal to see that all entries have been posted.
- *Trace all postings back to the journal.* Remember to place a check mark after each amount in the journal and ledger. Then check for unmarked amounts in the journal or ledger. An unmarked item in the journal may indicate that an entry was not posted. An unmarked item in the ledger may mean it was posted more than once. This is an example of where a good audit trail can really be useful.
- *Prepare a journal page proof of each journal page for the accounting period.* The total debits must equal the total credits for each page of the journal. The sample calculator tape in the margin shows how the numbers from page 1 of the journal for Exercise Plus would look.
- *Check journal entries with source documents.* If the entry is not found, then the source documents will have to be checked with the same journal.

Correcting Errors

A correction must be made for each error that is found. However, no erasures are made. Even pencil figures should not be erased on an accounting record. To correct an error in an amount, first draw a single line through the entire incorrect amount. Then write the complete correct amount above it. Erasures are not made in case there is any question about the entry. Finally, the person making the correction should put his or her initials opposite each correction. This means that any correction can be traced to the person responsible. See the illustration in the margin.

Errors Not Revealed by a Trial Balance

Are there some errors that can occur that are not shown on a trial balance? Yes, there are such errors. The fact that a trial balance is in balance does not mean that the accounting records are completely accurate. It only proves that the totals of the debit and credit balances in the ledger accounts are equal. The trial balance only checks the mathematical accuracy of the ledger.

Some errors on the trial balance do not create a difference between the totals of the debit balances and the credit balances. These errors include the following.

- *A transaction that is completely omitted from a journal.* Both debit and credit amounts are missing.
- *A transaction that is journalized more than once.* Both debits and credits increase by the same amount.
- *A transaction that is correctly journalized but not posted.* Both debit and credit amounts are missing.

- *A transaction that is correctly journalized but posted more than once.* Both debit and credit amounts increase by the same amount.
- *A transaction that is correctly journalized but posted to the wrong account.* For example, a debit to the Furniture account could have been posted as a debit to the Office Equipment account. The debit amount and the credit amount have been posted. The trial balance would still be in balance.
- *A transaction that is incorrectly journalized because the wrong account is debited or credited.* For example, a journal entry in which the Cash account has been debited by mistake instead of the Office Equipment account is incorrectly recorded. The debit amount still equals the credit amount.
- *A transaction that is incorrectly journalized or posted because the wrong amount is debited and credited.* Suppose a transaction for $50 is journalized as a $5 debit and a $5 credit. Both debit and credit amounts are equal.
- *Two errors for the same amount that cancel each other.* For example, a debit account balance is recorded that is $100 too much and a credit account balance is recorded that is $100 too much. Both the debit and credit total are increased by the same amount.

These errors emphasize the need for accuracy at all times in recording data, in analyzing transactions, in journalizing, and in posting. Time is lost if a person must look for errors.

Even though there are these limitations, the trial balance still serves a valuable purpose. It does show that the ledger is in balance, and it also summarizes the data for the financial statements.

Exercise F on page 173 may be completed at this point.

Information Not in the Trial Balance

Is all information about the operation of a business always available in the general ledger when the trial balance is prepared? Sometimes all the information is not available. For example, look at the trial balance for Exercise Plus on page 167. The value of supplies used by Exercise Plus during October has not yet been recorded. This is because certain account balances—Supplies and Supplies Expense, for example—are brought up to date at the end of the accounting period. Time is saved if use of each supply item does not have to be recorded.

Accountants update balances for accounts by means of adjustments. **Adjustments** are amounts added to or subtracted from account balances to bring the balances up to date. Account balances must be updated to ensure that current information is fully and accurately disclosed in the financial statements at the end of the accounting period.

In the case of Exercise Plus's supplies, how would the adjustment work? At the end of the October accounting period, Exercise Plus

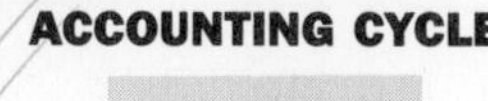

ACCOUNTING CYCLE

1 Originate data
↓
2 Journalize transactions
↓
3 Post entries
↓
4 Prove ledger

would determine the value of the supplies it had used during October. (The procedure for determining the value is explained in more detail in Topic 3.) The asset account Supplies is adjusted by decreasing that account by the value of the supplies that had been consumed. The account Supplies Expense is adjusted by increasing the account by the value of the supplies consumed. (The Supplies Expense account is used because supplies consumed are considered a cost of doing business.) The task of making adjustments might be difficult were it not for the availability of an accounting document known as a worksheet. In Topic 3, you will see that the preparation of a worksheet simplifies the task of planning and recording end-of-the-accounting-period adjustments.

The Accounting Cycle

The preparation of a trial balance is the fourth step in the accounting cycle. The steps discussed up to this point are as follows.

Step 1. Record the original data on a source document.
Step 2. Record the transactions in a journal.
Step 3. Post the journal entries to the ledger accounts.
Step 4. Prove the equality of the ledger.

DATA PROCESSING CYCLE

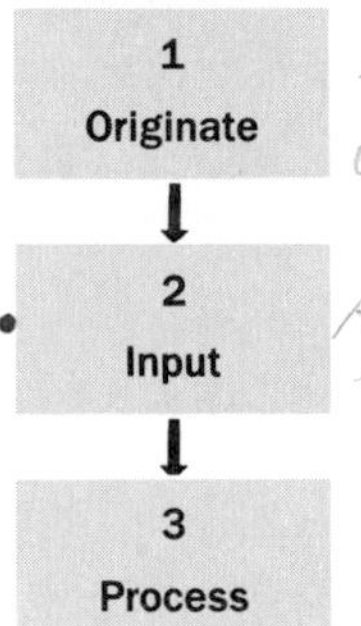

The Data Processing Cycle

In Chapter 5 you learned how the first two steps of the data processing cycle—origination of data and input of data—relate to the accounting cycle. Now we will see how Step 3 of the data processing cycle relates to the accounting cycle.

Step 3: Processing of Data After the data is put into the system, the data must be processed in order to produce the output (information) needed. **Processing** is undertaking a series of actions that will change or store data in order to bring about some result. In electronic data processing, the computer will perform these actions. In manual data processing, these actions are done by hand or with the help of some equipment.

In accounting, processing data involves taking the input from the journals, sorting it according to account title and number, updating the account balances, storing the data until the end of the accounting cycle, and then proving the ledger.

Concept: Full Disclosure
All relevant information that a user may need in making a decision should be disclosed and reported in the financial statements.

Principle: Updating Accounts
The generally accepted accounting principle is that certain accounts must be updated at the end of each accounting period. The procedure requires adjusting entries in order to reflect current account balances.

Exercise G on page 173 may be completed at this point.

TOPIC 2 EXERCISES

EXERCISE E. Answer the following questions about account balances and the trial balance. Refer to the text, margin notes, and illustrations on pages 166 and 167.

1. What are the first four steps of the accounting cycle?

2. Why is a trial balance prepared?

3. Are errors in accounting records corrected by erasures? Explain the procedure.

EXERCISE F. Indicate which of the following errors would be revealed by the trial balance. Write "yes" or "no" after the error, as appropriate.

EXAMPLE: Listing an incorrect account balance on the trial balance—yes

1. Posting a debit entry to the credit side of an account

2. Balancing an account incorrectly

3. Posting a journal entry (both the debit and the credit) more than once

4. Making two errors for the same amount

5. Failing to post a journal entry (both the debit and the credit)

6. Failing to post either a debit or a credit entry

7. Posting an entry to the wrong account

8. Omitting an account with a balance from the trial balance

9. Posting a debit entry for $260 instead of $620

10. Journalizing a debit to the wrong account

EXERCISE G. Match the steps in the manual accounting cycle in Column 2 with those steps in the data processing cycle listed in Column 1. Write your answers on a separate sheet of paper.

Column 1	Column 2
1. Origination of data	**a.** Prove ledger
2. Input of data	**b.** Journalize transactions
3. Processing data	**c.** Post entries
	d. Originate data

TOPIC 2 PROBLEMS

TOPIC PROBLEM 3. Prepare a formal trial balance for Ventura Travel Service on October 31. Use the ledger account balances from Topic Problem 1 in this chapter.

TOPIC PROBLEM 4. The trial balance prepared for Sunwest Photography on October 31 is shown on page 174.

Assume that the balance of each ledger account has been verified and that all the journal entries have been posted correctly. Thus, the error or errors must be in the trial balance.

a. Analyze each account carefully and correct any errors.

b. Prepare a new trial balance. (Assign appropriate account numbers to the accounts. Refer to the plan for the chart of accounts in Topic Problem 1 on page 166 for help in setting up the accounts.)

c. The trial balance should be in balance once you have completed this work. Are there any other errors which might still be present in the trial balance? Why or why not?

Sunwest Photography
Trial Balance
October 31, 19—

Cash	11,800 00	
Camera Equipment	1,000 00	
Accts. Pay./Ace Film	400 00	
Accts. Rec./Lake Wedding Chapel	2,400 00	
Salaries Expense	2,000 00	
Advertising Expense	200 00	
Land	3,600 00	
Building		14,850 00
Mortgage Payable		400 00
Leann Mason, Capital		31,450 00
Sales		3,600 00

TOPIC 3

Completing the Worksheet

Are the financial statements always prepared from the formal trial balance? No. There are times when the financial statements are prepared from a worksheet. The **worksheet** is a columnar form on which the accountant gathers data at the end of the accounting period. The data on the worksheet serves three purposes.

- First, the data is used to prepare a formal trial balance, if desired.
- Second, end-of-period adjustments to the accounts can be planned.
- Third, the data helps the accountant plan and prepare the financial statements.

In Chapter 4 you learned how financial statements are prepared from a trial balance. When businesses have only a few accounts, this is a good procedure to follow. However, when businesses have a larger number of accounts, it becomes worthwhile to prepare a worksheet.

The form of worksheet used in this chapter is shown on page 175. Note that the worksheet has ten money columns. The Trial Balance columns are used to gather trial balance data. The Adjustments columns are used to plan any changes for the end of the accounting period to the account balances. The Adjusted Trial Balance columns list all the account balances after adjustments, if any, have been included. The Income Statement and Balance Sheet columns are used to transfer

Exercise Plus
Worksheet
For the Month Ended October 31, 19—

ACCOUNT TITLE	ACCT. NO.	TRIAL BALANCE		ADJUSTMENTS		ADJUSTED TRIAL BALANCE		INCOME STATEMENT		BALANCE SHEET	
		DEBIT	CREDIT	DEBIT	CREDIT	DEBIT	CREDIT	DEBIT	CREDIT	DEBIT	CREDIT

the accounts listed on the adjusted trial balance to their appropriate financial statements.

The worksheet is not a financial statement. It does assist the accountant in preparing the financial statements. The worksheet is prepared in pencil so that the amounts can be erased and changed. Thus, the worksheet is often referred to as a "work sheet" or "working paper." The worksheet prepared for Exercise Plus on October 31 and shown on pages 176 to 178 will be used to show how the worksheet is completed.

■ Completing the Heading The heading of the worksheet answers the same three questions as do the headings on other financial documents.

- WHO? (the name of the business—Exercise Plus)
- WHAT? (a worksheet)
- WHEN? (the accounting period—For the Month Ended October 31, 19—)

The heading covers the accounting period because the net income (or net loss) for the period is computed on the worksheet.

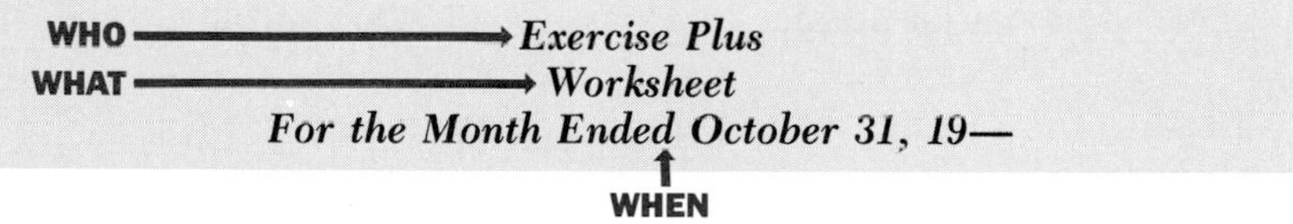

■ Completing the Trial Balance Columns The trial balance is prepared directly on the worksheet. Account titles, account numbers, and account balances are listed just as they are in a trial balance. The source of the trial balance data is the ledger. After the balances are entered, a single rule is drawn across both money columns and the amounts are totaled. If the amounts are equal, double rules are drawn under both money columns. If the amounts are not equal, the error must be found before the worksheet is completed. The process for finding the equality of debit and credit amounts is the same as the process in preparing a trial balance. Note that all accounts, whether or not they have balances, are entered in the trial balance. Thus, the Supplies Expense account is listed in the trial balance even though it has no balance before end-of-the-period adjustments have been made.

■ **Completing the Adjustments Columns** The Adjustments columns are placed on the worksheet to help the accountant adjust (update) accounts that need to be adjusted at the end of the accounting period. As discussed earlier, in some cases it is easier to adjust accounts once at the end rather than many times during the accounting period. For example, the amount of money a company has invested in supplies changes every time an item is used. If the accountant deducted from the Supplies account for every one of these items, time would be wasted. Therefore, a better method is to deduct the total amount of the supplies used at the end of the accounting period.

Exercise Plus purchased $600 worth of supplies during the month of October. On October 31, the accountant checked the supplies remaining and found that supplies costing $200 had been used. The Adjustments columns on the worksheet are used to compute the adjustment to the Supplies account. (A journal entry will be made later to correct the actual accounts.) The worksheet shown here illustrates the adjustment.

Exercise Plus
Worksheet
For the Month Ended October 31, 19—

	ACCOUNT TITLE	ACCT. NO.	TRIAL BALANCE		ADJUSTMENTS		ADJUSTED TRIAL BALANCE		INCOME STATEMENT		BALANCE SHEET		
			DEBIT	CREDIT	DEBIT	CREDIT	DEBIT	CREDIT	DEBIT	CREDIT	DEBIT	CREDIT	
1	*Cash*	101	12,100										1
2	*Accts. Rec./Carmen Saldi*	103	1,200										2
3	*Accts. Rec./Talbot Industries*	104	2,400										3
4	*Supplies*	108	600			200							4
5	*Furniture*	111	4,850										5
6	*Exercise Equipment*	112	13,000										6
7	*Accts. Pay./Shone Products*	201		350									7
8	*Accts. Pay./XYZ Repairs*	202		400									8
9	*Lisa Long, Capital*	301		32,000									9
10	*Income Summary*	399		—									10
11	*Sales*	401		3,600									11
12	*Repairs Expense*	504	200										12
13	*Salaries Expense*	505	2,000										13
14	*Supplies Expense*	506	—		200								14
15			36,350	36,350	200	200							15
16													16
17													17
18													18
19													19

NOTE: The cents columns have been omitted in order to show the entire worksheet.

The Supplies account is credited for $200 to decrease the balance to the current amount of supplies on hand ($400). The supplies that have been used become an expense for the business. Therefore, $200 is also debited to the Supplies Expense account.

Once all the adjustments have been made on the worksheet, the Adjustments columns are totaled to show that both the totals of the debits and credits in those columns are equal.

■ Completing the Adjusted Trial Balance Columns After the adjustments have been planned, the account balances are updated. The worksheet illustrated here shows the balances extended in the Adjusted Trial Balance columns.

Exercise Plus
Worksheet
For the Month Ended October 31, 19—

	ACCOUNT TITLE	ACCT. NO.	TRIAL BALANCE		ADJUSTMENTS		ADJUSTED TRIAL BALANCE		INCOME STATEMENT		BALANCE SHEET		
			DEBIT	CREDIT	DEBIT	CREDIT	DEBIT	CREDIT	DEBIT	CREDIT	DEBIT	CREDIT	
1	*Cash*	*101*	*12,100*				*12,100*						1
2	*Accts. Rec./Carmen Saldi*	*103*	*1,200*				*1,200*						2
3	*Accts. Rec./Talbot Industries*	*104*	*2,400*				*2,400*						3
4	*Supplies*	*108*	*600*			*200*	*400*						4
5	*Furniture*	*111*	*4,850*				*4,850*						5
6	*Exercise Equipment*	*112*	*13,000*				*13,000*						6
7	*Accts. Pay./Shone Products*	*201*		*350*				*350*					7
8	*Accts. Pay./XYZ Repairs*	*202*		*400*				*400*					8
9	*Lisa Long, Capital*	*301*		*32,000*				*32,000*					9
10	*Income Summary*	*399*		—				—					10
11	*Sales*	*401*		*3,600*				*3,600*					11
12	*Repairs Expense*	*504*	*200*				*200*						12
13	*Salaries Expense*	*505*	*2,000*				*2,000*						13
14	*Supplies Expense*	*506*	—		*200*		*200*						14
15			*36,350*	*36,350*	*200*	*200*	*36,350*	*36,350*					15
16													16
17													17
18													18
19													19

NOTE: The cents columns have been omitted in order to show the entire worksheet.

Notice that the Supplies account now shows a debit balance of $400 ($600 − $200). Supplies Expense has also been added to the Adjusted Trial Balance and shows a $200 debit balance. Once again, both the Debit and Credit columns are added to check for equality.

■ Completing the Balance Sheet and Income Statement Columns The worksheet was described as a "working paper." You will now see how the worksheet allows the accountant to plan the financial statements (the balance sheet and the income statement) before each is prepared.

Each balance in the Adjusted Trial Balance columns is now moved to one of the remaining four money columns. Thus, the accounts are sorted and classified according to the financial statement on which each will appear.

Exercise Plus
Worksheet
For the Month Ended October 31, 19—

	ACCOUNT TITLE	ACCT. NO.	TRIAL BALANCE		ADJUSTMENTS		ADJUSTED TRIAL BALANCE		INCOME STATEMENT		BALANCE SHEET		
			DEBIT	CREDIT	DEBIT	CREDIT	DEBIT	CREDIT	DEBIT	CREDIT	DEBIT	CREDIT	
1	*Cash*	101	12,100				12,100				12,100		1
2	*Accts. Rec./Carmen Saldi*	103	1,200				1,200				1,200		2
3	*Accts. Rec./Talbot Industries*	104	2,400				2,400				2,400		3
4	*Supplies*	108	600			200	400				400		4
5	*Furniture*	111	4,850				4,850				4,850		5
6	*Exercise Equipment*	112	13,000				13,000				13,000		6
7	*Accts. Pay./Shone Products*	201		350				350				350	7
8	*Accts. Pay./XYZ Repairs*	202		400				400				400	8
9	*Lisa Long, Capital*	301		32,000				32,000				32,000	9
10	*Income Summary*	399		—				—				—	10
11	*Sales*	401		3,600				3,600		3,600			11
12	*Repairs Expense*	504	200				200		200				12
13	*Salaries Expense*	505	2,000				2,000		2,000				13
14	*Supplies Expense*	506	—		200		200		200				14
15			36,350	36,350	200	200	36,350	36,350	2,400	3,600	33,950	32,750	15
16										2,400			16
17	*Net Income*									1,200		1,200	17
18											33,950	33,950	18
19													19

NOTE: The cents columns have been omitted in order to show the entire worksheet.

As you can see in the worksheet illustrated above, the asset, liability, and owner's equity Capital accounts are first moved to the proper Balance Sheet columns. These are the accounts that are numbered in the 100s, 200s, and 300s. The accounts that have debit balances (the asset accounts) are moved to the Debit column. The accounts that have credit balances (liabilities and the owner's equity Capital account) are moved to the Credit column.

The next step is to move the revenue and expense accounts to the proper Income Statement Debit or Credit column. These are the accounts that are numbered in the 400s and 500s. The revenue accounts are moved to the Credit column of the Income Statement section, and the expense accounts are moved to the Debit column. After each account listed in the Adjusted Trial Balance section is moved to the proper Balance Sheet or Income Statement column, the net income or the net loss is computed.

■ Computing the Net Income or Net Loss The net income or net loss for the accounting period is an important figure on both financial statements. On the income statement, net income or net loss shows profitability for the period. On the balance sheet, the net income or net loss shows the net increase or net decrease in owner's equity due to business activity. When the Balance Sheet columns are equal, it also proves the accountant's work.

In Chapter 2, you learned how net income or net loss was computed when using the accounting equation. You also learned how the net income or net loss was added to or subtracted from owner's equity to prove that assets equaled liabilities plus owner's equity. The steps you will learn next are similar. The difference is that all computations are made on the worksheet. Since the total of the Credit column of the Income Statement section is greater than the Debit column, the business has a net income.

■ Computing Net Income Each step for computing the net income is listed here. As you read a step, refer to the illustration at the right.

1. Place the total of the Income Statement Debit column beneath the total of the Credit column and subtract. The accounts entered in the Debit column of the Income Statement section are decreases in owner's equity. The amounts entered in the Credit column are increases in owner's equity. Since the increases (credits) in owner's equity are greater than the decreases (debits), the difference between the two totals is a net income.

2. Move the amount of the net income to the Credit column of the Balance Sheet section. This is done because a net income increases owner's equity, and owner's equity is increased on the credit side.

3. Add the net income to the total of the Credit column because a net income increases owner's equity. If all computations are correct, the total of the Credit column will now equal the total of the Debit column in the Balance Sheet section. The amounts must be equal after the net income is transferred because total debits must equal the total credits. The assets must equal the liabilities plus owner's equity.

INCOME STATEMENT		BALANCE SHEET	
DEBIT	CREDIT	DEBIT	CREDIT
2,400	3,600	33,950	32,750
	2,400	(2)	
	1,200		1,200
	(1)	33,950	33,950
		(3)	

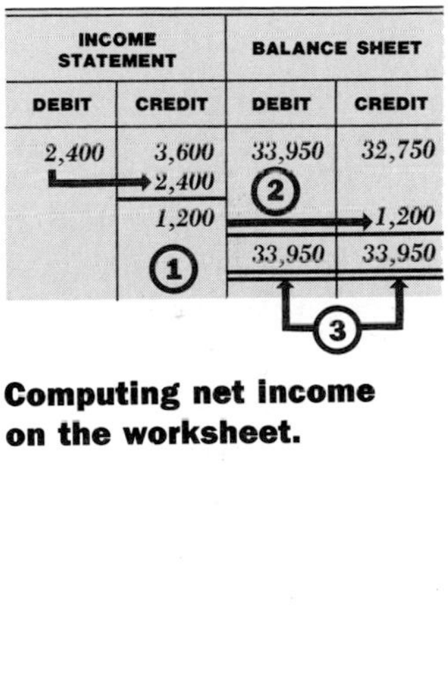

Computing net income on the worksheet.

If the totals agree, complete the worksheet. Draw double rules across the Balance Sheet columns. If the totals do not agree, recheck until the error is found. If the trial balance was correct, the error was made in moving the balances or computing the net income.

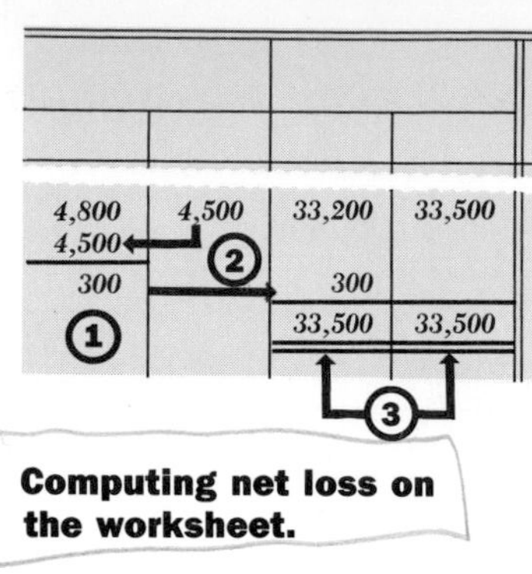

Computing net loss on the worksheet.

Exercises H and I on this page may be completed at this point.

■ Computing Net Loss If the total of the Debit column of the Income Statement section is greater than the Credit column, the business has a net loss. To complete the worksheet when the business has a net loss, follow these steps.

1. Place the total of the Credit column under the total of the Debit column and subtract. The difference is the net loss.
2. Extend the amount of the net loss to the Debit column of the Balance Sheet section. This is done because a net loss decreases owner's equity, and owner's equity is decreased on the debit side.
3. Add the net loss to the total of the Debit column. If no errors were made, the totals of the Debit and Credit columns of the Balance Sheet section will be equal. If the totals agree, complete the worksheet. If the totals do not agree, find your error.

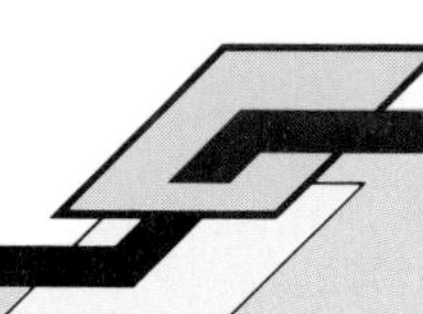

TOPIC 3 EXERCISES

EXERCISE H. Answer the following questions about completing a worksheet. Refer to the text on pages 174 to 180.

1. Why do accountants spend extra time preparing a worksheet?
2. What is the purpose of the Adjustments columns on the worksheet?
3. Which account balances are extended from the Adjusted Trial Balance columns to the Balance Sheet columns? To the Income Statement columns?
4. How can you tell when there will be a net income computed on a worksheet? A net loss?
5. Why is a net income added to the credit side of the Balance Sheet columns?
6. Why is a net loss added to the debit side of the Balance Sheet columns?

EXERCISE I. Indicate on a form similar to the one shown at the right what the net income or net loss will be by extending it to the correct Balance Sheet column.

	Income Statement		Balance Sheet	
	Debit	**Credit**	**Debit**	**Credit**
EX.	*$3,200*	*$4,650*	______	*$1,450*
1.	80	225	______	______
2.	1,695	1,550	______	______
3.	2,250	4,500	______	______
4.	-0-	3,310	______	______
5.	15,620	14,795	______	______

TOPIC 3 PROBLEMS

TOPIC PROBLEM 5. Complete a worksheet for the month ended August 31 for the Hilltop Repair Company. The accounts with ending balances for the month of August are listed at the right. For the purpose of making adjustments, assume that of $300 of supplies that were purchased, $75 worth were used during August.

NOTE: Save your work from this problem for further use in Topic Problem 1, Chapter 7.

Acct. No.	Account Title	Balance
101	Cash	$ 8,250 Dr.
102	Accounts Receivable/ Haussman, Inc.	275 Dr.
103	Accounts Receivable/ Levine and Sons	480 Dr.
104	Supplies	300 Dr.
111	Delivery Truck	7,200 Dr.
112	Repair Equipment	4,625 Dr.
201	Accounts Payable/ Downtown Supplies	1,225 Cr.
202	Accounts Payable/ Prell Parts, Inc.	150 Cr.
301	Joyce Popov, Capital	19,120 Cr.
399	Income Summary	-0-
401	Sales	4,485 Cr.
501	Repairs Expense	550 Dr.
502	Salaries Expense	2,000 Dr.
503	Supplies Expense	-0-
504	Truck Expense	1,300 Dr.

TOPIC PROBLEM 6. Complete a worksheet for the month ended July 31 for the Great Lakes Employment Agency. The accounts with ending balances for the month of July are listed at the right. For the purpose of making adjustments, assume that of the $2,000 of office supplies that were purchased, $500 worth were used during July.

NOTE: Save your work from this problem for further use in Topic Problem 2, Chapter 7.

Acct. No.	Account Title	Balance
101	Cash	$ 6,500 Dr.
102	Accounts Receivable/ Drake Company	1,500 Dr.
103	Accounts Receivable/ Ramirez Inc.	1,250 Dr.
104	Office Supplies	2,000 Dr.
111	Furniture	3,250 Dr.
112	Office Equipment	8,500 Dr.
201	Accounts Payable/ Hinton Furniture Co.	6,400 Cr.
202	Accounts Payable/ Mid-Central Supplies	2,000 Cr.
301	Luther Williams, Capital	11,025 Cr.
399	Income Summary	-0-
401	Sales	7,375 Cr.
501	Rent Expense	1,300 Dr.
502	Salaries Expense	2,000 Dr.
503	Supplies Expense	-0-
504	Telephone Expense	500 Dr.

CHAPTER SUMMARY

The third and fourth steps in the accounting cycle involve processing accounting data after it has been journalized.

In Step 3, data is posted from the journal to balance column ledger accounts. Each account lists all the changes in that account as well as a current balance. The use of posting reference numbers in the ledger accounts provides the accountant with an audit trail. All of the accounts make up the ledger.

In Step 4 of the accounting cycle, the balances in the ledger at the end of the accounting period are summarized. A trial balance is taken to prove the mathematical accuracy of the postings. That is, the debits posted to the ledger must equal the credits posted to the ledger.

In this chapter, the trial balance was prepared on a ten-column worksheet. The remaining columns of the worksheet were used to plan adjustments to the accounts and to sort the general ledger accounts for eventual placement on the income statement and the balance sheet.

THE LANGUAGE OF BUSINESS

Here are some terms that make up the language of business. Do you know the meaning of each?

posting
ledger account
balance ledger form
cross-referencing in posting
posting reference numbers
transposition
slide
adjustments
processing
worksheet

REVIEW QUESTIONS

1. Describe the procedure followed in posting an entry from the journal to the ledger.
2. Why are the journal and the ledger cross-referenced?
3. Why are audit trails used?
4. List two precautions that should be followed when posting an entry from the journal to the ledger.
5. What kinds of accounts have debit balances after all postings are made?
6. What kinds of accounts have credit balances after all postings are made?
7. Would the following errors show up on a trial balance? Explain each answer.
   a. A transaction is journalized by mistake as a debit for $100 to the Supplies account instead of the Office Equipment account.
   b. A journal entry is posted by mistake as a credit for $40 to the Cash account instead of the Accounts Receivable account.

8. What are the first four steps of the accounting cycle?
9. Why does the accountant prepare a worksheet?
10. Why is an Adjustments section on a worksheet useful?

CHAPTER PROBLEMS

Problems for Chapter 6 are given below. Write your answers to the problems on separate sheets of paper unless you are using the workbook for this textbook. If you are using the workbook, do the problems in the space provided there.

CHAPTER PROBLEM 6-1. Use the journal entries from Chapter Problem 5-1 on page 148, and do the following.

a. Open balance ledger form accounts in the ledger for each account. Assign appropriate account numbers.

b. Post the journal entries to the ledger.

c. Prepare a worksheet for the month ended October 31. Assume that supplies costing $850 were used during October.

NOTE: Save your work from this problem for further use in Chapter Problem 7-1.

CHAPTER PROBLEM 6-2. Use the ledger accounts from Chapter Problem 5-2 on pages 149 to 150, and do the following.

a. Open balance ledger form accounts in the ledger for each account.

b. Post the journal entries to the ledger.

c. Prepare a worksheet for the month ended May 31. Assume that supplies costing $75 were used during May.

NOTE: Save your work from this problem for further use in Chapter Problem 7-2.

SUPPLEMENTAL CHAPTER PROBLEM 6-3. If you are using the workbook for Part 1, do Supplemental Chapter Problem 6-3 in the space provided there.

MANAGEMENT CASES

The Ledger and Trial Balance. Many accountants consider the ledger the heart of the accounting records. In the ledger, debits and credits are posted, and accounts are kept up to date. The ledger has unique functions to perform in the accounting cycle. Accuracy of the ledger data is important because the ledger provides data to prepare financial statements. A trial balance is made to check the mathematical accuracy of the ledger. If an error is revealed by the trial balance, the source of the error must be found and corrected immediately. In many instances, a quick trial balance is made to check the equality of debits and credits.

CASE 6M-1. The May 31 trial balance of the ledger accounts for the United Wheel Company shows total debits of $63,720.45 and total credits of $63,720.50. The trial balance and the account balances were re-added and checked, but the error was not found. To find the error would require a check of each transaction. A detailed check would take about five hours unless the error was located early in the checking. The accounting clerk would have to work overtime at the rate of $8 per hour. Thus, it might cost as much as $40 to find the error.

a. Can the manager be sure that the error is only 5 cents?

b. If you were the manager, would you want to find the error or would you ignore it?

CASE 6M-2. The KTSD Radio Station owns and operates a radio station with four transmitting stations. It also owns several vehicles for station personnel, a garage for storing and repairing its trucks, broadcasting equipment, and a large central office. In addition, it has typewriters, calculators, computers, and other office machines in the central office.

In the ledger, only one equipment account is used to record all costs for equipment. Thus, when the balance sheet is prepared, only one amount is shown for all the equipment the company owns.

a. The president of the company believes that this plan does not provide enough detailed information. Why would the president want more detailed information about the equipment the company owns?

b. What changes in the accounting records would you suggest to provide the information the president wants?

CHAPTER

7

Output of Accounting Data

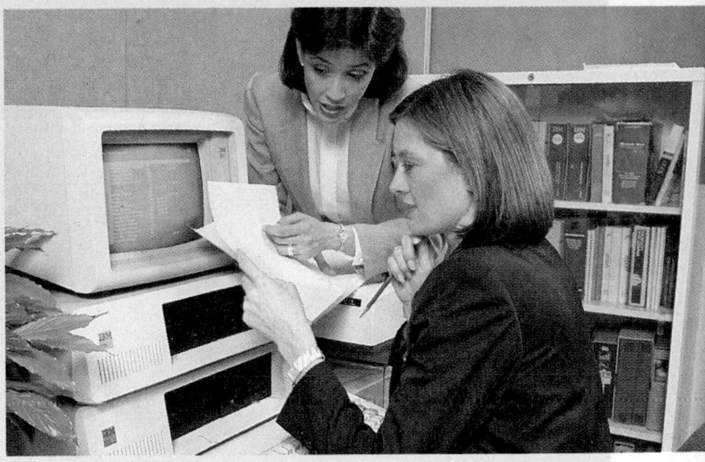

The worksheet provides the data to prepare the income statement and the balance sheet. It also has data for the adjusting and closing entries. You will now learn how to prepare financial statements at the end of the accounting period.

CHAPTER GOALS

After studying Chapter 7 you will be able to:

1 Define the terms listed in "The Language of Business" section on page 226.

2 Explain the accounting concepts and principles in this chapter related to preparing financial statements from a worksheet and to completing end-of-period activities.

3 Prepare an income statement and a balance sheet using information from a worksheet.

4 Update the owner's equity account by journalizing and posting the adjusting and closing entries.

5 Prepare a postclosing trial balance after the ledger accounts have been closed.

6 Interpret comparative income statements and balance sheets.

7 Compare the features of a single proprietorship, a partnership, and a corporation.

8 Identify the key differences in the preparation of financial statements for different forms of business ownership.

TOPIC 1

Preparing the Financial Statements

What is the fifth step in the accounting cycle? Step 5 of the accounting cycle is to prepare the financial statements at the end of the accounting period. Since the worksheet has been completed (see Chapter 6), the income statement and balance sheet can easily be prepared. The relationship between the worksheet and the two financial statements is shown below.

Exercise Plus
Worksheet
For the Month Ended October 31, 19—

	ACCOUNT TITLE	ACCT. NO.	INCOME STATEMENT DEBIT	INCOME STATEMENT CREDIT	BALANCE SHEET DEBIT	BALANCE SHEET CREDIT	
1	Cash	101			12,100		1
2	Accts. Rec./Carmen Saldi	103			1,200		2
3	Accts. Rec./Talbot Industries	104			2,400		3
4	Supplies	108			400		4
5	Furniture	111			4,850		5
6	Exercise Equipment	112			13,000		6
7	Accts. Pay./Shone Products	201				350	7
8	Accts. Pay./XYZ Repairs	202				400	8
9	Lisa Long, Capital	301				32,000	9
10	Income Summary	399				—	10
11	Sales	401		3,600			11
12	Repairs Expense	504	200				12
13	Salaries Expense	505	2,000				13
14	Supplies Expense	506	200				14
15			2,400	3,600	33,950	32,750	15
16			→	2,400			16
17	Net Income			1,200	→	1,200	17
18					33,950	33,950	18

Balance Sheet Accounts (lines 1–10)

Income Statement Accounts (lines 11–14)

NOTE: The cents columns have been omitted.

Exercise Plus
Income Statement
For the Month Ended October 31, 19—

Net Income		1,200 00

Exercise Plus
Balance Sheet
October 31, 19—

Owner's Equity	
Lisa Long, Capital $32,000.00	
Net Income 1,200.00	
Total Owner's Equity	33,200 00
Total	33,950 00

Net income is obtained from the worksheet and shown on the income statement and balance sheet.

In this topic, the basic standards used by accountants in preparing financial statements will be explained. You will be shown how the financial statements are prepared from information in the worksheet.

■ Standards for Preparing Financial Statements

In preparing financial reports, accountants are guided by certain basic standards or concepts. Among these are standards related to full disclosure, materiality, and consistency.

Full disclosure means that financial statements should disclose information fairly, accurately, and completely. The information should not be misleading. Otherwise, those who rely on the information may reach unsound judgments or make unwise decisions based on incomplete information.

Materiality means that financial statements should report only material, relevant, and important information. Unimportant information and minor details need not be reported.

Consistency means that once an accounting method is adopted, it should be applied consistently from one accounting period to the next. This makes comparisons of financial information more valid and reliable. (Topic 3 will discuss more about the ways comparisons of financial information are made.)

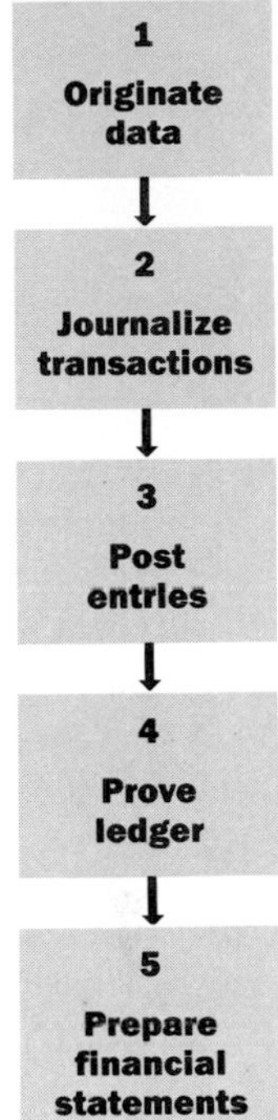

■ The Income Statement

The *income statement* is a financial statement reporting the revenue, expenses, and the net income or net loss of a business for a specific period of time. The types and amounts of the revenue and expenses and the net income (or loss) that are needed to prepare the income statement can be obtained from the Income Statement columns of the worksheet.

The income statement prepared for Exercise Plus from the worksheet for the month ended October 31 is illustrated below. It shows revenue of $3,600, expenses of $2,400, and a net income of $1,200 ($3,600 − $2,400).

Exercise Plus
Income Statement
For the Month Ended October 31, 19—

Revenue:		
Sales		3,600 00
Expenses:		
Repairs Expense	200 00	
Salaries Expense	2,000 00	
Supplies Expense	200 00	
Total Expenses		2,400 00
Net Income		1,200 00

Income statement shows types and amounts of revenue and expenses.

■ What the Income Statement Does Not Show

Previous discussions have emphasized what an income statement shows. (These items are presented in Chapter 4 on page 94.) There are a few things that an income statement does not show.

An income statement does not predict net income.

An income statement might not show all expenses.

Net income is not necessarily related to cash.

- Although it shows the net income or loss for the current accounting period, the income statement does not predict the net income for future periods. Managers and owners use it to make decisions.
- The income statement shows expenses matched against revenue, but it may not show all expenses for a period. For example, the expenses for an advertising campaign may have been paid in the October accounting period. Some people will see the advertising but will not buy any items until December. Thus, the revenue will be recorded in December and the expenses in October. This does *not* mean that the expenses are not matched against the revenue as much as is possible. (Remember the generally accepted accounting principle that revenue is matched against expenses.)
- The income statement shows net income or loss. However, the net income is not equated with cash. Revenue includes cash or receivables. The receivable may be recorded in one accounting period and the cash may be received in the next period when a customer pays his or her account. Remember that net income is the net increase to owner's equity as a result of matching revenue with expenses in an accounting period.

Exercise A on pages 191 and 192 may be completed at this point.

The Balance Sheet

What is the source of data used to prepare the balance sheet?

Like the income statement, the balance sheet is prepared from the worksheet. The balance sheet prepared for Exercise Plus as of October 31, 19—, is shown below. Note that the owner's equity section has the net income that was calculated on the worksheet ($1,200). Exercise Plus's balance sheet shows total assets of $33,950, total liabilities of $750, and total owner's equity of $33,200. The total of the assets

Exercise Plus
Balance Sheet
October 31, 19—

Assets				*Liabilities*			
Cash		12,100	00	*Accounts Payable:*			
Accounts Receivable:				*Shone Products*	*$350.00*		
Carmen Saldi	*$1,200.00*			*XYZ Repairs*	*400.00*		
Talbot Industries	*2,400.00*	3,600	00	*Total Liabilities*		750	00
Supplies		400	00				
Furniture		4,850	00	*Owner's Equity*			
Exercise Equipment		13,000	00	*Lisa Long, Capital*	*$32,000.00*		
				Net Income	*1,200.00*		
				Total Owner's Equity		33,200	00
Total		33,950	00	*Total*		33,950	00

Account form balance sheet: Assets are listed on the left. Liabilities and owner's equity are listed on the right.

($33,950) equals the total of the liabilities and owner's equity ($750 + $33,200).

■ Report Form Balance Sheet Until now, the balance sheets have been presented in the account form. The **account form balance sheet** lists all assets on the left side and the liabilities and owner's equity on the right side. This format is similar to that of the accounting equation, which has asset accounts on the left and liabilities and owner's equity accounts on the right. Another form of the balance sheet is called the report form. The **report form balance sheet** lists all assets in the upper portion and liabilities and owner's equity in the lower portion. The report form is illustrated here.

Exercise Plus
Balance Sheet
October 31, 19--

Assets			
Cash		$12,100.00	
Accounts Receivable:			
Carmen Saldi	$1,200.00		
Talbot Industries	2,400.00	3,600.00	
Supplies		400.00	
Furniture		4,850.00	
Exercise Equipment		13,000.00	
Total Assets			$33,950.00
Liabilities			
Accounts Payable:			
Shone Products		$ 350.00	
XYZ Repairs		400.00	
Total Liabilities			$ 750.00
Owner's Equity			
Lisa Long, Capital		$32,000.00	
Net Income		1,200.00	
Total Owner's Equity			33,200.00
Total Liabilities and Owner's Equity			$33,950.00

Report form balance sheet: Assets are listed in the upper portion. Liabilities and owner's equity are listed in the lower portion.

The report form is easier to prepare on a typewriter than the account form. There also is more space to include information. For example, notice that there is more space to prepare the owner's equity section. Also, there is another money column available for totals. It is much easier to identify quickly the total assets, total liabilities, and total owner's equity. All three section totals are shown in the last money column of the report form balance sheet.

Note that a double rule is drawn beneath the amount of the total assets on the report form. A double rule is also drawn beneath the amount of the total liabilities and owner's equity. The double rules indicate that the two amounts balance and that the balance sheet is completed.

■ Recording the Cost of Assets

A business's assets include cash, accounts receivable, supplies, and other items such as buildings, equipment, and land. Cash is the actual dollar amount available now. Accounts receivable is the actual dollar amount that will be received when the customers pay. The actual cost of supplies on hand is shown. Thus, cash, accounts receivable, and supplies are recorded on the balance sheet at their actual dollar amount.

Other assets such as buildings, equipment, and land are also recorded on the balance sheet at their cost to the business. This means that they are recorded at the amount that the business paid or promised to pay for them. For example, Exercise Plus bought conference tables for $700 on October 7 (see the journal entry on page 141). The $700 that Exercise Plus (the buyer) paid Shone Products (the seller) is the amount recorded as the cost of the asset (furniture).

Assets are recorded at their cost when acquired; they do not show present value.

The generally accepted accounting principle calls for assets to be recorded at their cost on the date acquired. This principle means that assets are recorded on the basis of the dollars that were used to acquire them. The recorded value of the assets on the balance sheet does not show what the assets can be sold for or what it would cost to replace them. Thus, the balance sheet shows that the total recorded value of the furniture owned by Exercise Plus on October 31 is $4,850. This was the cost of the furniture.

What a Balance Sheet Does Not Show

It is important to understand what a balance sheet shows. (These items are presented on page 99 in Chapter 4.) It also is important to understand what a balance sheet does not show.

- It shows the total claims of the creditors against the assets. It does not show claims against specific assets. For example, the October 31 balance sheet for Exercise Plus shows total liabilities of $750. It does not indicate that these claims are against cash, furniture, or any other specific assets.

A balance sheet does not show claims against specific assets.

- It shows the assets at the cost on the day they were acquired. It does not show the market value (what it could be sold for) or worth. The balance sheet shows furniture of $4,850. This was the cost when the furniture was purchased. The furniture could possibly be sold for more or less than that amount.

A balance sheet does not show market value or worth.

- It shows the amount of assets and liabilities on a specific date. The balance sheet does not show how these assets and liabilities changed during the accounting period. For example, the amount of cash was $12,100 on October 31. The balance sheet does not reveal whether the amount of cash increased or decreased during the period. As you know, you cannot assume that the amount of net income increased the amount of cash.

A balance sheet does not show how assets and liabilities changed during an accounting period.

- It shows owner's equity capital on a specific date. The balance sheet may not show how capital increased or decreased during the period. For example, on October 12 Lisa Long invested an additional $6,000, and on October 21 she withdrew $2,000. These changes are not shown on the balance sheet. The balance sheet for

Exercise Plus does, however, show the changes to owner's equity due to the net income earned during the period.

■ The Accounting Cycle

The preparation of the financial statements is the fifth step in the accounting cycle. The steps discussed up to this point are as follows.

Step 1. Record original data on a source document.
Step 2. Record the transactions in a journal.
Step 3. Post the journal entries to the ledger accounts.
Step 4. Prove the equality of the ledger.
Step 5. Prepare an income statement and a balance sheet.

Concept: Full Disclosure
All relevant information that a user may need in making a decision should be disclosed and reported in the financial statements.

Concept: Materiality
All information that may have a material, or significant, effect on a business decision should be included in the financial reports.

Principle: Basis for Recording Assets
The generally accepted accounting principle is that a balance sheet does not presume to show either the present values of assets to the business or the values that might be realized if the assets were sold. Assets are recorded at their cost on the date when they were acquired.

Concept: Recording Assets
Assets are recorded at their cost when acquired, not at their estimated sale or replacement value.

Exercise B on page 192 may be completed at this point.

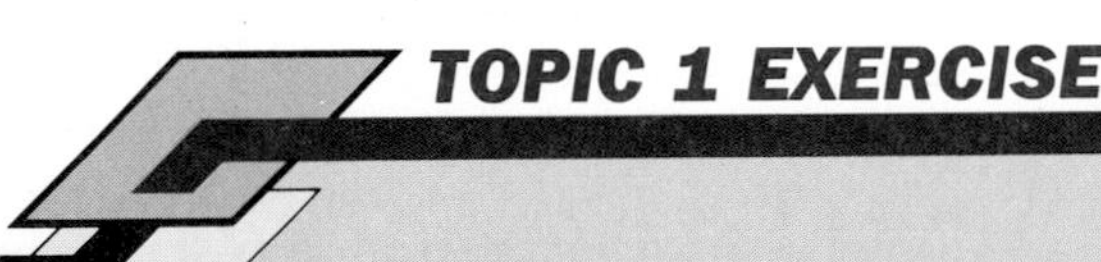

TOPIC 1 EXERCISES

EXERCISE A. Answer the following questions about preparing financial statements. Refer to the worksheet and income statement of Exercise Plus on pages 186 to 187.

1. What is the date of the worksheet?
2. What is the accounting period covered by the income statement?
3. From where is the information for the income statement obtained?
4. What is the revenue from sales?

5. What expenses arose during the month of October for Exercise Plus?
6. How was the net income determined for the income statement?
7. What amount shows the increase in owner's equity as a result of business operations during October?

EXERCISE B. Answer the following questions about the balance sheet. Refer to the worksheet on page 186 and balance sheet of Exercise Plus on page 188.

1. What is the total of the creditors' claims against Exercise Plus's assets?
2. Does the total of the liabilities and owner's equity on the balance sheet equal the total of the credit balances on the trial balance? Why or why not?
3. How much money is owed to Exercise Plus?
4. Does the total of the assets on the balance sheet equal the total of the debit balances on the trial balance? Why or why not?
5. How were the amounts shown for furniture and exercise equipment determined?
6. What does the amount shown for accounts receivable represent?
7. What is the difference between the account form balance sheet and the report form balance sheet?

TOPIC 1 PROBLEMS

TOPIC PROBLEM 1. Prepare the following financial statements for Hilltop Repair Company. Refer to your worksheet from Topic Problem 5 in Chapter 6.

a. Prepare an income statement for the monthly accounting period ended August 31.
b. Prepare a balance sheet in report form for August 31.

TOPIC PROBLEM 2. Use your worksheet from Topic Problem 6 in Chapter 6 to do the following for Great Lakes Employment Agency.

a. Prepare an income statement for the monthly accounting period ended July 31.
b. Prepare a balance sheet in account form for July 31.

TOPIC 2

Updating Accounts

What is the sixth step of the accounting cycle? The sixth step of the accounting cycle is to adjust and close the ledger. *Adjusting the ledger* involves recording in the journal and posting to the ledger any changes that were made at the end of the accounting period. *Closing the ledger* involves transferring the net income (or net loss) for the period from the temporary accounts to the owner's Capital account.

■ The Adjusting Procedure

In Chapter 6 you prepared a worksheet at the end of the accounting cycle. The worksheet included one adjusting entry to the Supplies account for supplies used during the month. Handling the adjustment to Supplies once at the end of the cycle was faster than recording many separate entries every time a piece of paper, paper clip, or pen was used.

To complete the adjusting procedure, adjusting entries must be made in the journal, using the information planned on the worksheet. Once the entries have been journalized, the information can be posted to the accounts and the account balances can be brought up to date.

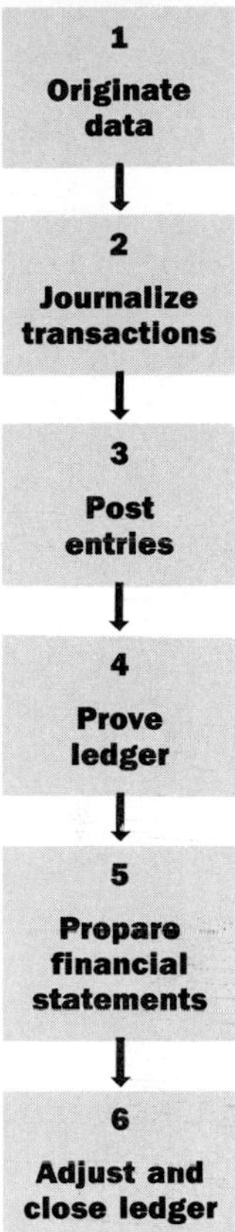

■ Journalizing and Posting the Adjusting Entry

The Adjustments columns for Exercise Plus on October 31 are shown here. Notice that the adjusting entry includes a debit to Supplies Expense for $200. The amount is for all supplies that have been used up during the month of October. The credit is to the asset account Supplies for $200. The credit reduces the Supplies account to the correct balance at the end of the month.

Exercise Plus
Worksheet
For the Month Ended October 31, 19—

	ACCOUNT TITLE	ACCT. NO.	ADJUSTMENTS DEBIT	ADJUSTMENTS CREDIT
1	*Cash*	*101*		
2	*Accts. Rec./Carmen Saldi*	*103*		
3	*Accts. Rec./Talbot Industries*	*104*		
4	*Supplies*	*108*		*200*
5	*Furniture*	*111*		
6	*Exercise Equipment*	*112*		
7	*Accts. Pay./Shone Products*	*201*		
8	*Accts. Pay./XYZ Repairs*	*202*		
9	*Lisa Long, Capital*	*301*		
10	*Income Summary*	*399*		
11	*Sales*	*401*		
12	*Repairs Expense*	*504*		
13	*Salaries Expense*	*505*		
14	*Supplies Expense*	*506*	*200*	
15			*200*	*200*
16				

NOTE: The cents columns have been omitted.

The journal entry showing the adjustments to the Supplies Expense and the Supplies accounts is shown on page 194.

The adjusting entry is posted to the Supplies and Supplies Expense accounts from the journal.

JOURNAL					Page 2
DATE		ACCOUNT TITLE AND EXPLANATION	POST. REF.	DEBIT	CREDIT
19—					
Oct.	31	Supplies Expense	506	200 00	
		Supplies	108		200 00

After posting the adjusting entry, the two accounts involved now show adjusted balances.

Supplies						Account No. 108	
DATE		EXPLANATION	POST. REF.	DEBIT	CREDIT	BALANCE	
						DEBIT	CREDIT
19—							
Oct.	6	Check 5	J1	600 00		600 00	
	31	Adjusting entry	J2		200 00	400 00	

Exercise C on page 204 may be completed at this point.

Supplies Expense						Account No. 506	
DATE		EXPLANATION	POST. REF.	DEBIT	CREDIT	BALANCE	
						DEBIT	CREDIT
19—							
Oct.	31	Adjusting entry	J2	200 00		200 00	

■ The Closing Procedure

In Chapter 4, you learned how to update the owner's equity Capital account and how to close the temporary accounts in a ledger with T accounts. This achieves two purposes.

- The temporary accounts end up with zero balances.
- Due to this procedure, the Capital account contains the owner's investment plus the net income (or net loss) for the accounting period.

The same procedure is followed in closing the ledger with balance ledger account forms. However, the entries must be journalized before the entries are posted to the ledger accounts. Use the worksheet information for your journal entries.

1. *Close all revenue accounts*. Close all revenue accounts in the Credit column of the Income Statement section of the worksheet. (The revenue accounts have numbers in the 400s.) The balances are transferred to the Income Summary account by debiting each revenue account and crediting the Income Summary account for the total of the balances of the revenue accounts.

Sales			401	Income Summary			399
19—		19—				19—	
Oct. 31	3,600	Oct. 31	3,600			Oct. 31	3,600

First closing entry transfers revenue account balances.

2. *Close all expense accounts.* Close all the expense accounts in the Debit column of the Income Statement section of the worksheet. (The expense accounts have numbers in the 500s.) The balances are transferred by debiting the Income Summary account for the total of the expense accounts and crediting each expense account for the account balance.

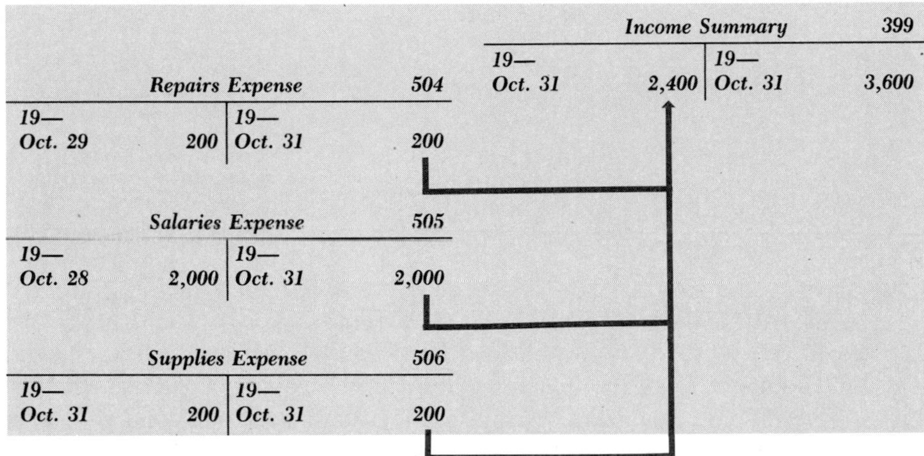

Second closing entry transfers expense account balances.

3. *Close the Income Summary account.* Close the Income Summary account. After the first two closing entries are posted, the balance of the Income Summary account is the net income (or net loss). This amount must agree with the amount on the income statement. The balance of the Income Summary account is transferred to the Capital account. A net income is transferred to the Capital account by debiting the Income Summary account and crediting the Capital account for the amount of the net income. A net loss is transferred to the Capital account by debiting the Capital account and crediting the Income Summary account for the amount of the loss.

Lisa Long, Capital			301	Income Summary			399
		19--		19—		19—	
		Oct. 31	32,000	Oct. 31	2,400	Oct. 31	3,600
		31	1,200	31	1,200		

Third closing entry transfers Income Summary account balance.

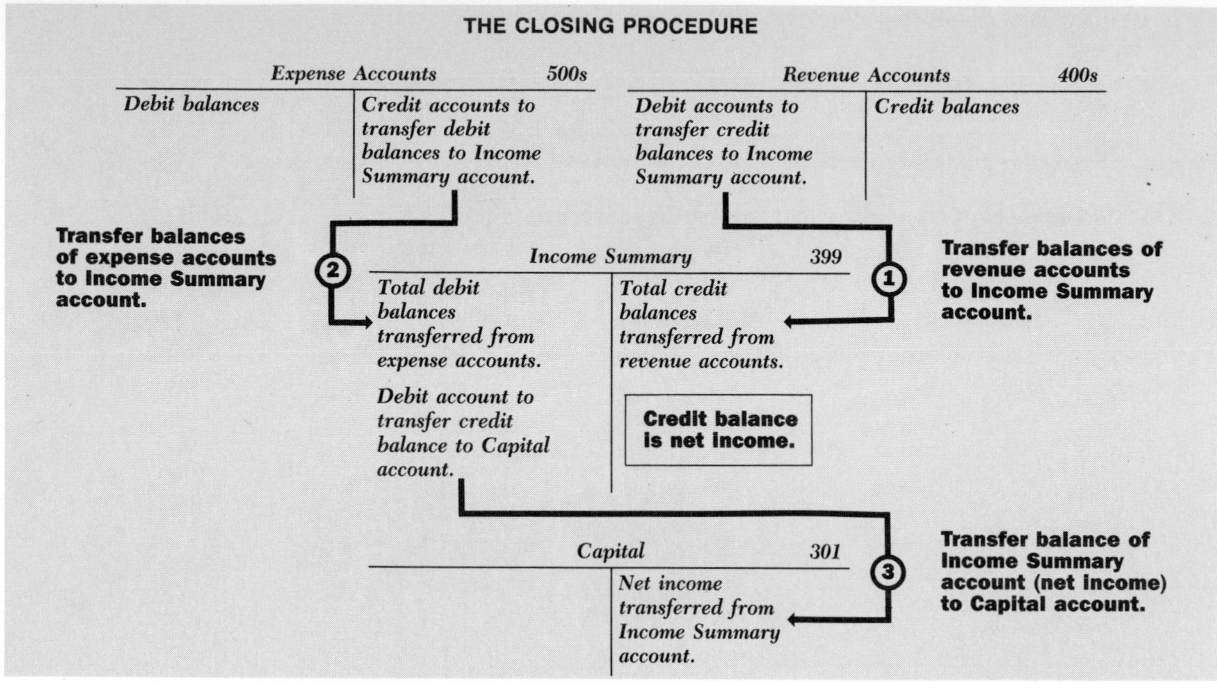
THE CLOSING PROCEDURE
Expense Accounts 500s
Debit balances
Credit accounts to transfer debit balances to Income Summary account.
Revenue Accounts 400s
Debit accounts to transfer credit balances to Income Summary account.
Credit balances
Transfer balances of expense accounts to Income Summary account.
Income Summary 399
Total debit balances transferred from expense accounts.
Total credit balances transferred from revenue accounts.
Debit account to transfer credit balance to Capital account.
Credit balance is net income.
Transfer balances of revenue accounts to Income Summary account.
Capital 301
Net income transferred from Income Summary account.
Transfer balance of Income Summary account (net income) to Capital account.
1
2
3

Journalizing and Posting the Closing Entries

Where is the data obtained for journalizing the closing entries? The balances of the revenue and expense accounts are obtained from the Income Statement columns of the worksheet. The amount of the net income (or net loss) is obtained from the worksheet, where it has been calculated, as illustrated here.

Net income (or net loss) is obtained from the worksheet.

Exercise Plus
Worksheet
For the Month Ended October 31, 19—

	ACCOUNT TITLE	ACCT. NO.	INCOME STATEMENT DEBIT	INCOME STATEMENT CREDIT
11	*Sales*	401		3,600
12	*Repairs Expense*	504	200	
13	*Salaries Expense*	505	2,000	
14	*Supplies Expense*	506	200	
15			2,400	3,600
16				2,400
17	*Net Income*			1,200

NOTE: The cents columns have been omitted.

The Income Summary account balance will be the same as the net income (or net loss).

The procedures for journalizing and posting the closing entries for the revenue, expense, and income summary accounts are discussed below. The closing entries for Exercise Plus are journalized and posted on October 31.

JOURNAL — Page 2

DATE		ACCOUNT TITLE AND EXPLANATION	POST. REF.	DEBIT	CREDIT	
19— Oct.						
	31	Sales	401	3,600 00		①
		Income Summary	399		3,600 00	
		Close revenue account.				
	31	Income Summary	399	2,400 00		
		Repairs Expense	504		200 00	②
		Salaries Expense	505		2,000 00	
		Supplies Expense	506		200 00	
		Close expense accounts.				
	31	Income Summary	399	1,200 00		
		Lisa Long, Capital	301		1,200 00	③
		Transfer net income.				

1. *Closing entries for revenue accounts*. The Sales account is the only source of revenue for Exercise Plus for the accounting period ended October 31, 19—. The data needed for the journal entry to transfer this $3,600 credit balance from the Sales account to the Income Summary account is in the Income Statement columns of the worksheet, which is the source document for this entry.

Sales — **Account No.** *401*

DATE		EXPLANATION	POST. REF.	DEBIT	CREDIT	BALANCE DEBIT	BALANCE CREDIT
19—							
Oct.	26	Invoices 106–110	J1		1,400 00		1,400 00
	27	Invoices 111–112	J1		2,200 00		3,600 00
	31	To Income Summary ...	J2	3,600 00			— 00

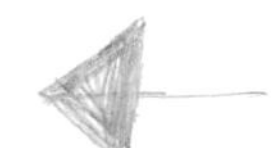

Sales balance is transferred to Income Summary account.

After this closing entry is posted, the Sales account has a zero balance. The total revenue of $3,600 has been transferred to the Income Summary account.

2. *Closing entries for expense accounts*. The three expense accounts of Exercise Plus have debit balances. A compound journal entry is required to transfer the balances of these expense accounts to the Income Summary account. This entry shows a credit to each of the three expense accounts and a debit for the total expenses to the Income Summary account.

This closing entry has reduced the expense account balances to zero and has transferred the total expenses of $2,400 to the Income Summary account. The worksheet is the source of information for this entry.

Repairs Expense **Account No.** *504*

DATE		EXPLANATION	POST. REF.	DEBIT	CREDIT	BALANCE DEBIT	BALANCE CREDIT
19—							
Oct.	29	Invoice 212	J2	200 00		200 00	
	31	To Income Summary	J2		200 00	— 00	

Repairs Expense balance is transferred to Income Summary account.

Salaries Expense **Account No.** *505*

DATE		EXPLANATION	POST. REF.	DEBIT	CREDIT	BALANCE DEBIT	BALANCE CREDIT
19—							
Oct.	28	Check 8	J2	2,000 00		2,000 00	
	31	To Income Summary	J2		2,000 00	— 00	

Salaries Expense balance is transferred to Income Summary account.

Supplies Expense **Account No.** *506*

DATE		EXPLANATION	POST. REF.	DEBIT	CREDIT	BALANCE DEBIT	BALANCE CREDIT
19—							
Oct.	31	Adjusting entry	J2	200 00		200 00	
	31	To Income Summary	J2		200 00	— 00	

Supplies Expense balance is transferred to Income Summary account.

As a result of these entries, the revenue and expense accounts of Exercise Plus are now closed. They have zero balances and are ready to accumulate new revenue and expense data during the next accounting period.

3. *Closing entry for the Income Summary account.* The Income Summary account is a convenient device for closing the revenue and expense accounts. Moreover, it shows the essential facts about the business's revenue and expenses during its accounting period. For example, the Income Summary account for Exercise Plus has a credit of $3,600 and a debit of $2,400 at this point. The account now has a credit balance of $1,200. This amount represents the net income that Exercise Plus earned during the accounting period ended October 31, 19—.

Net income increases owner's equity. The net income is transferred to the Capital account as a credit. This transfer closes the Income Summary account. The worksheet is the source document for this entry.

Income Summary — **Account No.** *399*

DATE		EXPLANATION	POST. REF.	DEBIT	CREDIT	BALANCE DEBIT	BALANCE CREDIT
19—							
Oct.	31	Revenue	J2		3,600 00		3,600 00
	31	Expenses	J2	2,400 00			1,200 00
	31	Net income	J2	1,200 00			— 00

Income Summary balance is transferred to Capital account.

Lisa Long, Capital — **Account No.** *301*

DATE		EXPLANATION	POST. REF.	DEBIT	CREDIT	BALANCE DEBIT	BALANCE CREDIT
19—							
Oct.	1	Opening entry	J1		28,000 00		28,000 00
	12	Remittance Slip RS-105	J1		6,000 00		34,000 00
	21	Check 7	J1	2,000 00			32,000 00
	31	Net income	J2		1,200 00		33,200 00

Capital account balance is identical with the total owner's equity on the balance sheet.

The Lisa Long, Capital account now has a balance of $33,200 ($32,000 + $1,200). The new balance in the Capital account is identical with the total owner's equity on the balance sheet for October 31. This is a result of closing the temporary accounts and transferring the net income into the permanent Capital account.

Exercise Plus
Balance Sheet
October 31, 19—

Owner's Equity		
Lisa Long, Capital	32,000 00	
Net Income	1,200 00	
Total Owner's Equity		33,200 00

Balance in the Capital account is identical with the total owner's equity on the balance sheet.

Two things result from closing Exercise Plus's Income Summary account.

- The Income Summary account has a zero balance.
- The Lisa Long, Capital account contains the net income for the month of October.

If Exercise Plus incurred a net loss, the Income Summary account would have shown a debit balance at the end of the accounting period. A debit balance would be transferred by debiting the Capital account and crediting the Income Summary account. The debit to the Capital account would then decrease the owner's equity by the amount of the net loss. (Remember that the normal balance of the Capital account is a credit balance.)

■ The Accounting Cycle

Making adjusting and closing entries is the sixth step in the accounting cycle. The six steps that have been discussed up to this point are as follows.

Step 1. Record original data on a source document.

Step 2. Record the transactions in a journal.

Step 3. Post the journal entries to the ledger accounts.

Step 4. Prove the equality of the ledger.

Step 5. Prepare an income statement and a balance sheet.

Step 6. Journalize and post the adjusting and closing entries.

Concept: Closing the Ledger

The revenue data and expense data for one accounting period must be clearly distinguished from that of another accounting period.

Exercise D on page 204 may be completed at this point.

■ Preparing a Postclosing Trial Balance

What is the seventh step in the accounting cycle? The seventh step in the accounting cycle is to prove (verify) that the ledger is in balance after all the closing entries have been posted. The *postclosing trial balance* is a proof that the ledger is in balance after all temporary accounts have been closed.

A postclosing trial balance is prepared like a trial balance. It can be prepared as a formal summary or as a quick check using a zero proof.

A formal postclosing trial balance prepared for Exercise Plus at the end of the one-month accounting period on October 31, 19—, is illustrated at the top of the next page. A formal postclosing trial balance is shown so that you can easily see what accounts are included in the proof.

The postclosing trial balance lists only those accounts that have *not* been closed. The accounts remaining open after the ledger has been closed are the permanent accounts. (These are the assets, the liabilities, and the owner's equity Capital account.) The temporary accounts have been closed and are not listed in the postclosing trial balance. (These are the revenue and expense accounts and the Income Summary account.)

Exercise Plus Postclosing Trial Balance October 31, 19—			
ACCOUNT TITLE	ACCT. NO.	DEBIT	CREDIT
Cash	101	12,100 00	
Accts. Rec./Carmen Saldi	103	1,200 00	
Accts. Rec./Talbot Industries	104	2,400 00	
Supplies	108	400 00	
Furniture	111	4,850 00	
Exercise Equipment	112	13,000 00	
Accts. Pay./Shone Products	201		350 00
Accts. Pay./XYZ Repairs	202		400 00
Lisa Long, Capital	301		33,200 00
		33,950 00	33,950 00

Formal postclosing trial balance shows permanent account balances.

Exercise Plus
Postclosing Trial Balance
October 31, 19–

```
      .00T
 12,100.00
  1,200.00
  2,400.00
    400.00
  4,850.00
 13,000.00
    350.00-
    400.00-
 33,200.00-
      .00T
```

Quick postclosing trial balance shows only amounts. Debits are added; credits are subtracted. Zero proof shows ledger is in balance.

The permanent accounts that are in the ledger of Exercise Plus are shown below and on the next page.

Permanent accounts are not closed.

Cash						Account No. 101	
DATE		EXPLANATION	POST. REF.	DEBIT	CREDIT	BALANCE	
						DEBIT	CREDIT
19—							
Oct.	1	Opening entry	J1	10,100 00		10,100 00	
	5	Remittance Slip RS-104	J1	700 00		10,800 00	
	6	Check 5	J1		600 00	10,200 00	
	12	Check 6	J1		1,500 00	8,700 00	
	12	Remittance Slip RS-105	J1	6,000 00		14,700 00	
	21	Check 7	J1		2,000 00	12,700 00	
	26	Invoices 106–110	J1	1,400 00		14,100 00	
	28	Check 8	J2		2,000 00	12,100 00	

Accts. Rec./Carmen Saldi						Account No. 103	
DATE		EXPLANATION	POST. REF.	DEBIT	CREDIT	BALANCE	
						DEBIT	CREDIT
19—							
Oct.	1	Opening entry	J1	700 00		700 00	
	5	Remittance Slip RS-104	J1		700 00	— 00	
	27	Invoice 111	J1	1,200 00		1,200 00	

Permanent accounts are not closed.

Accts. Rec./Talbot Industries **Account No.** *104*

DATE		EXPLANATION	POST. REF.	DEBIT	CREDIT	BALANCE DEBIT	BALANCE CREDIT
19—							
Oct.	1	Opening entry	J1	1,400 00		1,400 00	
	27	Invoice 112	J1	1,000 00		2,400 00	

Supplies **Account No.** *108*

DATE		EXPLANATION	POST. REF.	DEBIT	CREDIT	BALANCE DEBIT	BALANCE CREDIT
19—							
Oct.	6	Check 5	J1	600 00		600 00	
	31	Adjusting entry	J2		200 00	400 00	

Furniture **Account No.** *111*

DATE		EXPLANATION	POST. REF.	DEBIT	CREDIT	BALANCE DEBIT	BALANCE CREDIT
19—							
Oct.	1	Opening entry	J1	4,500 00		4,500 00	
	7	Invoice 9822	J1	700 00		5,200 00	
	8	Credit Mem. CM-67	J1		350 00	4,850 00	

Exercise Equipment **Account No.** *112*

DATE		EXPLANATION	POST. REF.	DEBIT	CREDIT	BALANCE DEBIT	BALANCE CREDIT
19—							
Oct.	1	Opening entry	J1	13,000 00		13,000 00	

Accts. Pay./Shone Products **Account No.** *201*

DATE		EXPLANATION	POST. REF.	DEBIT	CREDIT	BALANCE DEBIT	BALANCE CREDIT
19—							
Oct.	1	Opening entry	J1		1,500 00		1,500 00
	7	Invoice 9822	J1		700 00		2,200 00
	8	Credit Mem. CM-67	J1	350 00			1,850 00
	12	Check 6	J1	1,500 00			350 00

Accts. Pay./XYZ Repairs						Account No. 202	
DATE		EXPLANATION	POST. REF.	DEBIT	CREDIT	BALANCE	
						DEBIT	CREDIT
19—							
Oct.	1	Opening entry	J1		200 00		200 00
	29	Invoice 212	J2		200 00		400 00

Permanent accounts are not closed.

Lisa Long, Capital						Account No. 301	
DATE		EXPLANATION	POST. REF.	DEBIT	CREDIT	BALANCE	
						DEBIT	CREDIT
19—							
Oct.	1	Opening entry	J1		28,000 00		28,000 00
	12	Remittance Slip RS-105	J1		6,000 00		34,000 00
	21	Check 7	J1	2,000 00			32,000 00
	31	Net income	J2		1,200 00		33,200 00

Note that the accounts and the balances listed on the postclosing trial balance for Exercise Plus shown on page 201 now agree completely with the items on the balance sheet of October 31.

As a result of the closing entries, the balance of the Lisa Long, Capital account is now identical with the total owner's equity shown on the following balance sheet.

Exercise Plus
Balance Sheet
October 31, 19--

Assets			
Cash		$12,100.00	
Accounts Receivable:			
Carmen Saldi	$1,200.00		
Talbot Industries	2,400.00	3,600.00	
Supplies		400.00	
Furniture		4,850.00	
Exercise Equipment		13,000.00	
Total Assets			$33,950.00
Liabilities			
Accounts Payable:			
Shone Products		$ 350.00	
XYZ Repairs		400.00	
Total Liabilities			$ 750.00
Owner's Equity			
Lisa Long, Capital		$32,000.00	
Net Income		1,200.00	
Total Owner's Equity			33,200.00
Total Liabilities and Owner's Equity			$33,950.00

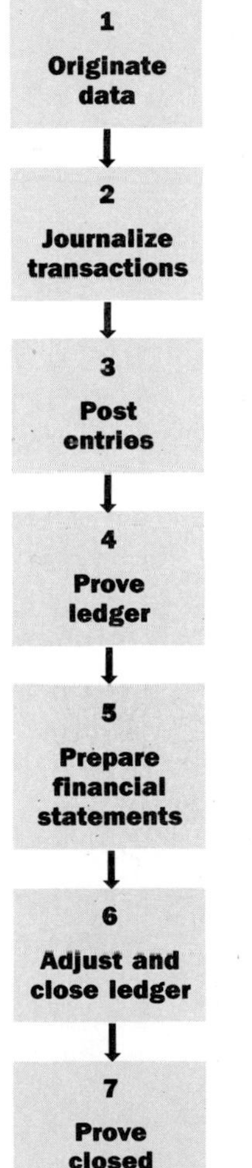

■ The Accounting Cycle

Proving the closed ledger is the seventh step in the accounting cycle. The steps discussed up to this point are as follows.

Step 1. Record original data on a source document.
Step 2. Record the transactions in a journal.
Step 3. Post the journal entries to the ledger accounts.
Step 4. Prove the equality of the ledger.
Step 5. Prepare an income statement and a balance sheet.
Step 6. Journalize and post the adjusting and closing entries.
Step 7. Prove the equality of the closed ledger.

Exercise E on page 205 may be completed at this point.

Concept: Postclosing Trial Balance

The equality of the total debits and the total credits in the ledger should be verified after the ledger has been closed.

TOPIC 2 EXERCISES

EXERCISE C. Answer the following questions about adjusting entries, using the information found on pages 193 to 194.

1. Where is the information found for making the adjusting entry in the journal?
2. Why is the Supplies account being adjusted?
3. Why are some accounts adjusted at the end of the accounting period rather than several times during the accounting period?
4. Why must all changes to the account balances come from the journal?

EXERCISE D. Answer the following questions about closing the revenue and expense accounts. Refer to the text and illustrations on pages 196 to 200.

1. What is the sixth step in the accounting cycle?
2. Which accounts are closed?
3. What does closing an account mean?
4. What is the entry to transfer a net loss amount?
5. What type of balances do revenue and expense accounts have at the beginning of the accounting period?
6. Is the Sales account debited or credited to close the account? Why?
7. Is the Repairs Expense account debited or credited to close it? Why?
8. To which account is the balance of the Repairs Expense account transferred?
9. What does the $2,400 debit in the Income Summary account represent?
10. What does the $3,600 credit in the Income Summary account represent?
11. Why is the Income Summary account debited to close it?
12. What is the October 31 balance of the Capital account after closing?

EXERCISE E. Answer the following questions about the postclosing trial balance prepared for Exercise Plus. Refer to pages 201 to 203.

1. What is the purpose of the postclosing trial balance?
2. Which ledger accounts are not listed on the postclosing trial balance? Why?
3. What does the debit total of the postclosing trial balance represent?
4. What does the credit total of the postclosing trial balance represent?
5. What is the date of the postclosing trial balance?

TOPIC 2 PROBLEMS

TOPIC PROBLEM 3. The worksheet for Inventronics on May 31 is shown here. The financial statements for the business have already been prepared.

a. Journalize and post the adjusting and closing entries for the month ended May 31, 19—.

b. Prepare a postclosing trial balance.

Inventronics
Worksheet
For the Month Ended May 31, 19—

	ACCOUNT TITLE	ACCT. NO.	TRIAL BALANCE		ADJUSTMENTS		ADJUSTED TRIAL BALANCE		INCOME STATEMENT		BALANCE SHEET		
			DEBIT	CREDIT	DEBIT	CREDIT	DEBIT	CREDIT	DEBIT	CREDIT	DEBIT	CREDIT	
1	*Cash*	*101*	*1,915 00*				*1,915 00*				*1,915 00*		1
2	*Accts. Rec./Astral Co.*	*102*	*275 00*				*275 00*				*275 00*		2
3	*Accts. Rec./Linden Inc.*	*103*	*100 00*				*100 00*				*100 00*		3
4	*Supplies*	*104*	*695 00*			*90 00*	*605 00*				*605 00*		4
5	*Truck*	*131*	*4,500 00*				*4,500 00*				*4,500 00*		5
6	*Accts. Pay./Sandy Hays*	*201*		*1,800 00*				*1,800 00*				*1,800 00*	6
7	*W. Dalzell, Capital*	*301*		*2,077 00*				*2,077 00*				*2,077 00*	7
8	*Sales*	*401*		*4,020 00*				*4,020 00*		*4,020 00*			8
9	*Supplies Expense*	*501*	*— 00*		*90 00*		*90 00*		*90 00*				9
10	*Truck Expense*	*502*	*412 00*				*412 00*		*412 00*				10
11			*7,897 00*	*7,897 00*	*90 00*	*90 00*	*7,897 00*	*7,897 00*	*502 00*	*4,020 00*	*7,395 00*	*3,877 00*	11
12										*502 00*			12
13	*Net Income*									*3,518 00*		*3,518 00*	13
14											*7,395 00*	*7,395 00*	14
15													15
16													16

TOPIC PROBLEM 4. Sometimes corrections to accounts are necessary even when it is not the end of the accounting period. Three pieces of information are given and two Accounts Receivable accounts are illustrated at the top of the next page. Apply the procedures for transferring amounts in accounts to correct the errors. Journalize on page 10 and post the entries given on July 31 for Consolidated Accounting Services, Inc. Be sure to post after every entry.

a. A sale for $500 on credit to Euclid Computer Company was incorrectly journalized as a debit to the Inglewood Computer Company.

b. A check for $850 received on account from the Inglewood Computer Company was incorrectly journalized as a credit to Euclid Computer Company.

c. The Lynn Corporation purchased the business of Euclid Computer Company and requested that the balance of $500 be transferred from the Accts. Rec./Euclid Computer Company account to a new account for the Lynn Corporation.

Accts. Rec./Euclid Computer Company — **Account No.** *102*

DATE		EXPLANATION	POST. REF.	DEBIT	CREDIT	BALANCE DEBIT	BALANCE CREDIT
19—							
July	*25*		*J9*		*850 00*		*850 00*

Accts. Rec./Inglewood Computer Company — **Account No.** *103*

DATE		EXPLANATION	POST. REF.	DEBIT	CREDIT	BALANCE DEBIT	BALANCE CREDIT
19—							
July	*7*		*J8*	*850 00*		*850 00*	
	9		*J8*	*500 00*		*1,350 00*	

TOPIC PROBLEM 5. The only accounts for the Jansen Company that still have balances after the closing procedures at the end of the accounting period are listed at the right. Use the accounts and figures given to prepare a post-closing trial balance for December 31. Use appropriate account numbers.

Cash	$3,715
Accts. Rec./George Supply	275
Accts. Rec./Roberts Company	130
Tools	345
Truck	2,500
Accts. Pay./Macon Supply	345
Accts. Pay./Spear Auto	3,330
M. Leskov, Capital	3,290

TOPIC 3

Interpreting Financial Information

What is the eighth step in the accounting cycle? Interpreting (using) accounting information is the last step in the accounting cycle. Remember that the interpretation of accounting information is a process that goes on continuously. It is listed here as the last step in the accounting cycle because all statements are now available for use. You have already studied the preparation of some of these statements. In this section you will study the uses of comparative financial statements. Such statements are used to compare the results of business operations at different times, usually for two successive accounting periods.

Some of the persons who want the information in these financial statements are persons outside of the business. These include creditors, potential investors in the business, bankers, and the state and federal tax departments. Other persons interested in the financial statements are those within the business. These are the managers who are responsible for making decisions within the business.

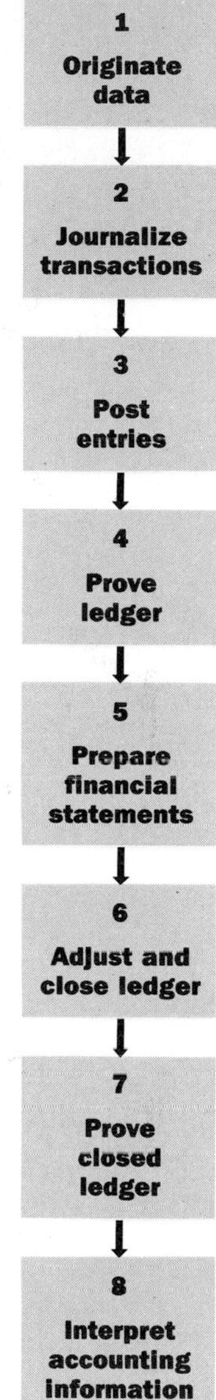

■ A Comparative Income Statement

Frequently, managers want to compare the earnings for two or more accounting periods. If Lisa Long wants to compare the revenues earned and the expenses incurred by Exercise Plus in October with those in September, the easiest way is to prepare a comparative income statement. A **comparative income statement** is an income statement that compares revenue and expense data for two or more accounting periods.

The income statements for the accounting period ended September 30 and the period ended October 31 and a comparative income statement are illustrated on page 208. The most recent income statement data is listed first because it shows the latest data available.

A third section has been added to the income statement. This section shows the increases and decreases in each item reported. Parentheses were placed around each amount that decreased.

Note how a single rule is placed below the Sales amounts and also the Total Expenses in the comparative income statement. This shows that these amounts are separated from those that follow. The net income is computed by subtracting the amount of Total Expenses from the amount of Sales. In some accounting forms there may not be enough space to group accounts in separate columns. The amounts must be placed in one column, as the amounts were in the comparative income statement. When this is done, it is acceptable to place a single rule above a group total and also a single rule under that total.

Now that a comparative income statement has been compiled, it is time for decision making. **Decision making** is the process of selecting a course of action from several alternatives. Thus, interpreting accounting data involves answering two questions.

- *What judgments can be made about the information?* Lisa Long compares the data on the income statements. She sees that total revenue for October ($3,600) is less than the total revenue for September ($6,100). She could interpret this as either a problem or an error. If she is concerned about accuracy, she could use an audit trail to verify the sales amount. The Sales account in the ledger would show the date and the Posting Reference number of each entry posted from the journal. The journal entry gives information to locate the source document. Since sales were less in the second accounting period, she should investigate the reasons.

Exercise Plus
Income Statement
For the Month Ended October 31, 19—

Revenue:		
Sales		3,600 00
Expenses:		
Repairs Expense	200 00	
Salaries Expense	2,000 00	
Supplies Expense	200 00	
Total Expenses		2,400 00
Net Income		1,200 00

Income statement for October.

Exercise Plus
Income Statement
For the Month Ended September 30, 19—

Revenue:		
Sales		6,100 00
Expenses:		
Repairs Expense	200 00	
Salaries Expense	2,900 00	
Total Expenses		3,100 00
Net Income		3,000 00

Income statement for September.

Exercise Plus
Comparative Income Statement
For the Months Ended October 31, 19-- and September 30, 19--

	Month Ended October 31, 19--	Month Ended September 30, 19--	Increase or (Decrease)
Revenue:			
Sales	$3,600.00	$6,100.00	($2,500.00)
Expenses:			
Repairs Expense	$ 200.00	$ 200.00	-0-
Salaries Expense.	2,000.00	2,900.00	($ 900.00)
Supplies Expense.	200.00	-0-	200.00
Total Expenses.	$2,400.00	$3,100.00	($ 700.00)
Net Income.	$1,200.00	$3,000.00	($1,800.00

Comparative income statement shows increases and decreases from one accounting period to the next.

Lisa Long also observes that there was a difference in expenses. Total expenses decreased during the second accounting period. On closer analysis, she observes that Repairs Expense stayed the same. Salaries Expense has decreased, meaning that employees worked fewer hours during the month. The fewer hours could have been caused by having fewer customers. The Supplies Expense account was also added to keep track of the supplies used by the business. Net income for the accounting period ended October 31 decreased $1,800 when compared with the net income of the previous accounting period. The decrease in net income was due to a decrease in revenue and not to an increase in expenses.

■ *What decisions can be made?* Based on her interpretation of data, Lisa Long makes several decisions concerning the future operation of her business. Her major decisions are to increase revenue from services, check on the usage of supplies over the next month, and supervise the work of employees.

Concept: Comparative Financial Statements
The information on the financial statements of a business should be compared at different times, usually for two successive accounting periods.

A Comparative Balance She

How would you compare the financial pos **another?** The financial position of a business by preparing a comparative balance sheet. A **comp** **sheet** is a balance sheet that compares the assets, liabili er's equity on two or more dates.

Suppose Lisa Long wants to compare her owner's equity in E Plus on October 31 with her equity on September 30. She needs reported on balance sheets for those dates.

Exercise Plus
Comparative Balance Sheet
October 31, 19-- and September 30, 19--

	October 31, 19--	September 30, 19--	Increase or (Decrease)
Assets			
Cash	$12,100.00	$10,100.00	$2,000.00
Accounts Receivable	3,600.00	2,100.00	1,500.00
Supplies	400.00	-0-	400.00
Furniture	4,850.00	4,500.00	350.00
Exercise Equipment	13,000.00	13,000.00	-0-
Total Assets	$33,950.00	$29,700.00	$4,250.00
Liabilities			
Accounts Payable	$ 750.00	$ 1,700.00	($ 950.00)
Total Liabilities	$ 750.00	$ 1,700.00	($ 950.00)
Owner's Equity			
Lisa Long, Capital	$32,000.00	$25,000.00	$7,000.00
Net Income	1,200.00	3,000.00	(1,800.00)
Total Owner's Equity	$33,200.00	$28,000.00	$5,200.00
Total Liabilities and Owner's Equity	$33,950.00	$29,700.00	$4,250.00

Comparative balance sheet shows increases and decreases from one date to the next.

A comparative balance sheet for September 30 and October 31 is illustrated above. The most recent balance sheet data is listed first because it shows the latest data available. (You can verify this data by checking the original balance sheets shown on page 100 and page 203.)

What judgments can be made about the information? When Lisa Long compares the balance sheets, she notes that total owner's equity on October 31 was $5,200 higher than total owner's equity on September 30. Her first interpretation is that net income was the cause of the increase in her equity. However, after further analysis, she has a second interpretation which is different than the first. On September 30 her total owner's equity was $28,000. On October 31 it was $33,200. This increase was due to two reasons. The business produced a net income and she made an additional investment in the business. A net income of $3,000 was reported for the accounting period ended September 30, 19—. A net income of only $1,200, however, was reported for the accounting period ended October 31, 19—.

What decisions can be made? Based on this interpretation of data, Lisa Long makes two decisions about the future operation of her business.

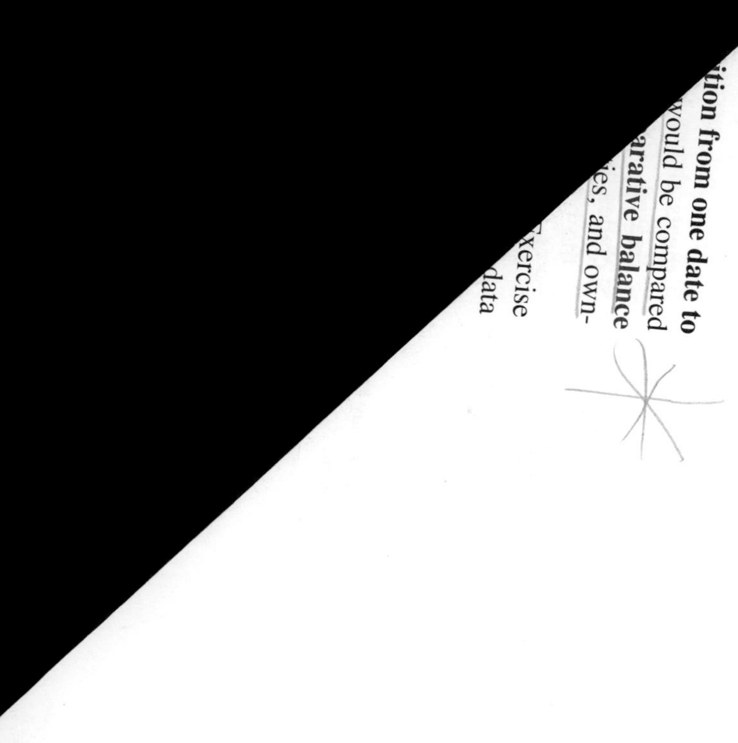

use of the business's resources to in- xample, further study of the balance sets increased and total liabilities de- resources. As a result, Lisa Long con- sources might improve the operation of

one additional cash investments until she formation for the next accounting period

pretation of information influences deci- of an accounting cycle. Interpretation of ntinuous process.

ycle

repeated each accounting period? The ated each accounting period.

data on a source document.

isactions in a journal.

l entries to the ledger accounts.

ility of the ledger.

ome statement and a balance sheet.

l post the adjusting and closing entries.

ality of the closed ledger.

Step 8. Interpret the accounting information.

All businesses follow the same steps of the accounting cycle to process their accounting data. However, they may use different methods, or accounting systems, to process their data. An **accounting system** is a specific method used to process data through the accounting cycle. The type of system used depends on the nature and size of the business and on the types of information needed.

■ Output

In the accounting cycle, the **input data** comes from transactions recorded on source documents (sales slips, purchase invoices, and so on). The input data is entered into the accounting system by journalizing the transactions. The **output data** is information about the results of business operations. This information is provided through such reports as the trial balance, the income statement, the balance sheet, and the postclosing trial balance. An accounting system takes input data from transactions. It then processes the data in different ways and by different means, such as the worksheet. Finally, an accounting system provides the desired output data to be used in making decisions.

The relationship between the data processing cycle and the accounting cycle is shown on the next page.

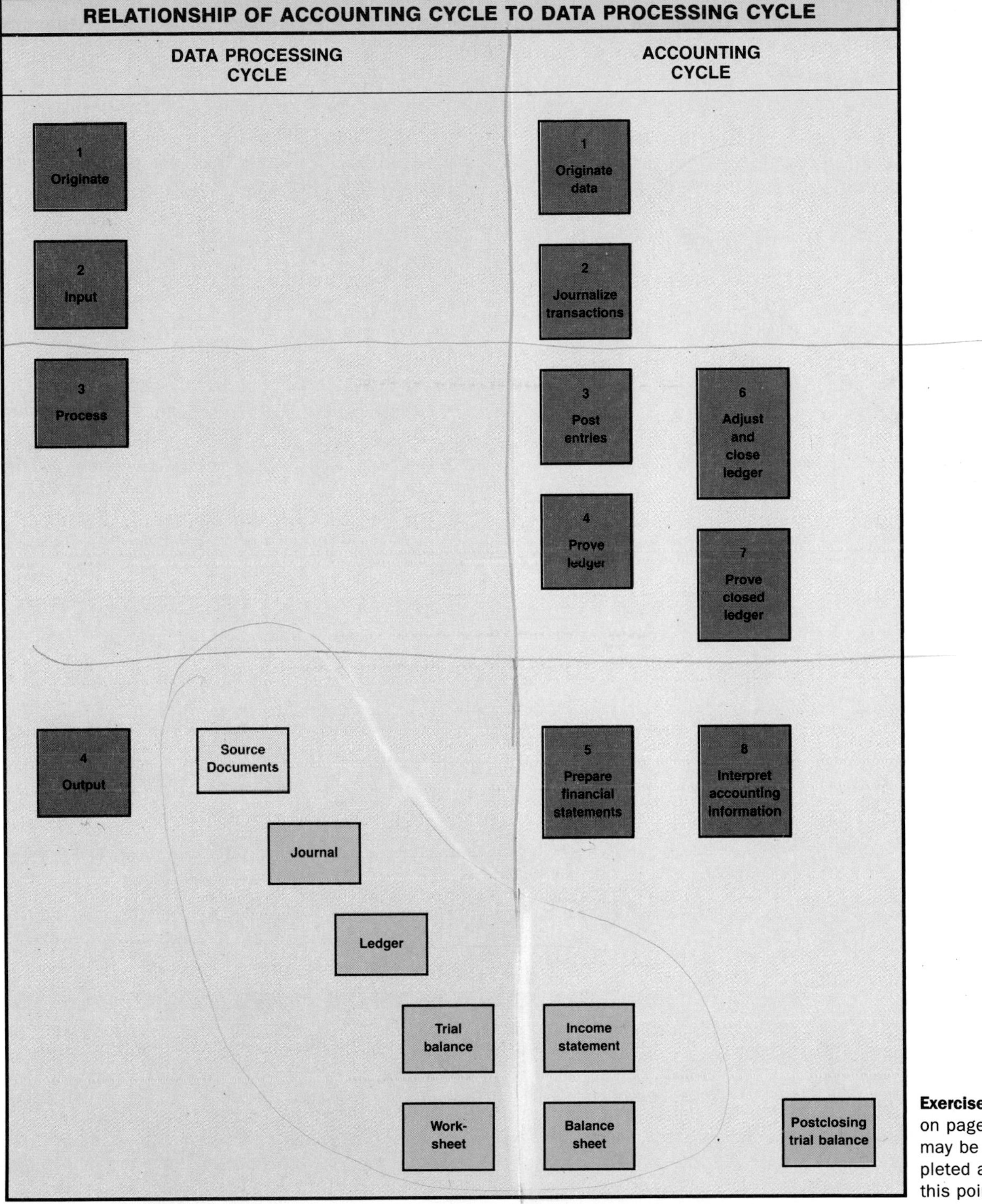

Exercise G on page 212 may be completed at this point.

Collecting data to be processed.

Changing and/or storing data to give the desired results.

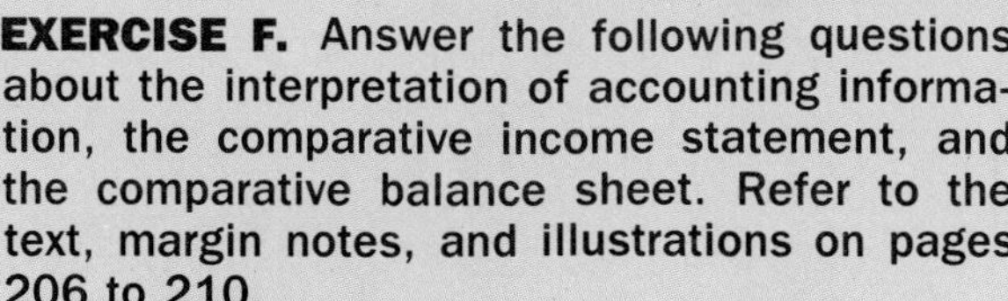

TOPIC 3 EXERCISES

EXERCISE F. Answer the following questions about the interpretation of accounting information, the comparative income statement, and the comparative balance sheet. Refer to the text, margin notes, and illustrations on pages 206 to 210.

1. Why is the interpretation of accounting information a continuous process?
2. Is the latest accounting period listed first on the comparative income statement? Why?
3. Is similar information shown on the comparative income statement and on the individual income statement? Explain.
4. What is the difference in net income between the accounting period ended October 31 and the period ended September 30?
5. What is the increase or decrease for each expense?
6. What is your opinion of the results of operations for the two accounting periods?
7. Is the latest accounting period listed first on the comparative balance sheet? Why?
8. Is similar information shown on the comparative balance sheet and on the individual balance sheets? Explain.
9. Why is this form of balance sheet more helpful to managers than the regular report form?
10. Did the amount of cash increase or decrease?
11. Did the owner's equity improve during this accounting period? Explain why or why not.

EXERCISE G. Answer the following questions on the accounting cycle and data processing cycle. Refer to the text and illustration on pages 210 and 211.

1. Are the eight steps in the accounting cycle repeated each accounting period?
2. What is the source of the input data?
3. Give four examples of output data.
4. Give four ways data is processed during the accounting cycle.
5. During which step is data put into the accounting cycle?

TOPIC 3 PROBLEMS

TOPIC PROBLEM 6. A partially completed comparative income statement for Alex's Shoe Repair is illustrated at the top of the next page. It shows the revenue, expenses, and net income for two accounting periods.

a. Complete the Increase or (Decrease) section of the comparative income statement.
b. What are the major factors that caused an increase in net income between the two accounting periods?

Alex's Shoe Repair
Comparative Income Statement
For the Months Ended April 30, 19— and March 31, 19—

	APRIL 30, 19—		MARCH 31, 19—		INCREASE OR (DECREASE)	
Revenue:						
Sales	60,000	00	55,000	00		
Expenses:						
Rent Expense	900	00	900	00		
Salaries Expense	26,000	00	28,000	00		
Supplies Expense	14,000	00	15,000	00		
Total Expenses	40,900	00	43,900	00		
Net Income	19,100	00	11,100	00		

TOPIC PROBLEM 7. A comparative balance sheet for the Erie Plumbing Company is illustrated below.

a. Complete the Increase or (Decrease) section of the comparative balance sheet.

b. What major factors caused a decrease in owner's equity?

c. Give an interpretation of what might have affected cash items.

Erie Plumbing Company
Comparative Balance Sheet
December 31, 19— and November 30, 19—

	DECEMBER 31, 19—		NOVEMBER 30, 19—		INCREASE OR (DECREASE)	
Assets						
Cash	2,200	00	3,500	00		
Accounts Receivable	275	00	175	00		
Supplies	1,020	00	1,100	00		
Equipment	4,900	00	5,500	00		
Truck	70,000	00	70,000	00		
Total Assets	78,395	00	80,275	00		
Liabilities						
Loans Payable	4,100	00	4,400	00		
Accounts Payable	1,775	00	1,625	00		
Total Liabilities	5,875	00	6,025	00		
Owner's Equity						
Gordon Howe, Capital	65,000	00	67,000	00		
Net Income	7,520	00	7,250	00		
Total Owner's Equity	72,520	00	74,250	00		
Total Liabilities and Owner's Equity	78,395	00	80,275	00		

TOPIC 4

Financial Statements for Partnerships and Corporations

What are the major forms of business ownership? The three major forms of business ownership are the single proprietorship, the partnership, and the corporation. As you learned in Chapter 1, a single proprietorship is owned by one person. All other forms of business ownership involve two or more persons. The form of ownership determines such things as how the net income is divided, who makes management decisions, and who is liable for the debts of the business.

Single Proprietorships

The simplest form of business ownership to organize and operate is a single proprietorship, or sole proprietorship. This is the most common form of ownership and is found in businesses such as small retail shops, service stations, shoe repair shops, and beauty salons. A **single proprietorship** is a business owned by one person.

A single proprietorship is owned by one person.

This form of business ownership has several advantages.

Advantages of a Single Proprietorship
- Simple to organize
- Owner makes all decisions
- Owner claims all profits
- Maximum personal incentive

- *Simple to organize*. A single proprietorship is simple to organize. Only one owner is involved.
- *Owner makes all decisions*. The owner is the only one in control and makes all the management decisions.
- *Owner claims all profits*. If the business is successful, the owner enjoys all the profits.
- *Maximum personal incentive*. The owner feels a strong need to be successful. If the business is successful, the owner gets all the profits. But many businesses are not successful. If a business fails, the owner suffers all the losses.

The single proprietorship form of ownership does have disadvantages. Among them are these.

Disadvantages of a Single Proprietorship
- Unlimited liability
- Limited resources
- Limited life
- Limited talent

- *Unlimited liability*. The owner has unlimited liability. **Unlimited liability** means that the owner is liable for all the debts of the business. If the business cannot pay its debts, the personal property of the owner (such as a house) can be legally taken to pay them.
- *Limited resources*. The amount of resources that the owner can raise is limited. Additional cash, for example, is usually limited to the amount of the owner's personal savings and to the amount that can be borrowed from other sources, including the owner's bank, friends, and relatives.
- *Limited life*. A single proprietorship has a limited life. **Limited life** means that the legal life of the business ends when the owner dies or withdraws from the business.
- *Limited talent*. The success or failure of the business depends mainly on the talents of one person, the owner.

Financial Statements for Single Proprietorships

Exercise Plus is a single proprietorship owned by Lisa Long. The total net income shown on the income statement is claimed by the owner. If there is a net loss, the owner suffers the entire loss.

Exercise Plus
Income Statement
For the Month Ended October 31, 19—

Revenue:		
Sales		3,600 00
Expenses:		
Repairs Expense	200 00	
Salaries Expense	2,000 00	
Supplies Expense	200 00	
Total Expenses		2,400 00
Net Income		1,200 00

Income statement for a single proprietorship. Owner claims all net income.

The balance sheet for a single proprietorship is illustrated here.

Exercise Plus
Balance Sheet
October 31, 19—

Assets			
Cash		12,100 00	
Accounts Receivable:			
Carmen Saldi	*$1,200.00*		
Talbot Industries	*2,400.00*	3,600 00	
Supplies		400 00	
Furniture		4,850 00	
Exercise Equipment		13,000 00	
Total Assets			33,950 00
Liabilities			
Accounts Payable:			
Shone Products		350 00	
XYZ Repairs		400 00	
Total Liabilities			750 00
Owner's Equity			
Lisa Long, Capital		32,000 00	
Net Income		1,200 00	
Total Owner's Equity			33,200 00
Total Liabilities and Owner's Equity			33,950 00

Balance sheet for a single proprietorship. Owner claims all net income.

The net income from the income statement is added to the owner's equity. Some of the disadvantages of the single proprietorship, however, can be seen on the balance sheet.

- The owner is liable for the liabilities of the business if it cannot pay its debts.
- The assets of the business are mainly limited by what the owner can raise.
- If the owner dies or withdraws from the business, the business ends.
- The success or failure of the business depends mainly on one person—the owner.

Exercise H on page 222 may be completed at this point.

Partnerships

A partnership is owned by two or more persons.

How does the ownership of a partnership differ from a single proprietorship? A **partnership** is a business owned by two or more persons. In a partnership, ownership is divided between two or more persons who agree to share their property and skills to start and operate a business. Each owner is called a *partner*.

Advantages of a Partnership
- Simple to organize
- Pooling of talents and skills
- Pooled resources
- Better credit rating
- High degree of personal incentive

Among the advantages of partnerships are these.

- *Simple to organize*. A partnership, like a single proprietorship, is simple to organize. A partnership agreement is made to show the amount of money and skill each partner will contribute, what responsibilities each will have, and how the profits and losses of the business will be divided. A **partnership agreement** is a legal agreement expressing the terms and conditions for running a partnership.
- *Pooling of talents and skills*. The talents and skills of several owners are shared. Each owner contributes his or her specialty. Thus, there is more than one person available to make decisions.
- *Resources are pooled*. Its owners can make a greater investment by pooling their property.
- *Better credit rating*. Credit is easier to get because the debt may be collected from any or all of the partners.
- *High degree of personal incentive*. Since the owners enjoy all the profits and suffer all the losses, they have a strong desire to be successful.

Disadvantages of a Partnership
- Unlimited liability
- Limited resources
- Limited life
- Divided authority

The partnership form of business also has several disadvantages. Among them are these.

- *Unlimited liability*. Each partner has unlimited liability for the debts of the business. Thus, a partner's personal property can be legally taken to pay these debts. In addition, one partner can be held fully responsible for all the business debts if the other partners cannot pay their shares.
- *Limited resources*. Even with several partners, the amount of money available is usually limited to what the partners can raise.

- *Limited life.* A partnership has limited life. The partnership is legally ended if one partner dies or withdraws from the business or if new partners are added.
- *Divided authority.* The authority in making decisions is divided among the partners. Thus, disagreements between the partners can result.

Financial Statements for Partnerships

The accounts used for a partnership are the same as in a single proprietorship, except the equity accounts. In a single proprietorship, only one Capital account is required. In a partnership, a separate Capital account is used for each partner.

Income Statement The income statement for a partnership is the same as the one for a single proprietorship, except in the Net Income (or Net Loss) section. It shows how the net income (or net loss) is distributed to the partners. For example, assume that Exercise Plus is a partnership owned by Lisa Long and George Steele. Assume also that the net income is shared equally by the partners. The income statement would show the net income of $1,200 being shared as in the following illustration.

Exercise Plus
Income Statement
For the Month Ended October 31, 19—

Revenue:				
Sales			3,600	00
Expenses:				
Repairs Expense	200	00		
Salaries Expense	2,000	00		
Supplies Expense	200	00		
Total Expenses			2,400	00
Net Income			1,200	00
Distribution of Net Income:				
Lisa Long	600	00		
George Steele	600	00		
Net Income Allocated			1,200	00

Income statement for a partnership. Distribution of net income is shown.

Balance Sheet The balance sheet for a partnership is the same as the balance sheet for a single proprietorship, except for the Partners' Equity section. The balance sheet for the partnership that is illustrated at the top of the next page shows the financial interest of each partner.

Exercise Plus Balance Sheet October 31, 19—			
Assets			
Cash		12,100 00	
Accounts Receivable:			
Carmen Saldi	$1,200.00		
Talbot Industries	2,400.00	3,600 00	
Supplies		400 00	
Furniture		4,850 00	
Office Equipment		13,000 00	
Total Assets			33,950 00
Liabilities			
Accounts Payable:			
Shone Products		350 00	
XYZ Repairs		400 00	
Total Liabilities			750 00
Partners' Equity			
Lisa Long:			
Capital	$16,000.00		
Net Income	600.00	16,600 00	
George Steele:			
Capital	$16,000.00		
Net Income	600.00	16,600 00	
Total Partners' Equity			33,200 00
Total Liabilities and Partners' Equity			33,950 00

Balance sheet for a partnership. Partners' equity section shows the equity for each partner.

Exercise I on pages 222 and 223 may be completed at this point.

Corporations

How does a corporation differ from single proprietorships and partnerships? A **corporation** is a business chartered under state law and owned by stockholders. A corporation may be owned by many people. It has its own name, in which it can buy, own, and sell property; make contracts; borrow money; and take court action. There are far fewer corporations than single proprietorships and partnerships combined. But corporations employ more employees than the other two, and they conduct the majority of the nation's business.

A corporation is usually owned by three or more persons.

Every corporation must be chartered under state law. A charter contains the terms and conditions for running a corporation. The corporation is supervised by a board of directors. The **board of directors** is the governing body of the corporation elected by the stockholders. The **stockholders**, or *shareholders*, are the owners of a corporation. A stockholder has one vote for each share of stock owned. The board of directors appoints officers to manage the corporation. A corporation holds at least one stockholders' meeting each year.

The corporation form of ownership has several advantages.

Advantages of a Corporation
- Ease of transferring ownership
- Continuous life
- Limited liability
- More resources
- Professional management

- *Ease of transferring ownership*. The ownership of a corporation is easily transferred. Each stockholder receives a stock certificate as evidence of ownership. This certificate is legally transferable from one person to another.
- *Continuous life*. A corporation has continuous life. **Continuous life** means that the life of the corporation does not end when stock is sold. The corporation remains intact no matter how often ownership of the stock changes.
- *Limited liability*. Stockholders have only limited liability. **Limited liability** limits the owner's liability for the debts of the business to the amount invested. Stockholders are not personally liable for the debts of the corporation. Thus, a stockholder's personal property cannot be taken for these debts.
- *More resources*. Corporations are able to raise large amounts of money by selling stock to many people.
- *Professional management*. Corporations do not have to depend on the talents of their owners. The officers are usually skilled professional managers.

The corporation form of ownership also has disadvantages.

Disadvantages of a Corporation
- Complicated and costly to organize
- More restrictions and regulations
- Double taxation

- *Complicated and costly to organize*. A corporation is more complicated and more costly to start.
- *More restrictions and regulations*. Many restrictions and regulations are placed upon it by state and federal laws.
- *Double taxation*. There is double taxation on a corporation's net income. A corporation pays an income tax on its net income. Then it distributes part of the net income to the stockholders as dividends. A **dividend** is a distribution of earnings to stockholders. Another tax must then be paid by the stockholders, who must declare the dividends as part of their personal income.

Financial Statements for Corporations

The major difference between the accounts for a corporation and a single proprietorship or a partnership is in the equity accounts. A Capital Stock account and a Retained Earnings account are used in a corporation. A **Capital Stock account** is an equity account used to show the stockholders' investment. A **Retained Earnings account** is an equity account used to show the net income kept by the corporation.

For a corporation, there is also a difference in the liability accounts. Single proprietorships and partnerships do not pay federal income taxes. The net income for the business is the owner's or partners' personal income. A corporation, however, must pay federal income

taxes. Thus, a corporation must have a liability account for the income taxes payable. The following illustration shows how the income taxes payable would appear in the Liabilities section of the balance sheet if Exercise Plus were a corporation.

Liabilities			
Accounts Payable:			
Shone Products	*$350.00*		
XYZ Repairs........................	*400.00*	750 00	
Income Taxes Payable		205 00	
Total Liabilities			955 00

A corporation that sells stock to the public must publish its financial statements for outsiders at least once a year.

■ Income Statement Some of the key characteristics of an income statement for a corporation are as follows.

1. A corporation usually includes the word "Corporation" or "Incorporated" as the last word of its name. (These words may be abbreviated as "Corp." or "Inc.") This reminds outsiders that the stockholders have limited liability and that the business is a legal entity. It has its own name and address, its own resources, its own continuous life, and the right to take court action. The corporation—not its owners—is responsible for its actions.

2. A corporation must pay income taxes on its net income. The amount of taxes owed is not known until the net income is computed on the income statement. Thus, the income taxes are not generally shown in the Expenses section of the income statement.

(1) → *Exercise Plus, Inc.*
Income Statement
For the Month Ended October 31, 19—

Revenue:		
Sales		3,600 00
Expenses:		
Repairs Expense	200 00	
Salaries Expense	2,000 00	
Supplies Expense	200 00	
Total Expenses		2,400 00
Net Income Before Income Taxes		1,200 00
(2) → *Provision for Income Taxes*		205 00
(3) → *Net Income After Income Taxes*		995 00

Income statement for a corporation. Provision for income taxes is shown.

Instead, income taxes are generally listed in the Net Income section. The amount is shown as a "Provision for Income Taxes" and is subtracted from the net income. The net income after income taxes is the amount carried forward to the balance sheet. The income statement on the previous page illustrates how income taxes would appear if Exercise Plus were a corporation. The rate of income taxes changes based on the total net income before taxes.

3. The net income in a single proprietorship or partnership is added directly to the owner's equity or partners' equity on the balance sheet. A corporation may or may not declare a dividend to the stockholders. The part of the net income that is not distributed to the owners is called **retained earnings**. For simplicity, we will assume that all the net income will be retained by the corporation. The retained earnings will be used to help the business grow.

■ **Balance Sheet** There are several differences between the balance sheet for a corporation and one for a single proprietorship or a partnership. These are illustrated below and discussed on the next page.

Exercise Plus, Inc.
Balance Sheet
October 31, 19—

Assets						
Cash		12,100	00			
Accounts Receivable:						
Carmen Saldi	*$1,200.00*					
Talbot Industries	*2,400.00*	3,600	00			
Supplies		400	00			
Furniture		4,850	00			
Exercise Equipment		13,000	00			
Total Assets				33,950	00	
Liabilities						
Accounts Payable:						
Shone Products	*$350.00*					
XYZ Repairs	*400.00*	750	00			
Income Taxes Payable		205	00			← ①
Total Liabilities				955	00	
Stockholders' Equity						
Capital Stock		32,000	00			← ②
Retained Earnings		995	00			← ③
Total Stockholders' Equity				32,995	00	
Total Liabilities and Stockholders' Equity				33,950	00	

Balance sheet for a corporation. Liability for income taxes is shown.

1. The Liabilities section of a balance sheet for a corporation shows the income taxes to be paid.
2. The Equity section of a balance sheet for a corporation shows the capital stock of $32,000. This capital stock is considered permanent capital. When one shareholder sells his or her shares to another, no change occurs on the balance sheet. Only the name of the owner of the shares changes.
3. The Retained Earnings account appears as the second equity item on the balance sheet. This amount represents the net income not distributed to the shareholders.

Concept: Reporting Net Income

An income statement reports the net income. When appropriate, it should also show the net income after income taxes and how the net income is distributed.

Concept: Reporting Equity

A balance sheet reports the total equity. When appropriate, it should also show how the equity is distributed and should separate the permanent investments from the retained earnings.

Exercise J on page 223 may be completed at this point.

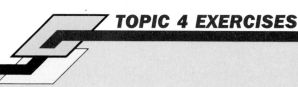

TOPIC 4 EXERCISES

EXERCISE H. Answer the following questions. Refer to the income statement and balance sheet for Exercise Plus on page 215.

1. How much of the net income is claimed by Lisa Long?
2. Suppose for some reason Exercise Plus could not pay its liabilities. For how much would Lisa Long have to pay from her personal property?
3. Suppose Lisa Long cannot borrow any money. How can she get more cash for the business?
4. Suppose the business had a net loss of $1,200 instead of a net income. How much of the net loss would Lisa Long suffer?

EXERCISE I. Answer the following questions about partnerships. Refer to the text and financial statements for a partnership on pages 216 to 218.

1. What is the accounting period?
2. What amount of the net income was allocated to George Steele?

3. What is the total partners' equity?
4. What is the total net income shown on the balance sheet for the partnership?
5. If Exercise Plus cannot pay its debts, who would be responsible for paying them?
6. Suppose that Exercise Plus cannot pay its debts and that Lisa Long cannot pay her share. How much of the $750 would George Steele be liable for?
7. Suppose George Steele decided to sell his share of the business. Would the partnership still be in existence? Explain.
8. How could the partnership raise more cash without borrowing it?
9. What advantages are there to Lisa Long's being in a partnership?
10. What disadvantages are there to Lisa Long's being in a partnership?

EXERCISE J. Answer the following questions about the financial statements for a corporation. Refer to the financial statements on pages 220 and 221.

1. How much money is owed by the corporation to the federal government? To the creditors? What are the total liabilities?
2. Are the liabilities of the corporation greater than the liabilities of the partnership? Why or why not?
3. What is the total net income of the corporation before taxes? After taxes?
4. How much money is the corporation keeping from its earnings (net income)?
5. What is the amount invested by the owners of the corporation? By the owners of the partnership?
6. What are the total assets of the corporation?
7. If the corporation cannot pay its debts, are the stockholders personally liable? Explain why or why not.
8. If the corporation wants to raise more cash, how can it do so without borrowing?

TOPIC 4 PROBLEMS

TOPIC PROBLEM 8. Use a form similar to the one below. List the main advantages and disadvantages for each form of business ownership given in the column headings of the form.

Single Proprietorship	Partnership	Corporation
Advantages: *EX.:* Simple to organize	Simple to organize	Limited liability of stockholders

TOPIC PROBLEM 9. Norman Isaacs worked for a number of years in a ceramics factory. He learned a great deal about the business during that time. After Isaacs had gained enough experience, he left the factory and started his own ceramics company. He invested his savings to start the business.

The financial information for Norman Isaac's firm at the end of its first year in business is listed on the table below.

Complete the equity section of the balance sheet for each of the situations listed at the right.

a. A single proprietorship owned by Norman Isaacs.

b. A partnership owned by Norman Isaacs and Joyce Lane. Assume that Norman Isaacs formed an equal partnership with Joyce Lane, and that the two partners agreed that the net income (or net loss, if any) would be distributed evenly between them.

c. A corporation. Assume that Norman Isaacs had formed a corporation and that the company must pay a corporate income tax of $1,518 on its net income for the year.

Cash	$ 6,000
Accts. Rec./Hall's Crafts	3,500
Accts. Rec./Brook's Galleries	2,350
Equipment	24,000
Accts. Pay./Creative Clay Company	150
Accts. Pay./Gomez Inc.	80
Capital	23,000
Net Income Before Taxes	12,620

TOPIC PROBLEM 10. The trial balance for the law firm of Gold and Logan as of July 31, 19—, is given below. The firm is a partnership, and the net income is divided equally between the two partners.

Use the data that is presented in the trial balance to complete the activities that are listed at the right.

a. Prepare an income statement for the month ended July 31.

b. Prepare a balance sheet in report form for July 31.

Gold and Logan
Trial Balance
July 31, 19—

ACCOUNT TITLE	ACCT. NO.	DEBIT	CREDIT
Cash	*101*	*11,500 00*	
Furniture	*111*	*2,700 00*	
Accts. Pay./Scott Furniture	*211*		*950 00*
Nathan Gold, Capital	*301*		*4,600 00*
Joan Logan, Capital	*302*		*4,600 00*
Fees	*401*		*5,025 00*
Rent Expense	*511*	*650 00*	
Travel Expense	*531*	*325 00*	
		15,175 00	*15,175 00*

TOPIC PROBLEM 11. From the data in the following trial balance, prepare (a) an income statement for the year ended December 31 and (b) a balance sheet in account form for December 31 for the Acme Landscape Corporation. Assume the provision for income taxes is $3,620.

Acme Landscape Corporation
Trial Balance
December 31, 19—

ACCOUNT TITLE	ACCT. NO.	DEBIT	CREDIT
Cash	101	18,000 00	
Accts. Rec./Northside Hospital	102	5,000 00	
Landscape Equipment	111	50,000 00	
Office Equipment	112	2,500 00	
Accts. Pay./Paris Nursery Company	201		7,000 00
Capital Stock	301		42,845 00
Sales	401		56,415 00
Maintenance Expense	501	9,870 00	
Miscellaneous Expense	502	690 00	
Salaries Expense	503	20,200 00	
		106,260 00	106,260 00

CHAPTER SUMMARY

Chapter 7 covers the final steps in the accounting cycle for a service business.

At the end of the accounting period after the entries for the period have been recorded and posted, a worksheet is prepared. This summarizes all the information needed for the remainder of the accounting cycle. The special Income Statement and Balance Sheet columns provide data to complete the financial statements. Adjusting and closing entries are also gathered on the worksheet. From there they can be recorded in the journal and posted to the ledger accounts.

The last step in the accounting cycle is to interpret all the accounting information compiled during the accounting period. Although interpretation is listed as the final step, it is carried out continually.

The three major forms of business ownership are the single proprietorship, the partnership, and the corporation. The form of ownership affects the way information is presented on the financial statements for a business.

THE LANGUAGE OF BUSINESS

Here are some terms that make up the language of business. Do you know the meaning of each?

account form balance sheet
report form balance sheet
comparative income statement
decision making
comparative balance sheet
accounting system
input data
output data
single proprietorship
unlimited liability
limited life
partnership
partnership agreement
corporation
board of directors
stockholders
continuous life
limited liability
dividend
Capital Stock account
Retained Earnings account
retained earnings

REVIEW QUESTIONS

1. Describe how the worksheet is prepared. What types of information are used from the worksheet in completing the end-of-the-accounting-period activities?
2. C & R Auto Wrecking had cash receipts of $50,000 and made cash payments of $37,000 during March. Can you assume the net income for the month was $13,000? Explain.
3. The Bell Company buys a truck for $2,500. The company believes it is worth $3,500. What amount will be on the balance sheet? Why?
4. What entries are needed to close the tempo-

rary owner's equity accounts at the end of the accounting period? What accounts are not affected by closing entries?

5. Why is an Income Summary account used?

6. Give two reasons for making closing entries.

7. On what statement would you find the amounts that appear on the postclosing trial balance? Why?

8. What is the purpose of comparative financial statements?

9. Describe the differences in the preparation of the income statements for a single proprietorship, a partnership, and a corporation.

10. Describe the differences in the preparation of the balance sheets for a single proprietorship, a partnership, and a corporation.

CHAPTER PROBLEMS

Problems for Chapter 7 are given below. Write your answers to the problems on separate sheets of paper unless you are using the workbook for this textbook. If you are using the workbook, do the problems in the space provided there.

CHAPTER PROBLEM 7-1. Using the worksheet prepared in Chapter Problem 6-1 on page 183, do the following for the Metro Copy Center.

a. Complete an income statement and a report form balance sheet.

b. Journalize and post the adjusting and closing entries.

c. Assist the owner and manager in decision-making activities by (1) estimating the supplies that will be used during the month of November, (2) estimating how much it will cost to pay off all of the accounts payable, and (3) estimating how much money will be received from the accounts receivable.

CHAPTER PROBLEM 7-2. Using the worksheet prepared in Chapter Problem 6-2 on page 183, do the following for Yvette's Veterinary Clinic.

a. Complete the income statement and a report form balance sheet.

b. Journalize and post the adjusting and closing entries.

c. Prepare the postclosing trial balance.

d. Assist the owner and manager in decision-making activities by (1) estimating the supplies that will be used during the month of June, (2) estimating how much it will cost to pay off all of the accounts payable, and (3) estimating how much money will be received from accounts receivable.

SUPPLEMENTAL CHAPTER PROBLEM 7-3. If you are using the workbook for Part 1, do Supplemental Chapter Problem 7-3 in the space provided there.

Comparative Financial Statements. By looking at photographs of a person taken over a period of time, you can see changes in the person's appearance. The same is true of a business. The income statement and the balance sheet are financial pictures of a business. The income statement can be combined into one statement covering two or more accounting periods. This statement is called a comparative income statement. Business managers study such statements carefully to determine (1) whether sales are increasing or decreasing, (2) whether expenses are increasing faster than sales, (3) which expense items are increasing, (4) the relationship between the amount spent for an expense and the revenue received, and (5) whether increased sales are resulting in increased net income.

The balance sheet, like the income statement, can be combined into one statement covering two or more accounting periods. By examining several consecutive balance sheets, management is able to note changes and trends.

CASE 7M-1. A comparative income statement prepared for Martin Travel Agency is illustrated below. It contains data for three consecutive accounting periods, which cover three quarters of the year.

Martin Travel Agency
Comparative Income Statement
For the Quarters Ended September 30, June 30, and March 31, 19—

	JULY, AUG., SEPT. (3rd QUARTER)		APR., MAY, JUNE (2nd QUARTER)		JAN., FEB., MAR. (1st QUARTER)	
Revenue:						
Sales		*75,000*		*64,400*		*60,000*
Expenses:						
Advertising Expense	*6,100*		*3,100*		*2,200*	
Miscellaneous Expense	*550*		*500*		*400*	
Office Expense	*7,500*		*6,000*		*5,500*	
Rental of Building	*900*		*900*		*900*	
Rental of Machines	*1,500*		*1,500*		*1,500*	
Salaries Expense	*29,500*		*29,300*		*28,500*	
Travel Expense	*3,900*		*7,400*		*7,000*	
Total Expenses		*49,950*		*48,700*		*46,000*
Net Income		*25,050*		*15,700*		*14,000*

a. The net income has shown a steady increase. What is the main reason for this increase?

b. On July 1, the management decided to increase its advertising. It also decided to change gradually from handling only airline tickets to a complete travel and tour service. It offers a special reduced price group travel. What effect have these policies had upon the business?

c. On July 1, the management changed its method of paying employees from a regular weekly wage to hourly pay. This change affected approximately 75 percent of the employees. The number of employees was reduced. How has the plan affected salaries expense?

d. Is there any expense item that the management should examine more carefully?

e. What is your general opinion of the results of the operations of the business as shown on the comparative income statement?

CASE 7M-2. Allison Carter owns Carter's Furniture Company. It is a store that sells furniture to homes and businesses. The comparative balance sheet below shows the financial position of the business on June 30 of this year and on December 31 of last year.

a. Is the financial position better on June 30 or on December 31? Give your reasons.

b. A large number of pieces of furniture were sold since the first of the year. Customers pay one-third of the total bill when the furniture is delivered, and they pay the balance in six equal monthly payments. Do the amounts on the balance sheet indicate that collections are being received from the customers? Explain your answer.

c. The business often rents a truck for deliveries at a very high fee. Ms. Carter can buy a truck for $6,500. She would have to pay $3,500 in cash now and $3,000 in six months. Could a truck be purchased safely now? Give your reasons.

d. The general office clerk buys office supplies without getting Ms. Carter's approval. Should Ms. Carter reexamine this policy? Give your reasons.

Carter's Furniture Company
Comparative Balance Sheet
June 30, 19— and December 31, 19—

	JUNE 30, 19—		DECEMBER 31, 19—	
Assets				
Cash	7,500 00		3,000 00	
Accounts Receivable	9,200 00		10,200 00	
Notes Receivable	2,500 00		4,500 00	
Office Supplies	750 00		125 00	
Equipment	15,200 00		16,000 00	
Total Assets		35,150 00		33,825 00
Liabilities				
Notes Payable	3,300 00		6,500 00	
Accounts Payable	2,000 00		2,250 00	
Total Liabilities		5,300 00		8,750 00
Owner's Equity				
Allison Carter, Capital		29,850 00		25,075 00
Total Liabilities and Owner's Equity		35,150 00		33,825 00

CHAPTER

8

Banking Activities

In the first seven chapters you learned how to process data through an accounting system. Many of the transactions were either cash receipts or cash payments. In this chapter you will find out how a business controls cash transactions by using a checking account, depositing cash receipts in a checking account, and paying bills by writing checks. You will also find out how a business compares its cash records with the cash records kept by the bank.

CHAPTER GOALS

After studying Chapter 8, you will be able to:

1. Define the terms listed in ''The Language of Business'' section on page 261.
2. Maintain a checkbook in which you complete checkbook stubs, determine new balances, and write checks.
3. Endorse checks using a blank endorsement, full endorsement, and restrictive endorsement.
4. Prepare a deposit ticket to deposit coins, currency, and checks.
5. Prepare a bank reconciliation statement.
6. Record entries in a petty cash register.
7. Prove a petty cash fund and total and rule a petty cash register.

TOPIC 1

Paying by Check

Why do businesses use checking accounts? Checking accounts are used for two reasons. First, a checking account is used to safeguard cash. In a checking account system, all cash is deposited in the bank and all bills are paid by writing checks. Thus, a business does not have to keep large amounts of cash on hand. Second, a checking account is a second record of cash. You have already studied how the Cash account is a record of cash receipts and payments. You will now see how writing checks and depositing cash in a checking account provide a second record of cash.

Signature Card

When opening a checking account, a signature card must be signed. A **signature card** is a card with signatures of persons authorized to draw or write checks on a certain bank account. Any signature on the card must be written exactly as it will appear on the checks. The bank keeps the signature card on file and can then compare the signature on the check with the signature on the card. The signature card shown below was prepared when Lisa Long opened a checking account at the Lincoln Bank for Exercise Plus.

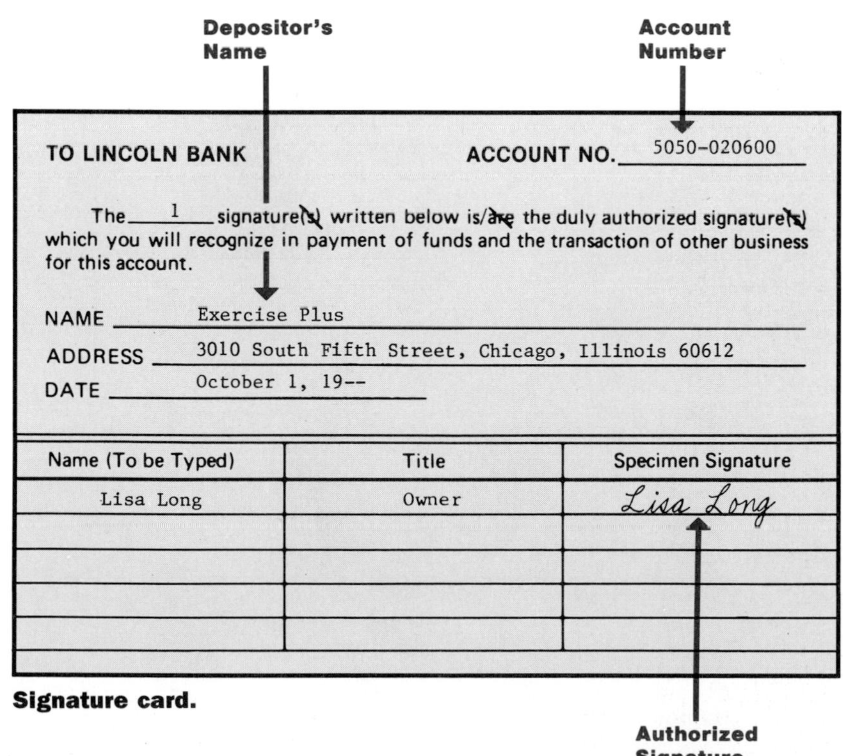

TO LINCOLN BANK ACCOUNT NO. 5050-020600

The 1 signature(s) written below is/are the duly authorized signature(s) which you will recognize in payment of funds and the transaction of other business for this account.

NAME Exercise Plus

ADDRESS 3010 South Fifth Street, Chicago, Illinois 60612

DATE October 1, 19--

Name (To be Typed)	Title	Specimen Signature
Lisa Long	Owner	Lisa Long

Signature card.

Drawing Checks

A **check** is a written order to pay a specific sum from a depositor's account to a payee. The depositor tells the bank to deduct a sum of money from his or her checking account and to pay that amount to the person, company, or organization named on the check. A **depositor** is an individual, business, or organization in whose name money is placed in the bank.

Three Parties to a Check
- Drawer
- Drawee
- Payee

There are three parties to a check. The signer (or maker) who writes the check is the **drawer**. The bank on which the check is drawn is the **drawee**. The individual, business, or organization to whose order the check is to be paid is the **payee**.

There are several advantages to paying all bills by check. The checkbook provides a record of cash paid out. The canceled checks provide proof that money has been paid to the person legally entitled to it. In addition, checks can be sent safely by mail.

The form of a check can vary with the bank and type of account used. Checks may be written in ink or typed, but *never* written in pencil, as the amount written in pencil could easily be changed. A variety of machines for preparing checks is available to depositors who issue many checks. One machine, for example, punches tiny holes in the check as it prints the amount. A machine such as this can make it impossible to change the amount of the check.

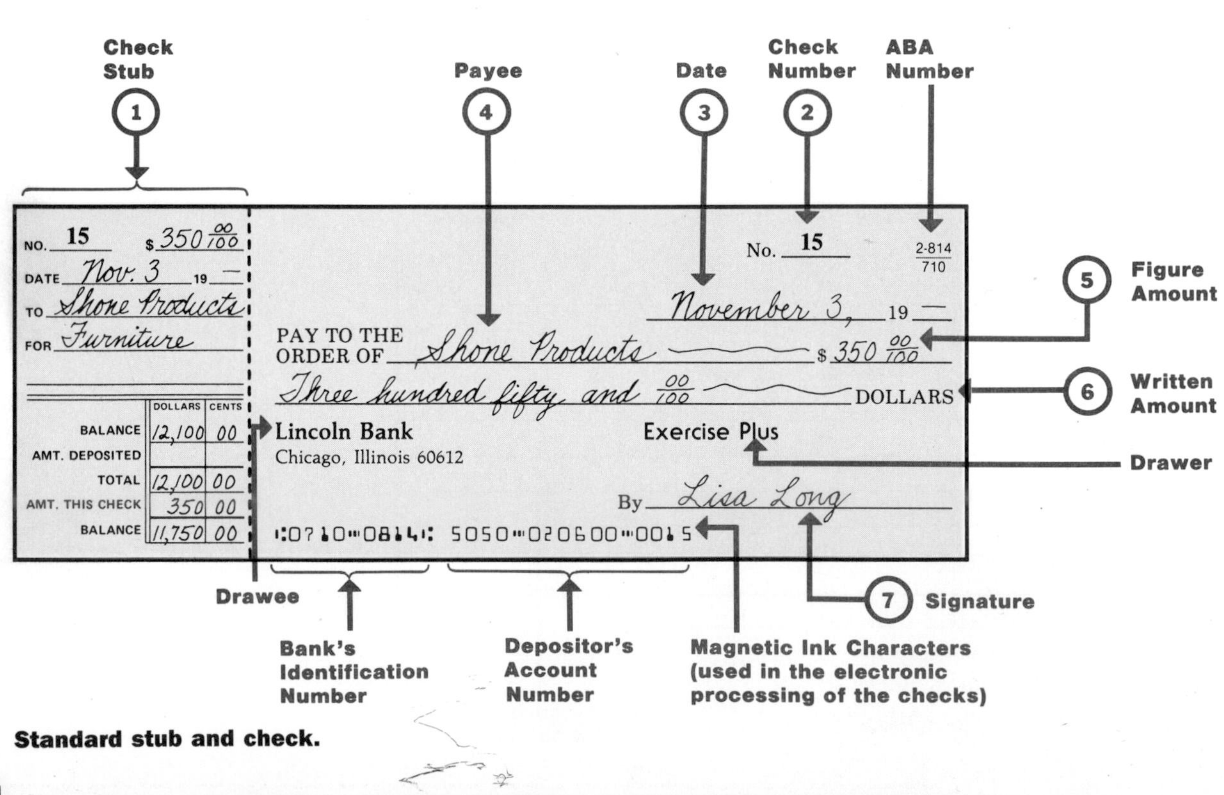

Standard stub and check.

The procedure for preparing a check is as follows.

1. *When using a standard checkbook, fill in the check stub first so that you will not forget it.* If the stub is not filled in, there will be no record of the check once it is removed from the checkbook. By filling in the data on the stub first, there is less chance of making an error when writing the check.

Before writing a check, update the checkbook balance in the stub section to make sure that there is money on deposit to cover the check. Add the amount of each deposit to the balance previously shown. Subtract the amount of each check from the balance as it is written and carry the balance forward to the next check stub.

After a check is removed from the checkbook, the check stub is the source document used to journalize the transaction.

2. *Write the check number if the check has not been prenumbered by the bank.* Banks usually have checks prenumbered when they are being printed. All checks must be numbered consecutively (in numeric order). If an error is made in preparing a check, write "Void" in large letters across the face of the check and on the check stub.

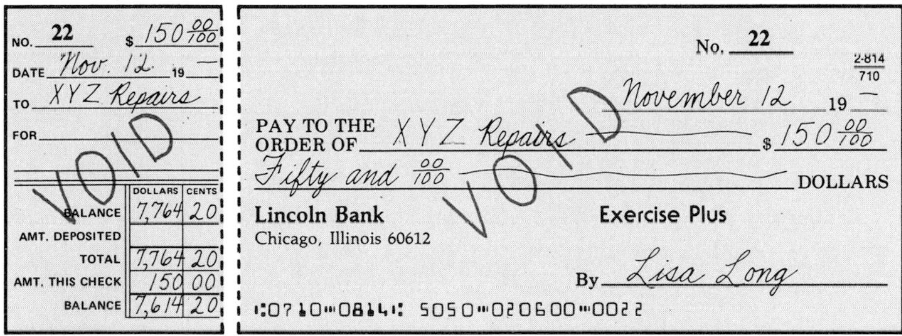

Voided check.

Do not destroy voided checks. Instead, file them until they can be sorted in numeric sequence with the canceled checks returned from the bank. In this way, all checks will be available for auditing, and it can be proven easily that the voided check was not issued.

3. *Write the date the check is issued.*

4. *Write the payee's name in full (starting at the extreme left), and spell it correctly.* Omit personal titles such as Mr., Mrs., Miss, Ms., or Dr. When making a check payable to a married woman, use her given first name whenever possible. For example, write "Anne Jones" rather than "Mrs. Jack L. Jones." After entering the payee's name, draw a line from the name to the dollar sign so that no one can change the name. If the check is typewritten, hyphens are typed on the check to fill in the space between the end of the payee's name and the dollar sign.

5. *In the space after the name of the payee, write the amount of the check in figures.* Be sure that the first digit is placed close to the

Handwritten: $72 $\frac{16}{100}$

Typewritten: $72.16

Expressing amounts in figures.

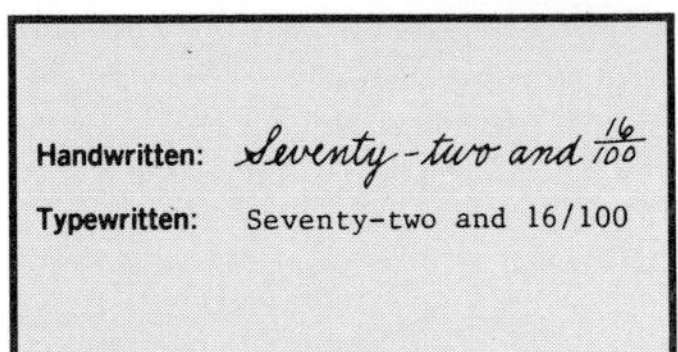

Expressing amounts in words.

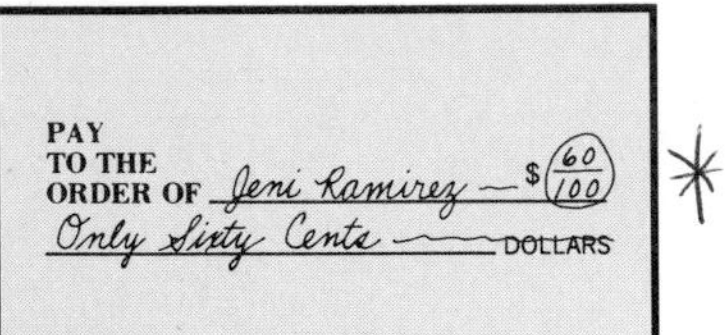

PAY TO THE ORDER OF Jeni Ramirez — $ $\frac{60}{100}$
Only Sixty Cents — DOLLARS

Expressing amounts for less than $1.

dollar sign so that no other digits can be added to increase the amount. Show the cents part of the amount as a fraction. For example, write 16 cents as "$\frac{16}{100}$." If the check is for an even dollar amount, write "$\frac{00}{100}$" or "$\frac{no}{100}$." If the check is typewritten, these amounts should be typed in the normal way—"$72.16." Amounts under $1.00 are circled, whether entered by hand or typewritten.

6. *In the space under the payee's name, write the amount in words.* Start at the extreme left of the line so that no words can be added to increase the amount. Separate the cents amount from the dollar amount by the word "and." Then write the cents as a fraction. For example, write "$\frac{16}{100}$" or "$\frac{00}{100}$." When the check is typewritten, the fraction for cents is typed as "16/100" or "00/100." Draw a line in the space between the fraction and the word "Dollars." If the check is typewritten, fill the space with hyphens. On checks for less than $1.00, write the amount as, for example, "Only Sixty Cents" and cross out the word "Dollars" at the end of the line.

The amount appears on a check twice, once in figures and once in words. This is done to make sure that the amount is stated correctly. If the amount written in figures is not the same as the amount in words, the bank will pay the amount in words. If the difference is too great, however, the bank may refuse to pay the check.

7. *The authorized person must sign the check.* A check may be filled out by anyone, but it must be signed only by an authorized person. For example, at Exercise Plus, the accounting clerk normally fills out the checks. However, the signature card shows that only Lisa Long is authorized to sign checks for the business. In the check shown on page 232, the name of the business has been printed above the signature line, and the signature itself reads "By Lisa Long." This emphasizes the fact that Lisa Long is acting for the business.

Processing Checks

The small fractional number in the upper right-hand corner of a check is the ABA number of the bank. (ABA stands for American Bankers Association.) Look at the example at the top of the next page. The ABA number identifies the bank and the Federal Reserve district. The first part of the number (2) identifies the city or state in which the bank is located; the second part (814) identifies the bank; and the third part (710) is the Federal Reserve designation.

Most banks use checks imprinted with magnetic ink characters. Magnetic ink is a special ink that can be read by machines. The characters are imprinted at the bottom of the checks.

The first group of eight magnetic ink characters identifies the bank on which the check is drawn. The first four characters in this group show the Federal Reserve designation number, and the other four characters show the bank number. The second group of magnetic ink characters identifies the depositor's account number. The account number for Exercise Plus is 5050-020600. The hyphen is shown by the symbol ⑈. A preprinted check number, such as 18, may also appear in magnetic ink characters following the account number (5050⑈020600⑈ 0018).

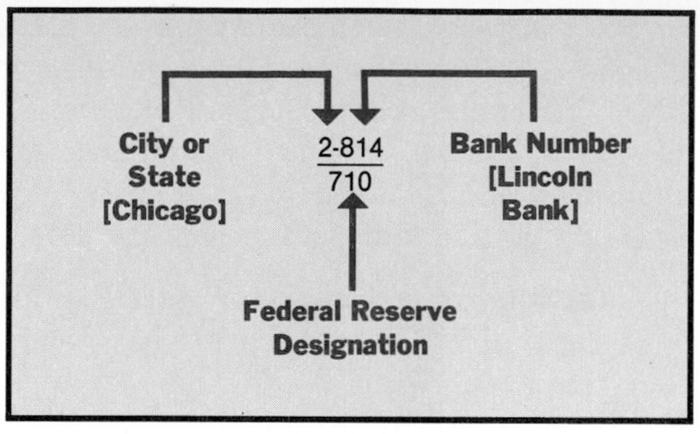

ABA number for Lincoln Bank.

When a check reaches a bank, a third group of magnetic ink characters is imprinted in the lower right-hand corner of the check. These characters contain the amount of the check. Zeros are added to the left of an amount with less than ten digits to fill the ten spaces. No commas, decimal points, or dollar signs are used. Thus, a check for $350 is imprinted as "0000035000."

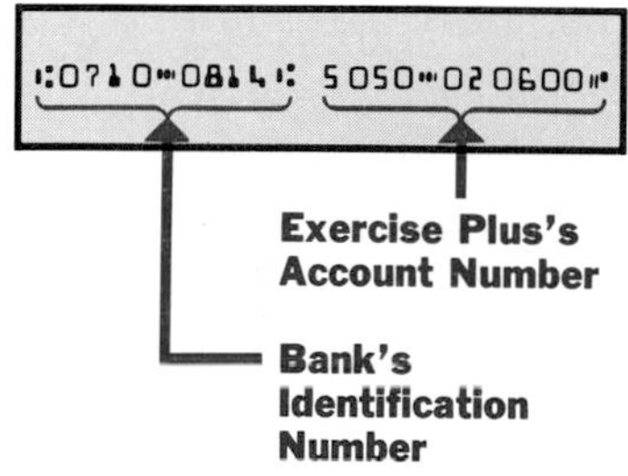

Magnetic ink characters.

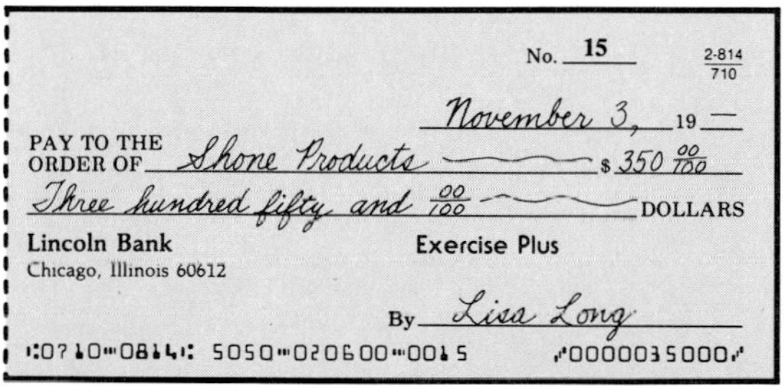

No. 15 2-814/710

November 3, 19__

PAY TO THE ORDER OF Shone Products $ 350 00/100

Three hundred fifty and 00/100 DOLLARS

Lincoln Bank
Chicago, Illinois 60612

Exercise Plus

By Lisa Long

⑆0710⑈0814⑆ 5050⑈020600⑈0015 ⑇0000035000⑇

Amount of Check in Magnetic Ink Characters

To process the checks deposited, the Lincoln Bank must sort the checks. It needs to know which checks are drawn on its own accounts and which must be forwarded to other banks for collection. A machine reads the magnetic code on each check. All checks with the magnetic code 0710-0814 will automatically be sorted into one group, since they are drawn on the Lincoln Bank. The checks drawn on other banks will be sorted into separate stacks according to the bank number in the code.

The stack of checks with the number of the Lincoln Bank is then sorted by depositors' account numbers. Any check with the magnetic code 5050-020600 will be classified as a claim against Exercise Plus's checking account. The amount, which is imprinted in magnetic code, will be deducted from the account.

MICR machine.

The machine used to read magnetic codes on checks and to sort the checks is called a *magnetic ink character recognition (MICR) machine*. This machine also transmits the data imprinted in magnetic code to other machines, which subtract the amount of the checks from the drawer's account and record the amount, the drawee's number, and the drawer's account number of each check.

Concept: Bank-Depositor Relationship

A contract exists between the bank and the depositor. The bank agrees to pay all checks drawn by the depositor as long as sufficient funds are on deposit to pay the checks.

Exercise A on pages 238 and 239 may be completed at this point.

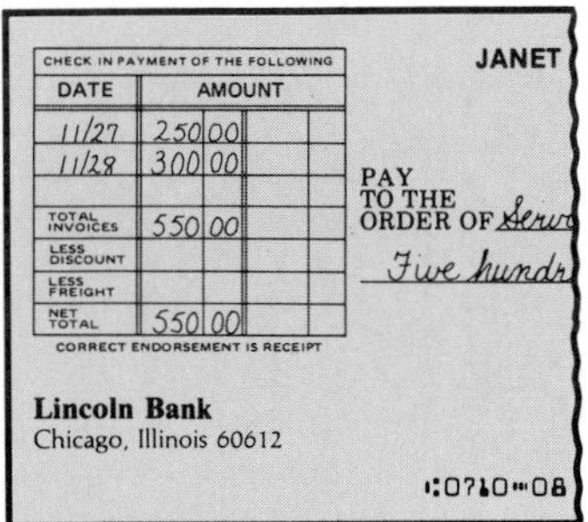
CHECK IN PAYMENT OF THE FOLLOWING

DATE	AMOUNT
11/27	250 00
11/28	300 00
TOTAL INVOICES	550 00
LESS DISCOUNT	
LESS FREIGHT	
NET TOTAL	550 00

CORRECT ENDORSEMENT IS RECEIPT

JANET

PAY TO THE ORDER OF Serv

Five hundr

Lincoln Bank
Chicago, Illinois 60612

⑆0710⑈08

Voucher check with voucher section on check.

Special Types of Checks

What other types of checks are used by businesses? In addition to the standard check, businesses use voucher checks and certified checks.

Voucher Checks Many businesses use a special check form called a voucher check. A **voucher check** differs from a standard check by showing the purpose for which the check is written. In one type of voucher check, the amounts for which the check is being issued are stated directly on the check.

Another type of voucher check is shown below. It is perforated so that it can be separated into two parts. One part is the check itself. The other part is the voucher, on which the purpose of the payment is

Voucher Section

NO. 782 American Design Studio 74 West Jackson Boulevard Chicago, Illinois 60604

REMITTANCE ADVICE

INVOICE NUMBER	INVOICE DATE MO. / DAY / YR.		GROSS AMOUNT	DISCOUNT	NET AMOUNT
1503	10 / 31 / --		$485.00		$485.00

DETACH BEFORE DEPOSITING CHECK

Check Section

NO. 782 American Design Studio 2-814/710

MO.	DAY	YR.
11 / 15 / --		

PAY TO THE ORDER OF Exercise Plus
3010 South Fifth Street
Chicago, Illinois 60612

AMOUNT $485.00

Four Hundred Eighty-Five and 00/100 ---------- DOLLARS

Dustin Hill
AUTHORIZED SIGNATURE

Lincoln Bank
Chicago, Illinois 60612

Thomas Cameron
AUTHORIZED SIGNATURE

⑆0710⑈0814⑆ 4370⑈971100⑈ 0782

Voucher check with detachable voucher.

written. The voucher is removed by the payee before depositing the check or transferring it to another person. This type of voucher check does not have a check stub. Instead, a carbon copy of the check is kept by the drawer as a record of the transaction.

■ Certified Checks In certain business transactions, such as those involving large sums of money, the payee of the check may want to be sure that the check will be paid without delay when presented to the bank. In this case the drawer obtains a certified check. A **certified check** is a depositor's check on which the bank guarantees payment. A certified check carries the guarantee of the bank that the depositor has enough cash to pay the check when it is presented.

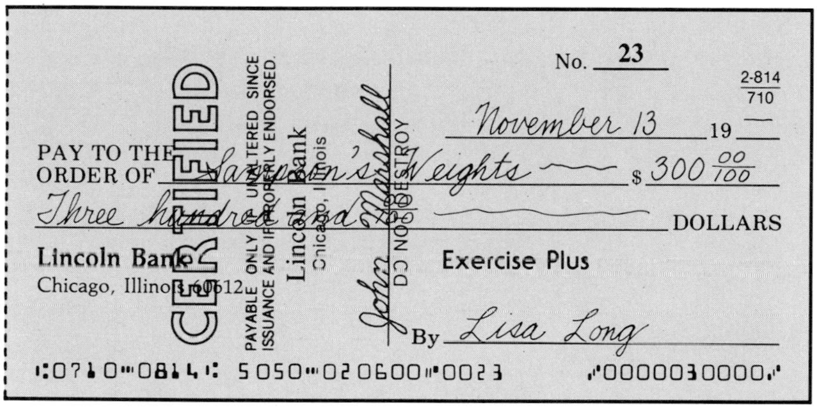

Certified check.

To have a check certified, the drawer writes the check in the usual way and takes it to the bank. The bank teller finds out whether the depositor has enough money in the account to meet payment of the check. If so, the teller stamps (or writes) the word "Certified" across the face of the check and signs it as a bank official. The amount of that check is deducted immediately from the depositor's account. Generally, the bank charges a fee for this service.

■ Stopping Payment on Checks

A **stop payment order** is an authorization by the drawer to the bank to not pay a check when it is presented for payment. Occasionally, a check that has been issued is lost or stolen. When this occurs, the drawer should telephone the bank at once, giving the information about the check and the reason for stopping payment. The drawer must then give the bank a written order or a letter authorizing the bank not to pay the check if it is presented for payment. The written order or letter that is issued to the bank to stop the check must contain a handwritten signature. An illustration of a stop payment order prepared by Exercise Plus is shown on the next page.

NO. 24 $1,500 00/100
DATE Nov. 20 19—
TO XYZ Repairs
FOR On account
Stopped payment

	DOLLARS	CENTS
BALANCE	9,125	00
AMT. DEPOSITED		
TOTAL	9,125	00
AMT. THIS CHECK	1,500	00
BALANCE	7,625	00

When a stop payment order has been issued, the accounting clerk writes "Stopped Payment" across the check stub. The amount of the check is added to the current checkbook balance. A new check can then be issued. If the old check is found after payment has been stopped, it is voided and filed.

The bank will usually charge a fee to the drawer of the check to stop payment. This fee is deducted from the depositor's account and recorded on the bank statement.

NO. 28 $1,500 00/100
DATE Nov. 25 19—
TO XYZ Repairs
FOR Replace Check 24 on account

	DOLLARS	CENTS
BALANCE	6,124	00
AMT. DEPOSITED (11/25 Stopped payment on Check 24)	1,500	00
TOTAL	7,624	00
AMT. THIS CHECK	1,500	00
BALANCE	6,124	00

To: LINCOLN BANK
Chicago, Illinois 60612

STOP PAYMENT ORDER

DATE November 30, 19--

Please stop payment of check No. 24 Dated November 20, 19--
for $ $1,500.00 in favor of XYZ Repairs
drawn by the undersigned on you.

Should the undersigned issue a duplicate check in place of this check bearing the same date, number, amount and payee, the undersigned agrees to mark such check "DUPLICATE" and such duplicate check may be honored when presented to you.

PLEASE PRINT CLEARLY — FROM ADDRESS OR LOCATION: Exercise Plus, 3010 South Fifth Street, Chicago, Illinois 60612

ACCOUNT No. 5050-020600

☒ REGULAR CHECKING ☐ SPECIAL CHECKING
☐ CHRISTMAS CLUB ☐ PERSONAL MONEY ORDER
☐ EMPLOYEE CHECKING

Lisa Long
AUTHORIZED SIGNATURE

REASON: Check lost

Stop payment order telling bank not to pay Check 24 if it is presented.

Exercise B on page 239 may be completed at this point.

TOPIC 1 EXERCISES

EXERCISE A. Answer the following questions about drawing and processing checks. Refer to the check and stubs illustrated on page 239.

1. What is the ABA number of the National Bank?
2. What is the amount of Check 17?
3. Why was Check 17 drawn?
4. Who is the payee of Check 17?
5. To whom was Check 21 drawn?
6. For how much was the June 26 deposit?
7. Which check was drawn on June 25? Why was it drawn?
8. What amount was brought forward on the stub of Check 29?
9. Who is the drawer of Check 29?
10. What is the total amount of the three checks?
11. Is a deposit added or subtracted on the stub? Why?

12. Is the amount of a check added or subtracted on the stub? Why?

13. Who is the drawee of Check 29?

14. What balance is carried forward from the stub of Check 29? To where is this balance carried forward?

NO. 17 $ 185 00/100
DATE June 24, 19—
TO B+B Ins. Co.
FOR Car insurance

NO. 21 $ 25 00/100
DATE June 25, 19—
TO East Coast Gas
FOR Gas

NO. 29 $ 48 00/100
DATE June 27, 19—
TO Mass. Power Co.
FOR Electricity

	DOLLARS	CENTS
BALANCE	741	15
AMT. DEPOSITED 6/26	210	25
TOTAL	951	40
AMT. THIS CHECK	48	00
BALANCE	903	40

No. 29

5-350/110

June 27, 19—

PAY TO THE ORDER OF Massachusetts Power Company $ 48 00/100

Forty-eight and 00/100 DOLLARS

National Bank
Boston, Massachusetts

Curtis Sampson

⑆0110⑈0350⑆ 200⑈0430⑈0029

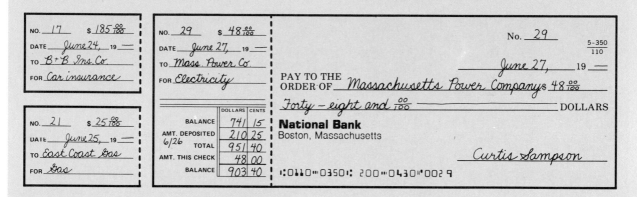

EXERCISE B. Answer the following questions about special types of checks. Refer to the voucher check, certified check, and stop payment order on pages 236 to 238.

1. What is the number of the invoice that the American Design Studio paid with Check 782? What was the date of the invoice?
2. What is the identification number for the Lincoln Bank?
3. What is the number of the American Design Studio's checking account?
4. Who is the payee of Check 23 issued by Exercise Plus?
5. How do you know that Check 23 is certified?
6. Why was the stop payment order issued?
7. What was the number and date of the check on which Exercise Plus stopped payment?
8. On what date was payment stopped?
9. Who is the payee of Check 24? The drawer? The drawee?

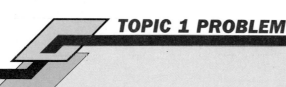

TOPIC 1 PROBLEM

TOPIC PROBLEM 1. Assume that you have a checking account at the National Bank, Columbus, Ohio. Your checkbook shows that after writing Check 54, you have a balance of $847. On the basis of the following cash transactions, record the appropriate information on the stub, carry forward the balance, and write the check.

Nov. 3 Deposited $295.50 in checking account.
4 Issued Check 55 for $260 to Sandra Mason on account.
5 Deposited $541 in checking account.
5 Issued check for $95 to Quick Health Supply for spa supplies.
6 Deposited $484 in checking account.
6 Issued check for $614 to Dole Brothers Transport Company for delivery service.

TOPIC 2

Depositing Cash

What should a business do with the cash it receives? A business should deposit all its cash receipts in the bank to provide an accurate record of the cash that has been received. By paying all its bills by check, the business also has an accurate record of how its cash has been spent. Two ways to control cash are to deposit all cash receipts in a bank and to pay all bills by check.

■ Preparing Cash for Deposit

The items deposited in the bank include all forms of cash—coins, currency, checks, and money orders.

The coins are sorted according to denomination (pennies, nickels, dimes, quarters, and half dollars). The coins are then counted and rolled in coin wrappers supplied by the bank. If there are not enough coins to fill a wrapper, they may be put in small coin envelopes which are supplied by the bank.

The currency is also sorted according to denomination. Bills are placed face up with the portraits on top. All bills face the same direction. The largest denominations are placed on top of the pile. The $20 bills come first, then the $10 bills, the $5 bills, and the $1 bills. The bank also supplies special paper bands to wrap the currency.

A check or money order must be endorsed before it can be deposited. An **endorsement** is a signature or stamp on the back of a check or money order that transfers ownership. The person or company whose name is written or stamped on the back of the check is the endorser. An endorsement on a deposited check or money order gives the bank a legal right to collect payment from the endorsee. The endorsee is a person or business to whom ownership of a check is transferred by endorsement. Any business paper that is a claim on cash and may be transferred legally by endorsement is a **negotiable instrument**.

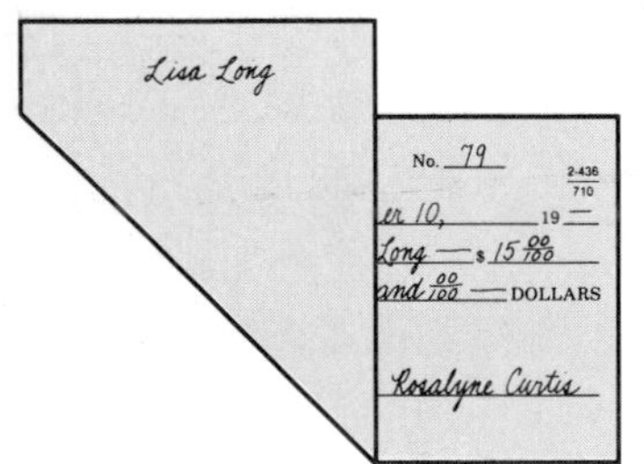

Blank endorsement.

The endorsement should be made across the back of the left end of checks and money orders. The illustrations shown below are types of endorsements commonly used.

■ Blank Endorsement A **blank endorsement** is endorsing a check with just the endorser's signature on the back of the check. This is the most common way of endorsing a check. A check with this type of endorsement is shown in the margin. It may be cashed by anyone who holds it. To prevent an endorsed check from getting into the hands of someone who might cash it illegally, an endorser should use a blank endorsement only when a check is being endorsed at the bank.

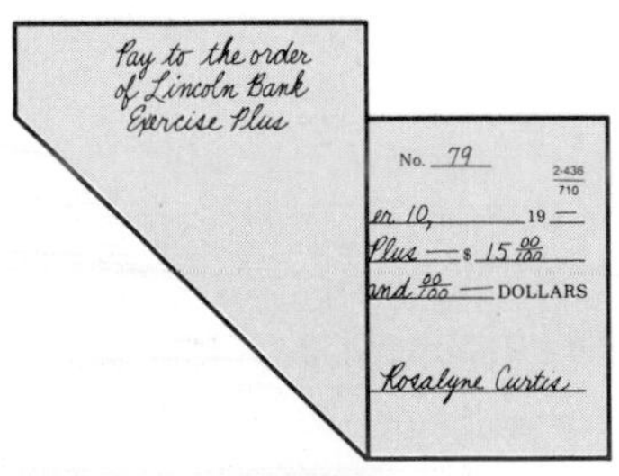

Full endorsement.

■ Full Endorsement A **full endorsement** is endorsing the check with the name of the party to whom the check is to be transferred. This is a safer endorsement than the blank endorsement. As shown in the margin on page 240, only the person or firm given in the full endorsement may cash or legally transfer the check to someone else.

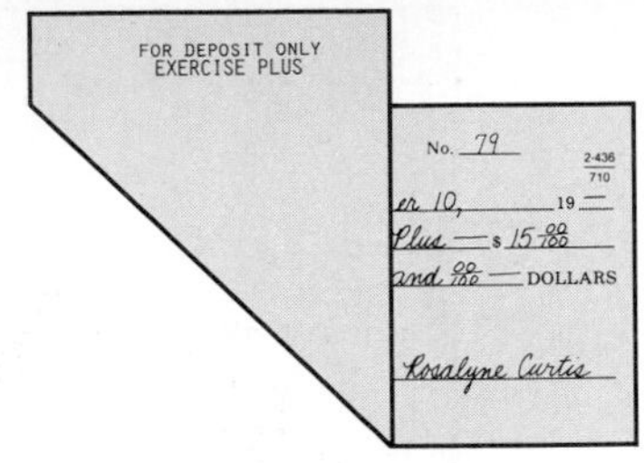

Restrictive endorsement, blank form.

■ Restrictive Endorsement A **restrictive endorsement** is endorsing the check with the purpose for which the money is to be used. This is the best endorsement for a business to use in making a deposit. A check endorsed "For Deposit Only" can only be deposited. It cannot be cashed. A restrictive endorsement can be a blank form or a full form. Many businesses use a rubber stamp to endorse checks with a restrictive endorsement.

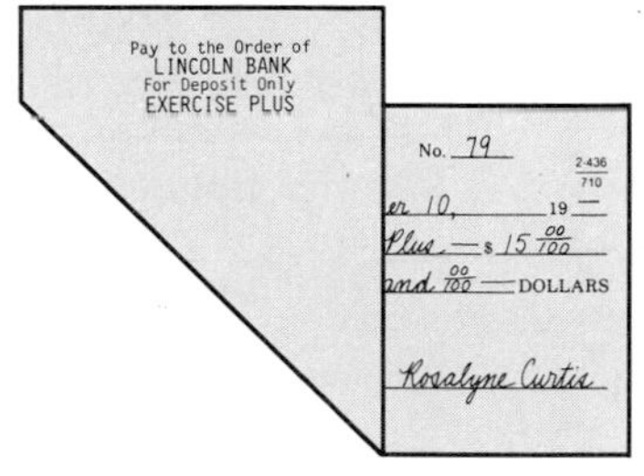

Restrictive endorsement, full form.

■ Making an Endorsement When a check is being endorsed for deposit, the endorsement must contain the name of the endorser. Thus all checks deposited in Exercise Plus's checking account must be endorsed with the name of Exercise Plus, not the name of the owner, Lisa Long. Checks endorsed with the name Lisa Long would be deposited in her personal account.

An endorser's name must be signed in the exact way in which it was written on the check or money order. If the endorser's name was written incorrectly on the check, the endorser's name must first be signed as it actually appears and then written correctly beneath.

For example, suppose Lisa Long receives a check incorrectly made out to "Exercise Spa." She must first endorse the check in the name "Exercise Spa." Then she endorses it correctly in the name "Exercise Plus." This kind of corrected endorsement may be made only in the case of an error.

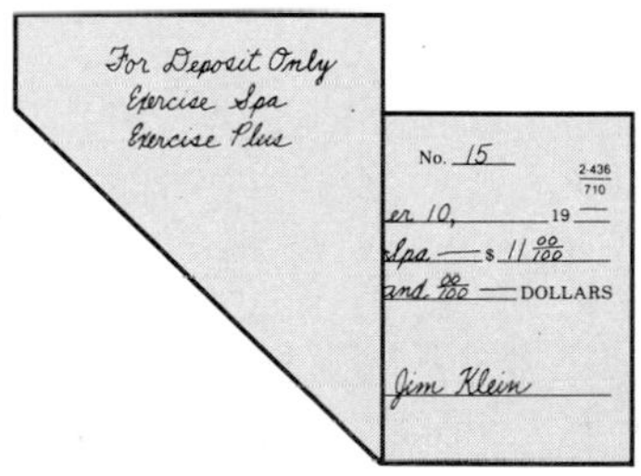

Corrected endorsement.

Exercise C on page 243 may be completed at this point.

Most businesses endorse checks "For Deposit Only" as soon as they are received. This restrictive endorsement protects the checks from being stolen and cashed.

Preparing a Deposit Ticket

How is a deposit ticket prepared? After the coins and currency have been sorted and the checks and money orders have been endorsed, a deposit ticket is filled out. A **deposit ticket** is a form listing coins, currency, checks, and money orders to be deposited. The deposit ticket, which is supplied by the bank, shows all the details of the deposit.

A duplicate copy of the deposit ticket should be made to show that all cash receipts have been deposited.

Many banks provide deposit tickets in unit sets, which consist of two or more copies of the deposit ticket fastened together with carbon paper between the copies. The form of the deposit ticket may vary, but most deposit tickets resemble the one shown on the next page.

Deposited In **Lincoln Bank**
Chicago, Illinois 60612

(1) Date *December 20, 19—*

(2) Deposit to Account of *Exercise Plus*
3010 South Fifth Street
Chicago, Illinois 60612

(3) 5050 ■ 020600
ACCOUNT NUMBER

		Dollars	Cents	
Currency		41	00	(4)
Coin		6	72	(4)
Checks	1	123	00	(5)
(List separately)	2	14	00	(5)
	3	78	65	(5)
	4	274	28	(5)
	5			
TOTAL		537	65	(6)

This deposit accepted under and subject to the provisions of the Uniform Commercial Code.

Deposit ticket.

The procedures for filling out a deposit ticket are as follows.

1. Write the date on the Date line.
2. Write the name and address of the depositor in the proper section. The name must appear exactly as it appears on the account.
3. Write the account number in the space provided. The number given to each account must be used on all deposit tickets to be sure that deposits will be posted to the right account.
4. Record the total amount of currency on the Currency line and the total amount of coins on the Coin line. Dollar signs and decimal points are not used.
5. List each check separately in the Check section. Be sure the checks are in the same order as they are listed on the deposit ticket. If many checks are deposited at the same time, a different form of deposit ticket is used or the bank permits the checks to be itemized on an adding machine. The adding machine tape is then clipped to the deposit ticket. The total on the tape is written on the first line in the Check section of the deposit ticket with the words "See list attached."
6. Compute the amount of the deposit and record this amount on the Total line. The amount must agree with the cash value of the items deposited.

Making the Deposit

How are deposits made and processed? When the deposit ticket and the cash items are presented for deposit, the bank teller gives the depositor some type of receipt as a record. Some banks provide a printed receipt that indicates the date and the amount deposited. A common practice is to have the deposit ticket prepared with carbon copies in unit sets. The teller stamps or initials a carbon copy and returns it to the depositor to keep as a record.

As long as a deposit does not include currency and coins, it can be mailed safely to the bank. The bank will mail back a duplicate deposit ticket or some other form of receipt. Banks generally have special forms for depositors who want to bank by mail.

Bank depositors who need to make deposits after the bank is closed can use the night depository. Deposits are placed in bank bags, and the bags are dropped through a chute into the vault.

■ Processing Deposits

When a depositor submits cash items for deposit, the bank uses the deposit ticket as the source document. The bank obtains from the deposit ticket the amount to be added to the account. To speed the processing of deposits and ensure accuracy, many banks now issue personalized deposit tickets, with the depositor's name and account number printed on them. The account number is imprinted in magnetic ink. The amounts of the deposits are later imprinted on these deposit tickets in magnetic ink characters enabling the deposit tickets to be automatically sorted. The amount of each deposit is then automatically added to each depositor's account.

Exercise D on this page may be completed at this point.

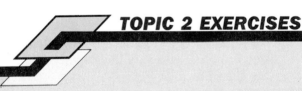

TOPIC 2 EXERCISES

EXERCISE C. Assume that you are Seth Schwartz and have a checking account at the Lincoln Bank. You have received a check for $65 from Gail Snow. Show how you would make the following endorsements on the check.

1. A blank endorsement
2. A full endorsement to transfer the check to Allyson Saunders
3. An endorsement to correct a check made out to Seth Schwarz
4. A blank form of restrictive endorsement to deposit the check in the Lincoln Bank
5. A full form of restrictive endorsement to deposit the check in the Lincoln Bank

EXERCISE D. Answer the following questions about processing the data from the deposit ticket shown on page 242.

1. What is the number of Exercise Plus's checking account?
2. Where is the account number written on the deposit tickets?
3. What is the amount of the deposit on December 20?
4. What source document does the bank use to add amounts to a depositor's account?
5. What source document does the bank use to deduct an amount from a depositor's account?

TOPIC 2 PROBLEM

TOPIC PROBLEM 2. Using today's date, prepare a deposit ticket for the Sea Shop, 10 Calgore Drive, Fresno, California 93705. The shop's account number at the First California Bank is 0544 002837. Use the information in the next column to prepare the deposit ticket.

Currency	Coins	Checks
Nine $20 bills	34 quarters	$98
Twelve $10 bills	14 dimes	47
Six $5 bills	43 nickels	—
Thirteen $1 bills	22 pennies	—

TOPIC 3

Verifying the Cash Balance and the Bank Balance

How do depositors know if their cash records agree with the bank's records? Periodically, each depositor should verify that the Cash account balance agrees with the checkbook balance and with the bank balance. This is usually done once a month. Exercise Plus's banking activities for the month of December are described below.

■ Verifying the Cash Balance

When cash is received and paid out, the transactions are recorded in the journal and posted to the ledger. Therefore, if all cash receipts are deposited and all payments are made by check, the balance of the Cash account should agree with the balance in the checkbook.

If the balances of the Cash account and the checkbook do not agree, then the ledger should be checked to see if it is in balance. If a trial balance shows that the ledger is in balance, the error is probably in the checkbook. The most common kinds of errors are these.

- Adding or subtracting amounts incorrectly on the check stubs.
- Carrying the wrong balance forward from one stub to another (for example, a balance of $7,350 carried forward as $7,530).
- Failing to subtract a check when it is drawn and journalized.
- Failing to deposit the cash receipts. In this case, the Cash account balance equals the cash in the bank plus the cash on hand.

Any adjustments or errors in the checkbook must be corrected on the latest check stub. For example, suppose a deposit for $220.40 was recorded by mistake as $202.40 on Stub 60. On the latest check stub, Stub 79, the difference of $18 ($220.40 − $202.40) would be added to the current balance in the checkbook to correct the error. The notation "Error, see Stub 60" would also be entered. A notation would be placed on Stub 60, stating that this error was corrected on Stub 79.

NO. 79 $ 24.00
DATE December 5 19 —
TO Franklin Stores
FOR Supplies

	DOLLARS	CENTS
BALANCE	17,086	00
AMT. DEPOSITED	18	00
Error, see Stub 60 TOTAL	17,104	00
AMT. THIS CHECK	24	00
BALANCE	17,080	00

These steps prove that the balances of the Cash account and the checkbook agree. The next step is to prove that the balance in the checkbook agrees with the balance on the bank statement.

■ The Bank Statement

Typically, the bank sends the depositor a bank statement once a month. A **bank statement** is an itemized list of additions to and subtractions from a depositor's account.

The bank statement shows the following.

- The balance at the beginning of the monthly period
- The deposits added during the month
- The checks and other charges subtracted during the month
- The balance at the end of the monthly period

A check paid from the depositor's account and returned to the depositor is called a **canceled check**. The checks paid during the month are returned with the bank statement.

Canceled checks are also paid checks.

The checks that are returned with the bank statement are perforated or stamped with the word "paid" and the date of payment. Canceled checks are valuable receipts. The endorsement on the check is evidence that the payee (individual or company) received the payment.

The bank statement should be checked as soon as it is received. This is done to verify that the balance shown by the bank agrees with the balance shown in the depositor's checkbook.

The procedures in checking the bank statement are as follows.

- Arrange the canceled checks in numeric order. Take any stop payment orders and voided checks from the files. Insert them in numeric sequence with the canceled checks.
- Compare each check (canceled or voided) with its check stub in the checkbook. If the check agrees with the stub, make a large check mark (✓) on the stub next to the check number. This mark shows that the check has been paid and returned by the bank, or that the check (if voided) is accounted for.

The December 31, 19— bank statement shown on page 246 was sent to Exercise Plus by the Lincoln Bank. The bank statement shows the following items.

- December 1 balance of $8,027.10 (beginning balance)
- Two deposits added during December (deposits)
- Six checks subtracted during the month (checks)
- Three additional charges subtracted during the month (charges)
- December 31 balance of $8,039.00 (ending balance)

The last checkbook stub for December (Stub 38) shows a balance of $7,829.20. This balance agrees with the balance in the Cash account in the ledger on December 31. However, the balance on the bank statement does not agree with the checkbook.

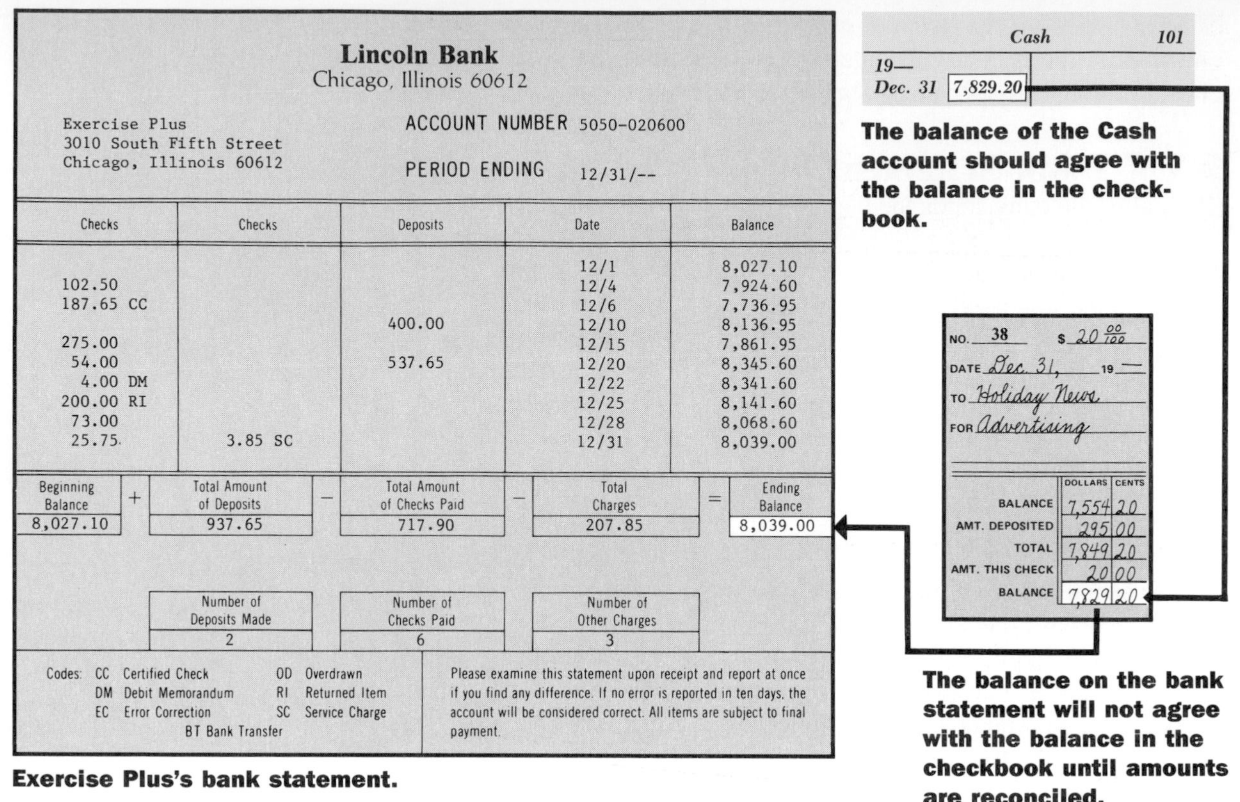

Lincoln Bank
Chicago, Illinois 60612

Exercise Plus
3010 South Fifth Street
Chicago, Illinois 60612

ACCOUNT NUMBER 5050-020600

PERIOD ENDING 12/31/--

Checks	Checks	Deposits	Date	Balance
			12/1	8,027.10
102.50			12/4	7,924.60
187.65 CC			12/6	7,736.95
		400.00	12/10	8,136.95
275.00			12/15	7,861.95
54.00		537.65	12/20	8,345.60
4.00 DM			12/22	8,341.60
200.00 RI			12/25	8,141.60
73.00			12/28	8,068.60
25.75	3.85 SC		12/31	8,039.00

Beginning Balance	+	Total Amount of Deposits	−	Total Amount of Checks Paid	−	Total Charges	=	Ending Balance
8,027.10		937.65		717.90		207.85		8,039.00

Number of Deposits Made	Number of Checks Paid	Number of Other Charges
2	6	3

Codes: CC Certified Check; DM Debit Memorandum; EC Error Correction; OD Overdrawn; RI Returned Item; SC Service Charge; BT Bank Transfer

Please examine this statement upon receipt and report at once if you find any difference. If no error is reported in ten days, the account will be considered correct. All items are subject to final payment.

Cash		101
19— Dec. 31	7,829.20	

The balance of the Cash account should agree with the balance in the checkbook.

NO. 38 $ 20 00/100
DATE Dec. 31, 19—
TO Holiday News
FOR Advertising

	DOLLARS	CENTS
BALANCE	7,554	20
AMT. DEPOSITED	295	00
TOTAL	7,849	20
AMT. THIS CHECK	20	00
BALANCE	7,829	20

The balance on the bank statement will not agree with the balance in the checkbook until amounts are reconciled.

Exercise Plus's bank statement.

This difference is not necessarily an error by either the depositor or the bank. The bank statement balance seldom agrees with the checkbook balance due to a delay by either the depositor or the bank in recording some of the items.

For example, a check is recorded in the checkbook when the check is written. However, the check is not subtracted from the depositor's account until the day the bank pays the check, causing a delay until the bank records the check. Here are some of the factors that can cause a difference between the balances.

■ **Outstanding Checks** A check that is not yet paid by the bank is called an **outstanding check**. Outstanding checks have been written against and subtracted from the depositor's checkbook but have not yet been presented to the bank for payment. When checks are outstanding, the bank statement will show a higher balance than the checkbook. This happens because the bank has not subtracted the checks from the depositor's account, but the checks have been subtracted from the checkbook balance. They will be subtracted from the bank balance when presented to the bank for payment.

■ Deposits in Transit A deposit not yet received by the bank is called a **deposit in transit**. These deposits have been added to the depositor's checkbook and mailed to the bank, but they are not listed on the monthly bank statement. When deposits are in transit, the bank statement will show a lower balance than the checkbook. This happens because the bank has not added the deposits to the depositor's account, but the depositor has added them to the checkbook balance. They will be added when received by the bank.

■ Dishonored Checks A person might endorse and deposit a check and later learn that the bank cannot collect on the check. A check that is not paid when properly presented to the bank is called a **dishonored check**. There are various reasons why a check may be dishonored.

- There are "not sufficient funds" (NSF) to cover the check in the account.
- The signature on the check might not be exactly the same as the one on the signature card.
- Payment on the check might have been stopped by the drawer.
- The check might have been altered or dated ahead.
- The endorsement might be missing or improper.

When a deposited check is dishonored, the bank subtracts the amount of the dishonored check from the depositor's account. This cancels the amount added when the check was originally deposited. The bank then returns the check to the endorser. Note that Exercise Plus's bank statement on page 246 shows a dishonored check for $200. This deduction is identified by the letters RI (meaning returned item).

■ Fees Banks sometimes charge a fee for collecting payment on certain kinds of negotiable instruments. In addition, most banks charge a fee to pay for the expenses involved in stopping payment on a check. A **debit memorandum** is a document explaining fees charged to the account. Fees are explained in detail on the debit memorandum. Fees are also shown on the bank statement. The debit memorandum below explains the December 22 fee of $4 on Exercise Plus's bank statement.

Lincoln Bank **Chicago, Illinois 60612** DEBIT MEMORANDUM	Date December 22, 19--	
Particulars	Amount	
Charge for processing stop payment order on Check 32, December 20, 19--	$4.00	
CHARGE ACCOUNT	By	Approved
Exercise Plus 3010 South Fifth Street Chicago, Illinois 60612 5050■0206 00 Number	*gc*	*T.M.P.*

Debit memorandum.

Service Charges Banks also charge for many of the special services they provide. Banks may collect a service charge to cover the expense of handling a checking account. A **service charge** is a fee charged by a bank for maintaining a checking account. Service charges may be calculated on the balance of the account, the number of checks paid, and the number of items deposited. A bank might also deduct from the depositor's account a charge for the use of the night depository or for the rental of a safe-deposit box.

Service charges are deducted directly from the depositor's account. They are identified on the bank statement by the initials SC (for service charge). Note that the bank statement for Exercise Plus shows a service charge of $3.85 for December.

Errors in Computations The checkbook balance might agree with the Cash account balance in the ledger, yet the checkbook balance might not agree with the bank statement balance. The difference might be due to one of the following errors.

- Writing a different amount on a check than on the stub
- Issuing a check, but not recording it on the stub or in the journal
- Not recording a deposit on the stub or in the journal

These errors in the depositor's records must be corrected.

Errors made by the bank should also be reported immediately. One bank error would be accepting a check on which someone had forged the depositor's signature (a loss to the bank, not to the depositor). Another bank error would be charging the depositor's account for another person's check by mistake.

Exercise E on page 252 may be completed at this point.

Concept: Bank Statement
The bank must account to the depositor for all money belonging to the depositor that comes into the bank's possession.

Reconciling the Bank Statement

How does a business determine the actual cash balance? The actual cash balance is determined by reconciling the bank statement. Reconciling the bank statement is the procedure used to find what causes the difference between the checkbook and bank statement balances. To reconcile the balances, the accountant prepares a bank reconciliation statement.

Bank reconciliation statements are used to analyze and reconcile differences between checkbook and bank statement balances.

A **bank reconciliation statement** is a statement verifying that the actual checkbook balance equals the actual bank statement balance. It is used to analyze the differences, to reconcile them, and to verify that the actual balances are equal. The bank reconciliation statement for Exercise Plus as of December 31 is illustrated on page 249. The form is printed on the back of the bank statement.

The procedure for preparing the bank reconciliation statement is as follows.

1. Complete the heading—WHO? WHAT? WHEN?
2. Find the ending balance shown on the bank statement and record it on the reconciliation statement. The ending balance on the December 31 bank statement is $8,039.
3. Compare the amounts of the deposits listed on the bank statement with the amounts of the deposits listed on the check stubs. Also, check last month's reconciliation statement to make sure that any deposits then in transit have been recorded on this month's statement. If any have not been recorded, notify the bank.

   On the reconciliation statement, list all deposits currently in transit. These are deposits that have been added in the checkbook but do not appear on the bank statement. In the case of Exercise Plus, a deposit of $295 is in transit. It appears on the check stub, but not on the bank statement.
4. Deposits in transit are then added to the ending bank statement balance because the bank will add these deposits when they are received. The sum of the ending bank statement balance and the total deposits in transit is entered as the subtotal on the left side of the reconciliation statement.
5. Take the canceled checks and any debit memorandums that are enclosed with the bank statement. Compare the amount on each item with the amount listed on the bank statement. If an amount

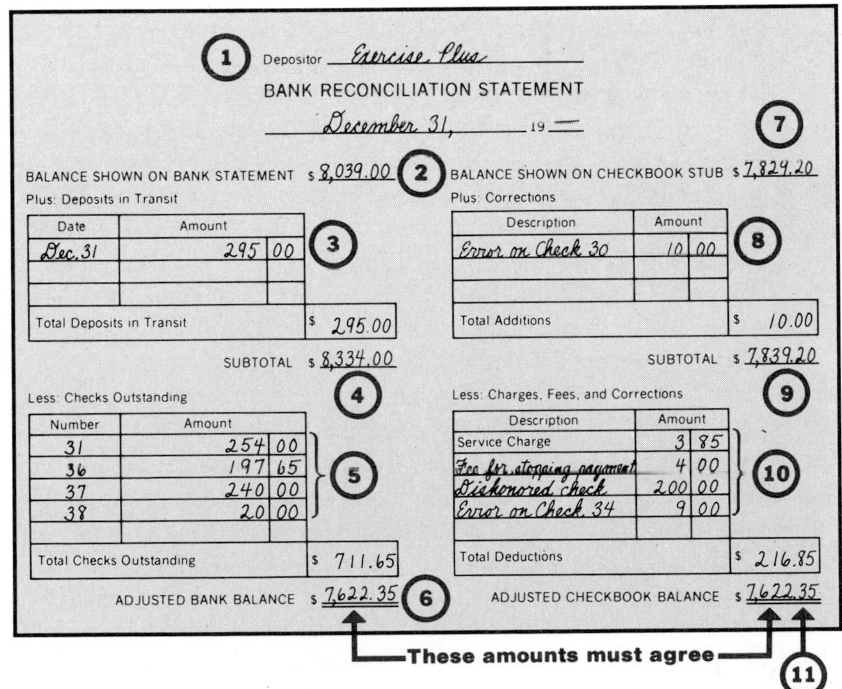

(1) Depositor *Exercise Plus*

BANK RECONCILIATION STATEMENT

December 31, 19__ (7)

BALANCE SHOWN ON BANK STATEMENT $ *8,039.00* (2)

Plus: Deposits in Transit

Date	Amount
Dec. 31	*295 00*

Total Deposits in Transit $ *295.00* (3)

SUBTOTAL $ *8,334.00* (4)

Less: Checks Outstanding

Number	Amount
31	*254 00*
36	*197 65*
37	*240 00*
38	*20 00*

(5)

Total Checks Outstanding $ *711.65*

ADJUSTED BANK BALANCE $ *7,622.35* (6)

BALANCE SHOWN ON CHECKBOOK STUB $ *7,824.20*

Plus: Corrections

Description	Amount
Error on Check 30	*10 00*

(8)

Total Additions $ *10.00*

SUBTOTAL $ *7,839.20* (9)

Less: Charges, Fees, and Corrections

Description	Amount
Service Charge	*3 85*
Fee for stopping payment	*4 00*
Dishonored check	*200 00*
Error on Check 34	*9 00*

(10)

Total Deductions $ *216.85*

ADJUSTED CHECKBOOK BALANCE $ *7,622.35*

These amounts must agree (11)

recorded on the bank statement is different from the amount on the check or the debit memorandum, notify the bank immediately. The statement must be corrected.

On the reconciliation statement, list all the numbers and amounts of the checks that have not been checked off on the check stubs. Also, check last month's reconciliation statement to make sure that checks then outstanding have now been returned. If these checks are still unpaid, list them as currently outstanding.

Certified checks that have not been returned with the bank statement should not be considered outstanding checks. The reason for this is that the bank deducts the amount of a certified check from the drawer's account at the time of certification. This deduction is shown on the bank statement, whether or not the canceled check is returned. The bank statement for Exercise Plus shows a $187.65 deduction on December 6 for a certified check (Check 33), identified on the bank statement by the code CC.

6. Subtract the total amount of checks outstanding from the subtotal shown above it on the reconciliation statement. The difference is the Adjusted Bank Balance. The Adjusted Bank Balance is the actual balance of the account.
7. Turn to the latest checkbook stub and record the current checkbook balance opposite ''Balance Shown on Checkbook Stub'' on the bank reconciliation statement.
8. List any corrections for errors that require increasing the balance of the checkbook. For example, Check 30 was issued to Shone Products on December 4 for $102.50 on account. It was recorded by mistake on the checkbook stub and in the journal as $112.50. The check was paid by the bank, returned with the December 31 bank statement, and listed correctly on the bank statement as a $102.50 deduction. The difference of $10.00, therefore, must be corrected in the checkbook; $10 too much was subtracted from the checkbook balance. Thus, $10 is listed in the section for amounts to be added to the checkbook balance.
9. Add the total additions ($10) to the checkbook balance shown at the top of the reconciliation statement ($7,829.20) and enter the sum as the subtotal ($7,839.20).
10. List any charges shown on the bank statement but not yet recorded in the checkbook, such as a service charge or a stop payment fee. These charges would decrease the checkbook balance, so they must be deducted from the checkbook balance. List the amount of any dishonored checks. This amount was added to the checkbook balance when it was deposited. It must now be deducted to show that the returned item cannot be collected. Also, list any errors that require decreasing the checkbook balance. For example, Check 34 was issued to pay $54 for furniture but was recorded on the check stub and in the journal as $45. The difference of $9

must be listed on the reconciliation statement as a deduction from the checkbook balance.

11. Subtract the total deductions ($216.85) from the subtotal shown above it ($7,839.20). The difference is the adjusted checkbook balance ($7,622.35). The adjusted checkbook balance is the actual balance of the account. This amount should be identical with the adjusted bank balance. If the amounts do agree, the balances are said to be reconciled. Reconciled balances are balances that are the same. If they do not agree, all the details must be rechecked until the error has been located and the balances agree. The double rules at the end of the reconciliation statement show that the balances agree and that the statement is complete.

Making Corrections and Entries After the Reconciliation

After the reconciliation statement has been completed, the balance on the last check stub must be brought into agreement with the adjusted checkbook balance shown on the reconciliation statement ($7,622.35). The check stub does not have to be adjusted for deposits in transit or outstanding checks. These items have already been entered in the checkbook. However, any additions and deductions shown on the right-hand side of the reconciliation statement must now be recorded in the checkbook. (Corrections for errors on check stubs should be cross-referenced; that is, make a note on the stub containing an error that the error has been corrected.)

After the corrections have been recorded in the checkbook, the balance on the last stub should agree with the adjusted checkbook balance on the reconciliation statement. The corrections must then be journalized and posted.

When the entries are posted, the balance in the Cash account will agree with the adjusted balance shown in the checkbook.

After reconciliation, corrections must be recorded on the latest check stub to adjust the checkbook balance, and journalized and posted to adjust the Cash account balance.

NO. 39 $ ____

DATE ____ 19 ____

TO ____

FOR ____

	DOLLARS	CENTS
BALANCE	7,829	20
12/31 ~~AMT. DEPOSITED~~	+10 / −216	00 / 85
Reconciliation Corrections TOTAL	7,622	35
AMT. THIS CHECK		
BALANCE		

JOURNAL — Page 4

DATE		ACCOUNT TITLE AND EXPLANATION	POST. REF.	DEBIT	CREDIT
19—					
Dec.	31	Cash	101	10 00	
		Accts. Pay./Shone Products	201		10 00
		Correct error on Check 30.			
	31	Accts. Rec./Carmen Saldi	103	200 00	
		Furniture	111	9 00	
		Miscellaneous Expense	503	7 85	
		Cash	101		216 85
		Returned check, error on Check 34, and bank charges.			

Cash — 101

Date	Debit	Date	Credit
19—		19—	
Dec. 31	7,829.20	Dec. 31	216.85
31	10.00		
	7,839.20		
7,622.35			

Exercise F on page 252 may be completed at this point.

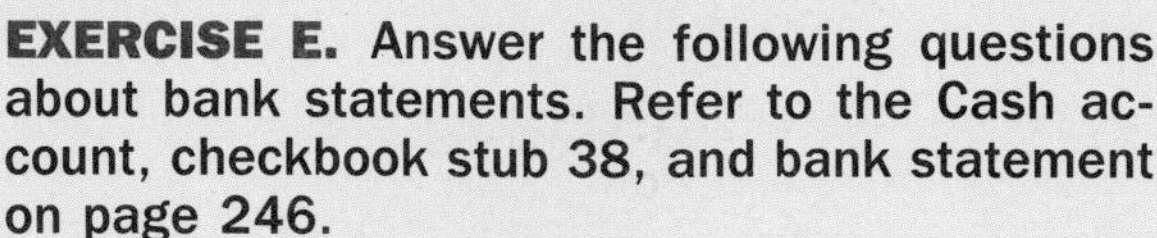

TOPIC 3 EXERCISES

EXERCISE E. Answer the following questions about bank statements. Refer to the Cash account, checkbook stub 38, and bank statement on page 246.

1. What is the account number?
2. What is the last date covered by the bank statement?
3. What is the bank balance at the beginning of the month?
4. How many deposits are shown on the bank statement?
5. What is the total of the deposits?
6. How many checks are paid by the bank?
7. What is the total of the checks paid?
8. How many other charges are made by the bank? What is the total?
9. What are the other charges made by the bank?
10. What is the bank balance at the end of the month? The Cash account balance?
11. Name some of the items that may cause a difference between the bank balance and the checkbook balance.

EXERCISE F. Answer the following questions about bank reconciliation. Refer to the bank reconciliation statement on page 249.

1. For what date is the reconciliation statement prepared?
2. Does $8,039 represent the bank balance at the beginning of the month or at the end of the month?
3. Why is the December 31 deposit not included in the bank balance?
4. What checks are outstanding?
5. How does Exercise Plus know these checks are outstanding?
6. Are outstanding checks added to or subtracted from the bank balance? Why?
7. What does the amount $7,829.20 represent?
8. Why is $10.00 added to $7,829.20?
9. What does the amount $3.85 represent?
10. Why is a $4 fee charged?
11. Why is a $200 charge made?
12. What is the $9 correction?
13. What does the amount $7,622.35 represent?
14. What does the amount $216.85 represent?
15. Should the adjusted bank balance and the adjusted checkbook balance agree? Why or why not?

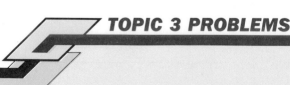

TOPIC 3 PROBLEMS

TOPIC PROBLEM 3. Information about banking activities for The Green Apple restaurant is shown on the next page. Use this information to do the following steps.

a. Prepare a bank reconciliation statement as of January 31.

b. Record any corrections in the checkbook and in the journal, page 10.

Bank balance as shown on bank statement: $2,752.40.
Checkbook balance: $2,801.95.
Deposit put in night depository on last day of month, recorded in checkbook but not shown on bank statement: $184.25.
Checks outstanding: Check 81, $124.60; Check 85, $55.35.
Service charge: $3.25.
Dishonored check: $42.00, received from James Davidson on account.

TOPIC PROBLEM 4. Use the given data to perform the following activities for The Green Apple restaurant.

a. Prepare a bank reconciliation statement as of April 30.

b. Record any corrections in the checkbook and in the journal.

Bank balance as shown on bank statement: $3,840.25.
Checkbook balance: $3,996.70.
Deposit put in night depository on last day of month, recorded in checkbook but not shown on bank statement: $250.00.
Checks outstanding: Check 128, $31.40; Check 131, $40.00; Check 132, $46.05.
Service charge: $3.90.
Dishonored check: $27.00, received from Rolanda Watts on account.
Fee for stopping payment on Check 126: $2.00.
Error on Check 124: Check was issued for $67, but the amount was recorded as $76 on the check stub, and the Maintenance Expense account was debited for $76 in the journal, page 11.

TOPIC 4

Petty Cash

Do businesses pay all bills by check? For the best control of cash, all cash receipts should be deposited in the bank and all bills should be paid by check. However, it is not practical to use checks for small cash transactions. As a result, most businesses usually keep a petty cash fund. A **petty cash fund** provides cash on hand to pay small amounts.

Some businesses use the petty cash fund to pay all bills of less than a certain amount, such as $5. In other businesses, all payments for such things as postage and small items of office supplies are paid out of the petty cash fund regardless of the amount.

Two methods for using a petty cash fund are described below—a petty cash fund with vouchers and a petty cash fund with a register.

Petty Cash Fund With Vouchers

A petty cashier is the individual who is responsible for establishing and maintaining the petty cash fund. (This individual is sometimes also referred to as a petty cash custodian.)

The discussion that follows describes the procedures that are used by a business that maintains a petty cash fund with vouchers.

■ Establishing the Petty Cash Fund The amount of money kept on hand as petty cash varies with the needs of the business. The fund should be large enough to cover petty cash payments for a specific period, such as on a monthly basis. The fund is started by drawing a check payable to the person responsible for the petty cash fund. The check is then endorsed and cashed. The money is placed in a petty cash box or drawer, which is usually kept apart from the cash receipts and secured by a lock. A separate record is kept of the flow of cash into and out of the fund.

■ Recording Disbursements A **cash disbursement** (sometimes referred to as a cash expenditure) is a payment from the petty cash fund. Each disbursement must be covered by some kind of receipt as evidence that cash was paid out of the fund. The receipt may be in the form of a bill marked ''Paid'' by the person receiving the money. Accountants, however, prefer to have businesses use special receipt forms called petty cash vouchers. A **petty cash voucher** is a form that provides evidence of a petty cash disbursement. One is shown below. The vouchers should be numbered at the time they are printed. If not, the vouchers should be numbered in sequence by the petty cashier. Normally, the voucher is signed by two persons—the person who has the authority to approve the disbursement and the person who receives the cash. The voucher is then put into the petty cash box as proof that the money was spent.

No. 1 Amount $ 4 75/100

PETTY CASH VOUCHER

Date Jan. 3, 19–

Paid to Regal Supply Co.

For Typewriter ribbon

Charge to Supplies

Exercise Plus

Approved by Lisa Long

Received by Stan Lowe

The total of the disbursements (as shown by the vouchers) plus the cash left in the fund must always equal the original amount of the petty cash fund. The procedure for checking that the total disbursements plus the remaining cash equals the original amount of the fund is called *proving the petty cash fund.*

For example, Exercise Plus set up a petty cash fund for $45. It requires a voucher for each disbursement. On January 15, the fund had vouchers for disbursements amounting to $42.95 and cash of $2.05. Total disbursements plus cash on hand equal $45 (the original amount of the fund), proving the fund is in balance.

Total disbursements ..	42	95
Cash on hand	2	05
Original amount of fund	45	00

■ Replenishing Petty Cash After the fund is reduced by disbursements to a certain amount (for example, $5), it is replenished. *Replenishing the petty cash fund* is restoring the fund to the original amount ($45). The procedure for replenishing the fund is as follows.

- Total the vouchers for disbursements from the fund.
- Prove the fund. The total of the vouchers plus the remaining cash should equal the original amount of the fund.
- Classify the types of accounts. For example, the petty cash disbursements might be classified into four kinds of accounts: Advertising Expense, Delivery Expense, Miscellaneous Expense, and Supplies.
- Draw a check payable to the order of the petty cashier for the amount of the total disbursements.
- Cancel the vouchers so that they cannot be used again.
- Attach the vouchers to the check, and submit the check to the proper person for signature.
- After the check is signed, file the vouchers in a dated envelope.
- Cash the check, and place the money in the petty cash fund. In this way the fund is replenished.

A **petty cash memorandum** is a form used to classify the petty cash disbursements according to the type of accounts. The petty cash memorandum in the margin classifies the petty cash disbursements for a two-week period. A petty cash memorandum is prepared unless a petty cash register is used.

Exercise Plus
Petty Cash Memorandum
January 2 to January 15, 19—

Advertising Expense ..	6	50
Delivery Expense	21	60
Miscellaneous Expense	8	00
Supplies	6	85
Total disbursements .	42	95
Cash on hand	2	05
Amount of fund	45	00

■ The Petty Cash Register

As an alternative way of controlling petty cash, accountants may use a petty cash register system. This is a systematic way of handling petty cash by using a memorandum book. A **petty cash register** (sometimes referred to as a memorandum or petty cash book) is a record of petty cash disbursements. All cash put into and taken out of the fund is recorded in the petty cash register. (A petty cash register is illustrated on page 256.)

■ Establishing the Petty Cash Fund The amount of cash used to establish the petty cash fund is recorded in the Received column of the petty cash register. The date and an explanation are recorded in the appropriate columns. A dash is placed in the Voucher Number column because no voucher is involved.

■ Recording Disbursements The amount of each voucher is recorded in the Paid Out column at the left. The amount is also recorded in at least one of the columns in the Distribution of Payments section at the right. The columns in the Distribution of Payments sec-

PETTY CASH REGISTER Page 1

Petty Cash Fund: Received	Petty Cash Fund: Paid Out	Date	Explanation	Voucher No.	Adv. Expense	Delivery Expense	Misc. Expense	Other Items: Account	Other Items: Amount
45 00		19— Jan. 2	Establish fund, Check 41	—					
	4 75	3	Typewriter ribbon	1				Supplies	4 75
	8 00	4	Snow removal	2			8 00		
	2 50	5	Ad in Express	3	2 50				
	7 50	7	Damon Trucking	4		7 50			
	2 10	8	Stationery	5				Supplies	2 10
	6 85	9	Damon Trucking	6		6 85			
	4 00	12	Ad in Express	7	4 00				
	7 25	15	Mountain Carriers	8		7 25			
45 00	42 95		Totals	—	6 50	21 60	8 00		6 85
	2 05	15	Cash on hand	—					
45 00	45 00								
2 05		Jan. 15	Cash on hand	—					
42 95		15	Replenish fund, Check 49	—					

tion help to classify disbursements according to the accounts in the ledger. The date, an explanation, and the voucher number are also recorded in the appropriate columns. The voucher is then placed in the petty cash box.

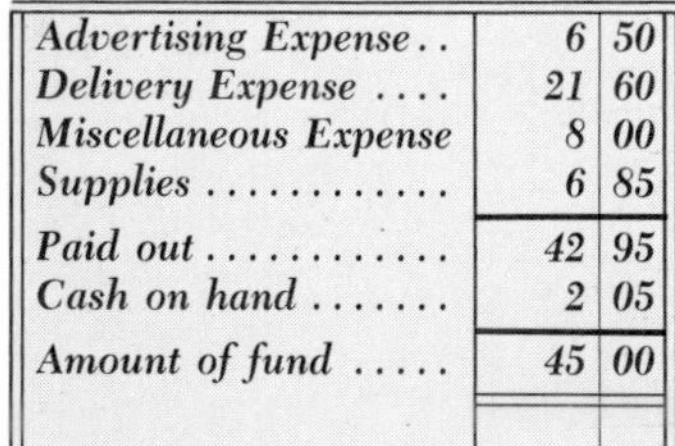

Advertising Expense	6 50
Delivery Expense	21 60
Miscellaneous Expense	8 00
Supplies	6 85
Paid out	42 95
Cash on hand	2 05
Amount of fund	45 00

Proof of petty cash register.

■ Recording the Replenishment of the Fund When the petty cash fund is replenished, the petty cash register is totaled and ruled using the following procedures.

- Draw a single rule across all the money columns.
- Pencil-foot the totals of the columns.
- Subtract the total cash paid out from the total cash received. The difference represents the cash on hand.
- Verify the amount of cash on hand by actually counting the cash left in the box or drawer.
- Verify that the totals of the Distribution of Payments columns equal the total of the Paid Out column.
- Verify that the total of the vouchers equals the total of the Paid Out column.
- Enter all the totals in ink.
- Draw a double rule across all money columns in the Distribution of Payments section.
- Enter the cash on hand balance in the Paid Out columns.
- Draw a single rule and total the Received and Paid Out columns.

- Verify that the totals of the Received column and the Paid Out column are equal. The total represents the original amount of the petty cash fund.
- Draw a double rule across the Received column, the Paid Out column, and the Date column. The double rule shows that the petty cash register is completed for this set of disbursements.
- Enter the balance of the cash on hand below the double rule in the Received column. This is the amount still in the fund.
- Enter in the Received column the amount of the check to replenish the fund.

The petty cash register is then ready for a new set of disbursements.

Exercises G and H on page 259 may be completed at this point.

Journalizing Petty Cash Entries

Is the information in the petty cash register posted to the ledger? No, entries are not posted from the petty cash register because the petty cash register is not a journal, a book of original entry. The petty cash register is simply a memorandum record.

The check to establish a petty cash fund must be recorded in the journal. From the journal, the transaction is posted to the accounts in the ledger.

The procedure to journalize petty cash entries is as follows.

A Petty Cash account is opened in the general ledger when a petty cash fund is established. This new account is used to show the transfer of cash from the Cash account to the Petty Cash account.

When Exercise Plus established its petty cash fund, a check was issued for $45. This transaction is journalized as a debit to the Petty Cash account and a credit to the Cash account. To increase the fund in the future, for example, to $75, a check is issued for $30. This transaction will be journalized as a debit to the Petty Cash account and a credit to the Cash account.

JOURNAL — **Page** 5

DATE		ACCOUNT TITLE AND EXPLANATION	POST. REF.	DEBIT		CREDIT	
19—							
Jan.	2	*Petty Cash*		45	00		
		Cash				45	00
		Establish the petty cash fund.					

Journal entry to establish petty cash fund.

Whenever cash is paid from the petty cash fund, an entry is recorded in the petty cash register, but not in the journal.

Whenever the petty cash fund is replenished, a check must be written for the total amount that has been paid out. This procedure is the same for either petty cash system. This check is recorded in the journal by making a compound journal entry. The individual accounts are debited for the totals of the columns in the Distribution of Payments section of the petty cash register. The Cash account is credited for the total amount. (The headings of the columns in the Distribution of Payments section should correspond to the titles of the accounts most frequently involved in the petty cash transactions.)

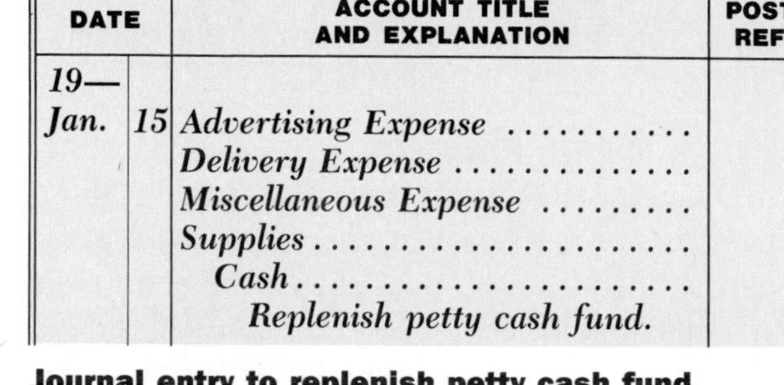

JOURNAL Page 6

DATE		ACCOUNT TITLE AND EXPLANATION	POST. REF.	DEBIT	CREDIT
19—					
Jan.	15	*Advertising Expense*		6 50	
		Delivery Expense		21 60	
		Miscellaneous Expense		8 00	
		Supplies		6 85	
		Cash			42 95
		Replenish petty cash fund.			

Journal entry to replenish petty cash fund.

A check for $42.95 was written to replenish the petty cash fund of Exercise Plus. This transaction is journalized by debiting the accounts for the appropriate amounts and crediting Cash for the total amount in the journal.

The Petty Cash account in the ledger will have only one amount in it as long as the fund stays at the original amount. The original amount for Exercise Plus was $45. The replenishment of the fund does not affect the Petty Cash account because the expenditures are debited to the individual accounts.

The petty cash fund should be replenished whenever it falls below a certain minimum. It must also be replenished at the end of an accounting period so that the expenditures are recorded during the accounting period in which they are made.

The Petty Cash account is an asset account. It is listed on the balance sheet directly after Cash. Since the petty cash fund is replenished at the end of the accounting period, the amount shown on the balance sheet is the fixed amount of the fund. What this means is that this amount is the amount of cash that is actually in the cash box or drawer. Replenishing the fund does not mean adding to the Petty Cash account in the ledger.

Concept: Petty Cash Fund

A petty cash fund is frequently kept for expenditures made in cash. From time to time, the fund is restored to its original amount by a transfer from the Cash account of a sum equal to the total disbursements.

Exercise I on pages 259 and 260 may be completed at this point.

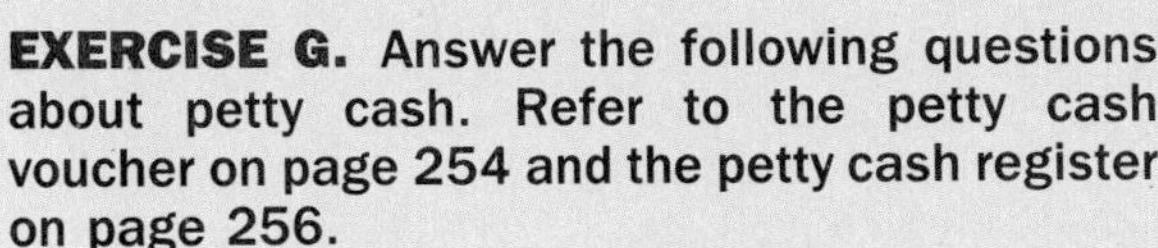

TOPIC 4 EXERCISES

EXERCISE G. Answer the following questions about petty cash. Refer to the petty cash voucher on page 254 and the petty cash register on page 256.

1. What information is provided by the petty cash voucher?

2. Who approved the expenditure for Voucher 1? Who received the cash?

3. Why is cash paid out on Voucher 1? What account is affected? How much is paid out?

4. When was the petty cash fund established?

5. Where is this information given?

6. Is any money paid from petty cash on January 3? If so, for what?

7. Is every expenditure entered in more than one column in the petty cash register? Why or why not?

8. What were the total petty cash expenditures from January 2 to 15? How is this amount determined and proved?

9. How much petty cash is left in the fund on January 15? How is this amount determined and proved?

10. When is the petty cash fund replenished? For what amount?

11. Why is the petty cash fund replenished for this amount?

12. After the petty cash fund is replenished on January 15, how much is there in the fund?

13. What are the total petty cash expenditures for advertising?

EXERCISE H. The petty cashier for Health Care Studios had the following transactions.

May 1 Received Check 58 for $50 to establish the petty cash fund.
4 Paid $8.75 for advertisement in the *News Gazette*.
6 Paid $3.50 for parcel post delivery.
8 Paid $5 for washing windows.
11 Paid $7.50 to repair chair (Repairs Expense).
14 Paid $4 for ad in track game program.
15 Paid $6 to have lawn cut.
18 Paid $4.50 to Winston Delivery Service for delivery.
19 Paid $3.60 for postage stamps (Office Expense).
20 Paid $3 to Delivery Express for delivery.

a. Record the transactions in the petty cash register. Number the petty cash vouchers consecutively, beginning with 1.

b. Pencil-foot the petty cash register as of May 21. Then complete a proof of the petty cash register. (There is $4.15 in the cash box on this date.)

c. Total and rule the petty cash register.

d. Record Check 73 to replenish the petty cash fund.

NOTE: Save your petty cash register for further use in Topic Problems 5 and 6.

EXERCISE I. Answer the questions here and on the next page about journalizing petty cash entries. Refer to the petty cash register on page 256 and the related journal entries on pages 257 and 258.

1. Which account is debited and which is credited when the petty cash fund is established?

2. Which accounts are debited and credited when the fund is replenished?

3. How many petty cash expenditures are made for supplies? How many times is the Supplies account debited? For what amount?

4. How many petty cash expenditures are made for advertising?

5. Which account is debited on January 4 for $8?

6. How can you be sure that you have not made an error in transferring the data from the petty cash register to the journal?

TOPIC 4 PROBLEMS

TOPIC PROBLEM 5. In Exercise H on page 259, you recorded transactions in the petty cash register for Health Care Studios. Now record the journal entries needed for these petty cash transactions.

a. Make the journal entry to record Check 58, which was issued to establish the fund on May 1.

b. Make the journal entry to record Check 73, which was issued to replenish the fund on May 21.

NOTE: Save your journal and the petty cash register for further use in Topic Problem 6.

TOPIC PROBLEM 6. Use the petty cash register from Exercise H on page 259. Record in the journal the entries to record the following transactions for Health Care Studios. Omit explanations in the journal.

May 22 Issued Check 74 for $15 to increase the fund to $65. (Debit Petty Cash. Enter amount in Received column of petty cash register.)
22 Paid $8.75 for ad in *News Gazette*.
25 Issued Check 75 for $600 to pay rent for June.
27 Paid $7.50 for adding machine tapes (Supplies).
June 4 Paid $9.50 for typewriter ribbons.
12 Paid $3.75 to Delivery Express for delivery of equipment.
16 Issued Check 76 for $525 for store equipment.
June 18 Issued Check 77 for $120 to Morris Equipment on account.
24 Paid $6.50 to Railway Express for delivery.
26 Issued Check 78 for $125 to pay the electric bill.

a. Record these transactions in the journal or the petty cash register.

b. Pencil-foot the petty cash register on June 30, the end of the accounting period.

c. Complete a proof of the petty cash register. (The petty cash box contains the following: three $5 bills, eight $1 bills, 10 quarters, 19 dimes, 24 nickels, and 40 pennies.)

d. Record Check 79 to replenish the petty cash fund.

CHAPTER 8 REVIEW

CHAPTER SUMMARY

In this chapter you studied banking activities and petty cash procedures. You learned that businesses use checking accounts to keep a second record of, and to safeguard, cash. You also learned how to properly complete and record a check and the procedures to follow when depositing cash and checks and when reconciling a bank statement.

To ensure speed and accuracy, banks use automated data processing equipment to handle checks and deposits.

Businesses do not pay all their bills by check. For small cash transactions, businesses usually keep a petty cash fund. This fund can be used either with vouchers or with a register.

THE LANGUAGE OF BUSINESS

Here are some terms that make up the language of business. Do you know the meaning of each?

signature card
check
depositor
drawer
drawee
payee
voucher check
certified check
stop payment order
endorsement
negotiable instrument
blank endorsement
full endorsement
restrictive endorsement
deposit ticket
bank statement
canceled check
outstanding check
deposit in transit
dishonored check
debit memorandum
service charge
bank reconciliation statement
petty cash fund
cash disbursement
petty cash voucher
petty cash memorandum
petty cash register

REVIEW QUESTIONS

1. Give several reasons why businesses use checking accounts.
2. What is the purpose of the magnetic ink characters printed at the bottom of deposit tickets and checks?
3. What three records are compared to verify the cash balance at the end of the month? In what order are they compared?
4. What information appears on a bank statement?
5. On June 30, a checkbook showed a balance of $420 and the bank statement showed a balance of $410. Give four factors that may have caused this difference.
6. Why is a bank reconciliation statement prepared? Describe in sequence the steps for preparing a bank reconciliation.

7. Which items on the bank reconciliation statement require journal entries?
8. Explain how a petty cash fund is established and operated.
9. What is the procedure for replenishing the petty cash fund?
10. The Petty Cash account of a business has a balance of $175. At the end of the accounting period, there is still $75 in the petty cash fund. Should the fund be replenished on the last day of the period? Why or why not?

CHAPTER 8 PROBLEMS

Problems for Chapter 8 are given below. Write your answers on a separate sheet of paper unless you are using the workbook for this textbook. If you are using the workbook, do the problems in the space provided there.

CHAPTER PROBLEM 8-1. Maria Larkin owns the New Sound Record Center. She has a checking account with the Security Bank. She uses a checking system to help her control cash payments and receipts for her business. The cash payments and cash receipts transactions shown below and on the next page occurred between January 15 and January 28.

Ms. Larkin records data about her cash payments and receipts transactions on checkbook stubs. Because the stubs are the source documents for journalizing cash payments and receipt transactions, this data must be recorded accurately. Assume that there is a balance of $1,337 in the New Sound Record Center's checking account before Maria issued Check 45. Using the data about the transactions below, prepare the stubs for Checks 45 to 53. Draw stubs like the one shown on page 232 on separate sheets of paper if you are not using the workbook for this textbook.

Complete the stubs, making sure to record amounts drawn on the checking account, record deposits, and carry the balance forward.

Jan. 15 Issued Check 45 for $340 to the King Corporation for cash purchase of stereo equipment.
15 Issued Check 46 to pay utilities expense (electric bill) of $88 to Clinton Power Company.
15 Deposited $384 received from cash sales. (Deposit recorded on the stub for Check 47.)
16 Issued Check 47 for $185 to pay Lunar Records on account.
18 Deposited $341 received from cash sales. (Deposit recorded on the stub for Check 48.)
19 Issued Check 48 for $234 to pay Sunrise Record Company on account.
20 Issued Check 49 for $200 made out to Maria Larkin as a withdrawal of funds for personal use.
22 Deposited $415 received from cash sales. (Deposit recorded on the stub for Check 50.)
23 Issued Check 50 for $32 to pay a telephone bill to Eastland Phone Company.

Jan. 24 Deposited $55 received from M-Market on account. (Deposit recorded on the stub for Check 51.)
25 Issued Check 51 to pay Hit Records $287 on account.
26 Issued Check 52 to Alan Baker Company for $304 for cash purchase of stereo equipment.
28 Deposited $350 received from J. Lopez on account. (Deposit recorded on the stub for Check 53.)
28 Issued Check 53 for $40 for the purchase of office supplies from Brady Supplies.

CHAPTER PROBLEM 8-2. Continue with Chapter Problem 8-1. Using the data about transactions in Chapter Problem 8-1 and the check stubs that you prepared, journalize the transactions for the New Sound Record Center which occurred between January 15 and January 28. Omit explanations in the journal entries.

CHAPTER PROBLEM 8-3. On January 31, Maria Larkin received the bank statement for the New Sound Record Center's checking account shown below. Enclosed with the bank statement were the following canceled checks: 45, 47, 48, 49, 50, 51, and 52. Use this statement and the checkbook stubs which you prepared for Chapter Problem 8-1 to prepare a bank reconciliation statement as of January 31. No check drawn before Check 45 is outstanding, and no deposit made before January 25 is in transit. To complete this problem on a separate sheet of paper, draw a bank reconciliation statement similar to the one shown on page 249.

SECURITY BANK
Chicago, Illinois 60612

New Sound Record Center
401 East Hamilton Lane
Chicago, Illinois 60606

ACCOUNT NUMBER 8606-308440

PERIOD ENDING 1/31/--

Checks	Checks	Deposits	Date	Balance
			12/31	1,445.00
175.00			1/5	1,270.00
295.00	235.00		1/10	740.00
		515.00	1/11	1,255.00
	405.00	487.00	1/14	1,337.00
340.00		384.00	1/17	1,381.00
234.00		341.00	1/19	1,488.00
185.00			1/20	1,303.00
		415.00	1/22	1,718.00
32.00			1/23	1,686.00
		55.00	1/24	1,741.00
304.00	200.00		1/27	1,237.00
287.00			1/29	950.00
3.00 SC			1/31	947.00

Beginning Balance	+	Total Amount of Deposits	−	Total Amount of Checks Paid	−	Total Charges	=	Ending Balance
1,445.00		2,197.00		2,692.00		3.00		947.00

Number of Deposits Made	Number of Checks Paid	Number of Other Charges
6	11	1

Codes: CC Certified Check; DM Debit Memorandum; EC Error Correction; OD Overdrawn; RI Returned Item; SC Service Charge; BT Bank Transfer

Please examine this statement upon receipt and report at once if you find any difference. If no error is reported in ten days, the account will be considered correct. All items are subject to final payment.

CHAPTER PROBLEM 8-4. On July 1, Maria Larkin issued Check 68 for $50 to establish a petty cash fund. On July 15, the cash on hand was 2 five-dollar bills, 3 one-dollar bills, 6 quarters, 5 dimes, and 3 nickels. Using the information provided below, prepare the petty cash vouchers that were issued between July 1 and July 15. If you are not using the working papers, draw vouchers like the one shown on page 254 on a separate sheet of paper. Maria Larkin approves all petty cash disbursements. You are the employee who receives the petty cash.

July 1 Paid $7.50 to Popular Music News for advertising circulars. Charge to Advertising Expense.
3 Paid $6.50 to Palen's Parcel Service for distribution of advertising circulars. Charge to Advertising Expense.
6 Paid $2.75 to Brady Supplies for pencils. Charge to Supplies.
11 Paid $8.00 to Rocky's Window Company for window washing. Charge to Miscellaneous Expense.
14 Paid $5.90 to Brady Supplies for price stickers. Charge to Supplies.
15 Paid $4.20 to the Post Office for stamps. Charge to Office Expense.

After you have completed the petty cash vouchers, do the following.

a. Record the entry to establish the petty cash fund.

b. Record the receipts and expenditures in the petty cash register.

c. Prove the petty cash register on July 16.

d. Record Check 84 issued on July 16 to replenish the fund.

e. Record the journal entries for the petty cash fund. (Assume the entries are to be recorded on page 96 of the journal.)

MANAGEMENT CASES

Safeguarding Cash. Every business runs the risk of robbery, embezzlement, and fraud. Some methods a business can use to protect itself against such losses are these.

- Use source documents as evidence of cash transactions.
- Use prenumbered forms.
- Deposit cash receipts in the bank one or more times each day.
- Use the night depository for deposits after the bank is closed.
- Place cash awaiting deposit in a safe.
- Vary the time of day and routine for going to the bank.
- Employ an armed-guard service to take the cash to the bank.
- Require identification when cashing checks for customers.
- Take out insurance against burglary and robbery.

CASE 8M-1. The Corner Market, owned and managed by Kim Brown, is open from 9 A.M. to 9 P.M. Monday through Saturday, and 10 A.M. to 6 P.M. on Sundays. The daily cash receipts amount to several thousand dollars and are placed in an office safe at the end of the day. These receipts are then deposited in the bank the next morning. The receipts for Friday, Saturday, and Sunday are deposited on Monday morning. Over the weekend there is usually $30,000 to $35,000 in the safe.

a. What safeguards might Kim Brown use to protect cash receipts during the day?

b. What safeguards can be taken to protect cash receipts during the evenings?

c. What safeguards can be taken to protect cash receipts during the weekends?

d. What safeguards can be taken to prevent losses due to robbery?

CASE 8M-2. Ralph McCabe owns a parking lot that Is open from 8 A.M. to 7 P.M. He charges a fee of $4 for a car, regardless of how long it is parked. Customers park their own cars and pay when they drive out of the lot. No parking ticket is issued to the customers. An attendant collects the money and deposits it in the bank once a day.

a. Mr. McCabe believes that he should install some plan to ensure that each person who parks a car pays the fee. What plan do you suggest?

b. Mr. McCabe also wants to ensure that all amounts collected by the attendant are deposited. What control system do you recommend?

GOLD STAR TOURS

On July 1, Judy Wells started Gold Star Tours. This single proprietorship plans group tours for high school and college students to historical sites around the country. Included in the service is transportation by minibus, guided tours, food, and lodging. The chart of accounts for the business is shown here.

GOLD STAR TOURS
CHART OF ACCOUNTS

101	Cash
103	Accts. Rec./Clinton High School
104	Accts. Rec./Ryder School
105	Accts. Rec./Sinclair College
108	Supplies
111	Minibuses
112	Office Equipment
201	Accts. Pay./Central Motors
202	Accts. Pay./Neal's Garage
301	Judy Wells, Capital
399	Income Summary
401	Sales
501	Advertising Expense
502	Maintenance Expense
503	Miscellaneous Expense
504	Office Expense
505	Salaries Expense
506	Supplies Expense

INSTRUCTIONS

Open the ledger accounts shown in this chart of accounts. (If you are not using the workbook, allow 17 lines for Cash; 4 lines for Judy Wells, Capital; 7 lines for Sales; and 4 lines for each of the other accounts.)

1. *Originating the data.* During the month of July, the business had the transactions listed at right and on page 267.

2. *Journalizing the transactions.* Record the transactions for July in the journal.

3. *Posting the transactions.* Post the journal entries.

4. *Proving the ledger.* Prepare a trial balance on a worksheet to prove the equality of the ledger.

5. *Preparing the financial statements.* Prepare the financial statements for the accounting period as follows.

   a. Complete the worksheet. A physical count showed that supplies costing $140 were used during the month.

   b. Prepare an income statement.

   c. Prepare a balance sheet.

6. *Adjusting and closing the ledger.* Journalize and post the adjusting and closing entries.

7. *Proving the closed ledger.* Prepare a postclosing trial balance to prove the equality of the ledger after it has been closed.

8. *Interpreting the financial information.* Based on the information in the financial records of Gold Star Tours, answer the following questions.

   a. Ms. Wells expects her revenue and expenses for August to be approximately the same as for July. However, she promised to pay the balance she owes to Central Motors for the minibuses by August 31. Do you think Gold Star Tours will have enough cash to pay its debt by August 31?

   b. If you think that Gold Star Tours does not have enough cash, explain how might the business handle the situation. If you think that it has extra cash, explain what the business might do with the funds.

TRANSACTIONS FOR JULY

July 2 Judy Wells started the business with a cash investment of $36,000.

3 Bought three used minibuses for $24,000 on credit from Central Motors.

5 Bought $620 worth of supplies from Apex Supplies with cash.

July 8 Judy Wells invested a typewriter costing $595 in the business.
8 Sold services for $1,250 on credit to Clinton High School.
8 Owed $360 to Neal's Garage for maintenance of the minibuses.
9 Paid $18 for an ad in *The Hightstown Herald.*
10 Paid $8,000 to Central Motors on account.
10 Bought office equipment for $800 with cash.
15 Sold services for $800 in cash.
16 Sold services for $1,680 on credit to Sinclair College.
18 Returned minibus bought for $8,000 on credit to Central Motors.
18 Received $350 from Clinton High School on account.
22 Sold services for $1,000 in cash.
23 Owed $95 to Neal's Garage for maintenance on the minibuses.

July 24 Returned office equipment bought for $455 in cash.
25 Judy Wells withdrew $2,500 from the business.
26 Paid $500 for maintenance on the minibuses.
26 Sold services for $1,800 on credit to Sinclair College.
26 Paid $4,000 for salaries.
29 Paid $65 for cleaning office (Office Expense).
29 Received $750 from Sinclair College on account.
30 Sold services for $1,600 on credit to the Ryder School.
30 Paid $20 to Overnight Couriers for next-day delivery of mail (Miscellaneous Expense).
31 Paid $27 for an ad in the *Mercer County News.*
31 Received $125 from the Ryder School on account.

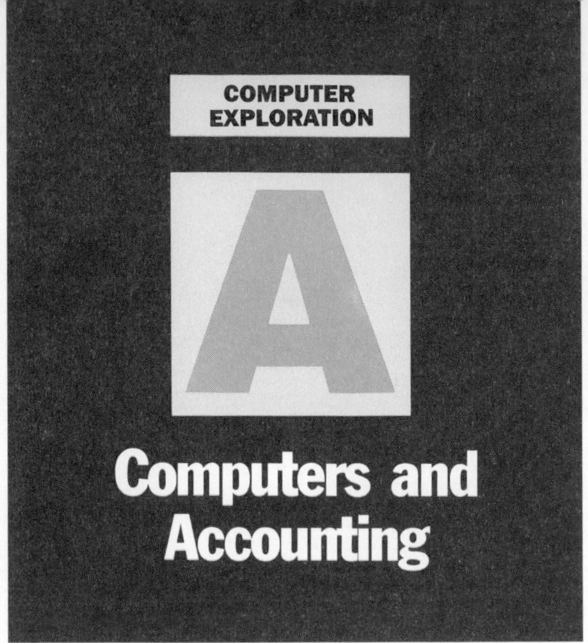

TOPIC 1

Computers and Computer Programs

A **computer** is an electronic device that can process data at rapid speeds by following instructions stored in its memory. A **computerized accounting system**, or electronic accounting system, processes accounting data through the use of computers. This method is much faster than processing data by manual techniques. A computer might complete in three seconds a task that could require three days if performed manually. Computers make it possible to obtain, process, and distribute large amounts of information about every facet of a business.

A computer can process data at rapid speeds.

Development of Computers

Many attempts have been made in the past to develop devices that would allow manual data processing tasks to be performed more quickly. These early devices that allowed for mechanical calculation, such as the ''analytical engine'' created by Charles Babbage in the 1830s, were not practical for widespread use.

The development of the modern computer is often spoken of as occurring in stages, or generations. Each new generation has come about as a result of technological advances. The first generation of computers was developed in the 1950s. These early models were huge and extremely expensive. They required large rooms filled with vacuum tubes and circuitry. Compared with later models, these computers were slow in processing data. A small portable computer of today is more powerful than the computers of the 1950s.

The invention of the transistor at Bell Laboratories in 1947 revolutionized computer design and introduced a new generation of computers. In the early 1960s, computers using transistors were developed that were much smaller, faster, and less expensive than the earlier computers.

In the early 1970s came the third and current generation of computers. (Some observers feel that since technology has advanced so much even since the 1970s, we are now using the fourth generation of computers.) Today's computers use integrated circuits—tiny assemblies of transistors placed on chips. With integrated circuits, computers have become even smaller, faster, less costly, and easier to use. Even small businesses can afford to purchase computers today.

The microcomputer has been called the "computer on a chip." A single silicon chip like the one shown here makes today's computers more powerful than the early models, which were so large that they filled one or more rooms.

■ Types of Computers

Today's computers are classified by cost, speed of processing data, storage capacity, and size. Generally, the larger the computer, the more it costs, the faster it processes data, and the more storage capacity it has. The three main categories of computers are microcomputers, minicomputers, and mainframe computers.

The **microcomputer**, which is also referred to as a personal computer, is the smallest and least expensive type of computer. Because they are so affordable, microcomputers are popular for both business and home use. A microcomputer is a complete computer on a single chip. Microcomputers use diskettes to store data for processing. Manufacturers of popular microcomputers include IBM, the Apple Corporation, and the Tandy Corporation.

A microcomputer system.

A **minicomputer** is a computer that operates with a stored program but has less storage capacity than a large computer. Minicomputers may be used by small and medium-sized businesses. Large businesses may also use minicomputers in different branch stores or production departments. When several minicomputers are used, they can be connected to a larger computer to form a computer network.

A mainframe computer is larger than the minicomputer or microcomputer. A **mainframe computer** is capable of storing and processing large amounts of data at fast speeds. Mainframes are usually placed in a centralized location where large volumes of data must be processed. Information processed with mainframe computers is often stored on magnetic disks similar to $33\frac{1}{3}$ records.

Minicomputers perform a variety of tasks in businesses.

Mainframe computers are capable of processing vast amounts of information.

■ Computer Equipment

The data entered into the computer system is processed so that information can be generated for decision making. As shown in the flowchart in the margin on the next page, the components of a computer correlate with the input-process-output steps of the data processing cycle.

The components of a microcomputer system typically include a keyboard, a central processing unit (CPU), one or two disk drives, a display screen, and a printer.

An optical character reader scans information and enters it automatically into the computer system.

■ Input Devices The keyboard is one means of entering data. Keyboarding information into the system converts data from human-readable to machine-readable form.

An **optical character reader (OCR)**, or optical scanner, is another way to enter data into a computer. This equipment can scan data and automatically enter it into the system. One place that makes extensive use of OCRs is the post office, which uses OCR equipment to read two-letter state abbreviations and ZIP codes on envelopes.

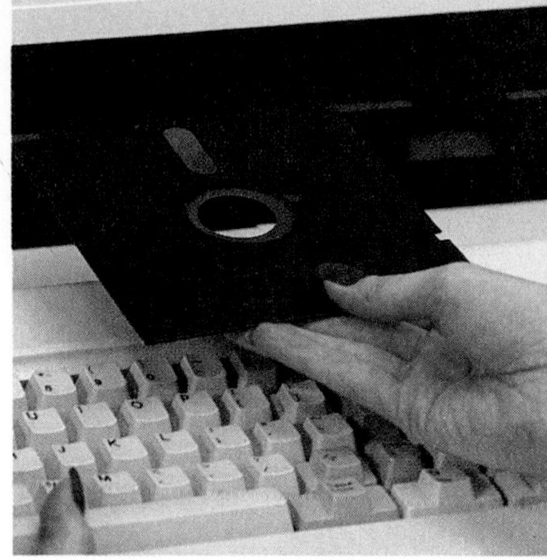

A floppy disk being inserted into a disk drive.

■ Central Processing Unit

The **central processing unit**, or CPU, is the device that actually processes the data. It contains the units that control the computer system, process information, and store data. The CPU contains the circuitry that enables the computer to operate.

A microcomputer has two forms of memory. There is built-in memory capacity, which is called *read-only memory* (ROM), and memory that can be changed, which is called *random access memory* (RAM). There is also external memory in the form of floppy disks, hard disks, or magnetic tape.

The basic unit of memory in a microcomputer is a *byte* (pronounced "bite"). Each byte holds one character. The common $5\frac{1}{4}$ inch, double-sided disk can store 368,640 characters (letters, marks of punctuation, and spaces), which is equivalent to approximately 180 typewritten, double-spaced pages.

Memory size is rated by kilobytes (K). One **kilobyte** is equal to 1,000 bytes. A computer with 256K (which is the amount of memory that may be found in an IBM PC with two disk drives) contains 256 kilobytes of memory.

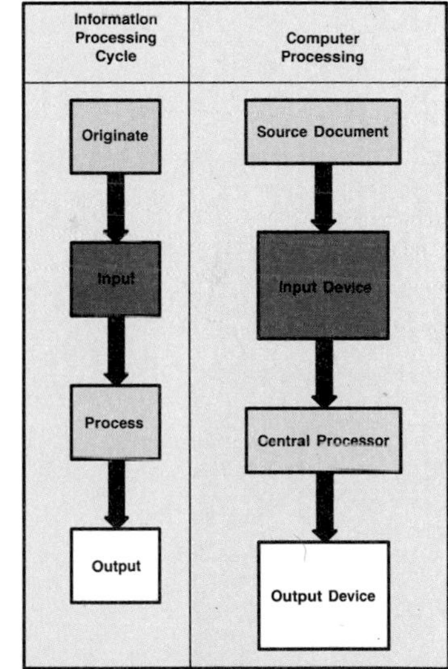

The components of a computer correlate with the input-process-output steps of the data processing cycle.

■ Output Devices

Several types of output devices are available. A **video display terminal**, also known as a *computer monitor* or a *cathode ray tube* (CRT), allows the user to display the information being processed.

A printer can be connected to a computer in order to produce a hard copy (printed copy) of the output. There are various types of printers.

- Dot matrix printers can print at fast speeds and can be used to produce reports and graphics.
- Letter-quality, or daisy-wheel, printers produce reports that look like they have been produced on a typewriter.
- Laser printers operate at very high speeds and can be used to produce brochures or books which combine text and graphics.

■ Telecommunications

Telecommunications allows computers to transmit information over the telephone. The device that connects a computer to a telephone is called a **modem**. All around the world, bank computers use modems to move trillions of dollars every year.

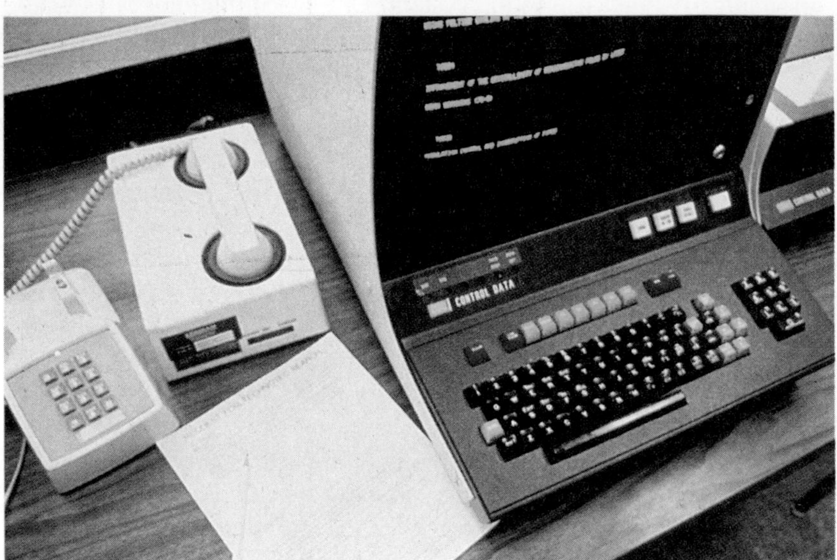

Modems like the one shown here allow computers to transmit information over the telephone.

■ Computer Programs

A computer operates by following a series of detailed instructions called a **program**. A program can be stored in the memory of the computer or on a floppy disk, a hard disk, or a magnetic tape. The instructions tell the computer, in a step-by-step sequence, exactly what to do and when to do it. A separate program must be prepared for each data processing job. For example, there may be a program for maintaining a general ledger, a program for updating accounts receivable, and a program for computing the payroll.

Once programmed, a computer can function with little human assistance and at speeds near the speed of light. Many processing jobs can be completed by a computer in seconds. An example of this is the posting step in the accounting cycle. You can immediately see how much faster posting is completed by the computer than by manual posting to the general ledger.

The person who prepares a computer program is called a **programmer**. To plan the most efficient computer program, the programmer uses a diagram called a flowchart, sometimes referred to as a *program flowchart* or *procedure flowchart*. A **flowchart** is an outline that shows the series of instructions the computer will follow in processing data. The flowchart helps the programmer detect unnecessary operations that would otherwise use valuable computer time. The programmer's job is to assess every possible thing that may happen when the program is being operated.

■ Applications Software

Programs that do specific jobs on the computer are known as **applications software**. An example of applications software is a general ledger program, which is discussed in detail in Topic 2.

Some other popular types of programs used in business today include spreadsheets, word processing, database management, graphics, and communications software. Applications software is discussed in more detail in ''Computer Exploration B: Computerized Accounting Systems,'' which starts on page 519.

■ Disk Operating Systems

A **disk operating system** allows an applications program to operate on the computer. For example, when using an IBM PC, an operating system called IBM DOS (disk operating system) needs to be loaded before starting the applications program. On the Apple computer, Apple DOS is used with most applications programs. The disk operating system is specific to the type of computer in use. Thus, IBM DOS cannot be used with the Apple computer, and Apple DOS cannot be used with the IBM computer.

A disk operating system is often necessary to run software on a microcomputer.

■ Mainframe Systems

Mainframe computers are capable of processing large amounts of data at very fast speeds with access to billions of characters of data. Large magnetic disks, called hard disks, are used for storage.

The uses of mainframe systems include the following.

- The automatic teller machines (ATMs) that are widely used by banks today are connected to mainframe computers. When an ATM card is placed in an automatic teller machine, the record of the deposit or withdrawal is provided by the mainframe system of that bank.

Automatic teller machines are widely used today.

- At the grocery store, an optical scanner may be used to read the universal product code (UPC) bars on a product. When the cashier enters a transaction at the cash register, the mainframe computer system at the grocery store is accessed to check the inventories of the product purchased. If inventories are running low on the item purchased, this information is given to the inventory control person so that the item can be replenished.
- Schools use mainframe systems for student recordkeeping. For example, when a request is made for a student's transcript, mainframe systems would be accessed to complete the search for the student's record.

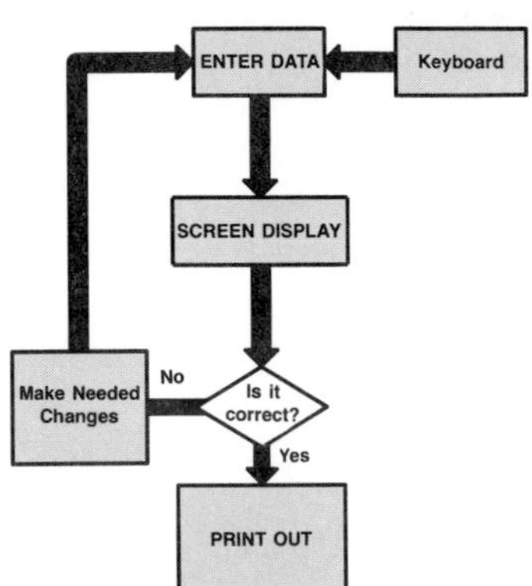

The same types of procedures are followed when using different types of accounting software.

TOPIC 2

Using General Ledger Software

General ledger software is one of the most frequently used types of accounting software in the business world today. It allows you to do all the steps in the accounting cycle easily, and it does some of them automatically.

There are many different general ledger programs available commercially, and they all differ somewhat in how they operate. However, many of them share similar basic features. The way in which a typical general ledger package operates is described in this topic.

These are just a few of the many general ledger software packages currently available.

Entering Data in the Chart of Accounts

Usually, the first step when using general ledger software generally is to enter the chart of accounts into the computer via the keyboard. Then the chart of accounts is displayed so that the accuracy of the input can be checked. If any changes are needed, enter the corrections and display the chart of accounts again to be sure it is correct. (Note that you can display data at almost any point when using general ledger software. The point at which you display or print out particular data depends on the software used and the information needed.)

When entering the chart of accounts, it is important to number the accounts correctly. Most general ledger software requires that different types of accounts be numbered within certain ranges, and some accounts may be assigned specific numbers. For example, the asset accounts may be numbered from 101 through 199, liability accounts from 201 through 299, owner's equity capital and income summary accounts from 301 through 399, revenue accounts from 401 through 499, and expense accounts from 501 through 599.

Many general ledger programs require that the chart of accounts be numbered in a specific way.

The reason for using a specific numbering system is simple: When the correct numbers are designated for accounts, the software can correctly handle the debit and credit entries and the account balances in the ledger. In addition, the software can then classify accounts for the financial statements. If asset, liability, and owner's equity accounts are numbered incorrectly, data will not be analyzed correctly by the program.

■ Recording in the Journal

After the chart of accounts has been entered, the journal entries are analyzed and entered at the computer. Display the journal entries on the screen so that you can check that each entry has been done correctly. Then you can make any corrections necessary before posting to the general ledger.

■ Posting to the General Ledger

Once the journal entries are recorded correctly, the next step is to post the entries to the general ledger. Posting to the general ledger can be done very quickly when accounting software is used. All the work of posting and calculating account balances for each general ledger account is done automatically when a computer is used.

The posting process is completed easily and automatically when a general ledger software program is used.

■ Generating a Trial Balance

After the journal entries have been recorded and posted, generate a trial balance in order to prove the equality of the ledger. The trial balance is calculated automatically. The computer does this job very quickly and accurately if the chart of accounts and journal entries were entered correctly.

■ Completing the End-of-the-Period Work

You can use general ledger software to complete the end-of-the-period work quickly and easily. First, record, correct, and post the adjusting entries for the period. Generate a new trial balance to prove the equality of the ledger. If it is in balance, you can use the computer to automatically generate an income statement for the period.

Next, record, correct, and post the closing entries. Again, check that the ledger is in balance by obtaining a trial balance. You can then prepare a balance sheet as of the end of the period.

CHAPTER SUMMARY

This chapter introduces you to computers and computer programs. After the first machines that performed mechanical calculations, computers developed in several stages as technology advanced from vacuum tube circuitry to transistors and finally to integrated circuits. The categories of computers, which are based on a number of factors such as speed, size, and cost, include mainframes, minicomputers, and microcomputers. The components of a microcomputer typically include a keyboard, a central processing unit, one or two disk drives, a display screen, and a printer.

Many types of computer programs are available. One of the most commonly used programs in the business world today is general ledger software. With a general ledger program, a user can complete all the steps in the accounting cycle.

THE LANGUAGE OF BUSINESS

Here are some terms that make up the language of business. Do you know the meaning of each?

computer
computerized accounting system
microcomputer
minicomputer
mainframe computer
optical character reader (OCR)
central processing unit (CPU)
kilobytes (K)
video display terminal
telecommunications
modem
program
programmer
flowchart
applications software
disk operating system

REVIEW QUESTIONS

1. What is a computer?
2. When and where was the transistor invented?
3. When did each of the three generations in the development of the computer begin? What advance in technology did each generation use?
4. What are the three types of computers? Describe each type.
5. What two forms of internal memory does a microcomputer have? What form of external memory?
6. Name the components of a microcomputer system.

7. What is the basic unit of memory for a microcomputer? How many typewritten pages can be stored on a 5¼ inch disk?
8. What are the three types of printers? Describe each type.
9. What is applications software? Give two examples of applications programs.
10. What steps in the accounting cycle can be completed using general ledger software?

MANAGEMENT CASES

Computerizing an Accounting System. Replacing an existing computer system or converting from a manual system to a computerized system are steps that should not be taken without a great deal of thought and planning. A business must decide what procedures should be computerized, what costs will be involved, and what kind of equipment and programs should be purchased. Current and future needs of the business must be evaluated. Staff members will require training, and new staff members may need to be hired.

CASE CAM-1. You are the manager of a supermarket with ten branches located within fifty miles. You have to make a decision about upgrading the computer equipment used in the supermarket. Currently, microcomputers are used mainly by the accounting staff and clerical staff. You have looked at minicomputers and microcomputers. The company wants this computer system to be installed for at least five years and wants to automate the checkout for their customers. Which computer system would you decide to purchase? Why?

CASE CAM-2. You are the manager of an accounting firm that has been in business for over 100 years. Most of the accountants use calculators and do most of their work manually. You have just taken a computerized accounting class and learned about various types of computers and computer software. You are convinced that automating the office would be a good idea. How would you convince your employees? What type of computer equipment would you recommend? What type of applications programs do you think they should know? How would you convince them?

PART

2

Accounting Subsystems and Special Procedures

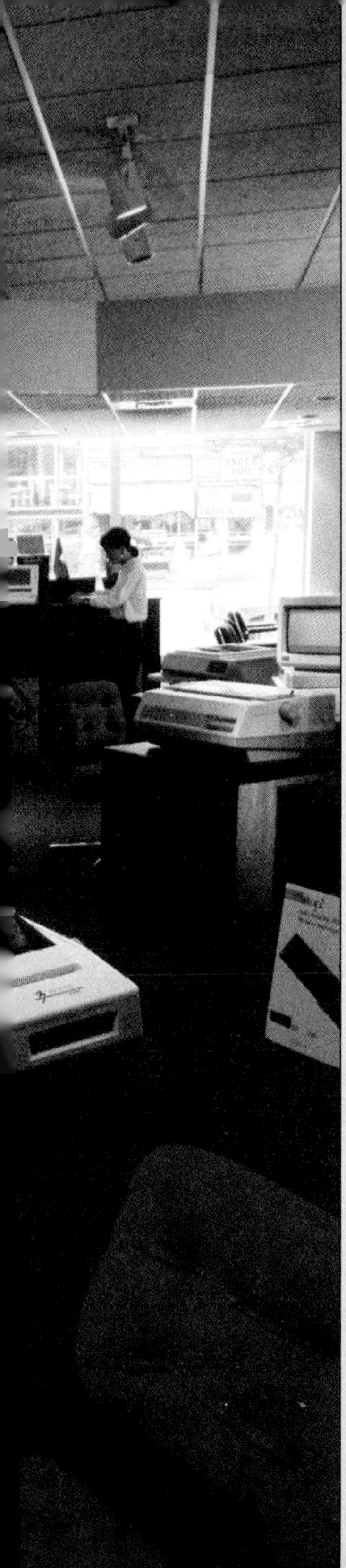

You have just completed your study of the accounting cycle for a service business. You have seen how data is processed when revenue is earned by providing a service. You will now learn about the accounting procedures for a merchandising business.

A *merchandising business* obtains revenue by selling goods. The goods are called *merchandise*. If the merchandising business sells to a customer, like yourself, it is known as a *retailer*. If the merchandising business sells to retailers, it is known as a *wholesaler*. The merchandise that retailers and wholesalers have in stock is known as *inventory*. In Part 2, you will be studying how businesses that earn revenue by selling merchandise process data.

Accounting systems vary. The system used is tailored to fit the type and size of the business, the nature of its operations, and the external and internal needs for information. No one accounting system fits the needs of every business.

In Chapters 9 to 14, you will study the accounting system used by Computer Age, a retail merchandising business that sells computer equipment and supplies. (The chart of accounts used by Computer Age is shown on page 280.) In an accounting system such as that used by Computer Age, there may be a number of subsystems. An *accounting subsystem* is a method used to process specific kinds of data in an accounting system. You will be studying six subsystems used in the Computer Age accounting system. The subsystems are cash receipts, cash payments, purchases, sales, personnel and payroll, and general accounting.

Some accounting subsystems make use of a special journal. A *special journal* is used to collect data about similar types of business transactions. The subsystems you will learn about in Chapters 9 to 14, the journals used in those subsystems, and the types of transactions each processes are listed below.

Subsystem	Journal	Transactions Recorded
Cash receipts	Cash receipts journal	All receipts of cash
Cash payments	Cash payments journal	All payments of cash
Purchases on credit	Purchases journal	All purchases of merchandise or services on credit
Sales on credit	Sales journal	All sales of merchandise or services on credit
Personnel and payroll	Payroll journal	All payroll and personnel expenses/liabilities
General accounting	General journal	All remaining transactions

As you study the accounting system of Computer Age, you will see that the components of any accounting system are the *people*, *forms*, *procedures*, and *equipment* needed to process data and provide information. An aspect of any accounting system that affects the people, forms, procedures, and equipment are *controls*. An accounting system must have controls to ensure accuracy, honesty, and efficiency and speed—three basic goals common to all accounting systems. You will see how controls are incorporated in an accounting system.

COMPUTER AGE
CHART OF ACCOUNTS

Assets

101 Cash
102 Petty Cash
103 Change Fund
111 Accts. Rec./Allied Display
112 Accts. Rec./Electro Computer
113 Accts. Rec./Hallmark Sales
114 Accts. Rec./Will's Appliance
115 Accts. Rec./Wing Computers
116 Accts. Rec./James Young
120 Merchandise Inventory
121 Prepaid Insurance
123 Supplies
132 Office Equipment
133 Stockroom Equipment

Liabilities

201 Loans Payable
211 Accts. Pay./Diskettes Plus
212 Accts. Pay./Johnson Supply
213 Accts. Pay./LCP Computer
214 Accts. Pay./Micro Components
216 Sales Tax Payable
221 Federal Income Taxes Payable
222 FICA Taxes Payable
223 State Income Taxes Payable
224 Federal Unemployment Taxes Payable
225 State Unemployment Taxes Payable
226 Salaries Payable
227 Insurance Premiums Payable
228 Union Dues Payable

Owner's Equity

301 Jason Booth, Capital
302 Jason Booth, Drawing
399 Income Summary

Revenue

401 Sales
402 Sales Returns and Allowances
403 Sales Discount

Costs and Expenses

501 Purchases
502 Transportation In
503 Purchases Returns and Allowances
504 Purchases Discount
511 Cash Short and Over
512 Advertising Expense
513 Delivery Expense
514 Insurance Expense
515 Miscellaneous Expense
516 Payroll Taxes Expense
517 Rent Expense
518 Salaries Expense
519 Supplies Expense
520 Utilities Expense

CHAPTER

9

A Cash Receipts Subsystem

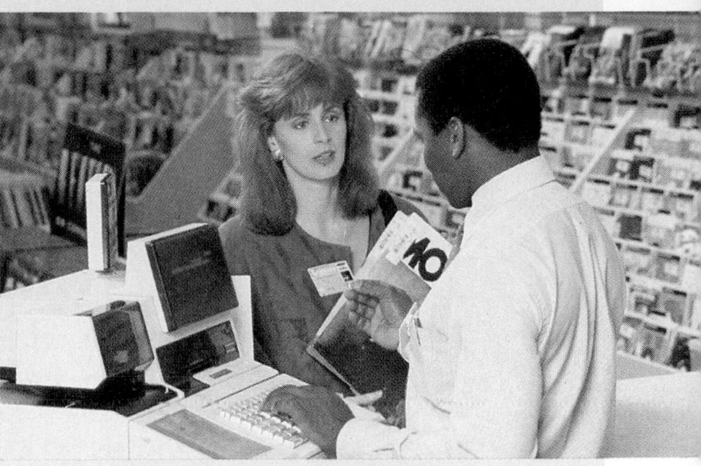

In a typical business, there are many daily transactions involving the receipt of cash. Money is received from cash sales, from charge customers, and from customers who owe money on notes. In this chapter you will study how people, forms, procedures, and equipment in a cash receipts subsystem are used to handle and record cash receipts. You will also learn about the key role played by the cashier.

CHAPTER GOALS

After studying Chapter 9, you will be able to:

1. Define the terms listed in ''The Language of Business'' section on page 301.
2. Explain the concepts and principles in this chapter related to accounting for cash receipts.
3. Use a flowchart to describe the relationship between people, forms, procedures, and equipment in a cash receipts subsystem.
4. Prepare a cash proof.
5. Journalize cash receipt transactions in a general journal and a cash receipts journal.
6. Post entries and a summary total from a cash receipts journal to ledger accounts.
7. Record bank credit card sales in a cash receipts journal.

TOPIC 1

Controlling Cash Receipts

What is a cash receipts subsystem? The people, forms, procedures, and equipment used to process cash receipts make up a **cash receipts subsystem**. The employee who processes cash receipts and prepares the necessary source documents is the **cashier**. There are two primary activities completed in any cash receipts subsystem. First, cash is received from customers, recorded on source documents, and proved. This activity is known as **handling cash receipts**. Second, the amounts of cash handled are journalized and posted in the accounting records. This activity is known as **recording cash receipts**. Because cash can be mishandled so easily, each activity—handling and recording cash receipts—is controlled by a set of procedures.

Controls for Cash Receipts
- Create source documents
- Use prenumbered source documents
- Prove cash frequently
- Deposit all cash intact
- Divide responsibility

Procedures for Controlling Cash Receipts

The procedures for the control of cash receipts are as follows.

- Creating source documents
- Using prenumbered source documents
- Proving cash frequently
- Depositing cash receipts intact
- Dividing responsibilities for handling and recording cash receipts

Creating Source Documents When cash is received, a cashier prepares the necessary source documents to record the transaction. These source documents should indicate the amount of cash, the date, why cash was received, who received the cash, and, in some cases, from whom cash was received. The source documents commonly used to record cash receipts are cash register tapes, prenumbered sales slips, and prenumbered remittance slips.

Cash Register Tapes A cashier usually uses a cash register to record the amount of cash received when goods or services are sold. The prices of items are entered and totaled in the cash register. The amounts are also displayed at the top of the machine as a control of the cashier's accuracy and honesty. The customer can then check the amounts entered with the price of each item. In addition, a permanent record of each cash receipt is usually made on a **cash register tape**, a source document produced on a cash register.

Two copies of the cash register tape are created. One copy is removed from the cash register and given to the customer as a receipt. A second stays in the register until it is removed and used as a source document.

Sales Slips A **sales slip** is a source document which may also be used to record the receipt of cash. An original sales slip and one or more copies are prepared. One copy is given to the accounting department as a source document describing the sale. Another is given to the customer as a receipt of the transaction. A third copy, if one is prepared, is kept as the record of all transactions that a particular cashier handles.

COMPUTER AGE
200 Girard Avenue
Denver, Colorado 80236

Date *August 15,* 19 —

Sold to *Allied Display*

Address *2 Camino de Oeste, Denver, Colorado, 80219*

Clerk	Cash	C.O.D.	Charge	On Acct.	Retd.	Paid Out
L.F.				✓		

QUANTITY	DESCRIPTION	PRICE	AMOUNT
	Received on account		*150.00*
		Total	*150.00*

No. 101 Received by *Brian Carlio*

Sales slip used as receipt.

Sales slips can be used instead of a cash register tape. There are also times when both a cash register tape and sales slips are used. A cash register tape does not include the customer's name and address. Thus, a sales slip or some other receipt is used whenever names and addresses must be recorded.

A form that is numbered when printed is a **prenumbered source document**. Prenumbered sales slips, which are prepared in duplicate or triplicate form, are available in a sales book, as single units, or filed in a forms register.

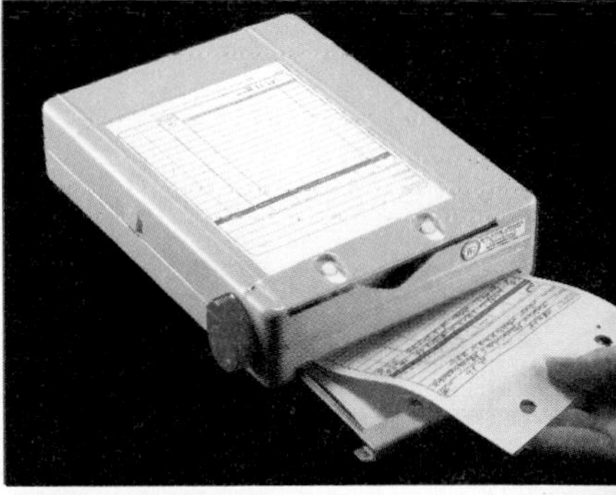

Forms register.

Forms registers come with or without cash drawers. When a forms register is used, at least two copies of the sales slip are prepared. One copy of the sales slip is removed from the register and given to the customer. The other copy remains locked inside the register until it is removed.

■ **Remittance Slips** Checks and money orders are often received by mail. The employee who opens the mail must record the transaction on a prenumbered remittance slip like the one shown on page 284. A **remittance slip** is used to record the amount of cash received from each customer. Completed remittance slips become source documents and are then sent to the accounting department.

COMPUTER AGE 200 Girard Avenue Denver, Colorado 80236		REMITTANCE SLIP RS-307
NAME: Hallmark Sales		
AMOUNT RECEIVED $600.00	CHECK NUMBER 182	CHECK DATE 8/22/—
EXPLANATION: Received on account.		
DATE RECEIVED 8/24/—		RECEIVED BY N.H.

Remittance slip.

■ **Using Prenumbered Source Documents** Prenumbering source documents makes it possible to keep track of the forms used. Voided forms should be kept on file in numeric sequence to account for each form. Prenumbered source documents provide a control for cash receipts transactions. Once either has been filled out, it is impossible to hide the fact that a transaction took place. A salesclerk must account for any slips missing from the numeric sequence.

■ **Proving Cash** The cash received should be proved frequently, usually at the end of each day. A supervisor (not the employee who prepares the source documents) should verify that the count of cash agrees with the total of the cash receipts recorded on the source documents. Both cash register tapes and sales slips are used in proving cash.

■ **Cash Register Tapes** When a cash register is used, the amount of cash in the drawer at the end of the day should equal the following.

- The amount of the **change fund** (the amount of cash put in the drawer to make change), plus
- The total cash sales recorded on the cash register tape, plus
- The total cash received on account from customers, less
- Any money paid out of the drawer. Usually, the only cash taken out of the drawer is the correct change given to customers. (The exception is when a customer returns goods bought for cash and wants a cash refund. The clerk must then record the amount on the cash register tape and take the cash refund from the cash drawer.)

The cash proof illustrated on page 285 shows how the supervisor verifies the receipts, refunds, and change fund handled by the clerk. The cash register tape for August 3 shows that total receipts from cash sales (TCa) amounted to $180. The total cash received on account

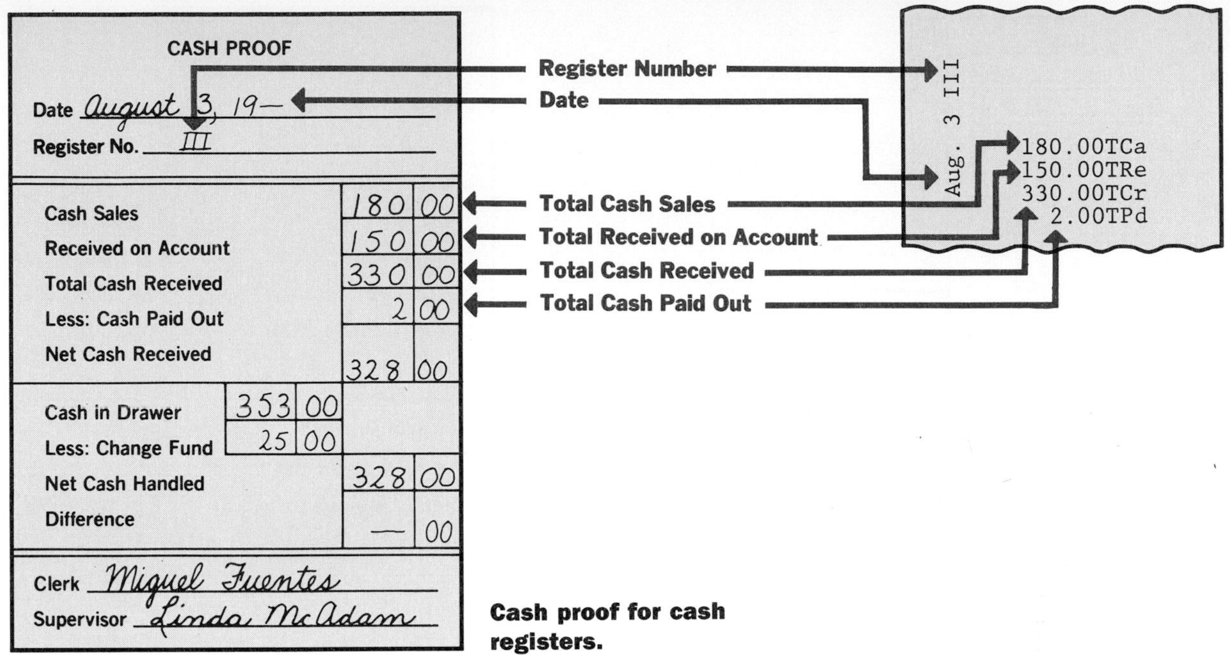

Cash proof for cash registers.

from customers (TRe) was $150. The total cash receipts (TCr) for August 3, therefore, is $330. The tape also shows that a total of $2 was paid out (TPd). The $2 must be subtracted to determine the net cash receipts for the day ($328). The supervisor counts the actual cash in the drawer ($353). The change fund ($25) is subtracted to arrive at the net cash handled ($328). The $328 agrees with the net cash receipts ($330 − $2) computed from the cash register tape.

■ **Sales Slips** When sales slips are used to record cash receipts, the supervisor first arranges the sales slips in numeric order (see the illustration on page 286) and makes sure that no slips are missing. (A missing slip suggests that a transaction was not recorded and cash was mishandled. But the salesclerk may have an explanation for the missing slip.) Second, the supervisor computes the total cash sales for the day by adding the cash sales slips on an adding machine or calculator. Third, the supervisor computes the total cash received on account from customers. The two totals are then added to find the total cash receipts for the day. Last, if cash was paid out, the supervisor would find the total amount paid out. The cash paid out would be subtracted from the total cash received.

The supervisor then counts the cash in the cash drawer and subtracts the amount of the change fund. The net amount of cash in the drawer should equal the total cash receipts recorded on the sales slips less any cash paid out.

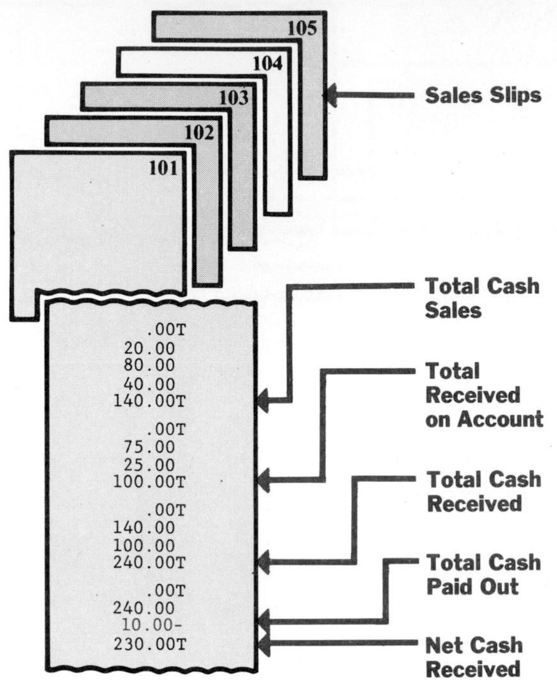

CASH PROOF

Date August 4, 19–

Sales Book No. 32

Cash Sales		140 00
Received on Account		100 00
Total Cash Received		240 00
Less: Cash Paid Out		10 00
Net Cash Received		230 00
Cash in Drawer	260 00	
Less: Change Fund	30 00	
Net Cash Handled		230 00
Difference		— 00

Clerk Miguel Fuentes

Supervisor Linda McAdam

Cash proof for sales slips.

■ **Remittance Slips** The cash proof is simplified when remittance slips are used to record cash received through the mail. The total amount on the remittance slips is compared with the total amount of cash in the cash drawer. As with sales slips, the prenumbering of remittance slips makes it easy to see if any slip is missing.

■ **Depositing All Cash Receipts Intact** The total bank deposits should equal the total cash receipts. Depositing all cash receipts intact provides one more check on the accuracy of cash procedures.

■ **Dividing the Responsibility** An important cash control procedure is to separate the handling of cash receipts from the recording of cash receipts. It is sometimes difficult to do so, but the best procedure is as follows.

- The employee who prepares the cash receipts source documents should not be the employee who makes the cash proof (comparing actual cash on hand with the source documents).
- The person who prepares the actual cash receipts for deposit should not be the person who prepares the source documents.
- The person who uses the cash receipts source documents to record the cash transactions in the journal should have no contact with the actual cash receipts.

Cashier: DOT 211.462-010
Receives cash, pays cash, and records transactions on source documents.

Exercises A and B on page 288 may be completed at this point.

Visualizing the Cash Receipts Subsystem

How are the handling and recording of cash related? The relationship between the two procedures involved in processing cash is illustrated by the flowchart below. It shows that the procedures for handling cash involve the customer, the cashier (or salesperson), the supervisor, and the bank.

A cash proof is prepared daily. The source documents are then sent to the accounting department to be journalized. All cash receipts are deposited intact in the bank. Thus, at the end of the month, the total deposits must equal the total of the cash debits recorded in the journal.

Exercise C on page 288 may be completed at this point.

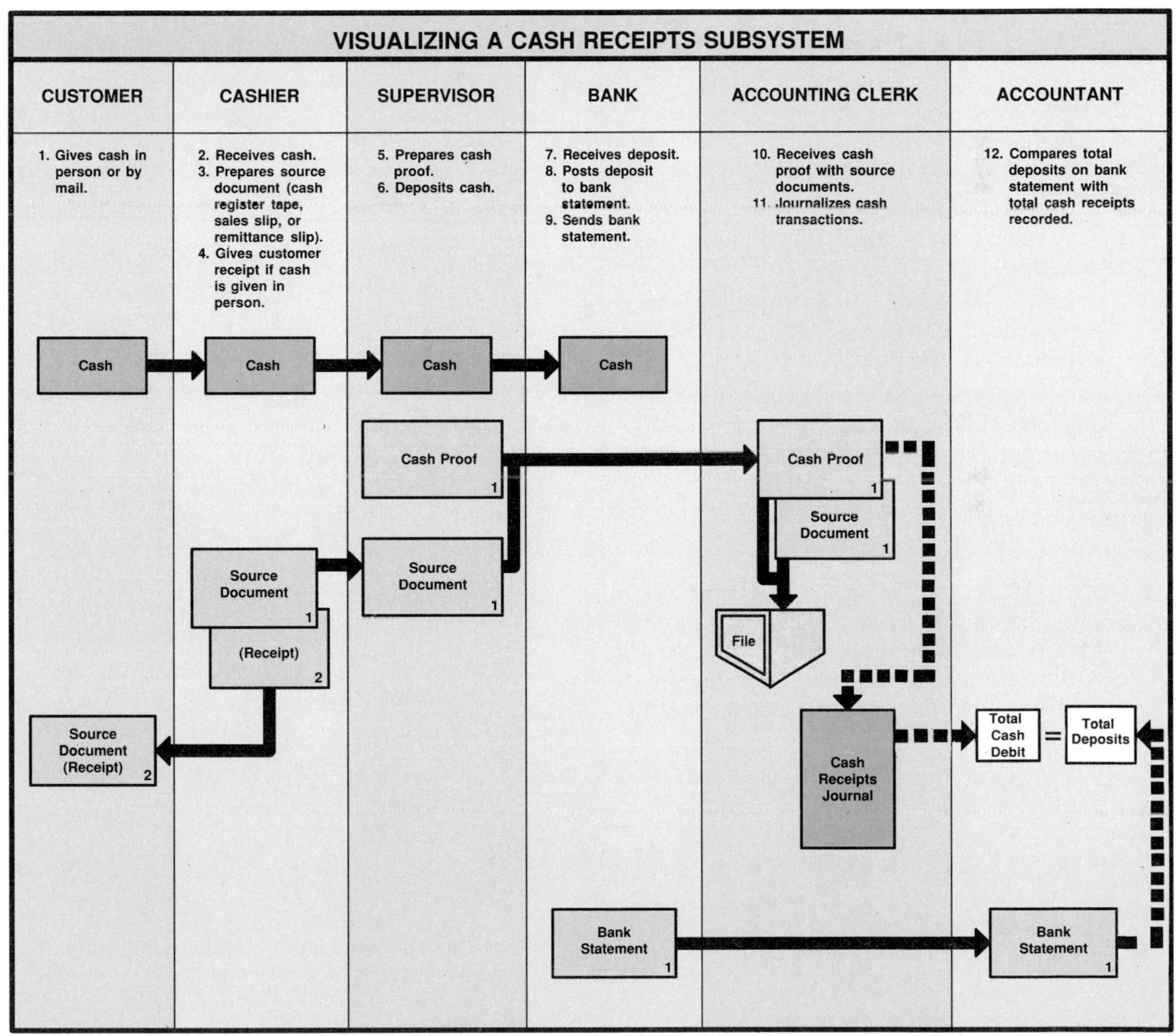

The numbers in the lower right corner of the document symbols show the copy number. The original copy is Copy 1. The duplicate copy is Copy 2.

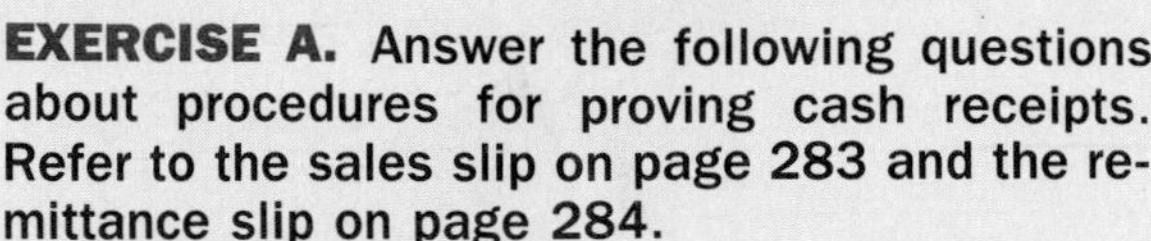

TOPIC 1 EXERCISES

EXERCISE A. Answer the following questions about procedures for proving cash receipts. Refer to the sales slip on page 283 and the remittance slip on page 284.

1. From whom is cash received on August 15? How much cash is received?
2. Why is the cash received from Hallmark Sales?
3. Who receives the cash on August 15?
4. When is cash received from Hallmark Sales? How much is received?
5. What is the date of the check received from Hallmark Sales?
6. What is the number of the cash remittance slip?
7. What would happen if the next completed sales slip were Sales Slip 103?

EXERCISE B. Answer the following questions on cash proofs. Refer to the cash proof for sales slips on page 286 and the cash proof for a cash register on page 285.

1. For which cash register is the cash proof prepared?
2. What is the total amount of cash sales recorded on the cash register on August 3? How much is the last cash sale?
3. What is the total amount received on account on August 3?
4. How much is the total cash paid out on August 3?
5. What is the total cash received on August 3? How much is in the cash drawer at the end of the day? Are the two amounts different? Why?
6. Who is the clerk operating Cash Register III? Who prepares the cash proof?
7. What are the total cash sales on August 4? How much is the last cash sale?
8. Is there a difference between the total cash received and the cash in the drawer on August 4? Why or why not?
9. What would change on the cash proof for August 3 if the Cash in Drawer were $350?

EXERCISE C. In a table similar to the one below, indicate who prepares or sends the following forms, to whom or where they are sent, and the purpose they serve. Refer to the flowchart of a cash receipts subsystem that is illustrated on page 287.

1. Source document: Copy 2
2. Cash proof: Copy 1 (with source documents)
3. Cash proof: Copy 1 (with source documents after journalizing)
4. Bank statement: Copy 1

Form	Prepared or Sent By	Sent To	Purpose
EXAMPLE: Source document: Copy 1	Cashier	Supervisor	As a record of all cash received and to provide the information needed to prepare a cash proof.

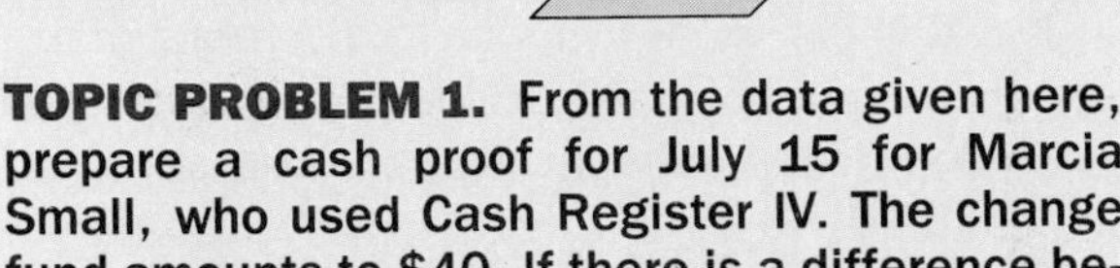

TOPIC 1 PROBLEMS

TOPIC PROBLEM 1. From the data given here, prepare a cash proof for July 15 for Marcia Small, who used Cash Register IV. The change fund amounts to $40. If there is a difference between the net cash received and the net cash handled, explain what could have caused the difference.

MONEY IN CASH REGISTER DRAWER

Currency	Coins	Checks
Fifty-four $20 bills	18 quarters	$300
Forty-two $10 bills	104 dimes	$ 80
Twenty-three $5 bills	45 nickels	$ 60
Eighty-two $1 bills	67 pennies	$ 50

July 15, IV

```
2,035.66TCa
  144.16TRc
2,179.82TCr
   15.00TPd
```

Cash register tape totals.

TOPIC PROBLEM 2. Using the following information, prepare Sales Slip 258: on October 9, salesclerk Paul Gomez received $36 on account from Ralph Baxter, 1 Poplar Road, Tucson, Arizona 85718. Prepare a cash proof for October 9 for Paul Gomez, who used Sales Book 84. Data for an additional 12 sales slips and the cash in the drawer is given below and in the next column. The change fund is $35. If there is a difference between the net cash handled, explain what could have caused the difference.

MONEY IN CASH REGISTER DRAWER

Currency	Coins	Checks
Nine $20 bills	14 quarters	$30
Seven $10 bills	21 dimes	$24
Thirteen $5 bills	14 nickels	$12
Thirty-three $1 bills	25 pennies	$45

No. 251 $43.80 Cash Sale	No. 257 $91.18 Cash Sale	No. 261 $70.00 On Account
No. 252 $18.65 Cash Sale	No. 254 $30.00 On Account	No. 255 $42.71 Cash Sale
No. 262 $52.71 Paid Out	No. 253 $9.24 Cash Sale	No. 260 $62.43 Cash Sale
No. 259 $40.90 Cash Sale	No. 263 $11.70 Cash Sale	No. 256 $26.65 Cash Sale

Prenumbered sales slips.

TOPIC PROBLEM 3. Prepare Remittance Slip RS-19 using the following information: $800 was received on account from Playtime Sales, Check 190, dated June 7 and received June 9.

TOPIC 2

Processing Cash Receipts

What kinds of transactions involve cash receipts? In general, there are three types of cash transactions that involve cash receipts.

- Customers paying cash for goods or services
- Debtors paying amounts they owe
- Owners making additional investments in their businesses

The number of cash transactions and the amount of cash received depend on the type and the size of the business. For example, a pharmacy has many cash sales. However, an average sale is probably under $15. An automobile dealer, on the other hand, might have only one cash transaction a day. But this sale could involve $10,000 or more.

Source documents are prepared when cash is received, as discussed in Topic 1. How these source documents are used to journalize and post cash receipts using the cash receipts journal is now discussed.

■ Journalizing Cash Receipts

Each journal entry to record a cash receipt includes a debit to the Cash account. The account credited depends on the source from which cash was received. For example, the Sales account is credited to record cash sales.

Each cash receipts entry recorded in a two-column general journal requires at least two lines. If an explanation is included, the entry requires at least three lines. Thus, ten cash receipts transactions in one day require 20 to 30 lines in the general journal. Also, when the ten transactions are posted, ten separate entries in the Cash account must be made.

A special journal is often used, which reduces the amount of space used in both the journal and the ledger. The **cash receipts journal** is a special journal used to record all receipts of cash using only one line for each entry. The cash receipts journal increases efficiency because all debits to the Cash account are posted in one amount at the end of the month. It also permits more than one person to work on the records at a time.

To illustrate how special journals and various methods of control are used, we will study the accounting system of Computer Age. Jason Booth is the owner of Computer Age, which is a business that sells computer equipment and supplies. The chart of accounts for Computer Age is shown on page 280.

The accounting system used by Computer Age provides that all cash sales are recorded on a cash register. Cash received through the mail is recorded on remittance slips. Because of the number of cash transactions, Jason Booth proves cash and makes a bank deposit once a week. Thus, the total bank deposit for any week must equal the weekly total on the cash register tape plus the weekly total of the remittance slips. The total deposit must also equal the cash receipts recorded in the journal for that week.

■ Using the Cash Receipts Journal Instead of the General Journal During August, Computer Age received $10,950. If the cash transactions were journalized in a two-column general journal, the entries would appear as shown on page 291.

Note that in this form of journal, the debit entry to the Cash account is repeated for each transaction. Cash is debited eight times to record the August transactions, and eight lines are required in the Cash account because each entry is posted separately.

The illustration at the bottom of this page shows how the August 3 transaction to increase the owner's equity by $6,000 would be journalized in a two-column general journal. The illustration also shows the same transaction in a cash receipts journal.

GENERAL JOURNAL — Page 1

DATE		ACCOUNT TITLE AND EXPLANATION	POST. REF.	DEBIT	CREDIT
19—					
Aug.	3	Cash	101	6,000 00	
		Jason Booth, Capital	301		6,000 00
		Additional investment.			
	6	Cash	101	800 00	
		Sales	401		800 00
		Cash sales for week.			
	8	Cash	101	400 00	
		Accts. Rec./Wing Computers	115		400 00
		Received on account.			
	13	Cash	101	700 00	
		Sales	401		700 00
		Cash sales for week.			
	15	Cash	101	150 00	
		Accts. Rec./Allied Display	111		150 00
		Received on account.			
	20	Cash	101	1,500 00	
		Sales	401		1,500 00
		Cash sales for week.			
	24	Cash	101	600 00	
		Accts. Rec./Hallmark Sales	113		600 00
		Received on account.			
	27	Cash	101	800 00	
		Sales	401		800 00
		Cash sales for week.			

Cash	101
6,000	
800	
400	
700	
150	
1,500	
600	
800	

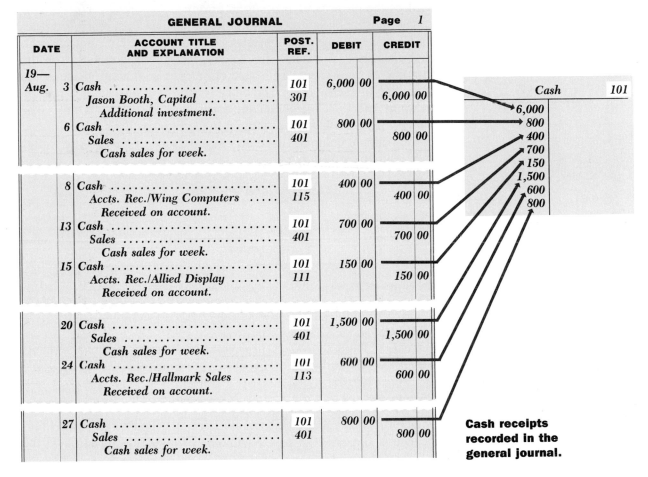

Cash receipts recorded in the general journal.

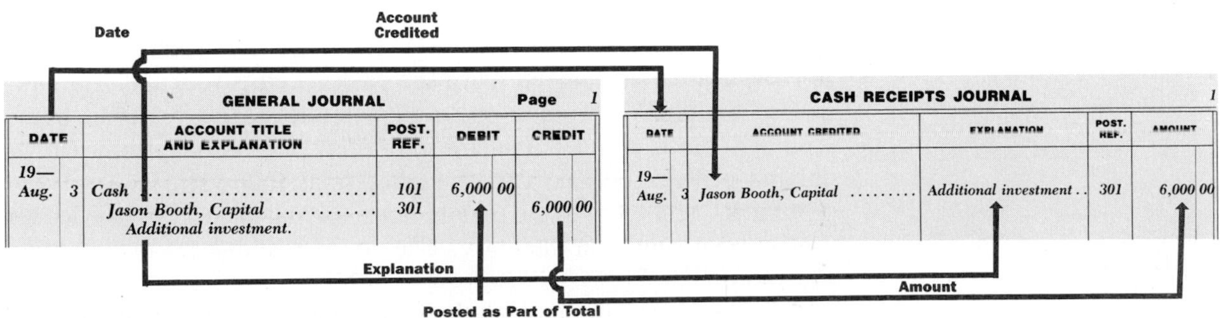

General journal compared to cash receipts journal.

Special journals save time in recording transactions, reduce posting activities, and allow employees to divide job duties.

When the cash receipts journal is used, the date, the account credited, the explanation, and the amount are all recorded on one line. Only the credit entry must be written. The account title Cash and the amount debited are not written. It is understood that there will be a debit entry to the Cash account for the total of all the credit entries in the cash receipts journal. Writing the amount only once saves time and reduces the chances of making an error.

The illustration below shows how the August cash receipts entries for Computer Age would appear in a one-column cash receipts journal. Note that the cash balance for August 1 ($8,400) is recorded on the first line of the journal. This type of entry is commonly made at the beginning of each month. The entry for the cash balance is a **memorandum entry**. A memorandum entry is an entry that is not to be posted. Thus, the balance is written in the Explanation column instead of the Amount column. Since no entry is made in the Posting Reference column, a dash is put in.

CASH RECEIPTS JOURNAL — **Page** *1*

DATE		ACCOUNT CREDITED	EXPLANATION	POST. REF.	AMOUNT
19—					
Aug.	*1*	*Cash Balance*	*$8,400*	—	
	3	*Jason Booth, Capital*	*Additional investment*		*6,000 00*
	6	*Sales*	*Cash sales for week*		*800 00*
	8	*Accts. Rec./Wing Computers*	*Received on account*		*400 00*
	13	*Sales*	*Cash sales for week*		*700 00*
	15	*Accts. Rec./Allied Display*	*Received on account*		*150 00*
	20	*Sales*	*Cash sales for week*		*1,500 00*
	24	*Accts. Rec./Hallmark Sales*	*Received on account*		*600 00*
	27	*Sales*	*Cash sales for week*		*800 00*

Concept: Accumulating Amounts
Debit amounts and credit amounts for an account can be accumulated and posted as totals without affecting the equality of the ledger.

Exercise D on page 295 may be completed at this point.

Posting From the Cash Receipts Journal

How are entries posted from the cash receipts journal? The procedure for posting from a one-column cash receipts journal to the ledger is much simpler than the procedure for posting from a two-column general journal. The procedure is as follows.

- Each credit entry in the cash receipts journal is posted to the ledger account shown in the entry. The credit postings are made during the month.
- At the end of the month, the cash receipts journal is totaled and ruled.

■ The total cash received during the month is then posted as a debit to the Cash account.

■ Posting the Credit Entries The letters *CR* are written in the Posting Reference column of the ledger account. This shows the amount was posted from the cash receipts journal. In the illustration below, CR1 shows that the $6,000 credit to the Capital account was journalized on page 1 of the cash receipts journal.

Jason Booth, Capital — **Account No.** *301*

DATE		EXPLANATION	POST. REF.	DEBIT	CREDIT	BALANCE DEBIT	BALANCE CREDIT
19—							
Aug.	1	Balance	—				19,000 00
	3		CR1		6,000 00		25,000 00

■ Totaling the Cash Receipts Journal The amount posted to the Cash account is the total of the entries in the cash receipts journal. To find the amount, use the following procedures.

1. Draw one line under the last amount in the Amount column.
2. Write the last date of the month in the Date column.
3. Write "Cash Debit" in the Account Credited column.
4. Write "Total receipts" in the Explanation column.
5. Add the amounts in the Amount column. Write the total in small pencil footings. Prove the addition. After proving the addition, write the total in ink beneath the single line.
6. Draw a double line under the Date, Posting Reference, and Amount columns to show that the journalizing for the accounting period is completed.

CASH RECEIPTS JOURNAL — **Page** *1*

DATE		ACCOUNT CREDITED	EXPLANATION	POST. REF.	AMOUNT
19—					
Aug.	1	Cash Balance	$8,400	—	
	3	Jason Booth, Capital	Additional investment	301	6,000 00
	6	Sales	Cash sales for week	401	800 00
	8	Accts. Rec./Wing Computers	Received on account	115	400 00
	13	Sales	Cash sales for week	401	700 00
	15	Accts. Rec./Allied Display	Received on account	111	150 00
	20	Sales	Cash sales for week	401	1,500 00
	24	Accts. Rec./Hallmark Sales	Received on account	113	600 00
	27	Sales	Cash sales for week	401	800 00 (1)
					10,950 00
(2)	31	(3) Cash Debit	(4) Total receipts	101	10,950 00 (5)
(6)					

Posting total cash receipts.

double line here

line is drawn double under post. ref. too

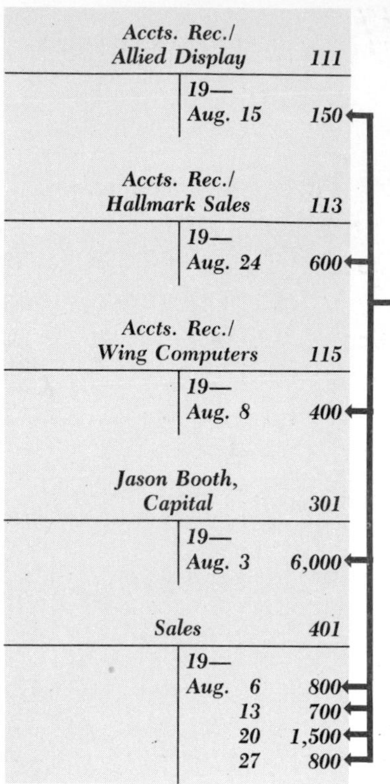

Accts. Rec./ Allied Display 111
19— Aug. 15 150
Accts. Rec./ Hallmark Sales 113
19— Aug. 24 600
Accts. Rec./ Wing Computers 115
19— Aug. 8 400
Jason Booth, Capital 301
19— Aug. 3 6,000
Sales 401
19— Aug. 6 800
13 700
20 1,500
27 800

Posting the Debit to Cash

After the cash receipts journal is totaled and ruled, the total is posted. The total amount of cash is posted to the debit side of the Cash account. Then the number of the Cash account is written in the Posting Reference column of the cash receipts journal.

Total Credits Posted: $10,950

CASH RECEIPTS JOURNAL Page *1*

DATE		ACCOUNT CREDITED	POST. REF.	AMOUNT
19—				
Aug.	31	Cash Debit	101	10,950 00

After all entries for August have been posted, as shown here, the Cash account will show only one debit—$10,950—for total cash receipts from August. The total credits posted from the cash receipts journal to the various accounts in the ledger also equal $10,950. Thus, the single debit posted to Cash equals the total credits posted.

Total Debits Posted: $10,950 →

Cash	*101*
19— Aug. 31 10,950	

Suppose a trial balance is prepared during the month. The ledger would be out of balance because only the credit entries from the cash receipts journal had been posted. The debit to the Cash account is not posted until the end of each month. Thus, if a trial balance is prepared during the month, the cash receipts journal must first be examined to determine the debits to Cash.

Recording the Memorandum Entry

The cash receipts journal is totaled, ruled, and posted at the end of the month. Thus, the current balance of the Cash account will be shown in the Cash account and is available as next month's memorandum entry. The procedures for verifying the Cash account balance are explained in the next chapter.

Recording an Opening Entry

All transactions involving the receipt of cash are recorded in a cash receipts journal. Thus, if an opening entry consists of a cash investment only, the opening entry is recorded in the cash receipts journal. If the owner invests other assets in addition to cash, the cash is recorded in the cash receipts journal and the other assets are recorded in the general journal.

Concept: Posting by Total
Posting by total should increase accuracy, efficiency, and speed because it reduces the number of times an amount is recorded.

Exercise E on page 295 may be completed at this point.

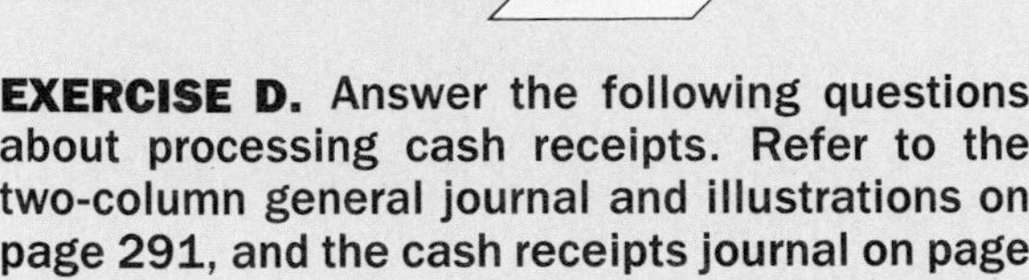

TOPIC 2 EXERCISES

EXERCISE D. Answer the following questions about processing cash receipts. Refer to the two-column general journal and illustrations on page 291, and the cash receipts journal on page 292.

1. How many lines are needed to journalize cash receipts for August in the two-column general journal? How many postings to the Cash account are needed?
2. How many lines are needed to journalize one entry in the cash receipts journal? In the general journal? How many lines are saved by journalizing a cash receipts transaction in a cash receipts journal?
3. Is the entry on August 3 a debit or a credit to Jason Booth, Capital?
4. What kind of entry is the cash balance entry on August 1? Is it posted?
5. What is the source of cash receipts journalized on August 6?
6. Why is the cash receipts journal described as a special journal?
7. How much cash is received on account for August? What are the cash sales for August?
8. Three sources of cash are recorded in August. What are the three sources?
9. What account is assumed to be debited for each entry in the cash receipts journal?

EXERCISE E. Answer the following questions about posting cash receipts. Refer to the cash receipts journal on page 293.

1. The August 1 cash balance is recorded as a memorandum entry in the cash receipts journal. From what other source can the cash balance be obtained?
2. Why is the amount of the August 1 cash balance shown in the Explanation column instead of in the Amount column?
3. Why is there a dash in the Posting Reference column for the cash balance?
4. What would the complete entry be if cash sales for the week of August 6 were recorded in a general journal?
5. Is the debit to the Cash account posted at the same time that the cash sales for the week of August 13 are posted? Why or why not?
6. When a $600 credit is posted from the cash receipts journal to the Hallmark Sales ledger account, is the debit to the Cash account posted at the same time? Explain.
7. On what date is $6,000 received? From what source?
8. What amount is posted to the Cash account on August 31? Is the amount debited or credited?
9. Is $8,400 a part of the cash debit on August 31? Why or why not?

TOPIC 2 PROBLEMS

TOPIC PROBLEM 4. Murray Motors is a small business owned by Roger Murray. The April transactions are listed on the next page.

a. Open ledger accounts and enter account balances for April for the general ledger accounts that are listed on the next page. Assign a proper number to each account.

Cash	$ 1,600
Accts. Rec./Ace Corporation	620
Accts. Rec./Kern Motors	370
Rental Equipment	30,000
Roger Murray, Capital	32,590
Sales	-0-

b. In the cash receipts journal, make a memorandum entry for the April 1 cash balance. Then journalize the transactions for the month. Post credit entries each week and on April 30.

c. Foot, prove, and rule the cash receipts journal.

d. Post the debit entry from the cash receipts journal.

e. Prepare a trial balance.

Apr. 5 Recorded cash sales of $1,120 for the week.
5 Posted credit entries for the week ended April 5.
8 Received $370 from Kern Motors on account.
12 Recorded cash sales of $1,360 for the week.
12 Posted credit entries for the week ended April 12.
17 Received $6,000 from Roger Murray as additional investment.
19 Recorded cash sales of $1,045 for the week.
19 Posted credit entries for the week ended April 19.
23 Received $200 from Ace Corporation on account.
26 Recorded cash sales of $1,180 for the week.
26 Posted credit entries for the week ended April 26.
29 Received $130 from Ace Corporation on account.
30 Received $1,200 for automobile (Rental Equipment) sold to Ronald Kroger.
30 Posted credit entries for transactions April 27–30.

TOPIC PROBLEM 5. Sandra Gallo started SG Services on August 1. During August, the business had the transactions listed below.

a. Open the ledger accounts for August 1 for the following accounts: Cash; Accts. Rec./Martin Company; Land; Sandra Gallo, Capital; and Sales.

b. Use a cash receipts journal and a general journal to journalize the transactions listed through August 17.

c. Post the entries from the general journal. Post the credit entries from the cash receipts journal.

d. Journalize the transactions for August 20–31.

e. Post the entries from the general journal. Post the credit entries from the cash receipts journal.

f. Foot, prove, and rule the cash receipts journal.

g. Post the debit entry from the cash receipts journal.

h. Prepare a trial balance.

Aug. 1 Sandra Gallo started the business with a cash investment of $11,500.
2 Sandra Gallo invested land of $20,000.
8 Sold shrubbery for $700 on account to Martin Company.
10 Recorded cash proof for the register showing cash sales of $875.
15 Received $450 from Martin Company on account.
17 Recorded the cash proof showing cash sales of $850.
20 Received $2,000 for land sold to Jack Birnbaum.
28 Received $100 from Martin Company on account.
31 Recorded the cash proof showing cash sales of $800.

TOPIC 3

Bank Credit Card Sales

How do businesses process bank credit card sales? Businesses process bank credit card sales as a special type of cash sale.

Processing Bank Credit Card Sales

A **bank credit card** is issued through a bank and can be used at any business accepting that card. The most widely used bank credit cards are VISA and MasterCard. Many businesses use credit card sales along with their cash and regular charge sales because they feel the advantages are greater than the disadvantages. Bank credit card sales have two primary advantages. First, total sales increase because many customers prefer to purchase with this type of credit card. Second, the business receives payment immediately from the issuing or cooperating bank. The primary disadvantage of a credit card sale is that the business must pay a fee to the bank that issues the card.

The following procedure is used to process bank credit card sales.

- The customer's credit card number is checked for validity.
- Source documents are prepared.
- Payment is obtained from the bank.

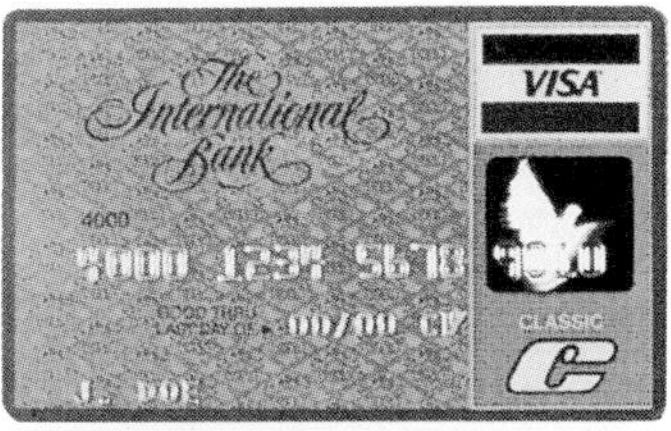

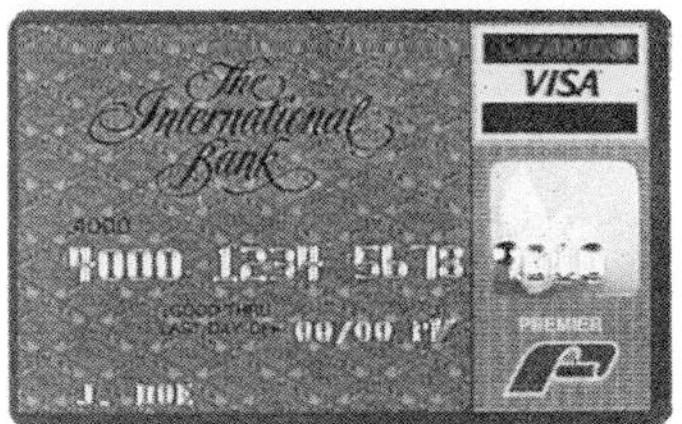

Bank credit cards.

Checking the Customer's Credit

To check a customer's credit, the salesclerk either places a telephone call to a central office or uses a special machine hooked up directly to a computer. If the transaction is approved, the salesclerk enters a credit authorization on the credit card sales slip.

Preparing Source Documents

After the customer's credit is verified, many businesses prepare two sales slips for each credit card sale. First, the salesclerk completes the sales slip that the business uses for regular cash sales. Then, the salesclerk prepares a special credit card sales slip preprinted with the name of the credit card (such as VISA). Both are illustrated on page 298.

The salesclerk places the credit card sales slip and the customer's plastic credit card in an imprinting device. This device prints the customer's name and credit card number on the sales slip. It also prints the business's name and identification number. When the sales slip is removed from the imprinting device, the customer is asked to sign the form.

Both the regular sales slip and the credit card sales slip consist of several copies. The customer receives one copy of each form. Other copies go to the accounting department. There, an accounting clerk verifies the accuracy of the amounts on the sales slips. A copy of the regular sales slip and a copy of the credit card sales slip are then filed.

4225 970 380 266

05/- 04/- BWC

DONNA WEEKS

COMPUTER AGE
4634305900 004
0070450903 467 5 9 -
3340507088 OH

CARDHOLDER SIGN HERE X *Donna Weeks*

The Issuer of the card identified on this item is authorized to pay the amount shown as TOTAL upon proper presentation. I promise to pay such TOTAL (together with any other charges due thereon) subject to and in accordance with the agreement governing the use of such card

CONVERSION RATE

CONVERSION AMOUNT

AUTHORIZATION NO. *97202*

DATE *5/9/-* CLERK *P.S.*

DESCRIPTION *Cable*

SALE	73 99
TAXES	
TIPS	
TOTAL	73 99

THIS FORM TO BE USED WITH VISA OR MasterCard

CUSTOMER COPY

TRAVEL & ENTERTAINMENT BANKCARD SALES SLIP

IMPORTANT: RETAIN THIS COPY FOR STATEMENT VERIFICATION

Credit card sales slip.

COMPUTER AGE
200 Girard Avenue
Denver, Colorado 80236

Date *May 9,* 19*—*

Sold to *Donna Weeks*

Address *108 Chain St., Denver, Colorado 80236*

Clerk	Cash	C.O.D.	Charge	On Acct.	Retd.	Paid Out
LJ			*✓VISA*			

QUANTITY	DESCRIPTION	PRICE	AMOUNT
1	*Cable*	*73.99*	*73.99*
		Tax	
		Total	*73.99*

No. **197** Received by *Pam Simon*

Sales slip.

Another copy of the credit card sales slip is kept in the accounting department until the bank deposit is prepared.

Obtaining Payment From the Bank When a bank deposit is prepared, an accounting clerk adds the totals of all the credit card sales slips on a calculator. The accounting clerk then lists the total on a special deposit form. This form is provided by the bank and is illustrated below.

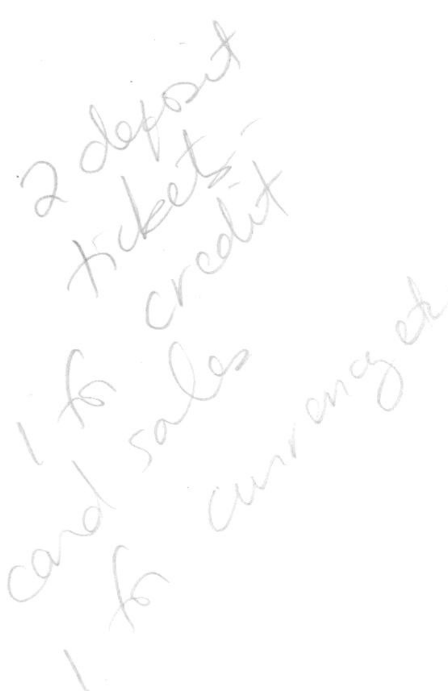

IMPRINT MERCHANT NAME AND NUMBER BELOW

COMPUTER AGE
7964 29 36

MERCHANTS BANK
Denver, Colorado

	NUMBER OF ITEMS	AMOUNT
TOTAL SALES DRAFT	*2*	*618.00*
PROC. FEE		*12.36*
TOTAL ▶		*605.64*

DATE *Nov. 1, 19—*

MERCHANT NAME *Computer Age*
200 Girard Avenue
Denver, Colorado 80236

CHECKING ACCOUNT NUMBER ▶ *7964 29 36*

SALES DRAFT TRASMITTAL/DEPOSIT SLIP

DEPOSIT TICKET

Deposit ticket for credit card sales.

The accounting clerk must also compute the processing fee. The **processing fee** is the fee that the bank deducts for handling the business's credit card sales. It is stated as a percentage of the business's credit card sales. For example, if the fee were 2 percent and total credit card sales were \$618, the amount of the fee would be \$12.36 (0.02 × \$618.00).

The accounting clerk then lists the fee and also the net amount of the credit card sales on the deposit form. The net amount, computed by subtracting the fee from the total of the credit card sales, is the amount the business receives from the bank. The net amount for the example described above would be \$605.64 (\$618.00 − \$12.36).

The accounting clerk attaches the calculator tape and a copy of each sales slip to the deposit ticket for credit card sales. Another deposit ticket is prepared for the currency, coins, and checks from cash receipts. Both deposits are taken to the bank. The bank adds the net amount of the credit card sales and the total of the other cash receipts to the balance in the business's checking account.

■ Recording Credit Card Sales

Bank credit card sales are treated as cash sales and are recorded in the cash receipts journal. The entry shown here would be made for the November 1 credit card sales described above.

CASH RECEIPTS JOURNAL — Page 3

DATE		ACCOUNT CREDITED	EXPLANATION	POST. REF.	GENERAL LEDGER CREDIT	SALES CREDIT	CREDIT CARD FEE EXPENSE DEBIT	NET CASH DEBIT
19—								
Nov.	*1*	*Sales*	*Bank credit card sales*			*618 00*	*12 36*	*605 64*

Recording bank credit card sales.

NOVEMBER 1: RECORDED CREDIT CARD SALES OF $618 LESS A PROCESSING FEE OF $12.36.		
What Happens	**Accounting Rule**	**Accounting Entry**
The asset Cash increases by $605.64.	To increase an asset, debit the account.	Debit: Cash, $605.64.
Credit Card Fee Expense decreases owner's equity by $12.36.	To decrease owner's equity, debit the account.	Debit: Credit Card Fee Expense, $12.36.
Credit card sales increase owner's equity by $618.	To increase owner's equity, credit the account.	Credit: Sales, $618.

There are two items you should focus on in this transaction. First, there is a new account called Credit Card Fee Expense. The **Credit Card Fee Expense account** is an operating expense that reduces owner's equity. The $12.36 is what the owner is willing to pay to increase sales (revenue) by $618. Second, special columns are added to the cash receipts journal to record the credit card sales. The addition of new columns is an example of how a business can design its accounting records to meet its needs. The amounts in the Credit Card Fee Expense and Sales columns will be posted as totals at the end of the month to the proper ledger accounts.

Some businesses set up a separate revenue account for credit card sales. This will allow management to see the amount that credit card sales contribute to the revenues each accounting period.

Exercise F on page 300 may be completed at this point.

TOPIC 3 EXERCISE

EXERCISE F. Answer the following questions about credit card sales. Refer to the text, margin notes, and illustrations on pages 297 to 299.

1. What is one advantage of a bank credit card sale? One disadvantage?
2. What is the processing fee percentage and the amount charged on the bank credit card sales?
3. How does a business obtain cash for bank credit card sales?
4. What accounts are debited when bank credit card sales are recorded? What account is credited?
5. What new columns have been added to the cash receipts journal to make the recording of bank credit card sales easier? How often are amounts in these columns posted?

TOPIC 3 PROBLEM

TOPIC PROBLEM 6. Friendly Motors sells auto supplies for cash and also accepts bank credit cards. On May 15, total sales were $2,000. Cash sales were $1,175.

a. Determine the bank credit card sales.

b. Compute the processing fee. (The fee is 2 percent.)

c. Prepare a bank credit card sales deposit ticket. (There were 27 credit card sales, and the checking account number is 12-7700.)

d. Record the sales and credit card fee expense in a four-column cash receipts journal.

CHAPTER 9 REVIEW

CHAPTER SUMMARY

The handling and recording of cash receipts are the two primary activities of a cash receipts subsystem. In this chapter, you learned about the specific procedures used to control cash receipts. These controls are necessary because cash can be mishandled so easily.

Transactions involving cash receipts need to be journalized and posted. These transactions can be journalized in either a general journal or a special cash receipts journal. The cash receipts journal is preferred because each entry can be recorded on only one line. This procedure also increases efficiency since all debits to the Cash account are posted in one amount at the end of the month and because more than one person can work on the records at a time.

A sale made using a bank credit card, such as MasterCard or VISA, is considered a special type of cash sale since there is a processing fee attached to it. The bank deducts this fee, which is stated as a percentage of the business's total credit card sales for handling the sale.

THE LANGUAGE OF BUSINESS

Here are some terms that make up the language of business. Do you know the meaning of each?

cash receipts subsystem
cashier
handling cash receipts
recording cash receipts
cash register tape
sales slip
prenumbered source document
remittance slip
change fund
cash receipts journal
memorandum entry
bank credit card
processing fee
Credit Card Fee Expense account

REVIEW QUESTIONS

1. List the procedures for the control of cash receipts. Why are these procedures important?
2. Explain the procedure followed for proving cash (a) when a cash register is used, (b) when sales slips are used, and (c) when remittance slips are used.
3. Why should a business deposit all cash receipts intact and pay all of its bills by check?
4. Why should the procedure for handling cash receipts be separated from the procedure for recording cash receipts?

5. Explain how the use of a cash receipts journal simplifies the journalizing and posting of cash receipts.
6. What procedure is followed to complete the cash receipts journal at the end of the month?
7. In which journal or journals is an opening entry recorded if the investment consists of cash only? If it consists of cash and other assets?
8. What are the major advantages of bank credit card sales?
9. Is there any expense connected with bank credit card sales? Explain.
10. In what way do good control procedures for cash receipts contribute to good employer-employee relations?

CHAPTER PROBLEMS

Problems for Chapter 9 are given below. Write your answers on separate sheets of paper unless you are using the workbook for this textbook. If you are using the workbook, do the problems in the space provided there.

CHAPTER PROBLEM 9-1. The cash receipts journal and the ledger accounts of Overnight Delivery are shown on the next page. They contain errors. Find the errors and describe them. Use a form similar to the ones shown below. As an example, the first error in the journal and the ledger is identified and described for you.

Errors in the Journal

Date	Description
EXAMPLE: May 1	Do not enter cash balance in money columns.

Errors in the Ledger

Acct. No.	Description
EXAMPLE: 101	May 31 entry should be $5,530, and the debit balance should be $9,170.

CASH RECEIPTS JOURNAL

Page 1

DATE		ACCOUNT CREDITED	EXPLANATION	POST. REF.	AMOUNT	
19—						
May	1	Cash Balance	$3,640	—	3,640	00
	3	Accts. Rec./Wendall Jones	On account	102	420	00
	15	Sales	Cash sales for two weeks	401	1,040	00
	28	Accts. Rec./Wendall Jones	On account		420	00
	30	Sales	Cash sales for two weeks	401	1,650	00
	31	William John, Capital ...	Additional investment ...	301	2,000	00
	31	Cash Credit	Total receipts	101	9,710	00

GENERAL LEDGER

Cash — Account No. 101

DATE		EXPLANATION	POST. REF.	DEBIT		CREDIT		BALANCE DEBIT		BALANCE CREDIT	
19—											
May	1	Balance	—					3,640	00		
	31	....	CR1	9,720	00			13,360	00		

Accts. Rec./Wendall Jones — Account No. 102

DATE		EXPLANATION	POST. REF.	DEBIT		CREDIT		BALANCE DEBIT		BALANCE CREDIT	
19—	1	Balance	—					750	00		
May	3	....	CR1			400	00	350	00		
	28	....	CR1	420	00			770	00		

William John, Capital — Account No. 301

DATE		EXPLANATION	POST. REF.	DEBIT		CREDIT		BALANCE DEBIT		BALANCE CREDIT	
19—											
May	1	....	—							4,020	00
	15	....	CR1			1,040	00			5,060	00
	31	....				2,000	00			7,060	00

Sales — Account No. 401

DATE		EXPLANATION	POST. REF.	DEBIT		CREDIT		BALANCE DEBIT		BALANCE CREDIT	
19—											
May	30	....	CR1			1,650	00			1,650	00

CHAPTER PROBLEM 9-2. On October 1, the accounts for Supreme Auto Repair had the following balances: Cash, $1,840; Accts. Rec./Steven Shelton, $840; Accts. Rec./Cynthia Smith, $300; and Craig King, Capital, $2,980. The prenumbered sales slips involving the cash receipts transactions for October are shown below.

a. Record the transactions from the source documents in a cash receipts journal.

b. Post the individual entries from the cash receipts journal.

c. Prove, total, and rule the cash receipts journal.

d. Post the total from the cash receipts journal.

e. Prepare a trial balance.

Supreme Auto Repair 843

Date Oct. 2, 19—

Mr. Steven Shelton

Address 29 Royal Place, Palo Alto, California

Clerk	Cash	Other	Charge	On Acct.	Retd.	Paid Out
J.H.				✓		

QUANTITY	DESCRIPTION	PRICE	AMOUNT
	Received on account		360.00

Supreme Auto Repair 846

Date Oct. 3, 19—

Ms. Edna Place

Address 19 North Street, Palo Alto, California

Clerk	Cash	Other	Charge	On Acct.	Retd.	Paid Out
J.H.	✓					

QUANTITY	DESCRIPTION	PRICE	AMOUNT
	Brakes repaired		100.00

Supreme Auto Repair 868

Date Oct. 14, 19—

Mr. Craig King

Address Mt. View, California

Clerk	Cash	Other	Charge	On Acct.	Retd.	Paid Out
R.M.		✓				

QUANTITY	DESCRIPTION	PRICE	AMOUNT
	Additional investment		4000.00

Supreme Auto Repair 886

Date Oct. 21, 19—

Ms. Cynthia Smith

Address 14 Bridge Street, Palo Alto, California

Clerk	Cash	Other	Charge	On Acct.	Retd.	Paid Out
J.H.				✓		

QUANTITY	DESCRIPTION	PRICE	AMOUNT
	Received on account		120.00

Supreme Auto Repair 892

Date Oct. 24, 19—

Mr. Steven Shelton

Address 29 Royal Place, Palo Alto, California

Clerk	Cash	Other	Charge	On Acct.	Retd.	Paid Out
J.H.				✓		

QUANTITY	DESCRIPTION	PRICE	AMOUNT
	Received on account		350.00

Supreme Auto Repair 910

Date Oct. 29, 19—

Mr. Anthony Bell

Address 18 King Avenue, Palo Alto, California

Clerk	Cash	Other	Charge	On Acct.	Retd.	Paid Out
J.H.	✓					

QUANTITY	DESCRIPTION	PRICE	AMOUNT
	Motor tune-up		84.00

MANAGEMENT CASES

Control of Cash Receipts. Many transactions of a business involve cash receipts and cash payments. Every business should set up safeguards to control cash because this asset is more likely to be mishandled than any other.

CASE 9M-1. In many large schools, the faculty members belong to the local, state, and national teachers' organizations. They pay their dues to an office clerk. The clerk issues a separate receipt for each payment of dues to any one of the three organizations. In order to reduce her work, the clerk at Wilson High School has requested that she be permitted to issue only one receipt to a person. (She would do this even when the dues are payable to more than one teacher's organization.)

a. Under the separate-receipt method, how would each of the three organizations obtain full information about the payment of dues and the members in good standing?

b. Under the one-receipt method, how would the same information be reported to each organization? How could each be sure that all dues collected were sent?

c. Design a receipt that can be used for all three organizations at one time.

CASE 9M-2. John Stewart owns the JS Service. Mr. Stewart has eight employees to repair TVs, stereos, refrigerators, and similar items in the customer's home or in the shop. Cash is received by Mr. Stewart in the following ways.

1. Charge customers send checks and, occasionally, small sums of money through the mail.
2. Charge customers pay their accounts in person.
3. Cash customers pay the employees who service appliances at their homes.
4. Cash customers pay cash to the cashier for work done in Mr. Stewart's shop.
5. Customers purchase tubes, extension cords, and other parts and pay the cashier in the shop.

Make suggestions that Mr. Stewart might consider when reviewing his procedures for controlling cash receipts. Specifically, describe how he should do the following things. When you develop your suggestions, refer to the procedures for controlling cash receipts on pages 282 to 286.

a. Handle checks and cash received through the mail.

b. Receive and record cash paid to the cashier for appliance services.

c. Control cash received by employees in the customers' homes.

d. Control cash received for the sale of parts.

CHAPTER

10

A Cash Payments Subsystem

In Chapter 9 you learned about the subsystem used by businesses in accounting for cash receipts. Each day businesses also are involved in numerous transactions requiring the payment of cash. In this chapter you will study the subsystem used by businesses in accounting for cash payments.

CHAPTER GOALS

After studying Chapter 10, you will be able to:

1. Define the terms listed in ''The Language of Business'' section on page 325.
2. Explain the concepts and principles in this chapter related to accounting for cash payments.
3. Identify the procedures used to ensure accuracy, honesty, and efficiency and speed in the control of cash payments.
4. Use a flowchart to describe the relationship between people, forms, equipment, and procedures in a cash payments subsystem.
5. Journalize cash payments in a one-column cash payments journal.
6. Post entries from the cash payments journal to the proper ledger accounts.
7. Define and use a change fund and a drawing account.
8. Demonstrate the techniques for proving cash.

TOPIC 1

Controlling Cash Payments

What is a cash payments subsystem? A **cash payments subsystem** uses people, forms, procedures, and equipment to control cash payments. As in the cash receipts subsystem, the cashier plays an important role. A second important person is the *cash payments bookkeeper,* who handles the cash payments portion of the financial records.

■ Procedures to Control Cash Payments

Controls for Cash Payments
- Verify and approve invoices
- Pay by check
- Use prenumbered checks
- Prove cash
- Divide responsibility

The control of cash payments includes procedures to ensure accuracy, honesty, efficiency, and speed in processing cash payments. These procedures include the following.

- Verifying and approving invoices
- Paying by check
- Using prenumbered checks
- Proving cash
- Dividing responsibilities for handling and recording cash payments

■ Verifying and Approving Invoices No invoice should be paid until it has been verified. This means that the goods or services listed on the invoice must have been ordered and received and that the amount of the invoice must be accurate. If the invoice is correct, then it can be approved for payment by an authorized employee.

■ Paying by Check All cash receipts should be deposited intact. No payments should be made from cash receipts. All payments (except petty cash payments) should be made by check. The check stub or a carbon copy of the voucher check becomes the source document for the data entered into the accounting system.

■ Using Prenumbered Checks Prenumbered checks should be used to keep track of the checks issued. Voided checks must be kept so that every check is accounted for in numeric order.

■ Proving Cash If all cash receipts are deposited in the bank and all bills are paid by check, then two separate records of cash receipts and cash payments are available. First, the business has a record of receipts. Second, the bank has a record of all deposits and withdrawals from the business's checking account. When the business receives a copy of its bank statement, it prepares a bank reconciliation to verify the cash receipts and cash payments records.

■ Dividing the Responsibilities It is wise to divide the responsibilities of verifying invoices, approving invoices, issuing checks, and recording checks among several employees. This way, the work of one employee can be checked against the work of another employee.

Visualizing the Cash Payments Subsystem

How is the handling and recording of cash payments related? The flowchart below illustrates the procedures to control the handling and recording of cash payments. The invoice is verified and approved before a check is issued. Prenumbered checks are used. The responsibilities to issue checks and journalize the payments are divided. Finally, the total of the checks written and the total of the cash payments are compared to see if they are equal.

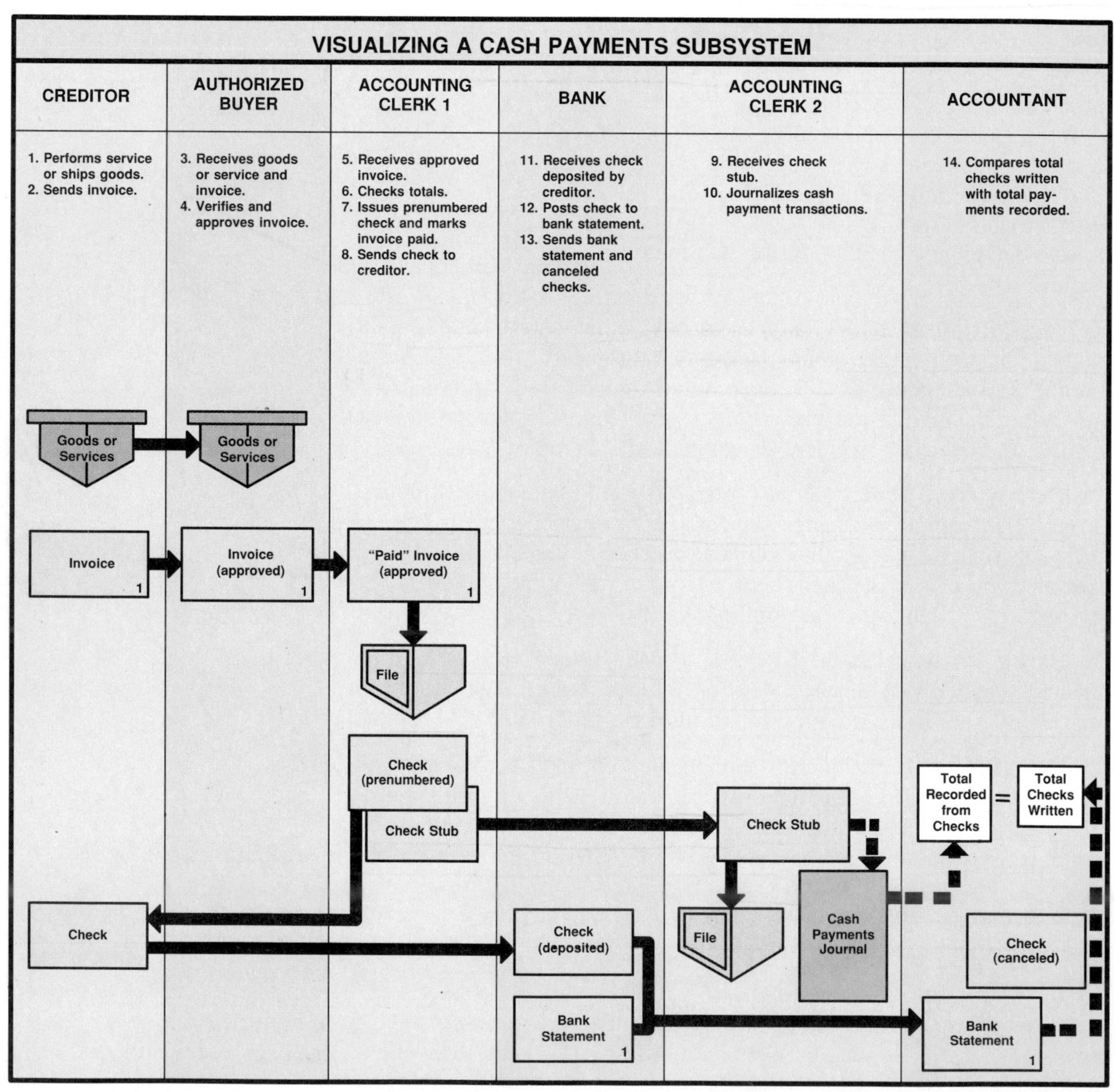

VISUALIZING A CASH PAYMENTS SUBSYSTEM
CREDITOR
1. Performs service or ships goods.
2. Sends invoice.
AUTHORIZED BUYER
3. Receives goods or service and invoice.
4. Verifies and approves invoice.
ACCOUNTING CLERK 1
5. Receives approved invoice.
6. Checks totals.
7. Issues prenumbered check and marks invoice paid.
8. Sends check to creditor.
BANK
11. Receives check deposited by creditor.
12. Posts check to bank statement.
13. Sends bank statement and canceled checks.
ACCOUNTING CLERK 2
9. Receives check stub.
10. Journalizes cash payment transactions.
ACCOUNTANT
14. Compares total checks written with total payments recorded.
Goods or Services
Goods or Services
Invoice
1
Invoice (approved)
1
"Paid" Invoice (approved)
1
File
Check (prenumbered)
Check Stub
Check Stub
Total Recorded from Checks
=
Total Checks Written
Check
Check (deposited)
File
Cash Payments Journal
Check (canceled)
Bank Statement
1
Bank Statement
1

Cash Payments Bookkeeper: DOT 211.382-018
Keeps cash payments portion of the financial records.

Concept: Safeguarding Cash
A bank account safeguards cash and serves as an external record for the control of cash.

Exercises A and B on this page may be completed at this point.

TOPIC 1 EXERCISES

EXERCISE A. Answer the following questions about the procedures to control cash payments. Refer to the text and margin notes on page 307.

1. What is meant by verifying and approving invoices?
2. What source documents are used when authorized payments are made by check?
3. What is the purpose of prenumbering checks?
4. When proving cash, what two records of cash receipts are available?
5. Why do businesses divide responsibilities among employees?

EXERCISE B. In a table similar to the one that follows, indicate who prepares or sends the following forms, to whom or where each one is sent, and the purpose each one serves. Refer to the flowchart of a cash payments subsystem on page 308 when completing this exercise.

1. Invoice (approved): Copy 1
2. Invoice (approved): Copy 1 after payment
3. Check
4. Check (to be deposited)
5. Check (deposited)
6. Check stub
7. Check stub (after journalizing)
8. Bank statement: Copy 1

Form	Prepared or Sent By	Sent To	Purpose
EXAMPLE: Invoice: Copy 1	Creditor	Person authorized to buy	As a bill for the service performed or the goods supplied.

TOPIC 1 PROBLEM

TOPIC PROBLEM 1. The Westin Company has asked you to study its cash payments subsystem and make recommendations for possible improvement. The company's procedures are given at the top of the next page. Based upon your study of Topic 1, indicate whether or not each procedure provides an adequate means of controlling cash payments. If you find a procedure inadequate, give the Westin Company your recommendation for changing that procedure.

1. Invoices are approved and paid by one employee.
2. Most payments are made by check. However, to save time, the Westin Company makes some purchases of supplies and merchandise in cash taken from the daily cash receipts.
3. The company does not prove its cash records with the bank's records. Westin's owner feels that the bank has expensive computers to do its work without error.
4. The checks are not prenumbered by the printer. However, the person who writes each check does number the checks consecutively.
5. One person handles all the accounting records for cash receipts and cash payments. This person counts the daily cash received, opens the mail, makes deposits, writes checks, makes the cash payments out of receipts, proves cash (when it is done), and files all paid checks received from the bank.

TOPIC 2

Processing Cash Payments

Why does a business make cash payments? Cash is usually used to pay expenses, to pay creditors, and to pay for assets. Cash is also withdrawn for the owner's personal use. The journalizing procedures for cash payments are now described.

Journalizing Cash Payments

When cash is paid, the asset Cash decreases. Thus, every cash payment involves a credit to the Cash account. The account debited depends on the purpose of the payment.

When cash payments are recorded in a two-column general journal, every debit entry must have a credit entry to the Cash account. For example, the illustration on page 311 shows the August cash payments for Computer Age recorded in the two-column general journal.

Many businesses prefer recording all cash payments in a special cash payments journal, as shown on page 311. In the **cash payments journal** only the debit entries are recorded and posted individually. The credit entries to the Cash account are totaled and posted as a single credit to the Cash account at the end of the month.

To see the advantages of using a one-column cash payments journal, look at the August 4 entry for payment of rent in the general journal. The entry requires three lines. The same entry in a one-column cash payments journal takes only one line, and the amount is written only once. A special column for recording check numbers is also provided in the cash payments journal, to account for all checks. Note that when a check is voided (Check 203, for instance), the number is listed, a line is drawn in the Account Debited, Posting Reference, and Amount columns, and the word "Voided" is written in the Explanation column.

GENERAL JOURNAL Page 1

DATE		ACCOUNT TITLE AND EXPLANATION	POST. REF.	DEBIT		CREDIT	
19—							
Aug.	4	Rent Expense	517	600	00		
		Cash	101			600	00
		August rent, Check 201.					
	8	Accts. Pay./Diskettes Plus	211	400	00		
		Cash	101			400	00
		On account, Check 202.					
	18	Office Equipment	132	240	00		
		Cash	101			240	00
		New adding machine, Check 204.					
	25	Change Fund	103	35	00		
		Cash	101			35	00
		Establish fund, Check 205.					
	31	Salaries Payable	226	1,200	00		
		Cash	101			1,200	00
		August 28 payroll, Checks 206–209.					
	31	Advertising Expense	512	20	00		
		Miscellaneous Expense	515	10	00		
		Cash	101			30	00
		Replenish petty cash, Check 210.					
	31	Jason Booth, Drawing	302	800	00		
		Cash	101			800	00
		Withdrawal, Check 211.					

Cash	101
	600
	400
	240
	35
	1,200
	30
	800

Cash payments recorded in a general journal.

CASH PAYMENTS JOURNAL Page 1

DATE		ACCOUNT DEBITED	EXPLANATION	CHECK NO.	POST. REF.	AMOUNT	
19—							
Aug.	4	Rent Expense	August rent	201		600	00
	8	Accts. Pay./Diskettes Plus	On account	202		400	00
	15	————	Voided	203	—	—	
	18	Office Equipment	New adding machine	204		240	00
	25	Change Fund	Establish fund	205		35	00
	31	Salaries Payable	August 28 payroll	206–209		1,200	00
	31	Advertising Expense	Replenish petty	210		20	00
		Miscellaneous Expense	cash fund	—		10	00
	31	Jason Booth, Drawing	Withdrawal	211		800	00

Each entry requires one line.

Cash payments recorded in a cash payments journal.

If an entry in the cash payments journal requires more than one debit, it is easily handled using two or more lines. The entry to replenish petty cash on August 31 is an example. Note that the date is not repeated and a dash is placed in the Check Number column to show that no check is missing.

In addition to the above, two entries were made in the August cash payments journal involving accounts that are new to you. The entry on August 25 (Check 205) is made to establish a *change fund,* money used for making change after a sale. The account for a change fund will be explained more fully in Topic 3. The entry on August 31 (Check 211) involves withdrawals of money or other assets by the owner using a Drawing account. This account will now be explained.

Exercise C on page 315 may be completed at this point.

Recording Withdrawals

When are withdrawals made? When cash and other assets are withdrawn from the business for the owner's personal use, the owner is said to have made a **withdrawal**. A withdrawal is made against the net income the owner expects to earn.

Withdrawals could be deducted from the owner's Capital account. However, withdrawals are usually recorded in a separate owner's equity account known as a Drawing account. The **Drawing account** is a temporary account used to record changes in owner's equity. For instance, when the owner Jason Booth withdraws $800 in cash for his personal use, the transaction is recorded in the cash payments journal. The Cash account is credited to show a decrease in assets. The Drawing account is debited to show a decrease in owner's equity.

Credit the Cash account to show a decrease in assets. Debit the Drawing account to show a decrease in owner's equity.

CASH PAYMENTS JOURNAL **Page** *1*

DATE		ACCOUNT DEBITED	EXPLANATION	CHECK NO.	POST. REF.	AMOUNT	
19—							
Aug.	*4*	*Rent Expense*	*August rent*	*201*		*600*	*00*
	31	*Jason Booth, Drawing*	*Withdrawal*	*211*		*800*	*00*

Temporary reduction of capital: Use Drawing account.

In the transaction on August 31, the owner made a withdrawal against expected net income. The entry would be different if the owner planned to permanently reduce the amount of investment in the business. A reduction of that kind would be debited to the Capital account (not the Drawing account), as illustrated on the next page.

When a Drawing account is used, only the following are recorded in the Capital account: the original investment, additional investments,

DATE		ACCOUNT DEBITED	EXPLANATION	CHECK NO.	POST. REF.	AMOUNT
19— Dec.	20	*Jason Booth, Capital*	*Reduce capital*	253		500 00

CASH PAYMENTS JOURNAL — Page 4

Permanent reduction of capital: Use Capital account.

and permanent withdrawals of investment. However, most withdrawals are against expected net income. Therefore, the Drawing account is used more often than the Capital account.

Exercise D on page 315 may be completed at this point.

Posting Cash Payments

How are entries posted from the cash payments journal? Each debit in the cash payments journal is posted individually to the proper ledger account. A *cash posting clerk* often plays a key role in this procedure. The posting takes place at various times during the month.

After an entry has been posted, the account number is entered in the Posting Reference column of the cash payments journal to show that an entry has been made. In the ledger account, the letters *CP* and the page number of the journal are written in the Posting Reference column. In the following illustration, the posting reference CP1 shows that the $600 debit to the Rent Expense account was posted from page 1 of the cash payments journal.

Rent Expense — **Account No.** 517

DATE		EXPLANATION	POST. REF.	DEBIT	CREDIT	BALANCE DEBIT	BALANCE CREDIT
19— Aug.	4	*Rent for August*	*CP1*	600 00		600 00	

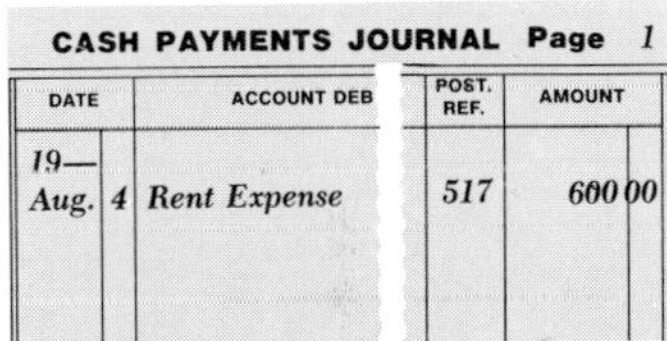

CASH PAYMENTS JOURNAL — Page 1

DATE		ACCOUNT DEB	POST. REF.	AMOUNT
19— Aug.	4	*Rent Expense*	517	600 00

CP: Cash payments journal.

Totaling the Cash Payments Journal

The credit amount posted to the Cash account at the end of the month is the total of the cash payments journal. To find this, the procedure described below is completed. Refer to the illustrations on page 314.

1. Draw a single rule under the last amount in the Amount column.
2. Write the last date of the month in the Date column.
3. Write "Cash Credit" in the Account Debited column.
4. Write "Total payments" in the Explanation column.
5. Add the amounts in the Amount column. Use an adding machine tape or the pencil-footing procedure to prove the addition. If the addition is accurate, write the total in ink beneath the single rule.
6. Draw a double rule under the Date, Posting Reference, and Amount columns to show that the journal is completed for the month.

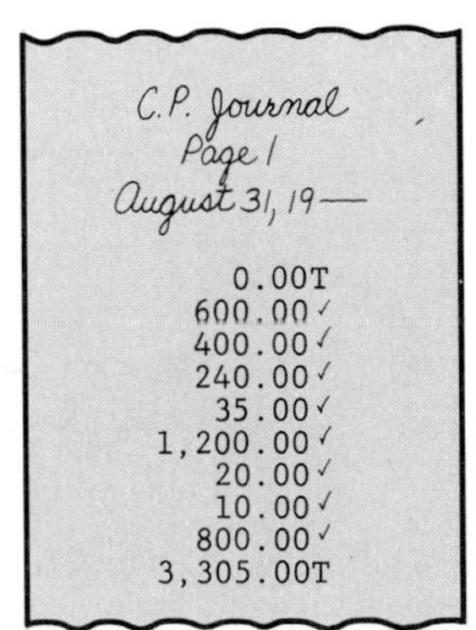

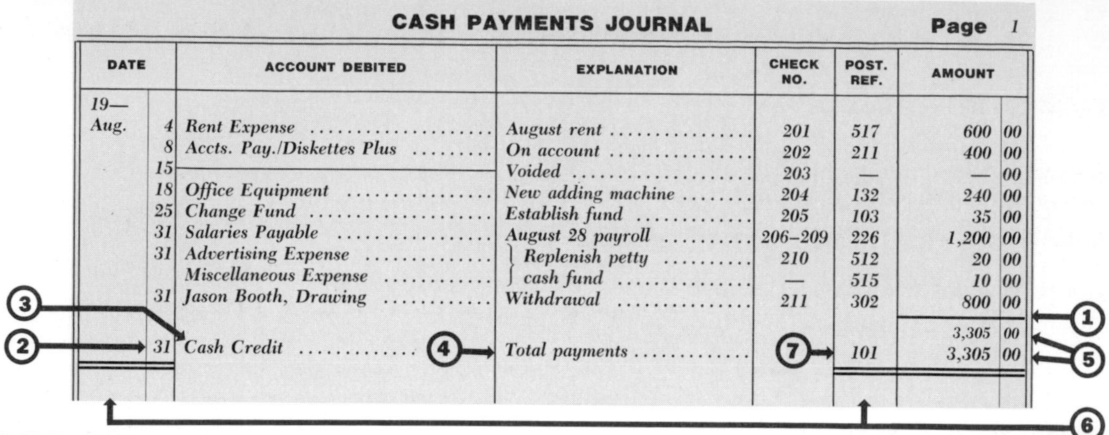

CASH PAYMENTS JOURNAL Page 1

DATE		ACCOUNT DEBITED	EXPLANATION	CHECK NO.	POST. REF.	AMOUNT
19—						
Aug.	4	Rent Expense	August rent	201	517	600 00
	8	Accts. Pay./Diskettes Plus	On account	202	211	400 00
	15		Voided	203	—	— 00
	18	Office Equipment	New adding machine	204	132	240 00
	25	Change Fund	Establish fund	205	103	35 00
	31	Salaries Payable	August 28 payroll	206–209	226	1,200 00
	31	Advertising Expense	Replenish petty	210	512	20 00
		Miscellaneous Expense	cash fund	—	515	10 00
	31	Jason Booth, Drawing	Withdrawal	211	302	800 00
						3,305 00
	31	Cash Credit	Total payments		101	3,305 00

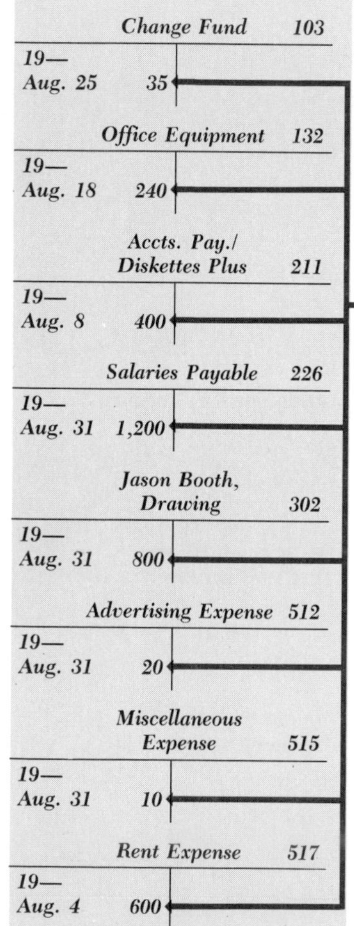

Cash — Account No. 101

DATE		EXPLANATION	POST. REF.	DEBIT	CREDIT	BALANCE DEBIT	BALANCE CREDIT
19—							
Aug.	1	Balance	—			8,400 00	
	31		CR1	10,950 00		19,350 00	
	31		CP1		3,305 00	16,045 00	

Total Debits Equal $3,305

Cash	101
	19— Aug. 31 3,305

Total Credit Posted: $3,305

7. Post the total credit of $3,305 to the Cash account. Finally, enter the number of the Cash account, 101, in the Posting Reference column of the cash payments journal.

After the credit to the Cash account is posted, the account appears as above. Note that the credit of $3,305 posted to the Cash account equals the total of the debits posted from the cash payments journal to the ledger accounts. (See the illustration.)

The credit to the Cash account is not posted until the end of the month. Thus, a trial balance taken during the month would be out of balance. Once the credit is posted, the trial balance should be in balance.

Exercise E on page 315 may be completed at this point.

Cash Posting Clerk: DOT 216.482-010
Performs a variety of computing, posting, and other accounting duties for cash receipts and/or cash payments.

TOPIC 2 EXERCISES

EXERCISE C. Answer the following questions about journalizing cash payments. Refer to the cash payments journal that is shown on page 311.

1. What would the complete entry be if the payment of rent on August 4 were recorded in a general journal instead of in the cash payments journal?
2. When the August 4 transaction is journalized in the cash payments journal, why is no credit entry to the Cash account recorded in the journal?
3. When the transaction involving office equipment is posted from the cash payments journal, is the credit to the Cash account for $240 posted at the same time? Why or why not?
4. Why is a check written on August 25?
5. On what date is the petty cash fund replenished?
6. How many checks are written on August 31? What is the total amount?
7. Why is Check 202 issued?
8. What happened to Check 203?
9. What is the purpose of Check 205?
10. What do you think is the best reason for using a cash payments journal?

EXERCISE D. Answer the following questions about withdrawals. Refer to the cash payments journal illustrated on page 312 and the text on pages 312 to 313.

1. What is meant by the term *withdrawal*?
2. Which account is credited to record a withdrawal? Why?
3. Which account is debited to record a withdrawal? Why?
4. If the owner's withdrawal of $800 on August 31 had been a permanent withdrawal of investment, which account would have been debited?

EXERCISE E. Answer the following questions about posting cash payments. Refer to the cash payments journal and to the Cash account on page 314.

1. What amount is posted to the Cash account from the cash payments journal on August 31? Is the account debited or credited?
2. Is $3,305 posted as a debit to any account on August 31? Why or why not?
3. Why is there a dash in the Posting Reference column of the Cash account for the August 1 entry?
4. What is the source of the August 31 debit of $10,950 in the Cash account?
5. What is the source of the August 31 credit of $3,305 in the Cash account?
6. What is the balance of the Cash account after the August 31 debit is posted?
7. Should the cash receipts or the cash payments journal be posted first? Why?

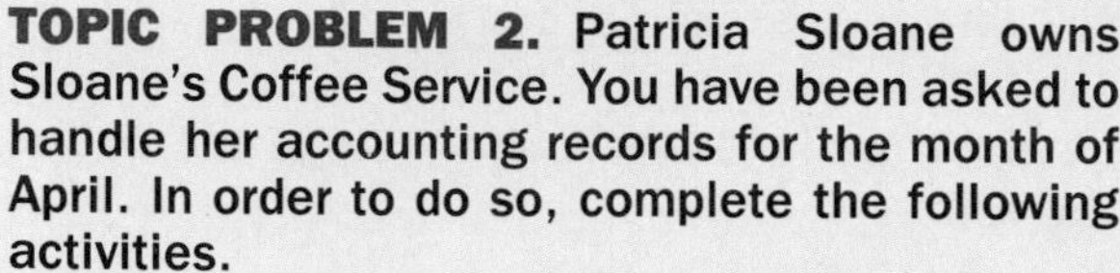

TOPIC 2 PROBLEMS

TOPIC PROBLEM 2. Patricia Sloane owns Sloane's Coffee Service. You have been asked to handle her accounting records for the month of April. In order to do so, complete the following activities.

a. Open accounts and record the April 1 balances for the following accounts: Cash, $7,200; Accts. Pay./Dave Kay, $800; Patricia Sloane, Capital, $6,400; Patricia Sloane, Drawing; and Advertising Expense. Assign an appropriate number to each account.

b. Record the transactions for April in a cash payments journal.

c. Post the debit entries from the cash payments journal.

d. Prove, total, and rule the cash payments journal.

e. Post the credit entry from the cash payments journal.

f. Prepare a trial balance.

Apr. 1 Issued Check 172 for $200 for advertising brochures.
8 Issued Check 173 for $400 to Dave Kay on account.
12 Issued Check 174 for $400 to Patricia Sloane, the owner.
18 Issued Check 175 for $80 to the *Daily Journal* for an advertisement.
27 Issued Check 176 for $200 to Dave Kay on account.
28 Issued Check 177 for $200 for advertisement in theater program.

TOPIC PROBLEM 3. You have recently been employed by All City Delivery Services, owned by Jay Werner. As the accounting clerk, you have been asked to do the following.

a. Open accounts and record the July 1 balances as follows: Cash, $9,800; Petty Cash; Automobile, $7,200; Accts. Pay./Ann White, $1,200; Jay Werner, Capital, $15,800; Jay Werner, Drawing; Automobile Expense; Delivery Expense; Telephone Expense. Assign a proper number to each account.

b. Record the transactions for July 1–19 in the cash payments journal.

c. Post the debit entries from the cash payments journal.

d. Record the transactions for July 23–31 in the cash payments journal.

e. Post the debit entries from the cash payments journal.

f. Prove, total, and rule the cash payments journal.

g. Post the credit entry from the cash payments journal.

h. Prepare a trial balance.

July 1 Issued Check 304 for $600 to Ann White on account.
6 Issued Check 305 for $75 to establish a petty cash fund.
10 Voided Check 306.
11 Issued Check 307 for $4,000 for a used car.
19 Issued Check 308 for $800 to Jay Werner, the owner (permanent withdrawal).

July 23 Issued Check 309 for $300 for car repairs.

25 Issued Check 310 for balance of Ann White account.

26 Issued Check 311 for $60 for monthly telephone bill.

27 Issued Check 312 for $16.50 for delivery expense.

July 31 Issued Check 313 for $500 to Jay Werner, the owner (withdrawal against net income).

31 Issued Check 314 for $47 to replenish petty cash fund (Automobile Expense, $42; Telephone Expense, $5).

TOPIC 3

Proving Cash

What is a cash proof? Any method used to verify that the amount of cash recorded equals the cash handled is known as a **cash proof** You know how a cash proof is made when the total on a cash register tape (the cash recorded) is compared with the total in the cash drawer (the cash handled). Another cash proof is when the checkbook is compared with the Cash account or with the bank statement.

Verifying the Cash Account and Checkbook Balances

The balance of cash can be found in three places when cash control procedures are used: the checkbook, the Cash account, and the monthly bank statement.

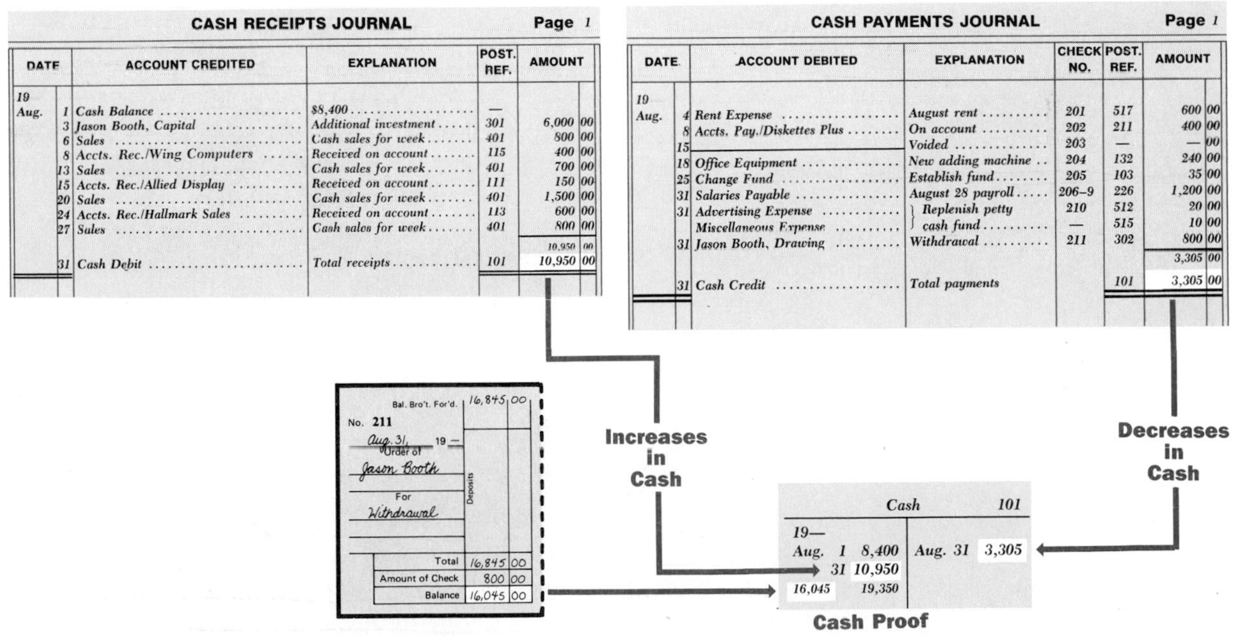

CASH RECEIPTS JOURNAL Page 1

DATE		ACCOUNT CREDITED	EXPLANATION	POST. REF.	AMOUNT
19					
Aug.	1	Cash Balance	$8,400	—	
	3	Jason Booth, Capital	Additional investment	301	6,000 00
	6	Sales	Cash sales for week	401	800 00
	8	Accts. Rec./Wing Computers	Received on account	115	400 00
	13	Sales	Cash sales for week	401	700 00
	15	Accts. Rec./Allied Display	Received on account	111	150 00
	20	Sales	Cash sales for week	401	1,500 00
	24	Accts. Rec./Hallmark Sales	Received on account	113	600 00
	27	Sales	Cash sales for week	401	800 00
					10,950 00
	31	Cash Debit	Total receipts	101	10,950 00

CASH PAYMENTS JOURNAL Page 1

DATE		ACCOUNT DEBITED	EXPLANATION	CHECK NO.	POST. REF.	AMOUNT
19						
Aug.	4	Rent Expense	August rent	201	517	600 00
	8	Accts. Pay./Diskettes Plus	On account	202	211	400 00
	15		Voided	203	—	— 00
	18	Office Equipment	New adding machine	204	132	240 00
	25	Change Fund	Establish fund	205	103	35 00
	31	Salaries Payable	August 28 payroll	206–9	226	1,200 00
	31	Advertising Expense	Replenish petty	210	512	20 00
		Miscellaneous Expense	cash fund	—	515	10 00
	31	Jason Booth, Drawing	Withdrawal	211	302	800 00
						3,305 00
	31	Cash Credit	Total payments		101	3,305 00

Proving cash at the end of the month.

The checkbook stub contains a record of all deposits and all checks written. Thus, the balance on the checkbook stub, for any date, should be the balance of cash for that date. Also, the checkbook stub should equal the Cash account balance for any date. The balances should be equal if the single debit total from the cash receipts journal and the single credit total from the cash payments journal have been posted. (During the month when their totals have not yet been posted, the Cash columns should be pencil-footed.) If there have been no errors in the entries or computations, the cash proof is easy—the checkbook stub balance will equal the Cash account balance.

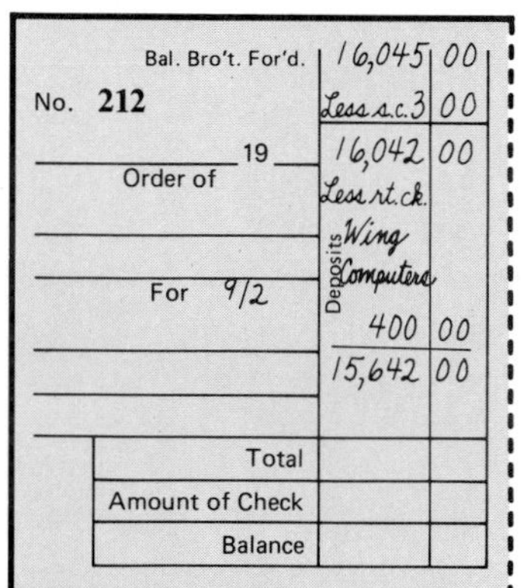

Check stub showing adjustments from bank reconciliation statement.

Verifying the Checkbook and the Bank Statement Balances

Effective cash control also requires that the checkbook balance equal the bank statement balance. The two balances are seldom in agreement because of outstanding checks, deposits in transit, dishonored checks, fees, service charges, and errors. The procedures for reconciling the two balances are described in Chapter 8.

Adjustments After the bank reconciliation is prepared, the balance on the last check stub must be brought into agreement with the "adjusted checkbook balance." This is done by transferring the adjustments from the bank reconciliation to the check stubs. Two adjustments to the checkbook balance are illustrated in the margin. The first adjustment is for a $3 service charge (s.c.). The second adjustment is for a $400 dishonored check (returned check or rt. ck.).

Adjustments that change the checkbook balance also change the Cash account balance. Thus, they must be recorded and posted. An entry recording a service charge of $3 is made in the cash payments journal. The account debited is the Miscellaneous Expense account. The $3 amount is included in the credit to the Cash account when the total of the journal is posted at the end of the month.

CASH PAYMENTS JOURNAL — **Page** 2

DATE		ACCOUNT DEBITED	EXPLANATION	CHECK NO.	POST. REF.	AMOUNT
19—						
Sept.	2	*Miscellaneous Expense*	*Bank service charge*	—		3 00

Entry to record bank service charge.

An entry recording the return of a dishonored check is made in the cash payments journal. The entry is not, strictly speaking, a cash payment. However, a dishonored check decreases cash and the entry "corrects" the original recording of the cash receipt. The entry is shown in the cash payments journal on the next page.

The dishonored check shown on the check stub in the margin on page 318 was received from Wing Computers on August 8 in partial payment of its account. An entry was made in the cash receipts journal when the check was received. See the illustration below at the left.

When the August 8 entry was posted, the Cash account was increased by $400. Accts. Rec./Wing Computers was decreased by the same amount. Now $400 must be deducted from the Cash account and added back to the Wing Computers account. This is done by making the entry shown in the cash payments journal below at the right.

Exercises F and G on pages 322 and 323 may be completed at this point.

CASH RECEIPTS JOURNAL — Page 1

DATE		ACCOUNT CREDITED	EXPLANATION	POST. REF.	AMOUNT
19— Aug.	8	Accts. Rec./Wing Computers	Received on account	115	400 00

Entry to record cash received on account.

CASH PAYMENTS JOURNAL — Page 2

DATE		ACCOUNT DEBITED	EXPLANATION	CHECK NO.	POST. REF.	AMOUNT
19— Sept.	2	Accts. Rec./Wing Computers	Ret'd check of Aug. 8.	—	115	400 00

Entry to record returned check.

Establishing, Using, and Replenishing Change Funds

What is a change fund? A change fund is the amount of money put in the cash drawer to make change. Computer Age established a change fund on August 25 for $35.

CASH PAYMENTS JOURNAL — Page 1

DATE		ACCOUNT DEBITED	EXPLANATION	CHECK NO.	POST. REF.	AMOUNT
19— Aug.	25	Change Fund	Establish fund	205		35 00

Entry to establish change fund.

Establishing the Change Fund

A check establishing a change fund is drawn on the Cash account. The check is made payable to the person responsible for the fund. The check is signed and cashed, and the money is placed in the cash register. The entry for the check includes a debit to the Change Fund account and a credit to Cash.

Using the Change Fund

The change fund is placed in the cash register each day to make change. As cash sales are made, the salesclerks put the cash into the cash register and make change. At the end of the day, the cash in the drawer is counted and the asset cash is proved. The amount of the change fund is subtracted from the total cash in the drawer to find the amount of net cash handled. This amount is then checked against the cash register tape or the net cash received on the cash proof.

Replenishing the Change Fund No check needs to be drawn to replenish the change fund. The cash needed to replenish the fund comes from the cash drawer. Therefore, no entry is made to replenish the change fund. An entry is made to establish the change fund or to adjust the fund if a greater or lesser amount is deemed necessary.

Concept: Proving Assets

The accuracy of the accounting records must be verified with the actual amounts at frequent intervals.

Exercise H on page 323 may be completed at this point.

Recording Cash Short and Over

What indicates that errors have been made in handling cash? The cash in the drawer and the amount recorded on the cash register tape sometimes differ. The cash in the drawer might be more or less than the amount shown on the tape. When the reason for the difference cannot be found, it is assumed that a mistake was made in making change. These mistakes are called *cash over* or *cash short*.

CASH PROOF		
Date *September 4, 19—*		
Register No. *III*		
Cash Sales		275 00
Less: Cash Paid Out		—
Net Cash Received		275 00
Cash in Drawer	312 00	
Less: Change Fund	35 00	
Net Cash Handled		277 00
~~Short or~~ Over		2 00
Clerk *Curtis Dawson*		
Supervisor *Linda Simms*		

Cash		?		Sales	
277			2		275

Cash Over A **cash overage** occurs when there is more cash in the drawer than there should be (according to the cash proof). For example, the cash register tape for September 4 shows that net receipts from cash sales are $275. The supervisor copies this amount on the cash proof form. The supervisor then counts the cash in the drawer ($312) and subtracts the amount of the change fund ($35). This leaves a balance of $277. The cash proof shows the clerk should have received only $275, but $277 is in the drawer. Thus, cash is over by $2. Since no error is found in the records, a mistake was made in making change.

The cash proof is then sent to the accounting department. It becomes the source document for a journal entry. The debit entry is clear. The Cash account must be debited for $277 because this amount will be deposited in the bank. The credit entry, however, should show the Sales account credited for only $275—the true dollar amount of sales. Thus, the overage of $2 must be credited to some other account, because the debit and credit amounts must always be equal.

An overage is treated as revenue because it increases owner's equity. Thus, the overage of $2 is credited to a new account called Cash Short and Over. The transaction is recorded in the cash receipts journal and posted to the proper accounts as follows.

Cash		Cash Short and Over		Sales	
277			2		275

CASH RECEIPTS JOURNAL — **Page 2**

DATE		ACCOUNT CREDITED	EXPLANATION	POST. REF.	AMOUNT
19—					
Sept.	4	Sales	Daily sales		275 00
	4	Cash Short and Over	Cash overage		2 00

The T accounts show that the equality of debits and credits is kept when a cash overage is treated as revenue and properly recorded.

CASH PROOF

Date *September 17, 19—*
Register No. *II*

Cash Sales		338 00
Less: Cash Paid Out		
Net Cash Received		338 00
Cash in Drawer	370 00	
Less: Change Fund	35 00	
Net Cash Handled		335 00
Short ~~or Over~~		3 00

Clerk *Shana Alberti*
Supervisor *Linda Simms*

■ Cash Short A **cash shortage** occurs when there is less cash in the drawer than there should be (as shown in the cash proof in the margin). If the net cash sales are $338 and the net amount of cash in the drawer is $335, cash is short by $3. If the money cannot be located, the shortage of $3 must be recorded.

The debit to the Cash account should be only $335. This is the amount that will be deposited in the bank. However, the $338 should be credited to the Sales account. This is the true revenue that was earned. Thus, the $3 shortage becomes an expense and is debited to Cash Short and Over.

If the transaction were recorded in a general journal, it would be entered as follows.

Sept.	*17*	*Cash*	*335 00*	
		Cash Short and Over	*3 00*	
		Sales		*338 00*

When special cash journals are used, the transaction must be recorded in a different way. Here is the procedure the accounting clerk would follow.

1. Record a $338 credit to Sales in the cash receipts journal. (The entry assumes a $338 debit to Cash.)

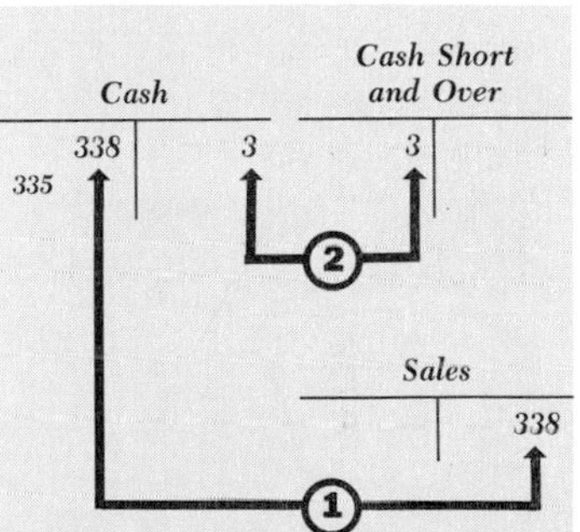

CASH RECEIPTS JOURNAL Page 2

DATE		ACCOUNT CREDITED	EXPLANATION	POST. REF.	AMOUNT
19—					
Sept.	*17*	*Sales*	*Daily sales*		*338 00*

2. Record the $3 shortage as a debit to Cash Short and Over in the cash payments journal. (The entry assumes a $3 credit to Cash.) Note that a dash is placed in the Check Number column to indicate that no check was issued.

CASH PAYMENTS JOURNAL Page 2

DATE		ACCOUNT DEBITED	EXPLANATION	CHECK NO.	POST. REF.	AMOUNT
19—						
Sept.	*17*	*Cash Short and Over*	*Cash shortage*	—		*3 00*

When the individual entries are posted, the balance of the Cash account would be $335. The Cash Short and Over account would have a $3 debit balance. The Sales account would have a $338 credit balance.

■ Uses of the Cash Short and Over Account The **Cash Short and Over account** shows the shortages and overages in making change during an accounting period. Thus, the balance of the Cash Short and Over account is viewed as either expense or revenue. When Cash Short and Over has a debit balance, it is shown as an expense on the income statement because it decreases owner's equity. When it has a credit balance, it is shown as revenue because it increases owner's equity.

Cash Short and Over	
Debit Balance *Expense*	*Credit Balance* *Revenue*

Expenses:		
Cash Short and Over	*3 00*	

Cash shortage shown on income statement as expense.

Revenue:		
Sales	*338 00*	
Cash Short and Over	*3 00*	
Total Revenue		*341 00*

Cash overage shown on income statement as revenue.

COMPUTER AGE CHART OF ACCOUNTS

Expenses
511 Cash Short and Over

The Cash Short and Over account is listed under expenses in the chart of accounts for Computer Age. If the account has a credit balance at the end of the accounting period, the balance will be considered revenue and not an expense. In either case, it is closed into the Income Summary account at the end of the accounting period.

The Cash Short and Over account is useful for balancing accounting records when differences in cash cannot be traced. This device, however, is not a substitute for locating errors. It is used only when absolutely necessary.

Exercise I on page 323 may be completed at this point.

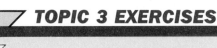

TOPIC 3 EXERCISES

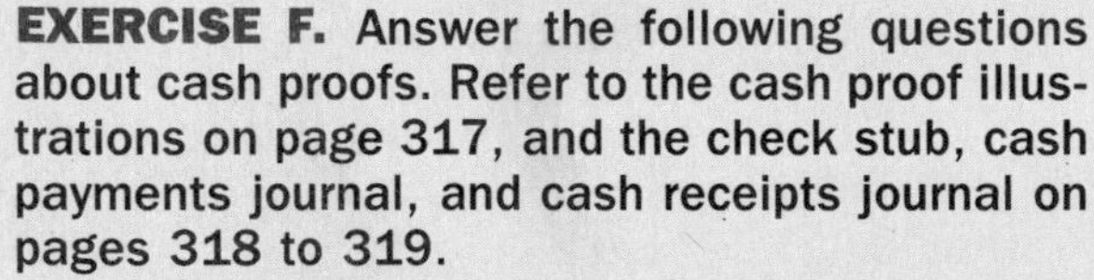

EXERCISE F. Answer the following questions about cash proofs. Refer to the cash proof illustrations on page 317, and the check stub, cash payments journal, and cash receipts journal on pages 318 to 319.

1. What does $10,950 in the cash receipts journal represent?
2. How does Computer Age arrive at the cash balance of $16,045 on August 31?
3. What is the cash proof amount for August 31?
4. What is the check stub balance on September 2?
5. Is a check for the $3 service charge recorded in the cash payments journal?
6. Would posting the September 2 entry increase or decrease the Wing Computers account? Why?
7. Why not accept the bank's balance for cash as the true balance and eliminate making cash proofs?
8. Why is a cash proof prepared?

EXERCISE G. Prepare a cash proof for Computer Age on August 19, showing the cash balance is the same as the checkbook balance for that date. The checkbook balance for August 19 is $15,210.

EXERCISE H. Answer the following questions about change funds. Refer to the text, margin notes, and illustrations on pages 319 to 320.

1. Which account is debited to establish a change fund? Which account is credited?

2. What is the amount of the change fund established on August 25?

3. What are the entries to replenish the change fund?

EXERCISE I. Answer the following questions about cash short and over. Refer to the cash short and cash over illustrations on pages 320 and 322.

1. What might have caused the cash overage on September 4?

2. Which account is credited for cash over?

3. What are the sales for September 4?

4. How much cash is received on September 4?

5. What might have caused the cash shortage on September 17?

6. Which account is debited for cash short?

7. How much cash is received on September 17?

8. How would you react to a company policy that deducts all cash shortages from an employee's paycheck?

TOPIC 3 PROBLEMS

TOPIC PROBLEM 4. John Ramos owns the Speedway Race Track. Visitors pay the admission price to the cashier, who records the sale on a cash register, which issues a ticket for the customer and lists the sale on a tape. You are to keep the cash records for the first two weeks of June.

a. Open balance ledger accounts and record the June 1 balances as follows: Cash, $6,000; Change Fund; Accts. Rec./Brooks Motors, Inc., $800; Race Equipment, $80,000; Accts. Pay./Tom's Repair Shop, $1,270; John Ramos, Capital, $85,530; John Ramos, Drawing; Admissions; Cash Short and Over; and Miscellaneous Expense.

b. Using a cash receipts journal and a cash payments journal, record the transactions below. First, record a memorandum entry for the June 1 cash balance.

c. Post the credit entries from the cash receipts journal and debit entries from the cash payments journal.

d. Prepare a cash proof for June 14. The checkbook shows a balance of $8,272.50.

June 2 Issued Check 81 for $25 to establish change fund.

5 Received $500 from Brooks Motors, Inc., on account.

June 6 Recorded the cash proof, showing admissions (revenue) of $1,784 and an overage of $7.

8 Issued Check 82 for $670 to Tom's Repair Shop.

9 Voided Check 83.

11 Issued Check 84 for $600 for timing clocks (debit: Race Equipment).

June 12 Issued Check 85 for $39 for tickets (Miscellaneous Expense).

13 Recorded the cash proof, showing admissions of $1,320 and a shortage of $4.50.

NOTE: Save your work from this problem for further use in Topic Problem 5.

TOPIC PROBLEM 5. Use the journals and ledger accounts prepared in Topic Problem 4 to keep the cash records for the Speedway Race Track for the last two weeks of June.

a. Record the following transactions.

b. Post the individual entries from the journals.

c. Prepare a cash proof for June 30. The checkbook shows a balance of $16,489.65.

d. Rule the journals, and post the totals to the ledger.

e. Prepare a trial balance.

June 15 Received $200 from Brooks Motors, Inc., on account.

16 Issued Check 86 for $200 to Tom's Repair Shop on account.

17 Issued Check 87 for $1,000 to John Ramos, the owner, for personal use.

June 18 Recorded service charge of $4.75 shown on bank statement.

18 Recorded the return by the bank of a dishonored check for $500 received from Brooks Motors, Inc., on June 5.

20 Recorded the cash proof, showing admissions of $1,750 and an overage of $18.

26 John Ramos invested an additional $5,000 in the business.

27 Recorded the cash proof, showing admissions of $1,400; no shortage or overage.

28 Received $800 from sale of a scoreboard.

30 Recorded the cash proof, showing admissions of $657 and a shortage of $3.10.

CHAPTER 10 REVIEW

CHAPTER SUMMARY

The cash payments subsystem uses forms, procedures, equipment, and people—especially the cashier and the cash payments bookkeeper—to control cash payments.

In this chapter, you learned how to journalize cash payments. To save space, time, and work, many businesses use a cash payments journal, which is a special journal in which only cash payments are recorded. It has advantages over the use of a general journal. Debit entries can be recorded and posted individually. Credit entries to the Cash account can be totaled and posted as a single credit to the Cash account at the end of the month. Thus, the credit entry can be completed using only one line in the cash payments journal. (If the general journal were used, many lines would be needed to record the same credit entries.) Journalizing in this way can also speed up the posting process. The accounts debited in the cash payments journal can be posted easily to proper accounts in the ledger.

You also learned how to establish, use, and replenish the change fund—the amount of cash a business keeps in its cash drawer for change. And, you learned how to use the Drawing account to record temporary withdrawals from the owner's equity account.

Finally, you studied the procedures for proving cash and for recording cash short and over. To make sure that cash on hand agrees with the cash balance obtained from the cash receipts and cash payments journal, a cash proof must be made. When the actual cash on hand is less than the cash balance, as shown in the cash journals, an entry debiting the Cash Short and Over account is made in the cash payments journal. When actual cash on hand is more than the cash balance, an entry crediting the Cash Short and Over account is made in the cash receipts journal. If a checking account is used to make cash payments, the proof is made by making sure that the checkbook balance equals the bank statement balance, and if it does not, then errors must be located and corrected.

THE LANGUAGE OF BUSINESS

Here are some terms that make up the language of business. Do you know the meaning of each?

cash payments subsystem
cash payments journal
withdrawal
Drawing account
cash proof
change fund
cash overage
cash shortage
Cash Short and Over account

REVIEW QUESTIONS

1. List and explain the procedures for the control of cash payments.
2. What source documents serve as the basis for the entries in the cash payments journal?

3. What procedure is followed to complete the cash payments journal at the end of the month?

4. How does the accountant know when to use the Drawing account and when to use the Capital account?

5. At the end of the accounting period, the Cash Short and Over account showed total debits of $4.80 and total credits of $3.90. Is the balance of this account considered revenue or an expense?

6. How is a cash shortage shown on the income statement? How is an overage of cash shown?

7. During the past month, the Cash Short and Over account had total debits of $97 and total credits of $3. The accountant feels that the procedure for handling shortages and overages should be investigated. Do you agree? Why?

8. Explain the procedures for verifying the Cash account balance and the checkbook balance at the end of the month and during the month.

9. Explain how the monthly bank statement provides an excellent external control of cash receipts and cash payments.

CHAPTER PROBLEMS

Problems for Chapter 10 are given below. Write your answers to the problems on separate sheets of papers unless you are using the workbook for this textbook. If you are using the workbook, do the problems in the space provided there.

CHAPTER PROBLEM 10-1. Tracey Li owns Music Video. You have been asked to handle her accounting records for the month of October.

a. Open accounts and record the October 1 balances as follows: Cash, $9,000; Accts. Pay./Kirk Phillips, $800; Tracey Li, Capital, $8,200; Tracey Li, Drawing; and Advertising Expense. Assign an appropriate number to each account.

b. Record the following transactions in a cash payments journal.

c. Post the debit entries from the cash payments journal.

d. Prove, total, and rule the cash payments journal.

e. Post the credit entry from the cash payments journal.

f. Prepare a trial balance.

Oct. 1 Issued Check 172 for $250 for advertising brochures.
2 Voided Check 173.
8 Issued Check 174 for $700 to Kirk Phillips on account.
12 Issued Check 175 for $500 to Tracey Li, the owner (withdrawal against net income).
18 Issued Check 176 for $90 to the *Tribune* for advertisement.
27 Issued Check 177 to Kirk Phillips for the balance of the amount owed.
28 Issued Check 178 for $30 for advertisement in play program.
30 Issued Check 179 for $600 to Tracey Li. The $600 is a permanent decrease in capital.

CHAPTER PROBLEM 10-2. Paul Bryant owns and operates the Seagate Theater. He uses a cash receipts journal and a cash payments journal to record all cash transactions. The Seagate Theater's chart of accounts and beginning balances on August 1 follows.

101 Cash, $6,040
111 Accts Rec./Cinema Supply Company, $2,900
121 Movie Equipment, $9,600
211 Accts. Pay./Carboni Film Company,$1,320
301 Paul Bryant, Capital,$17,220
302 Paul Bryant, Drawing
401 Theater Revenue
501 Cash Short and Over
502 Miscellaneous Expense
503 Rent Expense
504 Telephone Expense

a. Record the following transactions for August 1 to 13 in the appropriate journal.

b. Post the individual journal entries.

c. Prepare a cash proof for August 15. The checkbook shows a balance of $8,245.50.

d. Record the following transactions for the second half of the month.

e. Post the individual journal entries.

f. Prepare a cash proof for August 31. Assume that all data up to and including Check 167 has been recorded correctly on the check stubs.

g. Prove, total, and rule the cash receipts journal and the cash payments journal.

h. Post the totals from the journals to the ledger.

Aug. 1 Received $900 from Cinema Supply Company on account.
2 Issued Check 163 for $600 for monthly rent for August.
6 Recorded the cash proof showing theater revenue of $840 and a shortage of $9.50.
8 Received $350 from Cinema Supply Company on account.
9 Issued Check 164 for $340 for additional movie equipment.
13 Recorded the cash proof showing theater revenue of $1,050 and an overage of $15.
17 Issued Check 165 for $320 to Carboni Film Company on account.
18 Issued Check 166 for $900 to Paul Bryant, the owner, for personal use.
20 Recorded the cash proof showing theater revenue of $810.
29 Received $200 from Cinema Supply on account.
31 Recorded the cash proof showing theater revenue of $1,430 and an overage of $10.
31 Issued Check 167 for $58 for telephone bill.
31 Received the bank statement, which shows a service charge of $8. Record the appropriate entry in the journal and on a check stub.

NOTE: Save your work from this problem for further use in Chapter Problem 10-3.

CHAPTER PROBLEM 10-3. Continue with Chapter Problem 10-2. Verify that the balance of Seagate Theater's Cash account agrees with the cash proof and the checkbook balance on August 31. Then prepare a trial balance to verify that the ledger balances.

MANAGEMENT CASE

Control of Cash Disbursements. Many businesses lose large amounts of money through the theft or embezzlement of cash. Small sums taken by dishonest employees can add up to a sizable amount over a period of time. Reports of the embezzlement of large sums of cash are frequently reported in the news. A business should set up safeguards to control cash in order to (1) remove temptations to steal and (2) protect the reputations of all employees.

CASE 10M-1. The San Antonio Freight Company has branches in San Antonio and several other cities. Assume that you have been appointed manager of a branch. In addition to the drivers and their helpers, there are five people who work in the office: the manager (you), a secretary, an accounting clerk, and two office clerks. The secretary and the accounting clerk have been with the branch for a number of years. The following procedures are used in handling cash.

- Money is usually received through the mail and is opened by any office employee who has time. The person who opens the mail fills out a remittance slip for each amount received, gives the slip to the accounting clerk, and places all receipts in a locked box.
- Because the bank is a 30-minute drive from the office, deposits are usually made once a week. Any member of the office staff may be given the responsibility for taking the deposit to the bank. The average weekly deposit is $6,000.
- The manager, secretary, and accounting clerk are authorized to sign checks.
- All checks are prenumbered. When an error is made in preparing a check, the check is discarded and a note is made on the checkbook stub.
- All invoices are paid by check. The invoices are verified, approved, and paid by either the accounting clerk or the secretary, whoever has time. Since both are authorized to sign checks, they and the manager have access to the checkbook.
- A cash receipts journal and a cash payments journal are used. All receipts and payments are recorded in these journals by the accounting clerk only.
- Small expenditures are made from a petty cash fund. Although a careful record is kept of the amounts put in the fund, no record is kept of the disbursements from it. The fund is kept in a small box in the secretary's desk. Either the secretary, the accounting clerk, or the manager may take money from the box. (Each disburse-

ment is usually less than $1, but no policy has been set as to a maximum amount.) When the money in the box is gone, cash is taken from the bank deposit and placed in the petty cash box.

What recommendations would you make to improve the controls on the following cash procedures?

a. The receipt of cash and the preparation of source documents
b. The depositing of the cash
c. The writing of checks
d. The use of prenumbered checks
e. The payment of invoices
f. The recording of cash receipts and cash payments
g. The handling of petty cash

CHAPTER

11

A Purchases Subsystem

You will now study how the people, forms, procedures, and equipment in a purchases subsystem are used to control purchases on credit. You will also find out about the important jobs of the purchasing agent, inventory clerk, purchasing clerk, and receiving clerk in the purchases subsystem.

CHAPTER GOALS

After studying Chapter 11, you will be able to:

1. Define the terms listed in "The Language of Business" section on page 374.
2. Explain the concepts and principles in this chapter related to accounting for purchases of merchandise.
3. Use a flowchart to describe the relationship between people, forms, procedures, and equipment in a purchases subsystem.
4. Journalize and post from a purchases journal and multicolumn cash payments journal.
5. Calculate purchases discount, the end of the discount period, and the end of the credit period.
6. Explain the relationship between purchases, transportation in, purchases returns and allowances, and purchases discount.

TOPIC 1

Controlling Purchases: Ordering, Receiving, Accounting for, and Storing Merchandise

Procedures for Controlling Purchases on Credit

What is a purchases subsystem? The people, forms, procedures, and equipment used to control purchases on credit make up a **purchases subsystem**. Internal control is especially important in a purchases subsystem because purchases deal with large amounts of assets. The purchase of merchandise involves the following four activities.

- Ordering merchandise
- Receiving merchandise
- Accounting for merchandise
- Storing merchandise

Ordering Merchandise

Why is ordering an important activity in a merchandising business? To operate successfully, a merchandising business must maintain adequate quantities of every item it has for resale. These items are called **merchandise inventory**. The merchandise inventory must have a variety of sizes, styles, or models. If a merchandise business cannot provide a broad selection of items with fast delivery, it will lose customers. Thus, when an item in inventory drops below a minimum quantity, more merchandise must be ordered.

How is merchandise ordered? In a small business, merchandise may be ordered by the owner. In a large business, merchandise may be ordered by a purchasing agent in a special purchasing department. Regardless of its size, each business must decide what needs to be purchased, choose the supplier, and place the order.

■ Determining Needs In a very small business, a note from the owner could be the signal that some item needs to be ordered. In a larger business like Computer Age, the signal to order comes from inventory cards. An **inventory card** is a record of the stock of one item.

The inventory card in the margin is for boxes of computer diskettes (A82-B). The minimum (lowest) stock for them is 10. Thus, on September 23, when the inventory drops to 10, the inventory clerk knows it is time to order additional stock. The maximum (largest) stock of the diskettes (A82-B) is 28. Thus, the inventory clerk can quickly determine that 18 additional boxes of diskettes must be ordered to refill the stock. The minimum (10) and the maximum (28) are based on the average volume of sales and the time needed to get new stock.

INVENTORY CARD

No. A82-B
Item Computer Diskettes
Location: Aisle 3 Bin 4
Maximum 28 Minimum 10

Date	Quant. Rec'd	Unit Cost	Quant. Sold	Balance
19— 8/13	22	40.00		28
8/20			3	25
8/27			4	21
9/4			4	17
9/12			2	15
9/18			2	13
9/23			3	10

Inventory card showing maximum and minimum stock.

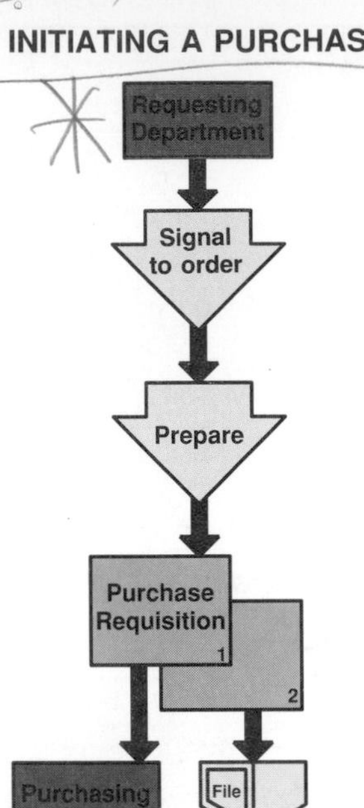

At Computer Age, each department manager requests merchandise that is needed on a purchase requisition. The **purchase requisition** is a prenumbered form from the department manager asking the purchasing agent to order merchandise.

The purchase requisition provides the following information, as illustrated in the form below.

- WHO is making the request
- WHAT is to be purchased
- WHEN it is needed

The prenumbered purchase requisition is signed by an authorized employee. The requisition is the source document that starts the purchasing activity and is sent to the purchasing agent.

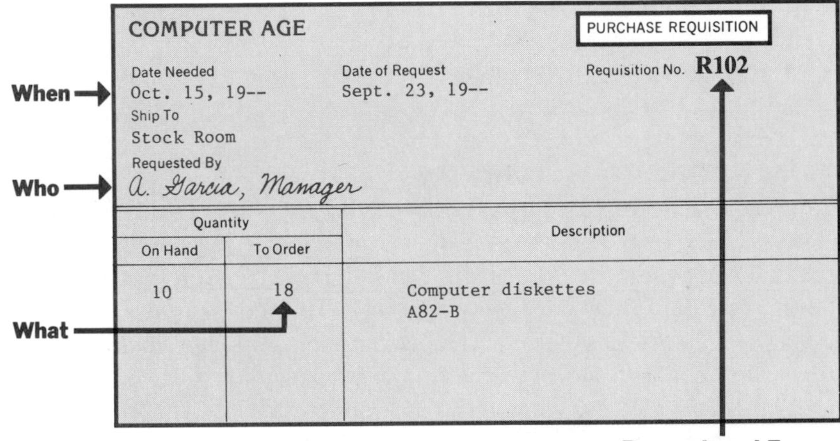

COMPUTER AGE — PURCHASE REQUISITION

Date Needed: Oct. 15, 19--
Date of Request: Sept. 23, 19--
Requisition No. R102
Ship To: Stock Room
Requested By: A. Garcia, Manager

Quantity On Hand	Quantity To Order	Description
10	18	Computer diskettes A82-B

Purchase requisition from department (WHO) asking purchasing agent to order diskettes (WHAT) to bring stock to maximum by October 15 (WHEN). Note use of prenumbered form.

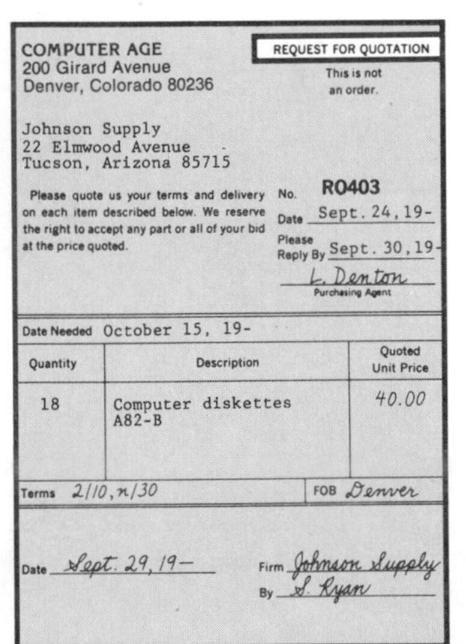

COMPUTER AGE
200 Girard Avenue
Denver, Colorado 80236

REQUEST FOR QUOTATION
This is not an order.

Johnson Supply
22 Elmwood Avenue
Tucson, Arizona 85715

Please quote us your terms and delivery on each item described below. We reserve the right to accept any part or all of your bid at the price quoted.

No. R0403
Date Sept. 24, 19-
Please Reply By Sept. 30, 19-
L. Denton, Purchasing Agent

Date Needed October 15, 19-

Quantity	Description	Quoted Unit Price
18	Computer diskettes A82-B	40.00

Terms 2/10, n/30 FOB Denver

Date Sept. 29, 19— Firm Johnson Supply By S. Ryan

Request for quotation from Computer Age answered by Johnson Supply.

■ **Selecting the Supplier** The purchasing agent selects the supplier who is best able to supply the merchandise. Before an order is placed, the purchasing agent might ask for prices from the suppliers if new items are requisitioned or new suppliers are needed.

The prices and quantities of merchandise are requested on a letter or a special form called a *request for quotation*. The form shown in the margin provides the following information.

- WHO is making the request for a quotation
- WHAT items and quantities are wanted
- WHEN the goods are needed

The request for quotation was issued by the purchasing agent of Computer Age. On it, Johnson Supply shows credit terms of 2/10, n/30. The term *2/10* means that the buyer can deduct 2 percent if the bill is paid within 10 days from the invoice date. In the term *n/30*, the *n* stands for net. Thus, *n/30* means that if the discount is not taken, the buyer has 30 days in which to pay the (net) full amount. (If the terms were *n/EOM*, the buyer would have until the end of the month to pay the net amount.) Many businesses take advantage of the discount offered and pay the invoice within the shorter period.

Johnson Supply also indicates that the goods will be shipped FOB Denver. **FOB (free on board)** is a shipping term that means that the seller pays shipping charges to that destination. Johnson Supply will pay the shipping charges from Tucson to Denver. (If the form showed FOB Tucson, Computer Age must pay the shipping charges.)

■ Placing the Order The purchasing clerk must now prepare a purchase order. The **purchase order** is the form on which the purchasing agent authorizes the supplier to ship merchandise and charge the

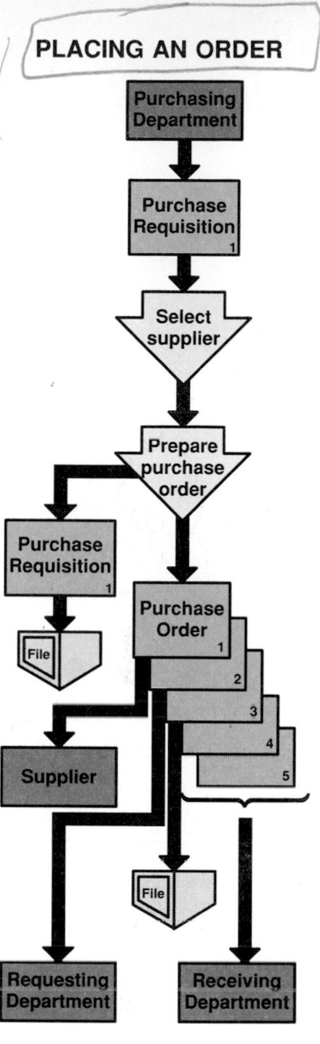

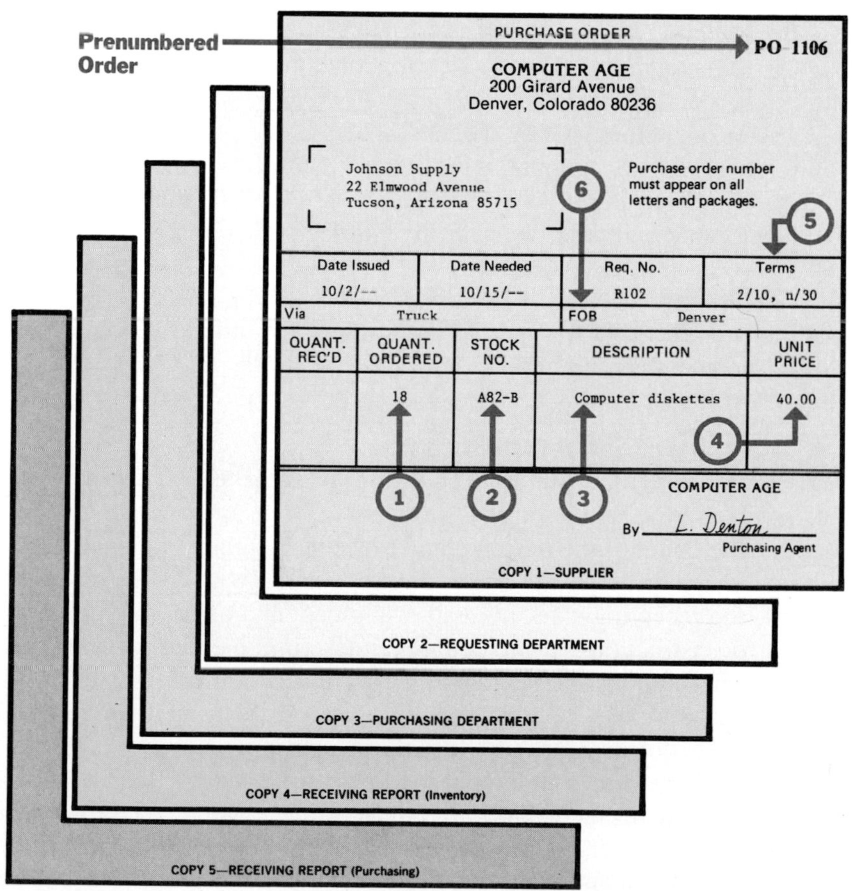

purchaser the quoted prices for the merchandise. The purchase order includes the following information.

1. The quantity ordered
2. A stock number, if known
3. A brief description
4. The unit price, taken either from the supplier's catalog or from the copy of the request for quotation
5. The terms
6. Shipping instructions

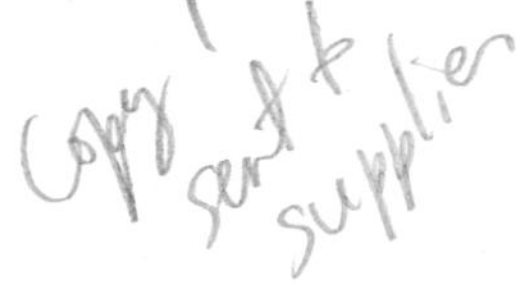

The number of copies of the purchase order varies with the size of the business. Computer Age prepares purchase orders on prenumbered forms. Each form contains five copies, as on page 333. Copy 1 is the order sent to the supplier who fills the order and ships it back to Computer Age. Copy 2 is sent to the department that initiated the purchase requisition to show that the needed merchandise is now on order. Copy 3 is kept by the purchasing department as a record of all purchase orders issued. Copies 4 and 5 are sent to the receiving department until the merchandise arrives.

Exercise A on page 340 may be completed at this point.

Purchasing Agent: DOT 162.157-038
Reviews requisitions, selects suppliers, and orders merchandise.

Inventory Clerk: DOT 222.387-026
Keeps record of amount, kind, and cost of merchandise on hand. May indicate items to be reordered. May count merchandise on hand. May compare physical inventories with records.

Purchasing Clerk: DOT 249.367-066
Prepares requests for quotation and purchase orders; keeps records of merchandise ordered.

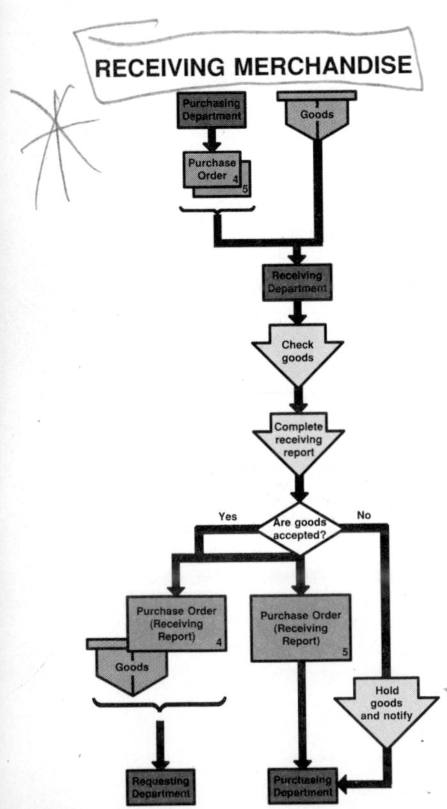

Receiving Merchandise

What happens when merchandise is received? The receiving clerk checks the items for any shortages, errors, or damages in shipment. The count of the items actually received is entered on Copy 4 of the purchase order. If the count does not agree with the quantity ordered, the receiving clerk holds the shipment and asks the purchasing agent for instructions. If the count and description agree with the purchase order and the merchandise is in good condition, the receiving clerk indicates that the shipment is accepted. The clerk initials the approval section of Copy 4—the receiving report.

Copy 4 serves as the source document for updating the inventory cards for the items received. In the illustration shown on the next page, the inventory card is updated to show the goods received in the receiving report. The quantity received (18) is added to the balance (4). The balance is now 22. The date received (10/10) and the unit cost ($40) are also recorded on the inventory card. The merchandise and Copy 4 are then sent to the stockroom or the department that requisitioned the items. There, the shipment is again counted and checked before being put into inventory.

The receiving department receives and checks the goods. The receiving clerk initials and approves the receiving report.

PURCHASE ORDER

PO–1106

COMPUTER AGE
200 Girard Avenue
Denver, Colorado 80236

Johnson Supply
22 Elmwood Avenue
Tucson, Airzona 85715

Goods Received 10/10/--
Quantity Checked S.G.
Quality Checked L.W.

Date Issued	Date Needed	Req. No.	Terms
10/2/--	10/15/--	R102	2/10, n/30

Via Truck FOB Denver

QUANT. REC'D	QUANT. ORDERED	STOCK NO.	DESCRIPTION	UNIT PRICE
18	18	A82-B	Computer diskettes	40.00

COMPUTER AGE

By L. Denton
Purchasing Agent

COPY 4—RECEIVING REPORT (Inventory)

INVENTORY CARD

No. A82-B
Item Computer Diskettes
Location: Aisle 3 Bin 4
Maximum 28 Minimum 10

Date	Quant. Rec'd	Unit Cost	Quant. Sold	Balance
19-- 8/13	22	40.00		28
8/20			3	25
8/27			4	21
9/4			4	17
9/12			2	15
9/18			2	13
9/23			3	10
9/28			2	8
10/2			3	5
10/8			1	4
10/10	18	40.00		22

Copy 5 carries the receiving clerk's initials of approval and is sent to the purchasing agent to show that the shipment has been received and accepted.

Receiving Clerk: DOT 222.387-050
Receives, unpacks, inspects, and verifies shipments; handles rejected merchandise; records merchandise and sends it to proper department.

Control: Accept merchandise in authorized quantities and quality only.

Accounting for Merchandise

What control procedures are used to account for merchandise? The purchasing agent must confirm that all items ordered have been received in good condition. To do so, the agent holds Copy 5 of the purchase order until an *invoice* (a bill) is received from the supplier. To the purchaser, the invoice is a **purchase invoice**. It lists the items purchased. To the supplier who has issued the bill, it is a sales invoice. It lists the items sold. The invoice shown on page 336 is a purchase invoice to the purchaser, Computer Age. It is a sales invoice to the supplier, Johnson Supply.

The purchasing agent verifies that the goods received are in good condition and checks the invoice.

Control: Verify invoices before approving payment.

PROCESSING A PURCHASE INVOICE

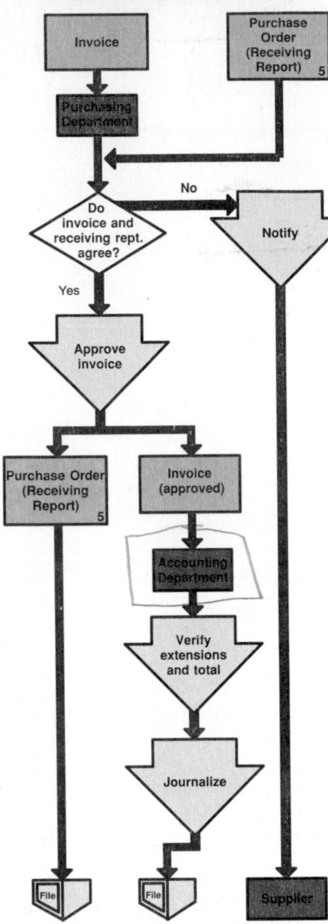

The accounting department receives the invoice for processing of payment.

APPROVED DATE	10/10/—
QUANTITIES RECEIVED	L. Denton
PRICES CHARGED	L. Denton
EXTENSIONS & TOTALS	M. Reiss
DATE PAID	10/18/—
CHECK NO.	308

"Approved" stamp to verify invoice.

The invoice contains almost the same information that is on the purchase order. It includes the following.

- The name and address of the seller and the purchaser
- The invoice number and the date
- The terms
- The purchase order number and date (for cross-reference)
- The method of shipment
- The quantity, description, and price of each item shipped
- The extensions

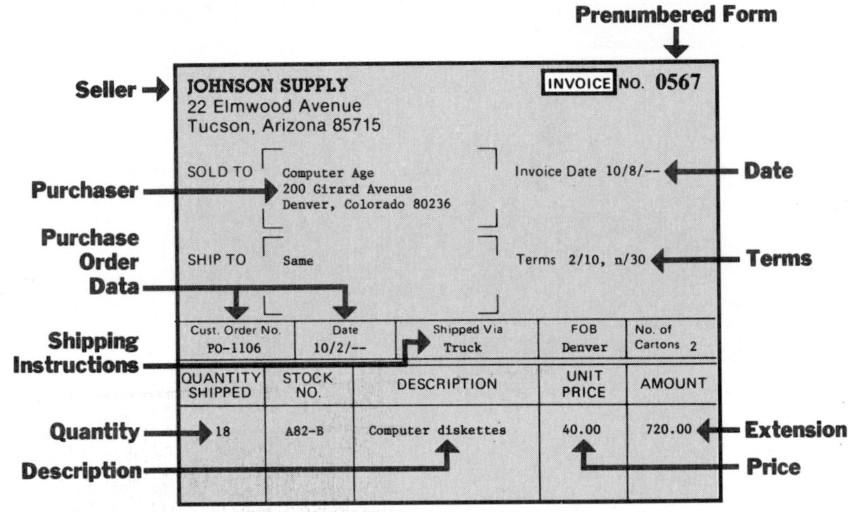

JOHNSON SUPPLY
22 Elmwood Avenue
Tucson, Arizona 85715

INVOICE NO. 0567

SOLD TO Computer Age
200 Girard Avenue
Denver, Colorado 80236

Invoice Date 10/8/--

SHIP TO Same

Terms 2/10, n/30

Cust. Order No.	Date	Shipped Via	FOB	No. of Cartons
PO-1106	10/2/--	Truck	Denver	2

QUANTITY SHIPPED	STOCK NO.	DESCRIPTION	UNIT PRICE	AMOUNT
18	A82-B	Computer diskettes	40.00	720.00

The invoice also shows how the amount owed was computed. Each amount in the Amount column is called an **extension**, which is found by multiplying the unit price of the item by the number of units shipped. The amount shown on the invoice above ($720) is computed by multiplying the unit price ($40) by the number of units shipped (18). If the invoice has more than one extension in the Amount column, the extensions are added to show the total amount owed.

The purpose of comparing the invoice with Copy 5 of the purchase order is to make sure that the business has been billed only for the items it received. If there are any differences, the purchasing agent contacts the supplier. If the invoice is correct, it is stamped with a special ''Approved'' stamp, as shown in the margin. The purchasing agent initials the checked and verified items to show they are correct. The invoice is then sent to the accounting department.

When the accounting department receives the invoice, the extensions and the total are rechecked. The invoice is then journalized. Finally, when the invoice is due, a check is issued for the correct amount. As the invoice is processed in the accounting department, the authorized employee initials the "Approved" stamp on the invoice to indicate the items have been checked and approved.

Exercise B on page 340 may be completed at this point.

Storing Merchandise

How do businesses keep track of inventory? Some businesses keep a daily record of each item in their inventory. Keeping a daily record of inventory is known as the **perpetual inventory procedure**. Most businesses that use this method generally sell small numbers of high-priced items.

Many businesses that handle a large number of low-priced items count their inventory less often but at regular intervals. For these businesses a different method is more useful. Using this method, which is called the **periodic inventory procedure**, the inventory is counted at regular intervals (perhaps once every six months or every year).

Inventory is taken to determine when more goods must be ordered and to help maintain the accuracy of the accounting records.

The actual counting of inventory is called *taking a physical inventory*. When a **physical inventory** is taken, every item is counted. The total inventory cost is computed by adding together the cost of each item.

A physical inventory serves several purposes.

- It is a check on the accuracy of the perpetual inventory records.
- It keeps track of how many items have been lost through theft or breakage by comparing the number of items on hand with the current balance on the inventory cards.
- It keeps track of how many goods have decreased in quality with the passing of time. For example, perishable items may have been left on the shelves too long.
- It helps a business correct its accounting records and have accurate financial statements.

Control: Prove inventory.

Inventory Loss

Why must merchandise be properly stored? Merchandise inventory must be properly stored so that customers are provided with the kinds of items desired and so that inventory loss is minimized. **Inventory loss** is a term used to describe a loss of items of inventory or a loss in the resale value of merchandise inventory. The loss could be due to deterioration, obsolescence, mishandling, or theft.

Deterioration *Deterioration* is the decrease in quality of goods with the passing of time. The most common examples of goods that deteriorate are food and other perishable items such as cosmetics or perfume. Inventory loss due to deterioration is controlled by the regular rotating of merchandise.

Obsolescence *Obsolescence* is the outdating of goods until they are not as useful as they were when new. Examples of goods that become obsolete are seasonal items such as clothing fashions or high-technology items like computers. Inventory loss due to obsolescence is controlled by following sound purchasing procedures and carefully determining which goods and how many goods should be purchased and in what quantities.

Mishandling and Theft *Mishandling* and *theft* are the improper handling and stealing of goods. Even though smaller goods are easier to mishandle and steal, all types of inventory are mishandled and stolen. Some statistics show that inventory is stolen every five seconds and that theft of inventory costs every consumer approximately $150 a year.

Inventory loss due to mishandling and theft is controlled by following strict internal control procedures. These procedures include locking storage areas and prohibiting unauthorized personnel from entering them, using surveillance systems (such as television monitors and double mirrors), and dividing the responsibilities among several employees.

Visualizing a Purchases Subsystem

How are the procedures in a purchases subsystem related to each other? The flowchart that is shown on the next page illustrates the procedures to control purchases in the purchases subsystem. The activities (which are numbered 1 to 22) are described briefly at the top and bottom of the flowchart. By reading the activities and following them on the flowchart, you can see how each relates to the other.

The subsystem for purchasing merchandise includes a number of procedures which ensure control over the activities of ordering, receiving, storing, and accounting for purchases of merchandise. A subsystem to control the purchase of merchandise includes the procedures listed below, which you studied in Topic 1.

- Identify merchandise needed.
- Initiate purchasing by authorized personnel.
- Use prenumbered forms.
- Divide responsibility.
- Purchase merchandise from approved suppliers.
- Accept merchandise only in approved quantities and quality.
- Verify quantities, terms, prices, and computations on invoices before approving payment.
- Verify quantities of merchandise in stock with inventory records.

In future topics in the chapter, you will learn about the following procedures for controlling inventory.

- Record data from completed purchase transactions.
- Obtain refunds or credits for all purchases returns and allowances.
- Pay invoices in time to take cash discounts.

Exercise C on page 340 may be completed at this point.

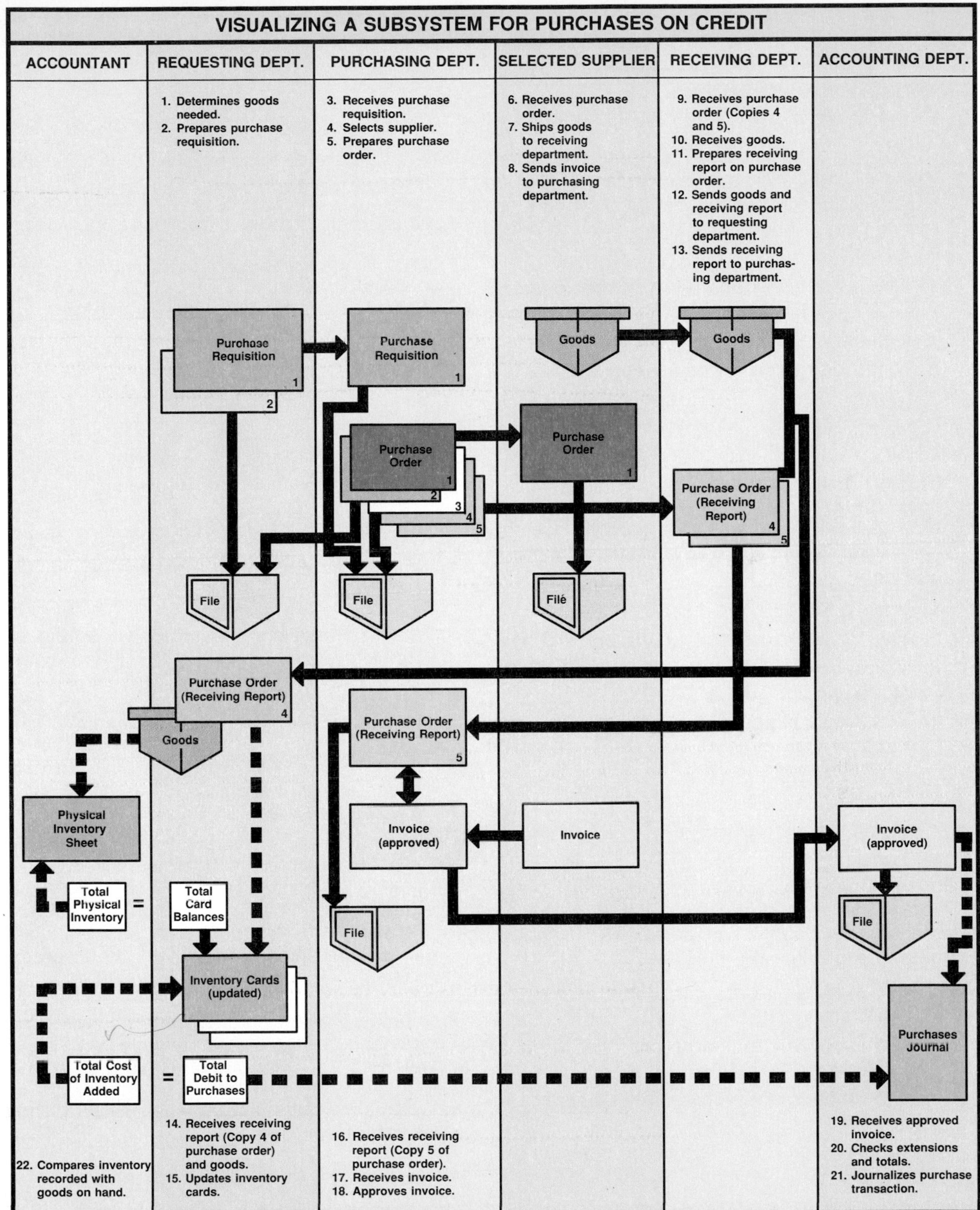

VISUALIZING A SUBSYSTEM FOR PURCHASES ON CREDIT
ACCOUNTANT
REQUESTING DEPT.
PURCHASING DEPT.
SELECTED SUPPLIER
RECEIVING DEPT.
ACCOUNTING DEPT.
1. Determines goods needed.
2. Prepares purchase requisition.
3. Receives purchase requisition.
4. Selects supplier.
5. Prepares purchase order.
6. Receives purchase order.
7. Ships goods to receiving department.
8. Sends invoice to purchasing department.
9. Receives purchase order (Copies 4 and 5).
10. Receives goods.
11. Prepares receiving report on purchase order.
12. Sends goods and receiving report to requesting department.
13. Sends receiving report to purchasing department.
Purchase Requisition
Purchase Requisition
Goods
Goods
Purchase Order
Purchase Order
Purchase Order (Receiving Report)
File
File
File
Purchase Order (Receiving Report)
Goods
Purchase Order (Receiving Report)
Physical Inventory Sheet
Invoice (approved)
Invoice
Invoice (approved)
Total Physical Inventory
=
Total Card Balances
File
File
Inventory Cards (updated)
Purchases Journal
Total Cost of Inventory Added
=
Total Debit to Purchases
22. Compares inventory recorded with goods on hand.
14. Receives receiving report (Copy 4 of purchase order) and goods.
15. Updates inventory cards.
16. Receives receiving report (Copy 5 of purchase order).
17. Receives invoice.
18. Approves invoice.
19. Receives approved invoice.
20. Checks extensions and totals.
21. Journalizes purchase transaction.

Note: Permanent inventory cards are kept in the accounting department.

compares physical inventory w/ inventory cards

TOPIC 1 EXERCISES

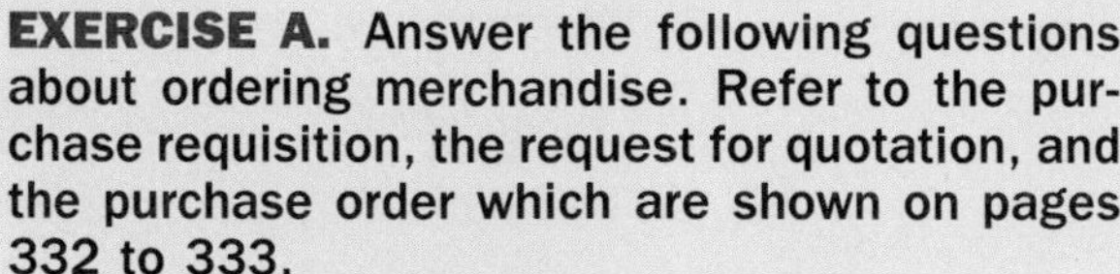

EXERCISE A. Answer the following questions about ordering merchandise. Refer to the purchase requisition, the request for quotation, and the purchase order which are shown on pages 332 to 333.

1. Where are the goods to be shipped?

2. What quantity is on hand? What quantity is requisitioned?

3. When are the diskettes needed by Computer Age?

4. What unit price for the diskettes is quoted by Johnson Supply?

5. What credit terms does Johnson Supply offer?

6. What is the purchase order number?

7. When is the purchase order issued?

8. Who approved the purchase order?

EXERCISE B. Answer the following questions about receiving and accounting for merchandise. Refer to the receiving report, inventory card, invoice, and approval stamp on pages 335 and 336.

1. When are the goods received?

2. How many boxes of diskettes are received?

3. Who checks the quantity of the goods? The quality?

4. What would happen if a customer wanted five boxes of diskettes on October 9 and would not take fewer than five?

5. What is the number of the invoice?

6. When is the invoice paid?

7. What is the number of the check to pay the invoice?

8. What is the total amount shown on the invoice?

9. What procedures for controlling purchases are illustrated by the approval stamp?

EXERCISE C. Using the flowchart on visualizing a subsystem for purchases on credit that is shown on page 339 and the text materials about storing merchandise on pages 337 and 338, answer the following questions.

1. How many steps are completed by the supplier?

2. What department journalizes the purchase transactions?

3. What department prepares the purchase requisitions?

4. The purchase requisition is the basis for preparing which document?

5. Does the purchasing department handle the goods?

6. Why does the accountant periodically compare the physical inventory with the inventory cards?

7. Should a business prenumber purchase requisitions, purchase orders, and checks? Why or why not?

8. What is the difference between perpetual and periodic inventory?

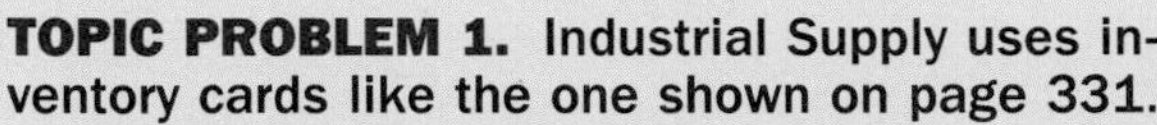

TOPIC 1 PROBLEMS

TOPIC PROBLEM 1. Industrial Supply uses inventory cards like the one shown on page 331.

a. Record these items on two inventory cards. Item 35: electric iron; aisle, 13; bin, 4; maximum, 72; minimum, 18; balance of 28 on April 1; unit cost, $28
Item 36: food processor; aisle, 15; bin, 8; maximum, 60; minimum, 12; balance of 17 on April 1; unit cost, $43

b. The transactions listed below were taken from receiving reports and shipping reports. Update the inventory cards.

c. List the dates on which purchase requisitions should be issued.

Apr. 3 Sold 8 of Item 35.
4 Sold 6 of Item 36.
9 Sold 8 of Item 35.
12 Received 49 of Item 36; unit cost, $43.50.
13 Sold 12 of Item 36.
16 Received 60 of Item 35; unit cost, $29.
17 Sold 12 of Item 35.
17 Sold 8 of Item 36.
18 Sold 12 of Item 35.
19 Sold 12 of Item 35.
19 Sold 12 of Item 36.
23 Sold 15 of Item 35.
24 Sold 18 of Item 36.
26 Sold 6 of Item 35.
May 1 Received 50 of Item 36; unit cost, $44.75.
3 Received 57 of Item 35; unit cost, $30.50.
6 Sold 8 of Item 36.
7 Sold 2 of Item 36.

TOPIC PROBLEM 2. An inventory card for one item sold by Hauer's Farm Supply is illustrated at the right.

a. Complete Purchase Requisition R111 to increase the quantity on hand to six units. The new units should be shipped to the warehouse. The current date is September 6 and the date the new units are needed is September 20.

b. Complete a request for quotation. The request should be sent to the Rural Till Company, 200 State Highway 33, East Windsor, New Jersey 08520. You need a reply by September 12.

c. Complete a purchase order. The Rural Till Company replies to your request for quotation and indicates that it can furnish the items by September 20 at a unit cost of $230; terms, 2/10, n/30, FOB Wheaton by Express Freight Lines. Your purchase order (Purchase Order C-444) should be dated September 12.

d. The invoice sent by the Rural Till Company to Hauer's Farm Supply for the items ordered on Purchase Order C-444 is on the next page. If

INVENTORY CARD

No. 180-S

Item Roto-Tiller, 3.5 HP, Easy-Till

Location: Aisle 3 Bin 14

Maximum 10 Minimum 3

Date	Quant. Rec'd	Unit Cost	Quant. Sold	Balance
19— 6/4	10	217.00		10
7/1			1	9
8/7			3	6
8/14			3	3
8/15	2	230.00		5
9/5			4	1

all the information on the invoice is correct, initial the "approved" stamp in the appropriate places. (Another accounting clerk will write the check.) If the information on the invoice is not correct, make a list of the incorrect information. Four items were received.

RURAL TILL COMPANY
200 State Highway 33
East Windsor, New Jersey 08520

INVOICE NO. 1762

Sold to: Hauer's Farm Supply
Fairfax Road
Wheaton, Illinois 60187

Invoice Date: September 20, 19--

Ship to: Same

APPROVED	DATE
QUANTITIES RECEIVED	
PRICES CHARGED	
EXTENSIONS & TOTALS	
DATE PAID	
CHECK NO.	

Customer Order No.	Date	Ship Via	Terms
C-444	9/12/--	Express	2/10, n/30

QUANTITY	DESCRIPTION	UNIT PRICE	AMOUNT
6	Roto-Tiller, 3.5 HP, Easy-Till	235.00	1,410.00

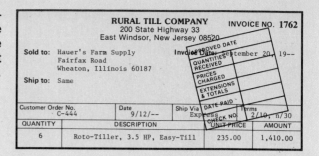

TOPIC PROBLEM 3. In a table similar to the one below, indicate who prepares or sends the forms listed at the right, to whom or where the forms are sent, and the purpose the forms serve. Base your answers on the flowchart of a purchases subsystem on page 339.

Forms

a. Copy 2 of purchase requisition
b. Copy 1 of purchase order
c. Copy 2 of purchase order
d. Copy 3 of purchase order

Form	Prepared or Sent By	Sent To	Purpose
EXAMPLE: Purchase Requisition: Copy 1	Requesting department	Purchasing department	To tell the purchasing agent what is needed, when, and by whom.

TOPIC 2

Processing Purchases

Does the purchase of merchandise affect a business's net income (or net loss)? Yes, the purchase of merchandise affects a business's net income (or net loss) because it affects its costs and gross profit. A *merchandising business* earns revenue through the sale of merchandise. The amounts paid for purchases of merchandise are called **costs.** The difference between revenue and costs is called **gross profit.** A business pays its expenses from gross profit. If the gross profit is greater than the expenses, the business has a net income. If the expenses are greater than the gross profit, the business has a net loss.

Determining Cost of Goods Sold

To make a gross profit, a merchandising business must sell goods at a price higher than it pays for them. For example, Computer Age bought disk drives for $120 and sold them for $150. In accounting terms, the revenue from the sale of goods was $150, and the cost of the goods sold was $120. The gross profit on the sale was $30. The gross profit of $30 is used to pay the expenses to operate the business.

Revenue increases owner's equity. Thus, revenue from the sale of goods is credited to a temporary owner's equity account called the **Sales account**. The cost of goods purchased for resale decreases owner's equity and is debited to a temporary owner's equity account called the **Purchases account**.

In a chart of accounts, accountants generally group the cost and expense accounts together because they both decrease owner's equity. They are called Cost and Expense accounts. The Purchases account is numbered 501 in the chart of accounts for Computer Age.

COMPUTER AGE CHART OF ACCOUNTS

Costs and Expenses
501 Purchases

Journalizing Purchases

How is the purchase of merchandise journalized? The procedures for journalizing purchases depend on whether the purchase is for cash or on credit.

Purchases for Cash

When a business pays cash for merchandise, the asset Cash is credited because cash decreases. The Purchases account is debited because there is a decrease in owner's equity.

The check stub is the source document for journalizing the purchase of merchandise for cash. The entry is recorded in the cash payments journal because the transaction involves a credit to the Cash account.

Purchases on Credit

When merchandise is purchased on credit, a liability is incurred. Thus, the liability account, Accounts Payable, is credited because liabilities increase. The Purchases account is debited because there is a decrease in owner's equity.

Control: Record all payables.

The journal entry recording the purchase of merchandise on credit cannot be made until the purchasing department approves the purchase invoice. Once approved, the purchase invoice is the source document that is the basis for a debit to the Purchases account and a credit to the creditor's account.

OCTOBER 10: COMPUTER AGE PURCHASES MERCHANDISE FROM JOHNSON SUPPLY FOR $720 ON CREDIT.

What Happens	Accounting Rule	Accounting Entry
Cost of merchandise decreases owner's equity by $720.	To decrease owner's equity, debit the account.	Debit: Purchases, $720.
The liability *Accounts Payable* increases by $720.	To increase a liability, credit the account.	Credit: Accts. Pay./Johnson Supply, $720.

The purchase invoice from Johnson Supply could be journalized in the general journal as shown on the next page.

Purchases of merchandise on credit recorded in general journal.

GENERAL JOURNAL — Page 5

DATE		ACCOUNT TITLE AND EXPLANATION	POST. REF.	DEBIT	CREDIT
19—					
Oct.	10	Purchases	501	720 00	
		Accts. Pay./Johnson Supply	212		720 00
		Invoice 0567; (10/8); 2/10, n/30.			
	11	Purchases	501	2,000 00	
		Accts. Pay./Diskettes Plus	211		2,000 00
		Invoice 82A; (10/10); n/EOM.			

Purchases 501	
19—	
Oct. 10 J5 720	
11 J5 2,000	

Accts. Pay./Diskettes Plus 211	
	19—
	Oct. 11 J5 2,000

Accts. Pay./Johnson Supply 212	
	19—
	Oct. 10 J5 720

When a business has many purchases of merchandise on credit, it is more efficient to use a special journal. The **purchases journal** is a special journal used to record the purchases of merchandise on credit only. Assets other than merchandise—such as office furniture—purchased on credit are recorded in the general journal. In that case the proper asset account—not the Purchases account—is debited for the amount of the invoice.

Each entry for a purchase of merchandise on credit involves a debit to the Purchases account. Only the credits to the individual creditors' accounts change. Thus, a one-column purchases journal is often used to record the name of the creditor for each purchase.

The purchases journal saves time and space because an entire entry is recorded on one line. The debits to the Purchases account are posted as a total at the end of the month.

Purchases of merchandise on credit recorded in purchases journal.

PURCHASES JOURNAL — Page 1

DATE		ACCOUNT CREDITED	INVOICE NO.	INVOICE DATE	TERMS	POST. REF.	AMOUNT
19—							
Oct.	10	Johnson Supply	0567	10/8	2/10, n/30		720 00
	11	Diskettes Plus	82A	10/10	n/EOM		2,000 00
	13	LCP Computer	P876	10/13	1/10, n/30		400 00
	20	Micro Components	106A	10/18	2/10, n/30		480 00
	23	Johnson Supply	0664	10/22	2/10, n/30		1,600 00
	26	LCP Computer	P903	10/25	1/10, n/30		152 00

Posting Purchases on Credit

How is posting done from the purchases journal? Posting entries from the purchases journal is similar to posting from other one-column journals. Each credit entry in the purchases journal is posted regularly to the proper creditor's account, as shown in the ledger accounts that are illustrated below. The credit postings are usually made daily so that the accountant will know the current amount owed to each creditor.

The account numbers that are placed in the Posting Reference column of the purchases journal show that the accounts have been posted. This is illustrated in the purchases journal on the next page. In the creditors' accounts, the letter *P* and the page number show that the amount has been posted from the purchases journal.

The invoice number is shown in the Explanation column of the account. Thus, it is easy to trace an entry to the invoice if a question about the purchase arises. (The invoice date and the terms are sometimes listed in the Explanation column to show the date the invoice should be paid.)

Accts. Pay./Diskettes Plus **Account No.** *211*

DATE		EXPLANATION	POST. REF.	DEBIT	CREDIT	BALANCE	
						DEBIT	CREDIT
19— Oct.	*11*	*Invoice 82A; (10/10); n/EOM*	*P1*		*2,000 00*		*2,000 00*

Accts. Pay./Johnson Supply **Account No.** *212*

DATE		EXPLANATION	POST. REF.	DEBIT	CREDIT	BALANCE	
						DEBIT	CREDIT
19— Oct.	*10*	*Inv. 0567; (10/8); 2/10, n/30*	*P1*		*720 00*		*720 00*

Purchases on credit posted to creditors' accounts from purchases journal.

At the end of the month, the purchases journal is totaled. The total is the debit amount to be posted to the Purchases account. The journal is then proved and ruled. The procedure is similar to that used for the cash receipts and cash payments journals. The only difference is that the words "Purchases Debit" are written in the Account Credited column.

After the purchases journal is totaled, proved, and ruled, the total amount of the purchases is posted as a debit to the Purchases account. When the amount is posted, the number of the Purchases account (501) is written in the Posting Reference column of the journal, as shown at the top of page 346.

DATE		ACCOUNT CREDITED	INVOICE NO.	INVOICE DATE	TERMS	POST. REF.	AMOUNT
19—							
Oct.	10	*Johnson Supply*	0567	10/8	2/10, n/30	212	720 00
	11	*Diskettes Plus*	82A	10/10	n/EOM	211	2,000 00
	13	*LCP Computer*	P876	10/13	1/10, n/30	213	400 00
	20	*Micro Components*	106A	10/18	2/10, n/30	214	480 00
	23	*Johnson Supply*	0664	10/22	2/10, n/30	212	1,600 00
	26	*LCP Computer*	P903	10/25	1/10, n/30	213	152 00
	31	*Purchases Debit*					5,352 00
						501	5,352 00

PURCHASES JOURNAL Page 1

Purchases journal totaled and ruled for month.

After the entries for October are posted, the Purchases account shows only one debit of $5,352 for all credit purchases made during the entire month. The credits posted from the purchases journal to the various creditors' accounts in the ledger also equal $5,352. Thus, the debit posted equals the total credits posted.

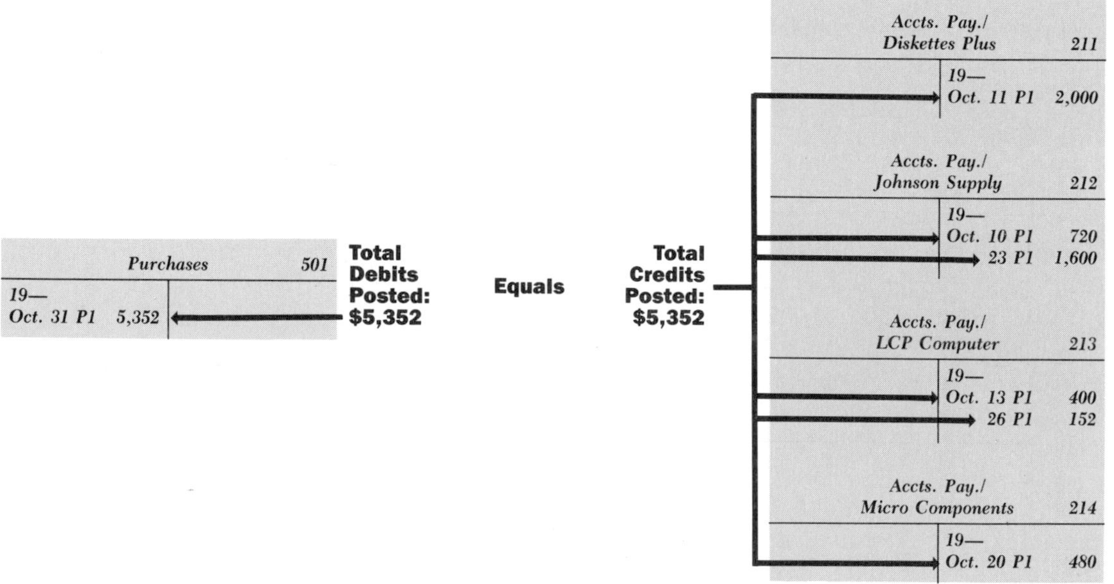

Using the purchases journal, like using the other special journals, saves time and space in journalizing and posting. It also allows for dividing responsibility among several people. One person might record all invoices in the purchases journal. Another might be responsible for the cash receipts journal. Another might work on the cash payments journal, and still another on the general journal.

Exercises D and E on page 347 may be completed at this point.

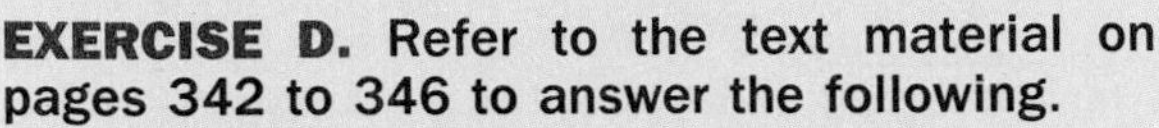

TOPIC 2 EXERCISES

EXERCISE D. Refer to the text material on pages 342 to 346 to answer the following.

1. How many lines are needed to record the October 10 and October 11 transactions in the general journal? In the purchases journal?
2. Which columns in the purchases journal are used to find the date the invoice is due for payment?
3. What are the terms of the purchase on October 26?
4. Would you rather record purchases of merchandise on credit in a general journal or in a purchases journal? Why?
5. Fill in the missing answers for a merchandising business.

   Revenues − __?__ = Gross Profit
   Gross Profit − __?__ = Net Income (Loss)

6. Why are cost accounts similar to expense accounts? How are they different?
7. When the October 11 entry is posted as a credit to Diskettes Plus, is a debit posted to the Purchases account at the same time? Why or why not?
8. What amount is posted to the Purchases account on October 31? Is the account debited or credited? Why?
9. What is the meaning of the "P1" in the Posting Reference column of the Johnson Supply account?
10. How many purchases are made from LCP Corporation during the month? From where does this information come?

EXERCISE E. On July 20, Kirshner Athletics received the invoice shown at right. It was checked and verified by the purchasing department and sent to the accounting department.

a. Verify the extensions and the totals. If there are any errors, give the correct amounts.
b. Which date will be used as the date for the journal entry?
c. What amount will be debited to the Purchases account?
d. What amount will be credited to Accts. Pay./Walker Sports?

WALKER SPORTS
922 South Main Street
Chicago, Illinois 60606

Invoice No. 1987

Sold to: Kirshner Athletics
365 South Fourth Street
River Forest, Illinois 60305

Date: July 19, 19--

Ship to: Same

Sales Clerk	Customer Order No.	Shipped Via	Terms
B. Brown	33233	Truck	2/10, n/30

Quantity	Stock No.	Description	Unit Price	Amount
12 doz.	30A80124	Hit-more tennis balls	11.20 doz.	134.40
18	30A34801	Mercury sleds, No. 127	12.30 ea.	221.40
15	30A24506	Flex-lite casting rods	32.50 ea.	487.50
6	30A24308	Mo Hill golf sets	88.00 ea.	528.00
30	30A73502	Tru-mold sets	1.98 doz.	59.40

TOTAL AMOUNT $1,430.70
INVOICE TOTAL $1,430.70

APPROVED DATE 7/20/—
QUANTITIES RECEIVED B. Herman
PRICES CHARGED A. Cohen
EXTENSIONS & TOTALS ________

TOPIC 2 PROBLEMS

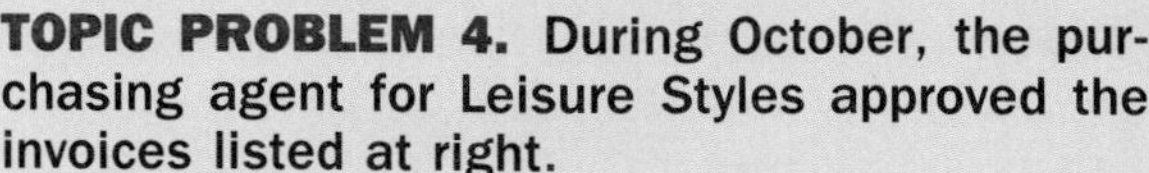

TOPIC PROBLEM 4. During October, the purchasing agent for Leisure Styles approved the invoices listed at right.

a. Open ledger accounts as follows: Accts. Pay./Highlight Clothing; Accts. Pay./Playwear Inc.; Accts. Pay./Sports Fashions; and Purchases. Assign an appropriate number to each account.

b. Journalize the invoices in a purchases journal on the date they were approved.

c. Post the credit entries from the purchases journal.

d. Prove and foot the purchases journal. Then rule the purchases journal.

e. Post the debit entry from the purchases journal.

Oct. 1 Invoice B73, dated September 29, from Sports Fashions for $400; terms n/30.
10 Invoice 3637, dated October 5, from Playwear Inc. for $620; terms n/60.
15 Invoice 237846, dated October 12, from Highlight Clothing for $220; terms 2/10, n/30.
23 Invoice B114, dated October 20, from Sports Fashions for $100; terms n/30.
27 Invoice 237910, dated October 24, from Highlight Clothing for $265; terms 2/10, n/30.

NOTE: Save the ledger for further use in Topic Problem 5.

TOPIC PROBLEM 5. During November the invoices listed at right were approved at Leisure Styles. Use the ledger accounts from Topic Problem 4 to do the following.

a. Journalize the invoices in the purchases journal.

b. Post the credit entries from the purchases journal.

c. Foot, prove, and rule the purchases journal.

d. Post the debit entry from the purchases journal.

e. Prepare a trial balance.

f. To which creditor is the largest balance owed on November 30?

g. From which creditor were the most number of purchases made?

h. What journal is used if a Leisure Styles supplier requires all purchases to be made for cash?

Nov. 5 Invoice 3702, dated November 1, from Playwear Inc. for $287; terms n/60.
11 Invoice B173, dated November 8, from Sports Fashions for $260; terms n/30.
16 Invoice 238004, dated November 13, from Highlight Clothing for $194; terms 2/10, n/30.
24 Invoice B202, dated November 21, from Sports Fashions for $87; terms n/30.
28 Invoice 3786, dated November 24, from Playwear Inc. for $126; terms n/60.

TOPIC 3

Controlling the Accounts Payable Ledger

Are all accounts kept in a single ledger? No, a single ledger is not practical for some businesses. A business may have hundreds of creditors. Its ledger would be very large if it contained accounts for each asset, liability, owner's equity, revenue, and expense account.

There are other problems with the single ledger. First, only one person at a time could do the posting work. Second, a trial balance prepared from the ledger would be very long. Third, if the trial balance were out of balance, all of the accounts would have to be checked to find the error. To avoid these problems, the ledger is usually divided into a general ledger and subsidiary ledgers. A **subsidiary ledger** is a group of similar accounts kept in a separate ledger.

■ Subsidiary Ledgers

To understand the need for subsidiary ledgers, look at the balance sheet for Computer Age below. Only the total of the accounts payable ($4,632) is used to compute the total liabilities. Thus, only one account—Accounts Payable—could be shown and the balance sheet would still be in balance.

Computer Age
Balance Sheet
October 31, 19—

Assets					
Cash		12,100	00		
Accounts Receivable:					
Allied Display	$130.00				
Electro Computer	90.00				
Hallmark Sales	25.00				
Wing Computers	160.00	405	00		
Land		6,000	00		
Building		20,000	00		
Office Equipment		7,200	00		
Stockroom Equipment		12,100	00		
Total Assets				57,805	00
Liabilities					
Loans Payable		4,000	00		
Accounts Payable:					
Diskettes Plus	$2,000.00				
Johnson Supply	1,600.00				
LCP Computer	552.00				
Micro Components	480.00	4,632	00		
Mortgage Payable		14,000	00		
Total Liabilities				22,632	00
Owner's Equity					
Jason Booth, Capital				35,173	00
Total Liabilities and Owner's Equity				57,805	00

Each creditor's account is then placed in a subsidiary ledger called the **accounts payable** (creditor's) **subsidiary ledger**. When creditors' accounts are placed in the accounts payable ledger, the Accounts Payable account in the general ledger is called a controlling account. A **controlling account** is an account in the general ledger that summarizes accounts in a subsidiary ledger. Thus, the Accounts Payable account summarizes the balances of all the individual creditors' accounts in the subsidiary ledger. It keeps the general ledger in balance, as shown in the illustration here.

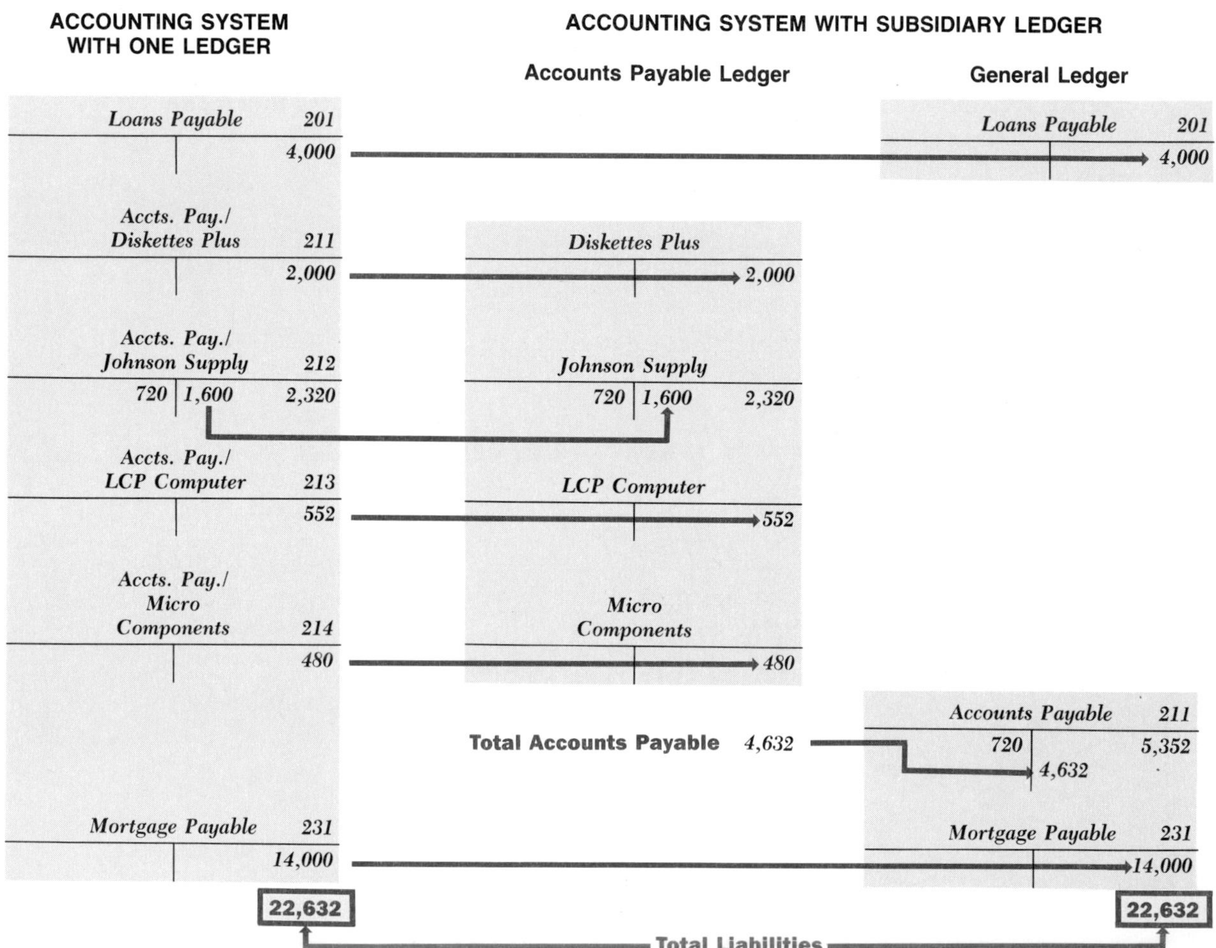

■ **Ledger Account Forms** Up to now, the balance ledger form with four money columns has been used. Many businesses, however, use a three-column balance ledger form for accounts in subsidiary ledgers, as illustrated at the top of the next page.

Name					
Address					
DATE	EXPLANATION	POST. REF.	DEBIT	CREDIT	CREDIT BALANCE

Three-column balance ledger form.

The **three-column balance ledger form** is a balance ledger that contains only one balance column. Creditors' accounts normally have a credit balance. Therefore, the three-column balance ledger form for these accounts contains a Credit Balance column. If a creditor's account has a debit balance, the balance is recorded in the Credit Balance column and circled, as shown in the margin.

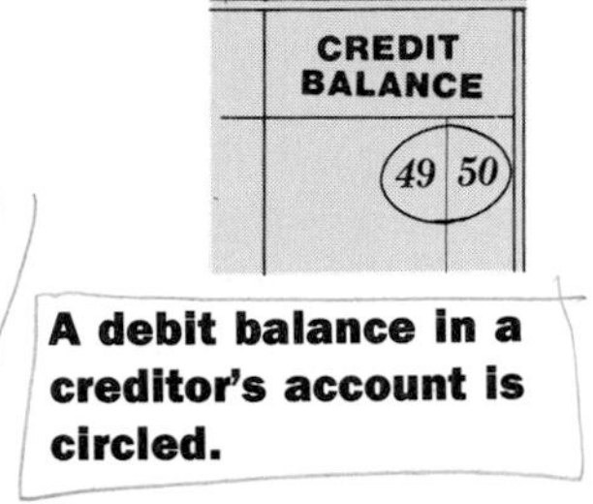

A debit balance in a creditor's account is circled.

The account for Johnson Supply shown here illustrates the use of the three-column balance ledger form.

Name *Johnson Supply*
Address *22 Elmwood Avenue, Tucson, Arizona 85715*

DATE		EXPLANATION	POST REF.	DEBIT	CREDIT	CREDIT BALANCE
19—						
Oct.	*10*	*Invoice 0567; (10/8); 2/10, n/30*	*P1*		720 00	720 00
	18		*CP3*	720 00		— 00
	23	*Invoice 0664; (10/22); 2/10, n/30*	*P1*		1,600 00	1,600 00
Nov.	*3*	*Invoice 0703; (11/1); 2/10, n/30*	*P2*		120 00	1,720 00

Three-column balance ledger form.

1. *October 10:* A purchase on credit for $720 is posted from the purchases journal to the Credit column of the account. The "P" in the Posting Reference column shows that the credit was posted from the purchases journal. The account now has a credit balance of $720.
2. *October 18:* Computer Age paid Johnson Supply $720 in cash. The creditor's account is debited. The payment reduces the balance owed to zero.
3. *October 23:* A purchase on credit for $1,600 is recorded. The account now has a credit balance of $1,600.
4. *November 3:* A purchase on credit for $120 increases the credit balance to $1,720. Additional credits are added to the account and debits are subtracted from the account. In this way the current balance is always shown.

Note that accounts in the accounts payable ledger contain the addresses of the creditors in the heading of each account. The creditors' accounts are usually kept on loose-leaf sheets in a binder or on file cards. This makes it easy to add or remove an account. The accounts are also placed in alphabetic order so that they can be located rapidly. No account numbers are assigned because Computer Age buys from a relatively small number of suppliers.

Posting to the Accounts Payable Ledger

What are the procedures for posting to the accounts payable ledger? The use of an accounts payable ledger does not change the journalizing of approved purchase invoices in the purchases journal. However, there is a difference in posting from the purchases journal to the ledger.

During the month, credit entries are posted from the purchases journal to the creditors' accounts in the subsidiary ledger. A check mark (✓) is used in the Posting Reference column of the purchases journal to show that the amount has been posted.

No postings are made to the general ledger until the purchases journal is totaled and ruled at the end of the month. At that time the total purchases for the month are posted as a debit to the Purchases account and a credit to the Accounts Payable controlling account in the general ledger. The credit amounts posted to the accounts payable ledger must equal the credit posted to the controlling account in the general ledger.

When the purchases journal is totaled, "Purchases Debit/Accts. Pay. Credit" is written in the Account Credited column. A diagonal line is drawn in the Posting Reference column to show that the total is posted to two accounts (the Purchases account and the Accounts Payable controlling account in the general ledger), as shown in the margin. The number of the Purchases account (501) is written above the diagonal line. The number of the Accounts Payable account (211) is written below the diagonal line. Thus, an account number in the Posting Reference column of the journal shows that the amount was posted to the general ledger. A check mark (✓) indicates that the amount was posted to the subsidiary ledger.

In summary, posting from the purchases journal to the subsidiary ledger and the general ledger is done in the following order.

- During the month, individual credits are posted to the creditors' accounts in the subsidiary ledger.
- At the end of the month, total purchases are posted as a debit to the Purchases account and a credit to the Accounts Payable controlling account in the general ledger.

When the balance ledger account form is used for the accounts payable ledger, the accounting clerk should post from the purchases journal before posting from the cash payments journal. Thus, credits are recorded in the accounts before the debits.

COMPUTER AGE CHART OF ACCOUNTS

Assets
101 Cash
102 Petty Cash
103 Change Fund
111 Accounts Receivable
130 Land
131 Building
132 Office Equipment
133 Stockroom Equipment

Liabilities
201 Loans Payable
211 Accounts Payable
216 Sales Taxes Payable
221 Federal Income Taxes Payable
222 FICA Taxes Payable
223 State Income Taxes Payable
224 Federal Unemployment Taxes Payable
225 State Unemployment Taxes Payable
226 Salaries Payable
231 Mortgage Payable

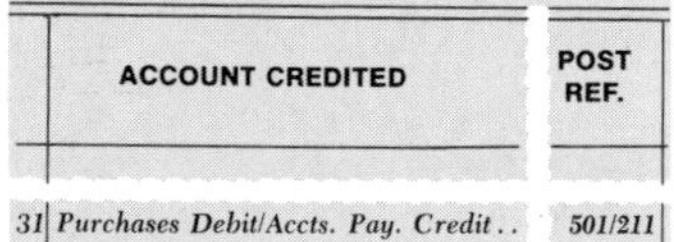

PURCHASES JOURNAL

	ACCOUNT CREDITED	POST REF.
31	*Purchases Debit/Accts. Pay. Credit . .*	501/211

A diagonal line is drawn in Posting Reference column when journal is totaled and ruled.

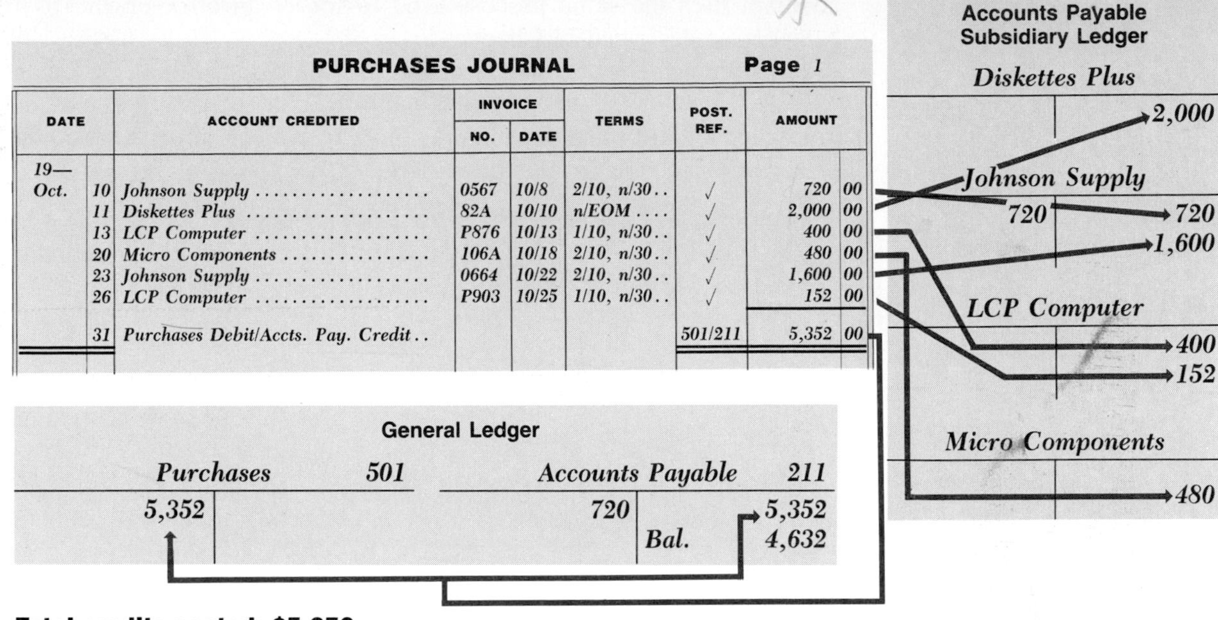

PURCHASES JOURNAL Page 1

DATE		ACCOUNT CREDITED	INVOICE NO.	INVOICE DATE	TERMS	POST. REF.	AMOUNT
19— Oct.	10	Johnson Supply	0567	10/8	2/10, n/30	√	720 00
	11	Diskettes Plus	82A	10/10	n/EOM	√	2,000 00
	13	LCP Computer	P876	10/13	1/10, n/30	√	400 00
	20	Micro Components	106A	10/18	2/10, n/30	√	480 00
	23	Johnson Supply	0664	10/22	2/10, n/30	√	1,600 00
	26	LCP Computer	P903	10/25	1/10, n/30	√	152 00
	31	Purchases Debit/Accts. Pay. Credit				501/211	5,352 00

Total credits posted: $5,352.

Accounts Payable Bookkeeper: DOT 210.382-018
Keeps accounts payable section of the financial records. May journalize accounts payable transactions and may post to subsidiary ledger.

Accounts Payable Clerk: DOT 214.362-026
Performs variety of computing, posting, and other accounting duties for accounts payable.

Proving the Accounts Payable Ledger

When is the accounts payable ledger proved? A proof of the equality of the subsidiary ledger and the controlling account is prepared at the end of the accounting period. The proof is done before the trial balance is prepared. This helps make any error correction on the trial balance easier.

The following procedure is followed to prove the subsidiary ledger. The balances of the creditors' accounts are added. If the individual creditors' names are not needed, the proof of the subsidiary ledger can be made on an adding machine tape, as shown in the margin. The total is then compared with the balance of the Accounts Payable controlling account.

If the total of the subsidiary ledger accounts does not agree with the balance of the controlling account, the error must be located and corrected before a trial balance is prepared. To locate the error, the ac-

Computer Age
Schedule of Accounts Payable
October 31, 19—

0.00T
2,000.00
1,600.00
552.00
480.00
4,632.00T

Proof of subsidiary ledger on adding machine tape.

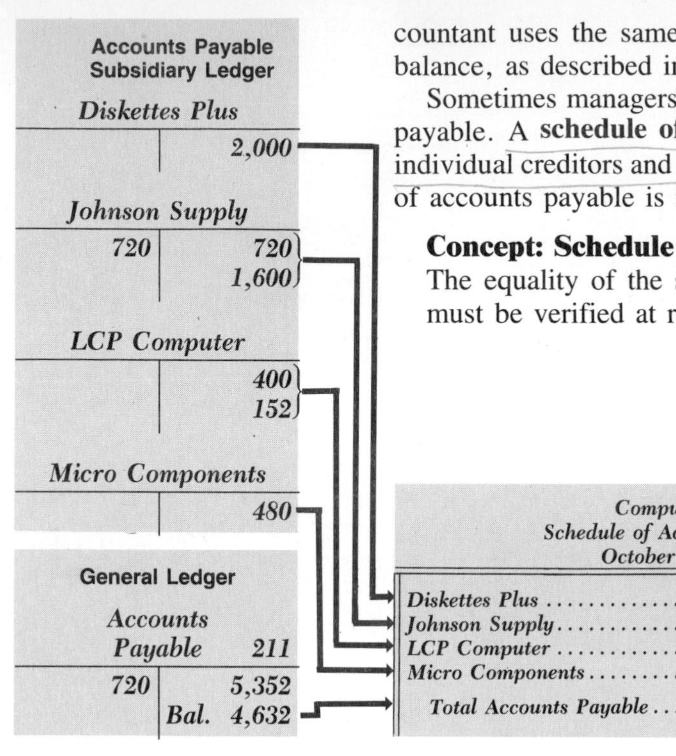

countant uses the same process used to locate an error on the trial balance, as described in Chapter 6.

Sometimes managers and owners will want a schedule of accounts payable. A **schedule of accounts payable** is a list of the names of individual creditors and the amounts owed to each creditor. A schedule of accounts payable is illustrated here.

Concept: Schedule of the Subsidiary Ledger
The equality of the subsidiary ledger and the controlling account must be verified at regular intervals.

Computer Age
Schedule of Accounts Payable
October 31, 19—

Diskettes Plus	*2,000*	*00*
Johnson Supply	*1,600*	*00*
LCP Computer	*552*	*00*
Micro Components	*480*	*00*
Total Accounts Payable	*4,632*	*00*

Proving the accounts payable ledger.

Exercise F on this page and page 355 may be completed at this point.

TOPIC 3 EXERCISE

EXERCISE F. Answer the following questions about subsidiary ledgers and proving the accounts payable ledger. Refer to pages 349 to 354.

1. How many liabilities does Computer Age have in the general ledger if it also uses an accounts payable ledger?
2. What is the dollar amount owed to the four creditors found in the subsidiary ledger?
3. What is the dollar amount of the total liabilities?
4. How much is owed to Johnson Supply on October 10? On October 23?
5. How much merchandise is purchased from Johnson Supply from October 10 to November 3?
6. What would the complete entry have been to record the October 13 purchases journal entry in a general journal?
7. When the October 20 entry is posted, is the credit posted to both the Accounts Payable account in the general ledger and the Micro Components account in the subsidiary ledger at the same time? Why or why not?
8. What does the check mark in the Posting Reference column of the journal for the October 20 entry mean?
9. What amount is posted to the Purchases account on October 31? Is this amount debited or credited? Why?
10. Is any account credited for $5,352 on October 31?

11. Is the Accounts Payable controlling account included on a trial balance? Are the individual subsidiary ledger accounts listed? Why or why not?

12. Where does the accounts payable clerk get the information for the schedule of accounts payable?

TOPIC 3 PROBLEMS

TOPIC PROBLEM 6. Jennifer Bauer, the owner of Bauer Medical Supplies, has received the invoices listed for merchandise purchased for resale.

a. Open general ledger accounts for Accounts Payable and Purchases. Also open subsidiary ledger accounts for the following creditors: Alan Chan, 2000 Clove Drive, Atlanta, Georgia 30324; Lynn Lewis, 27 Washington Road, Princeton, New Jersey 08540; and Miller Supplies, 26 Industrial Avenue, Lowell, Massachusetts 01851.

b. Journalize in a purchases journal the approved purchase invoices listed at the right.

c. Post the credit entries to the subsidiary ledger.

d. Foot, prove, and rule the purchases journal.

e. Post the total of the purchases journal to the general ledger.

f. Prepare a schedule of accounts payable. Compare the total of the schedule of accounts payable with the balance of the Accounts Payable controlling account.

Apr. 3 Invoice 3909, dated March 28, from Miller Supplies for $700; terms 2/10, n/30.

11 Invoice D176, dated April 6, from Alan Chan for $920; terms n/30.

16 Invoice 111, dated April 13, from Lynn Lewis for $684; terms n/60.

22 Invoice D197, dated April 17, from Alan Chan for $744; terms n/30.

28 Invoice 4186, dated April 23, from Miller Supplies for $600; terms 2/10, n/30.

NOTE: Save your ledgers for further use in Topic Problem 7.

TOPIC PROBLEM 7. Use the ledger accounts from Topic Problem 6 to do the following.

a. Journalize the approved purchase invoices listed at the right.

b. Post the credit entries to the subsidiary ledger.

c. Foot, prove, and rule the purchases journal.

d. Post the total of the purchases journal to the general ledger.

e. Prepare a schedule of accounts payable. Compare the total of the schedule of accounts payable with the balance of the Accounts Payable controlling account.

f. Prepare a trial balance.

May 5 Invoice 808, dated May 2, from Lynn Lewis for $840; terms n/60.

11 Invoice D237, dated May 6, from Alan Chan for $760; terms n/30.

16 Invoice 4306, dated May 12, from Miller Supplies for $540; terms 2/10, n/30.

22 Invoice 882, dated May 19, from Lynn Lewis for $1,104; terms n/60.

28 Invoice D296, dated May 23, from Alan Chan for $136; terms n/30.

TOPIC 4

Controlling Net Purchases

Does the Purchases account show all the costs of obtaining merchandise? No, the Purchases account does not show all the costs. It shows only the invoice cost of merchandise purchases. Other factors that might affect the cost of purchases include the following.

- Transportation (freight) charges for delivery of merchandise
- Return of merchandise to the seller or a cash allowance given by the seller
- Discount (reduced price) for paying promptly

Transportation In

The cost of merchandise should include any transportation (freight) charges for delivery to the purchaser. Depending on the terms of the sale, either the seller or the purchaser may pay the transportation charges. For example, when Computer Age purchased disk drives from Micro Components, the merchandise was shipped ''FOB Denver,'' as shown below. Computer Age is located in Denver. Thus, the shipment was made free on board (FOB) to the destination point. In other words, the seller (Micro Components) pays the transportation charges when merchandise is shipped **FOB destination**. Computer Age would make no journal entry for transportation charges when the terms are FOB destination.

Micro Components
16 Remington Street
Phoenix, Arizona 85011

Invoice No. **106A**

Sold To: Computer Age
200 Girard Avenue
Denver, Colorado 80236

Date October 20, 19--
Terms 2/10, n/30

Salesman	Your Order No.	Shipped By	FOB
Hunt	PO1135	Truck	Denver

QUANTITY	STOCK NO.	DESCRIPTION	UNIT PRICE	EXTENSION
2	84-576	Disk drives	240.00	480.00
			Invoice Total	480.00

In some businesses it is customary for a seller to send merchandise FOB shipping point. **FOB shipping point** means that the purchaser must pay the transportation charges. For example, the purchasing agent for Computer Age has the choice of buying storage racks from a local wholesaler for $80 each or buying the same racks in a distant city for $75. However, if the racks are bought from the more distant seller, Computer Age must pay $5 transportation charges for each rack.

In making the decision, the purchasing agent must consider the transportation charges as part of the cost of the storage racks. Thus, the delivered cost of the storage racks is the same from each supplier: $80 from the local wholesaler and $80 ($75 + $5) from the distant supplier who charges $5 for transportation. The generally accepted accounting principle when accounting for purchases and transportation charges is that the net cost of purchases includes the amount paid to the seller plus any transportation charges.

Journalizing Transportation Costs Computer Age purchased merchandise from Diskettes Plus with the terms FOB Dallas (shipping point). Computer Age paid $50 for the transportation charges on October 12. The account commonly used to record freight charges is the **Transportation In account** (sometimes referred to as the Freight In or Freight on Purchases account). Computer Age assigned account number 502 to Transportation In. The payment of the transportation charges is analyzed as follows.

COMPUTER AGE CHART OF ACCOUNTS

Costs and Expenses
501 Purchases
502 Transportation In

OCTOBER 12: COMPUTER AGE ISSUES CHECK 307 FOR $50 TO MAURO LINES FOR TRANSPORTATION CHARGES ON MERCHANDISE ORDERED FROM DISKETTES PLUS, FOB DALLAS.		
What Happens	**Accounting Rule**	**Accounting Entry**
Cost of transportation decreases owner's equity by $50.	To decrease owner's equity, debit the account.	Debit: Transportation In, $50.
The asset *Cash* decreases by $50.	To decrease an asset, credit the account.	Credit: Cash, $50.

The entry to record the payment of transportation charges is made in the cash payments journal because cash is paid.

CASH PAYMENTS JOURNAL **Page** *3*

DATE		ACCOUNT DEBITED	EXPLANATION	CHECK NO.	POST. REF.	AMOUNT
19—						
Oct.	*12*	*Transportation In*	*Mauro Lines*	*307*	*502*	*50 00*

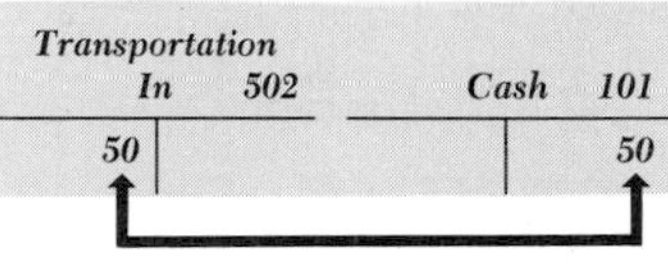

Recording transportation costs.

If payment for the transportation charges will be made on account at a later date, the entry is made in the general journal. The Transportation In account is debited. The Accounts Payable controlling account is credited. The creditor's account in the subsidiary ledger is credited.

Principle: Net Cost of Purchases
The generally accepted accounting principle is that the net cost of purchases includes the amount paid to the seller plus any transportation charges for delivery of the goods.

Exercise G on page 364 may be completed at this point.

Purchases Returns and Allowances

What are purchases returns and allowances? Purchases returns and allowances refers to the procedures used when the purchaser wants to return merchandise it has ordered. There are many reasons why a purchaser would want to return merchandise to the supplier. The merchandise might arrive in an unacceptable condition. It might be damaged. The quantity might be more or less than was ordered. The wrong items may have been sent. In other cases, the business might find that the items received were delivered too late or were not ordered.

For any of these reasons, the receiving department asks the purchasing department what to do with the merchandise. The purchasing agent normally has two choices when merchandise is unacceptable: return the merchandise or keep the merchandise with a reduction in the purchase price. For example, assume that one of the disk drives that Computer Age received from Micro Components was scratched in shipment. The receiving clerk notifies the purchasing agent of the damage. If the purchasing agent decides to return the disk drive, the transaction is called a purchases return. Thus, a *purchases return* is merchandise sent back to the supplier.

Control: Obtain refunds or credits for all purchases returns and allowances.

However, Micro Components may offer to reduce the purchase price of the scratched disk drive. Computer Age may then decide to keep the disk drive on these terms. In this case, the difference between the original price and the reduced price is a purchases allowance. A *purchases allowance* is a reduction in the purchase price for damage or other cause.

Receiving Cash for Purchases Returns and Allowances

General Ledger

Cash 101		*Purchases 501*	
	100	*100*	

Paying cash for a purchase of merchandise.

Purchases returns and allowances decrease cost of merchandise purchased.

A purchaser who has paid cash expects to have the cash returned when merchandise is returned or an allowance given. Suppose the supplier agrees to take back merchandise that Computer Age purchased for $100 in cash on October 2. To understand the transaction, let us review the original entry. The merchandise was purchased for cash, and the transaction was recorded in the cash payments journal. The entry resulted in a $100 debit to the Purchases account and a $100 credit to the Cash account.

CASH PAYMENTS JOURNAL — **Page** 3

DATE		ACCOUNT DEBITED	EXPLANATION	CHECK NO.	POST. REF.	AMOUNT
19—						
Oct.	*2*	*Purchases*	*Micro Components*.	*305*	*501*	*100 00*

Rather than crediting the Purchases account when merchandise is returned, it is better to keep a separate record of purchases returns and allowances. Purchases are recorded in one account and returns and allowances for purchases are recorded in another. Thus, information about each activity is readily available.

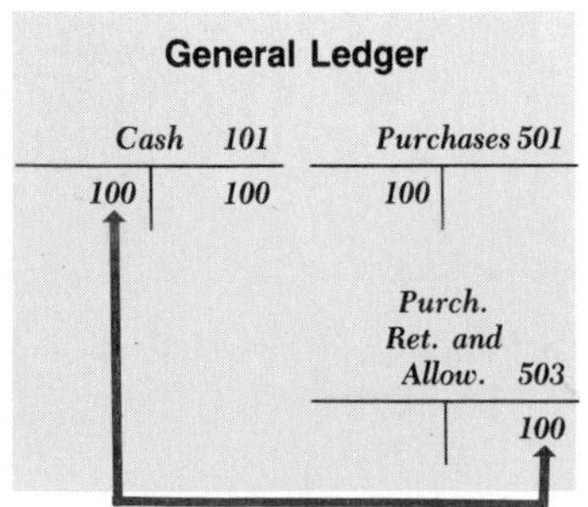

Receiving cash for a purchases return.

When Computer Age receives $100 in cash for the merchandise it returned, the Purchases Returns and Allowances account is credited. Since cash is received, the entry is in the cash receipts journal.

CASH RECEIPTS JOURNAL — **Page** 3

DATE		ACCOUNT CREDITED	EXPLANATION	POST. REF.	AMOUNT
19—					
Oct.	*10*	*Purchases Returns and Allowances*. . .	*Rets. to Micro Components*	*503*	*100 00*

The Purchases Returns and Allowances account, like the Purchases account, is a temporary owner's equity account. Its account number is 503 in the chart of accounts for Computer Age. The information in the Purchases Returns and Allowances account is used to help analyze the operations of the business. If the amount of the returns and allowances is large, the manager or owner might want to find out why. Are errors being made on purchase orders? Is poor merchandise being bought? Is too much merchandise arriving in damaged condition? By answering these questions, managers and owners can correct poor purchasing practices.

The **net purchases** are found by subtracting the balance of the Purchases Returns and Allowances account from the cost of delivered goods (Purchases plus Transportation In). This computation is illustrated in the margin.

COMPUTER AGE CHART OF ACCOUNTS

Costs and Expenses
501 Purchases
502 Transportation In
503 Purchases Returns and Allowances

Purchases	2,930	00
Add: Transportation In	50	00
Cost of Delivered Goods	2,980	00
Less: Purchases Returns and Allowances	240	00
Net Purchases	2,740	00

Receiving Credit for Purchases Returns and Allowances

When a purchaser has not paid for the merchandise returned, the supplier grants credit against the amount the purchaser owes. To understand the entry for a purchases return or allowance for credit, refer again to the transaction involving a damaged disk drive received from Micro Components. Suppose the purchasing agent tells Micro Components that the disk drive will be returned and Micro Components agrees to take the disk drive back. When the disk drive is returned, Micro Components issues a credit memorandum to Computer Age for $240, the net price of the disk drive. The credit memorandum shows that the amount owed by Computer Age to Micro Components for Invoice 106A ($480) is reduced by the price of the disk drive returned ($240).

Micro Components
16 Remington Street
Phoenix, Arizona 85011

CREDIT MEMORANDUM
Copy 1: Customer

No. 1254

To: Computer Age
200 Girard Avenue
Denver, Colorado 80236

Date October 27, 19--
Sold on Invoice No. 106A

Your Order No. P01135

We have credited your account as follows:

QUANTITY	DESCRIPTION	PRICE	AMOUNT
1	84-576 Disk drive Returned	240.00	240.00

A **credit memorandum** is the source document that grants credit to the purchaser for a purchase return or allowance. It also gives the reason for the credit. Thus, a credit memorandum is the source document for journalizing a purchase return or allowance. Occasionally, a business might use a special journal to record purchases returns and allowances. More often, the purchases returns and allowances are journalized in the general journal.

How the credit memorandum is journalized is better understood by reviewing the purchase from Micro Components.

An entry was made in the purchases journal for the amount of the invoice, \$480. Thus, Micro Components' account in the accounts payable ledger was credited for \$480 to show an increase in the amount owed to this creditor. Assume that this was the only entry made in the purchases journal during the month. Then, at the end of the month, a debit of \$480 was posted to the Purchases account in the general ledger and a credit of \$480 was posted to Accounts Payable.

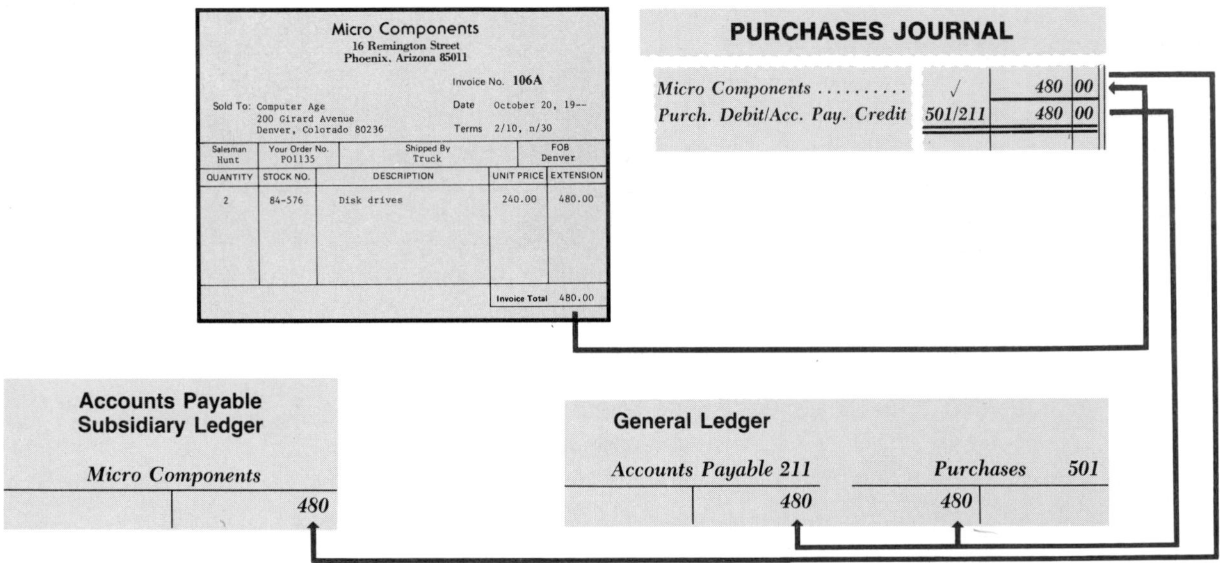

When the disk drive is returned, Micro Components sends a credit memorandum to Computer Age. The credit memorandum shows that Computer Age now owes \$240 less to Micro Components. This is the net price of one disk drive. The credit memorandum is then recorded in the general journal for the amount of the return, \$240. Thus, a debit of \$240 must be posted to Micro Components' account in the accounts payable ledger to show the decrease in the amount owed. Also, two entries are needed in the general ledger: a debit to the Accounts Payable controlling account and a credit to the Purchases Returns and Allowances account. The debit entry decreases the accounts payable liability. The credit entry reduces the total amount of purchases. This transaction is analyzed in the table at the top of the next page.

The diagonal line in the Posting Reference column of the general journal shows that the debit of \$240 is posted to two accounts—the controlling account in the general ledger and the creditor's account in the subsidiary ledger. The "211" in the Posting Reference column

OCTOBER 28: COMPUTER AGE RECEIVES A CREDIT MEMORANDUM FOR $240 FROM MICRO COMPONENTS FOR THE RETURN OF GOODS PURCHASED ON CREDIT.		
What Happens	**Accounting Rule**	**Accounting Entry**
The liability *Accounts Payable* decreases by $240.	To decrease a liability, debit the account.	Debit: Accounts Payable, $240 (also the creditor's account).
The reduction in costs caused by a return of a purchase increases owner's equity by $240.	To increase owner's equity, credit the account.	Credit: Purchases Returns and Allowances, $240.

shows that the debit has been posted to the Accounts Payable controlling account in the general ledger. The check mark (✓) shows that the debit has been posted to the Micro Components account in the subsidiary ledger. The posting of an entry to the controlling account in the general ledger and to an account in the subsidiary ledger is called **double-posting**. After the entries are posted, the total of the subsidiary ledger agrees with the balance of the controlling account.

The credit of $240 for the returned disk drive is posted to the Purchases Returns and Allowances account.

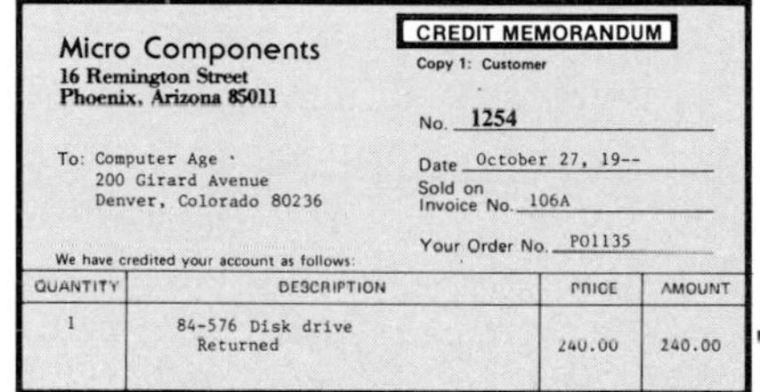
Micro Components
16 Remington Street
Phoenix, Arizona 85011

CREDIT MEMORANDUM
Copy 1: Customer

No. 1254

To: Computer Age
200 Girard Avenue
Denver, Colorado 80236

Date October 27, 19--
Sold on Invoice No. 106A
Your Order No. P01135

We have credited your account as follows:

QUANTITY	DESCRIPTION	PRICE	AMOUNT
1	84-576 Disk drive Returned	240.00	240.00

Recording a credit memorandum.

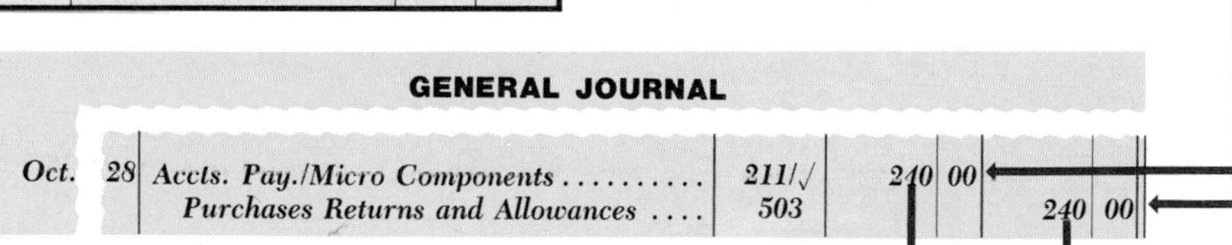
GENERAL JOURNAL

Oct.	28	*Accts. Pay./Micro Components*	*211/✓*	240 00	
		Purchases Returns and Allowances	*503*		240 00

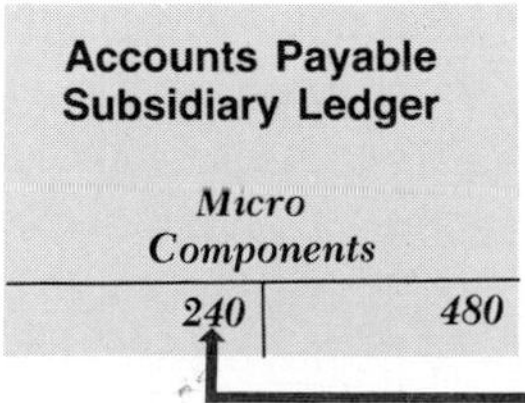
Accounts Payable Subsidiary Ledger

Micro Components	
240	*480*

General Ledger

Accounts Payable 211	
240	*480*

Purchases 501	
480	

Purchases Returns and Allowances 503	
	240

Concept: Types of Accounts

The number and type of accounts used depend on how detailed the information must be.

Purchase Discounts

When are invoices paid to the creditors? The terms on the purchase order and the invoice show when an invoice is to be paid. The terms given by a seller may vary from customer to customer. If the terms call for payment upon delivery of the merchandise, the invoice will be marked "Cash," "Net Cash," or "COD" (Cash on Delivery). A seller may demand immediate payment from some customers and offer other customers 30, 60, 90, or more days to pay an invoice. A customer who pays bills promptly will be given more generous credit terms than a customer who does not.

Credit Period

The period of time given to pay the invoice is called a **credit period**. The terms on the invoice will state the exact period of time covered in the credit period.

For most businesses, the credit period begins on the date of the invoice. If payment is due 30 days from the invoice date, the terms are shown as *n/30*. The *n* (for net) means that the full amount is due within 30 days after the invoice date. The term *n/EOM* means that the net amount on the invoice is due at the end of the month.

Cash Discounts

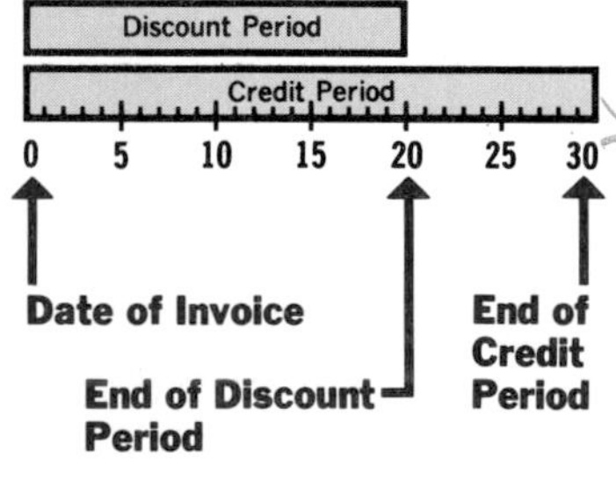

Many businesses try to encourage prompt payment of invoices. One method is to offer a cash discount. A *cash discount* encourages prompt payment by allowing the purchaser to deduct a certain amount from the total invoice if the invoice is paid in a specified period. The period of time in which a cash discount can be taken is the **discount period**. For example, suppose an invoice shows credit terms of 1/20, n/30. The *1/20* means that the purchaser may deduct 1 percent of the total invoice if payment is made within the 20-day discount period. The *n/30* means that if the invoice is paid within the last 10 days of the credit period, the full amount must be paid.

A cash discount on a purchase is called a **purchase discount**. The purchaser obtains the cash discount only if payment is made within the discount period. To understand purchase discounts, refer to the October 8 invoice from Johnson Supply for $720. The terms of the purchase are 2/10, n/30, as shown in the margin. Thus, if Computer Age mails its check on or before October 18 (10 days after the date of the invoice), it may deduct 2 percent of $720.00 ($14.40) from the invoice and pay $705.60 ($720.00 − $14.40). If Computer Age does not pay within the 10-day discount period, it must then pay the full amount of $720.00 by November 7. The business has a choice of paying early or not paying early. Thus, the discount is not recorded until after the check is drawn to pay the invoice. The procedure to compute a purchase discount is summarized here.

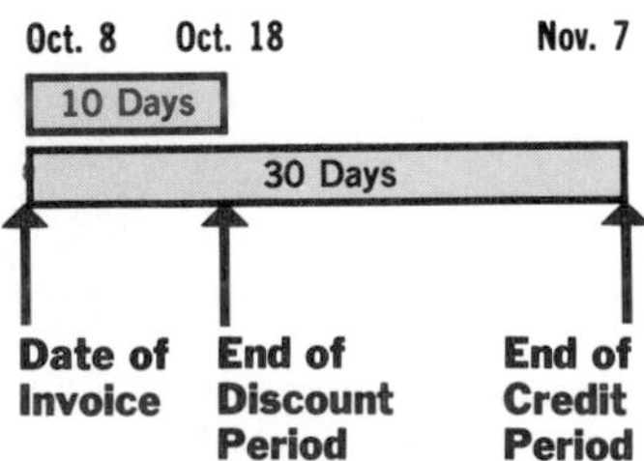

- The rate of the cash discount is listed. In this case it is 2 percent.
- The full amount of the invoice is multiplied by the rate of the cash discount to get the amount of the discount (0.02 × $720.00 = $14.40).
- The discount is subtracted from the full amount of the invoice to find the amount of payment ($720.00 − $14.40 = $705.60).

JOHNSON SUPPLY
22 Elmwood Avenue
Tucson, Arizona 85715

INVOICE NO. 0567
Invoice Date
Terms

SOLD TO Computer Age
200 Girard Avenue
Denver, Colorado 80236

Invoice Date 10/8/--

SHIP TO Same

Terms 2/10, n/30

APPROVED DATE	10/9/--
QUANTITIES RECEIVED	L. Denton
PRICES CHARGED	L. Denton
EXTENSIONS & TOTALS	M. Russ
DATE PAID	10/18/--
CHECK NO.	308

Cust. Order No.	Date	Shipped Via	FOB	No. of Cartons
PO-1106	10/2/--	Truck	Denver	2

QUANTITY SHIPPED	STOCK NO.	DESCRIPTION	UNIT PRICE	AMOUNT
18	A82-B	Computer diskettes	40.00	720.00

■ Tickler File

To take all available discounts and to keep a good credit rating, a business must have an efficient method of keeping track of when each invoice should be paid. One method is to use a tickler file. In a **tickler file**, each invoice is filed according to the date it must be considered for payment. A file folder is established for each day of the month (from 1 to 31). The accounting clerk then files each purchase invoice under the day it must be paid to obtain the cash discount. On that day the invoice is considered for payment. If the employee in charge of authorizing cash payments decides to pay the invoice, the discount is deducted from the invoice. A check is then drawn for the net amount. If it is decided not to pay the invoice, the invoice is then filed under the day that marks the end of the credit period.

Exercise H on page 364 may be completed at this point.

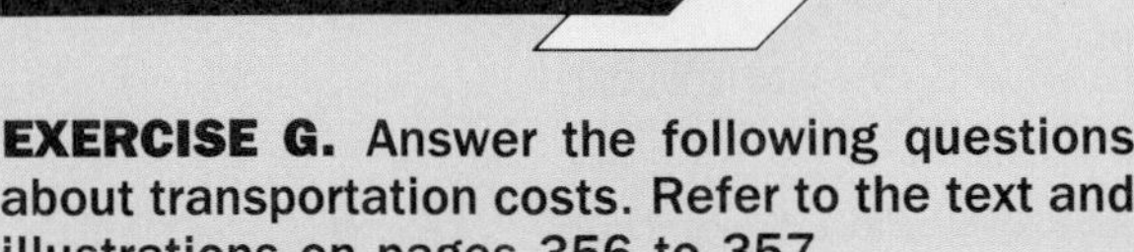

TOPIC 4 EXERCISES

EXERCISE G. Answer the following questions about transportation costs. Refer to the text and illustrations on pages 356 to 357.

1. Is the merchandise purchased from Micro Components shipped FOB destination or FOB shipping point? Explain.

2. Does Micro Components or Computer Age pay freight charges for the merchandise purchased on Invoice 106A?

3. Why is the transportation charge for merchandise purchased from Diskettes Plus recorded in the cash payments journal?

4. Is the merchandise from Diskettes Plus shipped FOB destination or FOB shipping point?

EXERCISE H. Answer the following questions about purchases returns and allowances and purchases discounts. Refer to the text and illustrations on pages 357 to 363.

1. Why is the credit memorandum issued?

2. What journal entry is made on October 28 to record the credit memorandum?

3. Why is 211 placed next to the check mark in the Posting Reference column of the general journal for October 28?

4. How much is owed to Micro Components after the October 28 entry is posted?

5. What is the date of Invoice 0567?

6. What is the credit period given on Invoice 0567? What is the discount period?

7. What is the amount of purchase discount offered on Invoice 0567?

8. Under what day would Invoice 0567 be filed in the tickler file to take the cash discount? What day for the end of the credit period?

TOPIC 4 PROBLEMS

TOPIC PROBLEM 8. For each of the invoices listed in the table at the right, find the following: the end of the discount period, the amount of payment if the invoice is paid within the discount period, and the end of the credit period.

Date	Amount	Terms
a. 8/20	$4,000	2/10, n/30
b. 7/14	3,400	3/10, n/30
c. 10/10	2,920	1/20, n/30
d. 1/15	3,792	n/EOM

TOPIC PROBLEM 9. During April, the Crossroads Market, owned by Tina Nash, received the invoices, transportation bills, and credit memorandums listed on the next page.

a. Open general ledger accounts, assign appropriate numbers, and record the April 1 balances as follows: Cash, $8,000; Store Equipment, $15,600; Accounts Payable; Tina Nash, Capital, $23,600; Tina Nash, Drawing; Purchases; Transportation In; and Purchases Returns and Allowances. Open subsidiary ledger accounts for Cane Inc., 200 Steven St., New Windsor, New York 12550; TM Supply, 950 Baker Avenue, Houston, Texas 77007; and Wheeler Company, Rydell Lane, Rye, New York 10580.

b. Record the transactions listed in a purchases journal, a cash payments journal, and a general journal.

c. Post the individual entries from the purchases journal, the cash payments journal, and the general journal.

d. Prove, total, and rule the special journals.

e. Post the totals from the special journals.

f. Prepare a schedule of accounts payable.

g. Prepare a trial balance.

April 2 Bought merchandise for $1,500 from Cane Inc.; Invoice 1250, dated April 1; terms FOB shipping point, 1/10, n/60.

2 Issued Check 192 for $27 to Lark Express for freight bill on merchandise from Cane Inc.

4 Bought a new refrigerator for store for $750 from TM Supply; Invoice 195, dated April 2; terms FOB destination, n/60.

5 Received Credit Memorandum 47 for $100 from Cane Inc., for returned goods.

9 Issued Check 193 for $130 to Pineview Farms for merchandise purchased for cash.

13 Bought merchandise for $720 from Wheeler Company; Invoice 22-84, dated April 10; terms FOB destination, 2/10, n/60.

22 Bought merchandise for $800 from Cane Inc.; Invoice 711, dated April 21; terms FOB shipping point, 1/10, n/60.

22 Issued Check 194 for $52 to Pen Freight Lines for delivering merchandise from Cane Inc.

25 Received Credit Memorandum 51 for $50 from TM Supply as allowance for damaged goods.

30 Issued Check 195 for $850 to Equipment, Inc., for a display unit purchased for cash.

30 Issued Check 196 for $1,500 to Tina Nash for personal use.

Note: Save your work from this problem for further use in Topic Problem 10.

TOPIC PROBLEM 10. Using the general journal and the ledgers prepared in Topic Problem 9, a purchases journal, and a cash payments journal, perform the following activities.

a. Record the entries for the transactions listed.

b. Post the individual entries from the journals.

c. Prove, total, and rule the special journals.

d. Post the totals from the special journals.

e. Prepare a schedule of accounts payable. Compare the total of the schedule of accounts payable with the balance of the Accounts Payable account.

f. Prepare a trial balance.

May 1 Issued Check 197 for $1,400 to Cane Inc., on account.

5 Bought merchandise for $832 from the Wheeler Company, Invoice 22-113, dated May 2; terms 2/10, n/60, FOB destination.

9 Received Credit Memorandum CM-15-2 for $200 from the Wheeler Company for returned merchandise.

17 Bought merchandise for $635 from Cane, Inc.; Invoice 802, dated May 16; terms FOB shipping point, 1/10, n/60.

17 Issued Check 198 for $75 to Lark Express for delivering merchandise from Cane, Inc.

21 Received Credit Memorandum CM-57 for $90 from Cane, Inc., as allowance for scratched merchandise.

28 Bought merchandise for $400 from the Wheeler Company, Invoice 22-137, dated May 25; terms FOB destination, 2/10, n/60.

TOPIC 5

Controlling Cash Payments on Account

When are payments for purchases journalized? Computer Age usually takes advantage of cash discounts when paying purchase invoices. However, there are times when payments for purchases are made at the end of the credit period instead of at the end of the discount period. The payment for each invoice must be journalized in the cash payments journal. The procedures for paying invoices are now described.

Control: Pay invoices in time to avoid loss of discounts.

For invoices paid at the end of the credit period
- Debit Accounts Payable.
- Credit Cash.

Journalizing Cash Paid on Account

Assume the accountant for Computer Age has to decide when to pay the invoice for the $720 purchase made on October 8. The decision is made to pay the invoice by the last day of the credit period (November 7). A check is drawn for $720, the full amount of the invoice. This procedure to journalize the transaction is shown here.

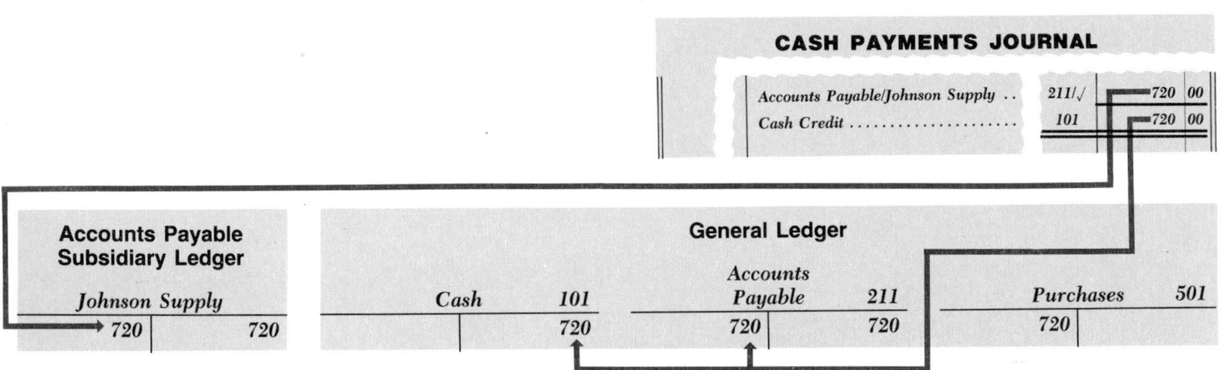

Suppose instead that the accountant has decided to pay the invoice within the discount period. Johnson Supply agrees to accept a check for $705.60 in full payment of the invoice for $720 if the check is sent within the discount period. Prior to October 18, therefore, the accountant has a check drawn for $705.60 and sends it to Johnson Supply. This transaction is described below and illustrated in the margin. (Checks should be mailed so that the creditor receives them by the end of the discount period.)

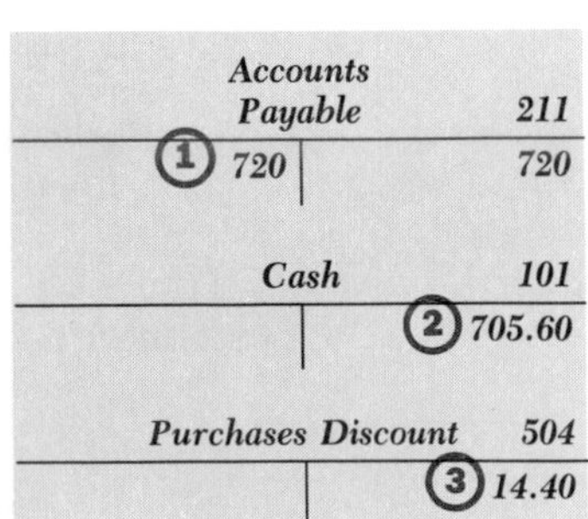

1. The creditor's account (Johnson Supply) has a credit balance of $720 and must be debited for $720 to show that the account has been paid in full. The Accounts Payable account is also debited for $720.
2. The check drawn to pay the debt amounts to $705.60. Thus, the Cash account must be credited for $705.60. This is the amount of cash paid.

3. The debit and credit amounts must be equal. The cash discount of $14.40 must be credited to some account. The discount reduces the cost of the merchandise. The merchandise is recorded at a cost of $720. However, Computer Age paid only $705.60 for the cassettes. Thus, the purchase discount reduces the cost of the merchandise by $14.40. The reduction in cost actually increases owner's equity. Thus, a new owner's equity account called Purchases Discount is credited for $14.40.

The credit entry to increase owner's equity could have been made in the Purchases account. However, it is a common accounting practice to record a purchase discount in a temporary owner's equity account called the **Purchases Discount account**. This practice gives managers and owners a record of all discounts taken. (Computer Age's account number for Purchases Discount is 504.)

The entry to record a purchase discount of $14.40 taken on a payment of $720 is analyzed here.

COMPUTER AGE CHART OF ACCOUNTS

Costs and Expenses
501 Purchases
502 Transportation In
503 Purchases Returns and Allowances
504 Purchases Discount

OCTOBER 18: COMPUTER AGE ISSUES CHECK 308 FOR $705.60 TO JOHNSON SUPPLY TO PAY AN INVOICE FOR $720.00, LESS A CASH DISCOUNT OF $14.40.

What Happens	Accounting Rule	Accounting Entry
The liability *Accounts Payable* decreases by $720.	To decrease a liability, debit the account.	Debit: Accounts Payable, $720 (also the creditor's account).
The asset *Cash* decreases by $705.60.	To decrease an asset, credit the account.	Credit: Cash, $705.60.
The cash discount on the purchase increases owner's equity by $14.40.	To increase owner's equity, credit the account.	Credit: Purchases Discount, $14.40.

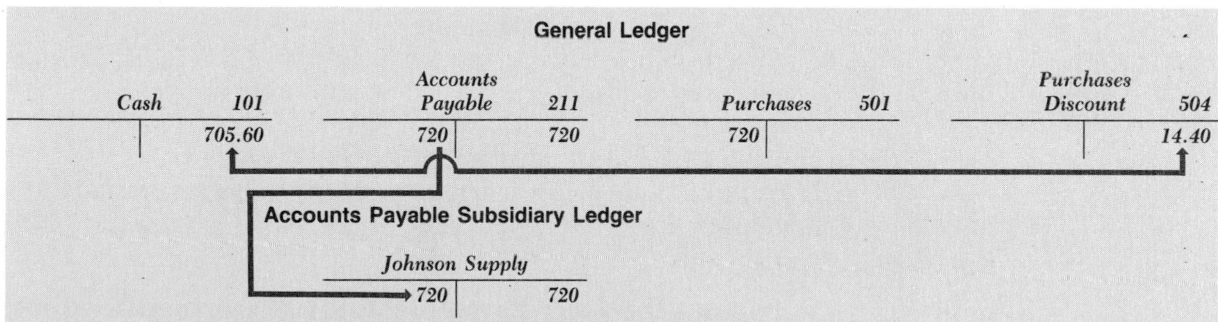

Recording Purchase Discounts in a Multicolumn Cash Payments Journal

All cash payments are recorded in the cash payments journal. The entry to record a payment within the discount period involves a debit to the Accounts Payable controlling account (and a debit to the individual creditor's account). The entry also involves a credit to the Purchases Discount account and a credit to the Cash account. This type of entry cannot be recorded in a one-column cash payments journal because it includes two credits. Thus, most businesses adapt the cash payments journal by adding a special column for credits to the Purchases Discount account. A journal with more than one money column is known as a *multicolumn journal*.

The special columns shown in the following multicolumn cash payments journal are often added to make the recording of cash payments easier.

CASH PAYMENTS JOURNAL — Page 3

DATE		ACCOUNT DEBITED	EXPLANATION	CHECK NO.	POST. REF.	GENERAL LEDGER DEBIT	ACCOUNTS PAYABLE DEBIT	PURCHASES DISCOUNT CREDIT	NET CASH CREDIT
19—									
Oct.	18	Johnson Supply ..	Invoice 0567.....	308			720 00	14 40	705 60

Recording cash payments.

The Net Cash Credit column is used to record the total cash paid. The Purchases Discount Credit column is used to record the purchase discounts taken. An entry in this column is a credit to the Purchases Discount account.

The Accounts Payable Debit column is used to record all debits to creditors' accounts. The amount entered in the Accounts Payable Debit column ($720) must be equal to the total amount of the credits ($705.60 + $14.40). The General Ledger Debit column is used for recording debits to any account for which there is no special column in the journal.

Concept: Purchase Discount
A purchase discount is a decrease in the cost of purchases. Costs and decreases in costs are not recorded until they are realized.

Posting Cash Payments

Is the cash payments journal posted during or at the end of the month? When to post the cash payments journal depends on the type of entry.

Posting the Cash Payments Journal During the Month

Each amount in the General Ledger Debit column of the cash payments journal is posted individually to the proper account in the general ledger. The account numbers in the Posting Reference column show that the amounts have been posted to the general ledger. These entries are posted during the month.

		CASH PAYMENTS JOURNAL						Page 3
DATE	**ACCOUNT DEBITED**	**EXPLANATION**	**CHECK NO.**	**POST. REF.**	**GENERAL LEDGER DEBIT**	**ACCOUNTS PAYABLE DEBIT**	**PURCHASES DISCOUNT CREDIT**	**NET CASH CREDIT**
19—								
Oct. 2	Mortgage Payable	October mortgage	304	231	450 00			450 00
2	Purchases	Fisher Company	305	501	100 00			100 00
4	Office Equipment	Typewriter	306	132	700 00			700 00
12	Transportation In	Mauro Lines	307	502	50 00			50 00
18	Johnson Supply	Invoice 0567	308	✓		720 00	14 40	705 60
24	LCP Computer	Invoice P876	309	✓		400 00	4 00	396 00
28	Diskettes Plus	Invoice 82A	310	✓		2,000 00		2,000 00
31	Salaries Payable	October 29 payroll	311–314	225	1,200 00			1,200 00
31	Advertising Expense	Replenish petty	315	512	12 25			26 00
	Miscellaneous Exp.	cash fund	—	515	13 75			— 00

Posting the cash payments journal during the month.

Debits posted during the month to accounts in general ledger.

Debits posted during the month to creditors' accounts in subsidiary ledger.

Amounts in these two columns are not posted separately during the month.

Each of the three entries in the Accounts Payable Debit column is posted to a creditor's account in the subsidiary ledger. A check mark (✓) is placed in the Posting Reference column. The check mark shows that the amount has been posted. None of the items in the Purchases Discount Credit column or Net Cash Credit column are posted individually during the month.

■ **Posting the Cash Payments Journal at the End of the Month** At the end of the month, all the money columns of the cash payments journal are pencil-footed. The equality of the debit and credit totals is also checked. To check the equality, add the totals of the two debit columns. Then add the totals of the two credit columns. The two sums must be equal. After the equality has been proved, the journal is totaled and ruled.

General Ledger Debit	2,526 00
Accounts Payable Debit	3,120 00
Total Debits	5,646 00
Purchases Discount Credit	18 40
Net Cash Credit	5,627 60
Total Credits	5,646 00

Proof of cash payments journal.

The total of the General Ledger Debit column is not posted. The amounts in this column have been posted during the month. A dash is

		CASH PAYMENTS JOURNAL						Page 3
DATE	**ACCOUNT DEBITED**	**EXPLANATION**	**CHECK NO.**	**POST. REF.**	**GENERAL LEDGER DEBIT**	**ACCOUNTS PAYABLE DEBIT**	**PURCHASES DISCOUNT CREDIT**	**NET CASH CREDIT**
19—								
Oct. 2	Mortgage Payable	October mortgage	304	231	450 00			450 00
31	Advertising Expense	Replenish petty	315	512	12 25			26 00
	Miscellaneous Expense	cash fund	—	515	13 75			— 00
31	Totals				2,526 00	3,120 00	18 40	5,627 60
					(—)	(211)	(504)	(101)

Posting the cash payments journal at the end of the month.

sums must be =

RECORDING TRANSACTIONS INVOLVING PURCHASES OF MERCHANDISE

TRANSACTION	SOURCE DOCUMENT*	JOURNAL	GENERAL LEDGER												ACCOUNTS PAYABLE LEDGER	
			Cash		*Accounts Payable*		*Purchases*		*Transportation In*		*Purchases Returns & Allowances*		*Purchases Discount*		*Individual Creditor's Account*	
Purchase for cash.	Check Stub	Cash Payments Journal		XXX			XXX									
Return or allowance for cash.	Remittance Slip	Cash Receipts Journal	XXX									XXX				
Purchase on credit.	Purchase Invoice	Purchases Journal				XXX	XXX									XXX
Transportation charge for cash.	Check Stub	Cash Payments Journal		XXX					XXX							
Return or allowance for credit.	Credit Memorandum	General Journal			XXX							XXX			XXX	
Payment with purchase discount.	Check Stub	Cash Payments Journal		XXX	XXX									XXX	XXX	
Payment without purchase discount.	Check Stub	Cash Payments Journal		XXX	XXX										XXX	

*Only one possible source document is shown.

placed in the column on the line beneath the double rule to show that the total is not posted.

The total of the Accounts Payable Debit column is posted as a debit to the controlling account in the general ledger. The individual amounts in this column were posted to the subsidiary ledger during the month. The account number (211) is recorded in the column beneath the double rule.

The total of the Purchases Discount Credit column is posted as a credit to the Purchases Discount account in the general ledger. The account number (504) is then recorded in the column beneath the double rule. The total of the Net Cash Credit column is posted to the credit side of the Cash account. The account number (101) is then recorded beneath the double rule.

Summarizing Transactions Involving Purchases

The various activities involved in purchasing merchandise are discussed earlier in this chapter. As a result of these activities, an approved purchase invoice was submitted to the accounting department for journalizing. In some cases, the full amount of the invoice was paid when due. In other cases, a deduction for a return or allowance was made from the total amount of the invoice. In still other cases, a deduction for a purchase discount was also made. The flowchart on page 370 summarizes these transactions.

Exercise I on this page and page 372 may be completed at this point.

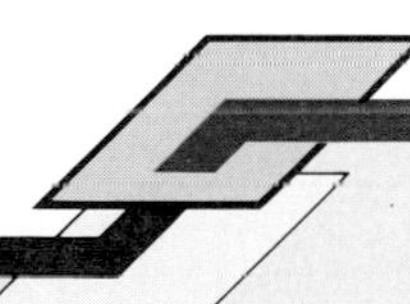

TOPIC 5 EXERCISE

EXERCISE I. Answer the following questions about journalizing and posting payments for purchases. Refer to the text, margin notes, and illustrations on pages 366 to 371.

1. Where are payments for purchases journalized?
2. How much is Johnson Supply willing to accept for the $720 invoice owed by Computer Age if paid within the discount period? How is the amount computed?
3. What accounts are debited and credited when the $720 invoice is paid within the discount period?
4. How many special columns are included in the cash payments journal on page 369?
5. Why is a purchase discount posted as a credit to the Purchases Discount account and not to the Purchases account?
6. What accounts and amounts are debited and credited in the entry made on October 24?
7. Why is a check mark placed in the Posting Reference column for the October 24 entry?
8. When the October 18 entry was posted as a debit to the Johnson Supply account, was the Accounts Payable controlling account in

the general ledger debited for $720 at the same time? If not, how will the amount be posted?

9. Why is a dash placed under the General Ledger Debit column?

10. Why is "(211)" placed under the Accounts Payable Debit column?

11. Is there any way to prove the amounts in the cash payments journal? How?

TOPIC 5 PROBLEMS

TOPIC PROBLEM 11. Find the cost of delivered goods and the net purchases for each of the following purchases.

Purchases	Trans. In	Purch. Ret. & Allow.	Purch. Disc.
a. $17,000	$225	$ 0	$300
b. 16,000	535	2,700	0
c. 6,500	0	700	350
d. 10,600	55	100	272

TOPIC PROBLEM 12. Process the following purchases data for the Haywood Nursery.

a. Open the general ledger accounts, assign appropriate numbers, and record the August 1 balances as follows: Cash, $30,200; Accounts Payable; Craig Conrad, Capital, $30,200; Craig Conrad, Drawing; Purchases; Transportation In; Purchases Discount; Rent Expense. Open accounts payable ledger accounts for the Ashley Nursery, 215 Main Street, Troy, New York 12180; and the Franklin Street Nurseries, Franklin Street, Nashua, New Hampshire 03061.

b. Using a purchases journal and a cash payments journal, record the entries for the listed transactions.

c. Post the individual entries from the journals.

d. Prove, total, and rule the journals.

e. Post the totals from the journals.

f. Prepare a schedule of accounts payable. Verify the total.

Aug. 1 Issued Check 204 for $360 for August rent.

5 Bought merchandise for $600 from the Franklin Street Nurseries; Invoice 482, dated August 2; terms FOB shipping point, 2/10, n/30.

5 Issued Check 205 for $52 to Van Express for delivering merchandise from the Franklin Street Nurseries.

8 Bought merchandise for $1,200 from the Ashley Nursery; Invoice R119, dated August 5; terms FOB destination, 1/10, n/60.

11 Issued Check 206 for $588 to the Franklin Street Nurseries to pay Invoice 482, less discount.

13 Issued Check 207 for $1,188 to the Ashley Nursery to pay Invoice R119, less discount.

13 Bought merchandise for $700 from the Ashley Nursery; Invoice R306, dated August 10; terms FOB destination, 1/10, n/60.

Aug. 18 Bought merchandise for $520 from the Ashley Nursery; Invoice R375, dated August 15; terms FOB destination, 1/10, n/60.

24 Issued Check 208 for $600 to Craig Conrad for personal use.

26 Bought merchandise for $160 from the Franklin Street Nurseries; Invoice 566, dated August 23; terms FOB shipping point, 2/10, n/30.

Aug. 26 Issued Check 209 for $64 to Van Express for delivering merchandise from the Franklin Street Nurseries.

NOTE: Save your ledgers for further use in Topic Problem 13.

TOPIC PROBLEM 13. Using the ledgers prepared in Topic Problem 11, complete the following work.

a. Record the listed entries for September in a purchases journal and a cash payments journal.

b. Post the individual entries from the journals.

c. Prove, total, and rule the journals.

d. Post the totals from the journals.

e. Prepare a schedule of accounts payable. Verify the total.

f. Prepare a trial balance.

Sept. 1 Issued Check 210 for $360 for September rent.

3 Issued Check 211 to the Ashley Nursery for Invoice R306.

5 Bought merchandise for $850 from the Franklin Street Nurseries; Invoice 624, dated September 2; terms FOB shipping point, 2/10, n/30.

Sept. 9 Issued Check 212 for $42 to Van Express for delivering merchandise from the Franklin Street Nurseries.

9 Issued Check 213 to the Franklin Street Nurseries to pay Invoice 624.

12 Bought merchandise for $1,100 from the Ashley Nursery; Invoice R402, dated September 9; terms FOB destination, 1/10, n/60.

18 Issued Check 214 to the Ashley Nursery to pay Invoice R402, less discount.

21 Issued Check 215 to the Franklin Street Nurseries to pay Invoice 566.

28 Bought merchandise for $580 from the Ashley Nursery; Invoice R490, dated September 25; terms FOB destination, 1/10, n/60.

FOB Destination - seller pays trans

FOB Shipping pt - buyer pays

CHAPTER SUMMARY

In this chapter, you learned that a purchases subsystem involves the ordering, receiving, accounting for, and storing of merchandise for a business.

The purchase of merchandise is recorded in a temporary owner's equity account called Purchases. Separate accounts are set up to record items that affect the cost of merchandise—transportation of goods, return of purchased merchandise, and purchases discounts.

Purchases of merchandise for cash are recorded in the cash payments journal. Purchases on account are usually recorded in a special journal called a purchases journal. In the general journal, a debit entry to the Purchases account and a credit entry to the creditor's account would be required for each purchase transaction. With a purchases journal, the effect of a purchase transaction can be summarized and recorded on just one line. At the end of the month the Purchases account is debited for the total amount credited to the various creditor's accounts.

In this chapter you also learned about the procedure for posting purchase transactions. A controlling account (Accounts Payable) is established in the general ledger. A subsidiary ledger (accounts payable ledger) is set up for individual creditor's accounts. At the end of the month the total purchases are posted in one entry to the debit side of the Purchases account and to the credit side of the Accounts Payable account in the general ledger.

THE LANGUAGE OF BUSINESS

The following terms make up the language of business. Do you know the meaning of each?

purchases subsystem
merchandise inventory
inventory card
purchase requisition
FOB (free on board)
purchase order
purchase invoice
extension
perpetual inventory procedure
periodic inventory procedure
physical inventory
inventory loss
costs
gross profit
Sales account
Purchases account
purchases journal
subsidiary ledger
accounts payable subsidiary ledger
controlling account
three-column balance ledger form
schedule of accounts payable
FOB destination
FOB shipping point
Transportation In account
purchases returns and allowances
net purchases
credit memorandum
double-posting
credit period
discount period
purchase discount
tickler file
Purchases Discount account

REVIEW QUESTIONS

1. What is merchandise inventory?
2. Why is it important to have control of purchases of merchandise?
3. Describe the four major purchasing activities.
4. What would be the effect on assets, liabilities, and owner's equity if the purchase of a typewriter was recorded in the purchases journal?
5. What is the purpose of preparing a schedule of accounts payable? In what ways is it like a trial balance?
6. Name and describe the source document for journalizing each of the following types of transactions.
   a. Purchases for cash
   b. Purchases on credit
   c. Purchases returns and allowances
   d. Transportation charges
   e. Purchases discounts
   f. Payments to creditors
7. Why are transportation charges not recorded in the Purchases account?
8. Why are purchases returns and allowances not recorded in the Purchases account?
9. Why are purchase discounts not recorded in the Purchases account?
10. How does a multicolumn cash payments journal simplify journalizing and posting?

CHAPTER PROBLEMS

Problems for Chapter 11 are given below. Write your answers to the problems on separate sheets of paper unless you are using the workbook for this textbook. If you are using the workbook, do the problems in the space provided there.

CHAPTER PROBLEM 11-1. The six purchase invoices that are shown on the next page were received by Warren Paints. Each invoice has been stamped, and the date of its receipt has been entered on the stamp. The invoices have been approved by the purchasing clerk, who checked the quantities and unit prices against the corresponding orders.

a. Verify the extensions and the total of each invoice. If there is an error, correct the amounts. If you are using a workbook, initial the "approved" stamp and make any necessary corrections on the purchase invoices.

b. Journalize each purchase in the purchases journal. (The date of the journal entry should be the date that the purchase invoice was received.)

c. Total and rule the purchases journal.

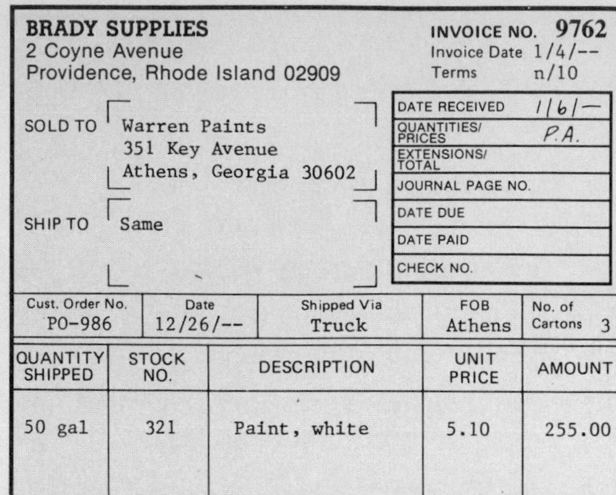

BRADY SUPPLIES
2 Coyne Avenue
Providence, Rhode Island 02909

INVOICE NO. 9762
Invoice Date 1/4/--
Terms n/10

SOLD TO Warren Paints
351 Key Avenue
Athens, Georgia 30602

SHIP TO Same

DATE RECEIVED	1/6/—
QUANTITIES/PRICES	P.A.
EXTENSIONS/TOTAL	
JOURNAL PAGE NO.	
DATE DUE	
DATE PAID	
CHECK NO.	

Cust. Order No.	Date	Shipped Via	FOB	No. of Cartons
PO-986	12/26/--	Truck	Athens	3

QUANTITY SHIPPED	STOCK NO.	DESCRIPTION	UNIT PRICE	AMOUNT
50 gal	321	Paint, white	5.10	255.00

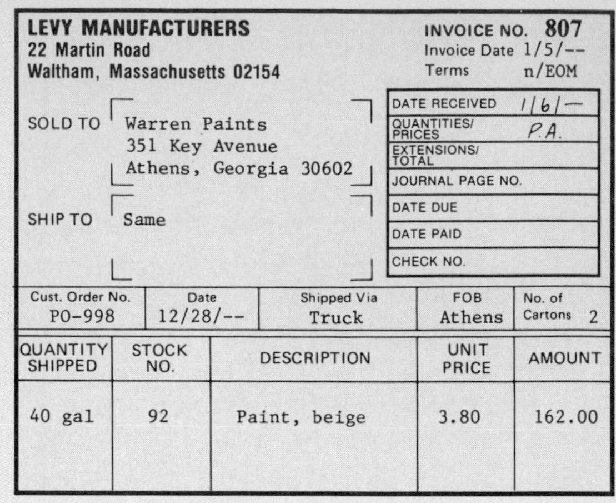

LEVY MANUFACTURERS
22 Martin Road
Waltham, Massachusetts 02154

INVOICE NO. 807
Invoice Date 1/5/--
Terms n/EOM

SOLD TO Warren Paints
351 Key Avenue
Athens, Georgia 30602

SHIP TO Same

DATE RECEIVED	1/6/—
QUANTITIES/PRICES	P.A.
EXTENSIONS/TOTAL	
JOURNAL PAGE NO.	
DATE DUE	
DATE PAID	
CHECK NO.	

Cust. Order No.	Date	Shipped Via	FOB	No. of Cartons
PO-998	12/28/--	Truck	Athens	2

QUANTITY SHIPPED	STOCK NO.	DESCRIPTION	UNIT PRICE	AMOUNT
40 gal	92	Paint, beige	3.80	162.00

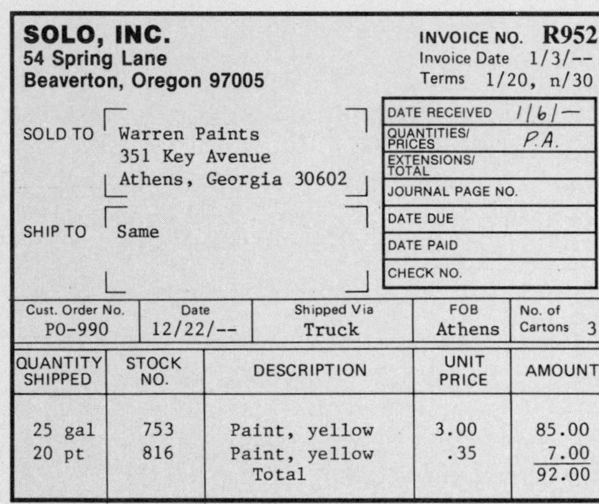

SOLO, INC.
54 Spring Lane
Beaverton, Oregon 97005

INVOICE NO. R952
Invoice Date 1/3/--
Terms 1/20, n/30

SOLD TO Warren Paints
351 Key Avenue
Athens, Georgia 30602

SHIP TO Same

DATE RECEIVED	1/6/—
QUANTITIES/PRICES	P.A.
EXTENSIONS/TOTAL	
JOURNAL PAGE NO.	
DATE DUE	
DATE PAID	
CHECK NO.	

Cust. Order No.	Date	Shipped Via	FOB	No. of Cartons
PO-990	12/22/--	Truck	Athens	3

QUANTITY SHIPPED	STOCK NO.	DESCRIPTION	UNIT PRICE	AMOUNT
25 gal	753	Paint, yellow	3.00	85.00
20 pt	816	Paint, yellow	.35	7.00
		Total		92.00

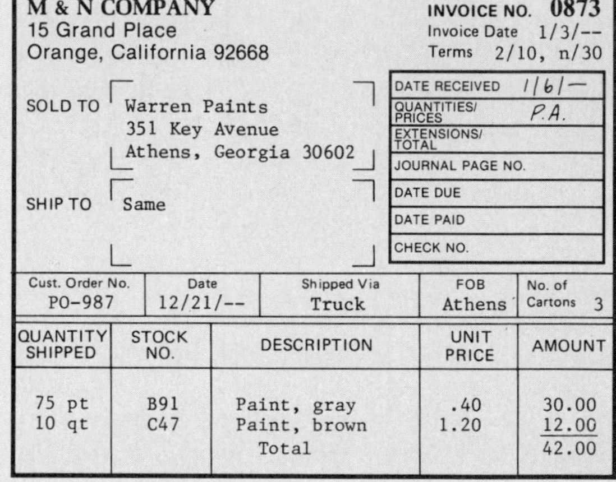

M & N COMPANY
15 Grand Place
Orange, California 92668

INVOICE NO. 0873
Invoice Date 1/3/--
Terms 2/10, n/30

SOLD TO Warren Paints
351 Key Avenue
Athens, Georgia 30602

SHIP TO Same

DATE RECEIVED	1/6/—
QUANTITIES/PRICES	P.A.
EXTENSIONS/TOTAL	
JOURNAL PAGE NO.	
DATE DUE	
DATE PAID	
CHECK NO.	

Cust. Order No.	Date	Shipped Via	FOB	No. of Cartons
PO-987	12/21/--	Truck	Athens	3

QUANTITY SHIPPED	STOCK NO.	DESCRIPTION	UNIT PRICE	AMOUNT
75 pt	B91	Paint, gray	.40	30.00
10 qt	C47	Paint, brown	1.20	12.00
		Total		42.00

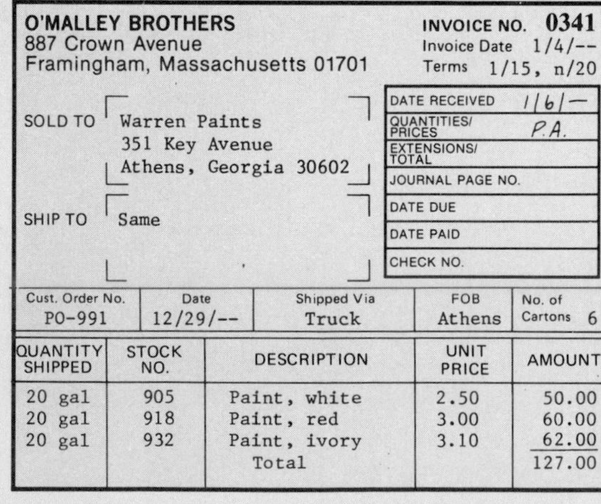

O'MALLEY BROTHERS
887 Crown Avenue
Framingham, Massachusetts 01701

INVOICE NO. 0341
Invoice Date 1/4/--
Terms 1/15, n/20

SOLD TO Warren Paints
351 Key Avenue
Athens, Georgia 30602

SHIP TO Same

DATE RECEIVED	1/6/—
QUANTITIES/PRICES	P.A.
EXTENSIONS/TOTAL	
JOURNAL PAGE NO.	
DATE DUE	
DATE PAID	
CHECK NO.	

Cust. Order No.	Date	Shipped Via	FOB	No. of Cartons
PO-991	12/29/--	Truck	Athens	6

QUANTITY SHIPPED	STOCK NO.	DESCRIPTION	UNIT PRICE	AMOUNT
20 gal	905	Paint, white	2.50	50.00
20 gal	918	Paint, red	3.00	60.00
20 gal	932	Paint, ivory	3.10	62.00
		Total		127.00

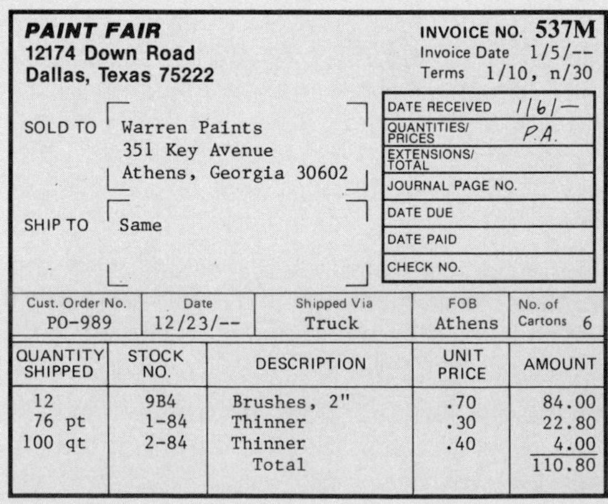

PAINT FAIR
12174 Down Road
Dallas, Texas 75222

INVOICE NO. 537M
Invoice Date 1/5/--
Terms 1/10, n/30

SOLD TO Warren Paints
351 Key Avenue
Athens, Georgia 30602

SHIP TO Same

DATE RECEIVED	1/6/—
QUANTITIES/PRICES	P.A.
EXTENSIONS/TOTAL	
JOURNAL PAGE NO.	
DATE DUE	
DATE PAID	
CHECK NO.	

Cust. Order No.	Date	Shipped Via	FOB	No. of Cartons
PO-989	12/23/--	Truck	Athens	6

QUANTITY SHIPPED	STOCK NO.	DESCRIPTION	UNIT PRICE	AMOUNT
12	9B4	Brushes, 2"	.70	84.00
76 pt	1-84	Thinner	.30	22.80
100 qt	2-84	Thinner	.40	4.00
		Total		110.80

CHAPTER PROBLEM 11-2. Use the purchase invoices shown in Chapter Problem 11-1 and the information provided below to carry out the following activities.

a. Compute the end of discount period.

b. Assuming that each invoice is paid one day before the end of the discount period, compute the cash discount and the amount to be paid for each invoice. (Assume that Checks 211 to 216 are issued to pay the invoices.)

c. Journalize each payment in the cash payments journal.

d. Prove, total, and rule the cash payments journal.

SUPPLEMENTAL CHAPTER PROBLEM 11-3. If you are using the workbook, follow the directions and write your answers in the space provided.

MANAGEMENT CASES

Trade Discounts. Many manufacturers and wholesalers publish catalogs showing the retail prices of their products. They frequently offer deductions from these list prices to their dealers. The reduction from list price is known as a trade discount. For example, a manufacturer advertises a certain $200 television set at a list price of $200 (the price to retail customers). However, it offers the same television set to dealers at a trade discount of 40 percent. This discount amounts to $80 (40 percent of $200). Thus, a dealer has to pay $120 ($200 − $80) for each set.

List Price ×	Rate of Trade Discount	=	Amount of Trade Discount
$200 ×	0.40	=	$80

List Price −	Amount of Trade Discount	=	Net Price
$200 −	$80	=	$120

Trade discounts are not entered in the accounting records because they are used only to find the net purchase price. The important price is what it costs the dealer for the item.

CASE 11M-1. Star Television buys color television sets for $500 each on credit terms of 1/10, n/30. The manufacturer pays the shipping cost. If the store buys a truckload of 120 television sets, a 10 percent trade discount is allowed.

Last year the store sold 100 color televisions. Sales have been increasing gradually, and the store expects a 20 percent increase next year. The store manager is considering buying a truckload of television sets and has asked for your opinion.

a. What is the trade discount? What amount is recorded in the purchases journal?

b. What amount is paid for 120 televisions if the store pays within ten days? Twenty days?

c. How much money will the store be tying up in inventory if it buys the truckload?

d. Would you recommend that the televisions be bought by the truckload? Explain.

CASE 11M-2. The Gallagher Shop bought a shipment of suits from the ABC Clothing Company. The invoice for the suits is for $5,000, is dated April 1, and has terms of 2/10, n/30. On April 11 the Gallagher Shop does not have enough cash to pay the invoice. It will have the money by May 1. In order to take advantage of the 2 percent cash discount, the owners are considering borrowing the money from a bank to pay the invoice within the discount period. The business has a good credit rating and can borrow the necessary amount at 10 percent interest.

a. How much will the owners have to borrow to pay the invoice on April 11?

b. For how many days will they have to borrow the money?

c. How much interest will they have to pay?

d. With the interest on the loan, what will the total cost of the suits be?

e. Would you recommend that the owners borrow the money and take advantage of the cash discount or that they pay the full amount of the invoice on April 30?

CHAPTER

12

A Sales Subsystem

In Chapter 11 you learned about the activities involved in purchasing merchandise. You will now study the forms, procedures, and equipment in a sales subsystem used to control sale of merchandise on credit. You will also learn about the jobs performed by accounting personnel within a sales subsystem.

CHAPTER GOALS

After studying Chapter 12, you will be able to:

1. Define the terms listed in "The Language of Business" section on page 422.
2. Explain the concepts and principles in this chapter related to accounting for the sale of merchandise.
3. Use a flowchart to describe the relationship of people, forms, procedures, and equipment in a sales subsystem.
4. Journalize and post from a sales journal and a multicolumn cash receipts journal.
5. Describe the relationship between sales, sales returns and allowances, and sales discounts.
6. Prepare a schedule of accounts receivable and prove its accuracy.
7. Prepare a statement of account and explain its function in billing customers.

TOPIC 1

Controlling Sales of Merchandise

Are the same procedures used to control cash sales and credit sales? No, somewhat different procedures are used. The procedures for cash sales are described in Chapter 9. The cash register tapes or sales slips for cash sales become source documents for entries in the cash receipts journal. When a retail or wholesale business sells merchandise on credit, however, the procedures are somewhat different. A subsystem must be set up with procedures to ensure accuracy, honesty, and efficiency and speed in handling sales on credit. A **sales subsystem** is, therefore, the people, forms, procedures, and equipment used to process sales of merchandise on credit. This subsystem involves procedures for receiving and approving customer orders, shipping and billing for merchandise, and accounting for sales on credit.

PROCESSING A CUSTOMER'S ORDER

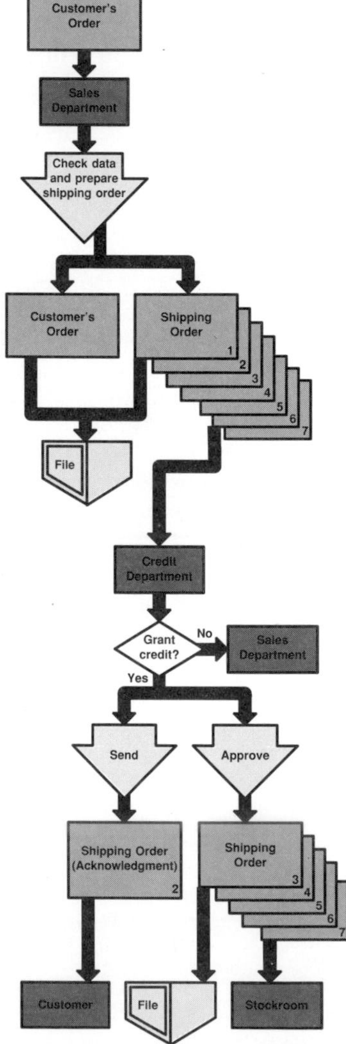

Receiving and Approving Customer Orders

What are the procedures for receiving and approving customer orders? Customer orders must be promptly approved or turned down when received. The procedures to do this include the following.

- Taking the order
- Preparing the shipping order
- Securing credit approval

Taking the Order Orders are received in many ways and on many forms. An order may come in on a purchase order or in a customer letter. An order may be jotted down on a sales slip by an order clerk who takes orders in person or over a telephone. Some businesses

PURCHASE ORDER

WILL'S APPLIANCE
16 Del Rey Drive
Denver, Colorado 80219

No. **69458**

- Purchase order numbers must appear on all papers and packages. Packing slip must accompany shipments.
- Terms of discount must be shown on invoice.
- Delivery schedule as indicated must be held.

TO Computer Age
200 Girard Avenue
Denver, Colorado 80236

Date	Items Needed By	Terms	Via	FOB
10/2/--	10/15/--	1/20, n/30	Truck Exp.	Denver

QUANTITY	DESCRIPTION	UNIT PRICE
12	Switches No. IR5	2.94
6	Wire Racks No. 3GK5	2.46
1	Stand, 3-section No. 84-3	11.72

Purchase order.

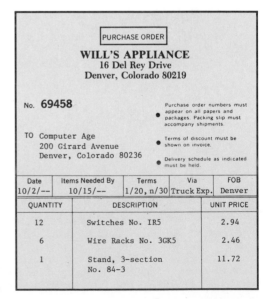

find it helpful to transfer each order received to a standard form called a shipping order. These shipping orders are usually prenumbered and printed in multiple copies. Use of the shipping order saves retyping and recopying at each step in the sales subsystem.

Control: Fill orders promptly.

Control: Use prenumbered forms.

■ Preparing the Shipping Order The shipping order shown here is prepared from a purchase order submitted by Will's Appliance to Computer Age. Some of the information on the purchase order is transferred without change. Other information is verified. For example, the order clerk must check the credit terms requested by the customer (1/20, n/30) before entering the terms on the shipping order. The clerk must also check the stock numbers and unit prices of items to be sure each is correct.

Control: Verify data on orders.

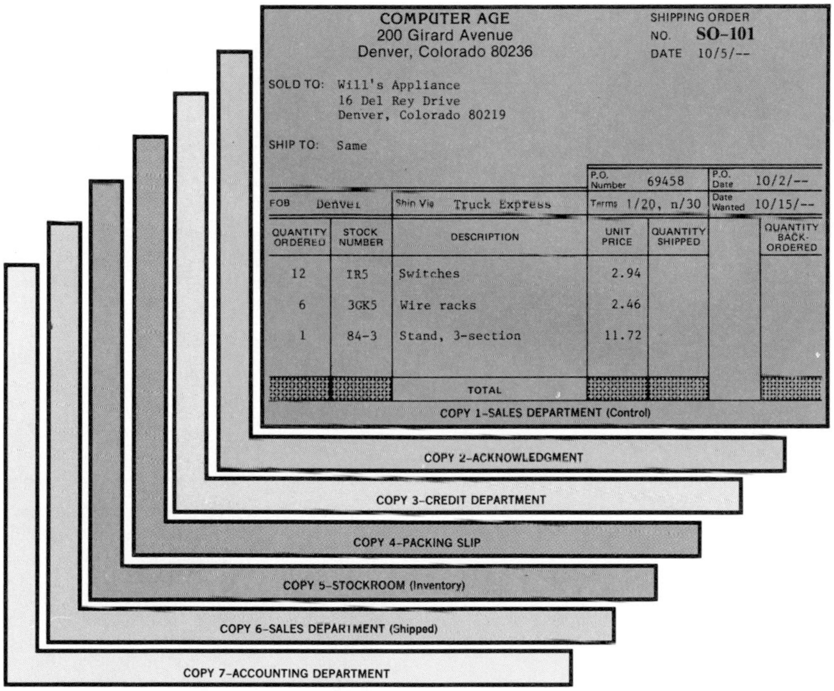

COMPUTER AGE
200 Girard Avenue
Denver, Colorado 80236

SHIPPING ORDER
NO. **SO-101**
DATE 10/5/--

SOLD TO: Will's Appliance
16 Del Rey Drive
Denver, Colorado 80219

SHIP TO: Same

P.O. Number 69458 | P.O. Date 10/2/--

FOB Denver | Ship Via Truck Express | Terms 1/20, n/30 | Date Wanted 10/15/--

QUANTITY ORDERED	STOCK NUMBER	DESCRIPTION	UNIT PRICE	QUANTITY SHIPPED		QUANTITY BACK-ORDERED
12	IR5	Switches	2.94			
6	3GK5	Wire racks	2.46			
1	84-3	Stand, 3-section	11.72			
		TOTAL				

COPY 1–SALES DEPARTMENT (Control)

COPY 2–ACKNOWLEDGMENT

COPY 3–CREDIT DEPARTMENT

COPY 4–PACKING SLIP

COPY 5–STOCKROOM (Inventory)

COPY 6–SALES DEPARTMENT (Shipped)

COPY 7–ACCOUNTING DEPARTMENT

When the order clerk completes the shipping order, Copy 1 is attached to the purchase order and is kept until the order is shipped and billed. This control copy is kept in the **unshipped orders file**. This is a file for orders that have not been shipped as yet. The other copies of the shipping order (Copies 2–7) are sent to the credit department.

■ Securing Credit Approval Before shipping the merchandise, the credit department must find out if the customer is a good credit risk. It must determine if the customer is likely to pay the bill when it comes due.

Control: Check customer's credit before shipping merchandise.

If the customer is a poor credit risk, the credit department usually returns the shipping order to the sales department. The salespeople must settle the problem with the customer. They either do not fill the order or work out a different method of payment. If the customer's credit is good, a credit clerk detaches Copy 2 and sends it to the customer. The customer then knows that the order has been received and is being processed. The credit clerk then signs the panel at the top of Copy 3 to show that the order has been approved for shipment, as shown below. (By means of interleaved carbon paper or specially treated paper, the clerk's signature is transferred to the other copies. Thus, anyone who uses one of the copies is sure that the customer's credit has been checked and approved.) The clerk then detaches Copy 3 of the shipping order for the credit department's files. Copies 4–7 are sent to the stockroom, where the merchandise is stored and orders are filled.

Control: Divide responsibility.

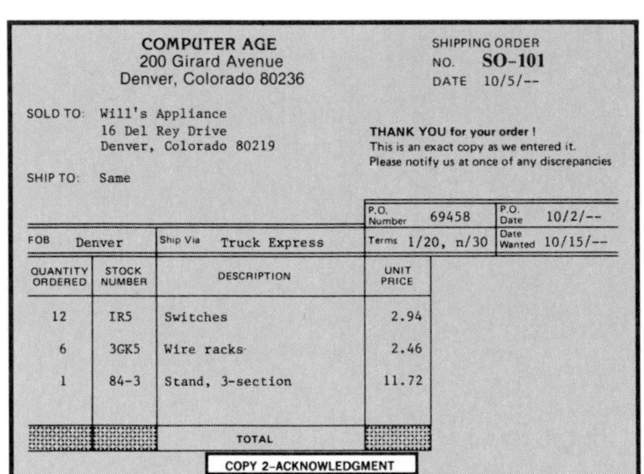

COMPUTER AGE
200 Girard Avenue
Denver, Colorado 80236

SHIPPING ORDER
NO. SO-101
DATE 10/5/--

SOLD TO: Will's Appliance
16 Del Rey Drive
Denver, Colorado 80219

THANK YOU for your order !
This is an exact copy as we entered it.
Please notify us at once of any discrepancies

SHIP TO: Same

P.O. Number 69458 | P.O. Date 10/2/--
FOB Denver | Ship Via Truck Express | Terms 1/20, n/30 | Date Wanted 10/15/--

QUANTITY ORDERED	STOCK NUMBER	DESCRIPTION	UNIT PRICE
12	IR5	Switches	2.94
6	3GK5	Wire racks	2.46
1	84-3	Stand, 3-section	11.72
		TOTAL	

COPY 2–ACKNOWLEDGMENT

Copy 2: Acknowledgment for customer.

Credit Signature

COMPUTER AGE
200 Girard Avenue
Denver, Colorado 80236

SHIPPING ORDER
NO. SO-101
DATE 10/5/--

Credit: D. Ruiz, 10/5/—

SOLD TO: Will's Appliance
16 Del Rey Drive
Denver, Colorado 80219

SHIP TO: Same

P.O. Number 69458 | P.O. Date 10/2/--
FOB Denver | Ship Via Truck Express | Terms 1/20, n/30 | Date Wanted 10/15/--

QUANTITY ORDERED	STOCK NUMBER	DESCRIPTION	UNIT PRICE
12	IR5	Switches	2.94
6	3GK5	Wire racks	2.46
1	84-3	Stand, 3-section	11.72
		TOTAL	

COPY 3–CREDIT DEPARTMENT

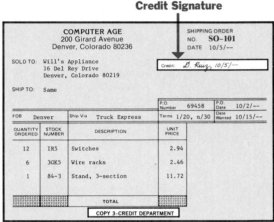

Copy 3: Shipping order with credit approval.

Order Clerk: DOT 249.367-054

Processes orders received by mail, telephone, or in person from customers.

Credit Clerk: DOT 205.367-022

Processes applications for loans and credit. Determines credit limit. May keep record of transactions with customers.

Exercise A on page 387 may be completed at this point.

Shipping Merchandise

What are the procedures for shipping merchandise? After the customer's order is approved, the merchandise must be shipped. The procedures include the following.

- A shipping clerk in the stockroom assembles and packs the items.
- The shipping clerk writes on Copy 4 (the packing slip copy) and all remaining copies whether the full quantity of each item is being sent.

- The shipping clerk fills in the shipping information on Copy 4.
- Copy 4 is then detached and enclosed in the package so that the customer can check the contents with the items listed on the packing slip.

COMPUTER AGE
200 Girard Avenue
Denver, Colorado 80236

SHIPPING ORDER
NO. **SO-101**
DATE 10/5/--

SOLD TO: Will's Appliance
16 Del Rey Drive
Denver, Colorado 80219

SHIP TO: Same

DETACH ALONG THIS LINE

Shipped by: S. Carson, 10/6/--
Weight: 30 lbs | No. of packages: 2

P.O. Number 69458 | P.O. Date 10/2/--
FOB Denver | Ship Via Truck Express | Terms 1/20, n/30 | Date Wanted 10/15/--

QUANTITY ORDERED	STOCK NUMBER	DESCRIPTION		QUANTITY SHIPPED		QUANTITY BACK-ORDERED
12	IR5	Switches		8		4
6	3GK5	Wire racks		6		0
1	84-3	Stand, 3-section		1		0
		TOTAL				

COPY 4–PACKING SLIP

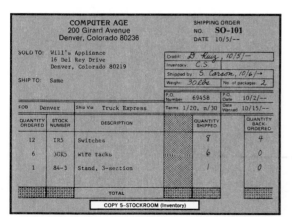

Copy 4: Packing slip sent with goods to customer.

The packing slip for Will's Appliance shows that all the items on the purchase order are being shipped except 4 of the switches. Only 8 of the 12 switches ordered can be supplied. The remaining 4 are listed in the Quantity Back-Ordered column. This column is for goods that cannot be shipped until a later time. (The quantity shipped plus the quantity back-ordered must agree with the customer's purchase order.) Therefore, the customer knows which items are not in the current shipment and which items will be sent when available. The shipping clerk then detaches Copy 5 (the inventory copy) for the stockroom's files. Copy 5 is used to subtract the number of items shipped from the inventory cards.

COMPUTER AGE
200 Girard Avenue
Denver, Colorado 80236

SHIPPING ORDER
NO. **SO-101**
DATE 10/5/--

SOLD TO: Will's Appliance
16 Del Rey Drive
Denver, Colorado 80219

SHIP TO: Same

Credit: D. Ruiz, 10/5/--
Inventory: C.S.
Shipped by: S. Carson, 10/6/--
Weight: 30 lbs | No. of packages: 2

P.O. Number 69458 | P.O. Date 10/2/--
FOB Denver | Ship Via Truck Express | Terms 1/20, n/30 | Date Wanted 10/15/--

QUANTITY ORDERED	STOCK NUMBER	DESCRIPTION		QUANTITY SHIPPED		QUANTITY BACK-ORDERED
12	IR5	Switches		8		4
6	3GK5	Wire racks		6		0
1	84-3	Stand, 3-section		1		0
		TOTAL				

COPY 5–STOCKROOM (Inventory)

Copy 5: Inventory copy to update inventory cards.

SHIPPING MERCHANDISE TO A CUSTOMER

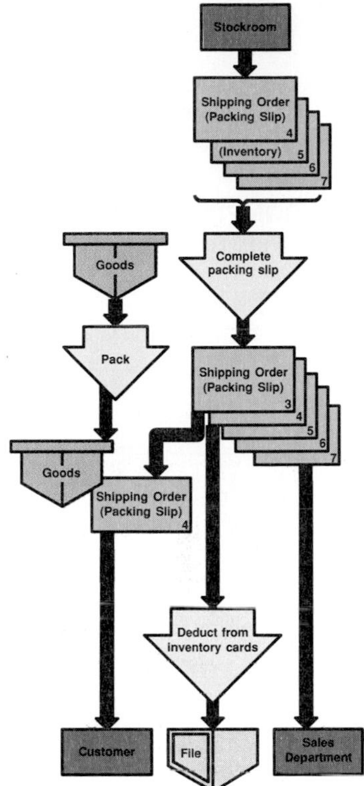

Control: Remove merchandise from stock only if there is proper authorization.

Shipping Clerk: DOT 222.387-050

Prepares merchandise for shipment and keeps records of the merchandise shipped.

Billing for Merchandise

What procedures are used to bill customers promptly for merchandise? Only after the merchandise is shipped should the customer be billed. Billing the customer requires completion of the shipping order, preparation of the sales invoice, and journalizing the sales invoice. To do so, the following steps are completed.

Control: Bill customers for all merchandise shipped.

- Copies 6 and 7 of the shipping order are returned to the sales department.
- A billing clerk takes Copy 1 (the control copy) out of the unshipped orders file. Copy 1 is then checked against the shipped copy (Copy 6) to see that no changes were made from the original order. If all merchandise has been shipped, Copy 1 is destroyed.
- On Copies 6 and 7, the billing clerk multiplies the quantity shipped by the unit price and records the extensions in the Amount column.

COMPLETING THE SHIPPING ORDER

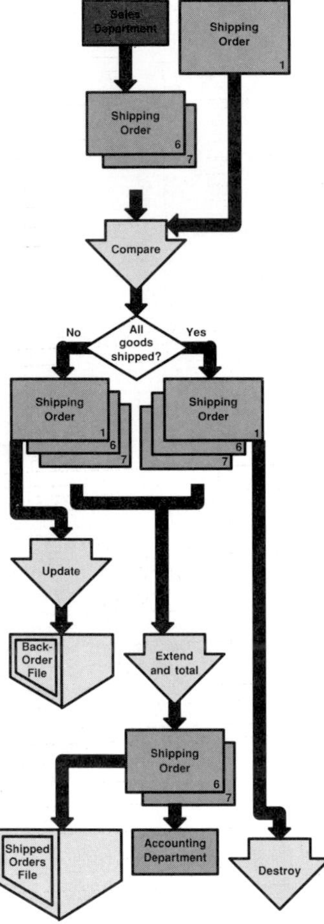

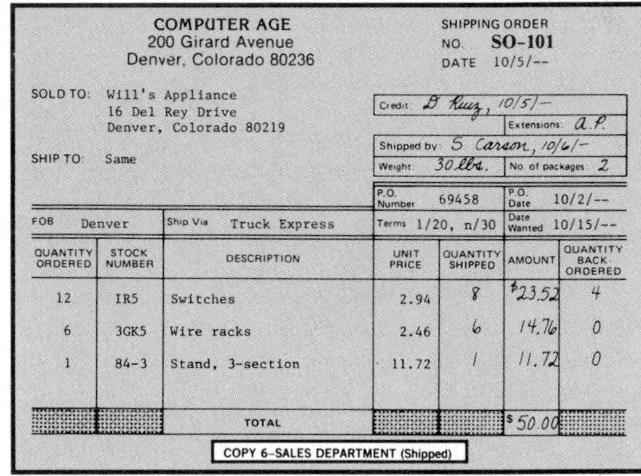

COMPUTER AGE
200 Girard Avenue
Denver, Colorado 80236

SHIPPING ORDER
NO. SO-101
DATE 10/5/--

SOLD TO: Will's Appliance
16 Del Rey Drive
Denver, Colorado 80219

SHIP TO: Same

Credit: D. Ruiz, 10/5/--
Extensions: a.P.
Shipped by: S. Carson, 10/6/--
Weight: 30 lbs.
No. of packages: 2

P.O. Number 69458 | P.O. Date 10/2/--
FOB Denver | Ship Via Truck Express | Terms 1/20, n/30 | Date Wanted 10/15/--

QUANTITY ORDERED	STOCK NUMBER	DESCRIPTION	UNIT PRICE	QUANTITY SHIPPED	AMOUNT	QUANTITY BACK-ORDERED
12	IR5	Switches	2.94	8	$23.52	4
6	3GK5	Wire racks	2.46	6	14.76	0
1	84-3	Stand, 3-section	11.72	1	11.72	0
		TOTAL			$50.00	

COPY 6–SALES DEPARTMENT (Shipped)

Copy 6: Shipped orders file copy with extensions and total computed.

COMPUTER AGE
200 Girard Avenue
Denver, Colorado 80236

SHIPPING ORDER
NO. SO-101
DATE 10/5/--

SOLD TO: Will's Appliance
16 Del Rey Drive
Denver, Colorado 80219

SHIP TO: Same

Verified: S.D.
Invoice Date: 10/7/--
Credit: D. Ruiz, 10/5/--
Extensions: a.P.
Shipped by: S. Carson, 10/6/--
Weight: 30 lbs.
No. of packages: 2

P.O. Number 69458 | P.O. Date 10/2/--
FOB Denver | Ship Via Truck Express | Terms 1/20, n/30 | Date Wanted 10/15/--

QUANTITY ORDERED	STOCK NUMBER	DESCRIPTION	UNIT PRICE	QUANTITY SHIPPED	AMOUNT	QUANTITY BACK-ORDERED
12	IR5	Switches	2.94	8	$23.52	4
6	3GK5	Wire racks	2.46	6	14.76	0
1	84-3	Stand, 3-section	11.72	1	11.72	0
		TOTAL			$50.00	

COPY 7–ACCOUNTING DEPARTMENT

Copy 7: Copy used to prepare sales invoice.

- The billing clerk then totals the extensions, initials the Extensions box, and separates Copies 6 and 7.
- Copy 6 is placed in a shipped orders file. A **shipped orders file** is a file containing shipping orders for items that have been sent out.

- Copy 7 is sent to the accounting department. Copy 7 is used to prepare a sales invoice (the customer's bill).

This procedure changes slightly for back orders. The billing clerk computes the extensions and total only for those items shipped. On Copy 1 the items not shipped are checked, and then Copy 1 is placed in a back order file. A **back order file** is a file of orders that will be filled later. When new stock is received, a new shipping order is filled out. The balance of the order is then shipped to the customer.

■ Preparing the Sales Invoice The sales invoice looks like the completed shipping order, as shown here. However, it lists only the amount that the customer owes for those items actually shipped.

COMPUTER AGE
200 Girard Avenue
Denver, Colorado 80236

INVOICE NO. 101

SOLD TO: Will's Appliance
16 Del Rey Drive
Denver, Colorado 80219

Invoice Date: 10/7/--

SHIP TO: Same

Terms: 1/20, n/30

Purchase Order No.	Date	Shipped Via	FOB	No. of Packages
69458	10/2/--	Truck Express	Denver	2

QUANTITY	STOCK NUMBER	DESCRIPTION	UNIT PRICE	AMOUNT
8	IR5	Switches	2.94	23.52
6	3GK5	Wire racks	2.46	14.76
1	84-3	Stand, 3-section	11.72	11.72
		TOTAL		50.00
		COPY 1-CUSTOMER		

Sales invoice prepared from shipping order (Copy 7).

BILLING FOR MERCHANDISE

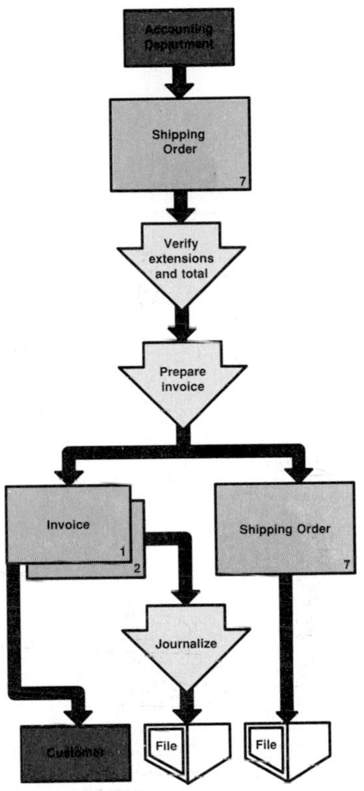

An accounting clerk first verifies the extensions and total amount on Copy 7 of the shipping order. At least two copies of the sales invoice are then prepared in the billing section of the accounting department. Copy 1 shown above is sent to the customer and is the customer's bill. Copy 2 of the invoice is kept in the accounting department. It is the source document for journalizing the sales transaction.

After the invoice is prepared, the invoice date is recorded at the top of Copy 7 of the shipping order to show that the customer was billed. Copy 7 is then filed in the accounting department.

Billing Clerk: DOT 214.482-010
Prepares invoices. Computes amounts due. May prepare statements of account—statements mailed periodically to customers showing the balances they owe.

Exercise B on page 387 may be completed at this point.

Visualizing Sales on Credit

How are the procedures to process sales related? The procedures for receiving and approving the customer's order, packing and shipping the merchandise, and billing for the merchandise are shown in the flowchart on the next page.

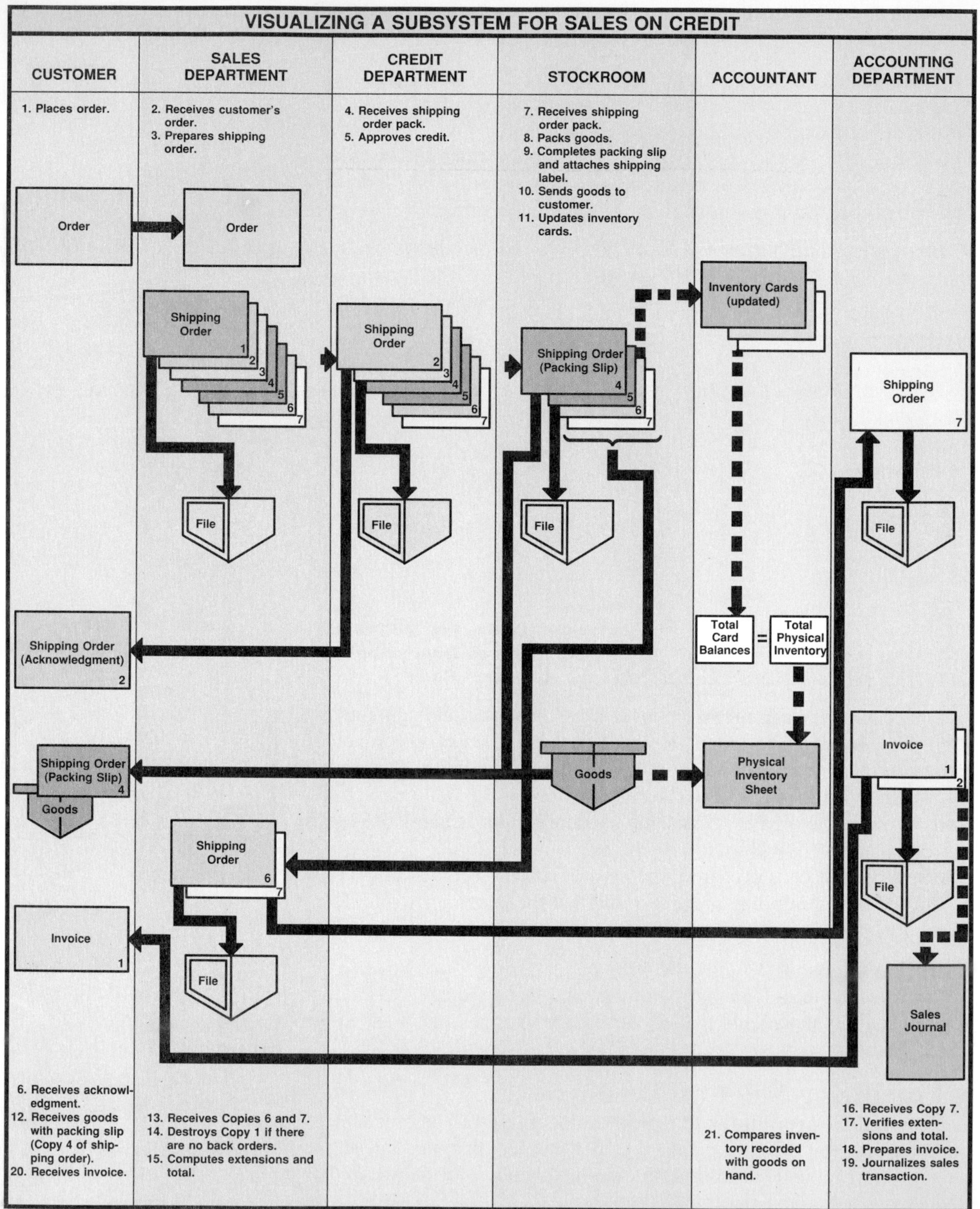
VISUALIZING A SUBSYSTEM FOR SALES ON CREDIT
CUSTOMER
SALES DEPARTMENT
CREDIT DEPARTMENT
STOCKROOM
ACCOUNTANT
ACCOUNTING DEPARTMENT
1. Places order.
2. Receives customer's order.
3. Prepares shipping order.
4. Receives shipping order pack.
5. Approves credit.
7. Receives shipping order pack.
8. Packs goods.
9. Completes packing slip and attaches shipping label.
10. Sends goods to customer.
11. Updates inventory cards.
Order
Order
Shipping Order
Shipping Order
Shipping Order (Packing Slip)
Inventory Cards (updated)
Shipping Order
File
File
File
File
Total Card Balances
=
Total Physical Inventory
Shipping Order (Acknowledgment)
Shipping Order (Packing Slip)
Goods
Goods
Physical Inventory Sheet
Invoice
Shipping Order
File
Invoice
File
Sales Journal
6. Receives acknowledgment.
12. Receives goods with packing slip (Copy 4 of shipping order).
20. Receives invoice.
13. Receives Copies 6 and 7.
14. Destroys Copy 1 if there are no back orders.
15. Computes extensions and total.
21. Compares inventory recorded with goods on hand.
16. Receives Copy 7.
17. Verifies extensions and total.
18. Prepares invoice.
19. Journalizes sales transaction.

These subsystems will run smoothly, however, only if employees use the following procedures to control for honesty, accuracy, and efficiency in processing sales on credit.

- Fill customers' orders promptly.
- Use prenumbered forms.
- Verify data on each order.
- Check the customer's credit before the merchandise is shipped.
- Divide responsibility.
- Remove merchandise from stock only if there is proper authorization.
- Bill customers for all merchandise shipped.

In addition, the sales subsystem will not work well unless the following control procedures are carried out effectively.

- Record receivables from completed sales transactions.
- Issue refunds and credits only for approved returns and allowances.
- Collect receivables as soon as possible.

These additional control procedures are discussed at greater length in the other topics in this chapter.

Exercise C on page 388 may be completed at this point.

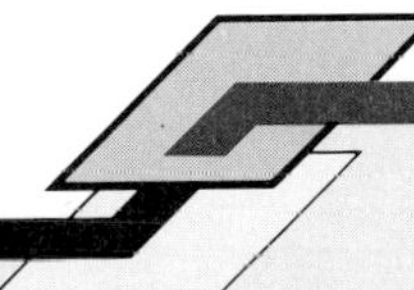

TOPIC 1 EXERCISES

EXERCISE A. Answer the following questions about receiving and approving customer orders. Refer to the illustrations on pages 380 to 382.

1. Who is the customer?
2. Which department receives the customer's order?
3. What happens if credit is not approved?
4. What credit terms are granted the customer?

EXERCISE B. Answer the following questions about shipping and billing for merchandise. Refer to the illustrations on pages 382 to 385.

1. Who ships the merchandise?
2. Which item is back-ordered? Why?
3. Who completed the extensions on shipping order SO-101?
4. What is the total amount of SO-101?
5. What are the differences between Invoice 101 and shipping order SO-101?
6. What is the last day on which Will's Appliance can take a 1 percent discount?
7. Who will receive Copy 1 of Invoice 101?
8. What happens to Copy 2 of the sales invoice?

EXERCISE C. Using the flowchart "Visualizing a Subsystem for Sales on Credit" on page 386 and the information provided in Topic 1, answer the following questions.

1. How many copies of the shipping order are prepared?
2. Which copy is sent to the customer to verify the order?
3. Why are the extensions and totals checked by people in two different departments?
4. What happens to the shipping order if there are no back orders?
5. Why does the sales department compare Copy 1 with Copy 6 of the shipping order?
6. Why is the customer's credit checked before the goods are prepared for shipment?
7. Should the sales invoice be sent before or after the order is shipped? Why?
8. What are the activities performed by the accounting department in the sales subsystem?

TOPIC 1 PROBLEMS

TOPIC PROBLEM 1. You are employed by MC Enterprises. Two purchase orders received on July 12 are shown below and at the right. Prepare a shipping order for each purchase order. The last shipping order number was 197.

RELIABLE SUPPLY, McAllen, Texas 78504

To: MC Enterprises
Box 3872
Industry, CA 91744

Invoice No. 206
Date: 7/10/--
Ship Via: Express
Terms: 2/10, n/30
Delivery Date: 7/21/--

QUANTITY	STOCK NO.	DESCIPTION	UNIT PRICE	AMOUNT
3	176-2	Tite-Belt sanders, Model 64D	40 00	120 00

Compass Hardware
East Kings Drive
West Covina, California 91791

PURCHASE ORDER NO. E717

TO: MC Enterprises
Box 3872
Industry, CA 91744

Date July 8, 19--
Terms 2/10, n/30
Ship Via Express
Required Delivery Date 7/20/--

QUANTITY	DESCRIPTION	UNIT PRICE	AMOUNT
4	Model No. 78 dustpans	2.20	8.80
3	D-17 garden hoses, 50', 3/8"	5.50	16.50
17 ctn.	30-amp fuses, H-11	2.40	40.80
	TOTAL		66.10

TOPIC PROBLEM 2. Prepare sales invoices for each of the shipping orders in Topic Problem 1. Assume the orders were shipped complete and the invoices were prepared on July 18.

TOPIC PROBLEM 3. Prepare a table to show who prepares or sends the following forms, to whom or where they are sent, and the purpose they serve. Use the flowchart on page 386.

1. Copy 1 of shipping order.
2. Copies 2–7 of shipping order.
3. Copy 2 of shipping order.
4. Copy 3 of shipping order.
5. Copies 4–7 of shipping order.
6. Copy 4 of shipping order (packing slip).
7. Copy 5 of shipping order.
8. Inventory cards (updated).
9. Copies 6 and 7 of shipping order.
10. Copy 1 of shipping order (after all merchandise is shipped).
11. Copy 6 of shipping order.
12. Copy 7 of shipping order.
13. Copy 1 of invoice.
14. Copy 2 of invoice.
15. Copy 7 of shipping order (after invoice is prepared).
16. Physical inventory sheet.

TOPIC 2

Processing Sales on Credit

What are the procedures for recording all receivables from sales transactions? The subsystem for sales usually includes the use of a special sales journal and an accounts receivable subsidiary ledger.

Journalizing Sales on Credit

In order to have information to journalize a credit sale, there must be a source document. In the case of credit sales, Copy 2 of the sales invoice can provide the information. The invoice shows the following.

1. The date of the transaction
2. The invoice number
3. The customer's name
4. The amount of the sale
5. The credit terms

The transaction can be recorded in the general journal. However, when a business has many sales on credit, it often uses a special journal for these transactions. The special journal saves time in journalizing and posting.

Control: Record all receivables.

COMPUTER AGE
200 Girard Avenue
Denver, Colorado 80236

INVOICE NO. 101

SOLD TO: Will's Appliance
16 Del Rey Drive
Denver, Colorado 80219

Invoice Date: 10/7/--

SHIP TO: Same

Terms: 1/20, n/30

Purchase Order No.	Date	Shipped Via	FOB	No. of. Packages
69458	10/2/--	Railway Exp.	Denver	2

QUANTITY	STOCK NUMBER	DESCRIPTION	UNIT PRICE	AMOUNT
8	IR5	Switches	2.94	23.52
6	3GK5	Wire racks	2.46	14.76
1	84-3	Stand, 3-section	11.72	11.72
		TOTAL		50.00
		COPY 2 - ACCOUNTING		

(1) Invoice date; (2) Invoice no.; (3) Sold to; (4) Total; (5) Terms

Sales invoice.

The Sales Journal

A **sales journal** is a special journal used only to record sales of merchandise on credit. The sale of any other asset sold on credit is recorded in the general journal. Any cash sale (of merchandise or another asset) is recorded in the cash receipts journal.

Computer Age makes two kinds of sales on credit. First, goods are sold to other businesses, which, in turn, sell the goods to consumers. Second, Computer Age sells goods directly to consumers. An invoice for each type of sale on credit is shown on page 390.

COMPUTER AGE INVOICE NO. **102**
200 Girard Avenue
Denver, Colorado 80236

SOLD TO: Hallmark Sales — Invoice Date: 10/7/--
17 Chaparral Boulevard
Tucson, Arizona 85718
SHIP TO: Same — Terms: 2/10, n/30

Purchase Order No.	Date	Shipped Via	FOB	No. of Packages
G1768	10/2/--	Railway Express	Tucson	4

QUANTITY	DESCRIPTION	UNIT PRICE	AMOUNT
2	G87 Disk drives	250.00	500.00
6	Monitors	180.00	1,080.00
1 ctn.	Cassette tapes	20.00	20.00
	TOTAL		1,600.00
	COPY 1-CUSTOMER		

Sales invoice for goods sold to a business.

COMPUTER AGE INVOICE NO. **105**
200 Girard Avenue
Denver, Colorado 80236

SOLD TO: James Young — Invoice Date: 10/15/--
200 Hinsdale Avenue
Englewood, Colorado 80112
SHIP TO: — Terms: n/30

Purchase Order No.	Date	Shipped Via	FOB	No. of Packages
Pick-up	--	--	--	1

QUANTITY	DESCRIPTION	UNIT PRICE	AMOUNT
1	Carlsbad 082 video display	700.00	700.00
	Sales Tax		45.50
	TOTAL		745.50
	COPY 1-CUSTOMER		

Sales invoice for goods sold to a consumer.

The sales on credit here are not the same. The sale to a consumer, James Young, includes a sales tax. The sale to a business, Hallmark Sales, does not. Both, however, are recorded in the same sales journal. The sales journal used by Computer Age is illustrated here.

SALES JOURNAL **Page**

DATE	INVOICE NO.	ACCOUNT DEBITED	TERMS	POST. REF.	ACCOUNTS RECEIVABLE DEBIT	SALES TAX PAYABLE CREDIT	SALES CREDIT
					(1)	(2)	(3)

Note that the sales journal used by Computer Age has three money columns. The columns are used as follows.

1. *Accounts Receivable Debit:* Accounts receivable represents money owed by customers. Each entry in the sales journal is a debit to Accounts Receivable because each sale on credit increases the asset Accounts Receivable.

2. *Sales Tax Payable Credit:* Sales Tax Payable is a liability account. Businesses must often collect a sales tax on each sale. Generally, sales made directly to the consumer are subject to a sales tax. Sales made to businesses that will resell the goods are not subject to sales tax. Amounts collected as sales tax must be sent periodically to the government. Thus, an amount in the Sales Tax Payable Credit column shows an increase in the liability Sales Tax Payable.

3. *Sales Credit:* Each sale on credit increases revenue. The revenue account used by many merchandising businesses is Sales. Thus, the Sales Credit column shows an increase in the revenue account Sales.

Now let us analyze the two entries in the sales journal. The first is the sale on credit to Hallmark Sales and does not include a sales tax.

OCTOBER 7: COMPUTER AGE ISSUES INVOICE 102 TO HALLMARK SALES FOR THE SALE OF MERCHANDISE ON CREDIT FOR $1,600.		
What Happens	**Accounting Rule**	**Accounting Entry**
The asset *Accounts Receivable* increases by $1,600.	To increase an asset, debit the account.	Debit: Accounts Receivable, $1,600. (Also debit the customer's account.)
Revenue increases owner's equity by $1,600.	To increase owner's equity, credit the account.	Credit: Sales, $1,600.

This entry increases both assets (Accounts Receivable) and revenue (Sales) by $1,600. Note the following.

1. The invoice number is recorded in the sales journal. Invoices are entered in numeric order to account for every invoice.
2. The credit terms are also entered in the sales journal. The credit terms will be transferred to the customers' accounts at the time of posting. For example, the sale made to Hallmark Sales was made on terms of 2/10, n/30. By having the terms in the customer's account, the accounting clerk can quickly compute the cash discount and the end of the discount period. The Terms column could be eliminated if the company offers the same credit terms to each customer.

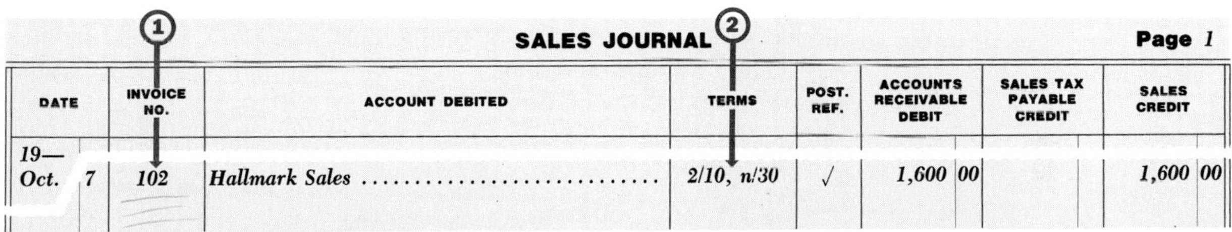

SALES JOURNAL — Page 1

DATE		INVOICE NO.	ACCOUNT DEBITED	TERMS	POST. REF.	ACCOUNTS RECEIVABLE DEBIT	SALES TAX PAYABLE CREDIT	SALES CREDIT
19— Oct.	7	102	*Hallmark Sales*	2/10, n/30	√	1,600 00		1,600 00

Recording sale on credit without sales tax.

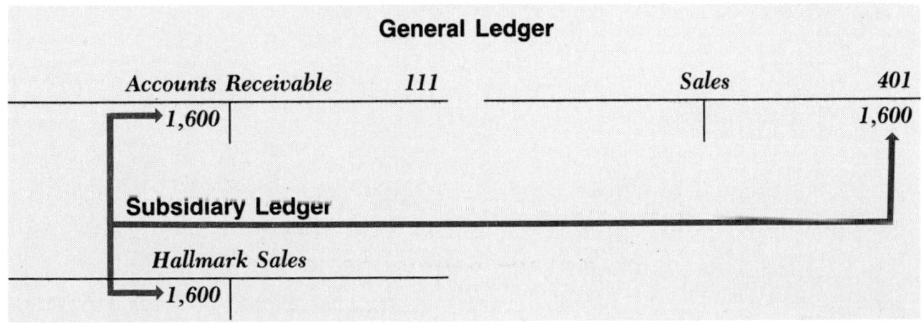

■ Journalizing Sales Taxes

Most states and many cities collect a sales tax. A sales tax is a tax charged on sales of merchandise to consumers. Some states also

COMPUTER AGE CHART OF ACCOUNTS

Liabilities
201 Loans Payable
211 Accounts Payable
216 Sales Tax Payable

charge sales taxes on sales of services. The seller collects the sales taxes and then sends them to the state or city government at specified times. [Notice that Computer Age uses a separate account (216) for recording sales taxes payable to the government.]

The October 15 sale on credit to James Young includes sales tax. The entry to record the sale of taxable merchandise with sales tax to James Young is analyzed as follows.

OCTOBER 15: COMPUTER AGE ISSUES INVOICE 105 TO JAMES YOUNG FOR THE SALE OF MERCHANDISE ON CREDIT FOR $700, PLUS SALES TAX OF $45.50.

What Happens	Accounting Rule	Accounting Entry
The asset *Accounts Receivable* increases by $745.50.	To increase an asset, debit the account.	Debit: Accounts Receivable, $745.50. (Also debit the customer's account.)
The liability *Sales Tax Payable* increases by $45.50.	To increase a liability, credit the account.	Credit: Sales Tax Payable, $45.50.
Revenue increases owner's equity by $700.	To increase owner's equity, credit the account.	Credit: Sales, $700.

This entry increases assets, liabilities, and revenue. The increase in assets (Accounts Receivable) is for the amount of the sale plus the amount of the sales tax. James Young must send $745.50 to Computer Age within 30 days. Computer Age will then send the amount of the sales tax collected from the Young account ($45.50) along with other sales taxes to the government. The journal entry is shown here.

SALES JOURNAL — **Page** *1*

DATE		INVOICE NO.	ACCOUNT DEBITED	TERMS	POST. REF.	ACCOUNTS RECEIVABLE DEBIT	SALES TAX PAYABLE CREDIT	SALES CREDIT
19—								
Oct.	15	105	*James Young*	n/30	√	745 50	45 50	700 00

Recording sale on credit with sales tax.

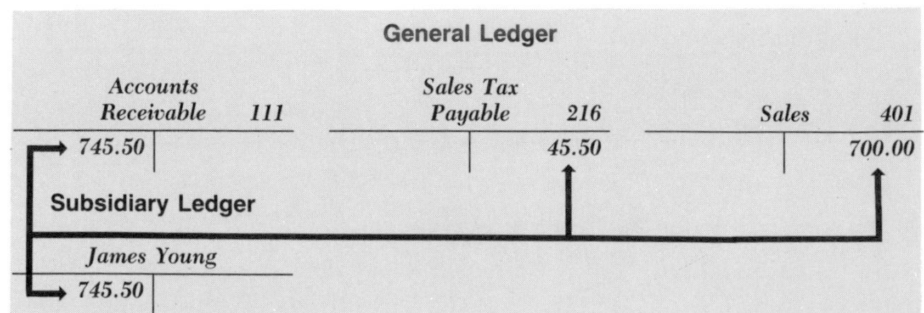

Exercise D on page 399 may be completed at this point.

The Accounts Receivable Ledger

Is there a subsidiary ledger for customers' accounts? Yes, there is. You learned that the creditors' accounts are often removed from the general ledger and placed in the accounts payable subsidiary ledger. It is also more efficient to remove the customers' accounts from the general ledger. They are often placed in alphabetic order in a subsidiary ledger called the accounts receivable ledger. An **accounts receivable ledger** is a subsidiary ledger for customers' accounts. Its use reduces the number of accounts in the general ledger. The general ledger is kept in balance by including an Accounts Receivable controlling account. (Notice that the controlling account for accounts receivable is 111 in the chart of accounts for Computer Age.) The balance of the Accounts Receivable controlling account must equal the total of all the customers' accounts in the accounts receivable ledger. This makes it easier to locate errors on the trial balance.

The balance ledger form is used for the accounts receivable ledger. Here is the accounts receivable ledger used by Computer Age.

COMPUTER AGE CHART OF ACCOUNTS

Assets
101 Cash
102 Petty Cash
103 Change Fund
111 Accounts Receivable
130 Land
131 Building
132 Office Equipment
133 Stockroom Equipment

Revenue
401 Sales

ACCOUNTS RECEIVABLE LEDGER

Name — **Credit Limit**
Address — **Telephone**

DATE	EXPLANATION	POST. REF.	DEBIT	CREDIT	DEBIT BALANCE
			①	②	③

Accounts receivable ledger account.

1. Increases in the customer's account balance are recorded in the Debit column.
2. Payments made by customers are recorded in the Credit column.
3. The customer's account balance is recorded in the Debit Balance column.

Exercise E on page 399 may be completed at this point.

Posting Sales on Credit

What are the procedures for posting from the sales journal? Entries to the customers' accounts should be posted daily to keep each account up to date. Current account balances are especially important to the credit manager. The credit manager determines if sales on credit should be approved and makes sure payments are made on time. If payments are not made promptly, the credit manager must see that the amounts are collected. In order to carry out their responsibilities, credit managers must have current account balances available to them.

Posting entries from the sales journal is similar to posting from other special journals. The procedure is described here.

- Each debit entry in the sales journal is posted to the customer's account in the accounts receivable ledger.

DATE		INVOICE NO.	ACCOUNT DEBITED	TERMS	POST. REF.	ACCOUNTS RECEIVABLE DEBIT	SALES TAX PAYABLE CREDIT	SALES CREDIT
SALES JOURNAL								Page 1
19—								
Oct.	7	101	Will's Appliance	1/20, n/30	✓	50 00		50 00

Posting a debit entry from the sales journal to the customer's account in the accounts receivable ledger.

Name *Will's Appliance* **Credit Limit** *$2,000*
Address *16 Del Rey Drive, Denver, Colorado 80219* **Telephone** *555-5510*

DATE		EXPLANATION	POST. REF.	DEBIT	CREDIT	DEBIT BALANCE
19—						
Oct.	7	Invoice 101; 1/20, n/30	S1	50 00		50 00

- A check mark (✓) is put in the Posting Reference column of the sales journal.
- The letter *S* and the page number are then written in the Posting Reference column in the customer's account to show that the amount was posted from the sales journal.
- At the end of the month, the sales journal is totaled to find the amounts posted to the general ledger. A single rule is drawn across all money columns.
- The money columns are then pencil-footed.
- The equality of the debits and credits is proved by adding the totals of the Sales Tax Payable Credit column ($55.25) and the Sales Credit column ($4,180). The sum must agree with the total of the Accounts Receivable Debit column ($4,235.25).
- After the equality is proved, the totals are written in ink.
- The last line is completed by writing the word *Totals* in the Account Debited column and drawing the double lines.
- The totals of the sales journal are then posted to the proper accounts in the general ledger. The account numbers are written beneath the double rules to show that the totals have been posted.

DATE		INVOICE NO.	ACCOUNT DEBITED	TERMS	POST. REF.	ACCOUNTS RECEIVABLE DEBIT	SALES TAX PAYABLE CREDIT	SALES CREDIT
SALES JOURNAL								Page 1
19—								
Oct.	7	101	Will's Appliance	1/20, n/30	✓	50 00		50 00
	7	102	Hallmark Sales	2/10, n/30	✓	1,600 00		1,600 00
	11	103	Allied Display	2/10, n/30	✓	160 00		160 00
	14	104	Will's Appliance	1/20, n/30	✓	800 00		800 00
	15	105	James Young	n/30	✓	745 50	45 50	700 00
	26	106	Allied Display	2/10, n/30	✓	320 00		320 00
	26	107	James Young	n/30	✓	159 75	9 75	150 00
	30	108	Hallmark Sales	2/10, n/30	✓	400 00		400 00
						4,235 25	55 25	4,180 00
	31		Totals			4,235 25	55 25	4,180 00
						(111)	(216)	(401)

Posting the totals of the sales journal.

ACCOUNTS RECEIVABLE LEDGER

Name *Allied Display* **Credit Limit** *$1,000*
Address *2 Camino del Oeste, Denver, Colorado 80219* **Telephone** *555-3031*

DATE		EXPLANATION	POST. REF.	DEBIT		CREDIT		DEBIT BALANCE	
19—									
Oct.	11	Invoice 103; 2/10, n/30	S1	160	00			160	00
	26	Invoice 106; 2/10, n/30	S1	320	00			480	00

The telephone number and credit limit are included in the accounts receivable ledger.

Name *Electro Computer* **Credit Limit** *$2,000*
Address *Canyon Road, Phoenix, Arizona 85040* **Telephone** *555-3210*

DATE		EXPLANATION	POST. REF.	DEBIT		CREDIT		DEBIT BALANCE	
19—									
June	15	Invoice 37; n/30	S1	25	00			25	00
Aug.	10	Invoice 76; n/30	S1	17	00			42	00
Sept.	5	Invoice 89; n/30	S1	26	00			68	00

Name *Hallmark Sales* **Credit Limit** *$4,000*
Address *17 Chaparral Boulevard, Tucson, Arizona 85718* **Telephone** *555-0701*

DATE		EXPLANATION	POST. REF.	DEBIT		CREDIT		DEBIT BALANCE	
19—									
Oct.	7	Invoice 102; 2/10, n/30	S1	1,600	00			1,600	00
	30	Invoice 108; 2/10, n/30	S1	400	00			2,000	00

Name *Will's Appliance* **Credit Limit** *$2,000*
Address *16 Del Rey Drive, Denver, Colorado 80219* **Telephone** *555-5510*

DATE		EXPLANATION	POST. REF.	DEBIT		CREDIT		DEBIT BALANCE	
19—									
Oct.	7	Invoice 101; 1/20, n/30	S1	50	00			50	00
	14	Invoice 104; 1/20, n/30	S1	800	00			850	00

Name *Wing Computers* **Credit Limit** *$800*
Address *1 Rockview Drive, Fort Collins, Colorado 80524* **Telephone** *555-3286*

DATE		EXPLANATION	POST. REF.	DEBIT		CREDIT		DEBIT BALANCE	
19—									
Aug.	30	Invoice 80; n/30	S1	126	00			126	00

Name *James Young* **Credit Limit** *$1,000*
Address *200 Hinsdale Avenue, Englewood, Colorado 80112* **Telephone** *555-2232*

DATE		EXPLANATION	POST. REF.	DEBIT		CREDIT		DEBIT BALANCE	
19—									
Oct.	15	Invoice 105; n/30	S2	745	50			745	50
	26	Invoice 107; n/30	S1	159	75			905	25

GENERAL LEDGER

Accounts Receivable **Account No.** *111*

DATE		EXPLANATION	POST. REF.	DEBIT		CREDIT		BALANCE DEBIT		BALANCE CREDIT	
19—											
Sept.	30							194	00		
Oct.	31		S1	4,235	25			4,429	25		

Sales Tax Payable **Account No.** *216*

DATE		EXPLANATION	POST. REF.	DEBIT		CREDIT		BALANCE DEBIT		BALANCE CREDIT	
19—											
Oct.	31		S1			55	25			55	25

Sales **Account No.** *401*

DATE		EXPLANATION	POST. REF.	DEBIT		CREDIT		BALANCE DEBIT		BALANCE CREDIT	
19—											
Oct.	31		S1			4,180	00			4,180	00

■ Proving the Accounts Receivable Ledger

At the end of the month, a proof is made to see if the accounts receivable ledger agrees with the Accounts Receivable controlling account in the general ledger. The subsidiary ledger can be proved by using a calculator with an adding machine tape. The balances of the customers' accounts are added. The total is then compared with the balance of the controlling account.

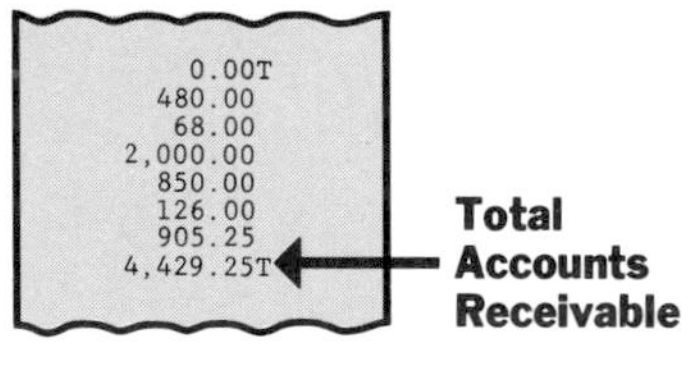

A more formal proof, called a **schedule of accounts receivable**, is a listing of the individual customers' names and the amounts owed. The owner or the credit manager will then use this information to control the amount of credit allowed each customer. A schedule of accounts receivable is illustrated at the top of the next page.

The proof must be prepared at the end of the accounting period before the trial balance is prepared. If the totals do not agree, the error must be located and corrected before the trial balance is prepared. To find an error on the schedule of accounts receivable, the accountant uses the same procedure that is used to locate an error on the trial balance.

You cannot be sure the books are accurate even if the schedule of accounts receivable and the Accounts Receivable controlling account agree. This shows only that the total of the balances in the subsidiary ledger is equal to the controlling account in the general ledger.

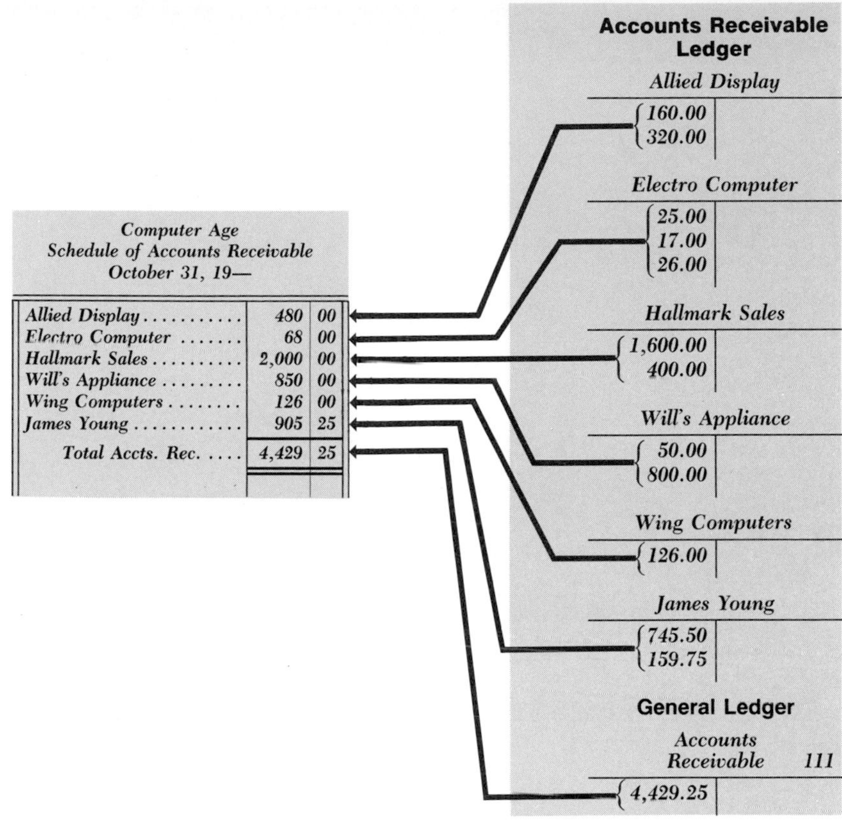

Accounts Receivable Bookkeeper: DOT 210.382-018
Keeps accounts receivable section of the financial records. May journalize accounts receivable transactions, and may post to subsidiary ledger.

Accounts Receivable Clerk: DOT 216.482-010
Performs variety of computing, posting, and other accounting duties for accounts receivable.

Concept: Schedule of Subsidiary Ledger
The equality of the subsidiary ledgers and the controlling accounts must be verified at regular intervals.

Exercise F on page 399 may be completed at this point.

Paying Sales Taxes

Where is the information for paying sales taxes found? The data for the sales tax return is found in the general ledger. For example, if Computer Age were required to file a sales tax return at the end of each month, the accountant would complete a return similar to the one shown at the top of the next page.

STATE OF COLORADO
DEPARTMENT OF REVENUE

DR 100 **COMBINED RETAIL SALES TAX RETURN** — DO NOT WRITE IN THIS SPACE

ACCOUNT NUMBER IS NON-TRANSFERABLE
If new owner, application form DR 594-A must be filed.

1. GROSS SALES AND SERVICES (include bad debts, previously deducted):				$ 4,180 00	
2. LESS DEDUCTIONS:					MAKE CHECKS OR MONEY ORDERS PAYABLE TO: COLORADO DEPARTMENT OF REVENUE
A. Sales to Other Licensed Dealers, For Resale			$ 1,330 00		
B. Other Deductions (must be itemized on reverse side)			$ 120 00		
C. Total Common Deductions			$ 1,450 00		
3. LINE 1 LESS 2C					
Common Net Taxable Sales	$ -0-	$ -0-	$ -0-	$ -0-	
A. Less Sales Out of Taxing Area	$ -0-	$ -0-	$ -0-	$ 2,000	
4. NET Taxable Sales for Each Tax	$ -0-	$ -0-	$ -0-	$ -0-	
COMPUTATION OF TAX	☐ COUNTY 20-31	☐ CITY 99-31	☐ RTD 62-31	☒ STATE 84-31	

16. ENTER TOTAL of All Applicable Columns and Attach Remittance for Total Amount Due $ 55 25

I hereby certify, under penalty of perjury in the second degree, that the statements made herein are to the best of my knowledge true and correct.

Computer Age	*Jason Booth*	Owner	October 31, 19—
NAME OF BUSINESS OR TAXPAYER	AGENT OR OFFICER	TITLE	DATE

General Ledger

Accounts Receivable	*111*
19— *Oct. 31 4,235.25*	

Sales	*401*
	19— *Oct. 31 4,180.00*

Sales Tax Payable	*216*
	19— *Oct. 31 55.25*

Sales tax return is completed from general ledger.

The amount of sales tax due ($55.25) is recorded in the Sales Tax Payable account. A check is drawn for this amount and is entered in the cash payments journal. Sales Tax Payable is debited for $55.25 because the liability account is decreased. After the entry is posted, the Sales Tax Payable account will have a zero balance.

CASH PAYMENTS JOURNAL — **Page** *4*

DATE		ACCOUNT DEBITED	EXPLANATION	CHECK NO.	POST. REF.	GENERAL LEDGER DEBIT	ACCOUNTS PAYABLE DEBIT	PURCHASES DISCOUNT CREDIT	NET CASH CREDIT
19— *Nov.*	*8*	*Sales Tax Payable . .*	*October return . . . . .*	*313*	*216*	*55 25*			*55 25*

Paying sales tax.

Sales Tax Payable	*216*
19— *Nov. 8 CP4 55.25*	*19—* *Oct. 31 S1 55.25*

The same procedure is used for sales taxes on cash sales. Of course, the sale and the sales tax are recorded in the cash receipts journal instead of the sales journal. Two entries are required in a one-column cash receipts journal to record the amounts because there are two credits. One credit is to the Sales account. The second credit is to the Sales Tax Payable account.

CASH RECEIPTS JOURNAL — **Page** *4*

DATE		ACCOUNT CREDITED	EXPLANATION	POST. REF.	AMOUNT
19— *Nov.*	*15*	*Sales . . . .*	*Cash sales for week . . . . . .*	*401*	*300 00*
		Sales Tax Payable.	*Taxes on cash sales . . . . . .*	*216*	*19 50*

Recording sales tax on cash sales.

Exercise G on page 399 may be completed at this point.

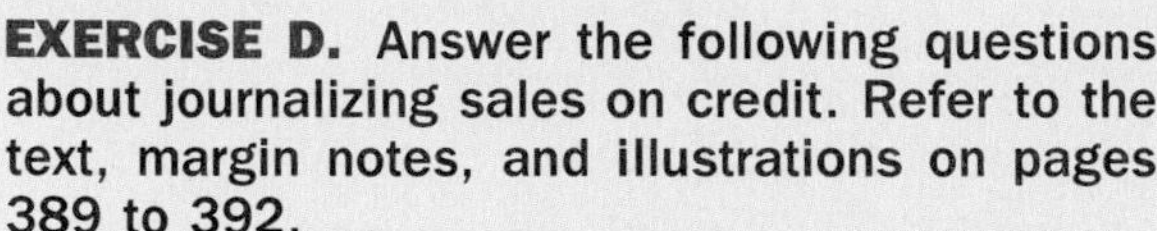

TOPIC 2 EXERCISES

EXERCISE D. Answer the following questions about journalizing sales on credit. Refer to the text, margin notes, and illustrations on pages 389 to 392.

1. What copy of the invoice is used as the source document for an entry in the sales journal?
2. In which journal would the sale of used office equipment on account be recorded?
3. An entry in the sales journal (without sales tax) means that three accounts are affected. What are these three accounts?
4. What types of entries are recorded in the sales journal?

EXERCISE E. Answer the following questions about the accounts receivable ledger. Refer to the text and illustrations on page 393.

1. Which accounts are placed in the accounts receivable ledger?
2. Which account is placed in the general ledger when a business uses an accounts receivable ledger?
3. How is the balance of each customer's account computed?

EXERCISE F. Answer the following questions about posting the sales on credit. Refer to the sales journal, subsidiary ledger accounts, and general ledger accounts shown on pages 393 to 397.

1. If the first October 7 sale had been entered in the general journal instead of the sales journal, what would the complete entry have been?
2. When the first October 7 sale was posted, was the Sales account credited for $50 at the same time? Why or why not?
3. What amount was posted to the Sales account on October 31? Was this amount debited or credited? Why?
4. If Allied Display wanted to pay its account on October 27, how much would it have to pay?
5. How is the accuracy of the accounts receivable subsidiary ledger proven?
6. Would proving the accounts receivable ledger identify a posting to Will's Appliance that should have been posted to Hallmark Sales? Why?
7. Are both the Accounts Receivable controlling account and the individual subsidiary ledger accounts listed on a trial balance? Why or why not?

EXERCISE G. Answer the following questions about paying sales taxes. Refer to the text and illustrations on pages 397 to 398.

1. What source of information is used to complete the sales tax return?
2. Which journal is used to record the payment of sales taxes?
3. What is the amount of sales tax due on October 31? On November 10?

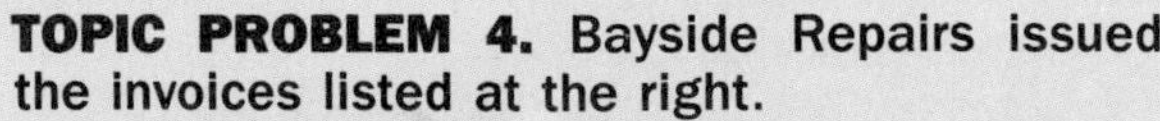

TOPIC 2 PROBLEMS

TOPIC PROBLEM 4. Bayside Repairs issued the invoices listed at the right.

a. Open general ledger accounts for Accounts Receivable, Sales Tax Payable, and Sales, and open subsidiary ledger accounts for the following customers.
General Distributors, 314 Lakeview Dr., Jackson, Mississippi 39205; credit limit, $1,500; phone, 555-9241
Maria Lopez, 15 Willow Dr., Jackson, Mississippi 39208; credit limit, $1,000; phone, 555-6143
Simpson Company, 47 Lorenz Dr., Jackson, Mississippi 39216; credit limit, $750; phone 555-3126

b. Record the sales transactions in the sales journal.

c. Post the debit entries from the sales journal.

d. Prove, total, and rule the sales journal.

e. Post the totals of the sales journal.

f. Prepare a schedule of accounts receivable. (Compare the total of the schedule with the balance of the Accounts Receivable controlling account.)

July 2 Invoice 710 to General Distributors for $500; terms 1/15, n/30.
11 Invoice 711 to Maria Lopez for $160 plus $8.00 sales tax; terms n/30.
15 Invoice 712 to Simpson Company for $380; terms 1/10, n/30.
23 Invoice 713 to Maria Lopez for $140 plus 5 percent sales tax; terms n/30.
28 Invoice 714 to Simpson Company for $240; terms 1/10, n/30.
30 Invoice 715 to Maria Lopez for $140 plus 5 percent sales tax; terms n/30.

TOPIC PROBLEM 5. The Garden Knit Shop must collect a 4 percent sales tax on all sales of merchandise. During May the store issued the invoices listed at the right.

a. Open general ledger accounts for Accounts Receivable, Sales Tax Payable, and Sales. Open subsidiary ledger accounts for Isaac Jones, Margo Yarns, Inc., and John Olson.

b. Record the transactions in a sales journal.

c. Post the individual entries from the sales journal.

d. Prove, total, and rule the sales journal.

e. Post the totals from the sales journal.

f. Prepare a schedule of accounts receivable. (Verify the total.)

g. In a multicolumn cash payments journal, record Check 216 issued on June 2 to remit the sales taxes for the month of May. Post the debit entry to the general ledger.

May 7 Invoice 430 to John Olson for $200; tax $8.00; terms n/30.
12 Invoice 431 to Margo Yarns, Inc., for $170 plus $6.80 tax; terms 1/10, n/30.
16 Invoice 432 to John Olson for $110 plus $4.40 tax; terms n/30.
22 Invoice 433 to Margo Yarns, Inc., for $80 plus $3.20 tax; terms 1/10, n/30.
29 Invoice 434 to Isaac Jones for $380 plus $15.20 tax; terms 1/15, n/30.

TOPIC 3

Controlling Net Sales

What is meant by net sales? Net sales is the difference between the amounts recorded in the Sales account and the total of sales returns and allowances plus sales discounts.

Sales Returns and Sales Allowance

When are refunds and credits issued for unacceptable merchandise? A subsystem must have controls to make sure that refunds and credits are given only for approved returns and allowances. The seller sometimes allows a customer to return unacceptable merchandise. As stated earlier, the reasons for returning merchandise vary. The merchandise may be damaged. The wrong items or quantities of items may have been sent. Or customers may find that the items do not meet their needs. In such cases, the seller generally allows a customer to return the items. The seller calls returned items **sales returns**.

Sometimes a customer agrees to keep the merchandise if he or she is given a reduction from the invoice price. Reductions from the sales price are called **sales allowances**.

In the previous chapter, returns and allowances are discussed from the customer's point of view as purchases returns and allowances. Now, returns and allowances are presented from the seller's point of view as *sales returns and allowances*.

Refunding Cash for Sales Returns and Allowances

Cash customers usually want returns and allowances refunded in cash. Cash refunds are made by taking the money out of the cash register or by drawing a check.

Control: Issue refunds and credits only for approved returns and allowances.

Refunds in Cash Cash refunds made from the cash register are shown on the cash proof. For example, the cash proof illustrated below shows the following.

1. $380 in cash was received from sales during the week.
2. $7 in cash was paid out of the drawer for returns and allowances.

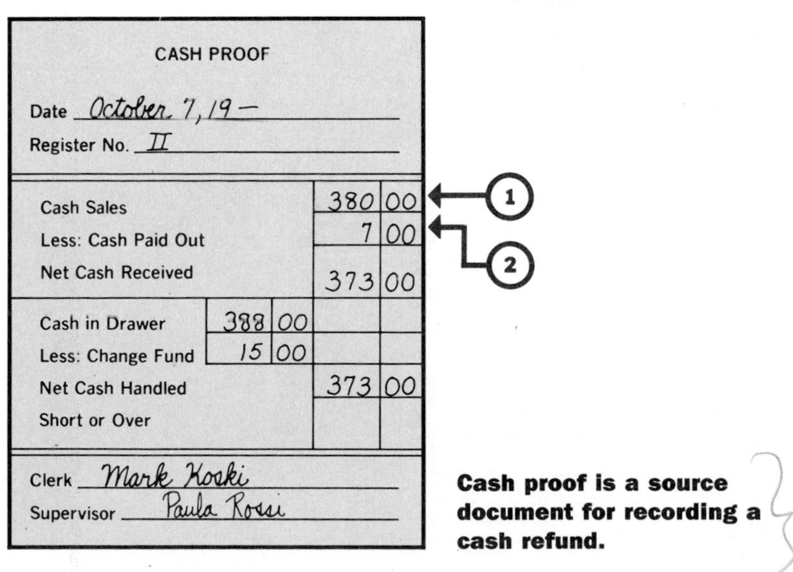

CASH PROOF

Date October 7, 19—
Register No. II

Cash Sales			380	00
Less: Cash Paid Out			7	00
Net Cash Received			373	00
Cash in Drawer	388	00		
Less: Change Fund	15	00		
Net Cash Handled			373	00
Short or Over				

Clerk Mark Koski
Supervisor Paula Rossi

Cash proof is a source document for recording a cash refund.

The entry to record the cash proof includes a debit for $380 to the Cash account to show the increase in assets. The Sales account is credited for $380 to show the increase in owner's equity caused by the revenue.

CASH RECEIPTS JOURNAL Page 3

DATE		ACCOUNT CREDITED	EXPLANATION	POST. REF.	AMOUNT
19—					
Oct.	7	Sales	Cash sales for week	401	380 00

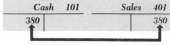

The amount of cash paid out for returns and allowances ($7) must also be recorded. The Cash account is credited to show the decrease in assets. Also, some of the revenue recorded in the Sales account has not been earned. Thus, the total amount of sales must be reduced. Sales could be reduced by debiting the Sales account. (Since sales increase owner's equity, sales returns decrease owner's equity.) However, it is a better practice to keep a record of sales returns and allowances in a separate temporary owner's equity account called the **Sales Returns and Allowances account**. In this way, information is available about the amount of sales and the amount and number of sales returns and allowances. (The Sales and the Sales Returns and Allowances accounts are closely related. Thus, the Sales account number is 401 and the Sales Returns and Allowances account number is 402.)

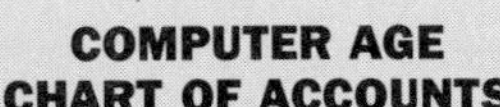

Revenue
401 Sales
402 Sales Returns and Allowances

The entry to record returns and allowances is a debit to the Sales Returns and Allowances account for $7 and a credit to the Cash account for $7. The entry is made in the cash payments journal.

CASH PAYMENTS JOURNAL Page 4

DATE		ACCOUNT DEBITED	EXPLANATION	CHECK NO.	POST. REF.	GENERAL LEDGER DEBIT	ACCOUNTS PAYABLE DEBIT	PURCHASES DISCOUNT CREDIT	NET CASH CREDIT
19—									
Oct.	7	Sales Ret. and Allow.	Returns for week	—	402	7 00			7 00

Recording cash paid for sales returns and allowances.

The result of posting all entries for the month, as shown here, is a net increase in the Cash account of $373 (a debit of $380 less a credit of $7). Also, there is a debit to the Sales Returns and Allowances account of $7. The credit is to the Sales account for $380.

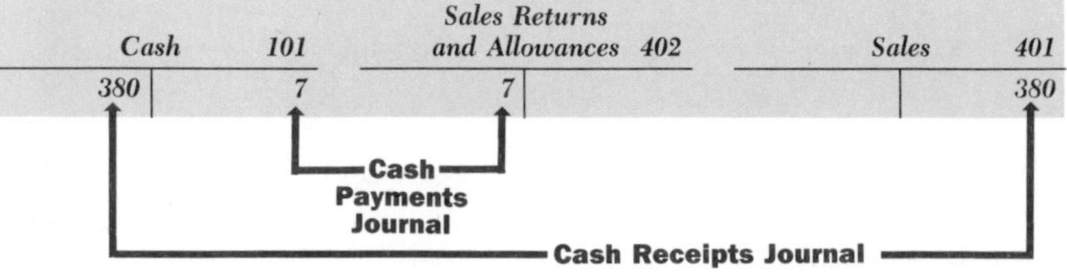

Effect of posting cash paid for sales returns and allowances.

Revenue From Sales:		
Sales	380	00
Less: Sales Returns and Allowances . .	7	00
Net Sales	373	00

Sales Returns and Allowances	
(Debit) For amount of all returns and allowances on merchandise sold.	

Sales	
	(Credit) For amount of all merchandise sold.

The Sales Returns and Allowances account, like the Sales account, is a temporary owner's equity account. Both accounts are included on the income statement. The amount of sales returns and allowances is subtracted from the amount of sales to find the net sales. Both the Sales Returns and Allowances and the Sales accounts are closed into the Income Summary account at the end of the accounting period.

The information in the Sales Returns and Allowances account is used to analyze the operations of the business. For example, if the amount of the returns and allowances becomes large, management should find out why. Are errors being made on shipping orders? Is the quality of the merchandise poor? Is the merchandise being packed so that damages occur in shipping?

Refunds by Check When a check is drawn to make the refund, the check stub is the source document for the journal entry. For example, on November 8 Computer Age issued Check 320 to refund $20 to John Weber. The entry is recorded in the cash payments journal shown below.

CASH PAYMENTS JOURNAL — Page 4

DATE		ACCOUNT DEBITED	EXPLANATION	CHECK NO.	POST. REF.	GENERAL LEDGER DEBIT		ACCOUNTS PAYABLE DEBIT		PURCHASES DISCOUNT CREDIT		NET CASH CREDIT	
19—													
Nov.	8	Sales Ret. and Allow.	J. Weber	320	402	20	00					20	00

Record check for sales returns and allowances.

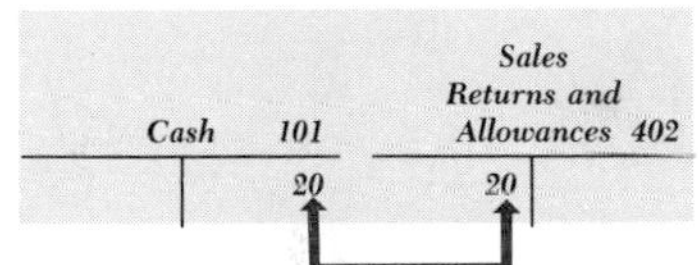

The effect of posting all the entries for the month is a debit to the Sales Returns and Allowances account and a credit to the Cash account for $20.

Exercise H on page 410 may be completed at this point.

Granting Credit for Sales Returns and Allowances

What happens when customers are given credit for returns and allowances? Customers who have not paid for merchandise are not given a cash refund for returns or allowances. Instead, the seller issues a credit memorandum to apply against the amount the customer owes.

Credit Memorandum A credit memorandum is issued by the seller and shows that the customer's account is being reduced. The credit memorandum states the customer's name, the amount of the credit, and the reason for the credit. For example, on October 7, Invoice 102 was issued for $1,600 to Hallmark Sales. The invoice is shown on page 404.

PROCESSING SALES RETURNS AND ALLOWANCES

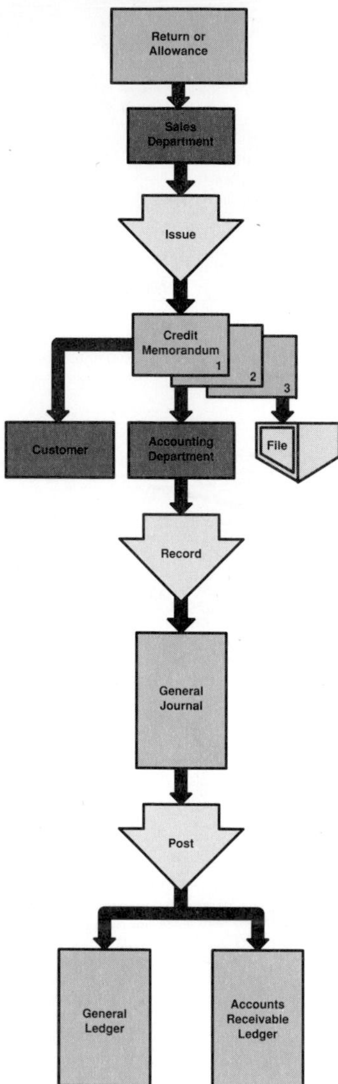

COMPUTER AGE INVOICE NO. **102**
200 Girard Avenue
Denver, Colorado 80236

SOLD TO: Hallmark Sales
17 Chaparral Boulevard
Tucson, Arizona 85718

Invoice Date: 10/7/--

SHIP TO: Same

Terms: 2/10, n/30

Purchase Order No.	Date	Shipped Via	FOB	No. of. Packages
G1768	10/2/--	Railway Express	Tucson	4

QUANTITY	DESCRIPTION	UNIT PRICE	AMOUNT
2	G87 Disk drives	250.00	500.00
6	Monitors	180.00	1,080.00
1 ctn.	Cassette tape	20.00	20.00
	TOTAL		1,600.00

COPY 1-CUSTOMER

Sales invoice.

When Hallmark Sales received the items ordered, they found the monitors were damaged. Hallmark Sales got permission to repair the monitors instead of returning them. In exchange, Computer Age reduced the total price for all six monitors by $100. The sales department of Computer Age then issued Credit Memorandum CM-12 for $100.

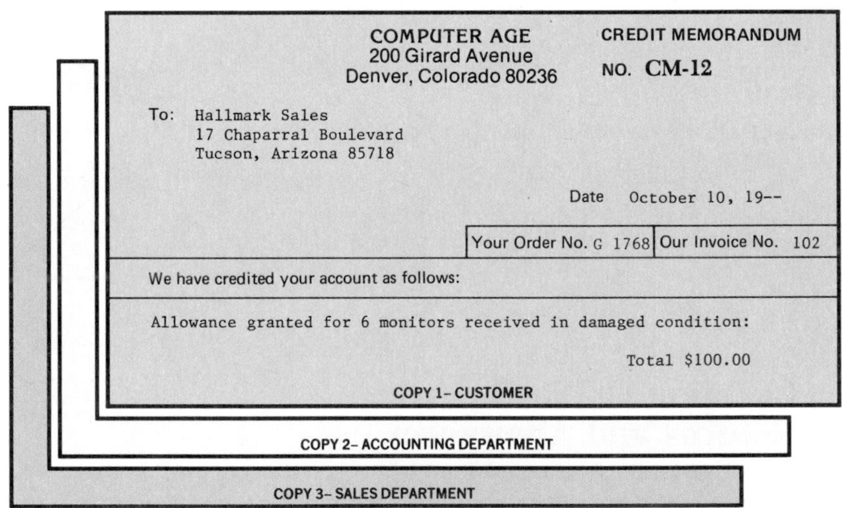
COMPUTER AGE
200 Girard Avenue
Denver, Colorado 80236

CREDIT MEMORANDUM
NO. **CM-12**

To: Hallmark Sales
17 Chaparral Boulevard
Tucson, Arizona 85718

Date October 10, 19--

Your Order No. G 1768 | Our Invoice No. 102

We have credited your account as follows:

Allowance granted for 6 monitors received in damaged condition:

Total $100.00

COPY 1- CUSTOMER

COPY 2- ACCOUNTING DEPARTMENT

COPY 3- SALES DEPARTMENT

Credit memorandum is a source document for recording credit for sales return or allowance.

The credit memorandum is prenumbered. It is issued in three copies. One copy goes to the customer. It becomes the customer's source document for an entry to decrease the account with Computer Age. The second copy goes to the seller's accounting department. It becomes the source document for crediting the customer's account. The third copy is kept by the sales department for its file. After the credit memorandum has been recorded by the seller and the customer, their records should agree on the amount owed.

■ Recording Sales Returns and Allowances The entry to record a credit memorandum reduces the revenue from sales and accounts receivable by the same amount. Thus, when the credit memorandum that has been issued to Hallmark Sales is recorded in the accounting records of Computer Age, an entry is made in the general journal to decrease the amount of the sale (a debit of $100) and the accounts receivable (a credit of $100).

Oct. 10 Computer Age issues Credit Memorandum CM-12 for $100 to Hallmark Sales for allowance on merchandise sold on credit.

The debit of $100 is posted to the Sales Returns and Allowances account in the general ledger. The credit of $100 must be double-posted. It is posted both to the Accounts Receivable controlling account in the general ledger and to the customer's account in the subsidiary ledger.

After this entry has been posted, the accounts in the general ledger are in balance, and the customer's account in the subsidiary ledger is updated.

GENERAL JOURNAL — Page 2

DATE		ACCOUNT TITLE AND EXPLANATION	POST. REF.	DEBIT		CREDIT	
19—							
Oct.	10	*Sales Returns and Allowances*	*402*	*100*	*00*		
		Accounts Receivable/Hallmark Sales	*111/√*			*100*	*00*
		Credit Memorandum CM-12.					

General Ledger

Accounts Receivable 111	
1,600	*100*

Sales 401	
	1,600

Sales Returns and Allowances 402	
100	

Subsidiary Ledger

Hallmark Sales	
1,600	*100*

Recording and posting credit memorandum.

A company that has many sales returns and allowances can use a special sales returns and allowances journal. The recording and posting procedures used for the sales returns and allowances journal are similar to those used for the sales journal.

■ Sales Taxes on Sales Returns and Allowances

In states and cities where sales taxes are collected, an additional entry must be made when sales returns and allowances are recorded. Recall the transaction of October 26, in which James Young bought merchandise on credit for $150 and was charged $9.75 in sales tax. The amount of the sale ($150) was credited to the Sales account. The amount of the sales tax ($9.75) was credited to the Sales Tax Payable account. The customer's account and the Accounts Receivable controlling account were debited for $159.75.

SALES JOURNAL — **Page** *1*

DATE		INVOICE NO.	ACCOUNT DEBITED	TERMS	POST. REF.	ACCOUNTS RECEIVABLE DEBIT	SALES TAX PAYABLE CREDIT	SALES CREDIT
19—								
Oct.	*26*	*107*	*James Young*	*n/30*	√	*159 75*	*9 75*	*150 00*

Assume that this was the only entry recorded in the sales journal during the month. The accounts would then show the amounts illustrated below at the end of the month.

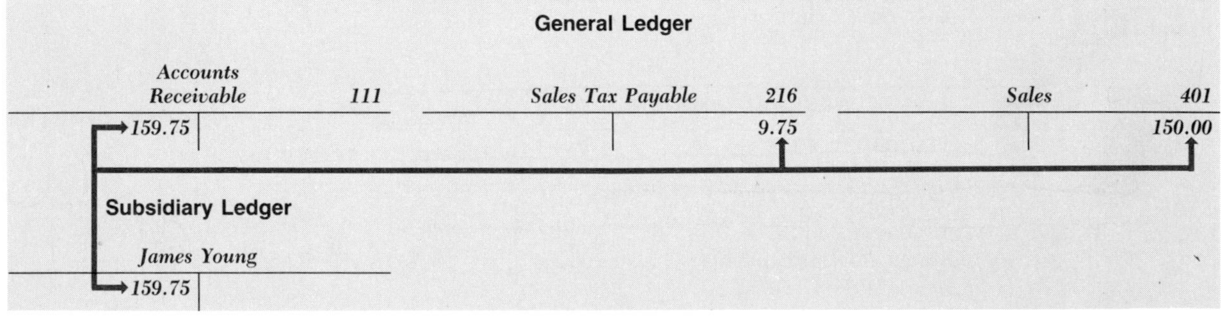

If the entire sale is returned, an entry must be made in the general journal to show the effect on all accounts. The necessary entries are illustrated here. The sales tax on the original sale is no longer payable to the governmental agency. Thus, the Sales Tax Payable account is reduced by the amount of the tax that was charged. Neither the customer nor the business must pay the tax.

Entry is double-posted.

GENERAL JOURNAL — **Page** 3

DATE		ACCOUNT TITLE AND EXPLANATION	POST. REF.	DEBIT	CREDIT
19—					
Oct.	*29*	*Sales Returns and Allowances*	*402*	*150 00*	
		Sales Tax Payable	*216*	*9 75*	
		Accounts Receivable/James Young	*111/√*		*159 75*
		Credit Memorandum CM-13.			

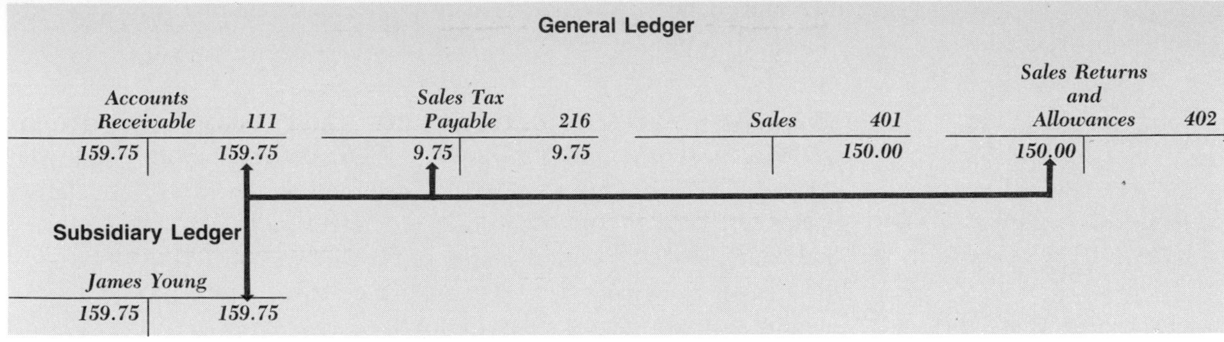

Recording credit memorandum with sales tax (entire sale returned).

If James Young returned only $50 of the merchandise, the following entry would be made.

GENERAL JOURNAL Page 3

DATE		ACCOUNT TITLE AND EXPLANATION	POST. REF.	DEBIT		CREDIT	
19—							
Oct.	29	*Sales Returns and Allowances*	402	50	00		
		Sales Tax Payable	216	3	25		
		Accounts Receivable/James Young	111/√			53	25
		Credit Memorandum CM-13.					

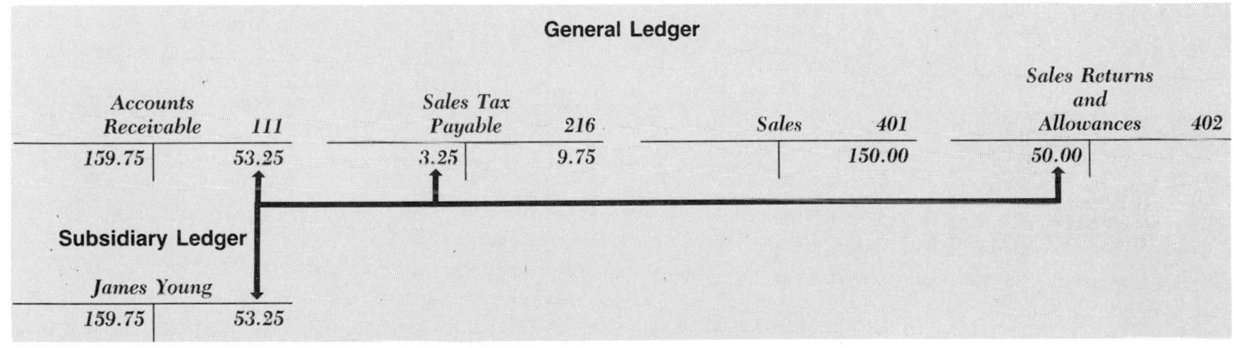

Recording credit memorandum with sales tax (part of sale returned).

In this entry, Sales Tax Payable was debited for $3.25 to cancel the amount of tax charged on $50 of merchandise (6.5 percent × $50). The balance of the Sales Tax Payable account is now $6.50, which is 6.5 percent of the actual sale ($100).

■ Delivery Charges

If the seller agrees to deliver the merchandise to the buyer, the shipping terms are FOB destination. Thus, on FOB destination sales, the seller considers any delivery payments to airlines or trucking companies as part of the expense to sell the merchandise. The amounts paid by the seller for making deliveries are debited to a separate expense

COMPUTER AGE CHART OF ACCOUNTS

Costs and Expenses
513 Delivery Expense

Exercise I on page 411 may be completed at this point.

account called Delivery Expense. (Remember that transportation charges on purchases are debited to Transportation In.)

Using Sales Discounts to Encourage Payment

Why is it important to collect accounts receivable promptly? Money owed to a business by its customers is "tied up." That is, it cannot be used for other purposes. It cannot be used to purchase new merchandise, to buy other assets, or to pay expenses. Thus, a business that is slow in collecting accounts receivable often has to borrow money at high interest rates to continue operations.

Control receivables as soon as possible by
- Recording customers' accounts
- Recording payments within discount period
- Informing customers with statements of account
- Determining if payments are made promptly

To encourage customers to pay their invoices quickly, some businesses offer cash discounts. To the customer a cash discount is a purchase discount. To the seller, a cash discount is a **sales discount**.

Look at the October 7 sales invoice issued to Will's Appliance for \$50. The terms on the sale are 1/20, n/30. Thus, if Will's Appliance pays on or before October 27 (20 days after October 7), it may deduct 1 percent of \$50 (\$0.50) from the invoice. Will's Appliance would then pay \$49.50 (\$50 − \$0.50). If Will's Appliance does not pay within the discount period, the full amount of \$50 will be due by November 6 (30 days after October 7).

Sales discount

COMPUTER AGE — INVOICE NO. **101**
200 Girard Avenue
Denver, Colorado 80236

SOLD TO: Will's Appliance — Invoice Date: 10/7/--
16 Del Rey Drive
Denver, Colorado 80219

SHIP TO: Same — Terms: 1/20, n/30

Purchase Order No.	Date	Shipped Via	FOB	No. of Packages
69458	10/2/--	Truck Exp.	Denver	2

QUANTITY	STOCK NUMBER	DESCRIPTION	UNIT PRICE	AMOUNT
8	IR5	Switches	2.94	23.32
6	3GK5	Wire racks	2.46	14.76
1	84-3	Stand, 3-section	11.72	11.72
			TOTAL	50.00
		COPY 1-CUSTOMER		

Sales invoice prepared from shipping order (Copy 7).

Receiving Payments

A sales discount is not recorded at the time the invoice is journalized. The seller does not know if the customer will pay within the discount period. Thus, when the sales invoice is recorded, the customer's account is debited for the amount of the invoice.

Assume Will's Appliance pays on November 6 the \$50 it owes to Computer Age on Invoice 101, dated October 7. The check must then be for \$50. Payment is received in the credit period but not in the discount period. The entry is recorded in the cash receipts journal and has the following effects.

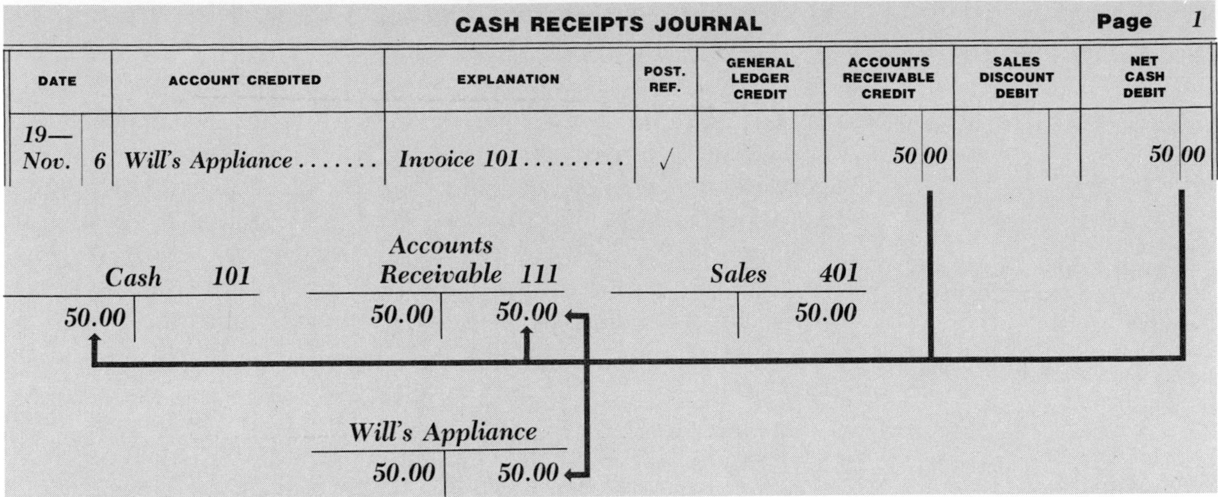

CASH RECEIPTS JOURNAL
Page 1
DATE
ACCOUNT CREDITED
EXPLANATION
POST. REF.
GENERAL LEDGER CREDIT
ACCOUNTS RECEIVABLE CREDIT
SALES DISCOUNT DEBIT
NET CASH DEBIT
19—
Nov. 6 Will's Appliance . . . .
Invoice 101 . . . .
✓
50 00
50 00
Cash 101
50.00
Accounts Receivable 111
50.00
50.00
Sales 401
50.00
Will's Appliance
50.00
50.00

Receiving cash from credit sales.

Suppose, however, that Will's Appliance pays the invoice within the discount period. The check would then be for $49.50. The cash receipt is analyzed as follows.

1. The customer's account shows a debit balance of $50. The account must be credited for $50 to show that the account has been paid.

2. The check amounts to $49.50. Thus, the Cash account must be debited for $49.50 because that is the amount of cash received.

3. The cash discount of $0.50 must be debited to some account. The discount reduces the revenue from the sale to Will's Appliance and at the same time decreases owner's equity. The debit entry to decrease owner's equity could be to the Sales account. However, it is common accounting practice to record a sales discount in a temporary owner's equity account called Sales Discount. The owner or manager then has a record of all discounts allowed and can see the reduction in revenue due to the discount policy.

Rate of cash discount = 1%
1% × $50 = $0.50 (amount of discount)
$50 − $0.50 = $49.50 (amount received)

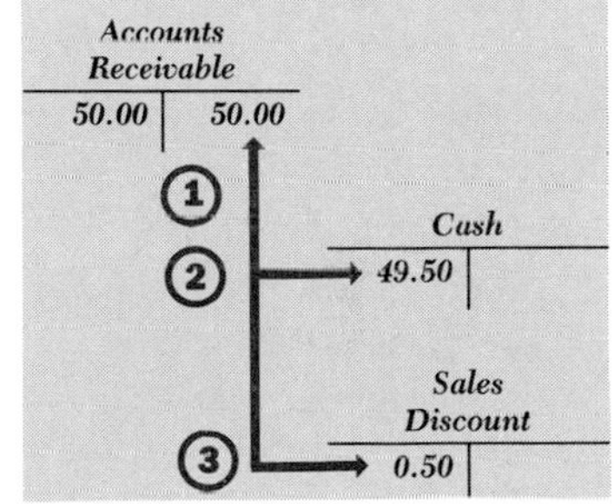

OCTOBER 26: COMPUTER AGE RECEIVES CASH FROM WILL'S APPLIANCE IN PAYMENT OF INVOICE FOR $50 LESS CASH DISCOUNT OF $0.50.

What Happens	Accounting Rule	Accounting Entry
The asset *Cash* increases by $49.50. The cash discount decreases owner's equity by $0.50. The asset *Accounts Receivable* decreases by $50.	To increase an asset, debit the account. To decrease owner's equity, debit the account. To decrease an asset, credit the account.	Debit: Cash, $49.50. Debit: Sales Discount, $0.50. Credit: Accounts Receivable, $50. (Also the customer's account.)

Net amount of invoice = $1,600 − $100 = $1,500
Rate of cash discount = 2%
2% × $1,500 = $30 (amount of discount)
$1,500 − $30 = $1,470 (amount received)

Amount of invoice = $160 + $10.40 = $170.40
Rate of cash discount = 2%
2% × $160 = $3.20 (amount of discount)
$170.40 − $3.20 = $167.20 (amount received)

Sales Taxes, Sales Returns and Allowances, and Sales Discounts

Sales discounts are given only on the net sales price. Sales discounts are not given on any amount for which a credit memorandum was given (sales return or allowance), or on any sales tax charged. For example, the entry of October 17 in the cash receipts journal shows that Hallmark Sales was allowed a sales discount of $30. The original amount of the invoice was $1,600 (Invoice 102 of October 7). However, the customer was granted a sales allowance of $100 on October 10 (Credit Memorandum CM-12). Hallmark Sales, therefore, was granted a discount on $1,500 ($1,600 − $100), which was the net amount of the sale.

Sales discounts are not given on any sales taxes. On a sale of $160 with terms of 2/10, n/30, for example, the sales tax of 6.5 percent charged to the customer would be $10.40. If the invoice is paid within the discount period, a sales discount is allowed on the $160 only—not on the $10.40. Thus, the sales discount would be $3.20 (2 percent × $160). The customer would have to pay $167.20 ($160 + $10.40 − $3.20).

COMPUTER AGE CHART OF ACCOUNTS

Revenue
401 Sales
402 Sales Returns and Allowances
403 Sales Discount

Revenue From Sales:		
Sales	4,180	00
Less: Sales Returns and Allowances . . $120.00		
Sales Discount 30.50	150	50
Net Sales	4,029	50

Finding Net Revenue

The amount of net revenue earned by a business is computed from the amount of sales. **Gross sales** is the amount of sales found in the Sales account.

To find the net revenue from gross sales, subtract the balance of the Sales Discount account from the Sales account. If Sales Returns and Allowances has a balance, it must also be subtracted from the Sales account. These three accounts are related, and they are assigned numbers 401, 402, and 403.

Exercise J on page 411 may be completed at this point.

TOPIC 3 EXERCISES

EXERCISE H. Answer the following questions on sales returns and allowances. Refer to the cash proof and cash receipts journal on pages 401 and 402 and the cash payments journals on pages 402 and 403.

1. What is the date of the cash proof?
2. How much are the cash sales?
3. How much cash is paid for returns and allowances?
4. What is the entry to record cash sales for the week ended October 7?
5. Is the Sales Returns and Allowances account a permanent or a temporary account?
6. Is the refund to John Weber made in cash or by check?

EXERCISE I. Answer the following questions about granting credit for sales returns and allowances. Refer to the credit memorandum on page 404 and the journals shown on pages 405 to 407.

1. What company receives the credit memorandum? Who is the seller?

2. In which journal is the credit memorandum recorded? Why?

3. How will the credit entry of October 20 be posted to the Accounts Receivable controlling account?

4. Why is the Sales Tax Payable account debited on October 29?

5. Why is the James Young account credited for $53.25 and not $50 on October 29?

6. What is the net sale to James Young?

7. How much sales tax will be paid by James Young?

EXERCISE J. Below you will find amounts for gross sales, sales returns and allowances, sales discounts, and net sales. Use these amounts to complete the following chart.

	Gross Sales	Sales Returns and Allowances	Sales Discounts	Net Sales
a.	$10,000	$ 350	$ 30	?
b.	?	550	150	$14,500
c.	30,000	600	?	28,800
d.	40,000	?	800	37,000
e.	35,000	1,500	0	?

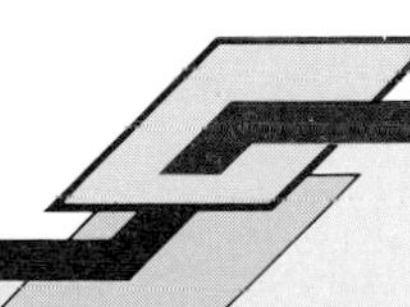

TOPIC 3 PROBLEMS

TOPIC PROBLEM 6. Perform the following accounting activities for TG Sales.

a. Open the general ledger accounts, assign appropriate numbers, and record the February 1 balances as follows: Cash, $18,400; Accounts Receivable; Sales Tax Payable; Thomas Gallo, Capital, $18,400; Sales; Sales Returns and Allowances; and Delivery Expense. Open accounts for Alvarez, Inc., and Bruce Roberts in the accounts receivable subsidiary ledger.

b. Record the transactions for February in a sales journal, a cash receipts journal, a cash payments journal, and a general journal.

c. Post the individual entries from the sales journal, cash payments journal, cash receipts journal, and general journal.

d. Prove, total, and rule the special journals.

e. Post the totals from the special journals.

f. Prepare a schedule of accounts receivable. (Verify that the total of the schedule of accounts receivable agrees with the Accounts Receivable controlling account.)

g. Prepare a trial balance.

Feb. 3 Sold merchandise for $720 on credit to Alvarez, Inc.; Invoice 255; terms 2/10, n/30.

Feb. 4 Recorded returns and allowances of $12 on the cash proof for the weekly cash sales. Sales were $700.

5 Issued $80 allowance to Alvarez, Inc., for returned merchandise costing $80; Credit Memorandum CM-251.

13 Sold merchandise for $680 plus $13.60 sales tax on credit to Bruce Roberts; Invoice 256; terms n/30.

13 Issued Check 86 for $50 to Rapid Express for delivering merchandise sold to Bruce Roberts, FOB destination.

Feb. 21 Sold merchandise for $600 on credit to Alvarez, Inc.; Invoice 257; terms 2/10, n/30.

25 Issued Check 87 for $40 to Kelly Nichols for returned merchandise sold for cash.

26 Issued $40 allowance to Alvarez, Inc., for scratched merchandise; Credit Memorandum CM-252.

TOPIC PROBLEM 7. During March, Multitronics had the sales on credit listed here. (Sales tax is 4 percent.)

a. Open accounts in the general ledger for Accounts Receivable, Sales Tax Payable, Sales, and Sales Returns and Allowances. Open accounts for Harold Brooks and Nicole Simms in the accounts receivable subsidiary ledger.

b. Record each of the transactions for March in a sales journal or in a general journal.

c. Post the individual entries from the sales journal and the general journal.

d. Prove, total, and rule the sales journal.

e. Post the totals from the sales journal.

f. Prepare a schedule of accounts receivable. (Verify the total.)

Mar. 6 Sold merchandise for $360 on credit to Nicole Simms; Invoice 896; terms 1/10, n/30; sales tax, $14.40.

7 Nicole Simms returned merchandise sold for $60; Credit Memorandum CM-247; sales tax, $2.40.

16 Sold merchandise for $865 on credit to Harold Brooks; Invoice 897; terms 2/10, n/30; sales tax, $34.60.

17 Issued allowance of $20 to Harold Brooks for imperfect merchandise; Credit Memorandum CM-248; sales tax, $0.80.

24 Sold merchandise for $250 on credit to Nicole Simms; Invoice 898; terms 1/10, n/30; sales tax, $10.00.

TOPIC 4

Controlling Cash Received on Account

How are cash receipts from sales on credit journalized? All cash receipts from credit sales are recorded in the cash receipts journal.

Journalizing Cash Received on Account

The entry to record the receipt of cash with a sales discount involves a debit to Cash, a debit to Sales Discount, and a credit to the Accounts Receivable controlling account (and the customer's account). The receipt of cash with a cash discount cannot be recorded in a one-column cash receipts journal. Two debits are involved—one to the Cash account and one to the Sales Discount account. Thus, most businesses add the column shown in the following illustration.

CASH RECEIPTS JOURNAL — Page 3

DATE		ACCOUNT CREDITED	EXPLANATION	POST. REF.	GENERAL LEDGER CREDIT	ACCOUNTS RECEIVABLE CREDIT	SALES DISCOUNT DEBIT	NET CASH DEBIT
19— Oct.	26	Will's Appliance	On account	√		50 00	50	49 50

Receiving cash on account, with a sales discount.

Cash	
49.50	

Sales Discount	
0.50	

Accounts Receivable	
	50.00

$49.50 + $0.50 = $50.00

The Net Cash Debit column is used to record the cash received. The Sales Discount Debit column is used to record the sales discount, if any. The Accounts Receivable Credit column is used to record all credits to customers' accounts from receipts. The amount entered in the Accounts Receivable Credit column ($50) must be equal to the total amount of the debits ($49.50 + $0.50). This column makes easier the double-posting that must be made to the Accounts Receivable controlling account and to the customer's account. The other credit column is the General Ledger Credit column. It is used for credits to any account for which there is no special column.

Posting Cash Receipts

How is the cash receipts journal posted during the month? Each amount in the General Ledger Credit column is posted during the

CASH RECEIPTS JOURNAL — Page 3

DATE		ACCOUNT CREDITED	EXPLANATION	POST. REF.	GENERAL LEDGER CREDIT	ACCOUNTS RECEIVABLE CREDIT	SALES DISCOUNT DEBIT	NET CASH DEBIT
19— Oct.	1	Cash Balance	$16,200	—				
	7	Sales	Cash sales for week	401	720 00			766 80
		Sales Tax Payable		216	46 80			— 00
	9	Office Equipment	Sold calculator	132	100 00			100 00
	11	Jason Booth, Capital	Additional investment	301	2,000 00			2,000 00
	14	Sales	Cash sales for week	401	580 00			617 70
		Sales Tax Payable		216	37 70			— 00
	17	Hallmark Sales	On account	√		1,500 00	30 00	1,470 00
	21	Sales	Cash sales for week	401	660 00			702 90
		Sales Tax Payable		216	42 90			— 00
	26	Will's Appliance	On account	√		50 00	50	49 50
	27	Allied Display	On account	√		160 00		160 00
	28	Sales	Cash sales for week	401	600 00			639 00
		Sales Tax Payable		216	39 00			— 00

① **Credits posted during the month to accounts in general ledger.**

② **Credits posted during the month to customers' accounts in subsidiary ledger.**

③ **Amounts in these two columns are not posted during the month.**

month to the general ledger. The account numbers in the Posting Reference column of the journal indicate the following.

1. The amounts have been posted to the general ledger.
2. Each of the three entries in the Accounts Receivable Credit column is posted to the proper customer's account in the subsidiary ledger. A check mark (✓) in the Posting Reference column means that the amount has been posted. Note that the entries for October 17 and 26 involve sales discounts. The entry for October 27 does not.
3. None of the items in the Sales Discount Debit column or the Net Cash Debit column are posted during the month.

ACCOUNTS RECEIVABLE LEDGER

Name *Allied Display* **Credit Limit** *$1,000*
Address *2 Camino del Oeste, Denver, Colorado 80219* **Telephone** *555-3031*

Receipt: October 27.

DATE		EXPLANATION	POST. REF.	DEBIT		CREDIT		DEBIT BALANCE	
19—									
Oct.	11	Invoice 103; 2/10, n/30	S1	160	00			160	00
	26	Invoice 106; 2/10, n/30	S1	320	00			480	00
	27	Cash	CR3			160	00	320	00

Name *Will's Appliance* **Credit Limit** *$2,000*
Address *16 Del Rey Drive, Denver, Colorado 80219* **Telephone** *555-5510*

Receipt: October 26.

DATE		EXPLANATION	POST. REF.	DEBIT		CREDIT		DEBIT BALANCE	
19—									
Oct.	7	Invoice 101; 1/20, n/30	S1	50	00			50	00
	14	Invoice 104; 1/20, n/30	S1	800	00			850	00
	26	Cash	CR3			50	00	800	00

Name *Hallmark Sales* **Credit Limit** *$4,000*
Address *17 Chaparral Boulevard, Tucson, Arizona 85718* **Telephone** *555-0701*

Receipt: October 17.

DATE		EXPLANATION	POST. REF.	DEBIT		CREDIT		DEBIT BALANCE	
19—									
Oct.	7	Invoice 102; 2/10, n/30	S1	1,600	00			1,600	00
	20	Allowance, Credit Mem. CM-12	J2			100	00	1,500	00
	17	Cash	CR3			1,500	00	—	00
	30	Invoice 108; 2/10, n/30	S1	400	00			400	00

Posting From the Cash Receipts Journal at the End of the Month

All the money columns in the cash receipts journal are pencil-footed at the end of the month. The journal is proved by adding the two debit totals and then adding the two credit totals. These two sums must be equal. After the equality of the debits and credits has been proved, the journal is totaled and ruled.

CASH RECEIPTS JOURNAL													Page 3
DATE		ACCOUNT CREDITED	EXPLANATION	POST. REF.	GENERAL LEDGER CREDIT		ACCOUNTS RECEIVABLE CREDIT		SALES DISCOUNT DEBIT		NET CASH DEBIT		
19— Oct.	1	Cash Balance	$16,200.............	—									
	28	Sales	Cash sales for week ..	401	600	00					639	00	
		Sales Tax Payable		216	39	00					—		
	31	Totals................			4,826	40	1,710	00	30	50	6,505	90	
					(—)		(111)		(403)		(101)		

Cash receipts journal totaled and ruled for month.

The total of the General Ledger Credit column is not posted. The amounts in this column were posted individually. Thus, a dash is placed in the General Ledger Credit column beneath the double rules.

The total of the Accounts Receivable Credit column is posted to the credit side of the controlling account in the general ledger. Each amount in this column was posted to the subsidiary ledger during the month. The controlling account number (111) is written beneath the double rules.

The total of the Sales Discount Debit column is posted as a debit to the Sales Discount account. The total of the Net Cash Debit column is posted as a debit to the Cash account. The account numbers (403 and 101) are written beneath the double rules.

Net Cash Debit	6,505	90
Sales Discount Debit.....	30	50
Total Debits	6,536	40
General Ledger Credit ...	4,826	40
Accounts Receivable Credit	1,710	00
Total Credits	6,536	40

Proof of cash receipts journal.

Exercise K on page 419 may be completed at this point.

Statements of Account

What is a statement of account? Most businesses send a statement of account to each customer periodically. A **statement of account** is prepared from the customer's ledger account and provides a summary of merchandise purchased and payments made, and other activities during the time covered by the statement. The statement of account sent to Will's Appliance, shown on the next page, includes the following data.

1. Beginning balance on October 1, $0.00
2. Sales made (charges)
3. Payments made (credits)
4. Ending balance on October 26 ($800)

Statements of account are used to keep customers informed about their accounts and to encourage prompt payment.

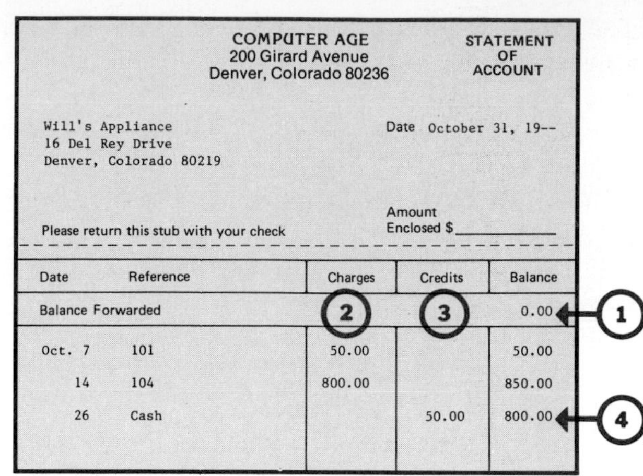

COMPUTER AGE
200 Girard Avenue
Denver, Colorado 80236

STATEMENT OF ACCOUNT

Will's Appliance
16 Del Rey Drive
Denver, Colorado 80219

Date October 31, 19--

Please return this stub with your check

Amount Enclosed $__________

Date	Reference	Charges	Credits	Balance
Balance Forwarded				0.00
Oct. 7	101	50.00		50.00
14	104	800.00		850.00
26	Cash		50.00	800.00

Statement of account showing dates, numbers, invoice totals, and payments.

Aging the Accounts Receivables

How does a business know if customers are paying their accounts promptly? Not all customers pay their accounts on time, even when they receive statements of account. To check that customers are not falling behind, businesses periodically age the accounts receivable. To age accounts receivable, a schedule is prepared listing the name of each customer and the balance of the customer's account, with balances classified according to the number of days since each invoice was issued. When all the balances have been classified, the schedule's columns are added to find the total of each age group. **Aging accounts receivable** is classifying the balance of each customer's account according to the age of the claim.

Computer Age gives every charge customer a credit period of 30 days. The schedule of accounts receivable for October 31 shows the age of the accounts according to the dates of the invoices. The schedule of accounts receivable by age is shown here.

Computer Age
Schedule of Accounts Receivable by Age
October 31, 19—

ACCOUNT WITH	BALANCE	1–30 DAYS	31–60 DAYS	61–90 DAYS	91–120 DAYS	OVER 120 DAYS
Allied Display	*320 00*	*320 00*				
Electro Computer	*68 00*		*26 00*	*17 00*		*25 00*
Hallmark Sales	*400 00*	*400 00*				
Will's Appliance	*800 00*	*800 00*				
Wing Computers	*126 00*			*126 00*		
James Young	*905 25*	*905 25*				
Totals	*2,619 25*	*2,425 25*	*26 00*	*143 00*		*25 00*

The information for aging the accounts is found in the accounts receivable ledger. The Allied Display account, for example, shows a balance of $320. None of this is over the 30-day credit period. Thus, the $320 balance is shown in the 1–30 Days column. The Electro Computer account shows a balance of $68. None of the $68 is current. The entire balance is past due because the credit period has expired and the amounts are past due 31 to over 120 days.

The owner and credit manager use the schedule of accounts receivable by age to control the credit allowed to various customers. The credit manager, for example, should contact Electro Computer before granting more credit to see why they are not paying the invoices. It is also easy to see which accounts need special collection action. The schedule, for example, shows that Wing Computers has owed $126 for 61–90 days. The credit manager needs to take steps to collect this amount. To keep close control over customers' accounts, a business usually prepares the schedule of accounts receivable by age at the end of each month.

The Electro Computer account shown below shows how an account is aged using the dates of the invoices. To age an account receivable, begin with the most recent *unpaid* invoice. Find how many days have passed since the date the invoice was issued. Then analyze the next latest invoice. Continue in this manner until all invoices that *have not been paid* have been analyzed.

Name *Electro Computer* **Credit Limit** *$2,000*
Address *Canyon Road, Phoenix, Arizona 85040* **Telephone** *555-3210*

DATE		EXPLANATION	POST. REF.	DEBIT	CREDIT	DEBIT BALANCE	
19—							③
June	15	Invoice 37; n/30	S1	25 00		25 00	②
Aug.	10	Invoice 76; n/30	S1	17 00		42 00	
Sept.	5	Invoice 89; n/30	S1	26 00		68 00	①

1. Invoice 89, the most recent invoice, is dated September 5 and has a credit period of n/30. The invoice is 56 days old (September 5 to October 31). Thus, the amount of the invoice ($26) is listed in the 31–60 Days column of the schedule of accounts receivable by age.

2. Invoice 76 is 82 days old (August 10 to October 31). Thus, the invoice amount ($17) is listed in the 61–90 Days column. The invoice amount is past due because the 30-day credit period has ended.

3. Invoice 37 is 138 days old (June 15 to October 31). The invoice amount ($25) is listed in the Over 120 Days column.

■ Summarizing the Transactions Involving Sales

The flowchart on page 418 summarizes the various types of transactions involved with sales.

Exercises L and M on page 419 may be completed at this point.

RECORDING TRANSACTIONS INVOLVING SALES

TRANSACTION	SOURCE DOCUMENT*	JOURNAL	GENERAL LEDGER: *Cash*	*Accounts Receivable*	*Sales*	*Sales Returns & Allowances*	*Sales Discount*	*Delivery Expense*	ACCOUNTS RECEIVABLE LEDGER: *Individual Customer's Account*
Sale for cash.	Cash Proof	Cash Receipts Journal	XXX │		│ XXX				
Return or allowance for cash.	Cash Proof	Cash Payments Journal	│ XXX			XXX │			
Sale on credit.	Cash Proof	Sales Journal		XXX │	│ XXX				XXX │
Delivery expense for cash.	Cash Proof	Cash Payments Journal	│ XXX					XXX │	
Return or allowance for credit.	Cash Proof	General Journal		│ XXX		XXX │			│ XXX
Receipt without sales discount.	Cash Proof	Cash Receipts Journal	XXX │	│ XXX					│ XXX
Receipt with sales discount.	Cash Proof	Cash Receipts Journal	XXX │	│ XXX			XXX │		│ XXX

***Only one possible source document is shown.**

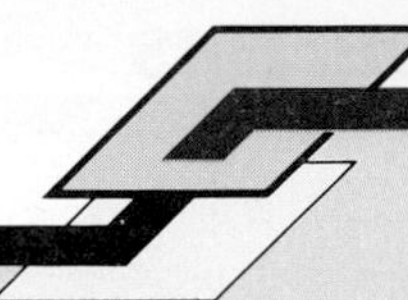

TOPIC 4 EXERCISES

EXERCISE K. Answer the following questions about journalizing cash received on account with a sales discount. Refer to pages 412 to 415.

1. In which journal(s) are sales discounts journalized? What accounts are involved?
2. By what amount did the sale and receipt of cash from Will's Appliance increase owner's equity?
3. What accounts and amounts are debited and credited in the October 26 entry in the cash receipts journal?
4. Why is a check mark placed in the Posting Reference column of the journal for the October 26 entry?
5. What account is credited on October 9?
6. When the October 9 credit is posted from the journal, is a $100 debit posted to Cash at that time? Why or why not?
7. When the Sales Discount column total is posted on October 31, is any other account credited for $30.50 at that time? Why or why not?
8. Is any account credited for $4,826.40 on October 31? Why or why not?
9. How does the accounting clerk prove the equality of debits and credits in the cash receipts journal?

EXERCISE L. Answer the following questions about collecting accounts receivable promptly and aging accounts receivable. Refer to pages 414 to 418.

1. What is the amount of the October 26 payment?
2. How much does Will's Appliance owe on October 26?
3. How much of the Will's Appliance account is past due on October 31?
4. What is the total amount that is past due for Electro Computer? For Wing Computers?
5. What is the total amount owed by all customers? How much is not past due?
6. What is the total amount past due from all customers? How much was not paid within 60 days after the invoices were issued?
7. When did the credit period end for Invoice 37? For Invoice 89?

EXERCISE M. The account shown here is taken from the accounts receivable ledger of Apex Builders. Age the account as of July 31 according to the dates of the invoices.

Name *Lee Cement, Inc.* **Credit Limit** *$750*
Address *Sky Boulevard, Cheyenne, Wyoming 82001* **Telephone** *555-2316*

DATE		EXPLANATION	POST. REF.	DEBIT	CREDIT	DEBIT BALANCE
19—						
Apr.	*1*	*Invoice 0971; n/30*	*S19*	*105 00*		*105 00*
	15	*Invoice 1121; n/30*	*S19*	*47 50*		*152 50*
	21	*Cash*	*CR21*		*47 50*	*105 00*
	26	*Invoice 2010; n/30*	*S19*	*132 00*		*237 00*
May	*3*	*Invoice 2460; n/30*	*S20*	*85 00*		*322 00*
	23	*Invoice 2910; n/30*	*S20*	*27 00*		*349 00*
June	*7*	*Invoice 3474; n/30*	*S20*	*118 00*		*467 00*
July	*25*	*Invoice 5609; n/30*	*S21*	*205 00*		*672 00*

TOPIC 4 PROBLEMS

TOPIC PROBLEM 8. Perform the following activities to process the cash receipts transactions for Advanced Graphics for the month of July.

a. Open general ledger accounts, assign appropriate numbers, and record the July 1 balances as follows: Cash, $14,400; Accounts Receivable; Store Equipment, $9,200; Karen Davis, Capital, $23,600; Karen Davis, Drawing; Sales; Sales Returns and Allowances; Sales Discount; Cash Short and Over; and Delivery Expense. Also open accounts receivable ledger accounts for Best Optics and King Camera.

b. Record each of the transactions listed for July 1–14 in a sales journal, a cash receipts journal, a cash payments journal, or a general journal.

c. Post the individual entries from the journals.

d. Record the transactions for July 18–31.

e. Post the individual entries from the journals.

f. Prove, total, and rule the special journals.

g. Post the totals from the special journals.

h. Prepare a trial balance.

July 1 Sold merchandise for $1,200 on credit to King Camera; Invoice 627; terms 2/10, n/30.

5 Sold merchandise for $1,260 on credit to Best Optics; Invoice 628; terms 1/10, n/30.

5 Karen Davis invested an additional $3,000.

6 Issued Check 45 for $18 to Midway Express for delivering merchandise sold.

July 9 Sold merchandise for $420 on credit to King Camera; Invoice 629; terms 2/10, n/30.

13 Sold merchandise for $600 on credit to Best Optics; Invoice 630; terms 1/10, n/30.

14 Received cash from Best Optics in payment of Invoice 628 dated July 5, less discount.

14 Recorded cash proof; cash sales, $1,800; sales returns, $24.

16 Issued Check 46 to Paula Cushing to pay for returned merchandise sold for cash, $60.

18 Sold merchandise for $360 on credit to King Camera; Invoice 631; terms 2/10, n/30.

19 Issued allowance of $140 for damage to merchandise sold to King Camera on Invoice 631; Credit Memorandum CM-19.

22 Sold merchandise for $330 on credit to King Camera; Invoice 632; terms 2/10, n/30.

25 Received $625 for used store equipment sold to Bruno Brothers.

27 Received cash from King Camera for Invoice 631 dated July 18, less allowance and discount.

29 Received cash from King Camera in payment of full amount of Invoice 629 dated July 9.

31 Recorded cash proof: cash sales, $1,830; sales returns, $20; cash overage, $6.25.

NOTE: Save your work for further use in Topic Problem 9.

TOPIC PROBLEM 9. Using the working papers from Topic Problem 8, perform the following activities for Advanced Graphics during August.

a. Journalize the transactions for August 1–14.

b. Post the individual entries from the journals.

c. Record the transactions for August 15–31.

d. Post the individual entries from the journals.

e. Prove, total, and rule the special journals.

f. Post the totals from the special journals.

g. Prepare a trial balance.

Aug. 1 Received cash from King Camera in payment of Invoice 632 dated July 22, less discount.
5 Sold merchandise for $960 on credit to King Camera; Invoice 633; terms 2/10, n/30.
7 Sold merchandise for $472 on credit to Best Optics; Invoice 634; terms 1/10, n/30.
11 Received cash from Best Optics in payment of full amount of Invoice 630 dated July 13.
13 Issued Check 47 for $3,000 to Karen Davis for withdrawal.
14 Recorded cash proof: cash sales, $2,020; sales returns, $16; cash shortage, $12.60.
15 Received cash from King Camera in payment of Invoice 633 dated August 5, less discount.

Aug. 16 Issued Credit Memorandum 20 to Best Optics for return of goods sold for $160 on Invoice 634.
20 Sold merchandise for $1,000 on credit to King Camera; Invoice 635; terms 2/10, n/30.
23 Issued Check 48 for $52 to Midway Express for delivering merchandise sold.
25 Sold merchandise for $20 on credit to King Camera; Invoice 636; terms 2/10, n/30.
29 Sold merchandise for $160 on credit to Best Optics; Invoice 637; terms 1/10, n/30.
31 Recorded cash proof: cash sales, $2,600.

NOTE: Save your accounts receivable ledger for further use in Topic Problem 10.

TOPIC PROBLEM 10. Using the accounts receivable ledger from Topic Problem 9, prepare a statement of account covering the August transactions that Advanced Graphics completed with Best Optics.

CHAPTER SUMMARY

A sales subsystem involves activities for receiving and approving customer orders, shipping merchandise, billing for merchandise, and accounting for credit sales.

Typically, if a business has many sales on account, the transactions are recorded in a special journal—a sales journal. Individual customer accounts are kept in the accounts receivable subsidiary ledger. A controlling account—Accounts Receivable—is kept in the general ledger. The balance of the controlling account must equal the balance of all the customer accounts in the subsidiary ledger. Sales, returns and allowances, sales discounts, sales taxes, and sales for cash are all involved in the sale of merchandise. The effect of each type of transaction must be recorded and posted.

Good accounting practice requires preparation of a schedule of accounts receivable. The schedule lists the balances of all customer accounts in the subsidiary ledger. The schedule serves as a proof that the total of the balances of the customer accounts agrees with the balance in the Accounts Receivable account in the general ledger.

It is common practice for a merchandising business to periodically send each customer a statement of account. This statement keeps customers informed about their accounts and is designed to encourage prompt payment of bills.

THE LANGUAGE OF BUSINESS

Here are some terms that make up the language of business. Do you know the meaning of each?

sales subsystem
unshipped orders file
shipped orders file
back-order file
sales journal
sales tax
accounts receivable ledger
schedule of accounts receivable
net sales
sales returns
sales allowances
Sales Returns and Allowances account
sales discount
gross sales
statement of account
aging accounts receivable

REVIEW QUESTIONS

1. List and explain the procedures for the control of sales on credit.
2. How does the use of the multicopy shipping order save time?

3. In what way does the credit department have a powerful control over the sales department? On what department does the credit department depend heavily for its information?

4. List and explain the advantages of a special sales journal.

5. Describe the procedure followed in posting from the sales journal.

6. Why is a separate account used for sales returns and allowances? How is the net revenue from sales computed?

7. Describe the procedure for posting the individual amounts and the totals from the four-column cash receipts journal.

8. When is a sales tax billed to a customer? Why is a liability account credited?

9. Why does aging the accounts receivable help a business to collect its accounts receivable more promptly?

10. A sale on credit to the Warren Stores was journalized correctly as $79 but was posted as $97 in the customer's account. When should this error be discovered? How might the customer detect the error?

CHAPTER PROBLEMS

Problems for Chapter 12 are given below. Write your answers to the problems on separate sheets of paper unless you are using the workbook for this textbook. If you are using the workbook, do the problems in the space provided there.

CHAPTER PROBLEM 12-1. Perform the following activities for the Wilson Shirt Company.

a. Open general ledger accounts, assign the appropriate account numbers, and record the opening balances for January as follows: Cash, $5,200; Accounts Receivable, $1,420; Sales Tax Payable; Marilyn Wilson, Capital, $6,620; Sales; Sales Returns and Allowances; and Sales Discount. Also open accounts receivable ledger accounts for Roberta Alford, 253 Melville Road, Farmingdale, NY 11735; credit limit, $2,000; telephone 555-2275; beginning balance, $600; and Craig Richards, 14 Grove Street, Buffalo, NY 14221; credit limit, $3,000; telephone 555-6539; beginning balance, $820.

b. Record each transaction below in a sales journal, a cash receipts journal, or a general journal.

Jan. 2 Received check for $5,000 from Marilyn Wilson as an additional investment.

3 Issued Invoice 1467 to Craig Richards; terms, 2/10, n/30; sales amount, $480; tax, $24.

9 Issued Invoice 1468 to Roberta Alford; terms 1/15, n/30; sale amount $260; tax, $13.

11 Received check for $494.40 from Craig Richards in payment of Invoice 1467 less discount.

12 Issued Invoice 1469 to Roberta Alford; terms 1/15, n/30; sale amount $420; tax, $21.

Jan. 16 Issued Invoice 1470 to Craig Richards; terms, 2/10, n/30; sale amount, $220; tax, $11.
18 Issued Credit Memorandum CM-49 to Craig Richards for returned merchandise of $20 and sales tax of $1 from Invoice 1470.
24 Received check for $206 from Craig Richards in payment of Invoice 1470 less return and discount.
27 Issued Invoice 1471 to Craig Richards; terms 2/10, n/30; sale amount, $320; tax, $16.
29 Received check for $100 from Roberta Alford on account.
31 Recorded $2,280 cash sales and $114 sales tax for the month.

CHAPTER PROBLEM 12-2. Verify the work done in Chapter Problem 12-1 by doing the following.

a. Prepare a schedule of accounts receivable on January 31 for the Wilson Shirt Company.

b. Prepare a trial balance on January 31 for the Wilson Shirt Company.

MANAGEMENT CASE

Returned Merchandise. It is expensive for a business to handle returned merchandise. Remember that there are many expenses involved in the sale of the merchandise. Salaries are paid to salespeople. There are expenses for wrapping and delivering the merchandise and for recording the transaction. When the merchandise is returned, there are more expenses for handling the complaint, inspecting the merchandise, recording the transaction, and placing the merchandise back in stock for resale.

CASE 12M-1. Debra Rothman owns the Shoe Place. Her net sales (sales less sales returns) for the year were $220,000. Her gross profit on sales ($88,000) was 40 percent of the net sales. The expenses of handling returned items cost the store $13,200 a year. Ms. Rothman is considering adopting a policy of "All Sales Final—No Returns" and reducing the selling price of her shoes.

a. What percent of the gross profit was the $13,200 in expenses for handling returns?

b. One line of shoes sells for $20 a pair. If Ms. Rothman allows no sales returns, what price would she have to charge for each pair of shoes to keep the same net income?

c. What factors should be considered before adopting an "All Sales Final—No Returns" policy?

d. Is it possible that Ms. Rothman might establish a policy of "All Sales Final" yet find that she actually has to increase the selling price of her shoes? How could this happen?

CHAPTER

13

A Personnel and Payroll Subsystem

A personnel and payroll subsystem controls the hiring of employees and payroll activities. This chapter discusses the roles of the personnel department in the employment process and the accounting department in preparing payroll records.

CHAPTER GOALS

After studying Chapter 13 you will be able to:

1. Define the terms listed in "The Language of Business" section on page 462.
2. Explain the concepts and principles in this chapter related to accounting for payroll.
3. Use a flowchart to describe the relationship of people, forms, procedures, and equipment in a personnel and payroll subsystem.
4. Compute employee earnings based on various payroll plans.
5. Determine from tax tables the amount of taxes withheld from employee earnings.
6. Record payroll data in a special payroll journal and post to both the general ledger and the employee earnings records.
7. Calculate, journalize, and post the employer's payroll taxes.
8. Complete payroll tax forms for taxes collected for and paid to government agencies.

TOPIC 1

Controlling Personnel and Payroll

What is the personnel and payroll subsystem? The **personnel and payroll subsystem** is the people, forms, procedures, and equipment that make up the subsystem in which the payroll for a business is processed. The people are the **employees** who perform services under the direction of an employer. An **employer** is an individual or a business for whom an employee performs a service.

Four primary activities are completed in any personnel and payroll subsystem.

- Hiring employees and officially terminating their employment
- Processing the payroll
- Paying the payroll
- Preparing and filing the payroll tax forms

The personnel department handles hiring and terminating employees. The payroll department processes and pays the payroll and prepares payroll tax returns for filing with government agencies.

These four activities are handled by two departments in the personnel and payroll subsystem—personnel and payroll. The two departments are separate but related because one must provide information for the other.

Personnel Department

The personnel department is responsible for recruiting and hiring employees, authorizing pay rates and deductions, and terminating the employee's service with the employer.

Recruiting and Hiring New Employees The recruiting and hiring of new employees is important in all businesses. This process usually begins with the request for a new employee. For instance, the accounting department might indicate the need for an accounting clerk. The request goes to the department manager, who either agrees or disagrees that a new employee is needed. If the request is accepted, the manager will authorize the personnel department to begin the recruiting process. The authorization to recruit will usually include a job description and pay rate.

The personnel department will then advertise for an employee. The advertisement might be posted inside the business for the benefit of all employees. A ''help-wanted ad'' might be placed in the newspaper. Examples of help-wanted ads are in the margin.

ACCOUNTING CLERK
Immediate opening in our downtown accounting office. No experience necessary, but accuracy and ability to work independently required. Please write:
Hallmark Sales
17 Chaparral Blvd.
Tucson, AZ 85718

CLERK - PAYROLL
We seek an individual for our payroll department. Must have ability to work with a calculator and knowledge of payroll reports. Should be able to work with minimal direction. Excellent salary and benefits. Please apply by sending a confidential resume to:
Will's Appliance
16 Del Rey Drive
Denver, CO 80219
Equal Opportunity Employer

ACCOUNTING CLERK: Permanent full-time position for an entry level accounting clerk. Duties include payables, typing, and general office work. Experience helpful but not required. Call 555-9067 between 9 a.m. and 5 p.m. for appointment.

The process at this point will vary from business to business. Many businesses will ask each person who answers the ad to complete an employment application. Part of a sample application is shown on the next page. Space is usually provided for items such as personal information, employment history, and educational background.

All applications are carefully screened and personal interviews are scheduled with potential recruits. Based on the applicant's interview and information provided on the application form, the most qualified

COMPUTER AGE
Employment Application

An Equal Opportunity Employer
Computer Age Policy and Federal Law Forbid Discrimination Because of Race, Religion, Age, Sex, Marital Status, Disability, or National Origin.

Date__________

Personal Data

Applying for position as __________ Salary required__________ Date available__________

Name: __________ (Last) (First) (Middle) (Maiden)

Present address __________ (Street) (City) (State) (Zip)

Permanent address __________ (Street) (City) (State) (Zip)

Telephone number__________ (Area code) Social Security number__________

Person to be notified in case of emergency:

Name__________ Telephone__________

Address__________

Reason for terminating

Partial job application.

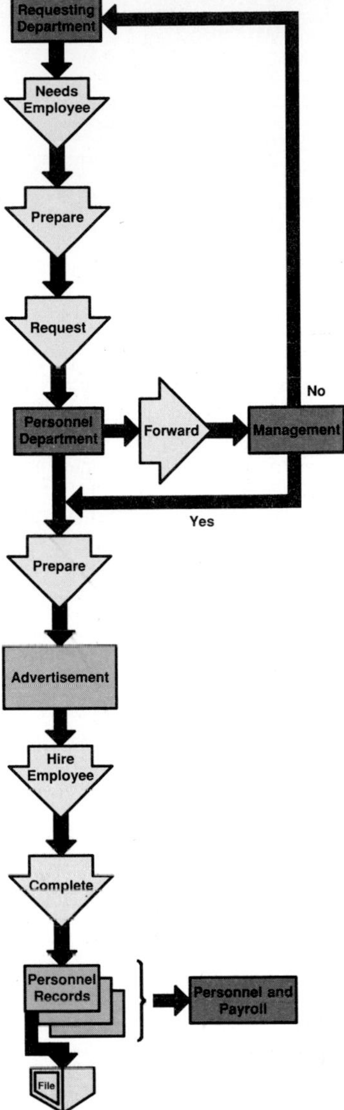

person is offered the position. If the person receiving the offer finds the salary, benefits, and working conditions acceptable, the hiring process is complete. A flowchart illustrating the hiring process is in the margin.

■ **Personnel Records** Before the new employee begins work, certain personnel records must be completed. Generally these records are the basis for deductions that will be made from the employee's gross pay. Gross pay and deductions are discussed in Topics 2 and 3.

■ **Personnel's Relation to the Payroll Department** The personnel department completes a series of activities prior to and at the beginning of employment. The personnel department must forward the following information to the payroll department.

- *The date of employment.* The payroll department then will know when to begin salary payments.
- *A copy of Form W-4.* The payroll department then will know the number of exemptions to which the employee is entitled.
- *The basis for computing net pay.* The payroll department then will know the hourly wage rate, the commission or bonus plan, or the salary to be earned by the employee.
- *The conditions of employment.* The payroll department then will know if the employee is entitled to overtime pay, when to begin overtime pay, and at what rate to pay overtime.

The records just described form the basis for the relationship between the personnel and payroll departments. All activities in the payroll department begin with the authorizations received from the person-

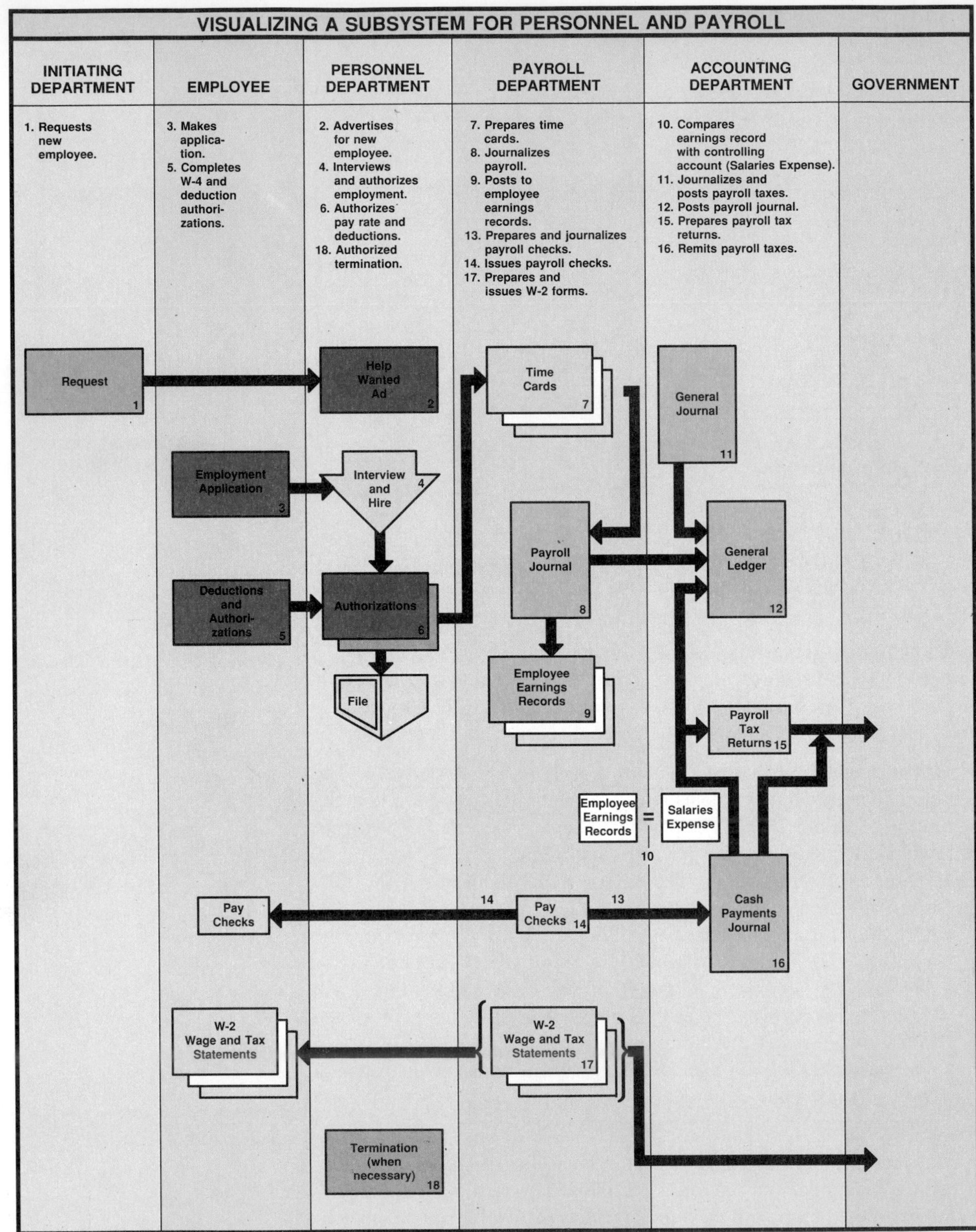
VISUALIZING A SUBSYSTEM FOR PERSONNEL AND PAYROLL
INITIATING DEPARTMENT
EMPLOYEE
PERSONNEL DEPARTMENT
PAYROLL DEPARTMENT
ACCOUNTING DEPARTMENT
GOVERNMENT
1. Requests new employee.
3. Makes application.
5. Completes W-4 and deduction authorizations.
2. Advertises for new employee.
4. Interviews and authorizes employment.
6. Authorizes pay rate and deductions.
18. Authorized termination.
7. Prepares time cards.
8. Journalizes payroll.
9. Posts to employee earnings records.
13. Prepares and journalizes payroll checks.
14. Issues payroll checks.
17. Prepares and issues W-2 forms.
10. Compares earnings record with controlling account (Salaries Expense).
11. Journalizes and posts payroll taxes.
12. Posts payroll journal.
15. Prepares payroll tax returns.
16. Remits payroll taxes.
Request 1
Help Wanted Ad 2
Time Cards 7
General Journal 11
Employment Application 3
Interview and Hire 4
Payroll Journal 8
General Ledger 12
Deductions and Authorizations 5
Authorizations 6
File
Employee Earnings Records 9
Payroll Tax Returns 15
Employee Earnings Records = Salaries Expense
10
Pay Checks
14
Pay Checks 14
13
Cash Payments Journal 16
W-2 Wage and Tax Statements
W-2 Wage and Tax Statements 17
Termination (when necessary) 18

nel department. Other information that the payroll department will need to know at some later time include the following.

- *Changes in the rate of pay*. The payroll department then will know when to increase or decrease an employee's gross earnings.
- *Notice of terminaton*. The payroll department then will know when to remove an employee from the payroll records.

■ Visualizing a Personnel and Payroll Subsystem The flowchart on page 428 shows how the activities between the personnel and payroll departments are related. It also shows how these departments are related to the accounting department. In smaller businesses some of these activities are combined.

In order for all these activities to run smoothly, companies need to establish and follow certain procedures, such as the following.

- Pay only authorized pay rates.
- Pay employees only for time worked or services rendered.
- Deduct authorized amounts from gross earnings.
- Maintain employee earnings records.
- Divide responsibility.
- Use prenumbered payroll checks.
- Designate authorized employees to sign checks.
- Pay only authorized employees.
- Secure the check-signing machine.

Payroll Clerk: DOT 215.482-010
Computes wages and posts wages to payroll records.

Concept: Payroll Records
The employer must maintain adequate payroll records.

Concept: Collection Agent
The employer acts as a collection agent for the government and for others designated by the employee or a court.

Exercise A on this page and page 430 may be completed at this point.

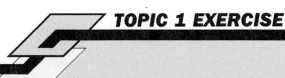

TOPIC 1 EXERCISE

EXERCISE A. Answer the following questions about activities in the personnel and payroll subsystem. Refer to the text on pages 426 to 429.

1. What begins the process for hiring a new employee?
2. Do all applicants receive a personal interview?
3. What records are completed in the personnel department for each new employee?
4. Can the payroll department operate without the personnel department?
5. In what steps of the flowchart on page 428 do you see a relation between the personnel and payroll departments?

6. How many activities are completed in the payroll department?
7. Which department prepares the paychecks? Which department prepares the W-2 forms?
8. How does the payroll department know how much to pay each employee?
9. Which journals are used in the accounting department? Which of the journals is new to you?
10. How does work completed in the payroll department act as a proof of work completed in the accounting department?

TOPIC 1 PROBLEM

TOPIC PROBLEM 1. On a table similar to the one below, indicate who prepares or sends the following forms, to whom or where the forms are sent, and the purpose for each form. Refer to the flowchart on page 428.

1. Form W-4
2. Deduction authorizations
3. Help-wanted advertisement
4. Time cards
5. Payroll journal
6. Paychecks
7. Prepared payroll tax returns
8. Checks that accompany payroll tax returns

Form	Prepared or Sent By	Sent To	Purpose
EXAMPLE: Request for new employee	Requesting Department	Personnel Department	Request new employee

TOPIC 2

Computing Gross Earnings

Control: Pay employees only for time worked or services rendered.
Control: Deduct authorized amounts from gross earnings.
Control: Maintain employee earnings records.
Control: Divide responsibility.

What kinds of records of employees' salaries and wages must an employer keep? The records of salaries and wages that an employer must keep are called *payroll records*. These records must provide several types of payroll data, including the following.

- The amount of wages or salaries paid to the employees
- The amounts deducted from the employees' earnings
- The classifications of wage and salary expenses
- The payroll taxes owed by the employer and the employees to the government agencies

Employee earnings are called salaries, wages, or commissions. *Salaries* are fixed amounts paid periodically to employees for their services. *Wages* are amounts paid to employees at a certain rate per hour, day, week, or unit of production. *Commissions* are amounts paid to employees according to the number or price of items sold. In practice, the terms wages and salaries often are used to mean the same thing. The Internal Revenue Service uses the term wages to cover all types of employee earnings.

The total earnings of all employees for a certain pay period is called the **payroll**. The pay period is usually weekly, biweekly (every two weeks), semimonthly (twice a month), or monthly.

■ Time Pay Plans

The amount an employee earns is known as his or her **gross earnings**. Various plans are used to determine an employee's gross earnings.

■ Salary Plan The **salary plan** is a payment based on a straight salary with a fixed amount for each pay period. If the gross earnings are stated for a period of time other than the pay period, some computations are needed to find the gross earnings for the pay period. To change a yearly salary to a weekly salary, divide the yearly salary by 52, since there are 52 weeks in a year. To change a yearly salary to a monthly salary, divide by 12, since there are 12 months in a year. To change a weekly salary into an hourly wage, divide the weekly amount by the number of hours in the work week. For example, Carlos Richard, who is an employee of Computer Age, is paid a salary of $200 per week. The amount of his gross weekly earnings is the amount of his salary—$200.

Salary Plan
Gross Earnings = Salary
$200 = $200

■ Hourly Rate Plan The **hourly rate plan** is a payment plan in which the employee is paid a set amount for each hour worked. To find the employee's gross earnings, multiply the hourly rate times the number of hours worked in the pay period. For example, Sonia Brouse, another employee at Computer Age, is paid $6 per hour. Her gross earnings for 40 hours are $240 (40 × $6). This plan is useful when the number of hours worked varies from one pay period to another.

Hourly Rate Plan
Gross Earnings = Hours × Rate
$240 = 40 × $6

■ Incentive Pay Plans

An **incentive plan** is a pay plan based on an employee's productivity or output. An incentive pay plan enables employees to increase their gross earnings by producing more. There are three plans that may be used in paying employees on a productivity or output basis.

■ Piece-Rate Plan The **piece-rate plan** is a payment plan in which an employee is paid a set amount for each item produced. For example, a presser in a clothing factory is paid $0.10 for every shirt pressed. The presser's gross earnings for pressing 2,250 shirts would be $225 (2,250 × $0.10).

Piece-Rate Plan
Gross Earnings = Items × Rate
$225 = 2,250 × $0.10

■ Commission Plan The **commission plan** is a payment plan based on the quantity of goods the salesperson sells. It is used by businesses to encourage salespeople to increase their sales. The com-

Commission Plan
Gross
Earnings = Percentage × Sales
$400 = 0.05 × $8,000

Salary-Commission Plan
Gross
Earnings = Salary + Commission
$340 = $100 + (0.03 × $8,000)
$340 = $100 + $240

Exercise B on pages 433 and 434 may be completed at this point.

mission is figured by multiplying the amount of sales made during the pay period by a certain percentage. For example, suppose a salesperson receives a commission of 5 percent on all sales. If the salesperson had sales of $8,000 in a week, the gross earnings would be $400 (0.05 × $8,000).

■ Salary-Commission Plan The **salary-commission plan** is a payment plan in which a basic salary plus a commission is paid. For example, assume that a salesperson is paid a salary of $100 a week plus a 3 percent commission on sales. In this plan, the salesperson's gross earnings in the above example would be $340 for weekly sales of $8,000 [$100 + (0.03 × $8,000)] or $100 + $240.

Wages and Hours of Work

What is a contract of employment? The wages employees are paid and the number of hours employees work depend upon their contract of employment and upon government legislation. In general, an employee's rate of pay is based upon an oral or written agreement between the employer and the employee. In businesses that have many employees, a contract of employment is usually written.

A **contract of employment** is an agreement between the employer and a union or bargaining agent, which represents the employees. The contract covers wages, hours of work, types of benefits offered (if any), and other working conditions. Such a contract must be followed by the employer and employee.

Fair Labor Standards Act

■ Overtime Pay Certain federal and state laws regulate the number of hours an employee may work and the employee's rate of pay. The Fair Labor Standards Act, also called the Wage and Hour Law, affects all firms engaged in interstate commerce. (*Interstate commerce* means that goods produced in one state are sold in other states.) Employers who are covered by the act must pay a minimum hourly rate of pay. The act also requires employers to pay overtime. **Overtime pay** is pay for over 40 hours in any week. The overtime rate is a minimum rate of 1½ times the regular rate. Thus, an employee who is paid a regular rate of $4 per hour would be paid an overtime rate of $6 (1½ × $4) per hour. The overtime rate of 1½ times the regular rate is commonly called *time and a half*.

Employers who are not subject to the Fair Labor Standards Act may still pay time and a half for overtime. They may do so because of a contract of employment with the union or to keep good relations with the employees. Some contracts call for employees to be paid for work on legal holidays and Sundays at double their regular rates.

Violations of the FLSA may lead to criminal and/or civil penalties. A fine of $10,000 or imprisonment for a term of up to six months, or both, can be imposed on employers who violate the act.

The Fair Labor Standards Act also requires that a complete record be kept of the hours worked by each employee. Businesses with many employees frequently use a time clock. Each employee has a time card to insert in the time clock upon arrival and again upon departure.

A **time card** is the source document for recording an employee's attendance at work to figure hours worked and wages. The time clock punches the time of the day on the card. At the end of the pay period, the payroll clerk collects all the time cards and figures total hours worked and gross earnings for each employee.

Salaried employees are also covered by the Fair Labor Standards Act and are eligible to receive overtime pay. An attendance record should be kept for salaried employees as well as for hourly employees. Such a record should show overtime hours and absences.

Name Dana Reese Employee No. 2

Week Ending April 5, 19--

Days	Regular				Other		Hours
	In	Out	In	Out	In	Out	
Thurs.	8:00	12:00	1:00	5:00			8
Fri.	8:58	12:00	12:59	5:00			7
Sat.							
Sun.							
Mon.	7:55	12:02	12:58	5:05	6:00	9:00	11
Tues.	8:05	12:01	12:59	5:01			8
Wed.	7:59	12:01	1:01	5:02	5:57	9:01	11

Extra Hours Approved		Hours	Rate	Earnings
	Regular	40	$ 4.00	$160.00
J. Evans	Overtime	5	$ 6.00	$ 30.00
Supervisor	Total Hours	45	Gross Earnings	$190.00

Total hours worked and gross earnings are computed on the bottom of the time card.

■ Determining Hours Worked

Most employers have an agreement with their employees regarding working hours. For example, employees might be required to work from 8 A.M. to noon. Noon to 1 P.M. may be set aside for lunch. Then the employees might work from 1 P.M. to 5 P.M. Some rules need to be made regarding lateness and the computation of time worked. Although the procedure for figuring time worked varies from business to business, the following procedure used by Computer Age is common.

- The employee is paid only for regular hours unless extra hours have been approved by the supervisor. For example, an employee receives no pay for work before 8 A.M., between noon and 1 P.M., and after 5 P.M. unless the work has been approved.
- Daily time is figured in hours and quarter-hours. Fractions of an hour less than 15 minutes are not counted.
- The nearest quarter-hour is used to figure the time for beginning and ending work. A quarter-hour begins and ends on the hour, 15 minutes after the hour, 30 minutes after the hour, or 45 minutes after the hour. Therefore, regardless of the time an employee punches in or out, the employee is given credit for working to the nearest quarter-hour. For example, 7:53 to 8:07 is considered as 8:00. However, 8:08 to 8:22 is considered as 8:15. Although lateness is discouraged, an employee is not penalized for being up to 7 minutes late.

TIME RECORDED	CONSIDERED AS
7:55, 8:05, 7:59	8:00
8:58	9:00
12:02, 12:01	12:00
12:59, 12:58, 1:01	1:00
5:05, 5:01, 5:02	5:00

Analysis of time.

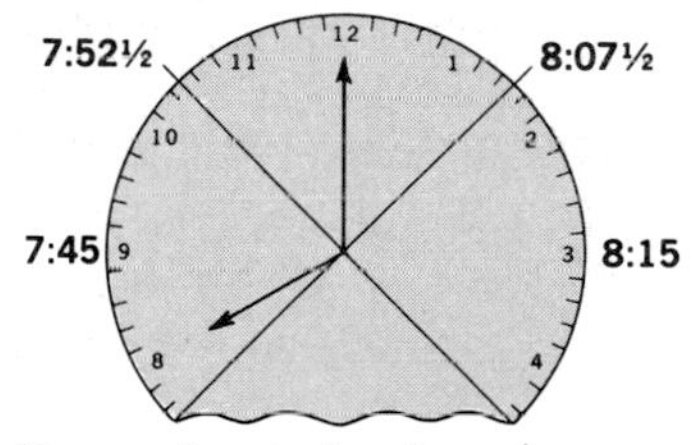

Nearest quarter hour.

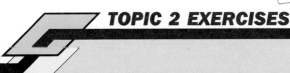

Exercise C on page 434 may be completed at this point.

TOPIC 2 EXERCISES

EXERCISE B. The Lincoln Company pays a rate of $4.00 per hour to all inexperienced employees. When employees have three months of experience, they are paid on a piece-rate basis. The production employees receive $0.50 for each unit they complete. The employees who pack the finished units for shipment receive $0.30 for each shipment they pack. Some of the employees of the Lincoln Company are listed here. Compute the gross earnings for each employee.

Inexperienced Employees		Production Employees		Packer Employees	
Employee	**Total Hours**	**Employee**	**Total Units**	**Employee**	**Total Shipments**
1. J. Cannon	38	**4.** J. Noonan	312	**7.** P. Moy	640
2. T. Liden	40	**5.** D. Bell	285	**8.** C. Krimsky	580
3. O. Malley	35	**6.** C. Diaz	270	**9.** T. Taylor	560

EXERCISE C. The time cards for the employees of the Seasons Corporation are given here. As payroll clerk for the business, perform the following activities.

1. Find the total number of hours worked each day by Robert Burke and Julie Laski. Regular hours are from 8 A.M. to noon and 1 to 5 P.M. Use the nearest quarter-hour to calculate the beginning and ending times. Figure the daily time in hours and quarter-hours.

2. Find the total hours worked during the week for each employee.

NOTE: Save your time cards for further use in Topic Problem 2.

Name Susan Dole Employee No. 4
Week Ending November 2, 19--

Days	Regular In	Regular Out	Regular In	Regular Out	Other In	Other Out	Hours
Thurs.	7^{59}	12^{00}	1^{00}	5^{00}			8
Fri.	8^{01}	12^{01}	1^{00}	5^{02}			8
Sat.							
Sun.							
Mon.	7^{58}	12^{00}	1^{00}	5^{00}			8
Tues.	7^{57}	12^{00}	1^{00}	4^{00}			7
Wed.	8^{00}	12^{00}	12^{59}	5^{01}			8

Extra Hours Approved		Hours	Rate	Earnings
	Regular			
	Overtime			
Supervisor	Total Hours		Gross Earnings	

Name James Montero Employee No. 7
Week Ending November 2, 19--

Days	Regular In	Regular Out	Regular In	Regular Out	Other In	Other Out	Hours
Thurs.	7^{56}	12^{00}	1^{00}	5^{04}			8
Fri.	7^{58}	12^{01}	1^{00}	5^{00}			8
Sat.							
Sun.							
Mon.	7^{59}	12^{00}	1^{01}	5^{00}			8
Tues.	8^{15}	12^{01}	1^{00}	5^{03}			$7\frac{3}{4}$
Wed.	7^{58}	12^{00}	1^{01}	5^{02}			8

Extra Hours Approved		Hours	Rate	Earnings
	Regular			
	Overtime			
Supervisor	Total Hours		Gross Earnings	

Name Robert Burke Employee No. 12
Week Ending November 2, 19--

Days	Regular In	Regular Out	Regular In	Regular Out	Other In	Other Out	Hours
Thurs.	7^{59}	12^{01}	1^{00}	5^{01}			
Fri.	8^{00}	12^{00}	1^{00}	5^{02}			
Sat.							
Sun.							
Mon.	7^{58}	12^{00}	1^{00}	5^{00}	6^{00}	9^{00}	
Tues.	8^{01}	12^{02}	12^{58}	5^{00}			
Wed.	7^{56}	12^{01}	1^{00}	5^{03}	6^{00}	8^{30}	

Extra Hours Approved		Hours	Rate	Earnings
	Regular			
S. O'Brien	Overtime			
Supervisor	Total Hours		Gross Earnings	

Name Julie Laski Employee No. 14
Week Ending November 2, 19--

Days	Regular In	Regular Out	Regular In	Regular Out	Other In	Other Out	Hours
Thurs.	7^{59}	12^{02}	1^{00}	5^{04}	6^{01}	9^{01}	
Fri.	7^{58}	12^{01}	1^{00}	5^{01}			
Sat.							
Sun.							
Mon.	7^{57}	12^{00}	1^{00}	5^{01}			
Tues.	7^{58}	12^{01}	1^{01}	5^{02}	6^{00}	7^{30}	
Wed.	8^{01}	12^{00}	1^{00}	5^{03}	6^{01}	8^{30}	

Extra Hours Approved		Hours	Rate	Earnings
	Regular			
S. O'Brien	Overtime			
Supervisor	Total Hours		Gross Earnings	

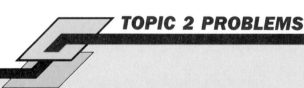

TOPIC 2 PROBLEMS

TOPIC PROBLEM 2. Use the time cards you prepared in Exercise C to perform the following duties as payroll clerk for the Seasons Corporation.

Figure the regular, overtime, and total gross earnings for each employee. The hourly rates are as follows: Burke, $3.50; Dole, $5.00; Laski, $4.00; and Montero, $4.60. Consider all hours in excess of 40 hours per week as overtime hours. Overtime hours are paid at the rate of $1\frac{1}{2}$ times the regular hourly rate.

NOTE: Save your time cards for further use in Topic Problem 4.

TOPIC PROBLEM 3. Steven Motors sells off-the-road vehicles and recreational vehicles, such as jeeps and motorcycles. The recreational vehicle salespeople are paid on a salary-commission plan. They receive a base salary of $600 per month and a 5 percent commission on their sales. The off-the-road vehicle salespeople are paid on a commission plan. They receive a 10 percent commission on their sales.

a. Compute the monthly gross earnings for each of the salespeople listed.

b. Which salespeople earn more money? Why?

c. What are the advantages and disadvantages of the two pay plans (salary-commission plan and commission plan)?

Off-the-Road Vehicle Salespeople	Total Sales	Recreational Vehicle Salespeople	Total Sales
1. B. Simpson	$10,750	**4.** M. Yee	$24,000
2. W. Harris	12,000	**5.** G. Mack	18,000
3. A. Chou	8,500	**6.** N. Wills	23,000

TOPIC 3

Deductions From Gross Earnings

Is there a difference between an employee's gross earnings and the amount actually given to an employee? Yes, various payroll deductions must be subtracted from an employee's gross earnings. A **payroll deduction** is an amount subtracted from gross earnings. Payroll deductions include deductions required by law, such as federal income tax, state income tax, and social security tax (FICA). They may also include voluntary deductions, such as group life insurance and hospitalization insurance premiums. In addition, some union contracts call for union deductions such as initiation fees and dues to be withheld from the employee's earnings.

Deductions Required by Law

An employer is required to withhold taxes from an employee's gross earnings. **Federal income tax** is a tax imposed by the federal government on personal and business income. Federal laws require the employer to withhold amounts for the employee's federal income tax and for the employee's share of the social security taxes. Many states and cities also require state income tax and city income tax to be withheld. In addition, courts of law can require employers to withhold money. The employer periodically sends the amounts withheld to the proper governmental or legal agency.

Federal Income Tax Withholding

The amount of federal income tax withheld depends upon the employee's gross earnings, marital status, and number of exemptions claimed.

An *exemption* is a government allowance that permits taxpayers to reduce their tax payment because they financially support qualified persons. In general, an employee is allowed the following exemptions.

- One exemption for the employee.
- One exemption for the employee's spouse unless he or she is working and claims a separate exemption.
- One exemption for each *dependent*. A dependent is a person supported by the taxpayer. A child under 19 or relatives receiving more than half of their support from the taxpayer are dependents. Children who are full-time students (at least five months per year) can be dependents regardless of their age or their earnings.

Each employee reports the number of exemptions claimed on an Employee's Withholding Allowance Certificate (Form W-4). **Form W-4** reports the number of exemptions the employee wants to claim. Every employee must give a completed and signed Form W-4 to the employer.

Form **W-4** Department of the Treasury—Internal Revenue Service
Employee's Withholding Allowance Certificate

1 Type or print your full name Sonia Brouse	2 Your social security number 201-26-8341
Home address (number and street or rural route) 16 Carmine Drive	3 Marital Status: ☐ Single ☒ Married ☐ Married, but withhold at higher Single rate **Note:** If married, but legally separated, or spouse is a nonresident alien, check the Single box.
City or town, state, and ZIP code Englewood, Colorado 80112	

4 Total number of allowances you are claiming (from line F of the worksheet on page 2) 3
5 Additional amount, if any, you want deducted from each pay . . . . . $
6 I claim exemption from withholding because (see instructions and check boxes below that apply):
a ☐ Last year I did not owe any Federal income tax and had a right to a full refund of **ALL** income tax withheld, **AND**
b ☐ This year I do not expect to owe any Federal income tax and expect to have a right to a full refund of **ALL** income tax withheld. If both a and b apply, enter the year effective and "EXEMPT" here . . . ▶ Year 19
c If you entered "EXEMPT" on line 6b, are you a full-time student? . . . . . ☐Yes ☐No

Under penalties of perjury, I certify that I am entitled to the number of withholding allowances claimed on this certificate, or if claiming exemption from withholding, that I am entitled to claim the exempt status.
Employee's signature ▶ *Sonia Brouse* **Date ▶** *January 2,* 19—

7 Employer's name and address **(Employer: Complete 7, 8, and 9 only if sending to IRS)**	8 Office code	9 Employer identification number
Computer Age 200 Girard Avenue Denver, Colorado 80236		42-1289370

The law requires employers to have a Form W-4 on file for each employee. Employees must file revised Form W-4s within ten days if their number of exemptions decreases. If their number of exemptions increases they may file revised Form W-4s if they wish. The federal income tax to be withheld from the earnings of an employee is determined by using wage-bracket tables or by computing the amount. The procedure commonly used is the wage-bracket method. The Internal Revenue Service provides tables for daily, weekly, biweekly, semimonthly, monthly, and miscellaneous payroll periods. Wage-bracket tables for single persons paid weekly and married persons paid weekly are shown on the next page.

To determine the amount of income tax to be deducted from each employee's gross earnings, use the following procedure.

- Locate the wage-bracket table for the pay period, such as weekly or monthly.

SINGLE Persons–**WEEKLY** Payroll Period

And the wages are–		And the number of withholding allowances claimed is–										
At least	But less than	0	1	2	3	4	5	6	7	8	9	10
		The amount of income tax to be withheld shall be–										
150	160	17	14	11	8	5	3	0	0	0	0	0
160	170	19	16	13	10	7	4	1	0	0	0	0
170	180	20	17	14	11	8	5	3	0	0	0	0
180	190	22	19	16	12	9	6	4	1	0	0	0
190	200	24	20	17	14	11	8	5	2	0	0	0
200	210	25	22	19	15	12	9	6	4	1	0	0
210	220	27	24	20	17	14	11	8	5	2	0	0
220	230	29	25	22	18	15	12	9	6	4	1	0
230	240	31	27	23	20	17	14	11	8	5	2	0
240	250	32	29	25	22	18	15	12	9	6	4	1
250	260	34	31	27	23	20	17	14	10	8	5	2
260	270	36	32	29	25	22	18	15	12	9	6	3
270	280	38	34	30	27	23	20	17	13	10	7	5
280	290	40	36	32	28	25	21	18	15	12	9	6
290	300	43	38	34	30	27	23	20	16	13	10	7
$390	$400	$67	$61	$56	$51	$46	$42	$38	$33	$30	$26	$22
400	410	69	64	59	54	49	44	40	35	31	28	24
410	420	72	67	61	56	51	46	42	37	33	29	26
420	430	75	69	64	58	53	49	44	39	35	31	27
430	440	77	72	66	61	56	51	46	41	37	33	29
440	450	80	74	69	64	58	53	48	44	39	35	31
450	460	82	77	72	66	61	55	51	46	41	37	33
460	470	85	80	74	69	63	58	53	48	43	39	35
470	480	88	82	77	71	66	61	55	51	46	41	37
480	490	91	85	79	74	69	63	58	53	48	43	39
490	500	94	88	82	77	71	66	60	55	50	46	41
500	510	97	91	85	79	74	68	63	58	53	48	43
510	520	100	94	87	82	76	71	66	60	55	50	45
520	530	103	97	90	84	79	74	68	63	57	52	48
530	540	106	100	93	87	82	76	71	65	60	55	50

Federal income tax wage-bracket table for single persons paid weekly.

MARRIED Persons–**WEEKLY** Payroll Period

And the wages are–		And the number of withholding allowances claimed is–										
At least	But less than	0	1	2	3	4	5	6	7	8	9	10
		The amount of income tax to be withheld shall be–										
92	94	5	2	0	0	0	0	0	0	0	0	0
94	96	5	3	0	0	0	0	0	0	0	0	0
96	98	5	3	1	0	0	0	0	0	0	0	0
98	100	5	3	1	0	0	0	0	0	0	0	0
100	105	6	4	1	0	0	0	0	0	0	0	0
105	110	6	4	2	0	0	0	0	0	0	0	0
110	115	7	5	2	0	0	0	0	0	0	0	0
115	120	8	5	3	1	0	0	0	0	0	0	0
120	125	8	6	3	1	0	0	0	0	0	0	0
125	130	9	6	4	2	0	0	0	0	0	0	0
210	220	21	18	15	12	9	7	4	2	0	0	0
220	230	22	19	17	14	11	8	6	3	1	0	0
230	240	24	21	18	15	12	9	7	4	2	0	0
240	250	26	22	19	16	14	11	8	6	3	1	0
250	260	27	24	21	18	15	12	9	7	4	2	0
260	270	29	25	22	19	16	13	11	8	5	3	1
270	280	30	27	24	21	18	15	12	9	7	4	2
280	290	32	29	25	22	19	16	13	10	8	5	3
290	300	34	30	27	24	21	18	15	12	9	7	4
300	310	35	32	28	25	22	19	16	13	10	8	5
360	370	46	42	38	35	31	28	25	22	19	16	13
370	380	48	44	40	36	33	30	26	23	20	17	14
380	390	49	46	42	38	35	31	28	25	21	19	16
390	400	51	47	44	40	36	33	30	26	23	20	17
400	410	53	49	46	42	38	35	31	28	25	21	18
410	420	55	51	47	44	40	36	33	29	20	23	20
420	430	58	53	49	45	42	38	34	31	28	24	21
430	440	60	55	51	47	43	40	36	33	29	26	23
440	450	62	57	53	49	45	42	38	34	31	28	24
450	460	64	60	55	51	47	43	40	36	33	29	26
750	760	145	138	131	125	120	114	108	102	97	91	86
760	770	148	142	135	128	122	117	111	105	99	94	89
770	780	152	145	138	131	125	119	114	108	102	96	91
780	790	155	148	141	134	128	122	116	111	105	99	94
790	800	158	151	145	138	131	125	119	113	108	102	96
800	810	162	155	148	141	134	128	122	116	110	105	99
810	820	165	158	151	144	138	131	125	119	113	107	102
820	830	168	161	155	148	141	134	128	122	116	110	104
830	840	172	165	158	151	144	137	130	125	119	113	107
840	850	175	168	161	154	147	141	134	127	122	116	110

Federal income tax wage-bracket table for married persons paid weekly.

- Refer to the table for the employee's marital status. Different tables are provided for single (including divorced, separated, or widowed) or married persons.
- Look down the wage columns (the first two columns at the left on each table). Ranges of wages are listed in these columns, which define various wage brackets. Locate the wage bracket that covers the amount of the employee's gross earnings.
- Follow across the line to the column for the number of withholding exemptions claimed on the employee's Form W-4.
- The amount in this block of the table is the income tax to be withheld from the employee's gross earnings.

For example, Sonia Brouse, a Computer Age employee, had gross earnings of $240 for the week ended April 6, 19—. She is married and claims three exemptions. Use the withholding table on page 437 for married persons paid weekly. Look down the wage columns for the bracket with $240 (at least $240, but less than $250). Follow this line across to the column for three exemptions. The amount in this block is $16.00.

Exercise D on page 442 may be completed at this point.

The Federal Insurance Contributions Act (FICA)

What does FICA require of employers and employees? The Federal Insurance Contributions Act (FICA) requires most employers and employees to pay taxes to support the federal social security programs. The **FICA tax** is a social security tax that is paid to the federal government for use in paying old-age, survivors, disability, and health insurance benefits. These are the principal federal social security programs.

- The old-age, survivors, and disability insurance program
- The federal health insurance program for the aged (Medicare)

The first program provides pensions to retired persons, disability payments to disabled persons, and benefits to dependents of insured workers who are disabled or deceased. This program and the Medicare program are operated by the federal government. Both programs are financed by taxes that are paid equally by both employers and employees.

The FICA tax is paid by both the employer and the employee. The tax is based only on the annual gross earnings of an employee up to a certain maximum amount paid during the calendar year (January 1 to December 31). As of this writing, the FICA tax is 7.15 percent and the maximum gross earnings subject to the tax is $42,000, and these are the figures used in the examples in this chapter. Annual gross earnings over $42,000 are not subject to the FICA tax. The present law provides for gradual increases in the FICA tax.

Let us see how the employee's share of the FICA tax is computed. Sonia Brouse had gross earnings of $240 for the week ended April 6. Since she earned $3,270 prior to this pay period, the entire amount of her gross earnings is subject to FICA tax. She has not earned $42,000 yet this year. To figure her FICA tax, multiply her gross earnings by 7.15 percent. The FICA tax is $17.16 (0.0715 × $240). The FICA tax can be found on the Social Security Employee Tax Table below.

Employee's FICA Tax

	Taxable	
FICA Tax =	Earnings ×	Rate
$17.16 =	$240 ×	7.15% (0.0715)

Social Security Employee Tax Table—Continued

7.15 percent employee tax deductions

Wages		Tax to be withheld	Wages		Tax to be withheld	Wages		Tax to be withheld	Wages		To to be withheld
At least	But less than		At least	But less than		At least	But less than		At least	But less than	
$ 99.66	$ 99.80	$ 7.13	$239.94	$240.07	$17.16	$279.66	$279.80	$20.00	$469.59	$469.73	$33.58
99.80	99.94	7.14	240.07	240.21	17.17	279.80	279.94	20.01	469.73	469.87	33.59
99.94	100.07	7.15	240.21	240.35	17.18	279.94	280.07	20.02	469.87	470.00	33.60
100.07	100.21	7.16	240.35	240.49	17.19	280.07	280.21	20.03	470.00	470.14	33.61
100.21	100.35	7.17	240.49	240.63	17.20	280.21	280.35	20.04	470.14	470.28	33.62
189.73	189.87	13.57	257.70	257.84	18.43	287.77	287.91	20.58	688.05	688.19	49.20
189.87	190.00	13.58	257.84	257.98	18.44	287.91	288.05	20.59	688.19	688.33	49.21
190.00	190.14	13.59	257.98	258.12	18.45	288.05	288.19	20.60	688.33	688.47	49.22
190.14	190.28	13.60	258.12	258.26	18.46	288.19	288.33	20.61	688.47	688.61	49.23
190.28	190.42	13.61	258.26	258.40	18.47	288.33	288.47	20.62	688.61	688.75	49.24
199.94	200.07	14.30	271.82	271.96	19.44	399.66	399.80	28.58	799.66	799.80	57.18
200.07	200.21	14.31	271.96	272.10	19.45	399.80	399.94.	28.59	799.80	799.94	57.19
200.21	200.35	14.32	272.10	272.24	19.46	399.94	400.07	28.60	799.94	800.07	57.20
200.35	200.49	14.33	272.24	272.38	19.47	400.07	400.21	28.61	800.07	800.21	57.21
200.49	200.63	14.34	272.38	272.52	19.48	400.21	400.35	28.62	800.21	800.35	57.22
214.62	214.76	15.35	275.60	275.74	19.71	415.60	415.74	29.72	824.69	824.83	58.97
214.76	214.90	15.36	275.74	275.88	19.72	415.74	415.88	29.73	824.83	824.97	58.98
214.90	215.04	15.37	275.88	276.02	19.73	415.88	416.02	29.74	824.97	825.11	58.99
215.04	215.18	15.38	276.02	276.16	19.74	416.02	416.16	29.75	825.11	825.25	59.00
215.18	215.32	15.39	276.16	276.30	19.75	416.16	416.30	29.76	825.25	825.39	59.01

The Internal Revenue Service provides a social security tax table that shows the amount of the FICA tax to be deducted from various wage amounts. Sometimes these tax amounts differ slightly from those figured by multiplying the earnings by 7.15 percent because of rounding to the nearest cent.

Suppose that you wish to compute the FICA tax for gross earnings not shown on the tax table. Remember that the FICA tax is levied on only $42,000 of the employee's gross earnings. Assume that Diane Sims has earned $41,600 prior to the current pay period. Now she has gross earnings of $450 during the current pay period. Only $400 of her gross earnings will be subject to FICA tax, because then she will have reached the maximum of $42,000 ($41,600 + $400). Her FICA tax, therefore, is $28.60 (0.0715 × $400). The FICA tax can be found on the social security tax table above.

Employee's FICA Tax

	Taxable	
FICA Tax =	Earnings ×	Rate
$28.60 =	$400 ×	7.15% (0.0715)

Every person covered by the federal social security law must have a social security account number. The social security account number is also used in many other ways. Taxpayers must supply their numbers with their federal income tax returns. Some banks use it as the depositor's bank account number. Many schools use it as the student's identi-

Social security card.

fication number. A person can get a social security card free of charge from the Social Security Administration.

■ State Income Tax

State income tax withholding is based on the same concept as federal income tax withholding. A certain amount is withheld from an employee's wages and paid to the state where the employee lives. The *state income tax* is a tax imposed by a state government on personal and business income. A state may also tax the income of nonresidents if the income is earned within that particular state.

While the federal tax law applies to all people in all states, state income tax law applies only to people in that specific state. Also, while some states have a personal income tax law, others do not. No one state follows the law of another state.

States that have state income tax withholding use different methods for figuring the tax. Some states use a percentage of the federal tax. Some use varying rates for different income brackets, with withholding tables similar to the federal income tax withholding tables. Others use a flat percentage rate. Below are examples of two state income tax withholding tables.

STATE INCOME TAX WITHHOLDING FOR WEEKLY PAYROLL PERIOD

Gross earnings minus $12.50 for each exemption claimed equals taxable earnings.

If taxable earnings are:

Earnings Range		Amount Withheld
More Than	**But Not Over**	**Amount to Be Withheld Is:**
$ 0	$ 96.15	$ .5% of such amount
96.15	192.31	.49 plus 1 % of excess over $ 96.15
192.31	288.46	1.45 plus 2 % of excess over $ 192.31
288.46	384.62	3.37 plus 2.5% of excess over $ 288.46
384.62	769.23	5.77 plus 3 % of excess over $ 384.62
769.23	—	17.31 plus 3.5% of excess over $ 769.23

MARRIED Persons — WEEKLY Payroll Period

AND THE WAGES ARE-		AND THE NUMBER OF WITHHOLDING EXEMPTIONS CLAIMED IS-										
AT LEAST	BUT LESS THAN	0	1	2	3	4	5	6	7	8	9	10 or More
		The Amount of Income Tax to be Withheld Shall Be-										
150	155	3.70	3.30	2.90	2.50	2.10	1.70	1.30	.90	.50	.10	
155	160	4.00	3.60	3.20	2.80	2.40	2.00	1.60	1.20	.80	.40	
160	165	4.20	3.80	3.40	3.00	2.60	2.20	1.80	1.40	1.00	.60	.20
165	170	4.50	4.10	3.70	3.30	2.90	2.50	2.10	1.70	1.30	.90	.50
170	175	4.70	4.30	3.90	3.50	3.10	2.70	2.30	1.90	1.50	1.10	.70
175	180	5.00	4.60	4.20	3.80	3.40	3.00	2.60	2.20	1.80	1.40	1.00
180	185	5.20	4.80	4.40	4.00	3.60	3.20	2.80	2.40	2.00	1.60	1.20
185	190	5.50	5.10	4.70	4.30	3.90	3.50	3.10	2.70	2.30	1.90	1.50
190	195	5.70	5.30	4.90	4.50	4.10	3.70	3.30	2.90	2.50	2.10	1.70
195	200	6.00	5.60	5.20	4.80	4.40	4.00	3.60	3.20	2.80	2.40	2.00
200	205	6.30	5.90	5.50	5.10	4.70	4.30	3.90	3.50	3.10	2.70	2.30
205	210	6.60	6.20	5.80	5.40	5.00	4.60	4.20	3.80	3.40	3.00	2.60
210	215	6.80	6.40	6.00	5.60	5.20	4.80	4.40	4.00	3.60	3.20	2.80
215	220	7.10	6.70	6.30	5.90	5.50	5.10	4.70	4.30	3.90	3.50	3.10
220	225	7.40	7.00	6.60	6.20	5.80	5.40	5.00	4.60	4.20	3.80	3.40

To illustrate the variations in income tax withholdings in two different states, assume that a married employee with three dependents has weekly gross earnings of $190. The state income tax withholding from the first table would be $1.05. From the second table, it would be $4.50.

For the purpose of completing exercises and problems in this chapter, the personal state income tax withholding will be computed using a flat rate of 2 percent. For the example above, the state income tax withholding on weekly gross earnings of $190 would be $3.80 (0.02 × $190).

■ Other Deductions Required by Law

In a few states, unemployment taxes and/or disability and sickness taxes must be deducted from an employee's gross earnings. The amounts to be deducted are specified by the laws in the various states. The procedure for figuring the amounts, however, is similar to the procedure described for the other taxes.

Another possible deduction is a garnishment. A **garnishment** is an amount ordered by a court to be deducted from an employee's earnings to pay a debt owed by that employee. Each pay period the employer withholds a set amount and sends it to the court until the debt has been paid.

■ Voluntary Deductions

An employee may ask to have voluntary deductions made for such items as safety or protective clothing, life insurance premiums, medical and hospitalization insurance premiums, pension plans, savings bonds, and donations to charity. The employee signs a written authorization for each deduction. These voluntary deductions are figured individually for each employee.

■ Union Deductions

Generally, employees who are members of a union must pay an initiation fee and union dues as a condition of employment. As part of the written agreement between the employer and the union, the employer usually withholds from an employee's earnings a certain amount for union dues.

The employer must have a written authorization from the employee before making a deduction for union dues, unless the deduction of union dues is a part of the contract between the employer and employees.

■ Computing Net Pay

All required, voluntary, and union deductions must be subtracted from the employee's gross earnings. The remainder is the employee's net pay. **Net pay** (commonly referred to as take-home pay) is the amount actually given to the employee.

The net pay for Sonia Brouse for the week ended April 27 is figured in the following way. Sonia Brouse's Form W-4 shows that she is married and claims three exemptions. Her time card shows that she worked 40 hours during the week. Her regular rate is $6.00 per hour. She has a voluntary deduction of $5 for group insurance premiums and a union deduction of $4 for dues.

Gross Earnings		−	Total Deductions		=	Net Pay
Regular .... 40 hours × $6.00 =	$240.00		Federal income tax withholding .	$21.00		
Overtime	36.00		State income tax withholding	5.52		
			FICA tax........................	19.73		
			Group insurance premiums.........	5.00		
			Union dues	4.00		
Gross earnings	$276.00	−	Total deductions	$55.25	=	Net pay.. $220.75

General Office Clerk: DOT 219.362-010
Performs variety of office duties, using knowledge of systems and procedures. May prepare payroll.

Concept: Tax Records
The employer is accountable to the government and to the employees for all amounts deducted from the employees' wages. The employer, therefore, must maintain adequate records of the amounts deducted.

Exercises E and F on this page and page 443 may be completed at this point.

TOPIC 3 EXERCISES

EXERCISE D. Find the amount to be deducted for federal income tax from the employees listed below. The gross earnings are for a weekly pay period. Refer to the federal income tax withholding tables on page 437.

Employee	Gross Earnings	Marital Status	No. of Exemp.	Employee	Gross Earnings	Marital Status	No. of Exemp.
1. B. Ali	$280	M	3	**5.** J. Reese	$470	S	5
2. J. Kruger	$272	S	1	**6.** D. Ryan	$800	M	6
3. A. Mingo	$416	M	2	**7.** H. Williams	$825	M	4
4. T. Moore	$288	S	1	**8.** R. Yannon	$400	M	3

EXERCISE E. Refer to the payroll information given in Exercise D to perform the following payroll activities. Find each employee's FICA tax by computing it at 7.15 percent. Prior to this pay period, D. Ryan had gross earnings of $41,800 and H. Williams had gross earnings of $43,000. All other employees had gross earnings of less than $30,000. Use $42,000 as the maximum amount of earnings subject to FICA tax. Check the taxes on the FICA tax table on page 439.

EXERCISE F. Refer to the payroll information in Exercise D to perform the following task. Find each employee's state income tax by using a tax rate of 2 percent.

TOPIC 3 PROBLEM

TOPIC PROBLEM 4. Use the payroll data you computed in Topic Problem 2 on page 434 to continue the duties of the payroll clerk for the Seasons Corporation. Compute the total deductions and net pay for the employees.

a. Use the time cards you prepared in Exercise C (page 434) to obtain the information about the earnings and hours of the four hourly-rate employees. The earnings and hours of the two salaried employees are as follows: Rose Casey earns $250 per week and works 40 hours; Daniel Blumberg earns $225 per week and works 40 hours.

b. Use the tables on page 437 for the federal income tax withholding to determine the tax withheld for the hourly-rate and salaried employees.

c. Compute the state income tax withholding by using a flat tax rate of 2 percent.

d. Compute the FICA tax. (All earnings are subject to a FICA tax rate of 7.15 percent. Multiply earnings times rate.)

e. Enter the deduction for insurance. Each employee has a deduction of $2 for insurance.

f. Enter the deduction for union dues. Each of the four hourly-rate employees has a deduction of $4 for union dues.

Empl. No.	Name	Marital Status	No. of Exemp.	Empl. No.	Name	Marital Status	No. of Exemp.
4	Susan Dole	S	5	14	Julie Laski	S	0
7	James Montero	S	5	20	Rose Casey	S	1
12	Robert Burke	S	1	24	Daniel Blumberg	M	3

TOPIC 4

Processing the Payroll

What are the steps used to process the payroll? Preparing the payroll includes these procedures.

- Journalizing the payroll
- Posting to the employee earnings records
- Posting to the general ledger accounts
- Recording and posting payroll taxes
- Recording and posting payment of the payroll and payroll taxes

Journalizing the Payroll

What is the payroll journal? The **payroll journal** is a special journal used to record payroll data for each pay period. The payroll journal used by Computer Age is illustrated here. The payroll data for each pay period for all employees is recorded in the payroll journal.

Control: Record all data from payroll transactions.

PAYROLL JOURNAL — Page *17*

For the Week Beginning *April 21,* 19 — **and Ending** *April 27,* 19 — **Paid** *April 29,* 19 —

Employee Data				Hours	Earnings			Deductions						Net Pay	
No.	Name	Marital Status	Exemp.		Regular	Overtime	Salaries Expense	Federal Income Taxes Payable	State Income Taxes Payable	FICA Taxes Payable	Insurance Premiums Payable	Union Dues Payable	Total	Salaries Payable	Ck. No.
1	S. Brouse	M	3	44	240 00	36 00	276 00	21 00	5 52	19 73	5 00	4 00	55 25	220 75	
2	B. Loren	S	1	38	190 00		190 00	20 00	3 80	13 59	5 00	4 00	46 39	143 61	
3	K. Mignon	S	2	40	200 00		200 00	19 00	4 00	14 30	5 00	4 00	46 30	153 70	
4	S. O'Brien	M	2	42	200 00	15 00	215 00	15 00	4 30	15 37	5 00	4 00	43 67	171 33	
5	C. Richard	M	1	20	100 00		100 00	4 00	2 00	7 15	5 00	4 00	22 15	77 85	
6	A. Vaughn	S	0	40	280 00		280 00	40 00	5 60	20 02	5 00	4 00	74 62	205 38	
	Totals				1,210 00	51 00	1,261 00	119 00	25 22	90 16	30 00	24 00	288 38	972 62	

Pay Period The beginning and ending dates of the pay period are entered at the top of the payroll journal. The Paid line is not completed until after the payroll has been paid. Although the pay period ends on April 27, the payroll will not be paid until April 29, as time is needed to prepare the payroll.

Employee Data The data for each employee—the number, name, marital status, and exemptions—is entered in the Employee Data section.

Control: Pay employees only for time worked or services rendered.

Earnings The total hours, regular earnings, overtime earnings, and total (gross) earnings of each employee are copied from the employee's time card into the Hours column and the Earnings section of the payroll journal. The accuracy of the Earnings section must be proved. The totals of the Regular Earnings plus Overtime Earnings columns must equal the amount of the Salaries Expense column, which is the total earnings.

Name Sonia Brouse Employee No. 1

Week Ending April 27, 19--

Extra Hours Approved		Hours	Rate	Earnings
	Regular	40	$6.00	$240.00
S. O'Brien	Overtime	4	$9.00	36.00
Supervisor	Total Hours	44	Gross Earnings	$276.00

Time cards provide the hours worked and gross earnings.

The column headings of the payroll journal, except for the Regular and Overtime Earnings and Total columns, name the account where the total of the column will eventually be posted. For example, the total in the Salaries Expense column ($1,261) will eventually be posted to that account. The total of the Salaries Expense account is the total expense for payroll for the pay period ended on April 27.

Control: Deduct authorized amounts from gross earnings.

■ Deductions In the Deductions section, each of the deductions is an amount withheld from the employee's earnings. Thus, each deduction is a liability to Computer Age. Each column heading in the Deductions section describes a different liability. For instance, amounts withheld for federal income taxes are recorded in the column Federal Income Taxes Payable. Amounts withheld for FICA taxes total $90.16 for the pay period ended April 27. Similar account titles are used for the other columns in the Deductions section. The Total column shows the total of each employee's deductions and the total of all deductions, but is not posted to any account.

■ Net Pay The last amount column—Salaries Payable—is the employer's liability for each employee's net pay. The total of the Salaries Payable column ($972.62) is the total liability for the net pay for the pay period ended April 27.

■ Proving the Payroll Journal After the data for each employee is entered in the payroll journal, the columns are pencil-footed. The payroll is then proved by adding and subtracting the columns as shown in the margin. When the journal is proved, the totals are written in ink and the columns are double-ruled.

Earnings:				
Regular	1,210	00		
Overtime	51	00		
Total			1,261	00
Deductions:				
Federal Inc. Taxes	119	00		
State Inc. Taxes	25	22		
FICA Taxes	90	16		
Insurance	30	00		
Union Dues	24	00		
Total			288	38
Net Pay			972	62

Proof of payroll journal.

■ Posting to the Employee Earnings Records

After the payroll journal is totaled and proved, the payroll information is posted to the employee earnings records. An **employee earnings record** shows the details of an employee's earnings and deductions for

EMPLOYEE EARNINGS RECORD FOR YEAR 19—

Name Sonia Brouse
Address 16 Carmine Drive
Englewood, Colorado 80110
Telephone No. 303-555-8346
Date of Birth June 14, 1959
Rate $6.00 Per Hour

Employee No. 1
Social Security No. 201-26-8341
Marital Status Married
Withholding Exemptions 3
Position Accounting Department
Date Employed January 2, 19—

DATE		HOURS	EARNINGS						DEDUCTIONS															
PERIOD ENDING	PAID		REGULAR		OVERTIME		TOTAL		FEDERAL INCOME TAX		STATE INCOME TAX		FICA TAX		INSURANCE PREMIUMS		UNION DUES		TOTAL		NET PAY		YEAR-TO-DATE EARNINGS	
19—																								
Apr. 6	4/8/—	40	240	00			240	00	16	00	4	80	17	16	5	00	4	00	46	96	193	04	3,510	00
13	4/15/—	42	240	00	18	00	258	00	18	00	5	16	18	45	5	00	4	00	50	61	207	39	3,768	00
20	4/22/—	40	240	00			240	00	16	00	4	80	17	16	5	00	4	00	46	96	193	04	4,008	00
27	4/29/—	44	240	00	36	00	276	00	21	00	5	52	19	73	5	00	4	00	55	25	220	75	4,284	00

the year. Federal law requires employers to keep all records of employee earnings and payroll taxes for at least four years.

Control: Maintain employee earnings records.

Employee Earnings Records as a Subsidiary Ledger

The employee earnings records are often viewed as a subsidiary ledger, and the Salaries Expense account in the general ledger is its controlling account.

The proof of the subsidiary ledger (employee earnings records) and the controlling account (Salaries Expense) is rather easy. The last amounts in the Year-to-Date Earnings column of each employee earnings record are added. The total is then compared to and must be the same as the balance of Salaries Expense in the general ledger. Any disagreement must be found and corrected.

Salaries Expense		*518*
19—		
Apr. 20	*19,352*	
27	*1,261*	
	20,613	

Year-to-date total for each employee as of 4/27/—

```
     0.00T
 4,284.00
 4,000.00
 4,774.00
 4,385.00
 1,998.00
 1,172.00
20,613.00T
```

Total Salaries Expense → 20,613.00T

COMPUTER AGE CHART OF ACCOUNTS

Liabilities
- 221 Federal Income Taxes Payable
- 222 FICA Taxes Payable
- 223 State Income Taxes Payable
- 224 Federal Unemployment Taxes Payable
- 225 State Unemployment Taxes Payable
- 226 Salaries Payable
- 227 Insurance Premiums Payable
- 228 Union Dues Payable

Costs and Expenses
- 516 Payroll Taxes Expense
- 518 Salaries Expense

Posting to the General Ledger Accounts

Details in the payroll journal are posted to the employee earnings records. The totals of the payroll journal provide the data for posting the payroll to the ledger accounts.

Posting From the Payroll Journal The date used to post from the payroll journal is the end of the pay period. In the journal shown on the next page, the end of the pay period is April 27. The amounts posted to the ledger accounts are the totals of the special columns.

"PR17" is written in the Posting Reference column for each ledger account to show that the amount was posted from page 17 of the payroll journal. (Pages in the payroll journal are numbered consecutively.) The proper ledger account number is written beneath each special column to show that an amount was posted.

The effect of posting the payroll journal for the pay period ended April 27 is described here.

- Salaries Expense is debited to decrease owner's equity by $1,261—the total of the salaries earned by the employees.

PAYROLL JOURNAL **Page** *17*

For the Week Beginning *April 21,* **19 —** **and Ending** *April 27,* **19 —** **Paid** *April 29,* **19 —**

EMPLOYEE DATA					EARNINGS			DEDUCTIONS						NET PAY	
NO.	NAME	MARITAL STATUS	EXEMP.	HOURS	REGULAR	OVERTIME	SALARIES EXPENSE	FEDERAL INCOME TAXES PAYABLE	STATE INCOME TAXES PAYABLE	FICA TAXES PAYABLE	INSURANCE PREMIUMS PAYABLE	UNION DUES PAYABLE	TOTAL	SALARIES PAYABLE	CK. NO.
1	*S. Brouse*	*M*	*3*	*44*	*240 00*	*36 00*	*276 00*	*21 00*	*5 52*	*19 73*	*5 00*	*4 00*	*55 25*	*220 75*	
	Totals				*1,210 00*	*51 00*	*1,261 00*	*119 00*	*25 22*	*90 16*	*30 00*	*24 00*	*288 38*	*972 62*	
							(518)	*(221)*	*(223)*	*(222)*	*(227)*	*(228)*		*(226)*	

Salaries Expense 518
PR17 1,261.00 |

Federal Income Taxes Payable 221
| *PR17 119.00*

State Income Taxes Payable 223
| *PR17 25.22*

FICA Taxes Payable 222
| *PR17 90.16*

Insurance Premiums Payable 227
| *PR17 30.00*

Union Dues Payable 228
| *PR17 24.00*

Salaries Payable 226
| *PR17 972.62*

- Each of the payable accounts is credited to increase the amount owed for each liability. In the payroll journal above, the accounts credited are Federal Income Taxes Payable, State Income Taxes Payable, FICA Taxes Payable, Insurance Premiums Payable, Union Dues Payable, and Salaries Payable.

Recording and Posting Payroll Taxes

Must employers pay payroll taxes? Yes, federal and state laws require employers as well as employees to pay payroll taxes.

Both the employer and the employee contribute to FICA; only the employer contributes to the federal and state unemployment taxes.

Employer FICA Tax Employers also pay taxes to the social security program. The employer's tax is at the same rate as the employee's FICA tax and is paid on the same earnings used to compute the employee's FICA tax (7.15 percent on a maximum of $42,000 for each employee).

None of the employees of Computer Age has earned over $42,000 before April 27. Thus, the business owes FICA tax of $90.16 ($1,261 × 0.0715).

Employer's FICA Tax

Tax	=	Rate	×	Taxable Earnings
$90.16	=	0.0715	×	$1,261

Federal Unemployment Compensation Tax (FUTA) The minimum FUTA tax is 0.8 percent* of the first $7,000 paid to each covered employee during a calendar year. The employees do not pay any FUTA tax. None of the employees of Computer Age earned over $7,000 before April 27. Thus, the business owes FUTA tax of $10.09 ($1,261 × 0.008) on the April 27 payroll.

FUTA Tax

Tax	=	Rate	×	Taxable Earnings
$10.09	=	0.008	×	$1,261

*The 0.8 percent is computed as follows. The FUTA tax rate is 6.2 percent. However, the employer may take a credit against this up to 5.4 percent for contributions paid to state unemployment funds. This leaves a 0.8 percent net federal tax.

SUTA Tax

Tax = Rate × Taxable Earnings
$68.09 = 0.054 × $1,261

■ State Unemployment Compensation Tax (SUTA)
Unemployment taxes vary among states. In general, employers are required to pay up to a 5.4 percent tax on the first $7,000 paid to each employee in a calendar year. This text uses the maximum rate for the state unemployment compensation tax (5.4 percent). At the maximum rate, the state unemployment compensation tax on the April 27 payroll of Computer Age would be $68.09 ($1,261 × 0.054).

5.4% on 1st $7,000 paid to each employee

Payroll taxes expense

■ Payroll Taxes Expense The employer's FICA tax and federal and state unemployment compensation taxes are expenses to the employer. A separate expense account can be kept for each tax, but usually they are combined. Thus, one amount is entered in one expense account, Payroll Taxes Expense. These individual taxes are liabilities until they are paid. A separate liability account is usually kept for each tax.

The entry to record the employer's payroll taxes for Computer Age is made in the general journal at the end of each payroll period. The April 27 entry is shown below.

GENERAL JOURNAL Page *17*

DATE		ACCOUNT TITLE AND EXPLANATION	POST. REF.	DEBIT		CREDIT	
19—							
Apr.	*27*	*Payroll Taxes Expense*	*516*	*168*	*34*		
		FICA Taxes Payable	*222*			*90*	*16*
		Federal Unemployment Taxes Payable	*224*			*10*	*09*
		State Unemployment Taxes Payable . .	*225*			*68*	*09*
		To record employer's payroll taxes.					

Record employer's payroll taxes.

Exercise G on pages 450 and 451 may be completed at this point.

■ Methods of Paying Employees
The method for paying employees depends on whether a business chooses to pay by cash, bank transfer, or check. Computer Age pays its employees by check.

■ Paying by Cash When the payroll is paid in cash, the payroll clerk must determine the number of bills and coins of each denomination needed for each employee's pay envelope. Then a *currency requisition* is prepared. It is a form that lists the denomination, quantity, amounts, and total cash needed. A check is then drawn for the total net pay. The check must agree with the total net pay shown in the payroll journal. When the check is cashed, the payroll clerk will receive the bills and coins in the denominations needed for the payroll.

Employers usually provide an employee pay statement to each employee. An **employee pay statement** is a summary of earnings and deductions for an employee for a pay period. An employee pay statement is given with each method of paying employees.

When the payroll is paid in cash, the employee pay statement is usually printed on the pay envelope and the employee may be asked to sign some kind of receipt.

Paying by Bank Transfer Some businesses pay their employees by bank transfer. A **bank transfer** is a method of transferring funds from one account to one or more other accounts. In this method, the employer gives the bank a check for the total net pay and a list showing the net pay for each employee. On payday, the bank deposits the net pay into each employee's bank account. Each employee receives a pay statement showing the gross earnings, the deductions, and the amount deposited in his or her account.

Paying by Check Most businesses prefer to pay their employees by check. This provides the employer with cancelled checks as proof that the employees have been paid. It also avoids having a large amount of cash on hand on paydays and sorting the cash into individual pay envelopes.

When paying the payroll, use prenumbered checks and designate authorized personnel to sign the checks.

Computer Age uses a voucher check for paying its employees. A **voucher check** consists of two parts, one of which is a check. The lower part of Computer Age's voucher check is a regular check. The upper part (or voucher part) is the employee pay statement and is kept by the employee as a record of gross earnings, deductions, and net pay for the pay period.

Period Ending	Date Paid	Hours Worked	Earnings: Regular	Earnings: Overtime	Earnings: Total	Deductions: Federal Withholding	Deductions: State Withholding	Deductions: FICA	Deductions: Insurance	Deductions: Union Dues	Deductions: Other	Deductions: Total	Net Pay: Amount	Net Pay: Ck. No.
Apr. 27	Apr. 29	44	240.00	36.00	276.00	21.00	5.52	19.73	5.00	4.00		55.25	220.75	188

Employee Pay Statement
Detach and retain for your records.

COMPUTER AGE
Denver, Colorado 80236

The voucher portion is kept by the employee.

COMPUTER AGE
200 Girard Avenue
Denver, Colorado 80236

Payroll Check

23-156
1020

No. 188

April 29, 19 --

Pay To The Order Of Sonia Brouse $ 220.75

Two hundred twenty and 75/100 Dollars

Merchants Bank
Denver, Colorado 80201

Jason Booth

⑆1020⑈156⑆ 5050⑈020600⑈

The check is cashed or deposited by the employee.

Recording a Payment of the Payroll

When the payroll is paid, the total amount of all the payroll checks is entered in the cash payments journal. The amounts are posted from the journal to the ledger accounts. The liability Salaries Payable is decreased and the asset Cash is decreased. The entry to pay the payroll for Computer Age is illustrated on page 450.

cash payment journal total amt of payroll checks

CASH PAYMENTS JOURNAL									Page 17
DATE		ACCOUNT DEBITED	EXPLANATION	CHECK NO.	POST. REF.	GENERAL LEDGER DEBIT	ACCOUNTS PAYABLE DEBIT	PURCHASES DISCOUNT CREDIT	NET CASH CREDIT
19—									
Apr.	*29*	*Salaries Payable .*	*April 27 payroll . .*	*188–193*	*226*	*972 62*			*972 62*

Cash	*101*	*Salaries Payable*	*226*
	972.62	*972.62*	*972.62*

Payment of the payroll.

The last step is to enter the check numbers for individual employee paychecks in the payroll journal, as shown below.

PAYROLL JOURNAL **Page** *17*

For the Week Beginning *April 22,* **19 — and Ending** *April 28,* **19 — Paid** *April 29,* **19 —**

EMPLOYEE DATA					EARNINGS			DEDUCTIONS						NET PAY	
NO.	NAME	MARITAL STATUS	EXEMP.	HOURS	REGULAR	OVERTIME	SALARIES EXPENSE	FEDERAL INCOME TAXES PAYABLE	STATE INCOME TAXES PAYABLE	FICA TAXES PAYABLE	INSURANCE PREMIUMS PAYABLE	UNION DUES PAYABLE	TOTAL	SALARIES PAYABLE	CK. NO.
1	*S. Brouse . . . .*	*M*	*3*	*44*	*240 00*	*36 00*	*276 00*	*21 00*	*5 52*	*19 73*	*5 00*	*4 00*	*55 25*	*220 75*	*188*

Enter check number.

Exercise H on page 451 may be completed at this point.

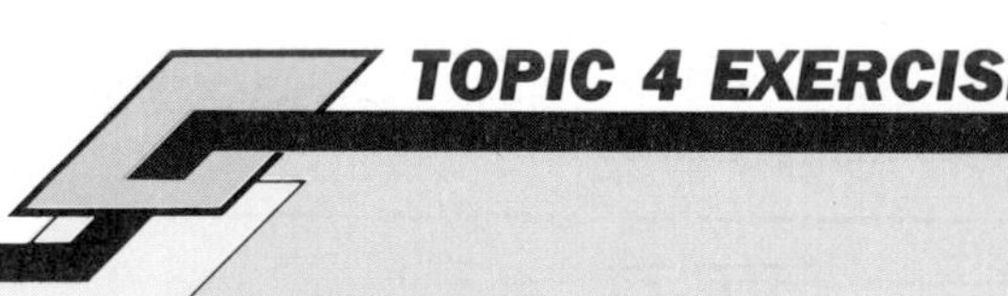

TOPIC 4 EXERCISES

EXERCISE G. Answer the following questions about processing the payroll. Refer to the text, margin notes, and illustrations on pages 443 to 448.

1. What is the source of payroll information posted to the general ledger?
2. By what amount did posting the payroll journal decrease owner's equity?
3. By what amount did posting the payroll journal increase total liabilities?
4. To what account was the total of the Regular Earnings column posted? Why?
5. How much does the employer owe for FICA taxes?
6. What is the total amount the employer owes for payroll taxes? In what journal is this amount recorded?
7. How much do the employees owe for federal unemployment taxes? State unemployment taxes? Why?

8. Why is the employer's FICA tax described as a "matching tax"?

9. In what journal is the entry recorded to pay the payroll?

10. What account is debited to record payment of the payroll? What account is credited?

EXERCISE H. Using the employee information and data about earnings for the week ended July 28 in the table below, compute the federal income tax withholding and FICA taxes for each employee. Use the tax tables on page 437. Set up a table similar to the one found here. No employee has reached the FICA maximum. If the FICA tax cannot be found on the Social Security Tax Table, multiply the earnings times 0.0715 to find the tax amount.

NOTE: Save your work for further use in Topic Problem 5.

Employee	Marital Status	No. of Exemp.	Federal Withholding	FICA Taxes	Data From Time Cards
1. J. Benedict	M	3	?	?	40 hours @ $7.45 = $298.00
2. H. Brown	M	5	?	?	40 hours @ $7.50 = $300.00
3. M. Coria	S	1	?	?	39 hours @ $5.75 = $224.25
4. I. Griesbaum	S	1	?	?	40 hours @ $5.30 = $212.00
5. P. Shea	S	1	?	?	37 hours @ $7.35 = $271.95

TOPIC 4 PROBLEMS

TOPIC PROBLEM 5. Use your work from Exercise H to complete the following payroll activities.

a. Record the payroll for the week ended July 28 in a payroll journal. The state Income tax rate is 2 percent of total earnings. Each employee has a deduction for insurance ($5.50) and union dues ($7.00) each week. In addition, both P. Shea and H. Brown have $12.50 deducted each week for United States savings bonds.

b. Total and prove your payroll journal.

c. Post the salaries expense and payroll liabilities to the general ledger.

NOTE: Save your work for further use in Topic Problem 6.

TOPIC PROBLEM 6. Payroll data for five employees is given here.

a. Record this data in employee earnings records.

1. Joseph Benedict: address, 245 North Third Street, Trenton, New Jersey 08602; telephone number, (609) 555-3807; date of birth, June 14, 1960; rate, $7.45 per hour; employee number, 1; social security number, 174-91-6532; marital status, married; withholding exemptions, 3; position, accounting supervisor; date employed, May 23, 1985; year-to-date earnings, $10,200.

2. Harlan Brown: address, Carter Road, Yardley, Pennsylvania 19067; telephone number, (215) 555-2891; date of birth, August 23, 1952; rate, $7.50 per hour; employee number, 2; social security number, 111-18-7091; marital status, married; withholding exemptions, 5; position, salesperson/full-charge bookkeeper; date employed, March 9 1978; year-to-date earnings, $12,300.
3. Maryann Coria: address, P.O. Box 719, Pennington, New Jersey 08534; telephone number, (609) 555-4382; date of birth, October 22, 1965; rate, $5.75 per hour; employee number, 3; social security number, 928-92-1100; marital status, single; withholding exemptions, 1; position, accounting clerk; date employed, March 13, 19—(current year); year-to-date earnings, $4,500.
4. Iris Griesbaum: address, 976 Carol Place, Washington Crossing, Pennsylvania 18977; telephone number, (215) 555-1759; date of birth, June 12, 1953; rate, $5.30 per hour; employee number, 4; social security number, 204-28-8623; marital status, single; withholding exemptions, 1; position, salesperson; date employed, August 7, 1980; year-to-date earnings, $8,200.
5. Patrick Shea: address, Blytine Avenue; Lawrenceville, New Jersey 08648; telephone number, (609) 555-3605; date of birth, February 14, 1954, rate, $7.35 per hour; employee number, 5; social security number, 204-28-6107; marital status, single; withholding exemptions, 1; position, payroll and accounting clerk; date employed, November 5, 1977; year-to-date earnings, $10,700.

b. Record the information from the payroll journal completed in Topic Problem 5.

c. Record and post the employer's payroll taxes.

d. Record and post the payment of the payroll. The next available check is No. 78.

e. Record the check numbers in the payroll journal.

f. Record the date on which the payroll was paid in the employee earnings records.

TOPIC 5

Preparing Payroll Tax Returns

Completing the payroll tax returns is an integral part of the activities performed by the payroll department.

What is the employer's responsibility for payroll taxes? Payroll tax returns must be prepared and the taxes paid on or before the due dates. The federal and state governments have time schedues for all employers to report and pay payroll taxes. The time schedules are based on the calendar year. What this means is that a business must use the calendar year for payroll tax purposes.

Paying Federal Taxes

The federal income taxes and the employees' and employer's shares of the FICA taxes must be paid to the Internal Revenue Service. The employer pays the taxes by depositing the amount due in a Federal Reserve bank or an approved commercial bank.

Federal Tax Deposit Coupon (Form 8109) **Form 8109** is the tax form that is used to deposit federal income taxes and FICA taxes. The due dates for depositing these taxes depend on the amount of undeposited taxes.

SCHEDULE OF DEPOSITS FOR FEDERAL INCOME TAX WITHHOLDING AND FICA TAXES

Effective Date	Amount	Deposit Due	Example
3d, 7th, 11th, 15th, 19th, 22d, 25th, or last day of any month	$3,000 or more	Within 3 banking days after effective date.	Undeposited taxes on April 22 are $3,100. Must deposit within 3 banking days after April 22.
Last day of any month of a quarter	$500 or more but less than $3,000	Within 15 days after end of month.	Undeposited taxes on February 28 are $600. Must deposit by March 15.
	Less than $500	Hold until the following month. Deposit at end of quarter.	Undeposited taxes on February 28 are $170. Hold until March 31. Rule below then shows April 30.
Last day of third month of a quarter (Mar., June, Sept., Dec.)	$500 or more but less than $3,000	By the last day of next month.	Undeposited taxes on June 30 are $575. Must deposit by July 31.
	Less than $500	May make deposit by last day of next month, or may file with quarterly tax return (Form 941).	Undeposited taxes on March 31 are $340. May either deposit or pay with tax return by April 30.

The undeposited taxes for Computer Age on April 30 are $1,272.17, as shown in the table in the margin. (The calendar quarter is April, May, and June.) The quarter ends on June 30. The undeposited amount of taxes is more than $500 but less than $3,000 for the first month of the quarter. Thus, the taxes must be deposited by May 15. The deposit must include a Federal Tax Deposit Coupon (Form 8109). Form 8109 is illustrated here.

Undeposited Payroll Taxes on April 30

Employees':	Federal income taxes	$ 650.00
	FICA taxes	311.09
Employer's:	FICA taxes	311.08
	Total	$1,272.17

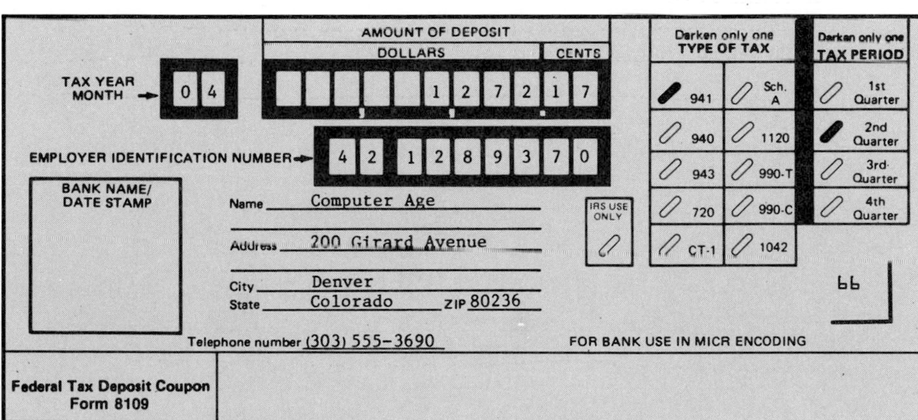

AMOUNT OF DEPOSIT — DOLLARS | CENTS: 1 2 7 2 | 1 7

TAX YEAR MONTH → 0 4

EMPLOYER IDENTIFICATION NUMBER → 42 1289370

Darken only one TYPE OF TAX: 941 (darkened), Sch. A, 940, 1120, 943, 990-T, 720, 990-C, CT-1, 1042

Darken only one TAX PERIOD: 1st Quarter, 2nd Quarter (darkened), 3rd Quarter, 4th Quarter

BANK NAME/ DATE STAMP

Name Computer Age

Address 200 Girard Avenue

City Denver

State Colorado ZIP 80236

IRS USE ONLY

66

Telephone number (303) 555-3690

FOR BANK USE IN MICR ENCODING

Federal Tax Deposit Coupon Form 8109

Form 8109 showing deposit of taxes on April payrolls.

On May 5, $1,272.17 was deposited in the Merchants Bank, which is a commercial bank qualified as a depository for federal taxes. The entry to journalize the check includes debits to the liability accounts because the liabilities are decreased. The Federal Income Taxes Payable account is debited for the amount of income taxes withheld ($650). The FICA Taxes Payable account is debited for $622.17. This is the total of the employees' FICA taxes withheld ($311.09) and the employer's FICA tax ($311.08). The Cash account is credited for $1,272.17.

CASH PAYMENTS JOURNAL — **Page** *18*

DATE		ACCOUNT DEBITED	EXPLANATION	CHECK NO.	POST. REF.	GENERAL LEDGER DEBIT	ACCOUNTS PAYABLE DEBIT	PURCHASES DISCOUNT CREDIT	NET CASH CREDIT
19—									
May	5	*Fed. Inc. Taxes Pay.* . .	*Deposit for April*	217	221	*650 00*			*1,272 17*
		FICA Taxes Payable . .			222	*622 17*			

Cash 101		*Federal Income Taxes Payable* 221		*FICA Taxes Payable* 222	
	19— *May 5* *1,272.17*	*19—* *May 5* *650.00*	*19—* *Apr. 30* *650.00*	*19—* *May 5* *622.17*	*19—* *Apr. 30* *622.17*

Entry for May 5 deposit of income taxes withheld and FICA taxes for April.

■ Employer's Quarterly Federal Tax Return (Form 941)

The employer must file an Employer's Quarterly Federal Tax Return (Form 941) with the Internal Revenue Service. The **Form 941** return shows the total federal income tax withheld and the total FICA taxes (employees' and employer's shares) for the quarter. Form 941 must be filed by the last day of the month following the end of the calendar quarter.

Form 941, illustrated on the next page, shows that Computer Age paid total wages subject to withholding in the amount of $15,800. Employee income tax withheld totals $1,460.00. The FICA tax for both employees and employer is $2,259.40 ($15,800 × 0.143). All taxes withheld and owed during the quarter total $3,719.40.

The three monthly payments deposited in a federal depository bank are $1,272.17, $1,134.12, and $1,313.11. These total $3,719.40 and are shown in the record of federal tax liability in the lower part of Form 941. Note that the total of the Tax Liability column which is shown on Line IV at the bottom of the form, equals the net taxes for the quarter on Line 16.

Form **941** Department of the Treasury Internal Revenue Service 4141

Employer's Quarterly Federal Tax Return

▶ For Paperwork Reduction Act Notice, see page 2.

Please type or print

Your name, address, employer identification number, and calendar quarter of return. (If not correct, please change.)

Name (as distinguished from trade name): Jason Booth — Date quarter ended: June 30, 19--

Trade name, if any: Computer Age — Employer identification number: 42-1289370

Address and ZIP code: 200 Girard Avenue, Denver, Colorado 80236

OMB No. 1545-0029 — T, FF, FD, FP, I, T

If address is different from prior return, check here ▶ ☐

IRS Use: 1 1 1 1 1 1 1 1 1 1 2 2 2 2 2 2 2 2 2 3 3 3 3 3 3 / 4 5 5 5 6 6 6 7 8 8 9 9 9 9 9 9 10 10 10 11 11 11 11 11 11 11 11 11 11

If you are not liable for returns in the future, check here ▶ ☐ Date final wages paid ▶

Complete for First Quarter Only

1a	Number of employees (except household) employed in the pay period that includes March 12th ▶		1a	
b	If you are a subsidiary corporation AND your parent corporation files a consolidated Form 1120, enter parent corporation employer identification number (EIN) ▶ 1b –			
2	Total wages and tips subject to withholding, plus other compensation ▶		2	15,800 00
3	Total income tax withheld from wages, tips, pensions, annuities, sick pay, gambling, etc. ▶		3	1,460 00
4	Adjustment of withheld income tax for preceding quarters of calendar year (see instructions) ▶		4	
5	Adjusted total of income tax withheld		5	1,460 00
6	Taxable social security wages paid $ 15,800 00	X 14.3% (.143)	6	2,259 40
7a	Taxable tips reported $	X 7.15% (.0715)	7a	
b	Tips deemed to be wages (see instructions) $	X 7.15% (.0715)	7b	
c	Taxable hospital insurance wages paid $	X 2.9% (.029)	7c	
8	Total social security taxes (add lines 6, 7a, 7b, and 7c)		8	2,259 40
9	Adjustment of social security taxes (see instructions for required explanation) ▶		9	
10	Adjusted total of social security taxes (see instructions)		10	2,259 40
11	Backup withholding ▶		11	
12	Adjustment of backup withholding tax for preceding quarters of calendar year		12	
13	Adjusted total of backup withholding		13	
14	Total taxes (add lines 5, 10, and 13) ▶		14	3,719 40
15	Advance earned income credit (EIC) payments, if any (see instructions)		15	
16	Net taxes (subtract line 15 from line 14). **This must equal line IV below** (plus line IV of Schedule A (Form 941) if you have treated backup withholding as a separate liability.)		16	3,719 40
17	Total deposits for quarter, including overpayment applied from a prior quarter, from your records ▶		17	3,719 40
18	Balance due (subtract line 17 from line 16). This should be less than $500. Pay to IRS ▶		18	-0-
19	If line 17 is more than line 16, enter overpayment here ▶ $ and check if to be: ☐ Applied to next return or ☐ Refunded.			

Record of Federal Tax Liability (Complete if line 16 is $500 or more) See the instructions under rule 4 for details before checking these boxes.

Check only if you made eighth-monthly deposits using the 95% rule ▶ ☐ Check only if you are a first time 3-banking-day depositor ▶ ☐

Date wages paid	First month of quarter		Second month of quarter		Third month of quarter	
1st through 3rd	A		I		Q	
26th through the last	H		P		X	
Total liability for month	I	1,272.17	II	1,134.12	III	1,313.11
IV Total for quarter (add lines I, II, and III) ▶						3,719.40

Under penalties of perjury, I declare that I have examined this return, including accompanying schedules and statements, and to the best of my knowledge and belief it is true, correct, and complete.

Signature ▶ *Jason Booth* Title ▶ Owner Date ▶ July 17, 19--

Form 941 reporting income taxes withheld and FICA taxes for the calendar quarter ending June 30. The quarter covers the April, May, and June payrolls. (If an employer owes less than $500 at the end of the quarter, the amount may be sent with Form 941.)

■ Paying Unemployment Compensation Taxes

The state unemployment compensation tax is paid quarterly. The date for paying the federal unemployment compensation tax depends on the amount of tax to be paid.

■ State Unemployment Compensation Taxes The form for the state unemployment compensation taxes return varies with each state. Usually the form asks for the names of the employees and their taxable earnings during the quarter.

The employer's payroll taxes are recorded when the payroll is paid. On June 30, the State Unemployment Taxes Payable account for Computer Age has a balance of $681. This amount is 5.4 percent of the

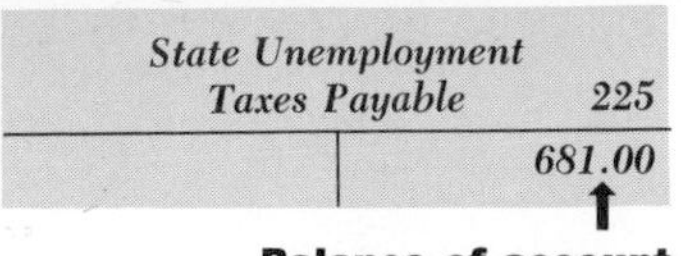

Balance of account on June 30 is amount due for quarter.

taxable salaries and wages paid during the quarter. The quarter covers the months of April, May, and June.

During the quarter, the employees of Computer Age had gross earnings of $15,800. However, some employees passed the $7,000 maximum gross earnings for these taxes. Thus, the earnings subject to unemployment compensation taxes are less than the gross earnings.

A payment of $681.00 was sent for the state unemployment taxes on July 17. The liability account State Unemployment Taxes Payable is debited because the liability is decreased. The asset account Cash is credited because the asset is decreased.

CASH PAYMENTS JOURNAL — Page *19*

DATE		ACCOUNT DEBITED	EXPLANATION	CHECK NO.	POST. REF.	GENERAL LEDGER DEBIT	ACCOUNTS PAYABLE DEBIT	PURCHASES DISCOUNT CREDIT	NET CASH CREDIT
19—									
July	*17*	*State Unempl. Taxes Payable . .*	*Second quarter taxes . . . .*	*280*	*225*	*681 00*			*681 00*

Cash 101	
	681.00

State Unemployment Taxes Payable 225	
681.00	*681.00*

Entry for second quarter's state unemployment taxes deposited on July 17.

Federal Unemployment Compensation Taxes

For deposit purposes, federal unemployment compensation taxes should be figured quarterly. If the amount owed is more than $100 for any quarter, that amount must be deposited by the last day of the month following the quarter. The deposit must be made in a federal depository bank. A Federal Tax Deposit Coupon (Form 8109) must be sent with each deposit.

Amounts of $100 or less do not have to be deposited until the quarter when the tax owed exceeds $100. The table here lists the schedule of deposits for federal unemployment taxes.

SCHEDULE OF DEPOSITS FOR FEDERAL UNEMPLOYMENT TAXES

Amount	Effective Day	Deposit Due
More than $100	Last day of quarter	Last day of following month
More than $100	Last day of year	January 31
Less than $100	Last day of quarter	Quarter when tax exceeds $100
Less than $100	Last day of year	January 31 or pay with Form 940

During the first quarter, Computer Age paid taxable salaries and wages of $22,300. None of the employees passed the maximum gross earnings during the quarter. Thus, all salaries and wages paid were subject to the federal unemployment compensation tax of 0.8 percent. Computer Age owed $178.40 ($22,300 × 0.008) for the first quarter. This exceeded $100, and the tax must be deposited.

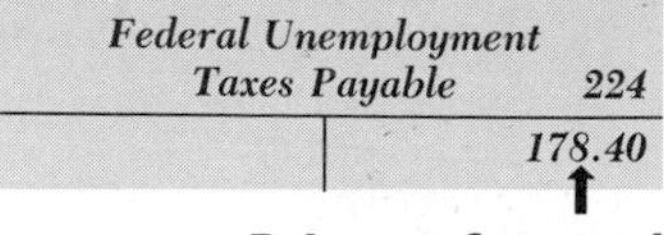

Balance of account on March 31 is amount due.

The deposit is made in a federal depository bank. The balance of the Federal Unemployment Taxes Payable account on March 31 shows the amount to be deposited.

Because the amount of taxes owed in the first quarter exceeds $100, the federal unemployment compensation taxes must be deposited in April, the first month following the quarter. A Federal Tax Deposit Coupon (Form 8109) must accompany the deposit.

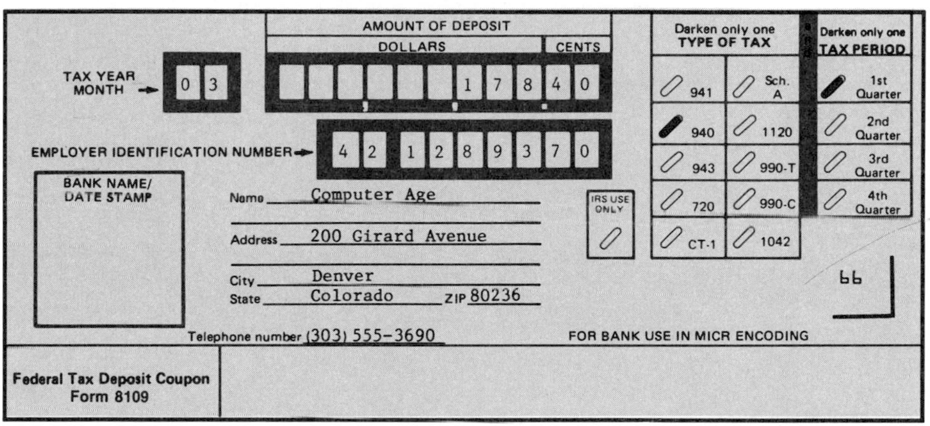

AMOUNT OF DEPOSIT
DOLLARS 178 CENTS 40

TAX YEAR MONTH → 0 3

EMPLOYER IDENTIFICATION NUMBER → 42 1289370

BANK NAME/ DATE STAMP

Name Computer Age

Address 200 Girard Avenue

City Denver

State Colorado ZIP 80236

Telephone number (303) 555-3690

IRS USE ONLY

Darken only one TYPE OF TAX: 941, Sch. A, 940 (darkened), 1120, 943, 990-T, 720, 990-C, CT-1, 1042

Darken only one TAX PERIOD: 1st Quarter (darkened), 2nd Quarter, 3rd Quarter, 4th Quarter

FOR BANK USE IN MICR ENCODING

Federal Tax Deposit Coupon Form 8109

The payment is recorded in the cash payments journal. The liability account Federal Unemployment Taxes Payable is debited because the liability is decreased. The asset account Cash is credited because the asset is decreased. The entry to record the deposit of federal unemployment compensation taxes on April 19 is presented here.

CASH PAYMENTS JOURNAL **Page** *17*

DATE		ACCOUNT DEBITED	EXPLANATION	CHECK NO.	POST. REF.	GENERAL LEDGER DEBIT	ACCOUNTS PAYABLE DEBIT	PURCHASES DISCOUNT CREDIT	NET CASH CREDIT
19—									
Apr.	*19*	*Fed. Unempl. Taxes Payable . .*	*First quarter deposit . . . .*	*68*	*224*	*178 40*			*178 40*

Cash	*101*
	178.40

Federal Unemployment Taxes Payable	*224*
178.40	*178.40*

Entry for federal unemployment taxes deposited on April 19.

Form W-2 is due to employees by January 31 or within 30 days if employee leaves.

Preparing Wage and Tax Statements

How are employees informed of yearly earnings? By January 31, the employer is required to give each employee a Wage and Tax Statement (Form W-2). **Form W-2**, which is illustrated below, is a federal tax form that shows the following information for the previous year.

- Federal income tax information, including the amount of federal income tax withheld from the employee and the total amount of the employee's earnings
- Social security information, including the FICA tax withheld from the employee's earnings and the total amount of the employee's earnings subject to FICA taxes
- State or local income tax information, including information regarding the wages paid and state or local taxes withheld

The information for Form W-2 is obtained from the employee earnings records, as shown below. The Yearly Totals section on the em-

1 Control number		OMB No. 1545-0008
2 Employer's name, address, and ZIP code Computer Age 200 Girard Avenue Denver, Colorado 80236	3 Employer's identification number 42-1289370	4 Employer's state I.D. number 42370
	5 Statutory employee ☐ Deceased ☐ Legal rep. ☐	942 emp. ☐ Subtotal ☐ Void ☐
	6 Allocated tips --	7 Advance EIC payment --
8 Employee's social security number 201-26-8341	9 Federal income tax withheld 1,196.00	10 Wages, tips, other compensation 14,200.00
	11 Social security tax withheld 1,015.30	
12 Employee's name, address, and ZIP code Sonia Brouse 16 Carmine Drive Englewood, Colorado 80110	13 Social security wages 14,200.00	14 Social security tips
	16	16a Fringe benefits incl. in Box 10
	17 State income tax 284.00	18 State wages, tips, etc. 14,200.00
	19 Name of state Colorado	
	20 Local income tax	21 Local wages, tips, etc.
	22 Name of locality	
Form **W-2 Wage and Tax Statement**	Copy B To be filed with employee's FEDERAL tax return This information is being furnished to the Internal Revenue Service.	Department of the Treasury Internal Revenue Service

Form W-2 showing data obtained from the employee earnings record.

EMPLOYEE EARNINGS RECORD FOR YEAR 19—

Name	*Sonia Brouse*	*Employee No.*	*1*
Address	*16 Carmine Drive*	*Social Security No.*	*201-26-8341*
	Englewood, Colorado 80110	*Marital Status*	*Married*
Telephone No.	*303-555-8346*	*Withholding Exemptions*	*3*
Date of Birth	*June 14, 1959*	*Position*	*Accounting Department*
Rate	*$6.00 per hour*	*Date Employed*	*January 2, 19—*

DATE		HOURS	EARNINGS			DEDUCTIONS						NET PAY	YEAR-TO-DATE EARNINGS
PERIOD ENDING	PAID		REGULAR	OVERTIME	TOTAL	FEDERAL INCOME TAX	STATE INCOME TAX	FICA TAX	INSURANCE PREMIUMS	UNION DUES	TOTAL		
		40	240 00		240 00	16 00	4 80	17 16	5 00	4 00	46 96	193 04	14,200 00
Totals			12,480 00	1,720 00	14,200 00	1,196 00	284 00	1,015 30	260 00	208 00	2,963 30	11,236 70	14,200 00

ployee earnings record for Sonia Brouse provided the information reported on Form W-2 prepared by Computer Age.

At least six copies of each Form W-2 are prepared. Three copies are given to the employee. (One is sent with the employee's federal income tax return. The second copy is sent with the state income tax return. The third is for the employee's file.) Another copy is for the employer's records. The employer sends a fifth copy to the federal government and a sixth copy to the state government.

If an employee leaves the job, the employer must give the employee Form W-2 within 30 days after the last payday.

Exercises I and J on this page may be completed at this point.

TOPIC 5 EXERCISES

EXERCISE I. Answer the following questions about preparing payroll tax returns. Refer to pages 452 to 459.

1. Which form is sent along with the deposit for federal income taxes withheld and FICA taxes?
2. How much is the total deposit?
3. The total balances of what ledger accounts equal the amount of the deposit?
4. What is the employer identification number of Computer Age?
5. What journal entry is made to record the deposit?
6. The deposit covers income taxes for what period of time?
7. What are the total taxable wages from April 1 to June 30?
8. How much is the total FICA tax for the 3 months? How much is withheld from the employees? How much does the employer have to pay?
9. What journal entry is made when Form 941 is filed? Why?
10. How many copies of Form W-2 are prepared, and who gets them?
11. What are Sonia Brouse's total wages for the year? What are her total FICA taxable wages for the year? Are these amounts the same? When would the amounts be different?
12. Which journal entry was made when Form W-2 was filed? Why?
13. When must employers give Form W-2 to current employees? To former employees?

EXERCISE J. Record the entries for depositing the taxes listed in the transactions at the right. Refer to the text, margin notes, and illustrations on pages 455 to 457.

Apr. 7 Deposited state unemployment compensation taxes of $567 (Check 451).
7 Deposited federal unemployment compensation taxes of $105 (Check 452).

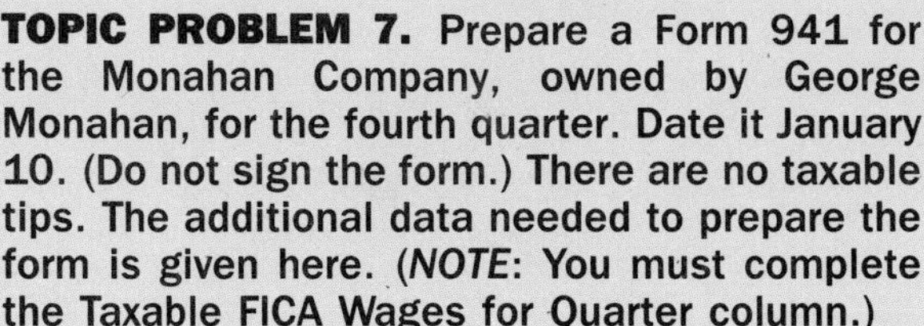

TOPIC 5 PROBLEMS

TOPIC PROBLEM 7. Prepare a Form 941 for the Monahan Company, owned by George Monahan, for the fourth quarter. Date it January 10. (Do not sign the form.) There are no taxable tips. The additional data needed to prepare the form is given here. (*NOTE*: You must complete the Taxable FICA Wages for Quarter column.)

The Federal Employee Income Taxes Payable account shows that the federal income taxes withheld from earnings for the quarter ended December 31 were $4,569.00. The total federal tax deposits were as follows: October, $2,108.85; November, $2,389.90; December, $3,595.20, for a quarterly total of $8,093.95. Complete lines 2, 3, 5, 6, 8, 10, 14, 16, 17, and 18 on Form 941.

Employee	Social Security Number	Year-to-Date Earnings (Dec. 31, 19—)	Total Wages Paid During Quarter	Taxable FICA Wages for Quarter
Joan Edwards	201-35-4461	$35,300	$7,600	?
Leonard Howell	246-78-2311	23,900	4,460	?
Walter Jones	997-87-9531	33,000	7,700	?
Scott King	548-74-3857	26,730	4,890	?

TOPIC PROBLEM 8. The credit balances on several dates are shown here for the FICA taxes Payable account, the Federal Income Taxes Payable account, and the Federal Unemployment Taxes Payable account.

a. For each date, determine the amount that must be deposited for the FICA taxes and income taxes and for the federal unemployment compensation taxes.

b. Determine the deadlines for making the deposits.

c. List the forms that must be included with deposits.

Date	FICA Taxes Payable	Federal Income Taxes Payable	Federal Unemployment Taxes Payable
Feb. 28	$ 832.00	$ 560.00	$ 80
Mar. 31	1,040.00	700.00	130
Apr. 7	1,560.00	1,550.00	75
July 31	41.60	145.60	8
Dec. 31	104.00	38.40	0

TOPIC PROBLEM 9. Part of the June 30 trial balance for the Corelli Repair Service is shown on the next page.

a. Compute the amount that is to be deposited in a federal depository for the employee income taxes and the FICA taxes for the month of June.

b. Record the entry to journalize Check 181, which was drawn on July 5 for the federal employee income taxes and FICA withholding deposit.

c. Record the entry to journalize Check 182 drawn on July 5 to remit the amount of the state unemployment compensation taxes.

d. Record the entry to journalize Check 183 drawn on July 5 to remit the amount of the federal unemployment compensation taxes.

e. Record the entry to journalize Check 184 drawn on July 5 to remit the amount of the insurance premiums to the Shield Insurance Company.

f. Record the entry to journalize Check 185 drawn on July 5 to remit the amount of the union dues to the United Union Local 18.

Corelli Repair Service
Trial Balance
June 30, 19—

ACCOUNT TITLE	ACCT. NO.	DEBIT	CREDIT
Federal Income Taxes Pay.	221		1,578 00
FICA Taxes Pay.	222		1,605 00
Federal Unemployment Taxes Pay.	223		240 00
Group Insurance Pay.	224		55 00
State Unemployment Taxes Pay.	225		1,372 00
Union Dues Pay.	226		96 00

CHAPTER SUMMARY

A personnel and payroll subsystem controls the hiring of employees and all activities involved in the payroll. The relationship between the two departments is very important. The personnel department recruits and hires all employees and determines the employees' rates and deductions. The payroll department processes and pays the payroll and prepares the payroll tax returns.

Federal laws regulate the amount of FICA taxes and income tax to be withheld from employees' gross earnings and the taxes to be paid by employers. State income tax laws vary from state to state. Employers are subject to payment of FICA tax and federal and state unemployment compensation taxes. The federal Fair Labor Standards Act and similar state wage and hour laws regulate the hours of work and wages paid to employees. Employers, as well as employees, should be aware of payroll legislation and the frequent changes in the tax rates and other provisions.

THE LANGUAGE OF BUSINESS

Here are some terms that make up the language of business. Do you know the meaning of each?

personnel and payroll subsystem
employee
employer
payroll
gross earnings
salary plan
hourly rate plan
incentive plan
piece-rate plan
commission plan
salary-commission plan
contract of employment
overtime pay
time card
payroll deduction
federal income tax
Form W-4
FICA tax
FUTA tax
garnishment
net pay
payroll journal
employee earnings record
employee pay statement
bank transfer
voucher check
Form 8109
Form 941
Form W-2

REVIEW QUESTIONS

1. What activities are completed in a personnel and payroll subsystem?
2. In a personnel and payroll subsystem, how does the personnel department relate to the payroll department?
3. Describe the various pay plans used to pay employees.
4. What data is needed to determine the amount of federal income tax to withhold from an employee's gross earnings?

5. What information is contained in the employee earnings records? How can the employee earnings record be used as a subsidiary ledger?

6. What is a commonly used source document for recording hours worked and computing an employee's gross earnings?

7. Which source document contains information about an employee's deductions for the year?

8. Describe three possible methods a business might use to pay employees.

9. What is the purpose of the entries to record and pay the payroll? The entries to record and pay the payroll taxes?

10. What information is shown on the Form W-2? Who receives copies of the form?

CHAPTER PROBLEMS

Problems for Chapter 13 are given below. Write your answers to the problems on separate sheets of paper unless you are using the workbook for this textbook. If you are using the workbook, do the problems in the space provided there.

CHAPTER PROBLEM 13-1. The payroll journal for the March 29 payroll of the Career Planning Institute shows the following totals: salaries expense, $2,500; withheld for federal income taxes, $350; withheld for FICA taxes, $178.75; withheld for group insurance premiums, $20; withheld for union dues, $40. No maximum for FICA, FUTA, or SUTA has been reached by any employee.

a. Post the payroll journal.

b. Record and post the following transactions.

Mar. 29 Record the employer's payroll taxes, FICA taxes (7.15 percent), federal unemployment compensation taxes (0.8 percent), and state unemployment compensation taxes (5.4 percent).
29 Post the employer's payroll taxes.
31 Record payment of the March 29 payroll (Checks 323–326).
Apr. 1 Deposited federal income taxes withheld and FICA taxes for the month of March (Check 354). Obtain amounts from the general ledger.
12 Deposited federal unemployment compensation taxes for the first quarter (Check 355).
12 Deposited state unemployment compensation taxes for the first quarter (Check 356).
12 Remitted group insurance premiums for the month of March (Check 357).
12 Remitted union dues for the month of March (Check 358).

CHAPTER PROBLEM 13-2. The Regency Gift Shop, which is owned by Alice Taylor, has three employees. Information about the hours worked, the hourly rate, the marital status, and the withholding allowances for the three employees for the week ended January 14 is given below.

1. Compute the gross earnings for each employee. Regular time is paid for the first 40 hours. Time and a half is paid for all hours over 40 hours. Enter this information in the payroll journal.
2. Compute the federal income tax withholding and FICA taxes for each employee. Use the tax tables on page 437, and a FICA rate of 7.15 percent. Enter this information in the payroll journal.
3. Complete the payroll journal for the week ended January 14. The state income tax rate is 2 percent of gross earnings. Each employee has a deduction of $4.50 for insurance and $6.00 for union dues.
4. Total and prove the payroll journal.
5. Post the salaries expense and payroll liabilities to the general ledger.

Employee	Hours Worked	Regular Hourly Rate	Marital Status	Withholding Allowances
Ann Abrams	42	$6.90	M	2
Paul Katz	39	$6.50	S	3
Ralph Lane	41	$7.20	M	1

MANAGEMENT CASES

Wage Increases. Management must decide whether or not a wage increase can be given to the employees. In making this decision, management determines whether the increase will allow the business to continue to price its product competitively. The increase in wages may make it necessary to raise prices so high that the product cannot be sold. If so, the business will soon be bankrupt. On the other hand, the increase in wages may decrease the net income enough so that it is unprofitable for the owner to keep an investment in the business. In this case, the owner will go out of business. Accounting records are used to help make decisions about wages.

CASE 13M-1. Braxton Disposal Service Incorporated charges $10 a month for trash and garbage pickup services. The company services 1,500 residences and employs six people. The income statement for the business shows the following information.

Braxton Disposal Service
Income Statement
For the Year Ended December 31, 19—

Revenues:				
Trash and garbage pickup service			*180,000*	*00*
Expenses:				
Wages Expense	*90,000*	*00*		
Truck Maintenance Expense	*7,000*	*00*		
Gas and Oil Expense	*45,000*	*00*		
Other Expenses	*13,000*	*00*		
Total Expenses			*155,000*	*00*
Net Income			*25,000*	*00*

In analyzing the costs, the accountant found that current labor costs are 50 percent of the trash service revenues. The employees have now asked for a wage increase that would total $18,000 a year. Upon studying the request, the accountant has determined that one of the following actions must be taken: (1) increase the pickup service fee, or (2) increase the number of residences that the company services without increasing the number of employees.

a. If the same number of residences are serviced, what increase in the pickup service fee is needed to absorb the wage increase? What would be the new trash pickup service fee? What would the percent of this increase be?

b. If the wage increases are granted, the pickup service fee remained the same, and all other operating expenses remained the same, how many additional residences must be serviced by Braxton Disposal Service Incorporated in order to maintain the same net profit?

c. As energy costs (specifically gas and oil) climb, what effects would a 20 percent increase in these costs have on Braxton Disposal Service Incorporated?

CASE 13M-2. Electra Company produces small electric motors. It sells all the motors at $4 each to the Hurricane Corporation, which manufactures electric fans. During the past year, Electra Company produced and sold 141,000 motors. Financial data for the year is shown here.

Sales	$564,000
Cost of Goods Manufactured	429,000
Gross Profit	$135,000
Operating Expense	52,500
Net Income	$ 82,500

The cost of goods manufactured includes labor costs of $352,500. The union is asking for a wage increase that would increase labor costs by 20 percent a year.

a. By approximately how much would Electra Company need to increase the price of its motors to cover the wage increase and maintain its present net income (assuming that no other costs could be reduced)?

b. Hurricane Corporation stated that it would stop purchasing the motors if Electra Company increased the price. A competing company can supply the motors for $4 each. Is it possible for Electra Company to grant the wage increase without incurring a net loss?

c. From the net income, Carla Owens, the owner, should receive $30,000 as an annual salary for managing the company. The remainder of the net income ($52,500) is a return on Ms. Owens' investment of $375,000. Is the current net income too high?

d. In your opinion, what is the maximum wage increase that the company can grant its employees if it can neither increase the selling price of the motors nor reduce other production costs?

e. If the requested wage increase is granted and the current selling price of $4 is maintained, what must be done to maintain the present net income?

CHAPTER 14

A General Accounting Subsystem

Cash receipts, cash payments, purchases, sales, and personnel and payroll are known as *special subsystems* because special information is processed in each. You will now see how this special information is combined at the end of the fiscal period into a general accounting subsystem and how the resulting information is analyzed, interpreted, and used in making business decisions.

CHAPTER GOALS

After studying Chapter 14, you will be able to:

1. Define the terms listed in "The Language of Business" section on page 510.
2. Explain the concepts and principles in this chapter related to processing of information through a general accounting subsystem.
3. Use a flowchart to show how financial data flows from special accounting subsystems through a general accounting subsystem.
4. Complete a worksheet with several adjustments.
5. Prepare a schedule of cost of goods sold and a statement of owner's equity.
6. Interpret accounting information using ratios and budgeting.

Steps in Accounting Cycle

1. Originate data
2. Journalize transactions
3. Post transactions
4. Prove ledgers and prepare worksheet
5. Prepare financial statements
6. Make adjusting and closing entries
7. Prepare postclosing trial balance
8. Interpret financial information

TOPIC 1

Controlling a General Accounting Subsystem

What is the general accounting subsystem? The **general accounting subsystem** combines the information from the special accounting subsystems in order to update the accounts and prepare financial reports. The first three steps of the accounting cycle—originate data, journalize transactions, and post transactions—are completed in the cash receipts, cash payments, purchases, sales, and personnel and payroll subsystems. Steps 4 through 8 in the accounting cycle are completed in the general accounting subsystem.

Procedures for Controlling Accounting Transactions

The majority of the procedures to control accounting transactions were studied as part of the special subsystems. Each control was designed to ensure accuracy, honesty, and efficiency and speed in handling and recording assets, liabilities, owner's equity, revenues, and expenses. Likewise, there must be procedures to control the activities within the general accounting subsystem.

Procedures to Control the General Accounting Subsystem There are two primary activities in the general accounting

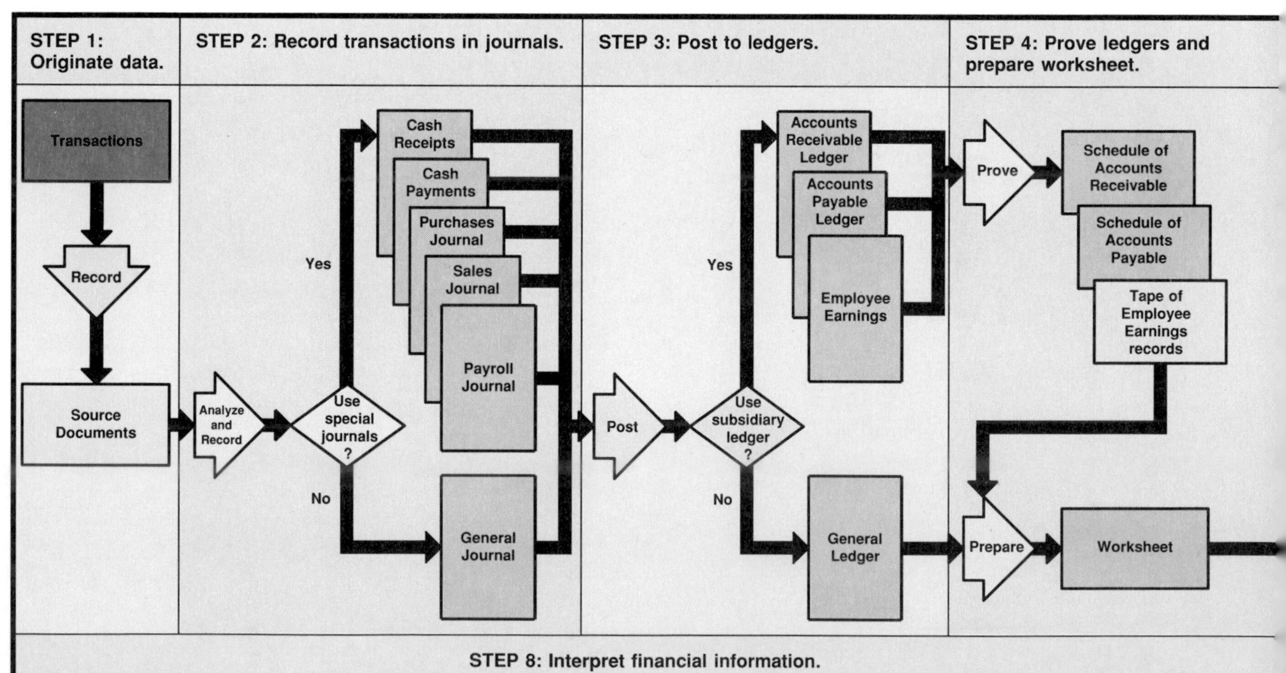

subsystem. The first activity is to prepare the accounts for the next accounting period. The second is to prepare the financial reports (statements) needed to make management decisions. It is important that special procedures are used to ensure the following.

- Prove equality of debits and credits in the ledger
- Prove agreement of the accounting records and actual amounts
- Properly match revenue and expenses
- Use proper cutoff date
- Accurately report the results of operations
- Accurately report financial position
- Separate revenue and expenses for accounting periods
- Divide responsibility

Visualizing the Accounting System

How does financial data flow from the special subsystems through the general accounting subsystem? The flowchart on page 468 and below shows how financial data flows through an accounting system—the eight steps of the accounting cycle. The first three steps in the accounting cycle are the following.

1. Originate data
2. Record transactions in journals
3. Post to ledgers

These three steps are completed primarily in the special accounting subsystems you studied in Chapters 9 to 13.

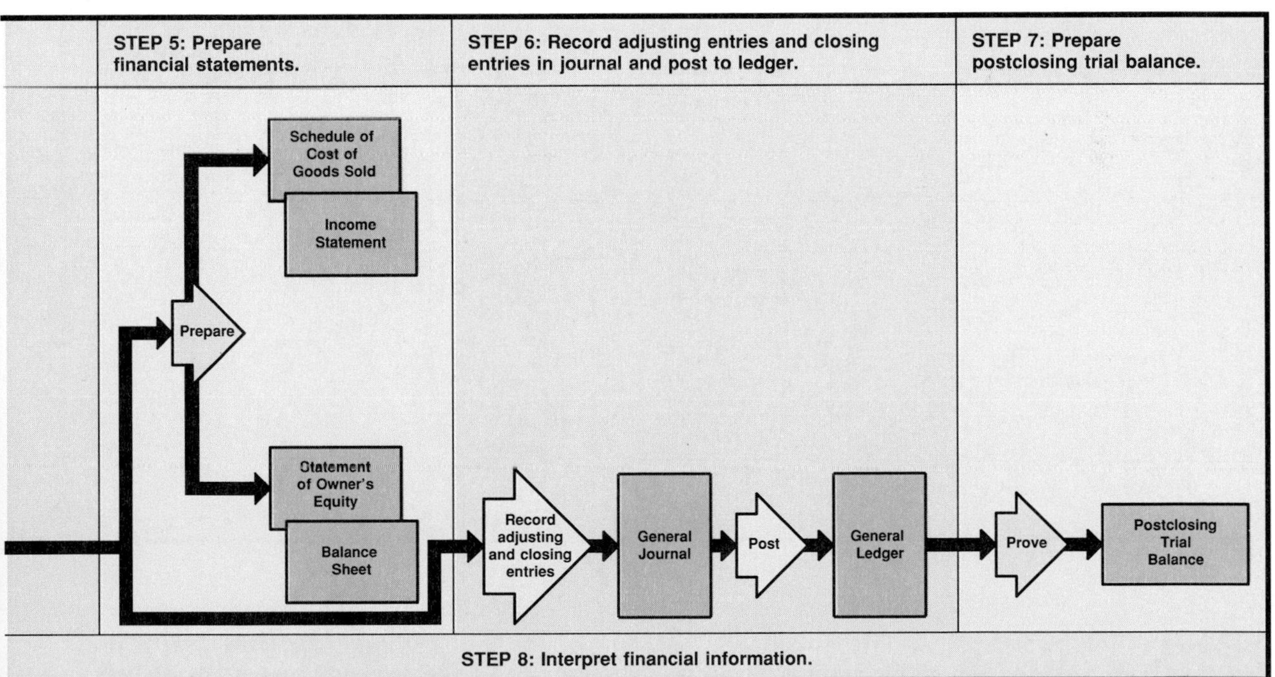

IMPORTANT

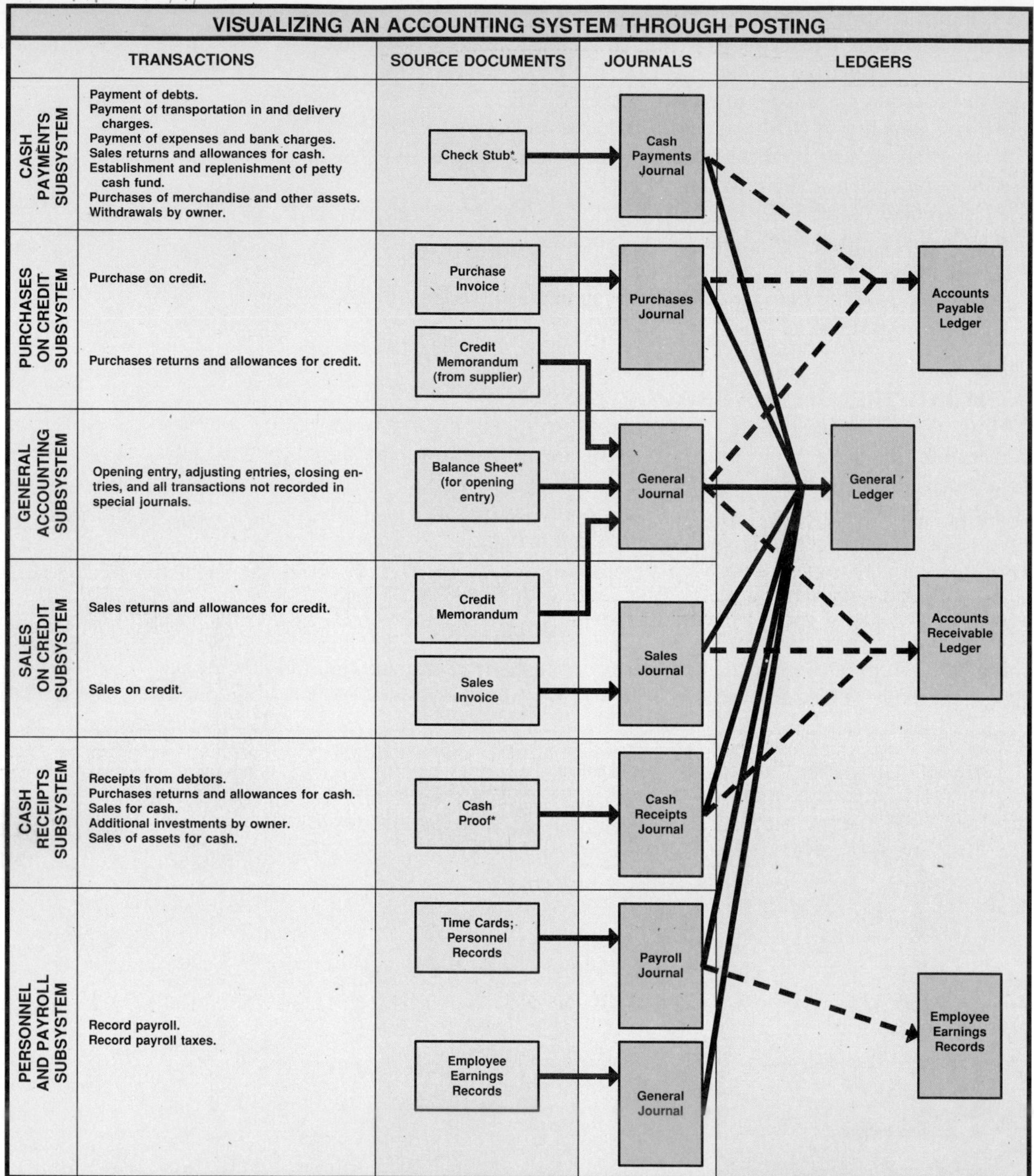

VISUALIZING AN ACCOUNTING SYSTEM THROUGH POSTING
TRANSACTIONS
SOURCE DOCUMENTS
JOURNALS
LEDGERS
CASH PAYMENTS SUBSYSTEM
Payment of debts.
Payment of transportation in and delivery charges.
Payment of expenses and bank charges.
Sales returns and allowances for cash.
Establishment and replenishment of petty cash fund.
Purchases of merchandise and other assets.
Withdrawals by owner.
Check Stub*
Cash Payments Journal
PURCHASES ON CREDIT SUBSYSTEM
Purchase on credit.
Purchases returns and allowances for credit.
Purchase Invoice
Credit Memorandum (from supplier)
Purchases Journal
Accounts Payable Ledger
GENERAL ACCOUNTING SUBSYSTEM
Opening entry, adjusting entries, closing entries, and all transactions not recorded in special journals.
Balance Sheet* (for opening entry)
General Journal
General Ledger
SALES ON CREDIT SUBSYSTEM
Sales returns and allowances for credit.
Sales on credit.
Credit Memorandum
Sales Invoice
Sales Journal
Accounts Receivable Ledger
CASH RECEIPTS SUBSYSTEM
Receipts from debtors.
Purchases returns and allowances for cash.
Sales for cash.
Additional investments by owner.
Sales of assets for cash.
Cash Proof*
Cash Receipts Journal
PERSONNEL AND PAYROLL SUBSYSTEM
Record payroll.
Record payroll taxes.
Time Cards; Personnel Records
Employee Earnings Records
Payroll Journal
General Journal
Employee Earnings Records

*Only one possible source document is shown.

Steps 4 through 8 of the accounting cycle are completed as part of the activities in the general accounting subsystem. Thus, Step 4 in the general accounting subsystem (prove ledgers and prepare worksheet) is

Step 4 in the accounting cycle. Accounting clerks and audit clerks, among other personnel, play key roles in completing these steps.

How each of the steps of the accounting cycle is completed in the general accounting subsystem is explained next.

Accounting Clerk: DOT 216.482-010
Performs variety of computing, posting, and other accounting duties. May be classified according to type of accounting performed, such as accounts receivable clerk.

Audit Clerk: DOT 210.382-010
Verifies accuracy of figures, computations, and postings pertaining to business transactions recorded by other workers.

Exercise A on this page may be completed at this point.

TOPIC 1 EXERCISE

EXERCISE A. Answer the following questions about the general accounting subsystem. Refer to the text, the margin notes in Topic 1, and the flowchart on visualizing the accounting system on pages 468 to 469.

1. What are the special subsystems you have studied?
2. What happens in the general accounting subsystem?
3. Which steps in the accounting cycle are completed primarily in the special subsystems? Which steps are completed in the general accounting subsystem?
4. List as many source documents as possible that are used in the various accounting subsystems you have studied.
5. What types of transactions are recorded in each of the six journals?
6. What does "proving the accounts receivable ledger" mean?

TOPIC 1 PROBLEM

TOPIC PROBLEM 1. For each of the transactions listed at right and on the next page, indicate the journal in which the transaction would be recorded and in which ledger or ledgers (general and/or subsidiary) it would be posted. If you need assistance, refer to the flowchart on page 470 and the text in Chapters 9 to 13.

1. Cash sales
2. Cash overage
3. Cash purchase
4. Cash investment by owner
5. Purchase on account

6. Return of merchandise sold on credit
7. Sale on account
8. Payment received on account
9. Check issued to pay insurance premium
10. Return of merchandise purchased on credit
11. Cash shortage
12. Cash withdrawal by owner
13. Employees' payroll
14. Payroll taxes

TOPIC 2

Proving the Ledgers and Completing the Worksheet

What happens after information is posted to the general ledger? Information posted to the general ledger is processed to prepare financial statements and prepare the accounts for the next accounting period. The first step after posting is Step 4 in the accounting cycle—proving the ledgers and preparing the worksheet. This step is explained in this topic.

Computer Age
Schedule of Accounts Receivable
November 30, 19—

Allied Display	*1,000*	*00*
Electro Computer	*280*	*00*
Hallmark Sales	*750*	*00*
Wing Computers	*—*	*00*
James Young	*970*	*00*
Total Accounts Receivable	*3,000*	*00*

Computer Age
Schedule of Accounts Payable
November 30, 19—

Diskettes Plus	*1,460*	*00*
Johnson Supply	*2,170*	*00*
LCP Computer	*680*	*00*
Micro Components ...	*1,190*	*00*
Total Accounts Payable	*5,500*	*00*

0.00T
560.00
600.00
470.00
663.00
276.00
231.00
2,800.00T

After all entries are posted, a proof must be made of the accuracy of the postings. First, a schedule of accounts receivable is prepared, as shown in the margin. Then, a similar schedule is prepared for the accounts payable ledger. The subsidiary ledgers are usually proved daily or monthly even if the accounting period is longer.

Next, the amounts related to payroll must be proved. The proof involves comparing amounts in the employee earnings records with amounts in the general ledger. To do this, a calculator tape is run of each employee's gross earnings. The total of this tape must equal the balance of the Salaries Expense account in the general ledger. Businesses can also use the amounts withheld for FICA taxes and employees' income taxes to verify the related credits to FICA Taxes Payable, Federal Income Taxes Payable, and State Income Taxes Payable accounts.

Proof	Ledger
Schedule of accounts receivable	Accounts receivable ledger
Schedule of accounts payable	Accounts payable ledger
Tape of gross earnings	Employee earnings records
Trial balance	General ledger

After each proof is verified, a worksheet is prepared for the general ledger accounts. In Chapter 7 you learned how to prepare a worksheet for a service business. Now you will see how a worksheet looks for a merchandising business.

Concept: Schedule of Subsidiary Ledgers
The equality of the subsidiary ledgers and the controlling accounts must be verified at regular intervals.

Step 4a: Preparing the Trial Balance Section

Why is the Trial Balance section of the worksheet prepared first? The Trial Balance section is a proof of the equality of the debits and credits in the ledger. Note that the Trial Balance columns of the worksheet for Computer Age contain all the accounts listed in the general ledger that you have seen previously. It also contains a new

COMPUTER AGE CHART OF ACCOUNTS

Assets
120 Merchandise Inventory
121 Prepaid Insurance
123 Supplies

Owner's Equity
399 Income Summary

Costs and Expenses
514 Insurance Expense
519 Supplies Expense

Computer Age
Worksheet
For the Month Ended November 30, 19—

	ACCOUNT TITLE	ACCT. NO.	TRIAL BALANCE		ADJUSTMENTS		ADJUSTED TRIAL BALANCE		INCOME STATEMENT		BALANCE SHEET		
			DEBIT	CREDIT	DEBIT	CREDIT	DEBIT	CREDIT	DEBIT	CREDIT	DEBIT	CREDIT	
1	Cash	101	9,500										1
2	Petty Cash	102	30										2
3	Change Fund	103	35										3
4	Accounts Receivable	111	3,000										4
5	Merchandise Inventory	120	7,000										5
6	Prepaid Insurance	121	480										6
7	Supplies	123	350										7
8	Land	130	8,000										8
9	Building	131	22,000										9
10	Office Equipment	132	1,800										10
11	Stockroom Equipment	133	2,700										11
12	Loans Payable	201		4,000									12
13	Accounts Payable	211		5,500									13
14	Sales Tax Payable	216		200									14
15	Federal Income Taxes Pay.	221		360									15
16	FICA Taxes Payable	222		220									16
17	State Income Taxes Pay.	223		140									17
18	Federal Unempl. Taxes Pay.	224		48									18
19	State Unempl. Taxes Pay.	225		176									19
20	Salaries Payable	226		—									20
21	Mortgage Payable	231		14,000									21
22	Jason Booth, Capital	301		29,232									22
23	Jason Booth, Drawing	302	1,200										23
24	Income Summary	399	—	—									24
25	Sales	401		12,600									25
26	Sales Returns and Allowances	402	190										26
27	Sales Discount	403	45										27
28	Purchases	501	6,800										28
29	Transportation In	502	80										29
30	Purchases Returns and Allow.	503		185									30
31	Purchases Discount	504		50									31
32	Cash Short and Over	511	6										32
33	Advertising Expense	512	100										33
34	Delivery Expense	513	120										34
35	Insurance Expense	514	—										35
36	Miscellaneous Expense	515	40										36
37	Payroll Taxes Expense	516	195										37
38	Salaries Expense	518	2,800										38
39	Supplies Expense	519	—										39
40	Utilities Expense	520	240										40
41			66,711	66,711									41

(4a)

NOTE: The cents columns have been omitted in order to show the entire worksheet.

account: Merchandise Inventory (120). This account will be explained in the sections that follow. The Trial Balance columns are balanced before the remainder of the worksheet is completed.

Step 4b: Updating the Trial Balance Section

What happens after the Trial Balance section is prepared? The Trial Balance section then must be analyzed and updated. To do this, the accountant asks this question about every account: Is the amount of the account on the trial balance accurate? If it is, the account is not changed. If it is not accurate, the accountant must make an adjustment of the account balance to update the trial balance.

Updating Merchandise Inventory Computer Age keeps items in inventory to sell to customers. The value of this inventory at the beginning of the accounting period is recorded in an account called **Merchandise Inventory**. The merchandise inventory owned by a business is considered an asset. As the inventory increases and decreases, these changes are recorded in the various purchases and sales accounts. (No additional entries are recorded in the Merchandise Inventory account.) A business needs merchandise on hand to satisfy its customers' needs. Thus, the business begins and ends each accounting period with merchandise in its inventory.

The amount of the merchandise on hand at the beginning of an accounting period is known as the **beginning inventory**. Inventory on hand at the end of a period is known as **ending inventory**. Accounting periods follow each other. Therefore, the ending inventory of one period is the beginning inventory of the next period.

The amount of merchandise on hand is always changing during the accounting period. Therefore, the income statement and the balance sheet cannot be prepared until the accountant finds the value of the ending inventory.

Computing the Value of the Ending Inventory At the end of the accounting period, a merchandising business takes a physical inventory. A physical inventory for Computer Age on October 31 showed the cost of the unsold merchandise to be $7,000. The cost of inventory on October 31 was computed by the following procedure.

- The quantity of each item was multiplied by the unit cost. For example, the unit cost of a box of computer diskettes was $40. This amount was multiplied by the number of boxes in stock (8) to find the total cost of $320.
- The total cost of the entire inventory was found by adding the cost of all the items. The total cost of the ending inventory for Computer Age on October 31 was $7,000. The $7,000 is also the beginning inventory of the next accounting period, which starts on November 1.

INVENTORY SHEET

COMPUTER AGE
200 Girard Avenue
Denver, Colorado 80236

Date October 31, 19— Sheet No. 12

Counted By M. West Recorded By J. Mann Figured By G. Rice

STOCK NO.	QUANTITY	UNIT OF COUNT	DESCRIPTION	UNIT PRICE	EXTENSION
A82-B	8	40 boxes	Computer Diskettes	40 00	320 00
937-R48	3	ea.	Disk Drive	125 00	375 00
			Total		7,000 00

Remember that no entries have been made to the Merchandise Inventory account during the accounting period. All changes were made to the Purchases and Sales accounts as merchandise was bought and sold. Thus, at the end of the accounting period, the Merchandise Inventory account still shows the inventory for the beginning of the period ($7,000). The physical inventory taken by Computer Age on November 30 shows the total cost of the unsold merchandise as $6,400. The Merchandise Inventory account must now be adjusted to show the actual inventory at the end of the period on November 30. To decrease the debit balance from $7,000 to $6,400, the Merchandise Inventory account must be credited for $600.

What account should be debited? At the end of the accounting period, Computer Age has $600 less merchandise on hand than it had at the beginning of the period. This means that $600 more merchandise was sold than was purchased during the period. The additional cost of $600 also affects owner's equity. Thus, $600 is transferred from the Merchandise Inventory account to the Income Summary account.

NOVEMBER 30: COMPUTER AGE MAKES AN ADJUSTING ENTRY TO DECREASE THE MERCHANDISE INVENTORY ACCOUNT BY $600.

What Happens	Accounting Rule	Accounting Entry
The decrease in merchandise inventory decreases owner's equity by $600.	To decrease owner's equity, debit the account.	Debit: Income Summary, $600.
The asset *Merchandise Inventory* decreases by $600.	To decrease an asset, credit the account.	Credit: Merchandise Inventory, $600.

Merchandise Inventory	120
7,000	600

Income Summary	399
600	

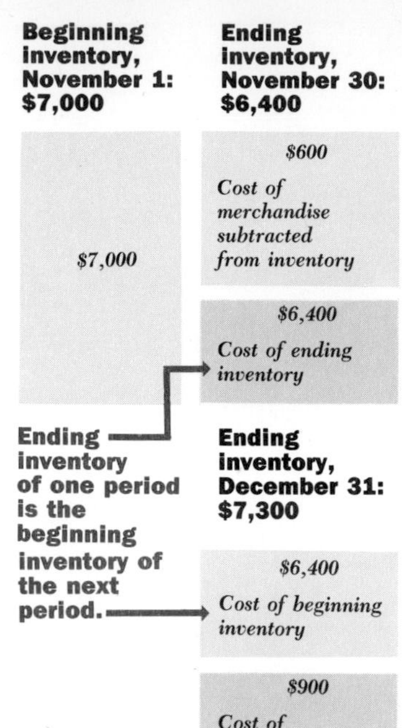

The adjustment on the worksheet to record the cost of the merchandise sold from the inventory is made by debiting the Income Summary account and crediting the Merchandise Inventory account. Later this adjustment will be recorded in the journal and posted to the ledger.

The merchandise counted on the last day of an accounting period is the merchandise inventory on the first day of the next period. On December 1 the balance of the Merchandise Inventory account is $6,400. Suppose on December 31 the business has an ending inventory of $7,300. Since the ending inventory is $900 more than the beginning inventory ($6,400), more merchandise was purchased than sold. An adjusting entry must be made to increase the Merchandise Inventory account by $900. Therefore, Merchandise Inventory will be debited and Income Summary will be credited.

DECEMBER 31: COMPUTER AGE MAKES AN ADJUSTING ENTRY TO INCREASE THE MERCHANDISE INVENTORY ACCOUNT BY $900.

What Happens	Accounting Rule	Accounting Entry
The asset *Merchandise Inventory* increases by $900. The increase in merchandise inventory increases owner's equity by $900.	To increase an asset, debit the account. To increase owner's equity, credit the account.	Debit: Merchandise Inventory, $900. Credit: Income Summary, $900.

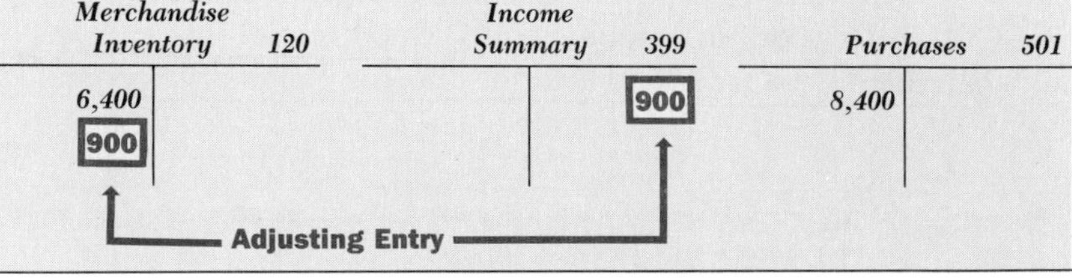

Exercise B on page 485 may be completed at this point.

Updating Prepaid Expenses

Updating Prepaid Expenses The cost of items and services bought for use in operating the business but not used by the end of the accounting period are called **prepaid expenses**. Supplies and prepaid insurance are examples of

Some business transactions cover more than one accounting period. For example, a business usually buys enough office supplies to last for several months. Remember that accountants follow a principle called "the matching principle." The matching principle means that the income statement for a business should show all expenses incurred in earning the revenue during that accounting period. For instance, only the expense for supplies that Computer Age used for November should be considered an expense for that period. Unused supplies should not be considered an expense until they are used in a future accounting period.

An income statement, however, must show all the revenues, costs, and expenses for the current accounting period—*none* for future accounting periods. To do this, there must be a *cutoff date* at the end of the accounting period when transactions cease to be recorded. Transactions after the cutoff date are recorded in the next accounting period. For example, the cutoff date used by Computer Age for its November accounting period is November 30. Adjustments must be made if certain prepaid expenses (supplies, for example) are used and others remain unused by the cutoff date of the accounting period. You will now learn how these adjustments are planned on the worksheet.

Updating Supplies Early in the November accounting period (November 4), Computer Age purchased supplies for $350, as illustrated below. The supplies were to last for several months.

NOVEMBER 4: COMPUTER AGE ISSUES A CHECK FOR $350 TO PAY FOR SUPPLIES, WHICH WILL LAST FOR SEVERAL MONTHS.

What Happens	Accounting Rule	Accounting Entry
The asset *Supplies* increases by $350. The asset *Cash* decreases by $350.	To increase an asset, debit the account. To decrease an asset, credit the account.	Debit: Supplies, $350. Credit: Cash, $350.

Cash	*101*	*Supplies*	*123*
	350	350	

Purchasing supplies.

COMPUTER AGE CHART OF ACCOUNTS

Assets
123 Supplies

Costs and Expenses
519 Supplies Expense

At the end of the accounting period on November 30, the supplies were counted. The physical inventory shows supplies of $300. This means that supplies of $50 ($350 − $300) were used during November. As was explained in Chapter 6, an adjustment is recorded on the worksheet to transfer the amount of the used supplies ($50) from the asset account to the Supplies Expense account. (See the worksheet illustrated on page 481.) Later, this entry will be made in the general journal and posted to the general ledger.

NOVEMBER 30: A PHYSICAL COUNT OF THE SUPPLIES ON HAND SHOWS UNUSED SUPPLIES OF $300.

What Happens	Accounting Rule	Accounting Entry
The expense *Repairs Expense* decreases owner's equity by $50. The asset *Supplies* decreases by $50.	To decrease owner's equity, debit the account. To decrease an asset, credit the account.	Debit: Supplies Expense, $50. Credit: Supplies, $50.

Cash 101		*Supplies* 123		*Supplies Expense* 519	
	350	*350*	50	50	

Adjusting supplies.

The effect of the adjusting entry is that Supplies now has a debit balance of $300. This is the amount of the asset shown on the balance sheet. In addition, the Supplies Expense account has a debit balance of $50. This is the amount of supplies used during the accounting period. Thus, the financial statements will show accurate amounts for the asset and the expense.

COMPUTER AGE CHART OF ACCOUNTS

Assets
121 Prepaid Insurance

Costs and Expenses
514 Insurance Expense

■ **Updating Prepaid Insurance** Assets of a business, such as equipment and buildings, are usually insured against loss due to theft, fire, flood, or storm. The total premium on an insurance policy is paid at the beginning of the insurance period, or paid in advance.

The amount paid for an insurance premium covering more than one accounting period is a prepaid expense. The amount of the premium is debited to the asset account Prepaid Insurance. As the insurance premium is used up, that portion becomes an expense.

When Computer Age pays a $480 premium for one year's fire insurance coverage, Cash is credited and Prepaid Insurance is debited for $480. This transaction is analyzed at the top of the next page.

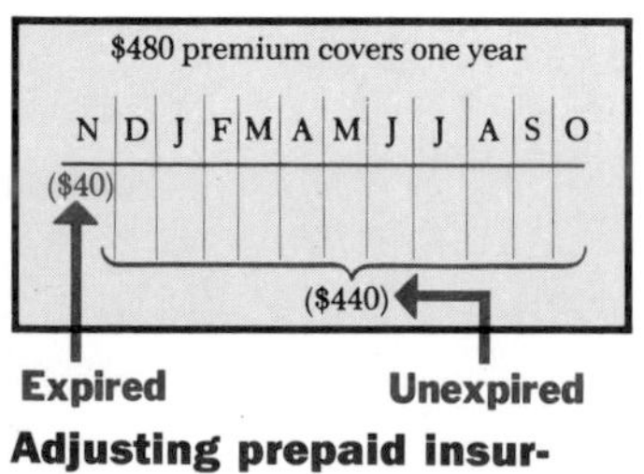

Adjusting prepaid insurance.

The premium of $480 provides a year's fire insurance coverage. However, each accounting period must be charged for the portion of the premium that expires during that period. Computer Age has an accounting period of one month. The cost of the insurance for the month of November would be one-twelfth of the annual premium of $480, or $40. At the end of November, an adjustment is made on the worksheet to transfer one month's insurance premium ($40) from the Prepaid Insurance account to the Insurance Expense account. (This is shown in the worksheet on page 481.) The worksheet adjustment will later be journalized and posted.

NOVEMBER 1: COMPUTER AGE ISSUES A CHECK FOR $480 TO PAY THE ANNUAL PREMIUM FOR FIRE INSURANCE COVERING ITS EQUIPMENT AND BUILDING.		
What Happens	**Accounting Rule**	**Accounting Entry**
The asset *Prepaid Insurance* increases by $480.	To increase an asset, debit the account.	Debit: Prepaid Insurance, $480.
The asset *Cash* decreases by $480.	To decrease an asset, credit the account.	Credit: Cash, $480.

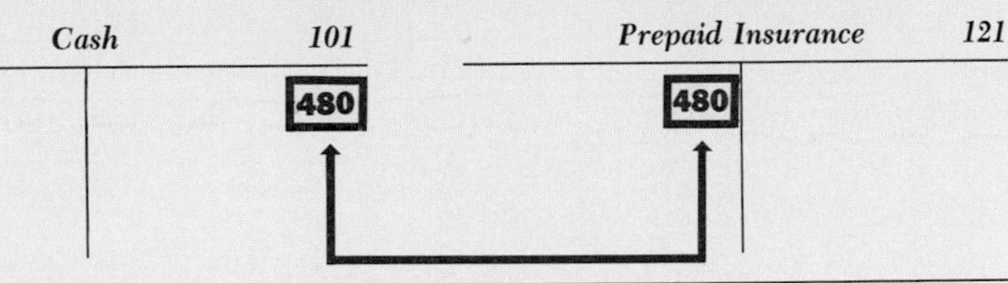

Purchasing insurance.

The balance of the Prepaid Insurance account on December 1 will be $440. This $440 represents the premium for 11 months' insurance that has not expired ($40 × 11). At the end of each month a similar adjusting entry will be made. The asset Prepaid Insurance will contain the amount of the unexpired insurance, and the Insurance Expense account will contain the amount of insurance that expired during the period.

NOVEMBER 30: COMPUTER AGE RECORDS THE AMOUNT OF INSURANCE EXPIRED DURING THE MONTH OF NOVEMBER.		
What Happens	**Accounting Rule**	**Accounting Entry**
Insurance expense decreases owner's equity by $40.	To decrease owner's equity, debit the account.	Debit: Insurance Expense, $40.
The asset *Prepaid Insurance* decreases by $40.	To decrease an asset, credit the account.	Credit: Prepaid Insurance, $40.

Cash 101

480

Prepaid Insurance 121

480 | 40

Insurance Expense 514

40

Adjusting Entry

Adjusting insurance.

Procedures to Adjust Prepaid Expenses
- Debit asset account when items are purchased.
- Determine unused portion at end of period.
- Debit expense account for portion used.
- Credit asset account for portion used.

■ Other Prepaid Expenses A business may have other prepaid expenses that are adjusted at the end of the accounting period. Examples include prepaid advertising and prepaid subscriptions.

■ Completing the Adjustments Section

The worksheet on the next page shows the adjustments for merchandise inventory, supplies, and prepaid insurance entered in the Adjustments section. Notice that letters in parentheses have been used to identify the debit and credit portions for each adjustment. For example, the adjustment for merchandise inventory is identified as *(a)*. The $600 debit to Income Summary is labeled *(a)*, and the $600 credit to Merchandise Inventory is also labeled *(a)*. The adjustment for supplies is labeled *(c)*, and the adjustment for prepaid insurance is labeled *(b)*.

Once all the debits and credits for the adjustments have been entered, a single line is drawn and the two columns are totaled. The total debits in the Adjustments section must equal the total credits. If there is an error, it must be located. When the two amounts agree, double rules are drawn under the totals.

Inventory Clerk: DOT 222.387-026
Keeps record of amount, kind, and cost of merchandise on hand. May count merchandise on hand. May compare physical inventories with records. May indicate items to be reordered.

Principle: Prepaid Expenses
The generally accepted accounting principle is that prepaid expenses—items or services that benefit more than one accounting period—are assets at first and become expenses only as they are used. Therefore prepaid expenses should be charged as expenses to future periods in which they are used.

Principle: Cutoff Date
The generally accepted accounting principle is that there must be a proper cutoff date for the recording of revenues, costs, and expenses in the accounting period.

Exercise C on page 485 may be completed at this point.

Step 4c: Completing the Adjusted Trial Balance Section

Where are the new balances found for the accounts that have been adjusted? The new balances for the accounts that have been adjusted are found by completing the Adjusted Trial Balance section of the worksheet. Each account balance in the Trial Balance section is combined with the adjustment, if any, in the Adjustments section. The adjustment is either added to or subtracted from the balance in the Trial Balance section. The new balance is moved to the Adjusted Trial Balance section.

Many of the accounts do not require an adjustment. The balances shown for these accounts in the Trial Balance section are simply

Computer Age
Worksheet
For the Month Ended November 30, 19—

	ACCOUNT TITLE	ACCT. NO.	TRIAL BALANCE		ADJUSTMENTS		ADJUSTED TRIAL BALANCE		INCOME STATEMENT		BALANCE SHEET		
			DEBIT	CREDIT	DEBIT	CREDIT	DEBIT	CREDIT	DEBIT	CREDIT	DEBIT	CREDIT	
1	Cash	101	9,500										1
2	Petty Cash	102	30										2
3	Change Fund	103	35										3
4	Accounts Receivable	111	3,000										4
5	Merchandise Inventory	120	7,000			(a) 600							5
6	Prepaid Insurance	121	480			(b) 40							6
7	Supplies	123	350			(c) 50							7
8	Land	130	8,000										8
9	Building	131	22,000										9
10	Office Equipment	132	1,800										10
11	Stockroom Equipment	133	2,700										11
12	Loans Payable	201		4,000									12
13	Accounts Payable	211		5,500									13
14	Sales Tax Payable	216		200									14
15	Federal Income Taxes Pay.	221		360									15
16	FICA Taxes Payable	222		220									16
17	State Income Taxes Pay.	223		140									17
18	Federal Unempl. Taxes Pay.	224		48									18
19	State Unempl. Taxes Pay.	225		176									19
20	Salaries Payable	226		—									20
21	Mortgage Payable	231		14,000									21
22	Jason Booth, Capital	301		29,232									22
23	Jason Booth, Drawing	302	1,200										23
24	Income Summary	399	—	—	(a) 600								24
25	Sales	401		12,600									25
26	Sales Returns and Allowances	402	190										26
27	Sales Discount	403	45										27
28	Purchases	501	6,800										28
29	Transportation In	502	80										29
30	Purchases Returns and Allow.	503		185									30
31	Purchases Discount	504		50									31
32	Cash Short and Over	511	6										32
33	Advertising Expense	512	100										33
34	Delivery Expense	513	120										34
35	Insurance Expense	514	—		(b) 40								35
36	Miscellaneous Expense	515	40										36
37	Payroll Taxes Expense	516	195										37
38	Salaries Expense	518	2,800										38
39	Supplies Expense	519	—		(c) 50								39
40	Utilities Expense	520	240										40
41			66,711	66,711	690	690							41
			4a		4b								

NOTE: The cents columns have been omitted in order to show the entire worksheet.

moved to the Adjusted Trial Balance section. For example, the first four accounts (Cash, Petty Cash, Change Fund, and Accounts Receivable) are not adjusted. Thus, the balances are moved to the Debit column of the Adjusted Trial Balance section. However, Merchandise Inventory (line 5) is adjusted. The Trial Balance section shows a debit of $7,000. The Adjustments section shows a credit adjustment of $600. The new balance is found by subtracting the $600 credit from the $7,000 debit, leaving a debit balance of $6,400. The adjusted balance is then entered in the Debit column of the Adjusted Trial Bal-

Obtaining Adjusted Trial Balance Amounts
Merchandise Inventory:
$7,000 − $600 = $6,400
Prepaid Insurance:
$480 − $40 = $440
Supplies:
$350 − $50 = $300

ance section. The same procedure is followed for the Prepaid Insurance and Supplies accounts.

The Income Summary account had no balance in the Trial Balance section. However, there is a $600 debit in the Adjustments section. The amount moved to the Adjusted Trial Balance section is, therefore, a debit balance of $600. The same procedure is used for the Insurance Expense and Supplies Expense accounts.

Computer Age
Worksheet
For the Month Ended November 30, 19—

	ACCOUNT TITLE	ACCT. NO.	TRIAL BALANCE		ADJUSTMENTS		ADJUSTED TRIAL BALANCE		INCOME STATEMENT		BALANCE SHEET		
			DEBIT	CREDIT	DEBIT	CREDIT	DEBIT	CREDIT	DEBIT	CREDIT	DEBIT	CREDIT	
1	Cash	101	9,500				9,500						1
2	Petty Cash	102	30				30						2
3	Change Fund	103	35				35						3
4	Accounts Receivable	111	3,000				3,000						4
5	Merchandise Inventory	120	7,000			(a) 600	6,400						5
6	Prepaid Insurance	121	480			(b) 40	440						6
7	Supplies	123	350			(c) 50	300						7
8	Land	130	8,000				8,000						8
9	Building	131	22,000				22,000						9
10	Office Equipment	132	1,800				1,800						10
11	Stockroom Equipment	133	2,700				2,700						11
12	Loans Payable	201		4,000				4,000					12
13	Accounts Payable	211		5,500				5,500					13
14	Sales Tax Payable	216		200				200					14
15	Federal Income Taxes Pay.	221		360				360					15
16	FICA Taxes Payable	222		220				220					16
17	State Income Taxes Pay.	223		140				140					17
18	Federal Unempl. Taxes Pay.	224		48				48					18
19	State Unempl. Taxes Pay.	225		176				176					19
20	Salaries Payable	226		—				—					20
21	Mortgage Payable	231		14,000				14,000					21
22	Jason Booth, Capital	301		29,232				29,232					22
23	Jason Booth, Drawing	302	1,200				1,200						23
24	Income Summary	399	—	—	(a) 600		600						24
25	Sales	401		12,600				12,600					25
26	Sales Returns and Allowances	402	190				190						26
27	Sales Discount	403	45				45						27
28	Purchases	501	6,800				6,800						28
29	Transportation In	502	80				80						29
30	Purchases Returns and Allow.	503		185				185					30
31	Purchases Discount	504		50				50					31
32	Cash Short and Over	511	6				6						32
33	Advertising Expense	512	100				100						33
34	Delivery Expense	513	120				120						34
35	Insurance Expense	514	—		(b) 40		40						35
36	Miscellaneous Expense	515	40				40						36
37	Payroll Taxes Expense	516	195				195						37
38	Salaries Expense	518	2,800				2,800						38
39	Supplies Expense	519	—		(c) 50		50						39
40	Utilities Expense	520	240				240						40
41			66,711	66,711	690	690	66,711	66,711					41
42													42
43	Net Income												43
44													44

4a 4b 4c

NOTE: The cents columns have been omitted in order to show the entire worksheet.

After all the account balances are entered in the Adjusted Trial Balance section, the columns are totaled. If the total debits equal the total credits, the columns are ruled. The accountant can then assume that there are no mathematical errors. The adjusted trial balance is the second trial balance prepared. It is used to check the equality of the debit and credit balances after the adjustments are made.

Concept: Trial Balance
The equality of the total debits and the total credits in the general ledger should be verified at regular intervals.

Step 4d: Completing the Financial Statement Sections

How does the accountant sort the balances in the Adjusted Trial Balance columns? Each balance in the Adjusted Trial Balance section is moved to one of the four remaining columns. Balance Sheet accounts are moved to the Balance Sheet columns. Temporary owner's equity accounts are moved to the Income Statement columns.

By moving the account balances into one of the final four columns, the accountant has also classified each account according to the financial statement on which it will appear. The financial statements can then be prepared easily from the worksheet. There is only one step left in completing the worksheet.

Determining the Net Income or Net Loss After each account balance has been moved to either the Income Statement section or the Balance Sheet section, a single rule is drawn across all money columns and the amounts are totaled. At this point the total debits in the Income Statement section do not equal the total credits because the business has a net income (increases in owner's equity are greater than decreases) or a net loss (decreases in owner's equity are greater than increases).

Net Income To find the net income (or net loss), begin with the Income Statement section. If the total of the Credit column is greater than the total of the Debit column, there is a net income. To find the amount of net income, follow this procedure.

1. Place the total of the Debit column beneath the total of the Credit column and subtract.
2. Move the amount of the net income to the Credit column of the Balance Sheet section.
3. Add the net income to the total of the Credit column. (This is done because a net income increases owner's equity.)

INCOME STATEMENT		BALANCE SHEET	
DEBIT	CREDIT	DEBIT	CREDIT
11,306	12,835	55,405	53,876
	11,306		
	1,529 (1)	(2)	1,529
		55,405	55,405
		(3)	(3)

Computing net income on the worksheet.

Computer Age
Worksheet
For the Month Ended November 30, 19—

ACCOUNT TITLE	ACCT. NO.	TRIAL BALANCE DEBIT	TRIAL BALANCE CREDIT	ADJUSTMENTS DEBIT	ADJUSTMENTS CREDIT	ADJUSTED TRIAL BALANCE DEBIT	ADJUSTED TRIAL BALANCE CREDIT	INCOME STATEMENT DEBIT	INCOME STATEMENT CREDIT	BALANCE SHEET DEBIT	BALANCE SHEET CREDIT
Cash	101	9,500				9,500				9,500	
Petty Cash	102	30				30				30	
Change Fund	103	35				35				35	
Accounts Receivable	111	3,000				3,000				3,000	
Merchandise Inventory	120	7,000			(a) 600	6,400				6,400	
Prepaid Insurance	121	480			(b) 40	440				440	
Supplies	123	350			(c) 50	300				300	
Land	130	8,000				8,000				8,000	
Building	131	22,000				22,000				22,000	
Office Equipment	132	1,800				1,800				1,800	
Stockroom Equipment	133	2,700				2,700				2,700	
Loans Payable	201		4,000				4,000				4,000
Accounts Payable	211		5,500				5,500				5,500
Sales Tax Payable	216		200				200				200
Federal Income Taxes Pay.	221		360				360				360
FICA Taxes Payable	222		220				220				220
State Income Taxes Pay.	223		140				140				140
Federal Unempl. Taxes Pay.	224		48				48				48
State Unempl. Taxes Pay.	225		176				176				176
Salaries Payable	226		—				—				—
Mortgage Payable	231		14,000				14,000				14,000
Jason Booth, Capital	301		29,232				29,232				29,232
Jason Booth, Drawing	302	1,200				1,200				1,200	
Income Summary	399	—	—	(a) 600		600		600			
Sales	401		12,600				12,600		12,600		
Sales Returns and Allowances	402	190				190		190			
Sales Discount	403	45				45		45			
Purchases	501	6,800				6,800		6,800			
Transportation In	502	80				80		80			
Purchases Returns and Allow.	503		185				185		185		
Purchases Discount	504		50				50		50		
Cash Short and Over	511	6				6		6			
Advertising Expense	512	100				100		100			
Delivery Expense	513	120				120		120			
Insurance Expense	514	—		(b) 40		40		40			
Miscellaneous Expense	515	40				40		40			
Payroll Taxes Expense	516	195				195		195			
Salaries Expense	518	2,800				2,800		2,800			
Supplies Expense	519	—		(c) 50		50		50			
Utilities Expense	520	240				240		240			
		66,711	66,711	690	690	66,711	66,711	11,306	12,835	55,405	53,876
									11,306		
Net Income									1,529		1,529
										55,405	55,405

NOTE: The cents columns have been omitted in order to show the entire worksheet.

If the totals agree, complete the worksheet. Draw double rules across the Income Statement and Balance Sheet sections. If the totals do not agree, recheck until the error is found. If the adjusted trial balance was correct, the error was made in moving the balances or computing the totals. A completed copy of the worksheet for Computer Age is shown above.

■ **Net Loss** If the total of the Debit column of the Income Statement section is greater than the Credit column total, the business has a net loss. To find the amount of the net loss, follow this procedure.

1. Place the total of the Credit column under the total of the Debit column and subtract.
2. Extend the amount of the net loss to the Debit column of the Balance Sheet section.
3. Add the net loss to the total of the Debit column. If no errors were made, the totals of the Debit and Credit columns will be equal.

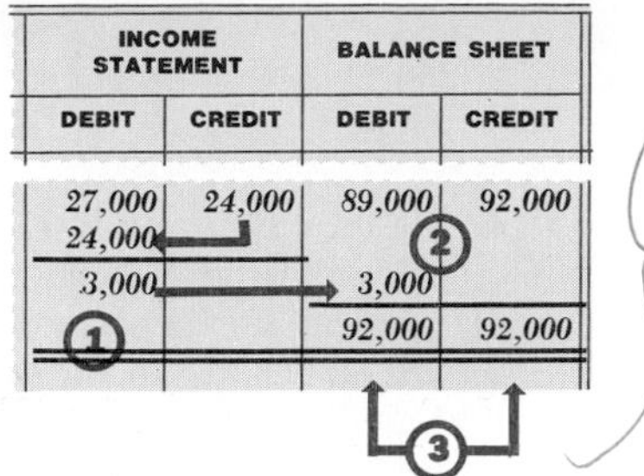

INCOME STATEMENT		BALANCE SHEET	
DEBIT	CREDIT	DEBIT	CREDIT
27,000	24,000	89,000	92,000
24,000			
3,000		3,000	
		92,000	92,000

Computing net loss on the worksheet.

Exercise D on this page and page 486 may be completed at this point.

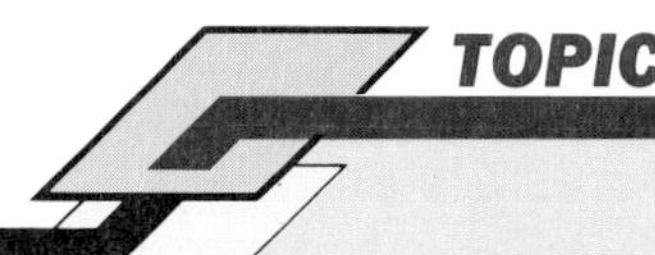

TOPIC 2 EXERCISES

EXERCISE B. Answer the following questions about updating the trial balance. Refer to the text, margin notes, and illustrations on pages 474 to 476.

1. Why is the Merchandise Inventory account credited for $600 on November 30?
2. What effect does the $600 adjustment have on owner's equity?
3. If the merchandise inventory had been larger on November 30 than it was on November 1, what adjusting entry would have been required?
4. Why is Merchandise Inventory debited for $900 on December 31?
5. What effect does the $900 have on owner's equity?
6. What will be the balance of Merchandise Inventory on January 1?

EXERCISE C. Answer the following questions about updating the trial balance. Refer to the text, margin notes, and illustrations on pages 476 to 480.

1. Why is it necessary to adjust the Supplies account on November 30?
2. What is the effect of the $50 credit to the Supplies account on November 30?
3. What is the effect on owner's equity of the debit to Supplies Expense?
4. Why is it necessary to adjust the Prepaid Insurance account on November 30?
5. What effect does the $40 credit to the Prepaid Insurance account have on the total assets of the business?

EXERCISE D. Answer the following questions about completing the worksheet. Refer to the text, margin notes, and illustrations on pages 480 to 485.

1. What is the adjusted trial balance amount for Prepaid Insurance? How was it found?
2. What is the adjusted trial balance amount for Mortgage Payable?

3. What is the effect of the credit to the Supplies account?

4. Is every balance in the Trial Balance section moved to the Adjusted Trial Balance section? If so, are the balances for the same account always identical? Why or why not?

5. What is the purpose of the small letters in the Adjustments section?

6. What is the amount of the net income? How is it determined?

7. Why is the $1,529 net income added to the total of the Credit column in the Balance Sheet section?

8. Does the amount of net income in the Income Statement section always have to be the same as the amount of the net income in the Balance Sheet section? Why or why not?

9. How can you tell that the $1,529 is net income and not a net loss?

10. Why is the $7,000 for Merchandise Inventory not moved to the Balance Sheet section?

TOPIC 2 PROBLEMS

TOPIC PROBLEM 2. For each of the adjustments listed below, give the following information: (1) the amount of the adjustment, (2) the account debited and the account credited, (3) the account balance after the adjustment is posted, and (4) whether the new account balance is a debit or credit balance.

a. Merchandise inventory at the beginning of the accounting period: $17,020. Merchandise inventory at the end of the accounting period: $20,612.

b. Merchandise inventory at the beginning of the accounting period: $12,261. Merchandise inventory at the end of the accounting period: $8,190.

c. Supplies at the beginning of the period: $610. Supplies at the end of the period: $115.

d. Supplies at the beginning of the period: $35. Supplies purchased during the period: $30. Supplies at the end of the period: $40.

TOPIC PROBLEM 3. For each of the adjustments listed below, give the following information: (1) the amount of the adjustment, (2) the account debited and the account credited, (3) the account balance after the adjustment is posted, and (4) whether the new account balance is a debit or credit balance.

a. Prepaid insurance at the beginning of the period: $680. Insurance purchased during the period: $180. Insurance expired during the period: $120.

b. Prepaid insurance at the beginning of the period: $1,025. Unexpired insurance at the end of the period: $320.

c. The premium for one year's insurance is $540. Adjust the account for one month of expired insurance.

d. Supplies at the beginning of the period: $720. No supplies were purchased during the period. Supplies at the end of the period: $730. (*Hint*: Discuss what could have happened to cause this situation.)

TOPIC PROBLEM 4. The accounts in the general ledger of Central Plains Equipment Company showed the balances given at the right on May 31. Listed below is data on the adjustments to be made for the month of May.

a. A physical inventory on May 31 showed merchandise on hand amounting to $8,790.

b. A physical inventory also showed unused supplies amounting to $120.

c. The amount of unexpired insurance as of May 31 is $480.

Using this information, complete a worksheet for the month ended May 31.

NOTE: Save your worksheet for further use in Topic Problem 6.

Central Plains Equipment Company
Trial Balance
May 31, 19—

ACCOUNT TITLE	ACCT. NO.	DEBIT	CREDIT
Cash	101	9,240 00	
Accounts Receivable	111	3,875 00	
Merchandise Inventory	112	12,653 00	
Prepaid Insurance	113	540 00	
Supplies	114	160 00	
Land	121	6,900 00	
Building	131	20,000 00	
Equipment	132	6,040 00	
Accounts Payable	211		1,783 00
Federal Income Taxes Payable	221		70 00
FICA Taxes Payable	222		62 00
Mortgage Payable	231		20,000 00
Mark Jeter, Capital	301		32,567 00
Mark Jeter, Drawing	302	800 00	
Income Summary	399		— 00
Sales	401		10,346 00
Sales Returns and Allowances	402	138 00	
Sales Discount	403	183 00	
Purchases	501	3,765 00	
Transportation In	502	45 00	
Purchases Returns and Allowances	503		87 00
Purchases Discount	504		76 00
Insurance Expense	511	— 00	
Miscellaneous Expense	512	21 00	
Payroll Taxes Expense	513	31 00	
Salaries Expense	514	600 00	
Supplies Expense	515	— 00	

TOPIC PROBLEM 5. The accounts in the general ledger of the Van Doren Company showed the balances listed at right on March 31. (Mr. Van Doren has no employees.) Here is data on the adjustments to be made.

a. A physical inventory on March 31 showed merchandise on hand amounting to $7,520.

b. A physical inventory also showed that the cost of the supplies used was $30.

c. The amount of expired insurance for March is $75.

Using this information, complete a worksheet for the month ended March 31.

NOTE: Save your worksheet for further use in Topic Problems 7 and 9.

Van Doren Company
Trial Balance
March 31, 19—

ACCOUNT TITLE	ACCT. NO.	DEBIT	CREDIT
Cash	101	3,521 00	
Change Fund	102	35 00	
Accounts Receivable	111	283 00	
Merchandise Inventory	112	6,213 00	
Prepaid Insurance	113	300 00	
Supplies	114	45 00	
Office Equipment	131	800 00	
Store Equipment	132	2,429 00	
Accounts Payable	201		86 00
Sales Taxes Payable	211		242 00
Carl Van Doren, Capital	301		14,696 00
Carl Van Doren, Drawing	302	140 00	
Income Summary	399		— 00
Sales	401		4,930 00
Sales Returns and Allowances	402	90 00	
Sales Discount	403	70 00	
Purchases	501	5,800 00	
Transportation In	502	23 00	
Purchases Returns and Allowances	503		45 00
Purchases Discount	504		120 00
Advertising Expense	511	140 00	
Insurance Expense	512	— 00	
Miscellaneous Expense	513	60 00	
Rent Expense	514	170 00	
Supplies Expense	515	— 00	

TOPIC 3

Preparing Financial Statements

What is the source of data that the worksheet supplies to prepare financial statements? The account balances have been sorted on the worksheet according to the statements on which the accounts appear. Also, the net income (or net loss) has been computed. It is now easy to prepare the financial statements—Step 5 in the accounting cycle.

Step 5a: Preparing the Schedule of Cost of Goods Sold and the Income Statement

What financial statements are prepared as part of Step 5 in the accounting cycle? Two statements are prepared at this time: the schedule of cost of goods sold and the income statement.

Schedule of Cost of Goods Sold

The **schedule of cost of goods sold** is a statement showing the computation of cost of goods sold during the accounting period. The schedule of cost of goods sold is prepared before the income statement because the amount of the cost of goods sold is needed to complete the income statement.

The schedule of cost of goods sold that was prepared for Computer Age for the month of November is shown on the next page. Note that the heading indicates that the schedule covers a period of time.

1. *Merchandise Inventory, November 1.* The inventory for November 1 is the cost of merchandise inventory on hand as of the beginning of the accounting period. The amount ($7,000) is found in the Trial Balance section of the worksheet.
2. *Net Purchases.* The data needed to compute the net purchases is found in the Income Statement section of the worksheet. During the month of November, Computer Age purchased merchandise costing $6,800. It also paid transportation charges of $80. The cost of delivered goods was $6,880 ($6,800 + $80). During the month, the business returned merchandise costing $185. It also took cash discounts of $50 offered by the suppliers. The two amounts reduced the net cost of the merchandise by $235 ($185 + $50). The amount of net purchases was $6,645 ($6,880 − $235).
3. *Cost of Goods Available for Sale.* This amount ($13,645) is the total of the inventory on hand at the beginning of the accounting period ($7,000), plus the net purchases ($6,645). The cost of goods available for sale is the total cost of goods that could have been sold if all the beginning inventory and purchases were sold. In practice, one would not expect to see all the beginning inventory and purchases sold.
4. *Merchandise Inventory, November 30.* The amount of the merchandise inventory at the end of the accounting period on November 30

is $6,400 and is found in the Balance Sheet section. This amount must be subtracted from the cost of goods available for sale in order to arrive at the cost of goods sold. Why must the ending inventory be subtracted from the cost of goods available for sale? An actual count of the inventory revealed that unsold merchandise costing $6,400 was still on the shelves and in storage at Computer Age. Since it was not sold, it cannot be included in the cost of goods sold.

5. *Cost of Goods Sold.* This amount ($7,245) is the dollar value of goods actually transferred to customers through business activity. It is found by subtracting the ending inventory ($6,400) from the cost of goods available for sale ($13,645).

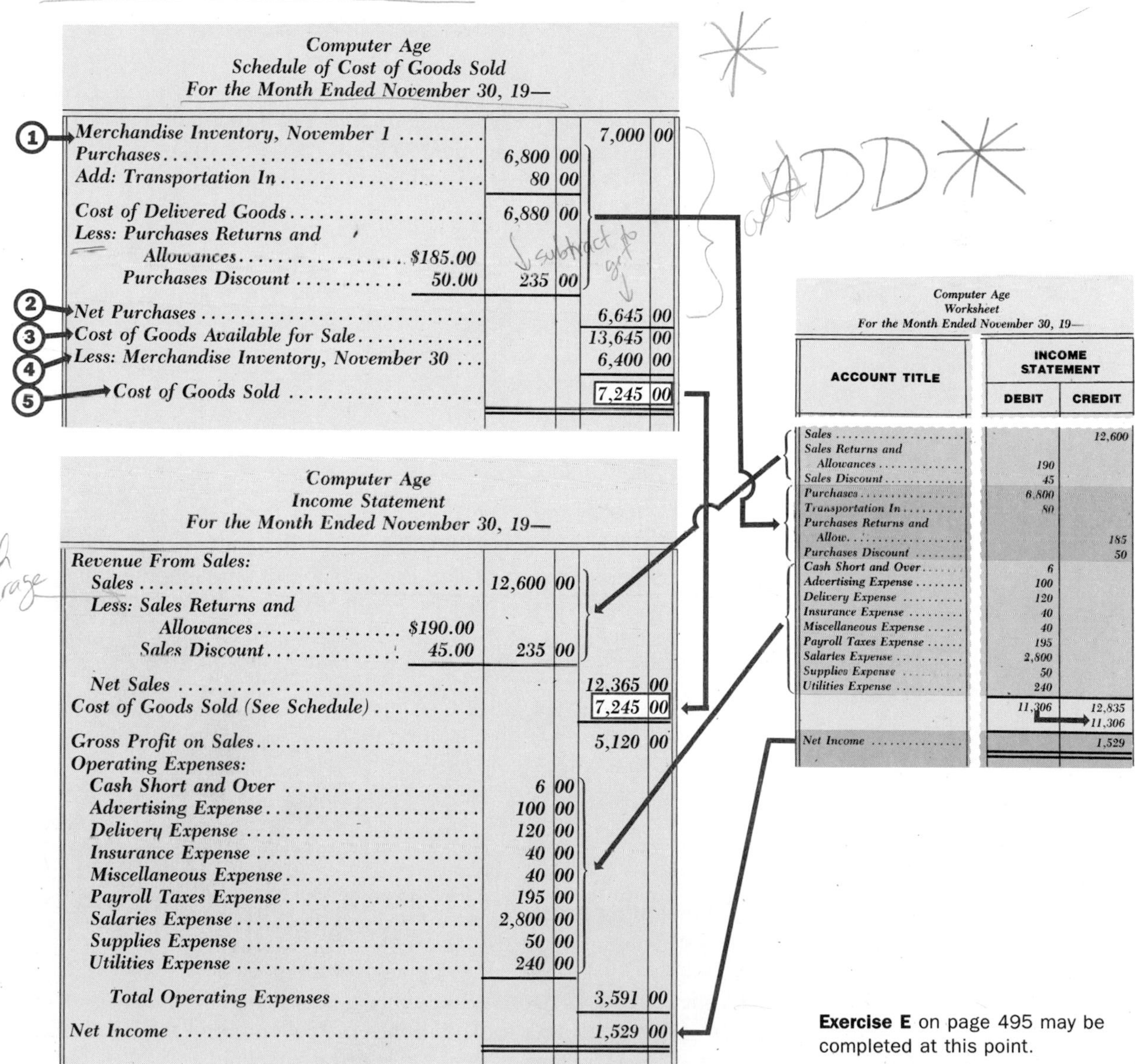

Computer Age
Schedule of Cost of Goods Sold
For the Month Ended November 30, 19—

① Merchandise Inventory, November 1			7,000 00
Purchases		6,800 00	
Add: Transportation In		80 00	
Cost of Delivered Goods		6,880 00	
Less: Purchases Returns and Allowances	$185.00		
Purchases Discount	50.00	235 00	
② Net Purchases			6,645 00
③ Cost of Goods Available for Sale			13,645 00
④ Less: Merchandise Inventory, November 30			6,400 00
⑤ Cost of Goods Sold			7,245 00

Computer Age
Income Statement
For the Month Ended November 30, 19—

Revenue From Sales:			
Sales		12,600 00	
Less: Sales Returns and Allowances	$190.00		
Sales Discount	45.00	235 00	
Net Sales			12,365 00
Cost of Goods Sold (See Schedule)			7,245 00
Gross Profit on Sales			5,120 00
Operating Expenses:			
Cash Short and Over		6 00	
Advertising Expense		100 00	
Delivery Expense		120 00	
Insurance Expense		40 00	
Miscellaneous Expense		40 00	
Payroll Taxes Expense		195 00	
Salaries Expense		2,800 00	
Supplies Expense		50 00	
Utilities Expense		240 00	
Total Operating Expenses			3,591 00
Net Income			1,529 00

Computer Age
Worksheet
For the Month Ended November 30, 19—

ACCOUNT TITLE	INCOME STATEMENT DEBIT	INCOME STATEMENT CREDIT
Sales		12,600
Sales Returns and Allowances	190	
Sales Discount	45	
Purchases	6,800	
Transportation In	80	
Purchases Returns and Allow.		185
Purchases Discount		50
Cash Short and Over	6	
Advertising Expense	100	
Delivery Expense	120	
Insurance Expense	40	
Miscellaneous Expense	40	
Payroll Taxes Expense	195	
Salaries Expense	2,800	
Supplies Expense	50	
Utilities Expense	240	
	11,306	12,835
		11,306
Net Income		1,529

Exercise E on page 495 may be completed at this point.

Revenue (from goods sold)
− Cost (of goods sold)

Gross Profit (on sales)
− Expenses (to operate business)

Net Income
(or Net Loss)

Income Statement The income statement for a merchandising business contains five sections: revenue from sales, cost of goods sold, gross profit on sales, operating expenses, and net income (or net loss). The two new sections—cost of goods sold and gross profit—are important. The net income (or net loss) of a merchandising business is found by subtracting both the cost of goods sold and expenses from revenue.

The income statement prepared for Computer Age for the month of November is an example of an income statement for a merchandising business. The amounts of the revenue, operating expenses, and net income are obtained directly from the Income Statement section of the worksheet. The cost of goods sold and the gross profit must be computed.

Revenue From Sales The total sales for the month ($12,600) is found in the Income Statement section of the worksheet. From this amount, the sales returns and allowances ($190) and sales discounts ($45) are deducted to obtain the net sales of $12,365.

Revenue From Sales:			
Sales		*12,600*	*00*
Less: Sales Returns and			
Allowances	*190.00*		
Sales Discount	*45.00*	*235*	*00*
Net Sales		*12,365*	*00*

Computing net sales.

Cost of Goods Sold The total cost of goods sold is shown on the income statement. The computation of the cost of goods sold is usually shown on a schedule that goes with the income statement. When a schedule of cost of goods sold supports the income statement, only the amount of the cost of goods sold ($7,245) appears on the income statement.

Gross Profit on Sales A gross profit on sales is made by selling merchandise for a higher price than was paid by the business. The amount of gross profit on sales ($5,120) is found by subtracting the cost of goods sold ($7,245) from the net sales ($12,365).

Net Sales	*12,365*	*00*
Cost of Goods Sold	*7,245*	*00*
Gross Profit on Sales	*5,120*	*00*

Computing gross profit.

Operating Expenses Each expense and the total expenses of operating the business for the month of November ($3,591) are found in the Income Statement section of the worksheet.

Net Income The net income is the amount remaining after total operating expenses are subtracted from the gross profit on sales. During November, Computer Age has a gross profit on sales of $5,120, operating expenses of $3,591, and a net income of $1,529 ($5,120 − $3,591). This is the same amount as the net income computed on the worksheet. If expenses had been greater than the gross profit on sales, there would have been a loss.

Gross Profit on Sales	5,120 00
Operating Expenses	3,591 00
Net Income	1,529 00

Computing net income.

Exercise F on page 495 may be completed at this point.

Step 5b: Preparing the Statement of Owner's Equity and the Balance Sheet

Why prepare a statement of owner's equity separately from the balance sheet? Up to this point, the owner's equity was shown in a section of the balance sheet. However, the owner's equity section can become too long, or the owner may want more details, or the owner may not want the details of his or her investment shown on the balance sheet. When this happens, a separate statement of owner's equity is prepared. The statement of owner's equity is prepared first because it is needed to complete the balance sheet.

Statement of Owner's Equity

A **statement of owner's equity** is a financial statement to report investments and withdrawals, as well as the net income (or net loss) for the period.

The owner's equity on November 1, the beginning of the accounting period, was $27,732. On November 30, the end of the accounting period, the owner's equity increased to $29,561. The increase of $1,829 was due to an additional investment of $1,500 and the net income of $1,529, less withdrawals of $1,200.

Computer Age
Statement of Owner's Equity
For the Month Ended November 30, 19—

Capital, November 1		27,732 00
Additional Investments		1,500 00
Total Investments		29,232 00
Net Income for the Month	1,529 00	
Less: Withdrawals	1,200 00	
Increase in Capital		329 00
Capital, November 30		29,561 00

If a statement of owner's equity is prepared, the owner's capital at the end of the accounting period is the only amount shown in the Owner's Equity section of the balance sheet. The November 30 balance sheet for Computer Age shows just one amount in the Owner's Equity section ($29,561).

Total Liabilities	24,644	00
Owner's Equity		
Jason Booth, Capital	29,561	00
Total Liabilities and Owner's Equity	54,205	00

If Computer Age had a net loss, a decrease in capital would be shown on the statement of owner's equity. For example, if there had been a net loss of $1,500 for November, the capital would decrease by $2,700 (net loss of $1,500 plus withdrawals of $1,200).

Capital, November 1		27,732	00
Additional Investments		1,500	00
Total Investments		29,232	00
Net Loss for the Month	*$1,500*		
Plus: Withdrawals	*1,200*		
Decrease in Capital		2,700	00
Capital, November 30		26,532	00

Showing a net loss.

Not all the information to prepare the statement of owner's equity is shown on the worksheet. The balance of the capital account at the beginning of the accounting period and the additional investments are found in the owner's capital account in the general ledger. The withdrawals and the net income (or net loss) are found in the Balance Sheet section of the worksheet.

COMPUTER AGE CHART OF ACCOUNTS

Current Assets
101 Cash
102 Petty Cash
103 Change Fund
111 Accounts Receivable
120 Merchandise Inventory
121 Prepaid Insurance
123 Supplies

■ Balance Sheet

The balance sheets up to this point have shown all assets in one group. All liabilities have also been shown in one group. For accounting purposes, however, assets and liabilities are usually classified into these groups: current assets, plant and equipment assets, current liabilities, and long-term liabilities.

■ Current Assets Cash, assets that will be changed into cash, and assets that will be used in the normal operations of the business within a year of the date of the balance sheet are classified as **current assets**. The four major types of current assets are cash, receivables, merchandise inventory, and prepaid expenses. The order on the balance sheet is determined by liquidity, that is, by how quickly each asset is expected to be changed into cash or used.

Cash is always listed first because it is available to pay debts. Petty Cash and Change Fund are listed next. Next are the *receivables,* such as Notes Receivable and Accounts Receivable. These are the amounts that customers owe the business. (Notes Receivable is usually listed before Accounts Receivable because notes have a definite collection date.)

Merchandise Inventory is listed next. It shows the cost of items the business has on hand and hopes to sell within the accounting period. Then come the *prepaid expenses,* such as Prepaid Insurance and Supplies. Prepaid expenses are current assets because they will be used in the near future.

The figure for the total current assets may be used for many purposes. For example, when a business applies for a loan, the bank often reviews the current assets to see if there will be cash to repay the loan. Also, the business may review its current assets to see if it can pay debts.

■ Plant and Equipment Assets that are expected to be useful to the business for a number of years are known as **plant and equipment**. Examples are land, buildings, furniture, and machinery. One way of listing plant and equipment on the balance sheet is to list the more permanent assets such as land and buildings first. Land has unlimited life. All other plant and equipment assets gradually lose their usefulness because they wear out and need replacement or become obsolete, or because more efficient items are needed.

COMPUTER AGE CHART OF ACCOUNTS

Plant and Equipment

130 Land
131 Building
132 Office Equipment
133 Stockroom Equipment

■ Current Liabilities **Current liabilities** are debts that must be paid within a year of the balance sheet date. Current liabilities are listed in the order that they must be paid. Those that must be paid first are shown first. (Loans Payable is generally listed before Accounts Payable because loans have a definite due date.)

■ Long-Term Liabilities Debts that are not due within a year are considered **long-term liabilities** (sometimes referred to as *fixed liabilities*). An example of a long-term liability is a mortgage on land and buildings.

COMPUTER AGE CHART OF ACCOUNTS

Current Liabilities

201 Loans Payable
211 Accounts Payable
216 Sales Tax Payable
221 Federal Income Taxes Payable
222 FICA Taxes Payable
223 State Income Taxes Payable
224 Federal Unemployment Taxes Payable
225 State Unemployment Taxes Payable
226 Salaries Payable

Long-Term Liabilities

231 Mortgage Payable

■ Classified Balance Sheet

If a business does not have one or more of the groups of assets or liabilities described here, it simply omits the classification or classifications from its balance sheet. A classified balance sheet prepared for Computer Age on November 30 is shown on page 494.

Computer Age
Balance Sheet
November 30, 19—

Assets				
Current Assets:				
Cash	9,500	00		
Petty Cash	30	00		
Change Fund	35	00		
Accounts Receivable	3,000	00		
Merchandise Inventory	6,400	00		
Prepaid Insurance	440	00		
Supplies	300	00		
Total Current Assets			19,705	00
Plant and Equipment:				
Land	8,000	00		
Building	22,000	00		
Office Equipment	1,800	00		
Stockroom Equipment	2,700	00		
Total Plant and Equipment			34,500	00
Total Assets			54,205	00
Liabilities				
Current Liabilities:				
Loans Payable	4,000	00		
Accounts Payable	5,500	00		
Sales Tax Payable	200	00		
Federal Income Taxes Payable	360	00		
FICA Taxes Payable	220	00		
State Income Taxes Payable	140	00		
Federal Unemployment Taxes Payable	48	00		
State Unemployment Taxes Payable	176	00		
Total Current Liabilities			10,644	00
Long-Term Liabilities:				
Mortgage Payable			14,000	00
Total Liabilities			24,644	00
Owner's Equity				
Jason Booth, Capital			29,561	00
Total Liabilities and Owner's Equity			54,205	00

Principle: Classifying Assets

The generally accepted accounting principle is that the assets reported on the balance sheet should be classified into at least two groups: current assets and plant and equipment.

Principle: Classifying Liabilities

The generally accepted accounting principle is that liabilities reported on the balance sheet should be classified into at least two groups: current liabilities and long-term liabilities.

Exercise G on page 495 may be completed at this point.

TOPIC 3 EXERCISES

EXERCISE E. Complete the following schedule of cost of goods sold.

Ridolfi Company
Schedule of Cost of Goods Sold
For the Quarter Ended March 31, 19—

Merchandise Inventory, January 1			*7,000 00*
Purchases		*7,315 00*	
Add: Transportation In		*60 00*	
Cost of Delivered Goods			
Less: Purchases Returns and Allow.	*$185.00*		
Purchases Discount	*120.00*		
Net Purchases			
Cost of Goods Available for Sale			
Less: Merchandise Inventory, March 31			*6,000 00*
Cost of Goods Sold			

EXERCISE F. Answer the following questions about preparing financial statements. Refer to pages 488 to 490.

1. How much is net purchases?
2. How is net purchases determined?
3. How much is the cost of goods sold? How is it obtained?
4. Where is the data obtained for preparing the income statement?
5. What is the amount of net sales?
6. Why is there a difference between gross profit and net income?

EXERCISE G. Answer the following questions about preparing financial statements. Refer to pages 491 to 494.

1. Does Jason Booth make any additional investments during the month? If so, how much?
2. Where is the net income obtained for the statement of owner's equity? Owner's withdrawals? Total investments?
3. Where is the data obtained for preparing the balance sheet and the statement of owner's equity?
4. Is the beginning or the ending merchandise inventory recorded on the balance sheet? Why?
5. Are there any prepaid expenses on the balance sheet? If so, what are the account titles and balances?

TOPIC 3 PROBLEMS

TOPIC PROBLEM 6. Using the data from the worksheet prepared in Topic Problem 4 on page 487, complete the following work for Central Plains Equipment Company for the month ended May 31. Mr. Jeter made additional investments of $5,000 during the period.

a. Prepare a schedule of cost of goods sold and an income statement.

b. Prepare a statement of owner's equity and a classified balance sheet.

TOPIC PROBLEM 7. Using the data from the worksheet that was prepared in Topic Problem 5 on page 487, complete the following work for the Van Doren Company for the month ended March 31, 19—. Mr. Van Doren made additional investments of $4,000 in the Van Doren Company during the period.

a. Prepare a schedule of cost of goods sold and an income statement.

b. Prepare a statement of owner's equity and a classified balance sheet.

NOTE: Save your worksheet for further use in Topic Problem 9.

TOPIC PROBLEM 8. Supply the missing amounts in the table below.

Beg. Inv.	Purchases	Transp. In	Cost of Delivered Goods	Purch. Ret.	Purch. Disc.	Net Purch.	Cost of Goods Available for Sale	End. Inv.	Cost of Goods Sold
a. $ 7,000	$8,000	$450	?	$800	$800	?	?	$7,000	?
b. $13,800	$4,800	?	$5,000	$200	?	$4,600	?	$8,700	?
c. $ 7,020	$7,600	$120	?	$340	$160	?	?	?	$9,740
d. $ 6,500	?	$840	$7,240	$260	$240	?	?	$3,000	?
e. ?	?	$ 70	?	$380	$120	$6,590	?	$6,400	$8,390
f. $ 3,800	$7,100	?	$8,200	?	$160	$7,800	?	$3,900	?

TOPIC 4

Adjusting and Closing the Ledger

Are the adjustments shown on the worksheet also recorded in the ledger? Yes, the ledger accounts—the permanent records—must be adjusted to contain the same balances shown on the worksheet. The procedure for bringing the ledger accounts up to date is known as *adjusting the ledger*. Also, a procedure known as *closing the ledger* is completed so that the ledger accounts for the next accounting period are prepared. Adjusting and closing the ledger is completed as a part of Step 6 in the accounting cycle.

Step 6a: Recording and Posting the Adjusting Entries

Why are end-of-period adjustments computed on the worksheet? The end-of-period adjustments are computed on the worksheet to provide correct account balances for the financial statements.

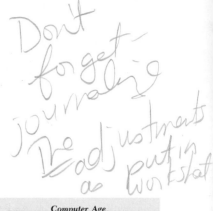

In the example of Computer Age, adjustments were needed for (a) Merchandise Inventory, (b) Prepaid Insurance, and (c) Supplies. These accounts in the general ledger, however, still show the incorrect balances. Thus, it is necessary to journalize the adjustments in the general journal and post the entries to the ledger. After journalizing and posting the adjustments, the accounts in the general ledger will agree with the amounts on the financial statements. The data for the adjusting entries is found in the Adjustments section of the worksheet.

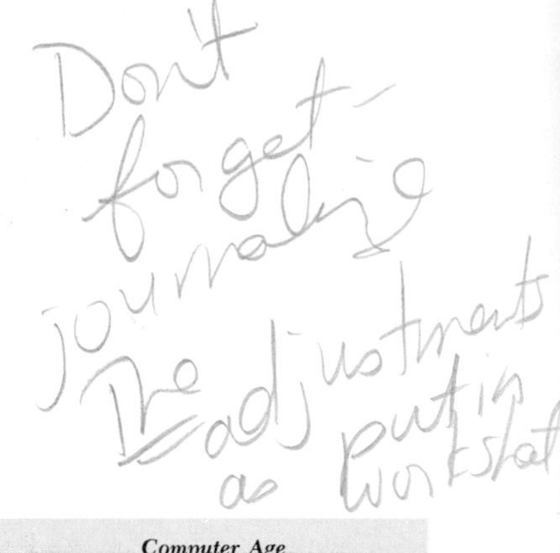

GENERAL JOURNAL Page 6

DATE		ACCOUNT TITLE AND EXPLANATION	POST. REF.	DEBIT	CREDIT
19—					
Nov.	30	Income Summary	399	600 00	
		Merchandise Inventory	120		600 00
		Adjust inventory.			
	30	Insurance Expense	514	40 00	
		Prepaid Insurance	121		40 00
		Record expired insurance.			
	30	Supplies Expense	519	50 00	
		Supplies	123		50 00
		Record supplies used.			

Adjustments recorded in the general journal.

Computer Age
Worksheet
For the Month Ended November 30, 19—

ACCOUNT TITLE	ADJUSTMENTS DEBIT	ADJUSTMENTS CREDIT
Merchandise Inventory		(a) 600
Prepaid Insurance		(b) 40
Supplies		(c) 50
Income Summary	(a) 600	
Insurance Expense	(b) 40	
Supplies Expense	(c) 50	

Worksheet: Source of adjustments.

Merchandise Inventory **Account No.** *120*

DATE		EXPLANATION	POST. REF.	DEBIT	CREDIT	BALANCE DEBIT	BALANCE CREDIT
19—							
Nov.	1	Balance	—			7,000 00	
	30	Adjustment	J6		600 00	6,400 00	

Income Summary **Account No.** *399*

DATE		EXPLANATION	POST. REF.	DEBIT	CREDIT	BALANCE DEBIT	BALANCE CREDIT
19—							
Nov.	30	Inventory adjustment	J6	600 00		600 00	

Prepaid Insurance **Account No.** *121*

DATE		EXPLANATION	POST. REF.	DEBIT	CREDIT	BALANCE DEBIT	BALANCE CREDIT
19—							
Nov.	1		CP6	480 00		480 00	
	30	Expired	J6		40 00	440 00	

Insurance Expense **Account No.** *514*

DATE		EXPLANATION	POST. REF.	DEBIT	CREDIT	BALANCE DEBIT	BALANCE CREDIT
19—							
Nov.	30		J6	40 00		40 00	

Supplies **Account No.** *123*

DATE		EXPLANATION	POST. REF.	DEBIT	CREDIT	BALANCE DEBIT	BALANCE CREDIT
19—							
Nov.	3		CP6	350 00		350 00	
	30	Used	J6		50 00	300 00	

Supplies Expense **Account No.** *519*

DATE		EXPLANATION	POST. REF.	DEBIT	CREDIT	BALANCE DEBIT	BALANCE CREDIT
19—							
Nov.	30		J6	50 00		50 00	

Ledger accounts after posting adjustments.

Step 6b: Recording and Posting the Closing Entries

What is the purpose of the closing entries? The closing entries are necessary to close the ledger. Closing the ledger prepares the accounts for the next accounting period. The first part of Step 6 is to journalize and post the adjusting entries. Next, all temporary owner's equity accounts—revenue, cost and expense, income summary, and drawing accounts—have to be closed. This is done by transferring the temporary account balances to other accounts. The temporary accounts then have zero balances and are ready for the next period's revenue and cost and expense data.

Four journal entries are made to transfer the balances of the temporary accounts. The procedures to do this are as follows.

Transfer temporary accounts with credit balances in the Income Statement section to the Income Summary account.

- *Close all the revenue and cost accounts in the Credit column of the Income Statement section of the worksheet.* The balances are transferred to the Income Summary account by debiting each account for the account balance and crediting Income Summary for the total of the balances.

Computer Age
Worksheet
For the Month Ended November 30, 19—

ACCOUNT TITLE	INCOME STATEMENT DEBIT	INCOME STATEMENT CREDIT
Sales		12,600
Purchases Ret. and Allow.		185
Purchases Disc.		50
		12,835

Worksheet: source of closing entry.

GENERAL JOURNAL Page 6

DATE		ACCOUNT TITLE AND EXPLANATION	POST. REF.	DEBIT	CREDIT
19— Nov.	30	Sales	401	12,600 00	
		Purchases Returns and Allowances	503	185 00	
		Purchases Discount	504	50 00	
		Income Summary	399		12,835 00
		Close accounts with credit balances.			

Journal entry to close accounts with credit balances.

Transfer temporary accounts with debit balances (except Income Summary) in the Income Statement section to the Income Summary account.

- *Close all the accounts (except the Income Summary account) in the Debit column of the Income Statement section of the worksheet.* The balances are transferred by crediting each account for the account balance and debiting the Income Summary account for the total of the balances. (The $600 debit was already transferred to the Income Summary account through an adjusting entry.)

Transfer Income Summary account balance to Capital account.

- *Close the Income Summary account.* After the first two closing entries are posted, the balance of the Income Summary account is the net income (or net loss). Income Summary is then transferred to the Capital account by debiting the Income Summary account and crediting the Capital account for the amount of the net income. A net loss is transferred to the Capital account by debiting the Capital account and crediting the Income Summary account for the amount of the net loss.

Close all the accounts (except Income Summary) in the Debit column of the Income Statement section of the worksheet.

GENERAL JOURNAL — Page 6

DATE		ACCOUNT TITLE AND EXPLANATION	POST. REF.	DEBIT	CREDIT
19—					
Nov.	30	Income Summary	399	10,706 00	
		Sales Returns and Allowances	402		190 00
		Sales Discount	403		45 00
		Purchases	501		6,800 00
		Transportation In	502		80 00
		Cash Short and Over	511		6 00
		Advertising Expense	512		100 00
		Delivery Expense	513		120 00
		Insurance Expense	514		40 00
		Miscellaneous Expense	515		40 00
		Payroll Taxes Expense	516		195 00
		Salaries Expense	518		2,800 00
		Supplies Expense	519		50 00
		Utilities Expense	520		240 00
		Close accounts with debit balances.			

Journal entry to close accounts with debit balances (except Income Summary).

Computer Age
Worksheet
For the Month Ended November 30, 19—

ACCOUNT TITLE	INCOME STATEMENT DEBIT	INCOME STATEMENT CREDIT
Sales Ret. and Allow.	190	
Sales Discount	45	
Purchases	6,800	
Transportation In	80	
Cash Short and Over	6	
Advertising Expense	100	
Delivery Expense	120	
Insurance Expense	40	
Miscellaneous Exp.	40	
Payroll Taxes Exp.	195	
Salaries Expense	2,800	
Supplies Expense	50	
Utilities Expense	240	

Worksheet: Source of closing entry.

Income Summary — Account No. 399

DATE		EXPLANATION	POST. REF.	DEBIT	CREDIT	BALANCE DEBIT	BALANCE CREDIT
19—							
Nov.	30	Inventory adjustment	J6	600 00		600 00	
	30	Closing entry	J6		12,835 00		12,235 00
	30	Closing entry	J6	10,706 00			1,529 00

Close the Income Summary account and transfer its balance to the Capital account.

GENERAL JOURNAL — Page 6

DATE		ACCOUNT TITLE AND EXPLANATION	POST. REF.	DEBIT	CREDIT
19—					
Nov.	30	Income Summary	399	1,529 00	
		Jason Booth, Capital	301		1,529 00
		Transfer net income.			

Closing entry to transfer net income to Capital account.

Computer Age
Worksheet
For the Month Ended November 30, 19–

ACCOUNT TITLE	INCOME STATEMENT DEBIT	INCOME STATEMENT CREDIT
	11,306	12,835
		11,306
Net Income		1,529

Income Summary — Account No. 399

DATE		EXPLANATION	POST. REF.	DEBIT	CREDIT	BALANCE DEBIT	BALANCE CREDIT
19—							
Nov.	30	Inventory adjustment	J6	600 00		600 00	
	30	Closing entry	J6		12,835 00		12,235 00
	30	Closing entry	J6	10,706 00			1,529 00
	30	Transfer net income	J6	1,529 00			— 00

Income Summary account closed.

Jason Booth, Capital — Account No. 301

DATE		EXPLANATION	POST. REF.	DEBIT	CREDIT	BALANCE DEBIT	BALANCE CREDIT
19—							
Nov.	1	Balance	—				27,732 00
	2	Additional investment	CR5		1,500 00		29,232 00
	30	Net income	J6		1,529 00		30,761 00

Capital account contains net income.

Transfer Drawing account balance to Capital account.

■ *Close the Drawing account*. The owner makes withdrawals against expected net income by debiting the Drawing account. At the end of the accounting period, the withdrawals are transferred to the Capital account. Thus, the withdrawals can be offset against the net income or loss. The $1,200 in the Drawing account is transferred to the Capital account. This data is in the Balance Sheet section of the worksheet.

Computer Age
Worksheet
For the Month Ended November 30, 19—

ACCOUNT TITLE	BALANCE SHEET	
	DEBIT	CREDIT
Jason Booth, Drawing	*1,200*	

Worksheet: Source of closing entry.

GENERAL JOURNAL Page 6

DATE		ACCOUNT TITLE AND EXPLANATION	POST. REF.	DEBIT	CREDIT
19—					
Nov.	*30*	*Jason Booth, Capital*	*301*	*1,200 00*	
		Jason Booth, Drawing	*302*		*1,200 00*
		Transfer to capital.			

Journal entry to close Drawing account.

Jason Booth, Capital Account No. *301*

DATE		EXPLANATION	POST. REF.	DEBIT	CREDIT	BALANCE DEBIT	BALANCE CREDIT
19—							
Nov.	*1*	*Balance*	—				*27,732 00*
	2	*Additional investment*	*CR5*		*1,500 00*		*29,232 00*
	30	*Net income*	*J6*		*1,529 00*		*30,761 00*
	30	*Transfer from drawing*	*J6*	*1,200 00*			*29,561 00*

Capital account contains net income and withdrawals.

Jason Booth, Drawing Account No. *302*

DATE		EXPLANATION	POST. REF.	DEBIT	CREDIT	BALANCE DEBIT	BALANCE CREDIT
19—							
Nov.	*23*	*Withdrawal*	*CP5*	*1,200 00*		*1,200 00*	
	30	*Transfer to capital*	*J6*		*1,200 00*	*— 00*	

Drawing account closed.

Concept: Closing the Ledger
The revenue data and the cost and expense data for one accounting period must be clearly distinguished from that of another accounting period.

Step 7: Preparing a Postclosing Trial Balance

What is the purpose of the postclosing trial balance? At the end of the accounting period, a trial balance was prepared to prove the equality of the debits and credits in the general ledger. After the adjustments were made on the worksheet, an adjusted trial balance was prepared to verify the equality of the debits and credits. Now, a postclosing trial balance is prepared to verify the equality of debits and credits of the accounts still open in the general ledger.

The postclosing trial balance prepared for Computer Age on November 30 is shown on page 501. (Notice that the postclosing trial balance shows the same balances for the asset, liability, and owner's equity accounts as the balance sheet.) When the postclosing trial balance is in balance, the accounts are ready for the next period.

Computer Age
Postclosing Trial Balance
November 30, 19—

ACCOUNT TITLE	ACCT. NO.	DEBIT	CREDIT
Cash	101	9,500 00	
Petty Cash	102	30 00	
Change Fund	103	35 00	
Accounts Receivable	111	3,000 00	
Merchandise Inventory	120	6,400 00	
Prepaid Insurance	121	440 00	
Supplies	123	300 00	
Land	130	8,000 00	
Building	131	22,000 00	
Office Equipment	132	1,800 00	
Stockroom Equipment	133	2,700 00	
Loans Payable	201		4,000 00
Accounts Payable	211		5,500 00
Sales Tax Payable	216		200 00
Federal Income Taxes Payable	221		360 00
FICA Taxes Payable	222		220 00
State Income Taxes Payable	223		140 00
Federal Unemployment Taxes Payable	224		48 00
State Unemployment Taxes Payable	225		176 00
Mortgage Payable	231		14,000 00
Jason Booth, Capital	301		29,561 00
		54,205 00	54,205 00

Concept: Postclosing Trial Balance
The equality of the total debits and the total credits in the general ledger should be verified after the ledger has been closed.

Exercise H on this page and page 502 may be completed at this point.

TOPIC 4 EXERCISE

EXERCISE H. Answer the following questions about adjusting and closing entries and the postclosing trial balance. Refer to pages 496 to 501.

1. Where is the data obtained for making the adjusting entries?
2. Why is Prepaid Insurance credited for $40? What is the new balance?
3. Why is Supplies credited for $50? What is the new balance?
4. Is the ending inventory less than the beginning inventory? By how much?
5. Why is the difference between the beginning inventory and the ending inventory transferred to the Income Summary account?

6. Where is the data obtained for making the closing entries?
7. How is the $12,835 credit to the Income Summary account obtained? Why is this entry made?
8. How is the $10,706 debit to the Income Summary account obtained? What is the purpose of this entry?
9. What is the Income Summary balance after the transfer of debit balances from temporary accounts? What does this amount represent?
10. What is the purpose of the $1,529 credit to the Capital account?
11. Why is the Drawing account credited for $1,200?
12. What makes up the $29,561 balance of the Capital account?
13. Why is the Capital account balance not the same on the postclosing trial balance and worksheet?

TOPIC 4 PROBLEMS

TOPIC PROBLEM 9. Using the data from the worksheet prepared in Topic Problem 5 and the financial statements prepared in Topic Problem 7, complete the following.

a. Journalize the adjusting entries and the closing entries.

b. During March, the Van Doren Company suffered a net loss. In analyzing the financial statements, what are some factors that should be considered in attempting to make a net income in April?

TOPIC PROBLEM 10. Refer to the worksheet and financial statements prepared for the Central Plains Equipment Company in Topic Problems 4 and 6. Journalize the adjusting and closing entries for the month.

TOPIC 5

Interpretation of Financial Information

A major purpose for keeping accounting records is to provide financial information that is needed to make business decisions. To facilitate interpretation, financial information is prepared and analyzed in a number of ways. Interpreting financial information is Step 8 of the accounting cycle.

Step 8: Interpreting Financial Information

When does the interpretation of financial information take place? Although interpreting financial information is listed as the last step in the accounting cycle, it occurs at any time that owners and managers use the accounting records to make business decisions. For example, you have already learned how the accounts receivable ledger is used to age receivables and how to analyze the due dates for accounts receivable. These are only two examples of how owners and managers interpret financial information whenever they have the need.

Financial information is interpreted at any time during or at the end of the accounting period.

Other extremely important tools to management—the use of ratios and budgets for decision making—are now discussed.

Using Ratios

How are ratios used to interpret financial information? Many financial decisions are based on the relationship between two amounts on the financial statements for one accounting period. This relationship is usually expressed in the form of ratios. For example, managers and owners might want to compare the amount of debts owed with the business's ability to pay the debts.

The numeric relation of one amount to another is called a **ratio**. A ratio may be expressed as a number, a percent, or a fraction. For example, if sales are $400,000 and net income is $40,000, the ratio can be expressed as follows.

$$\frac{\text{Sales}}{\text{Net Income}} = \text{Number Ratio}$$

$$\frac{\$400{,}000}{\$40{,}000} = 10$$

You can say that the ratio of sales to net income is 10 to 1, which is often written 10:1. A ratio can also be expressed as a percent.

$$\frac{\text{Net Income}}{\text{Sales}} = \text{Percent Ratio}$$

$$\frac{\$40{,}000}{\$400{,}000} = 0.10, \text{ or } 10\%$$

In this case you say that net income is 10 percent of sales. Ratios can also be expressed as fractions.

$$\frac{\text{Net Income}}{\text{Sales}} = \text{Fraction Ratio}$$

$$\frac{\$40{,}000}{\$400{,}000} = \frac{1}{10}$$

This ratio means that net income is one-tenth of sales.

The problem with interpreting financial information is deciding what ratio is satisfactory. Accountants look to different sources for comparative ratios. Sources include comparing current results with previous accounting periods, comparing results with similar businesses, and comparing results with government or investment guides.

Ratios computed for Computer Age follow. These ratios can be computed for any business and compared with the sources mentioned previously.

■ Ratios That Measure Current Position For accounting purposes, **working capital** is the difference between current assets and current liabilities. The working capital for Computer Age is computed in the margin.

$19,705	Current Assets
− 10,644	Current Liabilities
$ 9,061	Working Capital

A company has an idea of its ability to pay current debts by computing working capital. If there are more current assets than current liabilities, the company may be able to pay current debts and is described as **solvent**. If there are more current liabilities than current assets, the company will not be able to pay current debts and is described as **insolvent**.

Computing working capital is one way to determine debt-paying ability. The working capital can be interpreted in other ways.

The **current ratio** (sometimes referred to as the *working capital ratio*) is the number relation between current assets and current liabilities. The current ratio for Computer Age appears here.

$$\frac{\text{Current Assets}}{\text{Current Liabilities}} = \text{Current Ratio}$$

$$\frac{\$19{,}705}{\$10{,}644} = 1.85{:}1$$

The current ratio for Computer Age is expressed as 1.85:1. This means that the business owns $1.85 of current assets for each $1.00 of current liabilities. Computer Age is in a better position than a company with a ratio of 1.20:1 ($1.20 to $1.00).

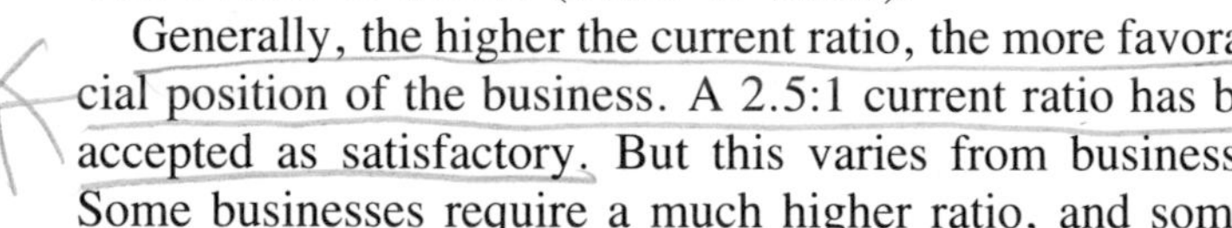

Generally, the higher the current ratio, the more favorable the financial position of the business. A 2.5:1 current ratio has been generally accepted as satisfactory. But this varies from business to business. Some businesses require a much higher ratio, and some can operate with a smaller ratio.

■ Ratios That Measure Operating Results Ratios such as the current ratio can be used to measure current position. Ratios can also be used to measure operating results. Two ratios used to determine a business's ability to earn a satisfactory net income are described here.

■ Return on Total Assets Ratio Computer Age earns a net income by putting assets to work. A **return on total assets ratio** is computed to see how effectively the assets are being used. The return on total assets ratio is computed by dividing net income by the total assets. The computation of this ratio for Computer Age for November is shown here.

$$\frac{\text{Net Income}}{\text{Total Assets}} = \text{Return on Total Assets}$$

$$\frac{\$1,529}{\$54,205} = 2.8\%$$

The net income ($1,529) and total assets ($54,205) were taken from the Computer Age financial statements for November. In this case, Computer Age earned 2.8 cents for each $1 in assets for one month—November. On a yearly basis, the return would be 33.6 percent (2.8% × 12 months = 33.6%, or $0.336 on each $1.00 of assets).

To interpret whether this is a sufficient return, the return must be compared with other investments. If the owner could earn more with another investment, then the second investment might be considered.

Return on Owner's Equity Ratio Perhaps the most important ratio for owners is the return on owner's equity. The **return on owner's equity ratio** shows the return on the owner's investment and is found by dividing net income by total owner's equity. The resulting percent is used to indicate profitability. The November return on owner's equity for Computer Age is illustrated here.

$$\frac{\text{Net Income}}{\text{Owner's Equity}} = \text{Return on Owner's Equity}$$

$$\frac{\$1,529}{\$29,561} = 5.2\%$$

The net income ($1,529) was taken from the income statement for November. The total owner's equity ($29,561) was taken from the balance sheet. The return on owner's equity is viewed as follows. The owner has invested cash and other resources, plus past earnings, of $29,561 in Computer Age. In return, the owner has earned 5.2 percent on the investment for one month. When deciding to continue operating Computer Age, the owner must compare the return on the investment, plus the advantages of business ownership, with other investment choices.

Exercise I on pages 508 and 509 may be completed at this point.

Budgeting

What is a budget? A **budget** is a plan for a future period, stated in money terms. The preparation of a budget has two purposes. First, it can act as a guide for operating a business. Second, it can be used to compare the actual results of business activity with the planned operations (the budget).

Jason Booth is the owner of Computer Age. He looks at the November income statement for the business and notes that the net income for the month was $1,529. He also notes that December is usually the best sales month for a business like Computer Age. Jason Booth feels that in December, Computer Age should double the net income it earned in November.

Computer Age
Income Statement
For the Month Ended November 30, 19—

Revenue From Sales:				
Sales	12,600	00		
Less: Sales Returns and Allowances . . . *$190.00*				
Sales Discount . . . *45.00*	235	00		
Net Sales			12,365	00
Cost of Goods Sold (See Schedule)			7,245	00
Gross Profit on Sales			5,120	00
Operating Expenses:				
Cash Short and Over	6	00		
Advertising Expense	100	00		
Delivery Expense	120	00		
Insurance Expense	40	00		
Miscellaneous Expense	40	00		
Payroll Taxes Expense	195	00		
Salaries Expense	2,800	00		
Supplies Expense	50	00		
Utilities Expense	240	00		
Total Operating Expenses			3,591	00
Net Income			1,529	00

In order to help ensure that net income doubles during December, Jason Booth decides to prepare a budget.

■ Preparing a Budget

The budget prepared by Jason Booth is shown on the next page. It was necessary to do the following to prepare the budget.

- Set goals for December.
- Prepare expected sales amounts.
- Prepare expected cost and expense amounts.
- Prepare the actual budget.

As you review the budget, note the following.

- The budget is actually an income statement with projected amounts.

Computer Age Projected Income Statement For the Month of December 19—			
Revenue from Sales:			
Sales		31,500 00	
Less: Sales Returns and			
Allowances	$1,000.00		
Sales Discounts	100.00	1,100 00	
Net Sales			30,400 00
Cost of Goods Sold			18,000 00
Gross Profit on Sales			12,400 00
Operating Expenses:			
Cash Short and Over		20 00	
Advertising Expense		1,000 00	
Delivery Expense		400 00	
Insurance Expense		40 00	
Miscellaneous Expense		50 00	
Payroll Taxes Expense		450 00	
Salaries Expense		6,000 00	
Supplies Expense		400 00	
Utilities Expense		500 00	
Total Operating Expenses			8,860 00
Net Income			3,540 00

- The projected net income is achieved because the expected sales amount ($31,500) is approximately 2½ times the November sales amount ($12,600).
- The projected cost of goods sold ($18,000) is approximately 2½ times the November amount.
- Some expenses are projected to increase much more than sales or cost of goods sold. For instance, advertising expense has increased 10 times over the November amount. This increase is a way of saying that Computer Age must advertise to increase sales. Note also that the salaries expense ($6,000) has a large projected increase. This increase indicates that the employees will be working long hours or that part-time help will be hired.
- The projected net income ($3,540) is approximately 2.3 times the November net income ($1,529). This means that it is projected to take 2½ times the amount of sales to produce 2.3 times the net income.

Comparison of Actual and Projected Amounts On December 1 the budget prepared by Jason Booth was a guide to operations for December. On December 31 the budget is used to evaluate performance for the month of December. Evaluation of performance is done by comparing the projected amounts with the actual amounts for December, as shown here.

Computer Age
Comparison of Projected and Actual Operations
For the Month of December 19—

		PROJECTED			**ACTUAL**	
Revenue From Sales:						
Sales		31,500 00			30,100 00	
Less: Sales Ret. and Allow.	$1,000.00			$1,100.00		
Sales Discounts	100.00	1,100 00		120.00	1,220 00	
Net Sales			30,400 00			28,880 00
Cost of Goods Sold			18,000 00			16,200 00
Gross Profit on Sales			12,400 00			12,680 00
Operating Expenses:						
Cash Short and Over		20 00			40 00	
Advertising Expense		1,000 00			990 00	
Delivery Expense		400 00			460 00	
Insurance Expense		40 00			40 00	
Miscellaneous Expense		50 00			45 00	
Payroll Taxes Expense		450 00			440 00	
Salaries Expense		6,000 00			5,880 00	
Supplies Expense		400 00			600 00	
Utilities Expense		500 00			560 00	
Total Operating Expenses			8,860 00			9,055 00
Net Income			3,540 00			3,625 00

The comparison of actual and projected operations is prepared from the projected income statement (budget) for December and the actual income statement prepared at the end of December. The columns labeled Projected are the budgeted figures. The columns labeled Actual are the results of operations for the month of December.

How would the performance for the month of December be evaluated? It appears that all the goals were realized. Actual sales ($30,100) fell a little short of the budget ($31,500). However, the gross profit ($12,680) exceeded the budget ($12,400) because Jason Booth was able to take advantage of some quantity purchases.

The advertising expense was right on the budget because Computer Age committed itself to spending $1,000 and would not exceed that commitment. As the rest of the expenses are reviewed, note that those that could be controlled did not exceed the budget. In a few instances, expenses over which there is little control slightly exceeded the budget (for example, the Utilities Expense).

Exercise J on page 509 may be completed at this point.

TOPIC 5 EXERCISES

EXERCISE I. Answer the questions on the next page about using ratios. Refer to the text, margin notes, and illustrations on pages 503 to 505.

1. Do the ratios illustrated compare financial information from one accounting period with information from another period? Explain.
2. Could a company have a current ratio of 0.8:1? Explain.
3. What is the source of information used to compute the current ratio?
4. What is the source of information used to compute the return on total assets for Computer Age?
5. Why is the return on owner's equity ratio so important?
6. Someone commented that the 5 percent return on owner's equity for Computer Age was not very good. The owner can get 10 percent in savings certificates. Do you agree that the 5 percent is not very good? Explain.

EXERCISE J. Answer the following questions about budgeting. Refer to the text, margin notes, and illustrations on pages 505 to 508.

1. What are the two purposes of a budget? Which of the two do you feel is most important?
2. What is the source of the projected sales, costs, and expenses?
3. What is the source of the actual sales, costs, and expenses?
4. By what amount did the projected net income exceed or fall short of the actual net income?

TOPIC 5 PROBLEM

TOPIC PROBLEM 11. The balance sheet prepared for Consolidated Finance on June 30 is illustrated. The net income for Consolidated Finance was $16,800 for the year ended June 30.

a. Compute the following, showing your computations.

1. A current ratio
2. Working capital
3. Return on total assets
4. Return on owner's equity

b. Do you think Consolidated Finance is a profitable business? Explain.

Consolidated Finance
Balance Sheet
June 30, 19—

Assets		
Current Assets:		
Cash	7,100 00	
Petty Cash	40 00	
Change Fund	30 00	
Accounts Receivable	1,600 00	
Merchandise Inventory	24,510 00	
Prepaid Insurance	2,200 00	
Supplies	280 00	
Total Current Assets		35,760 00
Plant and Equipment:		
Land	7,700 00	
Building	30,000 00	
Equipment	17,000 00	
Total Plant and Equipment		54,700 00
Total Assets		90,460 00
Liabilities		
Current Liabilities:		
Accounts Payable	18,000 00	
Sales Tax Payable	340 00	
Federal Income Taxes Payable	170 00	
FICA Taxes Payable	160 00	
Total Current Liabilities		18,670 00
Long-Term Liabilities:		
Mortgage Payable		16,000 00
Total Liabilities		34,670 00
Owner's Equity		
Robert Jeffers, Capital		55,790 00
Total Liabilities and Owner's Equity		90,460 00

CHAPTER SUMMARY

In Chapters 9 to 13 you covered each of the special accounting subsystems. These subsystems were used to summarize the majority of the journalizing and posting activities during the accounting period. Once the accounting period is over, the end-of-the-accounting period activities are completed in the general accounting subsystem. These activities include completing the worksheet, preparing the financial statements, adjusting and closing the ledger, preparing the postclosing trial balance, and interpreting financial information. Chapter 14 summarizes all of these activities for a merchandising business.

THE LANGUAGE OF BUSINESS

Here are some terms that make up the language of business. Do you know the meaning of each?

general accounting subsystem
Merchandise Inventory account
beginning inventory
ending inventory
prepaid expenses
schedule of cost of goods sold
statement of owner's equity
current assets
plant and equipment
current liabilities
long-term liabilities
ratio
working capital
solvent
insolvent
current ratio
return on total assets ratio
return on owner's equity ratio
budget

REVIEW QUESTIONS

1. What is the relationship between the special accounting subsystems and a general accounting subsystem?

2. What procedure is followed to record the purchase of a prepaid expense item? When and how is the expense recorded?

3. What is meant by the principle of matching revenue with expenses?

4. Describe the sequence that is followed in preparing the worksheet.

5. If no adjustment is made to transfer $50 from the Prepaid Insurance account to the Insurance Expense account, what will be the effect on net income? On total assets? On owner's equity?

6. Why does the total of the debits not equal the total of the credits in the Income Statement section of the worksheet? Why are the totals not equal in the Balance Sheet section?

7. Describe the procedure that is followed to find the cost of goods sold.
8. Describe the sequence of steps for journalizing the closing entries.
9. How does the work of the accounting clerk affect the accountant's ability to interpret financial information?
10. What is a budget?

CHAPTER PROBLEMS

Problems for Chapter 14 are given below. Write your answers to the problems on a separate sheet of paper unless you are using the workbook for this textbook. If you are using the workbook, do the problems in the space provided there.

CHAPTER PROBLEM 14-1. The trial balance for Kantell Sales for November 30 is shown below.

Kantell Sales
Trial Balance
November 30, 19—

ACCOUNT TITLE	ACCT. NO.	DEBIT		CREDIT	
Cash	101	9,300	00		
Accounts Receivable	102	2,187	00		
Merchandise Inventory	103	4,284	00		
Prepaid Insurance	104	348	00		
Supplies	105	155	00		
Equipment	121	1,630	00		
Tools	122	500	00		
Accounts Payable	201			1,382	00
Paul Masi, Capital	301			15,841	00
Paul Masi, Drawing	302	260	00		
Income Summary	399			—	00
Sales	401			6,510	00
Sales Returns and Allowances	402	110	00		
Sales Discount	403	90	00		
Purchases	501	3,820	00		
Transportation In	502	300	00		
Purchases Returns and Allowances	503			45	00
Purchases Discount	504			129	00
Cash Short and Over	511	64	00		
Delivery Expense	512	469	00		
Insurance Expense	513	—	00		
Rent Expense	514	390	00		
Supplies Expense	515	—	00		
		23,907	00	23,907	00

Using the trial balance, do the following.

a. Complete a worksheet. The physical inventory on November 30 showed (1) merchandise inventory of $4,742 and (2) supplies of $128. The amount of unexpired insurance as of November 30 is $261.

b. Prepare a schedule of cost of goods sold. Prepare an income statement for the month ended November 30.

c. Prepare a statement of owner's equity assuming the owner invested $5,000 during the month of November. Prepare a classified balance sheet on November 30.

d. Journalize the adjusting and closing entries for the month of November. (Posting of these entries is omitted to save space.)

e. Calculate the working capital, current ratio, return on total assets ratio, and the return on owner's equity ratio.

CHAPTER PROBLEM 14-2. The trial balance for AAA Appliance Sales for August 31 is shown below.

AAA Appliance Sales
Trial Balance
August 31, 19—

ACCOUNT TITLE	ACCT. NO.	DEBIT	CREDIT
Cash	*101*	*42,750 00*	
Accounts Receivable	*102*	*35,010 00*	
Merchandise Inventory	*103*	*115,000 00*	
Prepaid Insurance	*104*	*1,200 00*	
Supplies	*105*	*874 00*	
Store Fixtures	*121*	*3,620 00*	
Delivery Equipment	*122*	*12,210 00*	
Accounts Payable	*201*		*22,638 00*
Johanna Stern, Capital	*301*		*75,916 00*
Johanna Stern, Drawing	*302*	*2,000 00*	
Income Summary	*399*	*— 00*	
Sales	*401*		*186,003 00*
Sales Returns and Allowances	*402*	*2,175 00*	
Sales Discount	*403*	*1,225 00*	
Purchases	*501*	*68,250 00*	
Transportation In	*502*	*250 00*	
Purchases Returns and Allowances	*503*		*636 00*
Purchases Discount	*504*		*263 00*
Cash Short and Over	*511*		*20 00*
Delivery Expense	*512*	*312 00*	
Insurance Expense	*513*	*— 00*	
Rent Expense	*514*	*600 00*	
Supplies Expense	*515*	*— 00*	
		285,476 00	*285,476 00*

Using the trial balance, do the following.

a. Complete a worksheet. The physical inventory on August 31 showed (1) merchandise inventory of $112,950 and (2) supplies of $771. The amount of expired insurance for the month of August was $250.

b. Prepare a schedule of cost of goods sold. Prepare an income statement for the month ended August 31.

c. Prepare a statement of owner's equity assuming the owner made no investment during the month.

d. Journalize the adjusting and closing entries for the month of August. (Posting of these entries is omitted to save space.)

e. Calculate the working capital, current ratio, return on total assets ratio, and the return on owner's equity ratio.

MANAGEMENT CASES

Plant and Equipment. Business managers must maintain a relation between the amount invested in plant and equipment and the amount of current assets. One of the mistakes often made by a person going into business for the first time is to put too much money into plant and equipment (buildings and equipment). Usually, too little money is left for buying merchandise and supplies, for carrying accounts receivable, and for paying expenses. As a guide for small businesses, the U.S. Department of Commerce has compiled figures that show what percentage of total assets successful small businesses have invested in plant and equipment. An example follows.

Type of Business	Plant and Equipment as a Percentage of Total Assets
Automobile agencies	12%
Department stores	8%
Food and beverage stores	14%
Furniture stores	9%
Lumber and fuel companies	24%

CASE 14M-1. Phyllis Cutler, the owner of Cutler Beverages, has had difficulty in paying her debts when they become due. As a result, she has a poor credit rating and cannot get additional credit. The balance sheet for her business on July 31 is shown on the next page.

Cutler Beverages
Balance Sheet
July 31, 19—

Assets		Liabilities	
Cash	3,000 00	Accounts Payable	37,600 00
Accounts Receivable	27,000 00	Mortgage Payable	50,000 00
Inventory	24,000 00	Total Liabilities	87,600 00
Materials and Supplies	6,000 00		
Buildings and Storage Facilities	116,000 00	Owner's Equity	
Trucks	54,000 00	Phyllis Cutler, Capital	142,400 00
Total	230,000 00	Total	230,000 00

a. What percentage of the company's total assets is invested in plant and equipment?

b. What would you suggest the owner do to improve her credit situation?

c. Which of the assets are current assets? Plant and equipment?

d. Which of the liabilities are current liabilities? Long-term liabilities?

CASE 14M-2. Alex Ojeda has worked for a number of years in a small grocery and now wants to open his own business. He has found a house with an attached store in a residential section where he believes a small store would be successful. To meet the competition of other stores, he plans to purchase directly from suppliers in the area. He then expects to resell the products at lower prices than his competitors. To meet the competition of supermarkets, he plans to deliver telephone orders and to sell on credit. Mr. Ojeda believes that he will have to make an initial investment of $63,000 to start the business. A breakdown of the initial investment is as follows.

$45,000	Building
4,000	Remodeling
12,000	Store fixtures
2,000	Used delivery truck
$63,000	Total

Mr. Ojeda has total resources of $75,000 as follows.

$30,000	Savings
20,000	Bank mortgage
15,000	Small business loan from bank
10,000	Personal loan from relative
$75,000	Total cash resources

After the initial investment, Mr. Ojeda will have $12,000 ($75,000 − $63,000) cash to meet additional costs and expenses as he tries to get his business started.

a. Do you think that Mr. Ojeda will have sufficient funds to start the business as planned?

b. What would you suggest he do to improve his financial situation?

PROJECT 2

VILLAGE SOUND CENTER

You have been hired to keep the financial records of the Village Sound Center, which sells stereo equipment. It is owned and operated by Scott Harrison. He has three employees working for him at the store. The chart of accounts, the records used by the business, and the balance sheet as of May 31 are given on the following pages.

The subsidiary ledgers contain the following accounts: the Bentley Company and Glenco Enterprises are in the accounts receivable ledger, and Morgan Supplies Company and Atlas Distributing are in the accounts payable ledger. If you are not using the workbook, establish the general ledger and subsidiary ledger accounts and enter the June 1 balances.

VILLAGE SOUND CENTER
CHART OF ACCOUNTS

Assets
101 Cash
102 Petty Cash
103 Change Fund
111 Accounts Receivable
112 Merchandise Inventory
113 Prepaid Insurance
114 Store Supplies
121 Land
131 Building
132 Equipment

Liabilities
211 Accounts Payable
216 Sales Tax Payable
221 Federal Income Taxes Payable
222 FICA Taxes Payable
223 Salaries Payable
224 State Income Taxes Payable
225 Insurance Premiums Payable
226 Federal Unemployment Taxes Payable
227 State Unemployment Taxes Payable
231 Mortgage Payable

Owner's Equity
301 Scott Harrison, Capital
302 Scott Harrison, Drawing
399 Income Summary

Revenue
401 Sales
402 Sales Returns and Allowances
403 Sales Discount

Expenses
501 Purchases
503 Purchases Returns and Allowances
504 Purchases Discount
511 Cash Short and Over
512 Advertising Expense
513 Delivery Expense
514 Insurance Expense
515 Miscellaneous Expense
516 Payroll Taxes Expense
517 Salaries Expense
518 Store Supplies Expense
519 Telephone Expense

PAYROLL INFORMATION. Employees are paid biweekly. Insurance premiums are $10 for each biweekly pay period. All employees' wages are subject to FICA, FUTA, and SUTA taxes. The company has three employees. Alan Cole is single, claims two exemptions, and is paid $8 per hour. Susan Holt is single, claims one exemption, and is paid $8 per hour. Angela Warren is single, claims one exemption, and is paid $9 per hour. Employees are paid $1\frac{1}{2}$ times their hourly rate for hours in excess of 40 per week.

INSTRUCTIONS

1. *Originating the data.* Record the May 31 balances in the ledger. During June, the business had the transactions listed on pages 517 to 518.

2. *Journalizing the transactions.* Record the transactions for June in the appropriate journal or in the petty cash register. Prove, total, and rule the special journals at the end of the month.

Village Sound Center Records

Cash receipts journal
Cash payments journal
Payroll journal
Purchases journal
Sales journal
General journal
Petty cash register
General ledger
Accounts payable ledger
Accounts receivable ledger
Employee earnings records

Village Sound Center
Balance Sheet
May 31, 19—

Assets				
Current Assets:				
Cash	8,600	00		
Merchandise Inventory	35,000	00		
Store Supplies	270	00		
Total Current Assets			43,870	00
Plant and Equipment:				
Land	24,500	00		
Building	50,000	00		
Equipment	15,800	00		
Total Plant and Equipment			90,300	00
Total Assets			134,170	00
Liabilities				
Current Liabilities:				
Sales Tax Payable	440	00		
Federal Income Taxes Payable	176	00		
FICA Taxes Payable	165	00		
State Income Taxes Payable	58	00		
Federal Unemployment Taxes Payable	19	00		
State Unemployment Taxes Payable	73	00		
Total Current Liabilities			931	00
Long-Term Liabilities:				
Mortgage Payable			19,300	00
Total Liabilities			20,231	00
Owner's Equity				
Scott Harrison, Capital			113,939	00
Total Liabilities and Owner's Equity			134,170	00

3. *Posting the transactions.* Post the totals from the special journals to the appropriate ledger accounts. Remember to post the payroll journal for June 14 and June 28.

4. *Proving the ledgers.* Prove the ledgers as follows.

a. Prepare a schedule of accounts receivable by age. Verify the total.

b. Prepare a schedule of accounts payable. Verify the total.

c. Prepare a trial balance on a worksheet.

5. *Preparing the financial statements.* Prepare the financial statements for the accounting period as follows.

a. Complete the worksheet. A physical count of the merchandise on June 30 showed an inventory of $24,510, and a count of the store supplies showed an inventory of $280. An examination of the insurance policies showed unexpired insurance of $2,200.

b. Prepare a schedule of cost of goods sold and an income statement.

c. Prepare a statement of owner's equity and a classified balance sheet.

6. *Adjusting and closing the books.* Complete the books for the accounting period as follows.

a. Journalize and post the adjusting entries.

b. Journalize and post the closing entries.

7. *Proving the accuracy of the ledger.* Prepare a postclosing trial balance.

8. *Interpreting the financial information.* Based on the information in the financial records of the Village Sound Center, answer the following questions.

a. Scott Harrison wonders whether the accounts give him all the detailed information he needs. Do you think additional accounts are needed?

b. Are the accounts receivable being collected on time?

c. Are the current assets sufficiently greater than the current liabilities to pay current debts? (Bankers suggest that current assets should be approximately twice as large as the current liabilities.)

d. The Village Sound Center has been in business for one year. Many new businesses have a net loss during their first year of operations. Give some reasons why a new business like the Village Sound Center might lose money when it first opens.

TRANSACTIONS FOR JUNE

June 1 Recorded a memorandum entry for the cash balance in the cash receipts journal.

1 Issued Check 212 for $2,400 to pay annual insurance premium.

1 Received Invoice 516, dated May 31, from the Morgan Supplies Company for merchandise purchased for $700 on credit; terms 2/10, n/30.

1 Issued Check 213 for $30 to establish change fund.

2 Issued Invoice 402 to the Bentley Company for merchandise sold for $500 plus $25 sales tax on credit: terms 2/10, n/30.

2 Issued Check 214 for $440 to remit sales tax collected during May.

2 Deposited cash in bank; the checkbook balance is $5,730. Prepare a cash proof to compare checkbook balance with Cash account balance. (Remember that the entries have not been posted to the Cash account. Post the individual entries.)

4 Issued Check 215 for $40 to establish petty cash fund.

4 Received Invoice L15, dated June 2, from Atlas Distributing for merchandise purchased for $1,000 on credit; terms 1/10, n/30.

5 Received Credit Memorandum CM-C09 for $50 from Atlas Distributing for merchandise returned to them.

8 Issued Check 216 for $800 to Scott Harrison for personal use.

June 8 Paid $8 from petty cash for ad in baseball program.

8 Issued Check 217 to deposit federal income taxes withheld of $176 and FICA taxes of $165 for month of May.

9 Issued Invoice 403 to Glenco Enterprises for merchandise sold for $950 on credit; terms 2/10, n/30. (No sales tax since Glenco is out of state.)

9 Issued Check 218 for $686 to the Morgan Supplies Company to pay Invoice 516, less discount.

9 Paid $5 from petty cash for store supplies.

9 Issued Check 219 for $55 to pay telephone bill.

9 Recorded cash register proof showing weekly cash sales of $1,660, sales tax of $83, and an overage of $4.

9 Deposited all cash in bank; the balance in the checkbook is now $5,555. Prepare a cash proof. (Post the individual entries.)

11 Received Invoice 44405, dated June 10, from the Morgan Supplies Company for merchandise purchased for $850 on credit; terms 2/10, n/30.

11 Received check for $515 from the Bentley Company in payment of Invoice 402 of June 2, less discount (sales tax not included in computing discount).

11 Issued Check 220 for $58 to remit state income taxes withheld for May.

14 Recorded the biweekly payroll in the payroll journal. Angela Warren and Alan Cole worked 80 hours, and Susan Holt worked 84 hours. The amounts

withheld, in addition to the biweekly insurance premiums, were as follows. Alan Cole: federal income tax, $80; state income tax, $13; FICA tax, $46. Susan Holt: federal income tax, $99; state income tax, $14; FICA tax, $49. Angela Warren: federal income tax, $108; state income tax, $14; FICA tax, $51.

June 14 Recorded the employer's payroll taxes (FICA tax, $146; FUTA tax, $4; and SUTA tax, $30).

14 Issued Checks 221–223 in payment of the June 14 payroll.

15 Issued Invoice 404 to the Bentley Company for merchandise sold for $800 plus $40 sales tax on credit; terms 2/10, n/30.

16 Issued Credit Memorandum CM-41 to the Bentley Company for returned merchandise of $40 plus $2 sales tax.

16 Paid $9 from petty cash to Arrow Delivery Service for delivering merchandise to customers.

16 Recorded cash register proof showing weekly cash sales of $2,005, sales tax of $100, and a shortage of $5.

16 Deposited all cash in bank; the checkbook balance is $6,568. Prepare a cash proof. (Post the individual entries. Post to the employees earnings records.)

18 Received a $2,000 check from Scott Harrison as additional investment.

18 Issued Check 224 for $60 to the Brice Company for store supplies.

19 Received a check for $931 from Glenco Enterprises in payment of Invoice 403 of June 9, less discount.

19 Paid $1.00 from petty cash for phone call from pay phone.

22 Paid $3 from petty cash for coffee (Misc. Expense).

23 Issued Check 225 for $480 to the Webb Corporation for merchandise purchased for cash.

June 23 Recorded cash register proof showing weekly cash sales of $1,440, sales tax of $70, and sales returns of $27.

23 Deposited all cash in bank; the checkbook balance is $10,442. Prepare a cash proof. (Post the individual entries.)

25 Issued Invoice 405 to Glenco Enterprises for merchandise sold for $400 on credit; terms 2/10, n/30.

26 Received a check for $230 from the Webb Corporation for return of merchandise purchased for cash.

28 Recorded the biweekly payroll in the payroll journal. Angela Warren worked 80 hours, Alan Cole worked 90 hours, and Susan Holt worked 86 hours. The amounts withheld, in addition to the biweekly insurance premiums, were as follows. Angela Warren: federal income tax, $108; state income tax, $14; FICA tax, $51. Alan Cole: federal income tax, $107; state income tax, $15; FICA tax, $54. Susan Holt: federal income tax, $103; state income tax, $14; FICA tax, $51.

28 Recorded the employer's payroll taxes. (FICA tax, $156; there are no FUTA and SUTA taxes on this payroll.)

29 Issued Checks 226–228 in payment of the June 28 payroll.

30 Issued Check 229 for $950 to Atlas Distributing to pay Invoice L15, less returns.

30 Recorded cash register proof showing weekly cash sales of $2,100, sales tax of $105, a shortage of $3, and sales returns of $8.

30 Issued Check 230 to replenish petty cash fund. Amount in petty cash box is $14. Prove the petty cash fund.

30 Deposited all cash in bank; the checkbook balance is $10,245. Prepare a cash proof. (Post the individual entries. Post to the employees earning records.)

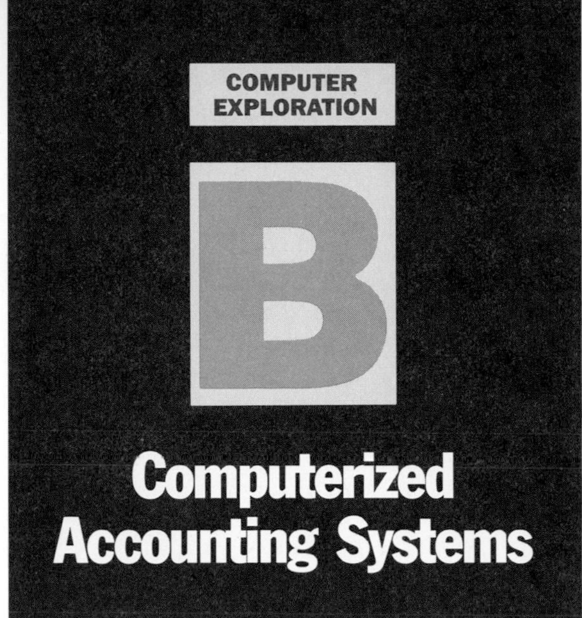

TOPIC 1

Computer Programs Used in Accounting

Computerized accounting is based on the same concepts as a manual accounting system. Only the equipment that is used and the procedures that are followed differ.

The use of computerized accounting systems as well as the use of computers for other business applications is continually increasing. This is in part because the cost has decreased in recent years. More and more businesses are finding that they can do their accounting work more quickly and efficiently on a computer.

Businesses that use computers for automated data processing can choose from a wide variety of accounting programs. There are hundreds of commercial software packages available for business use today, and software companies are always developing new programs. Thus, programs are available for almost every accounting task. The type of software selected depends upon the needs of the business.

■ Accounting Programs

Many software programs are available to handle the tasks and procedures involved in the accounting subsystems that you studied in Chapters 9 to 14. Some major types of accounting software and the features and capabilities commonly found in these programs are described on the following page.

■ General Ledger The general ledger is at the heart of every accounting system—manual or computerized. As you saw in Computer Exploration A, a general ledger program can be used to create and maintain the chart of accounts and the general ledger, to record and post journal entries, and to prepare financial statements.

Because posting is done automatically on a computer, the balances in the ledger are always current. The time-consuming work involved in manual posting is eliminated. A trial balance and financial statements can be generated instantly, without having to do manual calculations. Many general ledger packages allow a variety of reports to be generated that help managers evaluate the financial performance of their businesses. Of course, as with all accounting software, the output generated is only as accurate as the data that was entered.

A general ledger program may be all that is required by a small business. However, if a firm has large number of general ledger accounts and a wide variety of transactions, it will need to use subsidiary ledgers and special journals. In that case, a business may use other programs together with general ledger software. Several software applications that work together are called **integrated programs**.

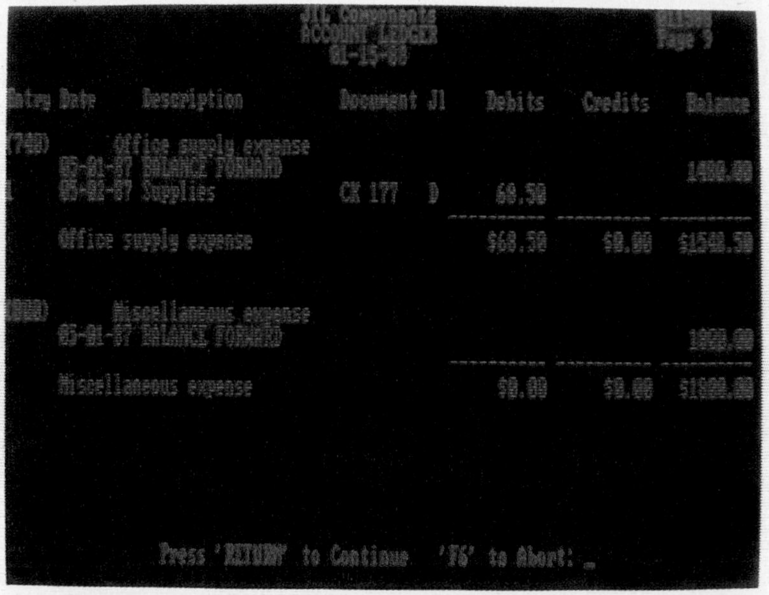

Automatic posting from the general journal to the general ledger is a time-saving feature of general ledger software.

■ Accounts Receivable With accounts receivable software, information about a company's credit sales and cash receipts can be recorded and reports involving these transactions can be generated.

Features of accounts receivable software differ, but most programs allow the user to record entries involving credit sales and cash receipts, maintain an accounts receivable ledger, and generate a variety of reports. For example, a program may produce sales analysis reports showing which customers are buying particular items, or sales returns reports that analyze what items are being returned. The software may print customer lists and mailing labels, maintain customer credit information, and create a schedule of accounts receivable. Because reports can be generated automatically with software, management can receive sales and credit information quickly. Management is then able to analyze and act on information in a timely manner.

■ **Sales Invoicing** If a sales invoicing program is used, it is generally integrated with accounts receivable. The major task of a sales invoicing program is to generate invoices and statements of account. When the necessary data is entered, a sales invoicing program can automatically compute unit prices and extensions and any sales commissions, sales taxes, shipping charges, or discounts involved in the sale. Sales invoicing programs may perform other tasks associated with sales such as producing credit memorandums, maintaining a back-orders file, or generating lists of product lines.

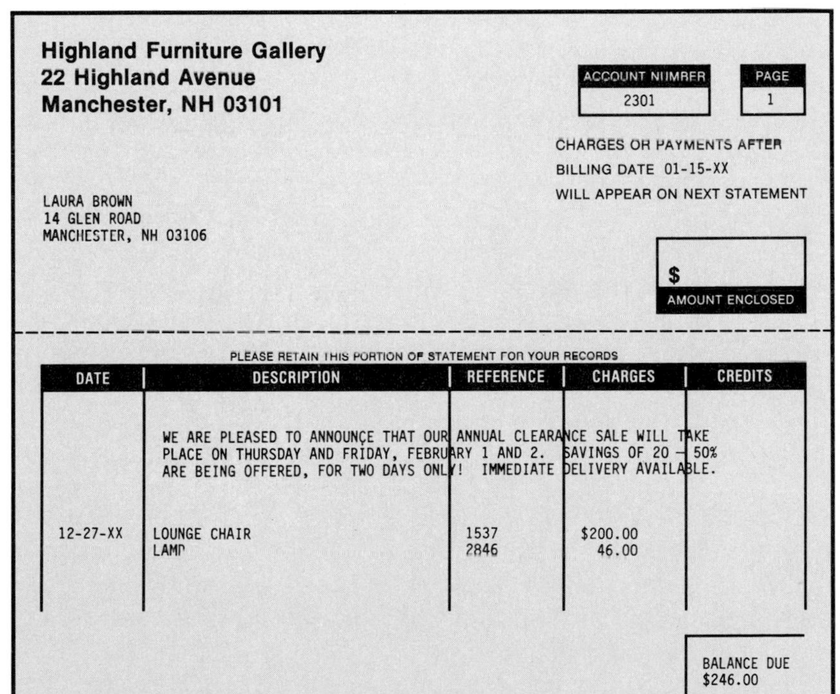

Highland Furniture Gallery
22 Highland Avenue
Manchester, NH 03101

ACCOUNT NUMBER	PAGE
2301	1

CHARGES OR PAYMENTS AFTER
BILLING DATE 01-15-XX
WILL APPEAR ON NEXT STATEMENT

LAURA BROWN
14 GLEN ROAD
MANCHESTER, NH 03106

$

AMOUNT ENCLOSED

PLEASE RETAIN THIS PORTION OF STATEMENT FOR YOUR RECORDS

DATE	DESCRIPTION	REFERENCE	CHARGES	CREDITS
	WE ARE PLEASED TO ANNOUNCE THAT OUR ANNUAL CLEARANCE SALE WILL TAKE PLACE ON THURSDAY AND FRIDAY, FEBRUARY 1 AND 2. SAVINGS OF 20 – 50% ARE BEING OFFERED, FOR TWO DAYS ONLY! IMMEDIATE DELIVERY AVAILABLE.			
12-27-XX	LOUNGE CHAIR	1537	$200.00	
	LAMP	2846	46.00	

BALANCE DUE
$246.00

Sales invoicing programs offer many advantages to businesses. For example, a customized message to customers can be printed on the monthly statements of account.

Accounts Payable Accounts payable software handles the activities involved with purchases of supplies and merchandise on account and payments for those purchases. Typical accounts payable software allows a user to record transactions involving purchases and payments on account, maintain an accounts payable ledger, generate checks for payment, and maintain a check register. Some systems generate purchase orders.

Many accounts payable systems will indicate when invoices must be paid in order to take advantage of discount periods, and will automatically track discounts earned or lost. With this feature, management can easily determine whether it is taking full advantage of discounts.

A time-saving feature of some accounts payable packages lets a user set the system up for payments that are made on a regular basis. For example, a program could automatically on the first of every month issue a check and prepare and post a journal entry for the monthly rent of the business.

Inventory You learned in Chapter 11 the importance of good control of merchandise inventory. Inventory software is available that automates many of the procedures involved in inventory control. For example, some inventory programs keep track of merchandise items by age, which is important information to a business that stocks merchandise that decreases in value over time. Many programs generate reports on overstocked and slow-moving items, and provide item-by-item sales analyses. Many keep track of the minimum number of units of an item that must be kept on hand and show when items must be reordered. Perpetual inventory records can be kept on a computer so that when physical inventory is recorded, the program can do an automatic comparison of the figures in the two sets of records.

Some businesses obtain sales or purchases programs that handle some tasks that can be performed by an inventory program. Or, a business may have an inventory program that is integrated with its sales and/or purchases program. For example, when a purchase of merchandise is recorded, the increase in merchandise automatically appears in the inventory records. When a sale of merchandise is recorded, the items are subtracted from the records.

Payroll Payroll work requires performing a wide range of activities and involves a great deal of time in recording information, preparing forms, and making calculations. Therefore, computerizing a payroll system can be very beneficial to a company since it cuts down on the time required for payroll work.

Most payroll programs can compute wages or salaries based on various pay plans such as hourly, weekly, salary, commissions, or piece-rate plans. Regular, overtime, and sick pay can all be calculated automatically, as well as federal, state, and local tax deductions and voluntary deductions such as savings bonds and union dues. Many payroll programs print payroll checks.

Payroll software that generates payroll forms and records can be helpful as well. For example, programs can be purchased that will print Forms 941 and W-2. A payroll program may be integrated with the general ledger system so that the necessary accounting entries are automatically posted to the general ledger.

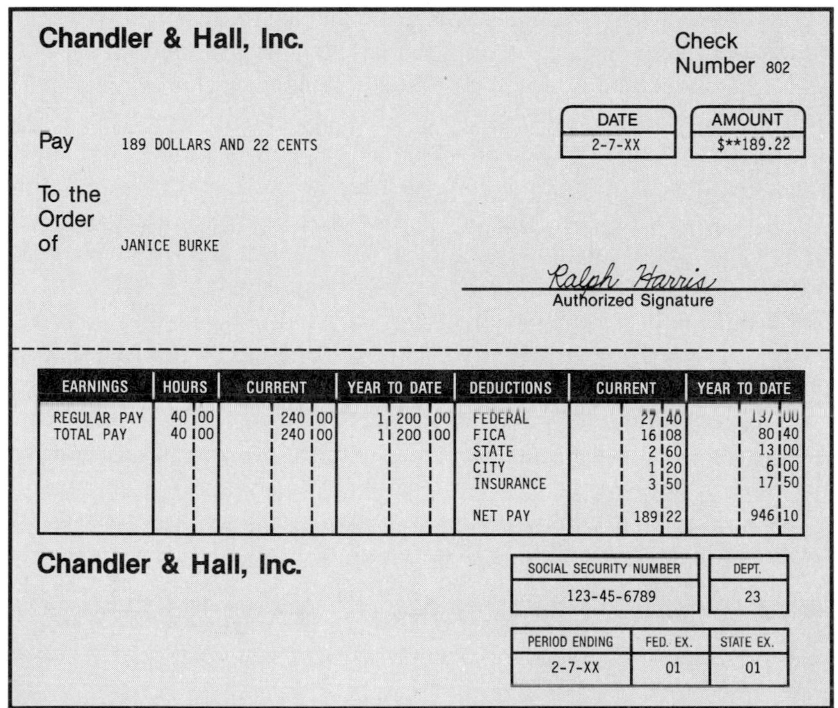

Chandler & Hall, Inc.

Check Number 802

DATE	AMOUNT
2-7-XX	$**189.22

Pay 189 DOLLARS AND 22 CENTS

To the Order of JANICE BURKE

Ralph Harris
Authorized Signature

EARNINGS	HOURS	CURRENT	YEAR TO DATE	DEDUCTIONS	CURRENT	YEAR TO DATE
REGULAR PAY	40 00	240 00	1 200 00	FEDERAL	27 40	137 00
TOTAL PAY	40 00	240 00	1 200 00	FICA	16 08	80 40
				STATE	2 60	13 00
				CITY	1 20	6 00
				INSURANCE	3 50	17 50
				NET PAY	189 22	946 10

Chandler & Hall, Inc.

SOCIAL SECURITY NUMBER	DEPT.
123-45-6789	23

PERIOD ENDING	FED. EX.	STATE EX.
2-7-XX	01	01

Many payroll programs can print voucher payroll checks like the one shown here.

■ Other Business Programs

The programs described above are designed specifically for accounting purposes. However, there are other business programs available that are frequently used by accounting personnel.

Electronic spreadsheets are tools for budgeting and forecasting.

■ Electronic Spreadsheet A **spreadsheet** may be thought of as a grid. Columns and rows of data can be entered in a spreadsheet and set up in the form of a table. What has made the electronic spreadsheet so popular for business use is its ability to perform large numbers of calculations and recalculations. The spreadsheet is able to do this by using formulas that the user enters into the computer. The formulas show the interrelationships of the numbers and data entered.

For example, an important function of many business owners and managers is budgeting and forecasting. Both of these tasks often require setting up possible scenarios and answering "what if" questions. The owner of a sports supply company may ask the accountant to show what will be the effect on the company's income for the year if the price of the Model 183 running shoe is raised 5 percent, 10 percent, or 15 percent. Of course, these calculations can be made by hand using paper, a pencil, and a calculator. However, if projections about the business's income are already entered in an electronic spreadsheet, the calculations required can easily be made by the program.

This is an example of some relatively simple recalculations, and it may seem easier to do them by hand. However, management might ask many "what if" questions that might require hours of manual recalculations. Information may be needed on the effects of prices rising, sales falling, salaries and rent increasing, and other expenses decreasing. The calculations for all of these factors can be done quickly and automatically using an electronic spreadsheet.

Here is another example involving the kind of work that you have done yourself. Look at the worksheet for Computer Age that is shown on page 481. Suppose that after completing the worksheet, the accountant rechecked the calculations and found that the amount of the adjustment should have been $80 instead of $50. The figures shown for Supplies and Supplies Expense in the Adjustments column and all of the following columns would need to be changed, as well as the totals for all of the columns.

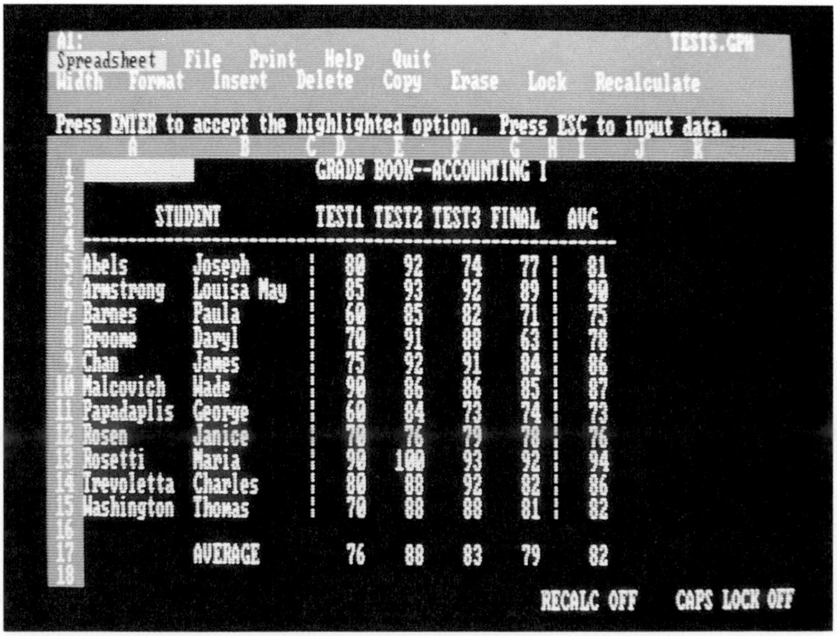

Electronic spreadsheets are set up in the form of a grid.

Suppose that instead, the accountant had entered the information for the worksheet on a computer using an electronic spreadsheet. All the accountant would need to do would be to enter the correct figures for the adjustment in the Adjustments column, and all of the other figures would be automatically corrected by the program.

The electronic spreadsheet is probably the most widely used software in the business world, even though its development is very recent. The first spreadsheet was introduced in 1979. It was called VisiCalc, which is short for "*visi*ble *calc*ulator." Many businesses purchased microcomputers for the first time after VisiCalc was developed because they wanted to take advantage of the power of the electronic spreadsheet.

The most widely sold spreadsheet today is Lotus 1-2-3, which was first sold in 1982. The name "1-2-3" refers to the three capabilities of the program: In addition to functioning as an electronic spreadsheet, Lotus can also perform graphic and database functions. You will learn about these types of programs below.

■ **Word Processing** With a **word processing** program, you can prepare, store, and print all types of written material. A first draft is created, and then corrections can be made for typographical errors, spelling, punctuation, and style. A new format can be created at the touch of the keys. For example, if a page has narrow margins and is single-spaced, it can be printed out again double-spaced and with wider margins.

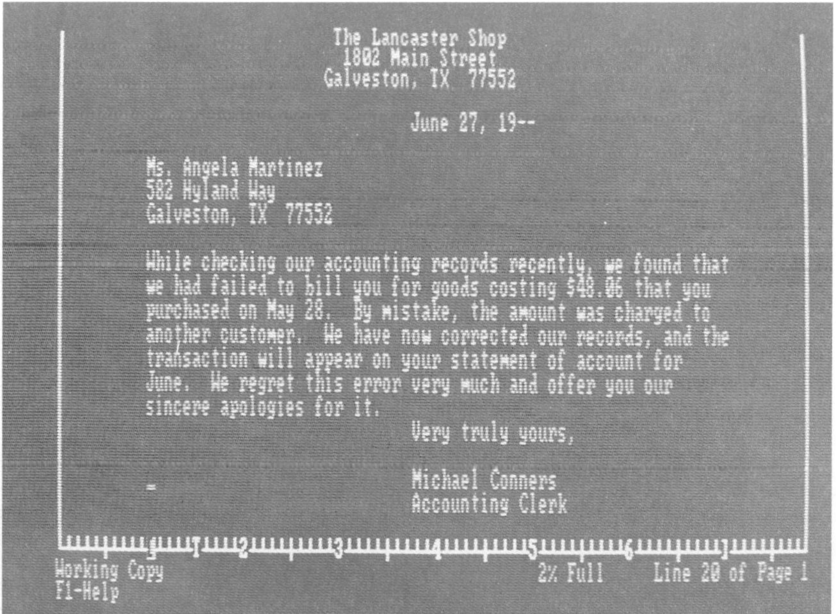

The Lancaster Shop
1802 Main Street
Galveston, TX 77552

June 27, 19--

Ms. Angela Martinez
582 Hyland Way
Galveston, TX 77552

While checking our accounting records recently, we found that we had failed to bill you for goods costing $48.06 that you purchased on May 28. By mistake, the amount was charged to another customer. We have now corrected our records, and the transaction will appear on your statement of account for June. We regret this error very much and offer you our sincere apologies for it.

Very truly yours,

Michael Conners
Accounting Clerk

Editing documents is simple when a word processing program is used.

Word processing makes writing easier because text can be edited heavily. The final printed copy shows no alterations, liquid correction fluid, or erasures. The editing itself is simple because words can be replaced or inserted. Whole paragraphs or blocks of text can be moved or changed with a few keystrokes. Some word processing programs will even flag or highlight misspelled words. A copy of the document can be stored for future editing and/or printing.

There are many word processing programs available to businesses. They vary somewhat in price and features, but most word processing programs share basic capabilities. In addition, businesses can purchase dedicated word processors—computer systems that are solely for word processing. Dedicated word processors have more sophisticated features—and are much more costly—than purchasing word processing software that is used on a microcomputer.

■ **Data Bases** The term **data base** refers to a group of records that share something in common. For example, a customer data base is a group of customer records, and a patient data base is a group of patient records. Data base software helps businesses manage the information contained in their files or data bases. After data bases are created, they can be easily revised and pulled out in alphabetic, numeric, or subject order, or in any other sequence desired. A data base is used to file records for a business and find them again when they are needed.

■ **Graphics** A software application that has become increasingly popular in the business world in recent years is the use of **graphics** or graphing—visual presentation of data. Visual displays can help make figures more meaningful to a user. For example, a graphics program integrated with a spreadsheet can present financial data in the form of pie charts, bar graphs, or line graphs. Color is often used to help enhance the visual presentation.

■ **Custom-Designed Programs** There are so many commercial software programs available today that most businesses are able to find packages with the capabilities and features they require. However, a large company or a firm with very specialized needs may decide that it requires specially developed programs. In this case, a company may hire a programmer to design its programs. Or, a company may hire a systems analyst, who would determine the needs of the company and design systems to meet those needs. The design would include the procedures to be followed by management and other employees as well as the types of computer programs that would be used.

A1: TESTS.GPH
Graph Data File Print Help Quit
Style Titles Values Display Reset

Press ENTER to accept the highlighted option. Press ESC to input data.

GRAPH TITLE : STUDENT GRADES, TEST 1, 2, & 3
Y-AXIS TITLE: POINTS
X-AXIS TITLE: TESTS
UNITS/X-AXIS: A5-A16

STYLE: Bar
BAR 1: TEST 1 D5-D16
BAR 2: TEST 2 E5-E16
BAR 3: TEST 3 F5-F16

GRADE BOOK--ACCOUNTING I

	STUDENT		TEST1	TEST2	TEST3	FINAL	AVG
5	Abels	Joseph	80	92	74	77	81
6	Armstrong	Louisa May	85	93	92	89	90
7	Barnes	Paula	60	85	82	71	75
8	Broome	Daryl	70	91	88	63	78
9	Chan	James	75	92	91	84	86
10	Crooke	Sharlene	85	100	93	91	92
11	Crowne	Dean	70	55	72	62	65
12	Densmore	Rhonda	60	80	60	71	68

CAPS LOCK OFF

Before a graph can be created using a graphing program, data for the graph must be entered, as shown here.

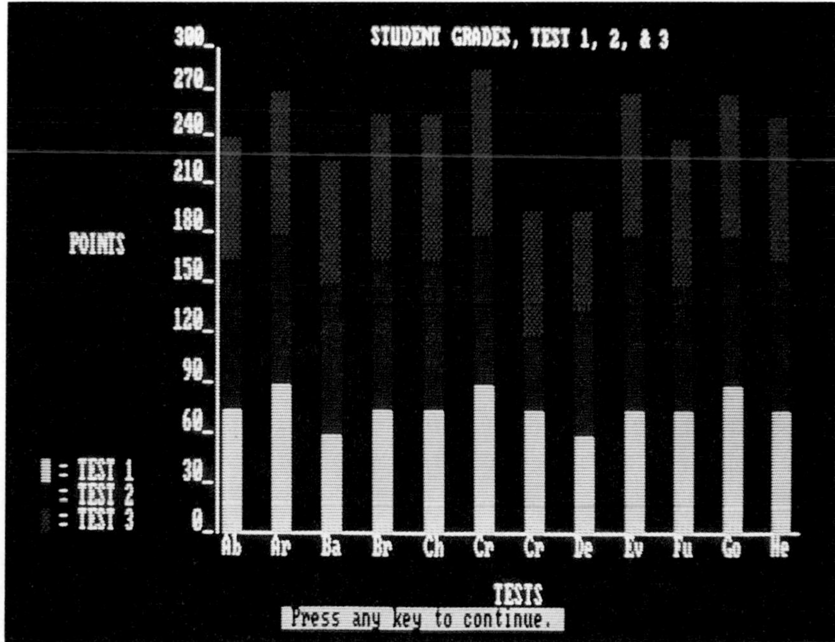

This graph was created from the data that was entered in the screen at the top of this page.

TOPIC 2

Controls for Computerized Accounting Systems

Computerized accounting systems must have the same basic controls as manual accounting systems in order to ensure accuracy, honesty, and efficiency and speed. However, automated accounting systems also require special controls. This is because one major disadvantage to computerized accounting systems is that there is a greater possibility for fraud and dishonesty than with a manual accounting system. Information that is kept on disks or tape can be altered or deleted without leaving any evidence. Stories in the newspapers about employees who are able to steal thousands and even millions of dollars in company money through computerized systems are not uncommon. Some of the controls that companies use to ensure that computerized records are not tampered with, whether accidentally or for dishonest purposes, are described here.

■ Organizational Controls

When a business sets up a computerized accounting system, it can organize the system in a way to ensure maximum controls. For example, computer equipment should be kept in a separate room that can be locked. Only employees who are authorized to use the system and the equipment should be allowed into the room.

Another control is dividing responsibility for the tasks required by the system among a number of employees. Of course, this can be difficult to do in a small business. However, when it is possible, businesses with computerized accounting systems set them up so that no one employee has responsibility for the entire system. For example, the person who designs the system or the procedures to be followed, the people who operate the computers, and the people in charge of the disks or tapes on which the programs are stored should all work separately from each other.

■ Program Controls

Certain controls can be built into the program itself. For example, some accounting programs require that a **password**—a special word or combinations of letters or numbers—be keyboarded into the computer before access can be made to the program. This is usually a code that prevents others from having access to the work that is being done. Passwords are used to protect confidential files or information. An example of a password is the personal identification number (PIN) issued by a bank for individual access to the automated teller machine (ATM) for cash withdrawals or deposits.

An **error report** is a control in which the computer is instructed not to process something. For example, the computer can be instructed not to write a check for more than $500. If a check request for $600 is processed, the computer will not issue the check. However, it will issue an error report and refer the request to management. This report alerts management to possible unauthorized attempts to use the program. This method is used to control cash payments.

Error reports are also used with an ATM. These 24-hour tellers (sometimes referred to as ''intelligent'' terminals) can be programmed to allow a maximum withdrawal of $200 for a single account in any one day. Any attempt to withdraw more than the allowed amount will result in an error message being printed on the screen or an error light flashing.

An **item count** is a control in which the computer is programmed to allow a specified number of items to be processed. For example, in processing payroll checks, the computer can be instructed to print out only a certain number of checks. As each is printed, a count is made. If the number of checks requested is different than the number of employees, the computer issues an alert.

Controls
- Passwords
- Error reports
- Item counts

TOPIC 3

Computer Applications

How does the computer decrease the amount of manual operations needed to process data? This question can best be answered by examining applications in which a computer is used to process data. One such application is described in this topic: updating accounts receivable.

Updating Accounts Receivable

A computer can decrease the amount of manual operations necessary to update accounts receivable. A computer helps in processing data from sales, remittances, and returns, and prepares monthly statements of account. A large business may have thousands of charge customers. The work involved in updating the accounts is highly repetitive.

Sales on Credit The Paragon Style Shop operates three suburban stores that sell casual clothes for men and women. Charge sales and remittances are made at all three stores. A computer center located in a central accounting office is used to keep the accounts receivable records for the 30,000 charge customers.

Origination The three stores use an electronic cash register system. The registers record sales transactions electronically and store sales and accounts receivable data on cassette tapes for processing by the computer. Two special features of this system are the bar-coded tag and the tag reader. A **bar-coded tag** contains bars of magnetic strips containing data. The tag contains the following information for each item of merchandise: color, size, style, price, and inventory number. A bar-coded tag is attached to each item of merchandise.

This electronic cash register is equipped with a tag reader. At the point of sale (POS), the tag reader records information such as price, size, color, style, and item number. This data is stored on a cassette tape and is later processed by the computer.

A **tag reader** is an optical scanning device used to read bar-coded tags. The tag reader looks like a pencil with a light at one end. It is connected to the cash register. By passing the tag reader over the bars on the tag, the salesclerk enters the merchandise data into the cash register automatically. The need to enter sales data manually is eliminated. This speeds up the recording of sales transactions and reduces the possibility of recording the wrong information. However, sales on credit require the salesclerk to enter the customer's account number into the cash register manually.

Each sales transaction entered in the cash register is stored in three places: on the customer's receipt, on an audit tape, and on a cassette tape. The cassette tape is in a unit called a data collector. The **data collector** is a unit for storing transactions until they are transferred to the computer center. At regular intervals during the day, sales data from three stores is transmitted by telephone lines to a cassette tape receiver in the central accounting office. Next, the sales data from all the cassette tapes is transferred to magnetic tape for computer processing. These procedures are shown at the top of the next page.

■ **Input** To update accounts receivable, the computer operator feeds the program entitled ''Updating Accounts Receivable—Charges to Accounts'' into the computer's memory. The magnetic tape containing the information about the current balances in the customers' ac-

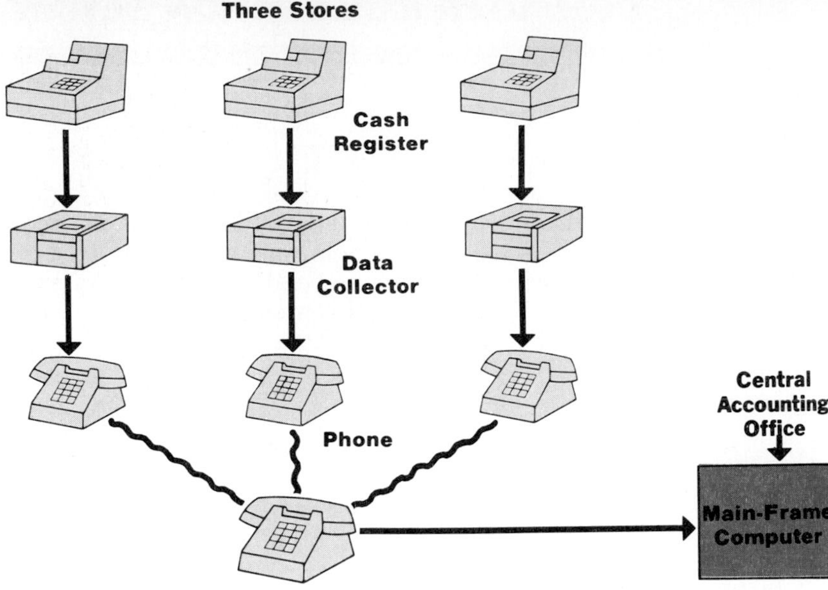

counts is placed in the magnetic-tape unit. Then the cassette tape containing the data from the three stores is fed into the computer.

■ **Processing** As the magnetic-tape reader communicates the data for each charge sale to the computer, the computer does the following.

- Searches its storage, finds the customer's account, and identifies the last balance in the account.
- Records the sale in the customer's account.
- Adds the amount of the charge to the old balance.
- Records the new balance in the storage location.

■ **Output** The output of this updating procedure is the new balances and data for the customer's accounts obtained in the fourth procedure of processing. This information is stored on magnetic tape.

■ **Remittances on Account and Returned Items** The same general procedure is followed in recording remittances from customers and credits for returned items. However, instead of adding, the computer subtracts the amount of the payment or credit from the previous balance of the customer's account to obtain the new balance.

■ **Daily Account Positions** Each morning the computer is used to print an alphabetic listing that shows each customer's name, address, account number, credit limit, and account balance.

The salesclerks must receive approval from the credit department of the central accounting office for all charge sales. To initiate an automatic credit check, the salesclerk enters the customer's account number and amount of the purchase into a cathode-ray-tube (CRT) display. The approval is immediately printed on the CRT display, provided the new account balance does not exceed the approved credit limit.

CHAPTER SUMMARY

In this chapter you learned about different types of programs that businesses use to computerize their accounting systems. You saw that many accounting procedures that you have learned to handle manually can also be done on a computer. You also learned about other software programs used in business that help to provide management with timely information. In addition, you learned some of the special controls required for computerized accounting systems. Finally, you were presented with a real-life application of a computerized sales and accounting system.

THE LANGUAGE OF BUSINESS

Here are some terms that make up the language of business. Do you know the meaning of each?

integrated programs
spreadsheet
word processing
data base
graphics
password
error report
item count
bar-coded tag
tag reader
data collector

REVIEW QUESTIONS

1. Is a computerized accounting system based on the same concepts as a manual accounting system? Explain.
2. Name some of the basic types of accounting programs that a business can purchase.
3. What is an integrated program?
4. Describe some of the tasks that a computerized payroll program can perform.
5. What is a spreadsheet? Why is it so popular in the business world?
6. How does a word processing program help with writing documents?
7. What is a data base? Give an example of a data base.
8. What special controls are needed for computerized accounting systems? Give examples of two steps companies can take to help control their computerized systems.
9. What is the purpose of passwords, errors reports, and item counts?
10. What are the four basic steps involved when monthly statements of account are updated by computer?

MANAGEMENT CASE

Selecting Computer Equipment. The selection of the right computer equipment is one of the more important decisions that management must make. Not only is a large sum of money involved, but the equipment selected will determine the types of information received from processing the data. Management must consider several factors before selecting computer equipment. These factors include the following.

- Management's need for information
- Source of needed information
- Cost and capacity of equipment
- Need for computer personnel to operate equipment
- Need for special facilities
- Availability of service on equipment
- Need for support equipment to use with computer

CASE CBM-1. Riley's Gourmet Foods originated as a small store serving the suburb of St. Louis. Over the years the store has grown and gone through remodelings as a result of population increases and good business practices. Christopher Riley, the owner, is now finalizing plans to move into a new building equipped with electronic cash registers. These cash registers will accumulate sales and inventory data on cassette tape that can be processed by a data processing service center. Each cash register will also have an optical scanner that will be built into the checkout station.

a. What types of reports should Christopher expect to receive from the data processing service center? How often should he expect these reports?

b. What will be a major advantage of the optical scanner unit built into each checkout station?

c. Can you think of a major disadvantage of the optical scanner unit? Do you think customers might complain that the checkout lines move too fast?

CHAPTER

15

Updating Accounts—Uncollectible Accounts and Depreciation

In Chapter 14, you studied adjustments that can be calculated with accuracy. However, the amounts of certain adjustments—such as expenses related to uncollectible accounts receivable—can only be estimated. In Chapter 15 you will learn how to estimate such adjustments and record them in the general journal.

CHAPTER GOALS

After studying Chapter 15, you will be able to:

1. Define the terms listed in ''The Language of Business'' section on page 565.
2. Explain the accounting concepts and principles in this chapter related to updating uncollectible accounts and the depreciation of plant and equipment assets.
3. Record adjusting entries for uncollectible accounts receivable using either the direct write-off method or the allowance method.
4. Record the collection of an account that has previously been written off as uncollectible.
5. Compute depreciation of a plant and equipment asset using the straight-line method.
6. Record adjusting entries for depreciation.
7. Compute the book value of plant and equipment assets.

TOPIC 1

Updating Accounts Receivable

Why are adjustments to Accounts Receivable necessary? The balance of the Accounts Receivable account represents the amount of money owed by customers of a business for merchandise sold on credit. In some cases, a few customers may not pay money owed to the business for one reason or another. An account that cannot be collected is called an **uncollectible account** (sometimes referred to as a *bad debt* or *doubtful account*). In this topic you will learn there are two methods used to account for uncollectible accounts receivable.

Losses From Uncollectible Accounts

A business wants to give credit only to those customers who can pay their debts. Yet despite the business's efforts to do this, some of its customers will not pay their debts when due. The reasons that credit customers do not pay their accounts vary. But the important point for the creditor is that the balance of the Accounts Receivable account may not be the actual value of the account. The actual or **realizable value of accounts receivable** is the amount a business can expect to receive from credit customers.

DURANT COMPANY
CHART OF ACCOUNTS

Current Assets

101	Cash
102	Petty Cash
103	Change Fund
111	Accounts Receivable
121	Merchandise Inventory
141	Prepaid Insurance
142	Supplies

The amount that cannot be collected will be determined uncollectible at a future date, usually in another accounting period. In fact, a year or more may pass before an account becomes uncollectible. One of two methods is used to record losses due to uncollectible accounts.

- The direct write-off method
- The allowance method

In the **direct write-off method**, an uncollectible expense is recorded at the time the customer's account is found to be uncollectible. In the **allowance method**, an estimate of uncollectible accounts expense is recorded before accounts are actually proven to be uncollectible.

Methods Used to Record Uncollectible Losses

- Direct write-off method
- Allowance method

Any business of any size may choose to use either of these two methods. The direct write-off method is the less complex of the two methods, and many small businesses may choose to use it for that reason. However, as you will learn, there are disadvantages to using the direct write-off method. Most medium-sized or larger businesses use the allowance method.

To show the differences between the two methods, we will now discuss a sales transaction that proved to be uncollectible. Let us begin with the credit sale. On December 1, 19X6, the Durant Company sells merchandise on credit for $200 to John Hayes. The credit terms are net 30 days, so payment is due by December 31. The Durant Company records the transaction in the sales journal.

The $200 is posted as a debit to the customer's account in the accounts receivable ledger. It is included in the total of $14,500 debited to the Accounts Receivable controlling account and credited to the Sales account. Since the amount is not paid by December 31, 19X6, the $200 appears on the balance sheet as part of the amount of Accounts Receivable in the Current Assets section. The two methods of accounting for uncollectible accounts will now be discussed.

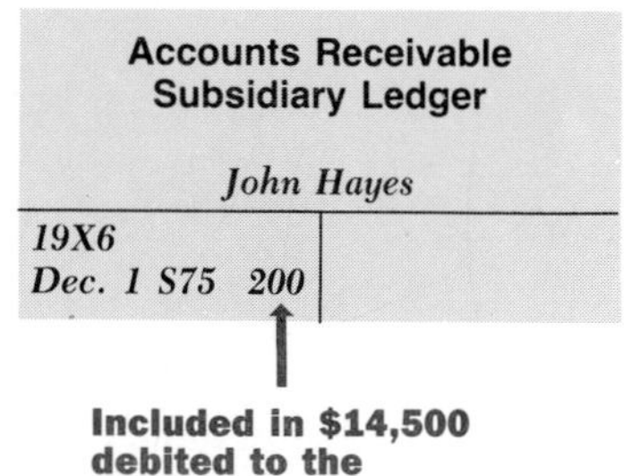

General Ledger

Accounts Receivable 111		Sales 401	
19X6 Dec. 31 S75 14,500			19X6 Dec. 31 S75 14,500

■ The Direct Write-Off Method

John Hayes did not pay the $200 he owed when it became due on December 31, 19X6. Attempts were made to collect the amount due, but Mr. Hayes still did not pay. The $200 remained part of the Accounts Receivable balance until June 15, 19X7. On June 15, 19X7, the Durant Company decides that the John Hayes account is uncollectible and must be written off as an expense. The direct write-off method will be used.

DURANT COMPANY CHART OF ACCOUNTS

Costs and Expenses
520 Uncollectible Accounts Expense

The entry made to record the write-off affects two elements in the accounting equation. When the original sale to John Hayes was recorded, owner's equity was increased because the Sales account was credited for $200. Since the $200 has not been collected, owner's equity must be decreased by debiting an expense account. And, the asset account Accounts Receivable is decreased because the Durant Company will not receive the $200 it is owed. The entry made to record the write-off in the general journal consists of a $200 debit to an account called Uncollectible Accounts Expense and a $200 credit to Accounts Receivable/John Hayes. The **Uncollectible Accounts Ex-**

GENERAL JOURNAL Page 36

DATE		ACCOUNT TITLE AND EXPLANATION	POST. REF.	DEBIT	CREDIT
19X7					
June	15	Uncollectible Accounts Expense . .	520	200 00	
		Accounts Receivable/John Hayes	111/√		200 00
		Write off the account as uncollectible.			

Accounts Receivable Subsidiary Ledger

John Hayes

19X6 Dec. 1 S75 200	19X7 June 15 J36 200 Uncollectible

Entry made to write off an uncollectible account using the direct write-off method.

General Ledger

Accounts Receivable 111		Uncollectible Accounts Expense 520	
19X6 Dec. 31 S75 14,500	19X7 June 15 J36 200	19X7 June 15 J36 200	

pense account is an account used to record the expense from credit sales that the business does not expect to receive. When the entry is posted, the account for John Hayes in the subsidiary ledger is reduced to zero, and the Accounts Receivable account in the general ledger is decreased by $200. The Uncollectible Accounts Expense account is increased by $200.

The direct write-off method of recording uncollectible accounts expense is often criticized by accountants because the revenue from the sale is recorded in one accounting period but the expense for the uncollectible account is recorded in another accounting period. This violates the accounting principle of matching revenue earned during an accounting period against expenses incurred in obtaining that revenue. The financial statements are affected in two ways.

1. On the income statement, net income is overstated for the accounting period in which the sale was recorded and understated for the accounting period in which the uncollectible expense is recorded.
2. On the balance sheet, the amount of the asset Accounts Receivable is overstated until the account is written off.

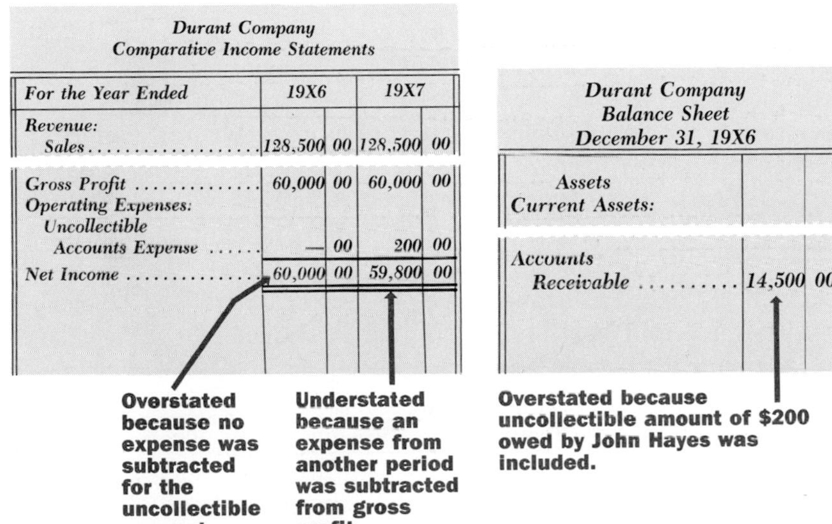

Durant Company
Comparative Income Statements

For the Year Ended	*19X6*		*19X7*	
Revenue:				
Sales	128,500	00	128,500	00
Gross Profit	60,000	00	60,000	00
Operating Expenses:				
Uncollectible Accounts Expense	—	00	200	00
Net Income	60,000	00	59,800	00

Durant Company
Balance Sheet
December 31, 19X6

Assets		
Current Assets:		
Accounts Receivable	14,500	00

Overstated because no expense was subtracted for the uncollectible account.
Understated because an expense from another period was subtracted from gross profit.
Overstated because uncollectible amount of $200 owed by John Hayes was included.

Exercise A on page 542 may be completed at this point.

The Allowance Method

When is the amount of uncollectible accounts determined using the allowance method? The allowance method provides for losses in the period when sales are made. The major disadvantage of the direct write-off method is that revenues earned during a period are not matched against the related expenses. The allowance method attempts to overcome that disadvantage. Since it cannot be determined at the end of the accounting period which accounts will not be collected, it is impossible to write off a particular account receivable at that time.

However, it is likely that some of the accounts receivable listed in the subsidiary ledger will not be collected. A firm's accountant can *estimate* an amount of accounts receivable that will be uncollectible and record an adjusting entry to reflect that estimate. As a result, when the allowance method is used, the uncollectible accounts expense will be matched to the sales transactions in the same accounting period in which sales were made.

■ Recording the Estimate

At the end of each accounting period, an estimate is made of the uncollectible accounts expense likely to result from making sales on credit. (Methods for determining the estimate are discussed in Topic 2.) The estimated expense is recorded in an adjusting entry. The amount of the estimated expense is debited to the Uncollectible Accounts Expense account. However, the Accounts Receivable account cannot be credited for the estimate because it is not known which account in particular will become uncollectible. Therefore, a new account is created called Allowance for Doubtful Accounts.

DURANT COMPANY CHART OF ACCOUNTS

Current Assets
111 Accounts Receivable
112 Allowance for Doubtful Accounts

The **Allowance for Doubtful Accounts account** is known as a contra asset account. A **contra account** is an account used to record deductions in the balance shown in some other account. (*Contra* means contrary to the normal balance.) A **contra-asset account** (sometimes called a *valuation account*, *minus asset account*, or *asset reduction account*) has a credit balance because it represents a deduction to another asset account. The balance of the contra-asset account is always subtracted from the balance of the asset account on the balance sheet to show the estimated realizable value of the asset. Therefore, the balance of Allowance for Doubtful Accounts will be deducted from the balance of Accounts Receivable on the balance sheet to show the estimated value of the Accounts Receivable account. The accountant for the Durant Company assigned number 112 to the Allowance for Doubtful Accounts account so that it would directly follow the Accounts Receivable account (111) in the current assets section of the chart of accounts.

Adjusting Entry for Uncollectible Accounts
Debit: Uncollectible Accounts Expense
Credit: Allowance for Doubtful Accounts

Using the contra account to record uncollectible accounts makes it possible to maintain the equality of the Accounts Receivable controlling account in the general ledger and the total of the customers' accounts in the accounts receivable ledger. The balance of the Allowance for Doubtful Accounts account shows the estimated amount of accounts receivable that may not be collected.

As you can see on the next page, the Accounts Receivable account shows that the total of the customers' accounts is $14,500. The Allowance for Doubtful Accounts account shows the estimated amount of accounts that will not be paid by customers as $600. The Uncollectible

Accounts Expense account shows the estimated expense recorded for the accounting period as $600.

DECEMBER 31, 19X6: THE DURANT COMPANY RECORDS AN ESTIMATED LOSS FROM UNCOLLECTIBLE ACCOUNTS OF $600 FOR THE ACCOUNTING PERIOD.

What Happens	Accounting Rule	Accounting Entry
The expense for uncollectible accounts decreases owner's equity by $600.	To decrease owner's equity, debit the account.	Debit: Uncollectible Accounts Expense, $600.
The realizable value of *Accounts Receivable* decreases by $600.	To decrease an asset, credit the account.	Credit: Allowance for Doubtful Accounts, $600.

Accounts Receivable 111		*Allowance for Doubtful Accounts* 112		*Uncollectible Accounts Expense* 520	
14,500			600	600	

Both Accounts Receivable and Allowance for Doubtful Accounts must be shown on the balance sheet to provide the correct information about the current assets. The amount shown for Allowance for Doubtful Accounts is the estimated decrease in the value of the asset Accounts Receivable. The difference between the accounts shows the realizable value of the accounts receivable.

realizable value

Durant Company
Balance Sheet
December 31, 19X6

Accounts Receivable	*$14,500*		
Less: Allowance for Doubtful Accounts	*600*	*13,900*	*00*

Allowance method: Realizable value of the accounts receivable.

■ Uncollectible Accounts on the Worksheet

The estimated uncollectible accounts expense is recorded as an adjusting entry at the end of the accounting period. The expense is calculated

ACCOUNT TITLE	ADJUSTMENTS	
	DEBIT	CREDIT
Allow. for Doubtful Accounts		(a) 600
Uncollectible Accounts Expense	(a) 600	

and then entered in the Adjustments section of the worksheet. This adjustment is entered on the worksheet in the same way as the adjustments you learned in Chapter 14. For example, the Durant Company has estimated its uncollectible accounts expense at $600. The adjustment to record the estimate involves a debit to the Uncollectible Accounts Expense account for $600 and a credit to the Allowance for Doubtful Accounts account for $600.

The adjustment is entered in the Adjustments section of the worksheet and later recorded in the general journal. Before the adjustment is made, both Uncollectible Accounts Expense and Allowance for Doubtful Accounts have a zero balance in the Trial Balance section of the worksheet. After the adjustment is made, both accounts have a balance of $600. The Allowance for Doubtful Accounts account shows a credit balance of $600, which will be carried to the Adjusted Trial Balance section and then to the Balance Sheet section of the worksheet. The Uncollectible Accounts Expense account shows a debit balance of $600, which will be carried to the Adjusted Trial Balance section and then to the Income Statement section of the worksheet.

Durant Company
Worksheet
For the Year Ended December 31, 19X6

	ACCOUNT TITLE	ACCT. NO.	TRIAL BALANCE DEBIT	TRIAL BALANCE CREDIT	ADJUSTMENTS DEBIT	ADJUSTMENTS CREDIT	ADJUSTED TRIAL BALANCE DEBIT	ADJUSTED TRIAL BALANCE CREDIT	INCOME STATEMENT DEBIT	INCOME STATEMENT CREDIT	BALANCE SHEET DEBIT	BALANCE SHEET CREDIT	
1	Cash	101	18,400				18,400				18,400		1
2	Petty Cash	102	30				30				30		2
3	Change Fund	103	35				35				35		3
4	Accounts Receivable	111	14,500				14,500				14,500		4
5	Allow. for Doubtful Accounts	112				(a) 600		600				600	5
23	Sales	401		128,500				128,500		128,500			23
24	Sales Returns and Allowances	402	7,000				7,000		7,000				24
25	Sales Discount	403	1,500				1,500		1,500				25
41	Uncollectible Accounts Expense	520			(a) 600		600		600				41

NOTE: The cents columns have been omitted in order to show the entire worksheet.

Uncollectible Accounts on the Financial Statements

The amount of the Uncollectible Accounts Expense account for the current accounting period is shown as an operating expense on the income statement. As a contra account, Allowance for Doubtful Accounts immediately follows its related asset account, Accounts Receivable, on the balance sheet. Its balance is subtracted from the balance for Accounts Receivable in order to find the realizable value of the accounts receivable. The realizable value of accounts receivable for the Durant Company is $13,900 ($14,500 − $600).

Durant Company Income Statement For the Year Ended December 31, 19X6		
Sales		128,500 00
Gross Profit on Sales		60,000 00
Operating Expenses:		
Uncollectible Accounts Expense	600 00	

Durant Company Balance Sheet December 31, 19X6		
Assets		
Current Assets:		
Cash		18,400 00
Petty Cash		30 00
Change Fund		35 00
Accounts Receivable	$14,500.00	
Less: Allow. for Doubtful Accounts	600.00	13,900 00

■ Uncollectible Accounts in Closing the Ledger

Like the other expense accounts, Uncollectible Accounts Expense is closed at the end of the accounting period and transferred to the Income Summary account. Allowance for Doubtful Accounts is an asset account and is not closed at the end of the accounting period.

GENERAL JOURNAL **Page** *30*

DATE		ACCOUNT TITLE AND EXPLANATION	POST. REF.	DEBIT	CREDIT
19X6					
Dec.	31	Uncollectible Accounts Expense	520	600 00	
		Allowance for Doubtful Accounts	112		600 00
		Record estimated loss.			

Entry to record Uncollectible Accounts Expense for the period.

At the beginning of the new accounting period, the Allowance for Doubtful Accounts account of the Durant Company has a credit balance of $600, and the Uncollectible Accounts Expense account has a zero balance.

Close the Uncollectible Accounts Expense account into the Income Summary account.

Allowance for Doubtful Accounts **Account No.** *112*

DATE		EXPLANATION	POST. REF.	DEBIT		CREDIT		BALANCE DEBIT		BALANCE CREDIT	
19X6											
Dec.	31	....	J30			600	00			600	00

Uncollectible Accounts Expense **Account No.** *520*

DATE		EXPLANATION	POST. REF.	DEBIT		CREDIT		BALANCE DEBIT		BALANCE CREDIT	
19X6											
Dec.	31	....	J30	600	00			600	00		
	31	To Income Summary ...	J31			600	00	—	00		

Exercise B on page 542 may be completed at this point.

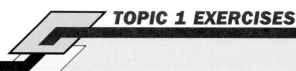

TOPIC 1 EXERCISES

EXERCISE A. Answer the following questions about uncollectible accounts. Use the information found on pages 535 to 537.

1. What two methods may be used to record losses due to uncollectible accounts?

2. Which of the two methods is the less complex? Why?

3. When an account is written off as uncollectible when using the direct write-off method, what account is debited?

4. When an account is written off as uncollectible when using the direct write-off method, what account is credited?

5. What is the major disadvantage in using the direct write-off method?

EXERCISE B. Answer the following questions about uncollectible accounts. Use the information found on pages 538 to 542.

1. What accounts are debited and credited when using the allowance method to write off an account as uncollectible?

2. When using the allowance method, at what point in the accounting period is the entry made to record the estimated loss from uncollectible accounts?

3. In which section of the worksheet is the estimated uncollectible accounts expense for the accounting period recorded?

4. Why is there a zero balance in the Trial Balance section of the worksheet for the Uncollectible Account Expense account?

5. To which worksheet column is the Allowance for Doubtful Accounts amount extended from the Adjusted Trial Balance section? Why?

6. To which worksheet column is the Uncollectible Accounts Expense amount extended from the Adjusted Trial Balance section? Why?

TOPIC 1 PROBLEMS

TOPIC PROBLEM 1. Lane's Department Store determines on July 1 that Michelle Carlin's account with them is uncollectible. Using the direct write-off method, record a journal entry to write off Carlin's account as uncollectible. Use the data in the T accounts below.

General Ledger

Accounts Receivable 111

19— Dec. 31 S86 23,450	

Subsidiary Ledger

Accounts Receivable/ Michelle Carlin

19— Nov. 6 S79 250	

TOPIC PROBLEM 2. Parts of the trial balance of December 31 for the Wainwright Electronics Shop are given at the right.

a. Enter this data on a worksheet for the month ended December 31.

b. Make the adjustments for the following items: estimated loss from uncollectible accounts, $350; ending merchandise inventory, $3,100; insurance explred, $100; and supplies used, $75.

c. Extend all amounts to their proper columns in the Income Statement or Balance Sheet sections of the worksheet.

d. Using the data given, show how the current assets would appear on the Wainwright Electronics Shop balance sheet.

ACCOUNT TITLE	ACCT. NO.	DEBIT	CREDIT
Cash	*101*	*4,200 00*	
Petty Cash	*102*	*50 00*	
Accounts Receivable	*121*	*5,700 00*	
Allowance for Doubtful Accounts	*122*		*— 00*
Merchandise Inventory	*131*	*5,000 00*	
Prepaid Insurance	*141*	*1,200 00*	
Supplies	*142*	*200 00*	
Income Summary	*399*		*— 00*
Sales	*401*		*20,000 00*
Sales Returns and Allowances	*402*	*300 00*	
Insurance Expense	*512*	*— 00*	
Miscellaneous Expense	*513*	*780 00*	
Rent Expense	*514*	*1,200 00*	
Supplies Expense	*515*	*— 00*	
Uncollectible Accounts Expense	*516*	*— 00*	

e. Record the general journal entries that would be made on December 31 for the adjustments.

TOPIC 2

Estimating and Writing Off Uncollectible Accounts

How is the amount of the uncollectible accounts estimated? The portion of Accounts Receivable estimated to be uncollectible is usually found by using one of two methods.

- The percentage of net sales method
- The percentage of aged accounts receivable method

Estimating Uncollectible Accounts
- Net sales method
- Aged accounts receivable method

The Percentage of Net Sales Method

When using the **percentage of net sales method** of estimating uncollectible accounts expense, the business assumes that a percent of net sales will not be collected. The percent used is usually based on the business's past experience with uncollectible accounts. If the business has many cash sales, only credit sales should be used to determine the expense resulting from uncollectible accounts.

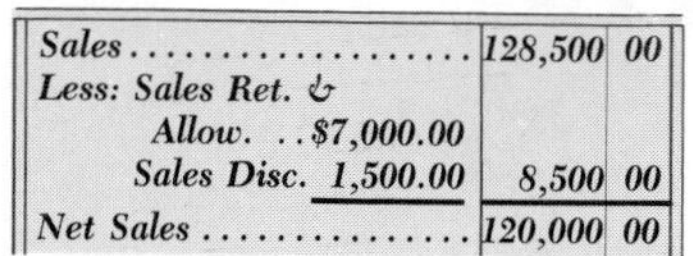

Sales	128,500	00
Less: Sales Ret. & Allow. . . $7,000.00		
Sales Disc. 1,500.00	8,500	00
Net Sales	120,000	00

Suppose that during the present year a business has gross sales of $128,500, sales returns and allowances of $7,000, and sales discounts of $1,500. Its net sales for the year, therefore, are $120,000. Based on past experience, the accountant estimates that the uncollectible accounts expense will be 0.5 percent of the net sales. This would make the amount of uncollectible accounts expense for the year $600 ($120,000 × 0.005).

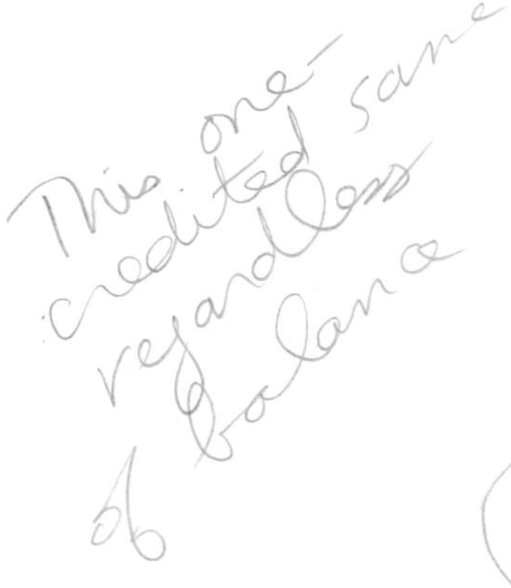

When the estimate of the uncollectible accounts expense is based on a percentage of net sales, the amount of the adjustment is the amount calculated *regardless* of the balance in the Allowance for Doubtful Accounts account. For example, if Allowance for Doubtful Accounts has a credit balance of $300 and the estimated uncollectible accounts expense for the accounting period is $600, the amount of the adjustment will be $600. The new balance of the Allowance for Doubtful Accounts is then $900 ($300 + $600).

Accounts Receivable 111		*Allowance for Doubtful Accounts 112*		*Uncollectible Accounts Expense 520*	
14,500			Balance 300	600	
			600		
			900		

Net sales method: Amount of adjustment is amount computed regardless of balance in Allowance for Doubtful Accounts.

Percentage of Aged Accounts Receivable Method

In the more accurate **percentage of aged accounts receivable method**, the estimated uncollectible accounts expense is determined by *aging* the accounts receivable. **Aging the accounts receivable** means assigning the balance of each customer's account to an age group according to the date the sale was made. Using this method, the accountant prepares a schedule of accounts receivable by age.

The schedule of accounts receivable by age shows a breakdown of the total accounts receivable by age groups. The estimated expense from uncollectible accounts is then found by taking a percentage of the total from each age group. The percentage varies from group to group because the older an account is, the less likely it is to be collected. For example, 50 percent of the accounts that are more than 120 days past

Durant Company
Schedule of Accounts Receivable by Age
December 31, 19X6

ACCOUNT WITH	BALANCE	1–30 DAYS	31–60 DAYS	61–90 DAYS	91–120 DAYS	OVER 120 DAYS
Allen & Brown	*1,700 00*	*1,500 00*		*200 00*		
Thomas Brent	*250 00*				*250 00*	
Chan Company	*300 00*	*300 00*				
Eric Ramos, Inc.	*400 00*					*400 00*
John Hayes	*200 00*	*200 00*				
McConnell Corporation	*2,400 00*	*1,800 00*	*400 00*		*200 00*	
Totals	*14,500 00*	*12,400 00*	*800 00*	*200 00*	*600 00*	*500 00*

due might be viewed as uncollectible, while only 1 percent of the accounts with a current balance might be viewed as uncollectible. The total estimated for the Durant Company is $560.

Age Group (in days)	Total	Estimated Percentage	Estimated Loss
1–30	$12,400	1%	$124
31–60	800	2%	16
61–90	200	10%	20
91–120	600	25%	150
Over 120	500	50%	250
	$14,500		$560

PERCENTAGE OF PROBABLE LOSSES	
1–30 days	1%
31–60 days	2%
61–90 days	10%
91–120 days	25%
Over 120 days	50%

Using this method, the adjusted balance of the Allowance for Doubtful Accounts must equal the amount of the estimated uncollectibles. If the Allowance for Doubtful Accounts account has a credit balance of $400 before the adjustment, the adjusting entry involves crediting Allowance for Doubtful Accounts for $160 and debiting Uncollectible Accounts Expense for the same amount.

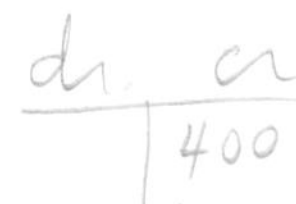

Accounts Receivable 111		*Allowance for Doubtful Accounts 112*		*Uncollectible Accounts Expense 520*	
14,500			*Balance 400*	*160*	
			160		
			560		

If the Allowance for Doubtful Accounts account has a debit balance of $300 before the adjustment, in the adjusting entry the account is credited for $860 ($300 + $560). The Uncollectible Accounts Expense account must be debited for the same amount. The Allowance for Doubtful Accounts account will have a debit balance any time the actual amount of uncollectible accounts written off is greater than the estimated allowance for uncollectible accounts.

Exercises **C and D** on pages 548 and 549 may be completed at this point.

Allowance for Doubtful Accounts 112		*Uncollectible Accounts Expense 520*	
Balance 300	*860*	*860*	
	560		

Recording Actual Uncollectible Accounts Expense

Writing Off Uncollectible Account
Debit: Allowance for Doubtful Accounts
Credit: Accounts Receivable/Customer's account

When a customer's account is found to be uncollectible, a journal entry is made to reduce the account to zero. The entry consists of a credit to Accounts Receivable and a debit to the Allowance for Doubtful Accounts account. The entry to write off the account of John Hayes for $200 under the allowance method is shown below.

GENERAL JOURNAL **Page** *36*

DATE		ACCOUNT TITLE AND EXPLANATION	POST. REF.	DEBIT		CREDIT	
19X7							
June	*15*	*Allowance for Doubtful Accounts*	*112*	*200*	*00*		
		Accounts Receivable/John Hayes	*111/√*			*200*	*00*
		Write off account as uncollectible.					

Entry to write off uncollectible account using allowance method.

It is important to note that writing off a customer's account under the allowance method does not affect the Uncollectible Accounts Expense account at all. It does not establish an expense. The debit to Allowance for Doubtful Accounts shows only that part of the estimate for uncollectible accounts expense has occurred.

GENERAL LEDGER

Accounts Receivable **Account No.** *111*

DATE		EXPLANATION	POST. REF.	DEBIT		CREDIT		BALANCE DEBIT		BALANCE CREDIT	
19X7											
June	*1*	*Balance*	—					*17,000*	*00*		
	15		*J36*			*200*	*00*	*16,800*	*00*		

Amount written off this period as uncollectible

Amount of uncollectible accounts expense estimated at end of previous period

Allowance for Doubtful Accounts **Account No.** *112*

DATE		EXPLANATION	POST. REF.	DEBIT		CREDIT		BALANCE DEBIT		BALANCE CREDIT	
19X7											
Jan.	*1*	*Balance*	—							*560*	*00*
June	*15*		*J36*	*200*	*00*					*360*	*00*

Amount still estimated after Hayes' account was written off

Uncollectible Accounts Expense					**Account No.** *520*	
DATE	**EXPLANATION**	**POST. REF.**	**DEBIT**	**CREDIT**	**BALANCE**	
					DEBIT	**CREDIT**

Amount written off does not appear as an expense for this period; it was recorded at the end of the previous period.

ACCOUNTS RECEIVABLE LEDGER

Name *John Hayes* **Credit Limit** *$300*
Address *1132 Peabody Street, Nashville, Tennessee 37203* **Telephone** *555-1121*

DATE		EXPLANATION	POST. REF.	DEBIT	CREDIT	DEBIT BALANCE
19X6						
Dec.	*1*	....	*S75*	*200 00*		*200 00*
19X7						
June	*15*	*Uncollectible*	*J36*		*200 00*	*— 00*

Customer's account in subsidiary ledger after posting the write-off.

Collecting Accounts Previously Written Off

What would happen if a customer paid the balance of an account after it has been written off? The account for John Hayes in the subsidiary ledger shows a zero balance because it was written off as uncollectible on June 15, 19X7. The entry consisted of a debit to the Allowance for Doubtful Accounts account and a credit to Accounts Receivable/John Hayes.

If John Hayes pays the $200 he owes on May 31, 19X8, the journal entry writing off the account of John Hayes must be reversed. A *reversing entry* serves to cancel the results of a previous journal entry. For example, a reversing entry in this instance would require a $200 debit to Accounts Receivable/John Hayes and a $200 credit to the Allowance for Doubtful Accounts account. This entry cancels the entry writing off the account of John Hayes as uncollectible. The account of John Hayes again shows a debit balance of $200.

GENERAL JOURNAL **Page** *46*

DATE		ACCOUNT TITLE AND EXPLANATION	POST. REF.	DEBIT	CREDIT
19X8					
May	*31*	*Accounts Receivable/John Hayes*	*111/√*	*200 00*	
		Allowance for Doubtful Accounts	*112*		*200 00*
		Reverse entry of June 15, 19X7 writing off this account, which was collected in full today.			

Since the Durant Company has received a $200 payment from John Hayes, an entry is recorded in the cash receipts journal in the usual manner.

CASH RECEIPTS JOURNAL — Page 80

DATE		ACCOUNT CREDITED	EXPLANATION	POST. REF.	GENERAL LEDGER CREDIT	ACCOUNTS RECEIVABLE CREDIT	SALES DISCOUNT DEBIT	NET CASH DEBIT
19X8 May	31	John Hayes........	On account	√		200 00		200 00

After the entries in the general journal and cash receipts journal are posted, the customer's account in the accounts receivable subsidiary ledger contains a complete record of all transactions and entries affecting the account.

ACCOUNTS RECEIVABLE LEDGER

Name *John Hayes* **Credit Limit** *$300*
Address *1132 Peabody Street, Nashville, Tennessee 37203* **Telephone** *555-1121*

DATE		EXPLANATION	POST. REF.	DEBIT	CREDIT	DEBIT BALANCE
19X6 Dec.	1	....	S75	200 00		200 00
19X7 June	15	Uncollectible	J36		200 00	— 00
19X8 May	31	Reverse write-off.....................	J46	200 00		200 00
	31	....	CR80		200 00	— 00

Exercise E on page 549 may be completed at this point.

TOPIC 2 EXERCISES

EXERCISE C. Answer the following questions about estimating uncollectible accounts expense. Refer to the information on pages 543 to 544.

1. What two methods can be used to estimate the uncollectible accounts expense?
2. Which of the two methods of estimating the uncollectible accounts expense is considered more accurate?
3. When using the percentage of net sales method of estimating uncollectible accounts, is the estimate based on gross sales or net sales?
4. Assume that the estimate of uncollectible accounts expense computed as a percentage of net sales is $300. What amount is credited to the Allowance for Doubtful Accounts account when it has a zero balance? When it has a credit balance of $300?

EXERCISE D. Answer the following questions about estimating uncollectible accounts expense. Refer to the information on pages 544 to 546.

1. What is meant by aging the accounts receivable?
2. Assume that the estimate of uncollectible accounts expense computed as a percentage of aged accounts receivable is $400. What amount is credited to the Allowance for Doubtful Accounts account when it has a credit balance of $400? A debit balance of $300?

EXERCISE E. Answer the following questions about recording uncollectible accounts expense. Refer to the text and illustrations involving the Durant Company on pages 546 to 548.

1. Whose account is written off as being uncollectible? What amount is written off?
2. What entry is made to write off the account?
3. After the account of John Hayes is written off on June 15, 19X7, what is the total amount billed but not yet paid by customers? How much is still estimated to be uncollectible? What is the estimated realizable value of the accounts receivable?
4. When the account of John Hayes is written off, what amount appears in the Uncollectible Accounts Expense account for 19X7?
5. What is the purpose of the general journal entry made on May 31, 19X8?
6. What is the purpose of the cash receipts journal entry of May 31, 19X8?

TOPIC 2 PROBLEMS

TOPIC PROBLEM 3. The Davis Company estimates its uncollectible accounts expense to be 1.5 percent of its net sales. The trial balance on December 31 shows these account balances: Sales, $65,200; Sales Returns and Allowances, $1,500; and Sales Discount, $700.

a. Record the adjusting entry for the uncollectible accounts expense in the general journal. The Allowance for Doubtful Accounts account has a zero balance.
b. Record the adjusting entry if the Allowance for Doubtful Accounts account has a credit balance of $80.
c. Record the adjusting entry if the Allowance for Doubtful Accounts account has a debit balance of $30.

TOPIC PROBLEM 4. The Perkins Fuel Company estimates its uncollectible accounts expense as a percentage of the aged accounts receivable. The breakdown of accounts receivable by age groups on October 31 is given in the table on page 550.

a. Compute the total amount of the expected uncollectible accounts expense. Use the percentage of probable losses shown on page 545.
b. Record the adjusting entry for the uncollectible accounts expense that is made if the Allowance for Doubtful Accounts account has a zero balance.
c. Record the appropriate adjusting entry for uncollectible accounts expense that is made

if the Allowance for Doubtful Accounts account has a credit balance of $150.

d. Record the adjusting entry if the Allowance for Doubtful Accounts account has a debit balance of $90.

Age Group	Total of Group
1–30 days	$12,000
31–60 days	7,400
61–90 days	2,400
91–120 days	1,500
Over 120 days	400
Total accounts receivable	$23,700

TOPIC PROBLEM 5. Perform the following activities involving the percentage of net sales method for estimating uncollectible accounts for the Computronics Corporation.

a. Open the general ledger accounts and record the May 31 balances as follows: Cash, $8,000; Accounts Receivable, $14,000; Allowance for Doubtful Accounts, $88 (credit balance); Income Summary; Uncollectible Accounts Expense. Also open the accounts receivable ledger accounts and record debit balances for the following subsidiary accounts: Angela Melendez, $100; Kelly Howard, $75.

b. Record an entry in the general journal on May 31 for an estimated expense of $340 from uncollectible accounts for the month. Post the entry to the appropriate ledger accounts.

c. Record an entry on May 31 to close the company's Uncollectible Accounts Expense account to the Income Summary account. Post the entry to the appropriate ledger accounts.

d. On June 10, Kelly Howard's account for $75 is determined uncollectible. Record the transaction in the general journal. Post the entry to the appropriate ledger accounts.

e. On June 15, the account of Angela Melendez for $100 is determined to be uncollectible. Record the transaction in the general journal. Post the entry to the appropriate ledger accounts.

f. Record the estimated uncollectible accounts expense of $320 for the month ended June 30. Post the entry to the appropriate ledger accounts.

g. Close the Uncollectible Accounts Expense account to the Income Summary account on June 30. Post the entry to the appropriate ledger accounts.

h. On July 15, Kelly Howard paid her account, which had been written off on June 10. Record the transaction in the appropriate journals. Post to the appropriate ledger accounts.

i. Record the estimated uncollectible accounts expense of $215 for the month ended July 31. Post the entry to the appropriate ledger accounts.

j. Close the Uncollectible Accounts Expense account to the Income Summary account on July 31. Post the entry to the appropriate ledger accounts.

TOPIC 3

Updating Plant and Equipment Assets

Are there other accounts for which the accountant must estimate the amount of the expense? Yes, another adjustment that must be estimated is one to *decrease* the recorded value of plant and equipment assets.

Allocating the Cost of Plant and Equipment Assets

A plant and equipment asset is an asset that will be used in a business over a number of years. Examples of plant and equipment assets include land, furniture, buildings, and machinery. Most plant and equipment assets have a limited useful life. That is, the asset will be of use to the business only for a limited number of accounting periods. The useful life of a plant and equipment asset is limited because it gradually deteriorates (wears out), becomes obsolete, or becomes inadequate because more efficient equipment is needed. The one exception is land. Land has an unlimited useful life because it can always be used for some purpose.

A business purchases a plant and equipment asset to produce revenue. As the plant and equipment asset produces revenue, a portion of the asset's cost should be matched against the revenue. This means that a portion of the plant and equipment asset's cost should be charged as an expense in each period in which the asset is used. The portion of the cost of a plant and equipment asset that is allocated to each accounting period in which revenue is produced is called **depreciation**.

Depreciation can be illustrated with an example. Paul Casey, the owner of the Durant Company, purchased a building at a cost of $150,000. He acquired the building in order to have a place to operate his business and earn revenue. The useful life of the building will be limited by deterioration from use, exposure to the sun and wind, and obsolescence. Mr. Casey estimates the total useful life of the building to be 30 years. He believes that the cost of the building should be charged as an expense over the 30-year period.

In effect, Paul Casey has purchased the use of the building for 30 years at a cost of $150,000. A portion of the cost will expire in each accounting period in which service is received from the asset. If the owner assumes that each year's operations should bear an equal share of the original cost of the building, the annual charge against revenue for depreciation will amount to $\frac{1}{30}$ of $150,000, or $5,000. In other words, $5,000 of the original cost of the building will expire each year for 30 years. The table at the top of page 552 shows how the original cost is spread over the first five years of the building's estimated useful life.

Depreciation is a process of allocating the cost of a plant and equipment asset over its useful life. Depreciation has nothing to do with any loss in the value of a plant and equipment asset that may have occurred. A part of the original cost of a plant and equipment asset must be matched with the revenue earned in each accounting period in which the asset is used. Failure to record depreciation expense causes the total operating expenses for the accounting period to be understated and results in the net income being overstated.

DEPRECIATION OF BUILDING DURING FIRST 5 YEARS OF 30-YEAR USEFUL LIFE							
Time of Purchase							
Original cost $150,000							Unexpired cost—$150,000
End of 1 Year		1					
Original cost .... $150,000 Expired cost $5,000		$5,000					Unexpired cost—$145,000
End of 5 Years		1	2	3	4	5	
Original cost .... $150,000 Expired cost $25,000		$5,000	$5,000	$5,000	$5,000	$5,000	Unexpired cost—$125,000

Net income is overstated if depreciation expense is not recorded.

Principle: Depreciation

The generally accepted accounting principle is that depreciation is a process of allocating (distributing) the cost of a plant and equipment asset over its expected useful life. Depreciation is a process of allocation, not of valuation.

■ Estimating Depreciation

When a plant and equipment asset is purchased, the accountant does not know exactly how long the asset will be useful. Nor is it known whether the asset will be sold, traded in for a new model, or scrapped because it is no longer useful. To estimate the amount of the depreciation, the accountant must make an estimate of the useful life of the asset and also of its disposal value. The **disposal value** (which is sometimes referred to as the *trade-in value* or *salvage value*) is the value of the asset at the end of its useful life. It is the amount that the asset might be sold for when it is no longer of use to the business. The estimates of the useful life and the disposal value are needed because the depreciation of a plant and equipment asset is figured in advance.

Needed to Compute Depreciation
- Cost (actual)
- Useful life (estimated)
- Disposal value (estimated)

Three amounts are needed to estimate the depreciation of a plant and equipment asset.

- The cost of the plant and equipment asset
- The number of years the asset is expected to be useful
- The estimated disposal value of the asset

The accountant may use depreciation guidelines published regularly by the Internal Revenue Service in estimating the useful life of the asset.

To see how the annual depreciation of a plant and equipment asset is computed, let us assume that the Durant Company purchases an electronic programmable calculator for $860. It has an estimated useful life of five years and an estimated disposal value of $110.

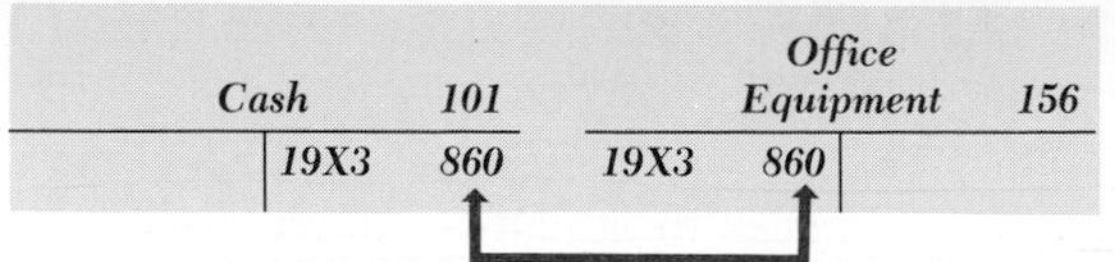

Purchase of a plant and equipment asset.

Cost	−	Disposal Value	=	Total Depr.
$860	−	$110	=	$750

Total Depr.	÷	Years of Use	=	Annual Depr.
$750	÷	5	=	$150

Annual Depr.	÷ 12 =	Monthly Depr.
$150	÷ 12 =	$12.50

The procedure to compute annual depreciation is as follows.

- Subtract the estimated disposal value from the cost to determine the total amount of depreciation.
- Divide the total depreciation by the years of estimated useful life to determine the annual depreciation. To determine depreciation for less than a year, find the annual depreciation and then divide that amount by the part of the year being considered. Monthly depreciation would then be determined by dividing the annual depreciation by 12.

It is also important to know how many months to use in calculating depreciation for less than a year. If a plant and equipment asset is purchased during the first half of the month, depreciation is computed from the first of that month. If, on the other hand, the asset is purchased during the second half of the month, depreciation is computed beginning with the first day of the following month. For example, if an item is purchased on May 7, depreciation for eight months will be recorded on December 31 (May through December). However, if the item is purchased on May 16, depreciation for only seven months will be recorded as the adjusting entry on December 31 (June through December).

After the electronic programmable calculator has been used for five years, it will have an estimated disposal value of $110, which is $750 less than its purchase price ($860 − $110). In effect, the business has purchased five years' use of the electronic programmable calculator at a total cost of $750. The $750 is the depreciable cost that should be spread over the five years that the electronic programmable calculator is used. The electronic programmable calculator would then have a depreciation rate of $150 per year ($750 ÷ 5), or a monthly depreciation rate of $12.50 ($150 ÷ 12).

The method just shown for computing depreciation is called the **straight-line method** because an equal amount of the cost of the plant and equipment asset is estimated as being used each year. There are several other methods that accountants may use to compute the amount of depreciation for each year. Among them are the sum-of-the-years'-digits method and the declining-balance method. These two methods are discussed in more detail in advanced accounting courses.

Recording Depreciation

How often is depreciation recorded? A portion of the total depreciation should be charged against revenue earned in each accounting period. The electronic programmable calculator is being used to earn revenue during the year, and \$150 (\$750 ÷ 5) should be charged against that annual revenue.

The amount of depreciation expense is recorded at the end of each accounting period. At that time, entries to adjust for depreciation are made for plant and equipment asset accounts (except land). The adjusting entry for depreciation is similar to the one for uncollectible accounts. The debit is to an expense account (for depreciation expense), and the credit entry is to a contra-asset account (for accumulated depreciation).

Adjusting Entry for Depreciation
Debit: Depreciation Expense
Credit: Accumulated Depreciation

A plant and equipment asset account is not credited directly because the amount of depreciation is only an estimate. Furthermore, if the plant and equipment asset account were credited, it would appear as though the business had disposed of part of the plant and equipment asset. The Accumulated Depreciation account will always show the total expired cost of the asset to that time.

The difference between the balance of the plant and equipment asset account and the balance of the Accumulated Depreciation account is the book value of the plant and equipment asset. The **book value** represents that portion of the cost of the asset that has not been recorded as a depreciation expense.

The first year's depreciation on the electronic programmable calculator purchased by the Durant Company would be recorded as follows.

DURANT COMPANY CHART OF ACCOUNTS

Plant and Equipment
156 Office Equipment
157 Accumulated Depreciation—Office Equipment

Costs and Expenses
514 Depreciation Expense—Office Equipment

DECEMBER 31, 19X3: THE DURANT COMPANY RECORDS DEPRECIATION OF \$150 ON THE CALCULATOR FOR THE FIRST YEAR.

What Happens	Accounting Rule	Accounting Entry
The expense for depreciation decreases owner's equity by \$150. The book value of the asset *Office Equipment* decreases by \$150.	To decrease owner's equity, debit the account. To decrease an asset, credit the account.	Debit: Depreciation Expense—Office Equipment, \$150. Credit: Accumulated Depreciation—Office Equipment, \$150.

Office Equipment 156		*Accumulated Depreciation—Office Equipment 157*		*Depreciation Expense—Office Equipment 514*	
860			150	150	

Depreciation for the first year.

The Depreciation Expense—Office Equipment account is an expense account and is debited to record the decrease in owner's equity. At the end of the accounting period, it is closed with the other expense accounts into the Income Summary account. The credit entry is recorded in the contra-asset account called Accumulated Depreciation—Office Equipment. This account shows the total amount of depreciation estimated and recorded for the first year ($150). The asset account Office Equipment shows the original cost of the plant and equipment asset ($860) and is not affected by the adjusting entry.

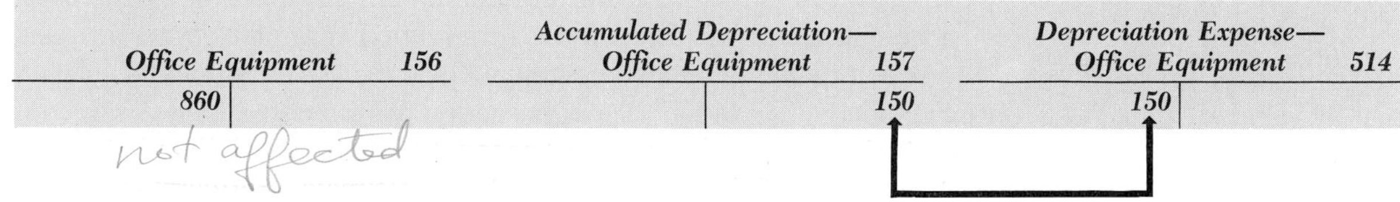

Depreciation for the first year.

Both the plant and equipment asset account and the accumulated depreciation account must be shown on the balance sheet to provide all information about the asset. If the electronic programmable calculator were the only piece of office equipment owned by the Durant Company, it would be listed under office equipment in the plant and equipment asset section of the balance sheet.

Office Equipment	*$860*	
Less: Accum. Depreciation ..	*150*	*$710*

Book value at the end of the first year.

Depreciation in succeeding years is recorded as follows. At the end of the second year, an adjusting entry is made to record the depreciation for that year as it was in the first year. Again, the Office Equipment account would not be affected by the adjusting entry.

Office Equipment			156
19X3	*860*		

Accumulated Depreciation— Office Equipment			157
		19X3	*150*
		19X4	*150*
		300	

Depreciation Expense— Office Equipment			514
19X4	*150*		

Depreciation for the second year.

The Office Equipment account still shows a balance of $860, the original cost of the electronic programmable calculator. The Accumulated Depreciation—Office Equipment account now has a balance of $300 ($150 × 2). The book value of the asset is now $560 ($860 − $300).

Office Equipment	*$860*	
Less: Accum. Depreciation ..	*300*	*$560*

Book value at the end of the second year.

If similar entries are made for each year, at the end of the fifth year the accounts will appear as shown.

Office Equipment			156
19X3	*860*		

Accumulated Depreciation— Office Equipment			157
		19X3	*150*
		19X4	*150*
		19X5	*150*
		19X6	*150*
		19X7	*150*
		750	

Depreciation Expense— Office Equipment			514
19X7	*150*		

Depreciation for the fifth year.

Office Equipment	*$860*	
Less: Accum. Depreciation ..	*750*	*$110*

Book value at the end of the fifth year.

The book value of the calculator at the end of the fifth year is $110 (original cost of $860 less total depreciation of $750). The $110 represents the disposal value of the calculator and is not depreciated regardless of how long the Durant Company keeps the calculator.

When a plant and equipment asset is sold, the cost of the asset must be removed from the plant and equipment asset account. Also, the accumulated depreciation must be removed from the contra account. Assume that the Durant Company sells the calculator for $110 in cash on January 2, 19X8. The transaction would require the following entry. The Cash account is debited for $110, the amount received for the sale. The contra account Accumulated Depreciation—Office Equipment is debited for $750, the total accumulated depreciation at the time of the sale. The asset account Office Equipment is credited for $860, the original cost of the asset. After the entry is posted, the balance of the Office Equipment account is reduced to zero (if the calculator is the only piece of office equipment), and the Accumulated Depreciation—Office Equipment account is also reduced to zero because the equipment is no longer owned.

Sale of Plant & Equipment Asset

GENERAL JOURNAL — **Page** 37

DATE		ACCOUNT TITLE AND EXPLANATION	POST. REF.	DEBIT	CREDIT
19X8					
Jan.	2	*Cash*	*101*	*110 00*	
		Accum. Depr.—Off. Equipment	*157*	*750 00*	
		Office Equipment	*156*		*860 00*

General journal entry to record sale of plant and equipment asset.

Cash 101

Debit		Credit	
19X8	*110*		

Office Equipment 156

Debit		Credit	
19X3	*860*	*19X8*	*860*

Accumulated Depreciation—Office Equipment 157

Debit		Credit	
19X8	*750*	*19X3*	*150*
		19X4	*150*
		19X5	*150*
		19X6	*150*
		19X7	*150*
	750		*750*

—0— —0—

Exercise F on page 563 may be completed at this point.

Subsidiary Ledger for Plant and Equipment Assets

Are separate accounts kept for each plant and equipment asset in the general ledger? To determine the amount of depreciation for each accounting period, the accountant needs information about each plant and equipment asset the business owns. The accountant needs to know the original cost, purchase date, number of years of useful life, and estimated disposal value of each asset. This information is necessary not only for estimating depreciation, but also for completing the required federal tax forms.

It is not practical to open a ledger account in the general ledger for each piece of furniture or machinery the business owns. The needed details are usually kept in a subsidiary ledger called the **plant and equipment ledger**. Each item is recorded on a separate card, similar to the plant and equipment record card shown below. The cards support the general ledger accounts for plant and equipment assets, which now become controlling accounts.

The plant and equipment record card was prepared for a TriStar calculator with the serial number X-9114. The title "Office Equipment" was written on the General Ledger Account line to show that this card supplements the Office Equipment account in the general ledger. When the calculator was purchased, the $860 debit was posted to the Plant and Equipment Account section because the Office Equipment account in the general ledger was debited for $860, the price at which it was purchased.

Depreciation Information

Controlling Account in General Ledger

PLANT AND EQUIPMENT RECORD

Item Calculator
Serial No. X-9114
Description TriStar
Cost When Acquired $860
Estimated Life 5 yrs.
General Ledger Account Office Equipment
Purchased From Colonial Office Supply
Location Accounting Department
Age When Acquired New
Estimated Scrap or Trade-In Value $110 *Annual Depreciation* $150

DATE			EXPLANATION	PLANT AND EQUIPMENT ACCT.			ACCUMULATED DEPRECIATION			BOOK VALUE
MO.	DAY	YR.		DEBIT	CREDIT	BALANCE	DEBIT	CREDIT	BALANCE	
1	2	X3	Purchased	860 00		860 00				860 00
12	31	X3						150 00	150 00	710 00
12	31	X4						150 00	300 00	560 00
12	31	X5						150 00	450 00	410 00
12	31	X6						150 00	600 00	260 00
12	31	X7						150 00	750 00	110 00
1	2	X8	Sold		860 00	— 00	750 00		— 00	— 00

Sold, Traded, or Scrapped to: Elaine Spradlin 1/2/X8 *Amount Received: $110*

Entries Affecting Plant and Equipment Account in General Ledger (Original Cost)

Entries Affecting Contra Account in General Ledger (Expired Cost)

Balance of Plant and Equipment Account Minus Accumulated Depreciation (Current Unexpired Cost or Book Value)

The entries recorded in the Accumulated Depreciation section of the plant and equipment record card were made each time the depreciation entry was posted to the contra account in the general ledger. The book value of the asset was calculated after each entry was posted.

When the calculator was sold, a credit of $860 was posted to the Plant and Equipment Account section of the card for the cost and a debit of $750 was posted to the Accumulated Depreciation section for the total accumulated depreciation. The Plant and Equipment and the Accumulated Depreciation account balances become zero, making the book value of the asset zero. At the time of disposal, the plant and equipment record card is removed from the subsidiary ledger.

To prove the subsidiary ledger for a plant and equipment account such as Office Equipment, the accountant adds the balance column of the Plant and Equipment Account section on each card for that asset. The total of all the balances must equal the balance of the asset account in the general ledger. The contra account is proved by adding the balance column of the Accumulated Depreciation section on each card. The total of all the balances must equal the balance of the contra account in the general ledger. The book value on all the cards is equal to the difference between the balance of the asset account and the balance of the contra account.

■ Depreciation on the Worksheet

The entries to record the depreciation for an accounting period are completed after the Trial Balance section of the worksheet has been prepared. The amount of depreciation must be found for each plant and equipment asset (except land). Then the adjustments are made in the Adjustments section of the worksheet, as shown below.

Durant Company
Worksheet
For the Year Ended December 31, 19X8

	ACCOUNT TITLE	ACCT. NO.	TRIAL BALANCE		ADJUSTMENTS		ADJUSTED TRIAL BALANCE		INCOME STATEMENT		BALANCE SHEET		
			DEBIT	CREDIT	DEBIT	CREDIT	DEBIT	CREDIT	DEBIT	CREDIT	DEBIT	CREDIT	
8	*Land*	151	60,000				60,000				60,000		8
9	*Building*	152	150,000				150,000				150,000		9
10	*Accumulated Depr.—Building*	153		10,000		(e) 5,000		15,000				15,000	10
11	*Delivery Equipment*	154	19,500				19,500				19,500		11
12	*Accumulated Depr.—Del. Eq.*	155		6,000		(f) 3,000		9,000				9,000	12
13	*Office Equipment*	156	12,000				12,000				12,000		13
14	*Accumulated Depr.—Off. Eq.*	157		2,000		(g) 1,000		3,000				3,000	14
41	*Depr. Expense—Building*	512			(e) 5,000		5,000		5,000				41
42	*Depr. Expense—Delivery Eq.*	513			(f) 3,000		3,000		3,000				42
43	*Depr. Expense—Office Eq.*	514			(g) 1,000		1,000		1,000				43

NOTE: The cents columns have been omitted in order to show the entire worksheet.

Building In 19X6, the Durant Company purchased land that cost $60,000 and a building that cost $150,000. The useful life of the building is estimated to be 30 years. At the end of that time, the building will be fully depreciated. Therefore, the yearly depreciation of the building is $5,000 ($150,000 ÷ 30). When a worksheet is prepared for the year ended December 31, 19X8, the contra account Accumulated Depreciation—Building has a credit balance of $10,000 ($5,000 depreciation was recorded in each of the previous two years).

Cost of building	*150,000*	*00*
Less: Disposal value .	—	*00*
Total depreciable cost	*150,000*	*00*

Adjustment (*e*) is made to record the depreciation for the current year. The Depreciation Expense—Building account is debited for $5,000 and the Accumulated Depreciation—Building account is credited for $5,000. The Adjusted Trial Balance section shows that the contra account now has a credit balance of $15,000 (the amount of depreciation for three years). The book value of the building is now $135,000 ($150,000 − $15,000).

Delivery Equipment The business owns three delivery trucks that were purchased for $6,500 each. Each truck is estimated to have a useful life of six years and a trade-in value (disposal value) of $500. Thus, each truck has annual depreciation of $1,000 ($6,500 − $500 = $6,000; $6,000 ÷ 6 = $1,000). The contra account in the Trial Balance section shows a $6,000 credit balance for the previous two years. The adjustment (*f*) to record the present depreciation ($3,000) debits the expense account and credits the contra account. The Adjusted Trial Balance section shows a $9,000 credit balance for the contra account, which represents depreciation for three years. This makes the book value of the three trucks $10,500 ($19,500 − $9,000).

Yearly depr. for each truck = $\frac{\$6,000}{6} = \$1,000$

Cost of truck	*6,500*	*00*
Less: Trade-in value .	*500*	*00*
Total depreciable cost	*6,000*	*00*

Office Equipment The cost of the office equipment is $12,000, and the depreciation recorded for past periods is $2,000. The book value of the office equipment is now $10,000 ($12,000 − $2,000). The plant and equipment record cards for the office equipment show the business owns several kinds of office equipment. The cards also indicate that the equipment was purchased at various times. To know what depreciation should be charged during this accounting period, the accountant must add the various amounts on the cards. Total depreciation for office equipment is $1,000, which is entered as adjustment (*g*) in the Adjustments section of the worksheet. Depreciation Expense—Office Equipment is debited for $1,000, and Accumulated Depreciation—Office Equipment is credited for $1,000.

As shown on the worksheet for the Durant Company on the previous page, there are contra accounts for each plant and equipment asset except land. The accumulated depreciation account remains as an open account as long as the plant and equipment asset is owned by the business. The book value of each group of plant and equipment assets is shown on the balance sheet by subtracting each contra account from its plant and equipment asset account.

Depreciation expense accounts are also set up for each group of plant and equipment assets, such as Depreciation Expense—Building, Depreciation Expense—Delivery Equipment, and Depreciation Expense—Office Equipment. The depreciation expenses are charged against current operations and are reported on the income statement. At the end of the accounting period, depreciation expense accounts are closed to the Income Summary account along with all other expenses.

■ Depreciation on the Financial Statements

The amounts of estimated depreciation for the current accounting period are reported as operating expenses on the income statement. On the balance sheet, the following three amounts are shown for each group of plant and equipment assets: cost, accumulated depreciation, and book value.

Durant Company
Income Statement
For the Year Ended December 31, 19X8

Revenue From Sales			200,000	00
Gross Profit on Sales			110,000	00
Operating Expenses:				
Depreciation Expense—Building.	5,000	00		
Depreciation Exp.—Del. Equip..	3,000	00		
Depreciation Exp.—Office Equip.	1,000	00		
Uncollectible Accounts Expense..	670	00		

Durant Company
Balance Sheet
December 31, 19X8

Assets				
Current Assets:				
Cash..............................	18,600	00		
Total Current Assets..............			53,000	00
Plant and Equipment Assets:				
Land	60,000	00		
Building................ *$150,000.00*				
Less: Acc. Depr. *15,000.00*	135,000	00		
Delivery Equipment...... *$ 19,500.00*				
Less: Acc. Depr. *9,000.00*	10,500	00		
Office Equipment .... *$ 12,000.00*				
Less: Acc. Depr. *3,000.00*	9,000	00		
Total Plant and Equipment			214,500	00
Total Assets..................			267,500	00

If no plant and equipment assets are sold during the next accounting period, and no additional plant and equipment assets are purchased, the cost of the plant and equipment assets will remain the same. However, the amount of accumulated depreciation for each group will increase, which means that the book value of the assets will decrease. Assume that no plant and equipment assets are sold or purchased during a four-year period and that the amount of the depreciation remains the same. The amounts shown for plant and equipment assets on the balance sheets for those four years will appear as illustrated on the comparative balance sheet at the top of the next page.

	19X6		19X7		19X8		19X9	
Plant and Equipment Assets:								
Land		*60,000*		*60,000*		*60,000*		*60,000*
Building	*150,000*		*150,000*		*150,000*		*150,000*	
Less Accumulated Depreciation	*5,000*	*145,000*	*10,000*	*140,000*	*15,000*	*135,000*	*20,000*	*130,000*
Delivery Equipment	*19,500*		*19,500*		*19,500*		*19,500*	
Less: Accumulated Depreciation	*3,000*	*16,500*	*6,000*	*13,500*	*9,000*	*10,500*	*12,000*	*7,500*
Office Equipment	*12,000*		*12,000*		*12,000*		*12,000*	
Less: Accumulated Depreciation	*1,000*	*11,000*	*2,000*	*10,000*	*3,000*	*9,000*	*4,000*	*8,000*
Total Plant and Equipment		*232,500*		*223,500*		*214,500*		*205,500*

The total of the plant and equipment assets decreases each year by $9,000 (from $232,500 to $223,500 to $214,500 to $205,500), the amount of the depreciation recorded each year.

Building	*5,000*	*00*
Delivery Equipment	*3,000*	*00*
Office Equipment	*1,000*	*00*
	9,000	*00*

Depreciation in Closing the Ledger

After the financial statements are prepared, the adjusting entries are recorded in the general journal. When the entries are posted, the plant and equipment asset accounts, accumulated depreciation accounts, and depreciation expense accounts appear as shown.

Depreciation Expense accounts are closed into the Income Summary account.

GENERAL JOURNAL — **Page** *46*

DATE		ACCOUNT TITLE AND EXPLANATION	POST. REF.	DEBIT		CREDIT	
19X8							
Dec.	*31*	*Depreciation Expense—Building*	*512*	*5,000*	*00*		
		Accumulated Depreciation—Building	*153*			*5,000*	*00*
		Record depreciation for year.					
	31	*Depreciation Expense—Delivery Equipment*	*513*	*3,000*	*00*		
		Accumulated Depr.—Delivery Equip.	*155*			*3,000*	*00*
		Record depreciation for year.					
	31	*Depreciation Expense—Office Equipment*	*514*	*1,000*	*00*		
		Accumulated Depreciation—Office Equip.	*157*			*1,000*	*00*
		Record depreciation for year.					

Adjusting entries for recording depreciation.

Debited for cost of land when purchased.

Land			*151*
19X6			
Jan. 1 Balance ✓	*60,000*		

No depreciation is recorded on land.

Debited for cost of building when purchased.

Building			*152*
19X6			
Jan. 1 Balance ✓	*150,000*		

To be credited for cost at time of disposal.

Debited for total amount of accumulated depreciation at time of disposal.

Accumulated Depreciation—Building			*153*
		19X8	
		Jan. 1 Balance ✓	*10,000*
		Dec. 31 *J46*	*5,000*

Credited for depreciation each accounting period until time of disposal or until book value equals disposal value.

Debited for cost of delivery equipment when purchased.

Delivery Equipment			154
19X6			
Jan. 1 Balance √	*19,500*		

To be credited for cost at time of disposal.

To be debited for total amount of accumulated depreciation at time of disposal.

Accumulated Depreciation—Delivery Equipment			155
		19X8	
		Jan. 1 Balance √	*6,000*
		Dec. 31 J46	*3,000*

Credited for depreciation each accounting period until time of disposal or until book value equals disposal value.

Debited for cost of office equipment when purchased.

Office Equipment			156
19X6			
Jan. 1 Balance √	*12,000*		

To be credited for cost at time of disposal.

To be debited for total amount of accumulated depreciation at time of disposal.

Accumulated Depreciation—Office Equipment			157
		19X8	
		Jan. 1 Balance √	*2,000*
		Dec. 31 J46	*1,000*

Credited for depreciation each accounting period until time of disposal or until book value equals disposal value.

Debited at end of accounting period for estimated depreciation for period.

Depreciation Expense—Building			512
19X8			
Dec. 31 J46	*5,000*		

To be closed to Income Summary account.

Debited at end of accounting period for estimated depreciation for period.

Depreciation Expense—Delivery Equipment			513
19X8			
Dec. 31 J46	*3,000*		

To be closed to Income Summary account.

Debited at end of accounting period for estimated depreciation for period.

Depreciation Expense—Office Equipment			514
19X8			
Dec. 31 J46	*1,000*		

To be closed to Income Summary account.

The balances of the Depreciation Expense accounts are closed to the Income Summary account with all other expenses. The plant and equipment asset accounts and the Accumulated Depreciation accounts appear on the postclosing trial balance.

Principle: Matching Revenue and Expenses

The generally accepted accounting principle is that revenue must be matched against the expenses incurred in obtaining that revenue. The result of matching revenue and expenses is net income (or net loss) for the accounting period.

Principle: Reporting Depreciation

The generally accepted accounting principle is that accumulated depreciation should be shown as a deduction from plant and equipment.

Principle: Cost
The generally accepted accounting principle is that plant and equipment assets are recorded on the balance sheet at their original cost.

Exercise G on this page and page 564 may be completed at this point.

TOPIC 3 EXERCISES

EXERCISE F. Answer the following questions about estimating and recording depreciation. Refer to the text and illustrations on pages 551 to 556.

1. What is the original cost of the building?
2. What is the annual amount of depreciation of the building?
3. What are the expired and unexpired costs after five years?
4. What are the expired and unexpired costs after 30 years?
5. What three elements are needed to compute depreciation?
6. What is the cost of the electronic programmable calculator? What is the disposal value? What is the total depreciation?
7. What method is used to compute the depreciation on the electronic programmable calculator?
8. When the adjustment is made for depreciation, which account is debited?
9. When the adjustment is made for depreciation, which account is credited?
10. Which account is debited to adjust for depreciation of the office equipment? Which account is credited? Why?
11. What general journal entry is made to record the estimated annual depreciation of office equipment?
12. What is the new book value of the office equipment after the first year?

EXERCISE G. Answer the following questions about recording depreciation. Refer to the text and illustrations on pages 558 to 562.

1. Are the entries to record depreciation made first on the worksheet or in the general journal?
2. In which section of the worksheet is the estimated annual depreciation of the building first entered?
3. What journal entry must be made to record the annual depreciation of the building?
4. To which worksheet column is the new total of the Accumulated Depreciation—Building account extended from the Adjusted Trial Balance section? Why?
5. Why is there no previous balance for Depreciation Expense—Building?
6. What is the new book value of the building?
7. What is the amount of Depreciation Expense—Building?
8. To which worksheet column is the amount of Depreciation Expense—Building extended from the Adjusted Trial Balance section? Why?
9. In which worksheet section is the estimated annual depreciation of the office equipment first recorded?
10. To which worksheet column is the new total of the Accumulated Depreciation—Office

Equipment account extended from the Adjusted Trial Balance column? Why?

11. What is the purpose of the small (*f*) before the amount in the Adjustments section of the worksheet?

12. To which worksheet column is the total of the Depreciation Expense—Office Equipment account extended from the Adjusted Trial Balance column? Why?

TOPIC 3 PROBLEMS

TOPIC PROBLEM 6. Instead of keeping plant and equipment record cards, the Western Star Corporation keeps a list of its plant and equipment assets and related information involving cost and depreciation. The list for the second year of the business's operations is shown here.

a. Supply the missing amounts.

b. Make the estimated semiannual entries in the general journal to record the estimated depreciation of the listed plant and equipment assets on June 30.

Asset	Cost	Disposal Value	Estimated Useful Life (in years)	Annual Depreciation	Monthly Depreciation	Current Book Value
(1) Automobile	$ 8,500	$ 1,000	5	$1,500	$125	$5,500
(2) Building	135,000	10,000	25	?	?	?
(3) Furniture	52,000	4,000	10	?	?	?
(4) Office equipment	4,800	-0-	5	?	?	?
(5) Tools	3,240	-0-	6	?	?	?
(6) Truck	49,900	7,000	3	?	?	?

TOPIC PROBLEM 7. Parts of the trial balance prepared for the Hyde Delivery Service are shown at the right.

ACCOUNT TITLE	ACCT. NO.	DEBIT	CREDIT
Cash	101	6,230 00	
Accounts Receivable	111	5,150 00	
Allowance for Doubtful Accounts	112		110 00
Prepaid Insurance	113	1,200 00	
Building	121	80,000 00	
Accumulated Depreciation—Building	122		12,000 00
Furniture	123	3,000 00	
Accumulated Depreciation—Furniture	124		800 00
Miscellaneous Expense	505	2,560 00	

a. Enter this data on a worksheet for the year ended December 31.

b. Make the adjustments for the following: estimated uncollectible accounts, $80 (based on a percentage of net sales); expired insurance, $600; estimated depreciation of the building, $6,000; and estimated depreciation of the furniture, $200.

c. Extend all amounts to the proper columns of the worksheet.

d. Record the adjusting entries in the general journal.

e. Show how each current asset, each plant and equipment asset, and each contra-asset account would appear on the balance sheet.

CHAPTER 15 REVIEW

CHAPTER SUMMARY

In this chapter you studied adjustments to accounts receivable and plant and equipment assets. There are two methods that businesses may use to account for uncollectible accounts: the direct write-off method and the allowance method. Under the allowance method, uncollectible accounts expense can be estimated in several ways: the percentage of net sales method or the percentage of aged accounts receivable method.

You learned how contra accounts—accounts with balances contrary to normal balances—are used to record uncollectible accounts and depreciation.

You studied the adjusting entries that must be recorded for all plant and equipment assets, except land. You also saw how to compute depreciation using the straight-line method, and how to record the adjusting entries for the annual depreciation at the end of the accounting period.

THE LANGUAGE OF BUSINESS

Here are some terms that make up the language of business. Do you know the meaning of each?

uncollectible account
realizable value of accounts receivable
direct write-off method
allowance method
Uncollectible Accounts Expense account
Allowance for Doubtful Accounts account
contra account
contra-asset account
percentage of net sales method
percentage of aged accounts receivable method
aging the accounts receivable
depreciation
disposal value
straight-line method
book value
plant and equipment ledger

REVIEW QUESTIONS

1. What are the two methods for writing off uncollectible accounts? Briefly describe each method.
2. If no allowance is made for uncollectible accounts, what effect does this have on revenue? On expenses? On net income?
3. Why is the amount of uncollectible accounts credited to a contra-asset account rather than to the Accounts Receivable controlling account?
4. Describe two methods of estimating losses from uncollectible accounts.
5. How is the amount of the debit to the Uncollectible Accounts Expense account obtained when the estimate is based on the percentage of net sales method? How does that differ when using the percentage of aged accounts receivable method?
6. Two years ago, the balance of the customer's account for Robert West was written off

as an uncollectible account. Describe the procedure used to record the check received from him today.

7. For which plant and equipment asset is no depreciation recorded? Why?
8. Why must the amount of depreciation on plant and equipment assets be recorded on the financial statements?
9. Why is the amount of depreciation credited to a contra account rather than credited directly to the plant and equipment asset account?
10. What is the effect upon owner's equity if no adjustment is made for depreciation? Why?

CHAPTER PROBLEMS

Problems for Chapter 15 are given below. Write your answers to the problems on separate sheets of paper unless you are using the workbook for this textbook. If you are using the workbook, do the problems in the space provided there.

CHAPTER PROBLEM 15-1. The uncollectible accounts expense for the King Fashions Company is estimated to be 6 percent of the total outstanding Accounts Receivable. The balance of the Accounts Receivable account as of December 31 is $14,375. Record in the general journal the adjusting entry for uncollectible accounts expense on December 31 for the company. For *a*, *b*, and *c*, assume that the uncollectible accounts expense is based upon the aged accounts receivable method.

a. Record the adjusting entry if the Allowance for Doubtful Accounts account has a zero balance.

b. Record the adjusting entry if the Allowance for Doubtful Accounts account has a credit balance of $619.

c. Record the adjusting entry if the Allowance for Doubtful Accounts account has a debit balance of $218.

CHAPTER PROBLEM 15-2. Use the following data from the Dennis Paxton Company's accounting records to complete the worksheet for the period ended May 31. The Trial Balance section of the worksheet is presented on the next page. The following data concerning the adjusting entries is provided here.

A physical count of the merchandise shows an inventory of $9,880 on May 31.

A physical count of the supplies shows an inventory of $110 on May 31.

The amount of unexpired insurance is $360 on May 31.

The estimated loss from uncollectible accounts is 1 percent of net sales.

Annual depreciation on equipment must be recorded. The equipment has an expected useful life of 5 years and an estimated disposal value of $2,000.

Annual depreciation on the truck must be recorded. The truck has a useful life of 3 years, and an estimated disposal value of $1,200.

a. Complete the worksheet.

b. Record the adjusting entries in the general journal.

	ACCOUNT TITLE	ACCT. NO.	TRIAL BALANCE			
			DEBIT		CREDIT	
1	*Cash*	*101*	*9,400*	*00*		
2	*Accounts Receivable*	*102*	*7,390*	*00*		
3	*Allowance for Doubtful Accounts*	*103*			*110*	*00*
4	*Merchandise Inventory*	*104*	*11,850*	*00*		
5	*Prepaid Insurance*	*105*	*480*	*00*		
6	*Supplies*	*106*	*356*	*00*		
7	*Equipment*	*107*	*14,500*	*00*		
8	*Accumulated Depreciation—Equipment*	*108*			*5,000*	*00*
9	*Truck*	*109*	*16,200*	*00*		
10	*Accumulated Depreciation—Truck*	*110*			*5,000*	*00*
11	*Notes Payable*	*201*			*1,200*	*00*
12	*Accounts Payable*	*202*			*937*	*00*
13	*Dennis Paxton, Capital*	*301*			*33,371*	*00*
14	*Dennis Paxton, Drawing*	*302*	*4,000*	*00*		
15	*Income Summary*	*399*			—	*00*
16	*Sales*	*401*			*27,240*	*00*
17	*Sales Returns and Allowances*	*402*	*340*	*00*		
18	*Sales Discount*	*403*	*300*	*00*		
19	*Purchases*	*501*	*7,100*	*00*		
20	*Purchases Returns and Allowances*	*502*			*170*	*00*
21	*Purchases Discount*	*503*			*135*	*00*
22	*Depreciation Expense—Equipment*	*506*	—	*00*		
23	*Depreciation Expense—Truck*	*507*	—	*00*		
24	*Insurance Expense*	*508*	—	*00*		
25	*Miscellaneous Expense*	*509*	*447*	*00*		
26	*Rent Expense*	*510*	*800*	*00*		
27	*Supplies Expense*	*511*	—	*00*		
28	*Uncollectible Accounts Expense*	*512*	—	*00*		
29			*73,163*	*00*	*73,163*	*00*

MANAGEMENT CASES

Credit Policies. Some businesses find it necessary to sell on credit to their customers. In businesses that sell furniture, for example, about 90 percent of the sales are made on credit. Under these circumstances, a furniture business may not be able to survive if it does not extend credit.

A new business must determine what is the best credit policy for it to follow in order to sell its products. With a strict credit policy, uncollectible accounts expense is low, but sales may also be low. With a lenient credit policy, both sales and uncollectible accounts expense will probably be high. Each business must decide which credit policy will yield the greater net income—more sales with more uncollectible accounts or fewer sales with fewer uncollectible accounts.

CASE 15M-1. Kenneth Olsen owns the Scandinavian Furniture Store. Mr. Olsen estimates that if the business follows an extremely liberal policy of extending credit to customers, the total credit sales for the year will be $300,000, and that uncollectible accounts will be 5 percent of the credit sales for that period. He figures that the gross profit after the deduction of the uncollectible accounts expense would be as follows.

Credit Sales	$300,000
Gross Profit (25% of sales)	$ 75,000
Uncollectible Accounts Expense (5% of Credit Sales)	−15,000
Gross Profit After Uncollectible Accounts Expense	$ 60,000

Mr. Olsen estimates that the business will have the following credit sales and uncollectible accounts expense if less liberal credit policies are used.

Very strict: Sales, $150,000; losses, ¼%
Strict: Sales, $175,000; losses, ½%
Moderate: Sales, $250,000; losses, 1%
Lenient: Sales, $275,000; losses, 3%

a. Based on each of Mr. Olsen's estimates, what gross profit would the business have after the uncollectible accounts are deducted?

b. What credit policy do you recommend that Mr. Olsen follow?

CASE 15M-2. The Northside Laundry Service owns a truck that it uses for picking up and delivering laundry. Last year, the truck traveled 75,000 miles and made 32,000 stops. Operating expenses for the truck were as follows: fuel, $9,000; repairs, $1,200; depreciation, $1,500; insurance, $650; license, $120; storage, $750; and driver's salary, $22,000. Diane Boyle, the owner, is thinking of selling the truck and either leasing a truck from the Stop & Go Company or using the Rapid Delivery Service.

The Stop & Go Company charges $500 per month for the truck. In addition to the monthly charge, the Northside Laundry Service must pay for fuel, insurance, storage, and the driver's salary. The Stop & Go Company pays for repairs and the license.

The Rapid Delivery Service will pick up and deliver the laundry in each delivery area once daily, at $2.10 per stop.

a. What decision would you make regarding the truck?

b. Are there other factors that should be considered in addition to the cost before making a decision?

CHAPTER

16

Updating Accounts for Accruals and Deferrals

In the preceding two chapters you learned to update various accounts at the end of the accounting period. In Chapter 16 you will learn how to account for transactions that affect more than one accounting period. You will learn how to record the transactions and update the accounts at the end of the accounting period.

CHAPTER GOALS

After studying Chapter 16, you will be able to:

1. Define the terms listed in ''The Language of Business'' section on page 589.
2. Explain the difference between the cash basis of accounting and the accrual basis of accounting.
3. Record the journal entries required when adjusting for accrued expenses and paying accrued expenses.
4. Record the journal entries required when adjusting for accrued revenue and receiving accrued revenue.
5. Record the journal entries required when receiving deferred revenue and adjusting for deferred revenue.

TOPIC 1

Accrued Expenses and Liabilities

What methods may a business use to process revenue and expenses? A business may use one of two procedures to process financial data: the cash basis of accounting or the accrual basis of accounting. The major difference between the two methods is when the business records (recognizes) revenue and expenses.

Under the **cash basis of accounting**, revenue is recorded in the accounting period when cash is received from customers. Expenses are recorded in the accounting period when cash is actually paid.

Many service businesses and professional people use the cash basis of accounting. For example, if a doctor uses the cash basis, the revenue recorded is only the revenue from fees actually collected throughout the accounting period. There may be fees owed by other patients. However, these fees are not recorded as revenue until the cash has been received.

Under the **accrual basis of accounting**, revenue is recorded during the accounting period in which merchandise is sold or a service is performed, whether the cash is received or not. Expenses are recorded during the period in which they are incurred, whether or not payment has been made for them. Businesses that have inventories of merchandise are required to use the accrual basis of accounting.

From an accounting point of view, the accrual basis is preferred over the cash basis. This is because the accrual basis complies with the matching principle. That is, under the accrual basis, revenue is recorded when it is earned, and expenses are recorded when they are incurred.

Accrued Expenses

How are most expenses paid and recorded? Most expenses, such as utilities or rent, are paid and recorded as expenses during the accounting period in which they are incurred. However, some expenses are incurred during the accounting period but will not be paid until a future accounting period. Adjusting entries must be made at the end of each accounting period for any unrecorded expenses.

An expense item incurred during an accounting period but not paid during that period is known as an **accrued expense**. For example, interest on a loan is charged for each day the borrower has the use of the money. However, the borrower does not pay the interest each day, and the interest is not recorded as an expense each day. In many cases, interest is not paid or recorded until the due date of the loan. For example, if an interest-bearing promissory note is not due to be paid until a future accounting period, the amount of the interest expense incurred during the present accounting period has not been recorded. An adjusting entry must be made at the end of the accounting period to record the accrued interest expense for that period.

■ Accrued Interest Expense On November 1, 19X7, the Star Computer Company gives a creditor a 90-day, 12 percent promissory note for $12,000 in payment of its account payable. The note is shown here.

A promissory note is a written promise to pay a sum of money at a fixed time in the future.

$ 12,000.00 November 1, 19 X7

Ninety days---------- after date I promise to pay to the order of Vanguard Supply Company----------

Twelve thousand and 00/100---------- Dollars

Payable at First National Bank----------

Value received with 12% interest Star Computer Company

No. 4 Date January 30, 19X8 John Alberts

The transaction is recorded as a debit to Accounts Payable and a credit to the liability account Notes Payable for $12,000, the **face value (principal)** of the note. The entry is shown here.

GENERAL JOURNAL **Page** *30*

DATE		ACCOUNT TITLE AND EXPLANATION	POST. REF.	DEBIT	CREDIT
19X7					
Nov.	*1*	*Accts. Pay./Vanguard Supply Co.* ...	*211/√*	*12,000 00*	
		Notes Payable	*202*		*12,000 00*
		Gave 90-day, 12% note.			

In counting the number of days a note has to run, begin counting the day after the note is issued since the note states "after date." The last day, however, is counted. The calendars in the margin show 90 days after November 1 as January 30.

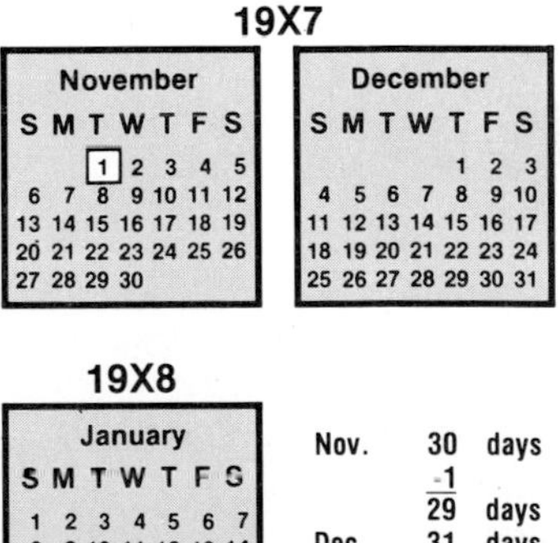

The interest on the note adds up daily over the 90-day period. However, the interest is not paid until the note is due to be paid. On January 30, 19X8, when the note falls due, the Star Computer Company must pay to the creditor a total of $12,360: $12,000 for the note plus $360 for the interest.

The accounting period for the Star Computer Company ends on December 31, 19X7. As of December 31, none of the interest on the loan has been paid. However, interest for a 60-day period has accrued. Therefore, the Star Computer Company must show in its accounting records that it has incurred this expense for the 60-day period from November 1 through December 31. If this expense is not recorded on

12% Interest on $12,000
$240 for 60 days
+120 for 30 days
$360 for 90 days

December 31, the accounting records will not show an accurate picture of the financial condition of the business. The results will be as follows.

- In 19X7, the net income for the year and the owner's equity will be overstated because interest accrued during the year has not been deducted.
- In 19X8, the net income and the owner's equity will be understated because interest accrued in 19X7 will be deducted from revenue earned in 19X8.

An adjusting entry is necessary at the end of the accounting period on December 31, 19X7, to record the expense for interest that has been incurred but not yet paid. This entry will help to make the financial statements for both 19X7 and 19X8 accurate.

Adjusting Interest Expense The amount of interest accrued on the $12,000 note payable for the last 60 days of 19X7 is $240. Since none of the interest has been recorded, the Interest Expense account must be debited for $240 to show the actual interest expense for 19X7. The interest will not be paid until the note becomes due on January 30, 19X8. As a result, a liability is created because the $240 is interest that is owed. The $240 is credited to a liability account called Interest Payable.

After the adjusting entry is posted, the three accounts related to the note show the following. The Notes Payable account shows the amount owed on the note ($12,000). The Interest Payable account shows the liability for interest incurred but not yet paid ($240). The Interest Expense account shows the amount of interest incurred during the present accounting period ($240).

STAR COMPUTER COMPANY CHART OF ACCOUNTS

Current Liabilities
202 Notes Payable
203 Interest Payable

Other Expenses
521 Interest Expense

DECEMBER 31, 19X7: THE STAR COMPUTER COMPANY RECORDS INTEREST EXPENSE OF $240 ACCRUED FOR 60 DAYS ON A NOTE PAYABLE.

What Happens	Accounting Rule	Accounting Entry
The expense for interest decreases owner's equity by $240.	To decrease owner's equity, debit the account.	Debit: Interest Expense, $240.
The liability *Interest Payable* increases by $240.	To increase a liability, credit the account.	Credit: Interest Payable, $240.

Notes Payable 202

Debit	Credit
	19X7 Nov. 1 12,000

Interest Payable 203

Debit	Credit
	19X7 Dec. 31 240

Interest Expense 521

Debit	Credit
19X7 Dec. 31 240	

Like other expenses, the Interest Expense account is closed into the Income Summary account at the end of the accounting period. The

Interest Payable and Notes Payable accounts remain open since they are liability accounts.

Paying the Interest When the note is paid on January 30, 19X8, the Star Computer Company sends $12,360 to the payee. This amount includes $12,000 to pay the note and $360 to pay the interest from November 1 through January 30. Of the $360 interest being paid, $240 (the amount that accrued from November 1 through December 31) has been recorded as an expense of the previous accounting period (19X7). The remaining $120 is an expense for the present accounting period (19X8).

Nov. 1 to Dec. 31		Jan. 1 to Jan. 30		
Previous Period	+	Present Period	=	Total Interest
$240 Interest Payable	+	$120 Interest Expense	=	$360

JANUARY 30, 19X8: THE STAR COMPUTER COMPANY SENDS $12,360 TO THE VANGUARD SUPPLY COMPANY, TO PAY PROMISSORY NOTE OF $12,000 AND INTEREST OF $360 FOR 90 DAYS.

What Happens	Accounting Rule	Accounting Entry
The liability *Notes Payable* decreases by $12,000.	To decrease a liability, debit the account.	Debit: Notes Payable, $12,000.
The liability *Interest Payable* decreases by $240.	To decrease a liability, debit the account.	Debit: Interest Payable, $240.
The expense for interest decreases owner's equity by $120.	To decrease owner's equity, debit the account.	Debit: Interest Expense, $120.
The asset *Cash* decreases by $12,360.	To decrease an asset, credit the account.	Credit: Cash, $12,360.

The entry to record the payment is made in the cash payments journal. The Notes Payable account is debited for $12,000, the original amount of the note that is now being paid. The Interest Payable account is debited for $240, the amount of interest that accrued in 19X7 and is now being paid. The Interest Expense account is debited for $120, the amount of interest accrued during the present accounting period. Finally, the Cash account is credited for $12,360, the total amount being paid.

Entry to Pay Accrued Liability
Debit: Liability account
Debit: Expense account
Credit: Cash

CASH PAYMENTS JOURNAL Page *81*

DATE		ACCOUNT DEBITED	EXPLANATION	CHECK NO.	POST. REF.	GENERAL LEDGER DEBIT	ACCOUNTS PAYABLE DEBIT	PURCHASES DISCOUNT CREDIT	NET CASH CREDIT
19X8									
Jan.	30	*Notes Payable*	*Note dated Nov. 1* .	275	202	12,000 00			12,360 00
		Interest Payable ...	*Interest for 60 days* .	—	203	240 00			
		Interest Expense ...	*Interest for 30 days* .	—	521	120 00			

After this entry is posted to the ledger, the balances of both the Notes Payable account and the Interest Payable account will be zero.

The Interest Expense account will have a balance of $120 until the account is closed at the end of the accounting period on December 31, 19X8.

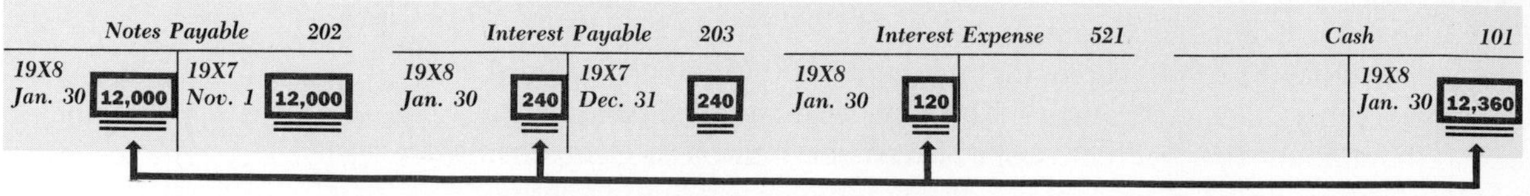

Exercise A on pages 577 and 578 may be completed at this point.

Accrued Salaries Expense Employees earn salaries each day they work, but the salaries expense is not recorded until the end of the pay period. For example, the pay period for the Star Computer Company ends each Wednesday. Suppose that December 31, the end of the accounting period, falls on a Saturday. The employees have earned salaries for two days since the previous payday. The Star Computer Company will not pay the employees for two days' work merely because it is the end of the accounting period. The employees will be paid next Wednesday (January 4). However, the company must show that the employees have earned two days' pay during the present accounting period. This will be done by recording an adjusting entry.

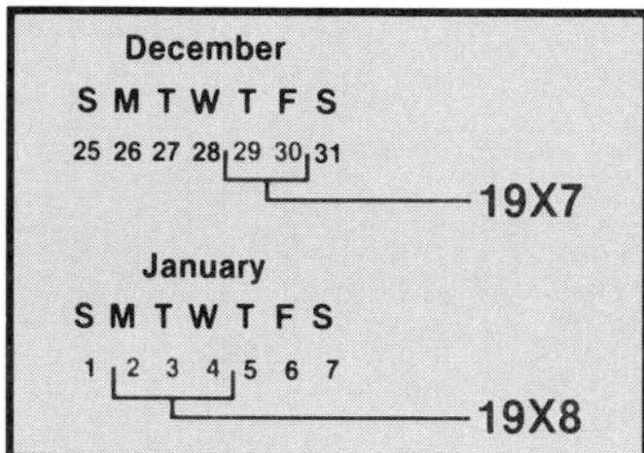

Adjusting Salaries Expense The total salaries are $300 a day, or $1,500 for five working days. The salaries for Thursday and Friday (December 29 and 30) amount to $600. The $600 represents the amount of salaries that has accrued during the current accounting period. The $600 is an expense for the current accounting period that will be paid during the next accounting period. The adjusting entry to record the accrued salaries for 19X7 consists of a debit to the Salaries Expense account for $600 and a credit to the Salaries Payable account for $600.

STAR COMPUTER COMPANY CHART OF ACCOUNTS

Current Liabilities
226 Salaries Payable

Costs and Expenses
518 Salaries Expense

Salaries Payable		*226*	*Salaries Expense*		*518*
	19X7		*19X7*		
	Dec. 31	600	*Dec. 31*	600	

When the closing entries are made on December 31, the Salaries Expense account will be closed into the Income Summary account. The Salaries Payable account will remain open until the salaries are paid on January 4, 19X8.

Paying the Salaries On January 4, 19X8, the Star Computer Company will pay the employees $1,500 for the five days worked. Of the $1,500, $600 was earned during the previous accounting period and $900 was earned during the present accounting period. The entry is recorded in the cash payments journal. The Salaries Payable account is debited for the $600. This decreases the liability for salaries incurred during the previous accounting period. The Salaries Expense account is debited for $900 to reflect the amount of salaries expense for the present accounting period. The Cash account is credited for $1,500.

Cash			*101*	*Salaries Payable*			*226*	*Salaries Expense*			*518*
		19X8		*19X8*		*19X7*		*19X8*			
		Jan. 4	*1,500*	*Jan. 4*	*600*	*Dec. 31*	*600*	*Jan. 4*	*900*		

Accounting for Accrued Expenses

Adjusting entries are needed for accrued expenses for the following reasons.

- To report all expenses incurred during the accounting period so that the correct net income will appear on the income statement.
- To report all liabilities on the balance sheet.
- To report the correct owner's equity on the balance sheet.

To record an accrued expense, debit the expense account to decrease the owner's equity for the current accounting period and credit the liability account to increase the liabilities.

Entry to Pay Accrued Liability
Debit: Liability account
Debit: Expense account
Credit: Cash

The entry to record the payment of an accrued expense involves debiting the liability account for the amount recorded as accrued in the previous accounting period. An expense account is also debited for the amount of the expense incurred during the current accounting period. Finally, the Cash account is credited for the total amount paid.

Exercise B on page 578 may be completed at this point.

Accrued Expenses on the Worksheet

When are accrued expenses recorded? As you have seen, the entries to record the accrued expenses for an accounting period are made as adjustments at the end of the period. At that time, the amounts of the accrued expenses are calculated and entered in the Adjustments section of the worksheet.

The Trial Balance section of the worksheet shows Interest Expense of $500 and Salaries Expense of $29,000 paid during the accounting period. The Interest Expense of $500 does not include the interest of $240 accrued from November 1 through December 31 on the $12,000 note due January 30, 19X8. The Salaries Expense of $29,000 does not include the $600 for the salaries accrued on December 29 and 30.

The adjustments to record the accrued expenses require debits to the expense accounts and credits to the liability accounts. The adjustments are shown as (*h*) and (*i*) on the worksheet illustrated on the next page.

Adjusting Entry for Accrued Expense
Debit: Expense account
Credit: Liability account

Accrued Interest Expense The amount of interest expense paid during the accounting period is $500. This is shown on the Trial Balance section of the worksheet. The $240 of interest that accrued from November 1 through December 31 must be added to this amount.

Star Computer Company
Worksheet
For the Year Ended December 31, 19X7

	ACCOUNT TITLE	ACCT. NO.	TRIAL BALANCE		ADJUSTMENTS		ADJUSTED TRIAL BALANCE		INCOME STATEMENT		BALANCE SHEET		
			DEBIT	CREDIT	DEBIT	CREDIT	DEBIT	CREDIT	DEBIT	CREDIT	DEBIT	CREDIT	
26	*Interest Payable*	*203*				*(h) 240*		*240*				*240*	26
27	*Salaries Payable*	*226*				*(i) 600*		*600*				*600*	27
30	*Salaries Expense*	*518*	*29,000*		*(i) 600*		*29,600*		*29,600*				30
33	*Interest Expense*	*521*	*500*		*(h) 240*		*740*		*740*				33

Interest Expense

Interest Paid	$500
Accrued Interest	+240
Total Interest Expense	$740

Therefore, the adjustment includes a debit to the Interest Expense account for $240 and a credit to the liability account Interest Payable to show the $240 that has not yet been paid.

The Adjusted Trial Balance section shows the actual amount of interest expense for the accounting period as $740 ($500 interest paid plus $240 interest accrued). This amount is then extended to the Income Statement section. The Adjusted Trial Balance section also shows Interest Payable of $240. Since this account is a liability, it is carried to the Balance Sheet section of the worksheet.

Salaries Expense

Salaries Paid	$29,000
Accrued Salaries	+600
Total Salaries Expense	$29,600

■ Accrued Salaries Expense The Trial Balance section shows that the amount of salaries paid during the accounting period was $29,000. The $600 of accrued salaries for December 29 and 30 must be added to this amount. Therefore, the adjustment includes a debit to the Salaries Expense account for $600 and a credit to the Salaries Payable account to show the $600 has not yet been paid.

The Adjusted Trial Balance section shows the Salaries Expense balance as $29,600. This represents the entire Salaries Expense for the accounting period ($29,000 paid during the period plus $600 accrued). The $29,600 is extended from the Adjusted Trial Balance section to the Income Statement section of the worksheet. The Adjusted Trial Balance section also shows the Salaries Payable account has a balance of $600. This represents the amount of salaries incurred but not yet paid during the accounting period. The Salaries Payable amount will be transferred to the Balance Sheet section with the other liabilities.

Accrued Expenses on the Financial Statements

Accrued expenses are reported on the income statement. Salaries Expense appears in the Operating Expenses section. However, Interest Expense does not appear in the Operating Expenses section because it is not incurred in the day-to-day operations of the business. As a result,

Interest Expense is reported in the Other Expenses section of the income statement.

If the accrued expenses are to be paid within a year, the liability accounts are listed in the Current Liabilities section of the balance sheet. However, if the accrued expenses are not due within a year, the liability accounts are listed in the Long-Term Liabilities section.

Star Computer Company
Income Statement
For the Year Ended December 31, 19X7

Revenue From Sales:				
Gross Profit on Sales ...			60,000	00
Operating Expenses:				
Salaries Expense	29,600	00		
Total Operating Expenses			42,000	00
Other Expenses:				
Interest Expense	740	00		

Star Computer Company
Balance Sheet
December 31, 19X7

Liabilities				
Current Liabilities:				
Notes Payable	12,000	00		
Interest Payable	240	00		
Accounts Payable	8,200	00		
Salaries Payable	600	00		
Total Curr. Liab. ..			21,040	00
Long-Term Liabilities:				
Mortgage Payable			20,000	00
Total Liabilities ..			41,040	00

■ Accrued Expenses in Closing the Ledger

The adjusting entries to record the accrued expenses are journalized along with the other adjustments in the general journal. The expense accounts (Interest Expense and Salaries Expense) are closed to the Income Summary account along with the other expense accounts.

The liability accounts (Interest Payable and Salaries Payable) are not closed because they are permanent accounts. The balances of these two accounts will appear on the postclosing trial balance and will remain open for the next accounting period, until the liabilities are paid.

Exercise C on page 578 may be completed at this point.

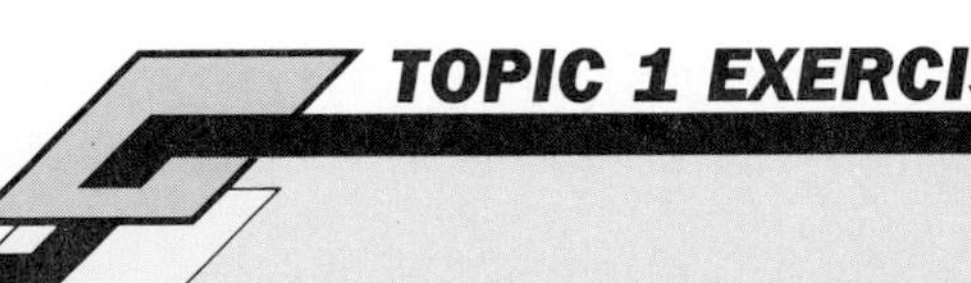

TOPIC 1 EXERCISES

EXERCISE A. Answer the following questions about accrued interest. Refer to the text and illustrations on pages 570 to 574.

1. Which of the two procedures to process financial data is preferred from an accounting point of view?
2. Under which basis of accounting are expenses recorded only in the accounting period in which cash is paid?
3. Under which basis of accounting are expenses recorded in the accounting period in which they are incurred, whether paid or not?

4. Why is Interest Expense debited for $240?

5. What account is credited for $240? Why?

6. What is the adjusting entry to record accrued interest?

7. What is the relationship between the entry for Interest Payable on January 30 in the cash payments journal and the adjusting entry for Interest Payable on December 31 in the general journal?

8. What is the relationship between the entry for the Interest Expense account on January 30 in the cash payments journal and the adjusting entry for the Interest Expense account on December 31 in the general journal?

EXERCISE B. Answer the following questions about accrued salaries. Refer to the text and illustrations on pages 574 to 575.

1. Why is Salaries Expense debited for $600?

2. Which account is credited for $600? Why?

3. What adjusting entry is made to record the accrued salaries?

4. Why is Salaries Payable debited for $600 on January 4?

5. Why is Salaries Expense debited for $900 on January 4?

EXERCISE C. Answer the following questions about accrued expenses on the worksheet and financial statements. Refer to the text and illustrations on pages 575 to 577.

1. What does the $500 balance in Interest Expense in the Trial Balance section represent?

2. What does the $240 debit in Interest Expense in the Adjustments section represent?

3. What does the $29,000 balance in Salaries Expense in the Trial Balance section represent?

4. What does the $600 debit to Salaries Expense in the Adjustments section represent?

5. To which section of the worksheet is the balance of Interest Payable transferred after the Adjusted Trial Balance section is completed?

6. To which section of the worksheet is the balance of Interest Expense transferred after the Adjusted Trial Balance section is completed?

7. In which section of the income statement is Interest Expense reported? Why?

8. In which section of the income statement is Salaries Expense reported? Why?

9. When will the Interest Payable account not appear in the Current Liabilities section of the Balance Sheet? Why?

TOPIC 1 PROBLEMS

TOPIC PROBLEM 1. Perform the following activities for Judy's Restaurant.

a. Open general ledger accounts and record the September 1 balances as follows: Notes Payable, $9,000; Interest Payable; Income Summary; and Interest Expense.

b. Record the adjusting entry in the general journal for accrued interest expense of $90 on September 30. Post the entry to the ledger.

c. Record the closing entry for Interest Expense on September 30. Post the entry to the ledger.

d. Record the following transaction in the cash payments journal: Issued Check 210 for $9,135 on October 15 to pay the $9,000 note payable dated September 1 plus $135 interest. Post the debit entries to the ledger.

TOPIC PROBLEM 2. Parts of the trial balance prepared for the Boyle Corporation on June 30 of the current accounting period are shown at the right.

a. Enter this data on a worksheet for the year ended June 30.

b. Make the adjustments for accrued interest of $60 on notes payable and accrued salaries of $1,450.

c. Extend all amounts to the proper columns of the Income Statement section or the Balance Sheet section of the worksheet.

d. Record the adjusting entries in the general journal.

Interest Payable	203		— 00
Salaries Payable	226		— 00
Purchases	501	51,750 00	
Purchases Returns and Allowances	502		925 00
Interest Expense	525	140 00	
Salaries Expense	527	7,230 00	

TOPIC PROBLEM 3. The Salaries Expense account below appeared in the general ledger of the Mini Service Station on April 30 of the current accounting period.

Salaries Expense — Account No. 527

DATE		EXPLANATION	POST. REF.	DEBIT	CREDIT	BALANCE DEBIT	BALANCE CREDIT
19— Apr.	7		CP18	650 00		650 00	
	14		CP18	700 00		1,350 00	
	21		CP19	700 00		2,050 00	
	28		CP19	700 00		2,750 00	

a. Open general ledger accounts for Salaries Payable, Income Summary, and Salaries Expense. (Include the entries just given.)

b. Record the adjusting entry in the general journal for accrued salaries of $460 on April 30. Post the entry to the ledger.

c. Record the closing entry for Salaries Expense on April 30. Post the entry to the ledger.

d. Record the following payment in the cash payments journal: Check 862 for $745 was issued on May 4 to pay the total salaries. Post the debit entries to the ledger.

TOPIC 2

Accrued Revenue and Assets

Are all revenue transactions recorded during the accounting period in which they are earned? Most revenue items, such as sales, are recorded during the accounting period in which they are earned. However, some revenue items may be earned during one accounting period but not recorded during the period. This is because the revenue will not be received until a future accounting period.

How and when to record revenue earned in one accounting period but received in a future accounting period are discussed in this topic.

Accrued Revenue

A revenue item earned during the current accounting period but not received until a future accounting period is known as **accrued reve-**

nue. One example of accrued revenue is the interest that accumulates on a note receivable. The interest is revenue to the payee (receiver) of the note and should be recorded as revenue for the accounting period in which it is earned.

When a note is received and due in the same accounting period, the interest revenue is recorded when the payee receives the cash for the note plus the interest. If the note is received in one accounting period, but is not due to be paid until a future accounting period, an adjusting entry must be made at the end of the current accounting period. This is done to show the interest earned but not yet received.

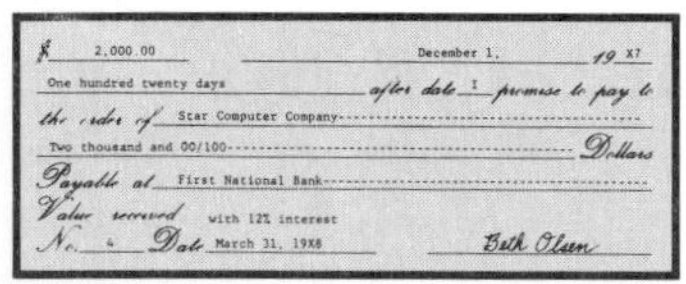

$ 2,000.00   December 1, 19 X7
One hundred twenty days after date I promise to pay to
the order of Star Computer Company
Two thousand and 00/100 Dollars
Payable at First National Bank
Value received with 12% interest
No. 4 Date March 31, 19X8   Beth Olsen

Accrued Interest Revenue On December 1, 19X7, Beth Olsen gives the Star Computer Company a 120-day, 12 percent note for $2,000 in payment of her account. When the Star Computer Company receives the note it records the transaction in the general journal in the following manner.

Notes Receivable 113	
19X7 Dec. 1 J30 2,000	

Date of Note		Due Date
Dec. 1	Dec. 31	Mar. 31
19X7	19X8	

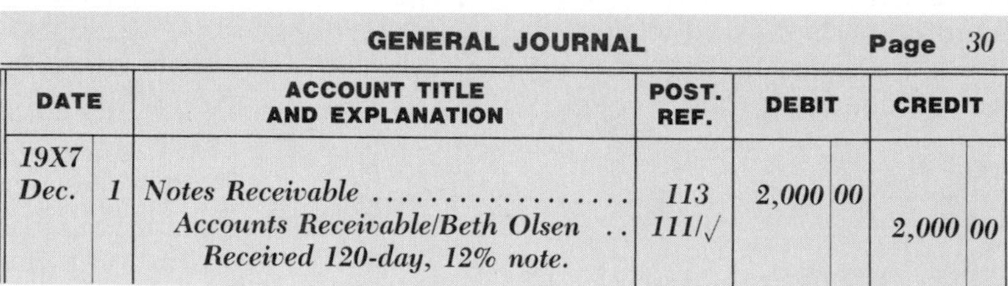

GENERAL JOURNAL   **Page** *30*

DATE		ACCOUNT TITLE AND EXPLANATION	POST. REF.	DEBIT		CREDIT	
19X7							
Dec.	*1*	*Notes Receivable*	*113*	*2,000*	*00*		
		Accounts Receivable/Beth Olsen	*111/√*			*2,000*	*00*
		Received 120-day, 12% note.					

The note receivable is recorded at its face value of $2,000 as a debit to the Notes Receivable account until it is due. The interest on the note is earned day by day but is not recorded each day. No interest will be received until the note is due. Thus, on March 31, 19X8, when the note is due, the Star Computer Company will receive $2,080 ($2,000 to pay the note and $80 to pay the interest) from Beth Olsen (the maker of the note). In this case, the interest has been earned in two accounting periods because the Star Computer Company has an accounting period that ends on December 31. Therefore, an adjusting entry must be made on December 31 to record the accrued interest revenue for 19X7.

December	31
	−1
	30 days
January	31 days
February	28 days
March (due)	31 days
	120 days

The amount of interest that has accrued on the $2,000 note receivable during the last 30 days of 19X7 is $20. If the interest revenue is not recorded in the 19X7 accounting period, both the net income and the owner's equity will be understated. In the next accounting period, the net income will be overstated because all the interest received on the note will be recorded as revenue for 19X8. An adjusting entry must be made in order to have the accrued revenue recorded in the accounting period in which it is earned.

12% interest on $2,000 for 30 days = $20

Adjusting Interest Revenue The amount of interest accrued on the $2,000 note receivable during 19X7 is $20. The Interest Revenue account must be credited for $20 in order to report all the interest earned during the period. Since none of the interest will be received until the note is due on March 31, 19X8, the $20 is a claim against the maker of the note until the maker pays the interest. In other words, Beth Olsen owes Star Computer Company $20 interest as of December 31, 19X7. The $20 owed to the company is considered a receivable, which is an asset.

A separate asset account, called Interest Receivable, is used to record the interest accrued on notes receivable. Because of its relationship with the Notes Receivable account, Interest Receivable is listed immediately after Notes Receivable in the Current Assets section of the Star Computer Company's chart of accounts. The Interest Receivable account is debited for $20 to show the increase in assets. The revenue account Interest Revenue is credited for $20 to show the increase in revenue during the accounting period.

STAR COMPUTER COMPANY CHART OF ACCOUNTS

Current Assets
113 Notes Receivable
114 Interest Receivable

Other Revenue
491 Interest Revenue

DECEMBER 31, 19X7: THE STAR COMPUTER COMPANY RECORDS INTEREST REVENUE OF $20 ACCRUED FOR 30 DAYS ON A NOTE RECEIVABLE.

What Happens	Accounting Rule	Accounting Entry
The asset *Interest Receivable* increases by $20.	To increase an asset, debit the account.	Debit: Interest Receivable, $20.
The revenue from interest increases owner's equity by $20.	To increase owner's equity, credit the account.	Credit: Interest Revenue, $20.

Notes Receivable 113

Debit		Credit	
19X7 Dec. 1	2,000		

Interest Receivable 114

Debit		Credit	
19X7 Dec. 31	20		

Interest Revenue 491

Debit		Credit	
		19X7 Dec. 31	20

After the adjusting entry is posted, the three accounts related to notes receivable show the following amounts. The Notes Receivable account shows the original amount of the note ($2,000). The Interest Receivable account shows the amount of the interest earned but not yet received ($20). The Interest Revenue account shows the amount of the interest earned during the current accounting period ($20).

The balance of the Notes Receivable account is the total amount to be received from the notes.

The balance of the Interest Receivable account is the total amount of interest earned but not yet received.

The balance of the Interest Revenue account is the total amount of revenue earned from interest.

When the closing entries are recorded, Interest Revenue is closed into the Income Summary account together with the other revenue accounts. Interest Receivable is a permanent account and remains open until the accrued interest has been received.

Receiving the Interest When the note comes due on March 31, 19X8, the Star Computer Company receives $2,080 in cash from Beth Olsen ($2,000 for the original amount of the note receivable and $80 for the interest from December 1 through March 31). Of the total interest received ($80), $20 has been recorded as revenue for the previous accounting period (19X7).

Dec. 1 to Dec. 31		Jan. 1 to Mar. 31		
Previous Period	+	Present Period	=	Total Interest
$20 Interest Receivable	+	$60 Interest Revenue	=	$80

The remainder of the interest ($60) is revenue for the present accounting period (19X8). Therefore, the Interest Revenue account must be credited for the $60 earned during the present accounting period. The Interest Receivable account must also be credited for $20. This must be done to decrease the asset that was recorded in the previous accounting period.

MARCH 31, 19X8: THE STAR COMPUTER COMPANY RECEIVES $2,080 IN CASH FROM BETH OLSEN FOR A NOTE RECEIVABLE OF $2,000 AND INTEREST OF $80.

What Happens	Accounting Rule	Accounting Entry
The asset *Cash* increases by $2,080.	To increase an asset, debit the account.	Debit: Cash, $2,080.
The asset *Notes Receivable* decreases by $2,000.	To decrease an asset, credit the account.	Credit: Notes Receivable, $2,000.
The asset *Interest Receivable* decreases by $20.	To decrease an asset, credit the account.	Credit: Interest Receivable, $20.
The revenue from interest increases owner's equity by $60.	To increase owner's equity, credit the account.	Credit: Interest Revenue, $60.

Notes Receivable 113

Debit		Credit	
19X7 Dec. 1	2,000	19X8 Mar. 31	2,000

Interest Receivable 114

Debit		Credit	
19X7 Dec. 31	20	19X8 Mar. 31	20

Interest Revenue 491

Debit		Credit	
		19X8 Mar. 31	60

Cash 101

Debit		Credit	
19X8 Mar. 31	2,080		

The entry to record the receipt of $2,080 by the Star Computer Company is recorded in the cash receipts journal. Three lines are required to record this transaction, as shown below.

CASH RECEIPTS JOURNAL **Page** *67*

DATE		ACCOUNT CREDITED	EXPLANATION	POST. REF.	GENERAL LEDGER CREDIT	ACCOUNTS RECEIVABLE CREDIT	SALES DISCOUNT DEBIT	NET CASH DEBIT
19X8								
Mar.	*31*	*Notes Receivable*	*Beth Olsen, Dec. 1* .	*113*	*2,000 00*			*2,080 00*
		Interest Receivable	*Interest for 30 days* .	*114*	*20 00*			
		Interest Revenue	*Interest for 90 days* .	*491*	*60 00*			

After the entry is posted, the balance of the Notes Receivable account is zero because the cash has been received for the note. The Interest Receivable account will also show a zero balance because the $20 interest accrued in 19X7 has been received. The Interest Revenue account shows a credit balance of $60, which is the interest revenue earned during the present accounting period.

Exercise D on page 587 may be completed at this point.

Deferred Revenue

Do businesses ever receive payment in advance? Yes, sometimes businesses receive payments for goods or services before the goods are delivered or the services are performed. Part of the payment may be revenue for the current accounting period, and part may represent revenue for a future accounting period.

Deferred revenue is first recorded as a liability.

Revenue received before it is earned is known as **deferred revenue** (sometimes referred to as *unearned revenue*). The term *deferred revenue* is used because recording the revenue must be deferred (postponed) until it is earned. Until then, the amount received is shown in the accounting records as a liability. It is shown as a liability because cash has been received and the business is now "liable" to provide the product or service or to refund the cash to the customer.

The following are examples of deferred revenue.

- A tenant pays rent in advance for December, January, and February. If the property owner has an annual accounting period that ends on December 31, only one month of the rent received will be earned during the present accounting period. The other two months' rent will be revenue for the next accounting period.
- A magazine publisher receives payment for a subscription in advance. This is deferred revenue until the magazines are sent to the subscriber.
- An insurance company requires the policyholder to pay the premium on a policy months or years in advance. The premiums are considered deferred revenue until they are actually earned.

Recording Deferred Revenue

To see how deferred revenue is recorded, assume that the Star Computer Company permits the Taylor Display Company to install an advertising billboard on its property for two years, from July 1, 19X7 to June 30, 19X9. In return for the use of the land, the Taylor Display Company agrees to pay $1,200 rent in advance for the two-year period. Since the Star Computer Company has received the money, it is obligated to rent the property to the Taylor Display Company for the entire two-year period.

Receiving Deferred Rental Revenue

When the $1,200 in cash is received for the rent, the transaction is recorded in the cash receipts journal. The Cash account is debited for $1,200. This amount covers more than one accounting period. Therefore, the rent cannot be recorded as revenue earned because the Star Computer Company has collected the rent but has not yet earned it. Since the $1,200 cannot be recorded as revenue, it must be recorded as a credit to a liability account called Unearned Rental Revenue. It is considered a liability because the Star Computer Company owes the Taylor Display Company the use of the property for two years. The entry is recorded as shown on the next page.

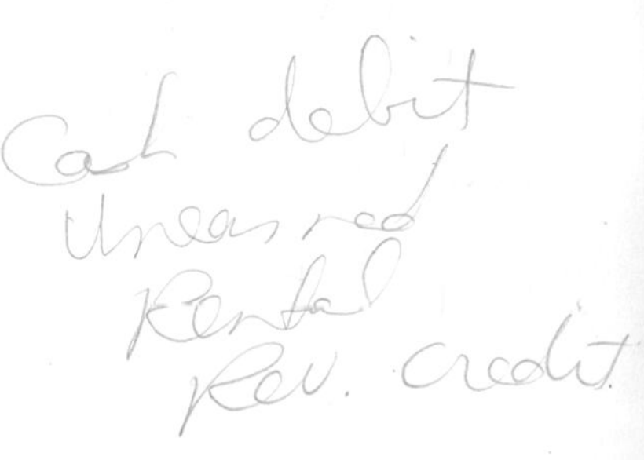

DATE		ACCOUNT CREDITED	EXPLANATION	POST. REF.	GENERAL LEDGER CREDIT		ACCOUNTS RECEIVABLE CREDIT		SALES DISCOUNT DEBIT		NET CASH DEBIT	
19X7												
July	1	Unearned Rental Rev.	Taylor Display Co., 2 yrs.' rent	227	1,200	00					1,200	00

CASH RECEIPTS JOURNAL — Page 65

Unearned Rental Revenue 227

	19X7 July 1 CR65 1,200

At the end of the accounting period on December 31, 19X7, an adjusting entry must be recorded to transfer the amount of revenue earned in 19X7 from the liability account to a revenue account. If this adjustment is not made, the liabilities will be overstated and the revenue will be understated for the accounting period. As a result, the owner's equity will also be understated.

■ **Adjusting Deferred Rental Revenue** At the end of the accounting period on December 31, 19X7, the Star Computer Company has earned six months' rent (July through December) from the Taylor Display Company. Since the rent for two years is $1,200, the amount earned for one month is $50 ($1,200 ÷ 24 months). Therefore, the revenue earned for 6 months is $300 ($50 × 6).

When deferred revenue is earned, it is transferred from a liability account to a revenue account.

The adjusting entry to transfer the revenue earned ($300) from the liability account to the revenue account on December 31, 19X7, is as follows. The liability account Unearned Rental Revenue is debited because the $300 has been earned during 19X7. A revenue account called Rental Revenue is credited because $300 in revenue has been earned. Since the revenue from the rental of the property is not connected directly with the operations of the business, rental revenue is classified as Other Revenue on the income statement. The Rental Revenue account is assigned number 492 in the Star Computer Company's chart of accounts.

STAR COMPUTER COMPANY CHART OF ACCOUNTS

Current Liabilities
227 Unearned Rental Revenue

Other Revenue
492 Rental Revenue

Unearned Rental Revenue = liability

DECEMBER 31, 19X7: THE STAR COMPUTER COMPANY RECORDS $300 OF DEFERRED RENTAL REVENUE AS RENT EARNED FOR SIX MONTHS.

What Happens	Accounting Rule	Accounting Entry
The liability *Unearned Rental Revenue* decreases by $300.	To decrease a liability, debit the account.	Debit: Unearned Rental Revenue, $300.
The revenue from rent increases owner's equity by $300.	To increase owner's equity, credit the account.	Credit: Rental Revenue, $300.

Unearned Rental Revenue 227

19X7 Dec. 31 **300**	*19X7 July 1* 1,200 900

Rental Revenue 492

	19X7 Dec. 31 **300**

After the adjusting entry is posted, the two accounts show the following balances. The Unearned Rental Revenue account shows the amount of deferred revenue ($900) not yet earned. The Rental Revenue account shows the amount of revenue earned during the current accounting period ($300).

When the closing entries are recorded, Rental Revenue is closed into the Income Summary account. Unearned Rental Revenue, liability account, is not closed at the end of the accounting period.

Accrued and Deferred Revenue on the Worksheet

The adjustments to record the amounts of the accrued revenue and deferred revenue earned during the accounting period are computed and entered in the Adjustments section of the worksheet. The adjustment to record accrued interest revenue is identified as adjustment (*j*), and the adjustment to record deferred rental revenue is identified as adjustment (*k*).

Star Computer Company
Worksheet
For the Year Ended December 31, 19X7

	ACCOUNT TITLE	ACCT. NO.	TRIAL BALANCE		ADJUSTMENTS		ADJUSTED TRIAL BALANCE		INCOME STATEMENT		BALANCE SHEET		
			DEBIT	CREDIT	DEBIT	CREDIT	DEBIT	CREDIT	DEBIT	CREDIT	DEBIT	CREDIT	
15	*Interest Receivable*	*114*			*(j) 20*		*20*				*20*		15
19	*Unearned Rental Revenue*	*227*		*1,200*	*(k) 300*			*900*				*900*	19
26	*Interest Revenue*	*491*		*56*		*(j) 20*		*76*		*76*			26
27	*Rental Revenue*	*492*				*(k) 300*		*300*		*300*			27

NOTE: The cents columns have been omitted in order to show the entire worksheet.

Accrued Revenue—Interest Revenue

The amount of interest revenue received during the accounting period is shown in the Trial Balance section of the worksheet as $56. In the Adjustments section, this amount is added to the accrued interest of $20 earned on the note receivable from Beth Olsen. As a result, the Adjusted Trial Balance section shows the actual amount of Interest Revenue earned for the accounting period as $76 ($56 interest received during the accounting period plus $20 interest accrued). The revenue amount ($76) is transferred to the Income Statement section. The adjustment for accrued interest revenue contains a debit to Interest Receivable for $20; this amount is transferred to the Balance Sheet section of the worksheet.

Deferred Revenue—Rental Revenue

As shown in the Trial Balance section of the worksheet, the unearned rental revenue received during the accounting period amounted to $1,200. When the $1,200 was received, it was credited to the liability account Unearned Rental Revenue because the amount received had not been earned.

The adjustment of $300 for the revenue earned is subtracted from the amount of Unearned Rental Revenue and transferred to the Adjusted Trial Balance section. Therefore, the balance of the Unearned Rental Revenue account in the Adjusted Trial Balance section is $900 ($1,200 − $300). The $900 is then extended to the Balance Sheet section of the worksheet. The Rental Revenue accounts shows $300 as rent earned during the accounting period. This amount is extended from the Adjusted Trial Balance section to the Income Statement section of the worksheet.

Accrued and Deferred Revenue on the Financial Statements

Accrued revenue is listed in the Other Revenue section of the income statement because it is revenue not earned from the regular operations of the business.

The amounts of the revenue earned are reported on the income statement. Both Interest Revenue and Rental Revenue appear in the Other Revenue section because they are not considered as being earned from the regular operations of the business. Other Expenses is generally shown as a subtraction from Other Revenue. Thus, only one amount appears on the income statement—either Net Other Revenue or Net Other Expense.

The amount of Interest Receivable ($20) is reported as a current asset on the balance sheet because the amount will be received within a year. The amount of Unearned Rental Revenue ($900) is reported as a current liability because the major part of it will be earned within the next year.

Star Computer Company
Income Statement
For the Year Ended December 31, 19X7

Revenue From Sales:		
...		
Net Income From Operations ...		29,550 00
Other Revenue:		
Interest Revenue $ 76.00		
Rental Revenue 300.00		
Total Other Revenue	376 00	
Other Expenses:		
Interest Expense	740 00	
Net Other Expense		364 00
Net Income		29,186 00

Star Computer Company
Balance Sheet
December 31, 19X7

Assets		
Current Assets:		
...		
Interest Receivable	20 00	
...		
Liabilities		
Current Liabilities:		
...		
Unearned Rental Revenue	900 00	

Accrued and Deferred Revenue in Closing the Ledger

The adjusting entries for accrued and deferred revenue are journalized with other adjustments in the general journal. The closing entries for accrued and deferred revenue are journalized with the other closing entries in the general journal.

Revenue accounts are closed into the Income Summary account.

The closing entries transfer the balances of the Interest Revenue account ($76) and the Rental Revenue account ($300) into the Income Summary account. The revenue accounts then have zero balances. The Interest Receivable account has a debit balance of $20 and will appear on the postclosing trial balance since it is a permanent account. The Unearned Rental Revenue account has a credit balance of $900 and will also appear on the postclosing trial balance because it is also a permanent account. Since the revenue accounts have been closed for the period, they do not appear on the postclosing trial balance.

Exercise E on this page may be completed at this point.

TOPIC 2 EXERCISES

EXERCISE D. Answer the following questions about accrued revenue and accrued assets. Refer to the text and illustrations on pages 579 to 582.

1. What adjusting entry is made on December 31?
2. Why is the adjustment made on December 31?
3. What is the effect of the December 31 entry on current assets? On owner's equity?
4. What entry is made on March 31?
5. Why is the entry recorded on March 31?
6. What is the effect of the March 31 entry on receivables? On cash?
7. What amount of the $80 interest is earned in 19X7? What amount of the interest is earned in 19X8?
8. What would be the effect on net income for 19X7 and 19X8 if $80 were recorded as interest earned only in 19X8?

EXERCISE E. Answer the following questions about deferred revenue. Refer to the text and illustrations on pages 583 to 587.

1. Has the $1,200 credited to the Unearned Rental Revenue account in the Trial Balance section of the worksheet already been received?
2. Why is the balance of Unearned Rental Revenue extended to the Balance Sheet section of the worksheet?
3. What adjusting entry is made to record earned rental revenue?
4. What amount of the $1,200 rental revenue is earned in 19X7?
5. What is the relationship between the July 1 entry in the cash receipts journal for Unearned Rental Revenue and the $1,200 amount for that account in the Trial Balance section of the worksheet?
6. In which section of the income statement would Interest Revenue or Rental Revenue be reported? Why?
7. Is the Unearned Rental Revenue account closed at the end of the accounting period? Why?
8. In which section of the balance sheet is Unearned Rental Revenue reported? Why?

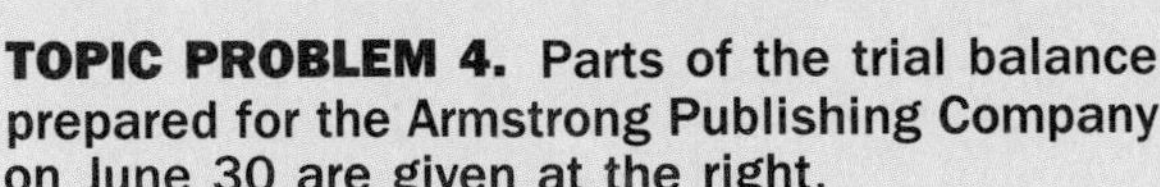

TOPIC 2 PROBLEMS

TOPIC PROBLEM 4. Parts of the trial balance prepared for the Armstrong Publishing Company on June 30 are given at the right.

a. Enter this data on a worksheet for the year ended June 30.

b. Make the adjustments for accrued interest of $40 on notes receivable and $2,200 of subscription revenue that was previously recorded as unearned but is now earned.

c. Extend all amounts to the proper columns of the Income Statement section or the Balance Sheet section of the worksheet.

Notes Receivable	*111*	3,000 00	
Interest Receivable	*112*		
Accounts Payable	*211*		2,340 00
Unearned Subscription Revenue	*215*		15,110 00
Subscription Revenue	*401*		24,000 00
Interest Revenue	*491*		
Miscellaneous Expense	*526*	248 00	

d. Record the adjusting entries in the general journal.

TOPIC PROBLEM 5. Western State College collects tuition from its students on a quarterly basis: in September, December, March, and June. On September 21 the Unearned Tuition Revenue account in the general ledger contained the information shown below.

a. Open general ledger accounts for Cash, Unearned Tuition Revenue (include the entries shown here), Income Summary, and Tuition Revenue. Enter the balance of $12,800 in the Cash account as of September 1.

b. On September 28, $12,300 in cash was received from tuition payments. Record this transaction in a four-column cash receipts journal.

c. Tuition earned for the period ended September 30 was $30,100. Record the adjusting entry for this deferred revenue item in the general journal.

d. Post the entries to the ledger.

e. Record and post the closing entry for Tuition Revenue on September 30.

f. Tuition earned for the period ended October 31 is $30,100. Record and post the adjusting entry on October 31.

g. Record and post the closing entry for Tuition Revenue on October 31.

h. Tuition earned for the period ended November 30 is $30,100. Record and post the adjusting entry on November 30.

i. Record and post the closing entry for Tuition Revenue on November 30.

Unearned Tuition Revenue **Account No.** *207*

DATE		EXPLANATION	POST. REF.	DEBIT	CREDIT	BALANCE DEBIT	BALANCE CREDIT
19—							
Sept.	*1*	*Balance*	—				*45,000 00*
	7		*CR42*		*10,000 00*		*55,000 00*
	14		*CR42*		*12,000 00*		*67,000 00*
	21		*CR43*		*11,000 00*		*78,000 00*

CHAPTER 16 REVIEW

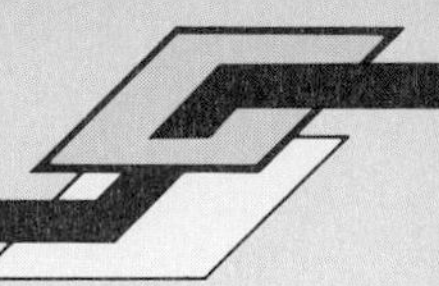

CHAPTER SUMMARY

Businesses use one of two procedures to process financial data: the cash basis of accounting or the accrual basis of accounting. Under the cash basis of accounting, revenues and expenses are recorded only when cash is received or paid. Under the accrual basis of accounting, revenue is recorded when it is earned, regardless of when cash is received. Expenses are recorded in the accounting period in which they are incurred, regardless of when cash is paid.

Under the accrual basis of accounting, transactions involving revenue and expenses that affect more than one accounting period must be handled in specific ways. Expenses that are incurred but not paid during an accounting period must be recorded through an adjusting entry for the period in which they are incurred. These expenses are known as accrued expenses. Revenue that is earned before it is received, which is known as accrued revenue, also must be recorded through an adjusting entry in the period in which it is earned. Revenue that is received before it is earned, which is called deferred revenue, must be reported as a liability until it is earned.

THE LANGUAGE OF BUSINESS

Here are some terms that make up the language of business. Do you know the meaning of each?

cash basis of accounting
accrual basis of accounting
accrued expense
face value
principal
accrued revenue
deferred revenue

REVIEW QUESTIONS

1. What is the primary difference between the cash basis of accounting and the accrual basis of accounting?
2. What type of account is Interest Payable? On which financial statement does it appear?
3. What is the difference between prepaid expenses and accrued expenses?
4. What is the difference between accrued revenue and deferred revenue?
5. In what respect are accrued expenses like accrued revenue? Prepaid expenses like deferred revenue?
6. How do the adjusting entries for accrued expenses relate to the matching principle?

7. Why is a deferred revenue item credited to a liability account rather than to a revenue account?

8. If no adjustment is made to record the accrued expenses for the current accounting period, what effect does this have on the net income? On the balance sheet accounts?

9. If no entry is made to adjust the deferred revenue for the current accounting period, what effect does this have on the net income? On the balance sheet accounts?

10. If no adjustment is made to record the accrued revenue for the current accounting period, what effect does this have on the net income? On the balance sheet accounts?

CHAPTER PROBLEMS

Problems for Chapter 16 are given below. Write your answers to the problems on a separate sheet of paper unless you are using the workbook for this textbook. If you are using the workbook, do the problems in the space provided there.

CHAPTER PROBLEM 16-1. From the following information, record the adjusting entries in the general journal of Baker Enterprises for the year ended December 31.

a. *Merchandise Inventory.* The trial balance shows a debit balance of $24,255 for Merchandise Inventory. An actual count on December 31 showed merchandise inventory costing $21,145 on hand.

b. *Prepaid Expenses.* The trial balance shows a debit balance of $210 for Prepaid Insurance. The unexpired insurance on December 31 is $70.

c. *Uncollectible Accounts.* The estimated uncollectible accounts expense is $220. Baker Enterprises uses the percentage of net sales method to estimate uncollectible losses.

d. *Depreciation.* The estimated depreciation is $4,000 per year on a building and $1,100 per year on a truck.

e. *Accrued Revenue.* The accrued revenue from interest is $30.

f. *Accrued Expense.* The accrued expense for salaries is $2,100.

g. *Deferred Revenue.* The trial balance shows a credit balance of $1,800 for Unearned Rental Revenue. During the current accounting period, $600 of this rent has been earned.

CHAPTER PROBLEM 16-2. The trial balance for the Stern Business School for December 31 is shown on the next page. From the information provided enter the adjustments on the worksheet. Once the adjustments are recorded, complete the remainder of the worksheet.

	ACCOUNT TITLE	ACCT. NO.	TRIAL BALANCE	
			DEBIT	CREDIT
1	*Cash*	*101*	*18,050*	
2	*Notes Receivable*	*111*	*4,000*	
3	*Interest Receivable*	*112*		
4	*Accounts Receivable*	*121*	*12,100*	
5	*Allowance for Doubtful Accounts*	*122*		*416*
6	*Prepaid Insurance*	*131*	*600*	
7	*Supplies*	*132*	*450*	
8	*Equipment*	*141*	*16,700*	
9	*Accumulated Depreciation—Equipment*	*142*		*6,680*
10	*Notes Payable*	*201*		*1,000*
11	*Interest Payable*	*202*		
12	*Accounts Payable*	*211*		*705*
13	*Federal Income Taxes Payable*	*221*		*210*
14	*FICA Taxes Payable*	*222*		*160*
15	*Salaries Payable*	*223*		—
16	*Unearned Tuition Revenue*	*231*		*52,410*
17	*David Stern, Capital*	*301*		*28,526*
18	*David Stern, Drawing*	*302*	*5,000*	
19	*Tuition Revenue*	*401*		—
20	*Interest Revenue*	*491*		*200*
21	*Depreciation Expense—Equipment*	*502*	—	
22	*Insurance Expense*	*503*	—	
23	*Interest Expense*	*504*	*80*	
24	*Miscellaneous Expense*	*505*	*170*	
25	*Payroll Taxes Expense*	*506*	*657*	
26	*Rent Expense*	*507*	*6,000*	
27	*Salaries Expense*	*508*	*26,500*	
28	*Supplies Expense*	*509*	—	
29	*Uncollectible Accounts Expense*	*510*	—	
30			*90,307*	*90,307*

a. *Supplies.* A physical inventory of supplies on December 31 shows supplies costing $295 on hand.

b. *Prepaid Insurance.* The $600 balance represents the insurance premium for a three-month period. It was paid on December 1. Therefore, one month's insurance has expired.

c. *Uncollectible Accounts.* The estimated loss from uncollectible accounts is $109.

d. *Depreciation.* The estimated depreciation on equipment is 10 percent of the original cost per year.

e. *Accrued Revenue.* The accrued revenue from interest is $100.

f. *Accrued Expense.* The accrued expense for salaries is $350.

g. *Accrued Expense.* The accrued expense for interest is $20.

h. *Deferred Revenue.* Tuition revenue earned during the accounting period is $48,760.

NOTE: Save this problem for work in Chapter Problem 16-3.

CHAPTER PROBLEM 16-3. During January, the Stern Business School had the following transactions that relate to the adjustments made in Chapter Problem 16-2. Record the transactions in the appropriate journal. When necessary, refer to the data provided in Chapter Problem 16-2.

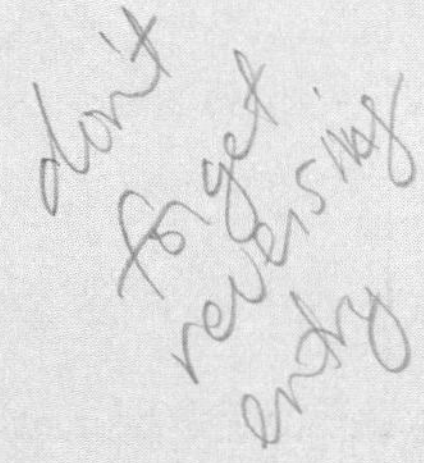

Jan. 7 Issued Check 1436 for $150 to purchase supplies.
7 Kim Bond's account for $275 was determined to be uncollectible.
8 Issued Check 1437 for $535 to pay salaries for the weekly payroll. ($350 of the salaries has been recorded as an accrued expense.)
8 Issued Check 1438 for $200 for the semiannual premium on theft insurance.
9 Issued Check 1439 for $1,965 for a new microcomputer.
11 Received $31,260 for tuition from students for the coming semester.
11 Mary Hodge's account for $75 was determined to be uncollectible.
11 Received $275 from Kim Bond, whose account was written off as uncollectible on January 7.
15 Issued Check 1440 for $1,030 to the Hudson Company in payment of a note for $1,000 plus interest. (Interest of $20 has been recorded as an accrued expense.)
15 Received $4,160 from Richard Rendell in payment of a note for $4,000 plus interest. (Interest of $100 has been recorded as accrued revenue.)

MANAGEMENT CASES

Cash Basis vs. Accrual Basis. Federal income tax regulations give the individual taxpayer the option of reporting revenue and expenses on a cash basis or on an accrual basis.

If the *cash basis* is used, the taxpayer reports as revenue only those amounts actually received and deducts as expenses only those amounts actually paid.

When the taxpayer uses the *accrual basis*, the reported revenue for the period is all revenue earned whether or not it has actually been received during the period. The taxpayer reports as expenses for the period all expenses incurred whether or not they have actually been paid during the period.

The taxpayer must be consistent from one year to the next in the method of reporting. A change cannot be made from the cash basis to the accrual basis or vice versa without the consent of the Internal Revenue Service. Furthermore, the taxpayer must report tax data in the manner in which the records are kept.

CASE 16M-1. Lisa Morton plans to start a medical practice in a small rural community. She will be the only doctor in the area and will be expected to handle all calls and treat all patients. Some patients will be unable to pay any of her fee. Others will pay only part of her fee. She expects to accumulate a large number of accounts receivable, many of which she will never collect. Dr. Morton also knows she will receive payments from her patients on an irregular basis. Some patients will pay immediately. Others will wait before paying.

Would you advise Dr. Morton to keep her accounting records on a cash or accrual basis? Why?

CASE 16M-2. The Wayne Advertising Agency specializes in preparing videotape advertisements. The agency prepares the tapes under contracts with various businesses that advertise their products on television. The standard contract provides for the agency to be paid in full upon completion and delivery of each series of tapes. Frequently, the tapes are in process for several months before they are ready and can be delivered. The accounting records for the agency have been kept on a cash basis. The tax reports have been prepared on this basis.

Do you agree with the agency's use of the cash basis? Why?

CHAPTER

17

The Combination Journal

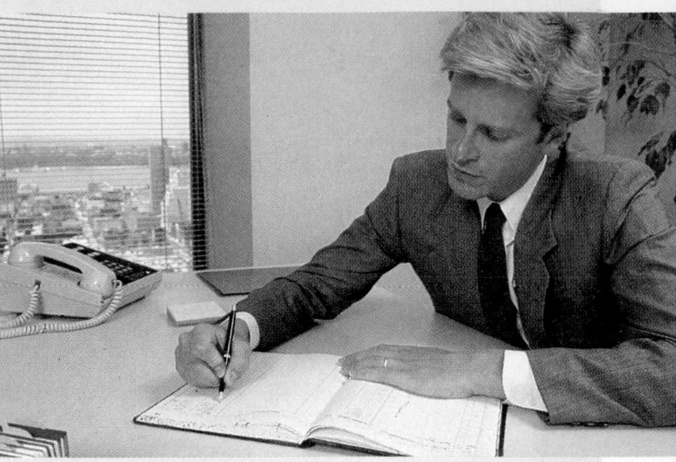

You have learned how to record transactions in various special journals. Now you will learn how to record transactions in a combination journal. The combination journal is a consolidation of the special journals and the general journal. All transactions recorded in those journals can be consolidated in one journal. The combination journal is generally used by small businesses with a limited number of accounts.

CHAPTER GOALS

After studying Chapter 17, you will be able to:

1. List the advantages and disadvantages of processing data using a combination journal.
2. Record transactions in a combination journal.
3. Prepare a proof of the combination journal.
4. Post transactions from a combination journal to the general ledger and the subsidiary ledgers.
5. Design the columns of a combination journal to meet the special needs of a business.

TOPIC 1

Using the Combination Journal

What is a combination journal? A **combination journal** is a multicolumn journal that combines the features of the general journal with the features of the special journals. The accounts that are used most frequently, such as Cash, Accounts Receivable, Accounts Payable, Sales, and Purchases, are provided individual columns in the combination journal. For accounts used less frequently, a general ledger column is provided.

■ Designing a Combination Journal

The number of columns and the choice of headings in a combination journal depend upon the needs of the business. A business needs to analyze its transactions to determine how often accounts are used when recording the transactions. For example, if a business were to grant many sales discounts, it would require a Sales Discount column in the combination journal. Another business may not offer sales discounts, but it may collect sales tax quite frequently. This business would include a Sales Tax Payable column in its combination journal. Combination journals must include general ledger columns for debits and credits to accounts for which no special columns are provided.

Combination journals are designed to meet the needs of a business.

The columns of the combination journal can be arranged to suit the individual business. In most businesses, the Cash account is used more than any other account. In the combination journal shown on pages 596 and 597, the Cash columns are at the extreme left. Other combination journals may have more money columns at the left or all money columns at the right.

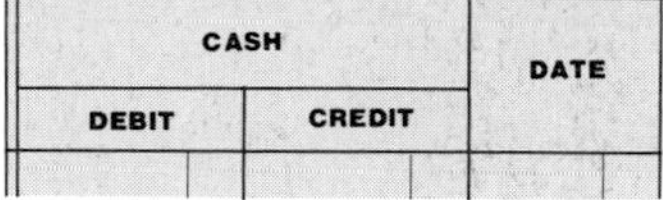

CASH		DATE
DEBIT	CREDIT	

Although any number of columns can be included, the combination journal becomes cumbersome to use if there are too many columns.

■ Advantages of the Combination Journal

The combination journal has the time-saving, space-saving, and error-reducing advantages of special journals because special money columns are used for similar transactions. The combination journal is often used by professionals such as doctors or accountants whose businesses call for only a few types of transactions. The combination journal, however, is not adequate for a service or merchandising business unless the business's transactions are limited and do not affect a great variety of accounts. If transactions are numerous or too varied, the special journals would be more efficient for a business to use.

The combination journal can be extremely useful to small businesses. However, the chances of making an error by placing an amount in the wrong column are increased because of the large number of

COMBINATION JOURNAL

	Cash Debit	Cash Credit	Date		Account Title and Explanation	Ck. No.	Post. Ref.	General Ledger Debit	General Ledger Credit
			19—						
1			April	1	Cash Balance, $4,080		—		
2	700 00			2	Sales		—		
3	121 50			3	Lucy Garcia		√		
4		490 00		4	Graham Electronics—Invoice 1120	211	√		
5				5	Tyson Co.—Invoice 421A; (4/1); 2/10, n/30		√		
6				6	B & J Co.—Invoice 140; 1/20, n/30		√		
7				8	Purch. Ret. and Allow./Tyson Co.—CM-1307		503/√		100 00
8				9	Store Equip./Thorne Office Equip.—Inv. 6111; (4/5); n/30.		134/√	85 00	
	2,000 00	1,300 00						800 00	1,210 00
30	2,000 00	1,300 00		19	Carried Forward		—	800 00	1,210 00

Special Columns

End of Page

Post. ref. numbers and check marks are entered when individual amounts are posted, and dashes for amounts not posted or not posted individually.

General Columns

It is easier to make errors in a combination journal because there are more columns than in a general or special journal.

money columns. Also, since only one person can record an entry at a time, the use of the combination journal prevents division of responsibility.

Recording Entries in the Combination Journal

Each transaction must be analyzed to determine the accounts to be debited and credited. Then the transaction is recorded by entering the debit and credit amounts in the correct money columns. Thus, the amounts are sorted according to the accounts affected.

To show how entries are recorded in a combination journal, we will now examine the April transactions of the Jensen Supply Company. The April entries are shown in the combination journal above.

Apr. 1 At the beginning of the month, a memorandum entry is made to record the cash balance. This entry is similar to the memorandum entry made in the cash receipts journal at the beginning of the month.

	Date		Account Title
	19—		
1	April	1	Cash Balance, $4,080

On line 1 of the combination journal, the memorandum entry is the first entry recorded for the month of April. The cash balance is shown in the Account Title and Explanation column. No amounts are written in any money columns. The dash (—) is placed in the Posting Reference column to show that the entry is not to be posted to the ledger.

Apr. 2 Sold merchandise for $700 in cash during the week.

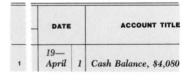

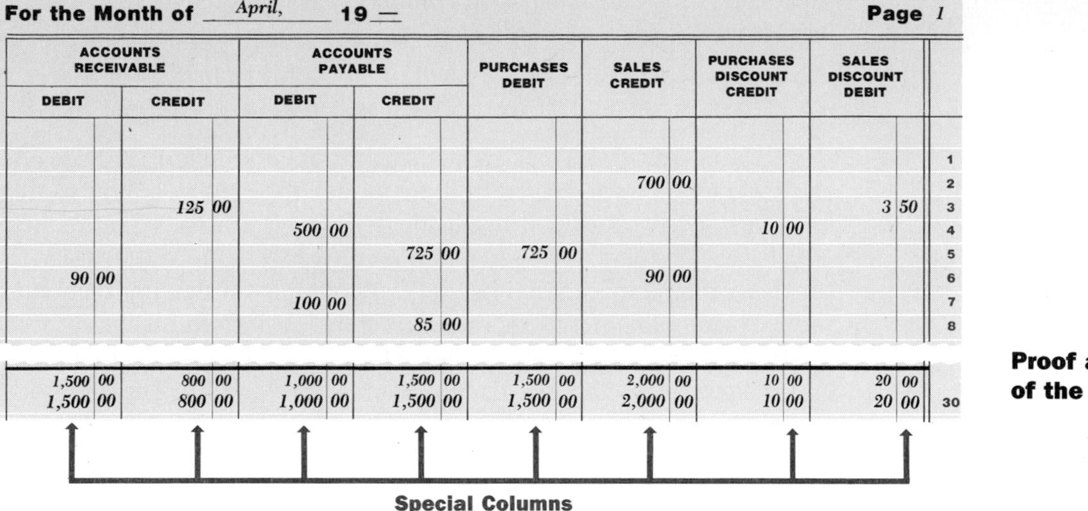

For the Month of *April,* 19 — Page *1*

Accounts Receivable Debit	Accounts Receivable Credit	Accounts Payable Debit	Accounts Payable Credit	Purchases Debit	Sales Credit	Purchases Discount Credit	Sales Discount Debit	
								1
					700 00			2
	125 00						3 50	3
		500 00				10 00		4
			725 00	725 00				5
90 00					90 00			6
		100 00						7
			85 00					8
1,500 00 1,500 00	800 00 800 00	1,000 00 1,000 00	1,500 00 1,500 00	1,500 00 1,500 00	2,000 00 2,000 00	10 00 10 00	20 00 20 00	30

Proof at the end of the page.

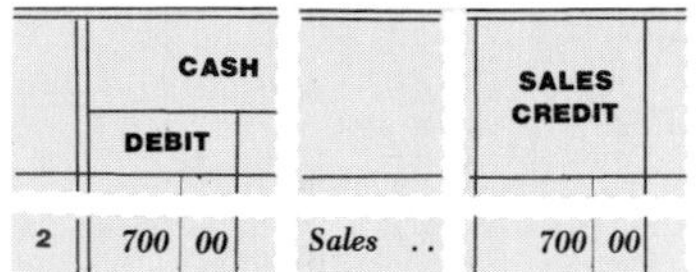

	Cash Debit		Sales Credit
2	700 00	*Sales* ..	700 00

The entry for this transaction involves a debit to the Cash account and a credit to the Sales account for $700. Special columns are provided in the combination journal for both the Cash and Sales accounts.

Notice on line 2 of the combination journal that $700 has been recorded in the Cash Debit column and in the Sales Credit column. The amounts in the Cash Debit column accumulate during the month just as in the cash receipts and cash payments journals. Unlike the cash receipts or cash payments journals, columns are provided for both debits and credits to the Cash account. At the end of the month, the totals of the Debit and Credit columns are posted to the Cash account. The total of the Sales Credit column is posted at the end of the month to the Sales account. The Sales Credit column contains all credits for sales transactions—both sales for cash and sales on credit. The word "Sales" is written in the Account Title and Explanation column to provide a brief explanation for the entry. Without the explanation, each money column would have to be examined to learn why the entry was made.

Apr. 3 Received $121.50 in cash from Lucy Garcia in payment of Invoice 60 for $125, less a sales discount of $3.50.

The entry for this transaction involves three accounts: a debit to Cash for $121.50, a debit to Sales Discount for $3.50, and a credit to Accounts Receivable for $125.

The combination journal contains special columns for each of the three accounts. The entry is journalized in the combination journal (see line 3) by recording $121.50 in the Cash Debit column, $125 in the Accounts Receivable Credit column, and $3.50 in the Sales Discount Debit column. The customer's name, Lucy Garcia, is recorded in the

	Cash Debit	Accounts Receivable Credit	Sales Discount Debit	
3	121 50	125 00	3 50	3

Account Title and Explanation column for use in posting the credit to the accounts receivable ledger.

Apr. 4 Issued Check 211 for $490 to Graham Electronics in payment of Invoice 1120 for $500, less a purchase discount of $10.

	CASH CREDIT	ACCOUNTS PAYABLE DEBIT	PURCHASES DISCOUNT CREDIT
4	490 00	500 00	10 00

Graham Electronics was granted a 2 percent discount of $10 because the $500 invoice was paid within the discount period. The transaction therefore involves a debit to Accounts Payable for $500, a credit to Purchases Discount for $10, and a credit to Cash for $490.

The combination journal has special columns for this transaction as well. The amount of $490 is recorded in the Cash Credit column, $500 is recorded in the Accounts Payable Debit column, and $10 is recorded in the Purchases Discount Credit column (see line 4). The creditor's name, Graham Electronics, is recorded in the Account Title and Explanation column for use in posting the entry to the accounts payable ledger. The invoice number (1120) is entered in the Account Title and Explanation column. This serves as a reference to the original transaction. The check number (211) is entered in the Check Number column.

Apr. 5 Bought merchandise for $725 on credit from Tyson Company, Invoice 421A.

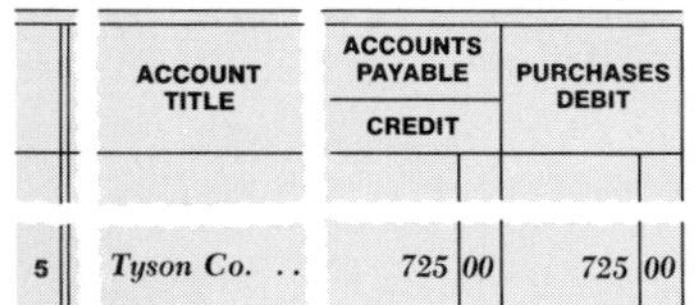

	ACCOUNT TITLE	ACCOUNTS PAYABLE CREDIT	PURCHASES DEBIT
5	*Tyson Co.* . .	725 00	725 00

The transaction involves a debit to the Purchases account and a credit to the Accounts Payable account. Here again, the combination journal provides special columns for the accounts affected by this transaction. The debit to the Purchases account for $725 is recorded in the Purchases Debit column. The credit to the Accounts Payable account for $725 is recorded in the Accounts Payable Credit column (see line 5). The creditor's name (Tyson Company), invoice number (421A), date of invoice (April 1), and terms (2/10, n/30) are written in the Account Title and Explanation column for use in posting to the accounts payable ledger.

Apr. 6 Issued Invoice 140 for $90 to B & J Company for a sale on credit.

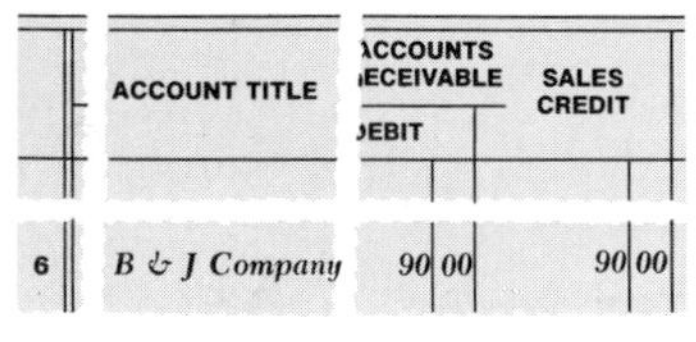

	ACCOUNT TITLE	ACCOUNTS RECEIVABLE DEBIT	SALES CREDIT
6	*B & J Company*	90 00	90 00

This transaction requires a debit to the Accounts Receivable account for $90 and a credit to the Sales account for $90. The debit of $90 is entered in the Accounts Receivable Debit column and the credit is entered in the Sales Credit column. The customer's name (B & J Company), the invoice number (140), and the terms (1/20, n/30) are entered in the Account Title and Explanation column.

Apr. 8 Received Credit Memorandum 1307 for $100 from Tyson Company for the return of merchandise purchased on credit.

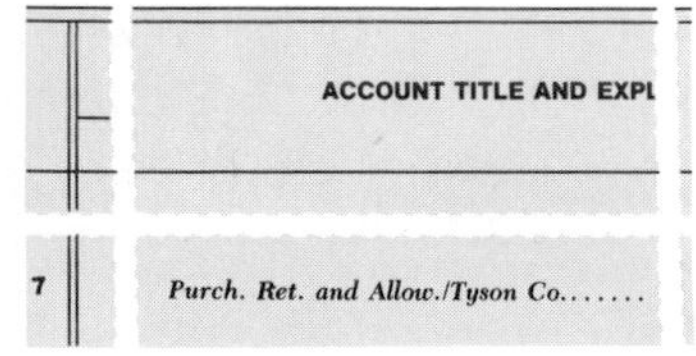

	ACCOUNT TITLE AND EXPL
7	*Purch. Ret. and Allow./Tyson Co.* . . . . . .

The entry for the transaction requires a debit to the Accounts Payable account for $100 and a credit to the Purchases Returns and Allowances account for $100. The debit of $100 to Accounts Payable is recorded in the Accounts Payable Debit column. Since no special column is provided for credits to the Purchases Returns and Allowances account, the credit of $100 must be recorded in the General Ledger Credit column. To provide the necessary information for posting the entry, "Purch. Ret. and Allow./Tyson Co.—CM-1307" is written in the Account Title and Explanation column. The title of the Purchases Returns and Allowances account is recorded so that the $100 credit can be posted from the General Ledger Credit column to the correct account in the general ledger. The creditor's name is written so that the debit in the Accounts Payable Debit column is posted to the correct subsidiary account in the accounts payable ledger. A diagonal line is placed in the Posting Reference column to show that this entry is double-posted.

	General Ledger Debit	General Ledger Credit	Accounts Payable Debit	Accounts Payable Credit
7		100 00	100 00	

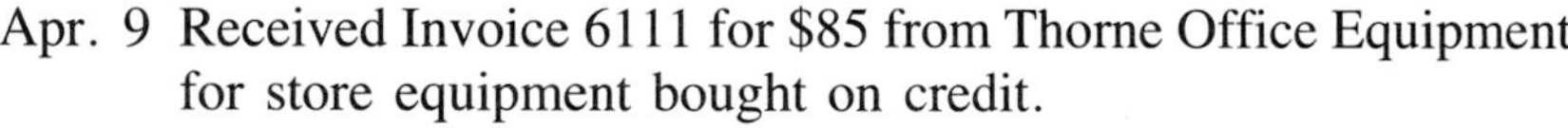

Apr. 9 Received Invoice 6111 for $85 from Thorne Office Equipment for store equipment bought on credit.

This transaction for the purchase of an asset involves a debit to the asset account Store Equipment and a credit to the liability account Accounts Payable for $85.

The debit of $85 is entered in the General Ledger Debit column because no special column is provided for store equipment (see line 8). The credit of $85 is entered in the Accounts Payable Credit column. The titles of the two accounts (Store Equipment and Thorne Office Equipment) are written in the Account Title and Explanation column. A diagonal line is drawn between the account titles. Store Equipment must be written in this column so that the correct asset account is debited when posting to the general ledger. Thorne Office Equipment must also be written in this column so that the correct subsidiary account is credited in the accounts payable ledger.

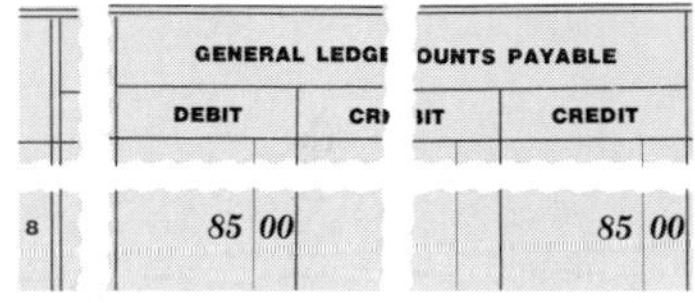

	General Ledger Debit	General Ledger Credit	Accounts Payable Debit	Accounts Payable Credit
8	85 00			85 00

Exercises A and B on this page and page 600 may be completed at this point.

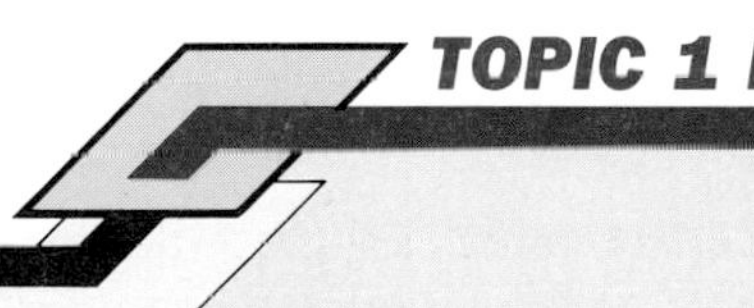

TOPIC 1 EXERCISES

EXERCISE A. Answer the following questions about the combination journal. Refer to the text and illustrations on pages 595 to 599.

1. How are the accounts that appear in the combination journal columns selected?
2. Is a general ledger column required in the combination journal? Why or why not?
3. In what ways does using a combination journal save time?
4. Why is the April 1 cash balance entered in the Account Title and Explanation column?
5. Is each transaction recorded in more than one money column? Why?
6. When is the first credit sale made? To whom is it made? How much is it?
7. How many special money columns are there? How many general ledger accounts have special money columns?

EXERCISE B. Answer the following questions about the combination journal. Refer to the text and illustrations on pages 595 to 599.

1. Is cash received or paid on April 3? From whom or to whom?
2. Is a cash discount recorded in the entry for April 3? If so, how much?
3. What is the difference between the April 5 transaction with the Tyson Company and the April 8 transaction?
4. In the transaction on April 8, which account(s) is (are) debited? Why?
5. Is the April 2 entry for a cash sale or a credit sale?
6. What account is debited for the transaction on April 9? Why is the Purchases account not debited?

TOPIC 1 PROBLEM

TOPIC PROBLEM 1. The Rosebud Flower Shop is a small business owned and operated by Linda Miller.

a. Open general ledger accounts, assign appropriate numbers, and record the May 1 balances as follows: Cash, $6,700; Accounts Receivable; Merchandise Inventory, $890; Store Equipment, $4,200; Accounts Payable; Sales Tax Payable, $210; Linda Miller, Capital, $11,580; Linda Miller, Drawing; Sales; Sales Returns and Allowances; Purchases; Purchases Returns and Allowances; Purchases Discount; Delivery Expense; and Rent Expense. Open the accounts in the accounts receivable ledger for Oswego Bank and the Welcome Club. Open accounts in the accounts payable ledger for Diane's Greenhouse and the Trident Company.

b. Journalize the following transactions in a combination journal.

May 1 Recorded the memorandum entry for the cash balance.
- 2 Issued Check 69 for $700 to Swan Realty to pay May rent.
- 3 Received Invoice 820, dated May 1, from Diane's Greenhouse for merchandise purchased for $400 on credit; terms 2/10, n/30.
- 3 Recorded the cash proof showing weekly cash sales of $700 plus sales tax of $35.
- 4 Received $3,000 from Linda Miller as an additional investment in the business.
- 9 Received Invoice 132M, dated May 7, from the Trident Company for a cash register purchased for $1,850 on credit; terms n/30.
- 10 Issued Invoice 181 to the Welcome Club for merchandise sold on credit for $110 plus $5.50 sales tax.
- 10 Recorded the cash proof showing weekly cash sales of $615 plus sales tax of $30.75.
- 11 Received Invoice 898, dated May 9, from Diane's Greenhouse for merchandise purchased for $240 on credit; terms 2/10, n/30.
- 12 Issued Check 70 for $392 to Diane's Greenhouse to pay Invoice 820, less discount.
- 15 Received Credit Memorandum CM-108 from Diane's Greenhouse for $30 as an allowance for damaged merchandise purchased on Invoice 898.

NOTE: Save your journal and ledgers for further use in Topic Problem 2.

TOPIC 2

Proving and Posting From the Combination Journal

How is the combination journal proved? The total of the debit money columns should equal the total of the credit money columns in a combination journal. Because of the number of columns in a combination journal, it is easier to make an error when recording an entry in a combination journal than when recording the entry in the general journal or one of the special journals. Therefore, at a minimum, a proof should be made when recording in a combination journal at the end of each page and at the end of the month.

■ Proof at the End of the Page

To prove the combination journal at the end of a page (see the combination journal on pages 596 and 597), leave one blank line after the last transaction recorded and follow this procedure.

- Pencil-foot all money columns. Then prove the equality of the debit columns and the credit columns, as shown at right.
- After the money columns are proved, draw a single rule under the last entry and record the current date in the Date column. Then write "Carried Forward" in the Account Title and Explanation column. Place a dash in the Posting Reference column. Finally, enter the totals in ink on the last line.
- Bring the totals forward to the first line of the next page (see the illustration on pages 602 and 603). Enter the date in the Date column. Write "Brought Forward" in the Account Title and Explanation column. Place a dash in the Posting Reference column. Then, record the amounts in the proper money columns.

	DEBITS		CREDITS	
Cash	2,000	00	1,300	00
General Ledger	800	00	1,210	00
Accounts Receivable	1,500	00	800	00
Accounts Payable	1,000	00	1,500	00
Purchases	1,500	00		
Sales			2,000	00
Purchases Discount			10	00
Sales Discount	20	00		
Totals	6,820	00	6,820	00

Proof of combination journal at the end of a page.

Follow this procedure for each page of the combination journal. To prove the journal before the end of the page, pencil-foot all money columns and prove the equality of the debits and credits. This may be done by adding all debits together and adding all credits together. Then compare the totals. Or, a zero proof can be prepared by subtracting all credits from all debits.

The totals brought forward are included in the totals for each new page of the combination journal. At the end of the month, the total of each column on the last journal page for the month will include all amounts entered in the column during the month.

■ Proof at the End of the Month

To prove the combination journal at the end of the month, use the procedure that follows. (Refer to the combination journal on pages 602 and 603.)

COMBINATION JOURNAL

	CASH		DATE		ACCOUNT TITLE AND EXPLANATION	CK. NO.	POST. REF.	GENERAL LEDGER	
	DEBIT	CREDIT						DEBIT	CREDIT
			19—						
1	2,000 00	1,300 00	April	19	*Brought Forward*		—	800 00	1,210 00
2		60 00		20	*Utilities Expense*	380	518	60 00	
23				30	*Sales Ret. and Allow./Lucy Garcia—CM-27*		402/√	20 00	
24	4,400 00 4,400 00	2,800 00 2,800 00		30	*Totals*		—	1,800 00 1,800 00	2,600 00 2,600 00
	(101)	(101)						(—)	(—)

- Pencil-foot all money columns and prove the equality of the debit and credit columns.
- Draw a single rule in the money columns under the last entry.
- Enter the last day of the month in the Date column.
- Write "Totals" in the Account Title and Explanation column.
- Place a dash in the Posting Reference column.
- Enter the totals in ink.
- Draw double rules under all columns with the exception of the Account Title and Explanation column and the Check Number column.

Exercise C on pages 604 and 605 may be completed at this point.

Posting From the Combination Journal

Posting from the combination journal is similar to posting from the special journals.

Posted During the Month
- Accounts receivable ledger
- Accounts payable ledger
- General ledger debit and credit

Posted at the End of the Month
- Special column totals

What is the procedure for posting from the combination journal? The procedure for posting from the combination journal is similar to posting from the special journals. The entries in the Accounts Receivable and Accounts Payable columns are posted to the customers' and creditors' accounts in the subsidiary ledgers during the month. In addition, the entries in the General Ledger columns are posted to the appropriate accounts in the general ledger during the month. At the end of the month, the totals of the special columns are posted to the general ledger account listed in the title of the column. None of the totals should be posted to the general ledger until the combination journal has been proved.

Posting From the General Ledger Columns To post from the General Ledger columns, post each amount in the General Ledger Debit column to the debit side of the account shown in the Account Title and Explanation column. Write the account number in the Posting Reference column of the combination journal to show that the amount has been posted. The page number of the combination journal is then written in the Posting Reference column of the general ledger account. Only the number must be written in the ledger account. Letters such as *CJ* are not needed because the combination journal is the only journal

For the Month of *April* 19— Page 2

ACCOUNTS RECEIVABLE		ACCOUNTS PAYABLE		PURCHASES DEBIT	SALES CREDIT	PURCHASES DISCOUNT CREDIT	SALES DISCOUNT DEBIT	
DEBIT	CREDIT	DEBIT	CREDIT					
1,500 00	800 00	1,000 00	1,500 00	1,500 00	2,000 00	10 00	20 00	1
								2
	20 00							23
3,430 00 3,430 00	1,800 00 1,800 00	2,200 00 2,200 00	3,500 00 3,500 00	3,350 00 3,350 00	4,500 00 4,500 00	22 00 22 00	42 00 42 00	24
(111)	(111)	(211)	(211)	(501)	(401)	(504)	(403)	

Proof at the end of the month.

used by the business. The same procedure is followed when posting the credit entries from the General Ledger Credit column.

■ **Posting From the Accounts Receivable Columns** When posting from the Accounts Receivable Debit and Credit columns, each amount is posted to the customer's account in the accounts receivable ledger. A check mark is placed in the Posting Reference column to indicate that the amount has been posted to the subsidiary ledger. At the end of the month, the Accounts Receivable Debit and Credit column totals are posted to the Accounts Receivable controlling account in the general ledger.

■ **Posting From the Accounts Payable Columns** Each amount in the Accounts Payable Debit and Credit columns is posted to the creditor's account in the accounts payable ledger. A check mark is placed in the Posting Reference column. The column totals are posted to the controlling account in the general ledger at the end of the month.

■ **Double-Posting** Some entries in the combination journal require double-posting. For example, when the entry for merchandise returned for credit is journalized (see the entry on April 30), a diagonal line is drawn in the Posting Reference column. When the debit is posted to the general ledger, the Sales Returns and Allowances account number (402) is placed to the left of the diagonal line. When the credit is posted to the customer's account in the subsidiary ledger, a check mark is written to the right of the diagonal line.

■ **Making Other Entries** When no debit or credit amount for an entry is posted individually, place a dash in the Posting Reference column. For example, when merchandise is sold for cash, the amount is recorded in the Cash Debit column and the Sales Credit column. Since both amounts are posted as part of the column totals at the end of the month, neither is posted individually. Therefore, a dash is placed in the Posting Reference column. This dash indicates that the amounts will be posted as part of the column totals at the end of the month. It is important that a check mark, account number, or dash appears for each entry in the combination journal. This assures that all entries have been posted to the appropriate ledger.

Posting the Column Totals After the combination journal is totaled and ruled, post the totals to the appropriate accounts in the general ledger. The total of each column—except the General Ledger columns—is posted as a debit or credit to the account named in each column heading.

Write the account number in parentheses below the double rule to show that the column total has been posted. For example, after the totals of the Cash Debit and Credit columns are posted, the number of the Cash account (101) is recorded under each column.

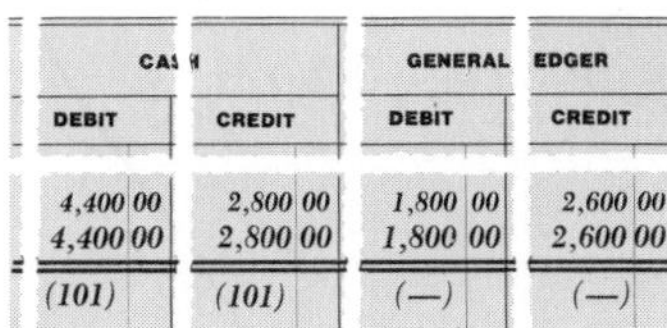

CASH		GENERAL LEDGER	
DEBIT	CREDIT	DEBIT	CREDIT
4,400 00	2,800 00	1,800 00	2,600 00
4,400 00	2,800 00	1,800 00	2,600 00
(101)	(101)	(—)	(—)

Posting the column totals.

The totals of the General Ledger columns are not posted because each amount in the columns has been posted individually. Dashes are placed under the double rule of the two General Ledger columns. The dashes indicate that the amounts in the General Ledger columns have been posted individually and that the totals of the columns are not posted to any specific account.

Exercise D on page 605 may be completed at this point.

Concept: Posting by Total
Posting by total increases accuracy and efficiency and speed because it reduces the number of times an amount is recorded.

TOPIC 2 EXERCISES

EXERCISE C. Answer the following questions about proving the combination journal. Refer to the text and illustrations on pages 601 to 602.

1. In what way do you prove a combination journal?
2. What must be done to prove the journal at the end of the page?
3. When proving the combination journal at the end of the month, when are the totals entered in ink?

4. When proving the end of a page, what is written in the Account Title and Explanation column?
5. What is written in the Account Title and Explanation column on a new page?
6. What symbol is written in the Posting Reference column when proving the end of a page?
7. When proving the end of a page (not at the end of the month) is a double rule drawn under the totals? Why or why not?
8. When proving the combination journal at the end of the month, is a double rule drawn under the totals of the columns? Why or why not?
9. Are the totals brought forward from one page of the combination journal included in the totals for the next page?

EXERCISE D. Answer the following questions about posting from the combination journal. Refer to the text and illustrations on pages 602 to 604.

1. How are the General Ledger columns posted from the combination journal?
2. How are the Accounts Receivable columns posted from the combination journal?
3. How are the Accounts Payable columns posted from the combination journal?
4. What does a dash in the Posting Reference column mean?
5. Why is an account number written in parentheses under some column totals?
6. Why is a dash written in parentheses under the General Ledger columns?

TOPIC 2 PROBLEMS

TOPIC PROBLEM 2. Using the combination journal and ledgers prepared in Topic Problem 1, perform the following activities.

a. Post the individual entries from the combination journal to the ledgers.

b. Foot and prove the combination journal.

NOTE: Save your journal and ledgers for further use in Topic Problem 3.

TOPIC PROBLEM 3. Using the combination journal and ledgers prepared in Topic Problem 1, perform the following activities.

a. Journalize the following transactions.

b. Post the individual entries from the combination journal.

c. Foot and prove the combination journal. Then total and rule the journal.

d. Post the totals from the combination journal.

e. Prepare a schedule of accounts receivable and a schedule of accounts payable. Prove the totals.

f. Prepare a trial balance.

May 16 Issued Invoice 182 to Oswego Bank for merchandise sold for $180 plus $9 sales tax on credit.

17 Issued Credit Memorandum CM-14 to Oswego Bank for an allowance on mer-

chandise sold for $20 plus $1 sales tax on Invoice 182.

May 17 Recorded the cash proof showing weekly cash sales of $680 plus sales tax of $34.

23 Received $115.50 from the Welcome Club in payment of Invoice 181.

24 Recorded the cash proof showing weekly cash sales of $445 plus sales tax of $22.25.

24 Issued Check 71 for $95 to Pacific Florists for merchandise purchased for cash.

25 Issued Check 72 for $65 to Petrocelli Delivery Service for the delivery of flowers to customers.

26 Issued Invoice 183 to Oswego Bank for merchandise sold for $42 plus $2.10 sales tax.

May 28 Issued Check 73 for $1,250 to Linda Miller for her personal use.

29 Received $168 from Oswego Bank in payment of Invoice 182, less allowance.

29 Issued Check 74 for $210 to Diane's Greenhouse to pay Invoice 898, less allowance.

31 Recorded the cash proof showing weekly cash sales of $980 plus sales tax of $49.

31 Received Invoice 1078, dated May 29, from Diane's Greenhouse for merchandise purchased for $830 on credit; terms 2/10, n/30.

CHAPTER 17 REVIEW

CHAPTER SUMMARY

Businesses use a variety of accounting records and procedures to process information about business activities. Some small businesses record all of their transactions in a single multicolumn journal called a combination journal. The combination journal combines the features of the general journal with the features of the special journals.

The combination journal can be designed to meet the needs of a particular business. Columns are set up for the accounts that are most frequently used by a business. The combination journal is thus generally suited to small businesses with a limited number of accounts. If transactions for a business are numerous or varied, it would be more efficient to use special journals.

Using a combination journal can be very useful to a small business, and can save more time than using a general journal. However, the chances of making an error by placing an amount in the wrong column are increased because of the large number of money columns.

The procedures for recording transactions in the combination journal and posting entries from the combination journal to the ledger accounts are similar to those used for the special journals.

THE LANGUAGE OF BUSINESS

Here is a term that makes up the language of business. Do you know its meaning?

combination journal

REVIEW QUESTIONS

1. What is a combination journal?
2. What size business normally uses a combination journal?
3. How is the design of a combination journal determined?
4. What are some advantages of using a combination journal?
5. What are some disadvantages of using a combination journal?
6. When using a combination journal, is each transaction recorded in more than one money column? Why or why not?
7. Give an example of an entry in the combination journal that requires double-posting.
8. Is the combination journal proved only at the time of totaling and ruling?
9. What is the procedure for posting from the combination journal?
10. Would a department store be likely to use a combination journal? Why or why not?

Problems for Chapter 17 are given below. Write your answers to the problems on a separate sheet of paper unless you are using the workbook for this textbook. If you are using the workbook, do the problems in the space provided there.

CHAPTER PROBLEM 17-1. The David Weiss Company uses a combination journal. On March 12, page 14 of the journal showed the following totals.

Cash Debit, $6,148
Cash Credit, $4,325
General Ledger Debit, $371
General Ledger Credit, $2,900
Accounts Receivable Debit, $3,950
Accounts Receivable Credit, $1,945
Accounts Payable Debit, $2,100
Accounts Payable Credit, $950
Purchases Debit, $2,430
Sales Credit, $4,868
Purchases Discount Credit, $52
Sales Discount Debit, $41

a. Bring forward the above totals to page 15 of the combination journal.

b. Record the following transactions in the combination journal.

Mar. 12 Sold merchandise for $750 on credit to Thomas Quinn; Invoice 1520; terms 2/10, n/30.
13 Issued Check 182 for $700 to pay the rent.
13 Purchased merchandise for $1,250 on credit from the Wilson Company; Invoice M317 dated March 12; terms 2/10, n/30.
15 Sold merchandise for $780 cash; Invoice 1521.
18 Issued Check 183 for $65 for repair of typewriter (debit Office Expense).
19 Received a check from Thomas Quinn in payment of Invoice 1520 dated March 12, less discount.
20 Issued Check 184 to the Wilson Company to pay Invoice M317 dated March 12, less discount.
20 Purchased equipment for $75 on credit from the Jet Supply Company.
21 Sold merchandise for $1,145 on credit to Sandra Ryan; Invoice 1522; terms 2/10, n/30.
22 Issued Credit Memorandum CM-13 for a $145 allowance to Sandra Ryan for damaged merchandise sold on Invoice 1522.
22 Purchased merchandise for $280 on credit from Betts & Carr; Invoice 71M dated March 21; terms 1/10, n/30.
23 Issued Check 185 for $500 to David Weiss, the owner, for withdrawal for personal use.

Mar. 25 Received $20 allowance from Betts & Carr for defective merchandise purchased on Invoice 71M.
27 Issued Check 186 for $126 to pay the telephone bill.
29 Received a check from Sandra Ryan in payment of Invoice 1522, less allowance and discount.
29 Issued Check 187 to Betts & Carr to pay Invoice 71M dated March 21, less allowance and discount.

c. Prove, total, and rule the combination journal.

CHAPTER PROBLEM 17-2. Ken Hendricks owns a small gift shop. During the past three months, the gift shop had the following types of transactions.

Advertising expense (paid monthly by check)
Cash sales (most sales are made for cash)
Cash short and over (cash is proved daily)
Delivery expense (usually paid out of petty cash)
Electric and telephone bills (paid monthly by check)
Investments by the owner (about once a year)
Miscellaneous expenses (usually paid by check about three times a month)
Payment of accounts payable (some with purchases discounts)
Payment of rent (once a month)
Payroll (one person paid on a biweekly basis)
Petty cash (replenished once a week)
Purchases of equipment (various types are purchased once every two weeks)
Sales on credit (few sales are made on credit)
Sales returns and allowances (cash refunds are given for most returns and allowances)
Selling expenses (paid by check about three times a month)
Supplies expense (usually paid once a month by check)
Transportation in (usually paid out of petty cash)
Withdrawals by the owner (about once a month)

Mr. Hendricks has decided to use a combination journal. He purchased journal paper with 12 money columns. Analyze the above types of transactions and decide the appropriate titles for the various money columns. Write the column headings that can be used to efficiently record the transactions of the gift shop.

MANAGEMENT CASES

Designing Journals. Journals should be adapted to meet specific needs of a business. Most businesses add special columns to their journals to handle the specific types of transactions which occur frequently. The special columns speed up the posting process and decrease the possibility of making errors when posting. This is possible because the special columns permit posting of column totals instead of individual amounts. Special money columns can be added to any journal: the general journal, the special journals, or the combination journal.

CASE 17M-1. Trudy Ellison owns and operates an accounting service. One of her customers is Donald Diaz, a doctor. The most frequently recurring transactions for Dr. Diaz' medical practice are the following: cash from fees received from patients, cash paid to creditors, cash paid for utilities and miscellaneous expenses, purchases of medical supplies, and cash withdrawals by the owner.

Design a combination journal with eleven special money columns that can be used to efficiently record the transactions from Dr. Diaz' medical practice.

CASE 17M-2. Another of Ms. Ellison's customers is Charles West, a farmer. The most frequently recurring transactions for Mr. West's farm are the following: cash received from sales of livestock and produce, purchases on credit of gasoline and oil for the truck and tractor, cash paid to creditors, and cash paid for repairs and miscellaneous expenses.

Design a combination journal with eleven special money columns that can be used to efficiently record the transactions from Mr. West's farm.

Index

***NOTE:* Entries in boldface type refer to accounting concepts or principles.**